Third Parties

Third Parties

Victims and the Criminal Justice System

LESLIE SEBBA

Ohio State University Press / Columbus

Copyright © 1996 by the Ohio State University Press.
All rights reserved.

Library of Congress Cataloging-in-Publication Data
Sebba, Leslie.
  Third parties : victims and the criminal justice system / Leslie
Sebba.
    p. cm.
  Includes bibliographical references and index.
  ISBN 0-8142-0664-6 (cloth : alk. paper)
  1. Victims of crimes—United States.   2. Victims of crimes—Legal
status, laws, etc.—United States.   3. Criminal justice,
Administration of—United States.   I. Title.
HV6250.3.U5S4 1996
362.88'0973—dc20   95-50577
                                                                        CIP

Text and jacket design by Nighthawk Design.
Type set in Trump Medieval by Huron Valley Graphics.
Printed by Thomson-Shore, Inc.

The paper used in this publication meets the minimum requirements of American National Standard for Information Sciences—Permanence of Paper for Printed Library Materials. ANSI Z39.48-1992. ∞

9 8 7 6 5 4 3 2 1

For my children

Contents

Part IV   *Integration: Past, Present, and Future Remedies*

Acknowledgments

The volume has been in the process of formulation and crystallization over an extensive period of time, and there is hardly a criminologist, victimologist, or jurist of my acquaintance who has not provided me with some source or idea during this period. I regret my inability to thank them all by name. However, I wish specifically to mention certain colleagues who invested time and trouble in reading and commenting on sections of the manuscript, namely, Malcolm Feeley, Edna Erez, Hugo Adam Bedau, Leroy Lamborn, and Avi Kaye—and my co-editors on the *International Review of Victimology*, David Miers and Joanna Shapland. Others whose encouragement proved to be invaluable at various stages of the enterprise include Marvin Wolfgang and Pat Langan (at the early stages), Si Dinitz (at the later stages), and Wes Skogan and Eliahu Harnon (at all stages).

Among the institutions that have provided support for my research, my primary debt is to the National Institute of Justice, which in the years 1981/82 awarded me a visiting fellowship (grant no. 81-IJ-CX-0026) to develop my ideas in this area. This resulted in a report submitted to the NIJ entitled *Wrongdoers, Victims and Justice*. While the structure of that report formed the basis for the current volume, the meteoric pace of developments in the field—and in the literature—in subsequent years required a substantial revision and reorientation of the text. Needless to say, the NIJ is in no way responsible for the ideas expressed here.

Other institutions to which I am indebted for providing assistance include NOVA, the National Victim Center, the National Criminal Justice Reference Service, the Bureau of Justice Statistics, the libraries of the Max Planck Institute of Criminal Law and Criminology in Freiburg, the

Institute of Criminology at Cambridge, and the CESDIP in Paris, as well as the Law Library at the Hebrew University of Jerusalem.

My thanks also for the patience shown by the editors of the Ohio State University Press and to their editorial staff for their painstaking cooperation.

Last but not least I wish to thank Varda for her encouragement (and gentle insistence), particularly at the final stages of editing.

Part I

Background

Introduction

Over the past two decades considerable interest has developed in the subject of the victims of crime. This interest reached a peak in 1982 with the establishment and report of the President's Task Force on Victims of Crime (1982), which made numerous recommendations for legislative, executive, and other institutional action on both the federal and state levels, including an amendment to the United States Constitution. However, the momentum continued. Subsequent developments have included the establishment of an Office for Victims of Crime in the Office of Justice Programs, a flurry of legislative activity across the nation, and the declaration of National Crime Victims' Rights weeks with the participation of the U.S. president. The interests of victims have been taken up not only by special organizations established for the purpose, such as the National Organization of Victims' Assistance (NOVA), the Victims' Assistance Legal Organization in Virginia, and the National Victim Center (founded in honor of Sunny von Bulow), as well as more narrowly focused groups such as MADD (Mothers against Drunk Driving), but also by such mainstream professional bodies as the American Bar Association (ABA), the National Association of Attorneys General, the National Conference of the Judiciary, the American Psychological Association, and the National Institute for Mental Health. Landmark legislation at the federal level includes the Victim and Witness Protection Act of 1982, the Victims of Crime Act of 1984, and the Victims' Rights and Restitution Act and other related provisions of the Crime Control Act of 1990. (See also the Attorney-General's Guidelines for Victim and Witness Assistance, issued in pursuance of the 1982 and the 1990 acts.) A review of victim-oriented legislation both at the federal and at the state levels, conducted by the Bureau of Justice Statistics

1

in 1984, reproduced 1,489 pages of such legislation (Bureau of Justice Statistics, 1984). Additional legislative updates were compiled annually by the National Organization for Victim Assistance (see, e.g., NOVA, 1989).

Similar trends have begun to emerge in other countries (see, e.g., Joutsen, 1987; Melup, 1991). In 1990 Britain issued its "Victim's Charter" to coincide with European Victims Day (Hannaford, 1991). National organizations on behalf of victims have become the norm. Some examples are the Canadian Organization for Victim Assistance (COVA), the National Association of Victim Support Schemes (NAVSS) in Britain, the Weisser Ring in Germany, and the National Institute for Assistance for Victims (INAVEM) in France.

Campaigns on behalf of crime victims have also been launched on the international level (Bassiouni, 1988). The World Society of Victimology and the World Federation of Mental Health, as well as national bodies and individuals, were instrumental in pressing for a United Nations declaration on victim rights; and following a recommendation on the part of the Seventh United Nations Congress on the Prevention of Crime and the Treatment of Offenders in 1985, the General Assembly adopted the *Declaration of Basic Principles of Justice for Victims of Crime and Abuse of Power* in the same year. This, in turn, appears to have further stimulated national legislation (Melup, 1991).

Among the specific proposals calculated to ameliorate the situation of the victim which have been raised and in many cases adopted are the following: provision for crisis intervention, protection orders, victim/witness-assistance programs, informal mechanisms of dispute resolution, victim participation in plea bargaining and sentencing procedures, victim-impact statements, victim compensation programs, restitution, escrow laws, and third-party liability. These concepts and proposals will be elaborated below.

Background to Contemporary Interest in Victims

An attempt to offer an explanation or explanations for these developments might be considered somewhat speculative: the study of social movements is a complex topic (Etzioni, 1976), and the "victim movement" seems to be no exception (Rock, 1986: esp. chap. 3; Mawby and Gill, 1987:35). Nevertheless, some of the developments that appear to be associated with this movement will be briefly considered here, partly because of their intrinsic interest, and partly because in the course of the evaluation to be undertaken in subsequent chapters of the various programs and proposals designed to ameliorate the situation of crime victims, it may be relevant to consider which social forces gave rise to these programs and proposals (cf. Casper and Brereton, 1984).

While surveys of the development of the victim movement (Elias, 1986: chap. 2; Rock, 1986: chap. 3; Joutsen, 1987: chap. 2; Van Dijk, 1988; Karmen, 1990: chap. 1)[1] diverge somewhat in their analysis, it seems that at least seven developments pertaining to recent sociolegal history may be relevant in considering the current focus on the victim.

The Rise of Victimology

The term *victimology* has been credited to Beniamin Mendelsohn in the early 1940s (Mendelsohn, 1974). In the postwar years a number of criminologists (von Hentig, 1948; Ellenberger, 1955; Wolfgang, 1957; Fattah, 1967; Amir, 1971; Curtis, 1974) devoted considerable attention to the role played by the victim in the commission of the offense, while academic debate on this issue took place in Japan (Mendelsohn, 1963:243–44). Additionally, a cry was sporadically raised in favor of better treatment for victims of crime, in particular for financial compensation (Fry, 1959; Schafer, [1960] 1970), and an example was set in this respect by government-sponsored schemes in New Zealand in 1963 and Great Britain in 1964. These two fields of interest converged in 1973, when the First International Symposium in Victimology was held under the auspices of the International Society of Criminology, resulting in the publication of five volumes of proceedings (Drapkin and Viano, 1974–75). Since that time, international symposia have been held on a triennial basis, two journals of victimology have been founded, the World Society of Victimology has been established, and a proliferation of literature has emerged.[2]

This duality of themes which gave rise to the development of victimology—interest in the victim-offender relationship on the one hand, and in victim welfare on the other—is not without significance. To some extent these foci of interest remain distinct today, contributing in part to the fragmentation of this area of study—other facets of which will be noted subsequently. Moreover, while these two areas continue to be discussed within the same organizational framework, namely, "victimology," victim welfare seems to have superseded the first topic (victim-offender interaction) as the dominant area of interest. This has in turn led to an orientation toward policy formulation on the part of victimologists as well as political activism directed at the enhancement of the victim's rights (Fattah, 1974; Rock, 1986: chap. 3; Joutsen, 1987: chap. 2).

Victimization Surveys

Since the pioneering surveys conducted in the 1960s by Ennis and Biderman on behalf of the President's Commission for Law Enforcement and the Administration of Justice (1967), victimization surveys have become a routinized procedure in the United States as a source of criminological.data. The invention and institutionalization of victimization surveys may have been even more significant, both academically and politically, than the rise of victimology. In a sense, this development, too, is part of victimology, in that the surveys are extensively referred to and relied upon in the literature. To this extent they constitute a third focal area, in addition to the two mentioned above—the victim-offender relationship and victim welfare. However, the surveys were developed primarily as a contribution to the more traditional areas of criminology, for they serve as a source of data for the dimensions of criminality, complementary to or substituting for police statistics. Indeed, the National Crime Survey in the United States, and equivalent surveys elsewhere, now constitute the primary source for measuring trends in criminality. These surveys offer a persuasive response to the traditional criticism of criminologists, that the official criminal statistics ignore the "dark figures" of crime. Only rarely or marginally, however, do such surveys provide meaningful information regarding the individual victims.[3] Nonetheless, some researchers have endeavored to develop theories of criminal victimization (such as the "lifestyle" theory) based upon macro data derived from the surveys (cf. Fattah, 1991: chap. 12), thereby creating an analytical link with the early victimologists, with their focus on victim-offender relationships.

The political, as opposed to the academic, importance of the victimization surveys derives from the fact that the surveys have indicated that a considerable amount of crime goes unreported. This has led to a number of conclusions being drawn by policy makers as well as by academicians, to the effect that *(a)* crime rates are really much higher than indicated by previous assessments, based upon police or FBI statistics; *(b)* victimization is a very widespread phenomenon,[4] and thus victims constitute a considerable constituency; and *(c)* the failure of many victims to report crimes suggests a degree of malaise either on the part of these victims or in the system as a whole.

"Law and Order"

In recent years there have been vociferous demands for more stringent law enforcement measures against offenders. These demands seem to have been stimulated by the general belief that crime, in particular violent crime, was on the rise, leading to an increasingly pervasive "fear of crime." They may also be seen as a "backlash" (Brownell, 1976), a reaction against the liberal extensions of the constitutional guarantees bestowed by the U.S. Supreme Court on suspects and defendants in the 1960s.[5] The conservative Republican administrations of Presidents Nixon and Reagan were particularly sympathetic to such demands,[6] which found academic respectability in the views of James Q. Wilson (1975), Ernest van den Haag (1975), and others, with respect to the merits of deterrent punishment and incapacitation.

This development resulted in proposals for restrictions on the granting of bail, the abolition or modification of the exclusionary rule, limitations on the collateral attacks on conviction by means of habeas corpus proceedings, mandatory and sometimes enduring prison terms, demands for increased prison building, and the reintroduction of the death penalty. Many of these proposals were placed on the agenda of the Reagan administration by the Attorney General's Task Force on Violent Crime (1981) and paved the way for somewhat repressive and impersonal penal policies (Feeley and Simon, 1992).

It is a short step from the advocacy of harsher measures against offenders to the demand for greater protection for the victim. Indeed, in many instances the latter is seen as the direct justification for the former. Detention before trial, higher conviction rates, longer prison sentences, and the abolition of parole are thought by their advocates to prevent victimization and are sometimes advocated specifically in these terms. The interrelationship of these causes is well illustrated by the Attorney General's Task Force referred to above, which, while focusing on the violent criminal, made a number of proposals for the benefit of victims (see recommendations 13, 14, 62, 63, and 64). Conversely, Frank Carrington's book *The Victims* (1975) advocated a number of the above-mentioned measures directed at offenders—as did the President's Task Force on Victims of Crime (1982) and California's "Proposition 8" (Ranish and Shichor, 1985). Even more explicitly, one victim-advocate group bears the name "Victim Advocates for Law and Order" (VALOR).

Further, the "fear-of-crime" syndrome, coupled with the statistics drawn from the victimization surveys (see, e.g., Attorney General's Task

Force, 1981:87), undoubtedly produced a large constituency sympathetic to victim-oriented policies. Moreover, this dual trend of increasing toughness toward offenders coupled with victim protection measures seems to have been little affected either by the falling off in crime rates (Zawitz et al., 1993:7–8) or by the advent of a Democratic administration, traditionally more liberal on law and order issues. President Clinton's Crime Act has incorporated both mechanisms for the incapacitation of offenders ("three strikes and you're out") and new measures for the protection of victims—in particular, women (educational programs to prevent sex abuse, domestic violence hotlines, etc.). Harsher sentences continue to be perceived as a means of victim protection (see, e.g., the provisions for the protection of the elderly).

Feminist and Other Grassroots Movements

One of the main focal concerns of the women's movement has been the sexual exploitation of women, notably in the context of rape (see, e.g., Brownmiller, 1975). Attention has been drawn to the discrepancy between the presumed high rates of victimization and the low reporting rates, attributed to the social definitions applied to sexual assault and social pressures exerted on the victims. The feminist critique also alluded to the absence of appropriate assistance following the trauma, and to the harrowing experiences undergone by complainants during the investigatory and judicial processes. Women activists have pressed for and secured reformed rape laws and police and judicial procedures and the establishment of rape crisis centers. A similar interest has been shown in the area of domestic violence, attention being drawn to the reluctance of the law enforcement system to classify victimized women as "true" victims and to the absence of legal or social remedies. These developments stimulated considerable research on the topic of women victims (e.g., Holmstrom and Burgess, 1978; Chapman and Gates, 1978) and led to the establishment of special services for this constituency. Thus, even though not all feminists identify their exploited gender as "victims,"[7] there can be little doubt that the wider movement in favor of assisting victims generally, as epitomized by the National Organization of Victims' Assistance, benefited from this highly motivated special-interest group.

Similarly, other grassroots organizations have labored on behalf of battered children, elderly victims, and the victims of drunken drivers (cf. Karmen, 1990:36–38; Rock, 1986:90). In addition, there have been contributions by individual "moral entrepreneurs," such as Irvin Waller in Canada (Rock, 1986: chap. 3) and Marlene Young of NOVA, who have been instrumental in translating the aims of the pressure groups into policy.

Radicalism

The victim movement has not generally been identified with political or social radicalism. Victimologists have in the past generally been identified with positivist criminology and thus either ignored by radicals or criticized for their methodology or focal interests (Quinney, 1974; Bruinsma and Fiselier, 1982; Falandysz, 1982). More particularly, the victim movement is often perceived as part of the "war against crime," as reflected in the law-and-order camp, whereas radicals have tended to regard those waging the war as the aggressors and the offenders as the oppressed. Recently, however, a new emphasis may be discerned in radical thinking. Victimization surveys have shown that the so-called underclass—the poor and in particular poor blacks—suffers relatively high rates of victimization in respect of violent crimes (Skogan and Maxfield, 1981; Zawitz et al., 1993). Indeed, some observers (Jones et al., 1986) claim that *initially* there was an emphasis on such findings, with their implicit concern to radicals. Thus Ramsay Clark is cited as having noted as early as 1970 that the poor, black, urban slum dweller "faces odds five times greater" than the average citizen of being a victim of violent crime (ibid., 1); Jones et al. detect here "a sentiment . . . which pervades the work of the new radical, realist approach to crime today" (ibid., 7). They argue that the victimization issue was subsequently appropriated by the political right and so-called administrative criminology, which advocated increased punitiveness and other conservative solutions. Whatever their historical contribution, contemporary radicals—particularly in England—have become involved in victim surveys, while radicals have generally been active in various community-oriented victimization prevention programs (Hudson, 1987:177–79).

Moreover, studies of the criminal justice system, including the application of the death penalty, indicate that the victimization of blacks and other minorities is treated by the system as though it were less serious than that of whites, indicating to civil rights activists that society discriminates in the level of protection it provides for different groups (Karmen, 1990:34–36). Such activists thus have an interest in promoting certain aspects of victims' rights. Conversely, it has been argued that victims have benefited from some of the civil rights or civil liberties successes of the 1960s in such areas as equal protection under law and improved services (ibid., 36).

Another area of interest to some radicals is the potential for developing an interrelationship between criminal victimization and socioeconomic or political oppression or human rights abuses. This is the theme of Robert Elias's *The Politics of Victimization* (1986), which he subtitled *Victims, Victimology and Human Rights*. The same focus led to pressure on the international level to extend the application of the United Nations declaration on the rights of crime victims to "victims of abuse of power."

Finally, there often is a radical component both in the grassroots movements referred to in the previous section and in the move toward informalism discussed below.

The "Just-Deserts" Philosophy

The next development to be discussed under the present heading has a more tenuous causal connection with the rise of the victim movement, if indeed it has any such connection. As is by now well known, criminologists have in recent years become disillusioned with their traditional objective of rehabilitation of the offender, following the researches of Martinson (1974) and others, who argued that rehabilitation programs did not work, and of more radical groups who argued that rehabilitative penal systems were oppressive and discriminatory (see, e.g., American Friends' Service Committee, 1971). This led to advocacy of the so-called justice or just-deserts model of punishment (Fogel, 1975; von Hirsch, 1976), based on a notional balance between the seriousness of the offense and the severity of the punishment. The implications here regarding victims are twofold. First, criminologists were released from their hitherto dominant mission of searching for the optimal methods of rehabilitating the offender and could devote some of their displaced energies to the advantage of the victim. Second, the just-deserts model sought measures for determining the seriousness of the offense, or the offender's "desert"; and the degree of harm inflicted on the victim was proposed as an appropriate measure for this purpose (see, e.g., Wolfgang, 1976). Whether the debt was owed by the offender to society as a surrogate for the victim was left ambiguous. (These issues will be discussed below.) As noted, whether this revolution in penal philosophy had any direct effect on promoting the victim movement or victim welfare is unclear, but that it has far-reaching conceptual implications regarding the role of the victim in the criminal justice system is incontrovertible.

Informalism

While the just-deserts movement has advocated a formalized criminal justice system, with the almost inexorable application of predetermined penalties, another movement has developed contemporaneously in the opposite direction, namely, in support of informal processes of justice. This movement has been supported by traditionalist rehabilitationists and adherents of labeling theory, who have sought to maximize the offender's reformation, or to minimize the stigma incurred, by means of diversion and "community corrections" rather than more punitive penal sanctions. While on the face of it this movement (like the justice movement) is not directly related to victims, some of the informal procedures (which will be expanded upon in subsequent chapters) involve restitution for or reconciliation with the victim—objectives that are assumed to benefit the victim as well as the offender. At the same time, some advocates of "informalism" (such as Nils Christie)[8] have been concerned primarily with the victim. They have noted the victim's inferior status in the formal criminal justice system and seek to enhance his or her role by means of civil-law, "abolitionist," or informal procedures.

These developments, which coincidentally have all taken place within the last 20 to 25 years, seem to have contributed in varying degrees to the present interest in the victims of crime, and thus also to the proliferation of victim-related policy reforms and legislative measures. Some in-depth studies have emerged of the evolution of these measures in particular settings. Thus Smith and Freinkel (1988) and Sayles (1991) have commented upon the importance of coalitions of divergent groups in securing reforms on the federal level and in Florida, respectively. McCoy has also referred to the "confluence of conditions" that led to California's famous (infamous?) Proposition 8, but mainly to the "manipulation by a dedicated group of right-wing entrepreneurs" (1987:44–45), although these same proponents perceived their activity as "a grassroots outpouring of frustration against insensitive officialdom" (ibid., 18). Rock (1988), in his detailed studies of the development of victim reforms in Canada and Britain, noted the relative significance in this context of *(a)* government policies, *(b)* voluntary associations, and *(c)* moral entrepreneurs—central government policies having played the main role in Canada, voluntary associations in Britain. However, the identification of such factors in these particularist studies is not necessarily inconsistent with the seven "macro" influences noted above; indeed, it is in some cases illustrative of these influences.

Analysis of the dynamics of victim-related reforms is not, however, the main objective of the present study. Suffice it for present purposes to note that the plethora of victim-related programs and proposals (to be elaborated in chap. 1) were novel, were speedy in their development, and were the product of a constellation of influences.

Aims of the Present Study

It is evident from the foregoing that considerable energy has been devoted to the development of new ideas and new programs for the benefit of victims. However, because of the novelty of these proposals and programs, and the dynamics of their implementation, progress has been somewhat hasty and unreflecting. The precise objectives of these programs have not always been carefully defined, nor has much attention been devoted to their conceptual analysis and implications. Joutsen (1987) has presented a paradigm according to which victimological theory led to scientific research, the results of which "were then marshalled by the victim movement and criminal justice practitioners for reforming the operation of the criminal justice system" (51). This seems at best to be an idealization of the process that has been taking place; the political and emotional (or moral) forces for change have surely been at least as powerful as the scientific ones, and possibly considerably stronger (Landau and Sebba, 1991). Adequate evaluation has been wanting with respect both to the novel programs themselves and to the underlying needs they are designed to meet, although considerable progress on this last topic is evidenced in recent research publications (see, e.g., Lurigio et al., 1990). Subject to this welcome development, however, it is still probably true that "to date, there has been no comprehensive, systematic effort to view the problems, and the needs involved from the standpoint of the victims" (Victims of Crime, 1985:56). Certainly there has been none that endeavors to consider at the same time the needs and the interests of other relevant parties (see below).

Further, little thought has been given to the relationships among the various programs, either conceptually or in practice. As one legal scholar has observed, the victims' movement "raises fundamental issues about the purposes of criminal law, its sanctions and remedies" (Goldstein, 1982:529); and while the paucity of scholarly literature in this area noted by Gittler (1984) has been partially rectified, the emphasis has been upon action and legislation rather than upon conceptualization and evaluation.

Of course, literature relating to the victim and the criminal justice system is not lacking. Indeed the last years have produced something of an avalanche. Following the seminal work of Schafer (1968), which presented the historical background, MacDonald (1976) and his fellow contributors considered many of the (then) current developments. Ziegenhagen (1977) analyzed some of the conceptual issues related to victims and social control. The problems encountered by victims in the criminal justice system were studied by INSLAW (Hernon and Smith, 1983), while comparable studies were conducted in Canada (Hagan, 1980) and Britain (Shapland et al., 1985). The American Bar Association, too (following their review of the then-prevailing legislation—see ABA, 1981), commissioned some papers in this area, leading to the publication of a special issue of the *Pepperdine Law Review* in 1984, to be followed by further special issues of the *Wayne Law Review* in 1987, the *Pepperdine Law Review* in 1989, and the *International Review of Victimology* in 1994. A most comprehensive (particularly in the geographical sense) multivolume review of the victim and the criminal justice system has recently been published by the Max Planck Institute for Foreign and International Penal Law in Freiburg (Kaiser et al., 1991). In the area of victim needs and services, pioneering studies were published by Knudten et al. (1976) and Salasin et al. (1981), the latter emphasizing mental health issues. Further publications have emerged in connection with New York City's Victim Services Agency, evaluations having been conducted or supported by the Vera Foundation or the National Institute of Justice. The latter has also supported evaluations both of specific programs and of general overviews of particular areas. Included in this last category are works by Carrow (1980), McGillis and Smith (1983), and Parent et al. (1992) on victim compensation programs; Hudson et al. (1980) on restitution programs; and Cronin and Borque (1981), Finn and Lee (1983), and Skogan et al. (1990) on victim/witness-assistance programs. Other recent evaluations of this last topic include Roberts (1990) and, in Britain, Maguire and Corbett (1987) and Mawby and Gill (1987). A vast literature is also available on alternative mechanisms for dispute resolution (see, e.g., Alper and Nichols, 1981; Tomasic and Feeley, 1982; Abel, 1982a, 1982b; Marshall, 1985; Matthews, 1988; Galaway and Hudson, 1990).

The above overview is confined to full-length volumes and reports, to the exclusion of numerous journal articles. Also useful are the wide-ranging edited volumes of Hudson and Galaway (1975), Galaway and Hudson (1981), Fattah (1986, 1989, 1992), Maguire and Ponting (1988), and Lurigio et al. (1990), as well as a special issue of *Crime and Delinquency* (1987), the proceedings of the international symposia of the International Society of

Criminology and the World Society of Victimology (Drapkin and Viano, 1974–75; Schneider, 1982; Separovic, 1989; Miyazawa and Ohya, 1986; Ben-David and Kirchhoff, 1992), and student textbooks by Karmen (1984, 1990) and Doerner and Lab (1995) in the United States and by Walklate (1989) in Britain, and textbooks in other countries. Other publications are directed at a broader public, such as *The Crime Victim's Book* of Bard and Sangrey (1979) and the *American Civil Liberties Union Handbook* (Stark and Goldstein, 1985).

However, in spite of this vast literary outpouring, integrative analysis of the field under discussion has generally been lacking, although two attempts to undertake such analyses must be noted, the one from a political science perspective (Elias, 1986), and the other having a criminal justice orientation (Joutsen, 1987; see also Ashworth, 1986).

The Structure of This Book

The first aim of the present study will be to provide an overview of the reforms that have been adopted or are currently being proposed, accompanied by an attempt to place them in a more meaningful perspective (chap. 1). This will be followed by a review of our knowledge of the role of the victim in the traditional criminal justice system (chap. 2), with a view to ascertaining the backdrop against which these reforms are being developed. Part 2 will attempt to identify the parameters of a justice system which any reforms should take into consideration (chap. 3) and then to examine these parameters in depth (chaps. 4–6). In this way, the criteria for evaluating the appropriateness and the success of any reforms will be established. These criteria then, in part 3, will be applied to the new proposals and programs, insofar as sufficient data are available for this purpose (chaps. 7–11). Part 4 will endeavor to integrate the analysis conducted in the preceding chapters, considering (in chap. 12) the implications of the various reforms reviewed for the type of criminal (or noncriminal!) justice system which might emerge, and developing a dichotomy of alternative models into which most of the reforms or proposals can be integrated. Chapter 13 briefly considers some developments indicative of a possible third model. Some final reflections will be presented in chapter 14.

1

An Overview of Victim-Oriented Reforms

The remedies proposed for the amelioration of the victim's lot—some now widely adopted, others still at the experimental stage[1]—are diffuse in character. As noted in the previous chapter, scant consideration has been devoted to analysis of the theoretical foundations of the different proposals, of the relationships between these proposals, or of the degree to which they are conceptually consistent with the prevailing criminal justice system. An essential preliminary is to evolve a taxonomy of the remedies or proposals under consideration.

A fourfold classification may tentatively be suggested:

1. Proposals concerned with improving upon the traditional criminal process from the victim's standpoint.
2. Proposals concerned with providing alternatives to the traditional processes of the criminal law.
3. Proposals designed to ameliorate the victim's situation without impinging upon the nature of the criminal process.
4. "Catch-all" remedies.

The reforms or proposals falling within each category will be briefly reviewed here with a view to clarification of the subject matter of this study; their detailed analysis will form the basis of part 3 below.[2]

Proposals for Modifying the Criminal Process

Since the desire for change derives primarily from the perception that the victim has fared badly under the traditional criminal justice system, it is hardly surprising that the main focus of reform has been on the introduction of modifications to this system. The reforms proposed may be classified in the following ways: (1) according to the extent to which emphasis is placed upon changing the *procedures* involved as compared with changing the *outcome* of the process, (2) according to the degree of activism it is sought to attribute to the victim's role within the framework of the reform, and (3) according to the stage of the proceeding it is sought to reform. Although in subsequent chapters considerable emphasis will be placed on the first two modes of classification, it will be convenient at this point to list the proposed reforms by employing the last-mentioned framework of analysis, namely, according to the stage of the criminal process to which the reform relates.

Bail Hearing. Historically, the bail hearing dealt with the issue of the risk that a suspect or defendant might not appear for trial. In recent years it has been asserted that the danger of the defendant committing "further offenses" (bearing in mind that the offense for which he or she has been apprehended has not yet been proven) is also a legitimate consideration in determining bail, hence the concept of "preventive detention." Since the victim of the suspect's alleged offense may again be at risk in the case of a repeat offense, it may also be pertinent to consider this particular risk at the bail hearing. Moreover, there may be an additional risk here—that the suspect will attempt to intimidate the victim (or any other witness) in order to inhibit him or her from testifying at the trial. It is thus seen to be proper for the judge to take these factors into account in determining the bail decision. In spite of the constitutional objections to the placing of limitations on bail, it has been recommended that "bail be conditioned on the defendant's having no access to victims or prosecution witnesses" (National Conference of the Judiciary on the Rights of Victims of Crime, 1983:11; see also sec. 8 of the Federal Victim and Witness Protection Act of 1982). Further, following a recommendation of the President's Task Force on Victims of Crime, the Bail Reform Act was enacted to allow federal judges and magistrates to consider danger to the community when determining whether a defendant is eligible for pretrial release (Office of Justice Programs, 1986:15). Many states also require that the victim be notified of bail or pretrial release (NOVA, 1989:14).

Moreover, the use of both criminal sanctions and civil "restraining orders" has been sanctioned by the Federal Victim and Witness Protection Act of 1982, as well as by state legislation (see ABA, 1981:31ff.; Bureau of Justice Statistics, 1984:11). Similarly, "protection orders" are particularly recommended in cases of domestic violence (ABA, 1981:63–66; Finn and Colson, 1990). While these proposals are not necessarily related to bail proceedings, this appears to be the optimal stage of the proceedings for considering issues of risk and intimidation.

Plea Negotiation. In the majority of criminal cases the outcome is determined in the course of a plea bargain conducted between defendant's counsel and the prosecuting attorney and generally ratified subsequently by the judge. (For the variations in participants and dynamics, see Miller et al., 1978.) The result is generally a guilty plea, whether to a lesser charge than the one originally specified, or in exchange for an understanding that a relatively lenient penalty will be sought. It thus becomes unnecessary to call witnesses for the prosecution—including the victim. Not only will the latter have no opportunity to express his or her views as to the appropriate sentence, but the case will be determined without the court receiving any direct impression of the victim or the true extent of his or her injury or suffering.

To remedy this situation it was suggested by Norval Morris (1974) that victims—and indeed the defendants themselves—should be enabled to participate in the plea-bargaining process. Experiments of this nature were conducted in Florida and other states (Kerstetter and Heinz, 1979; Heinz and Kerstetter, 1980; Buchner et al., 1983), and by 1988, 24 states had made express legislative provision for such participation (NOVA, 1989:12), while an even larger number of states required that the victim be notified (ibid., 14).

Victim-Impact Statements. An alternative method of assuring that the court has a complete picture of the nature of the injury inflicted upon the victim,[3] and one that would also apply to cases that went to trial, is for the court to request a special report on this facet of the case. In the Victim and Witness Protection Act of 1982, Congress introduced the "victim-impact statement" (VIS), whereby in federal courts the presentence report would include "information concerning any harm, including financial, social, psychological harm, done to or loss suffered by any victim of the offense." By 1988, 48 states had made some provision for victim input in sentencing, mostly by means of the victim-impact statement (ibid., 10). Such statements may be submitted to the court as part of the presentence report, as under the federal legislation, or directly, by the victim or by an advocate on the victim's behalf. (The model provisions drafted by the National Association of Attorneys General and the American Bar Association would allow for both methods in combination; see NAAG/ABA, 1986, sec. 105.)

A separate issue is whether the victim should be enabled to express an opinion as to his or her attitude toward the offender and as to the decisions to be made by the various agencies, in this case the court. Many states now allow for a "victim statement of opinion" (VSO), which may be submitted orally—called the "right of allocution"—or in writing. This type of reform raises fundamental issues regarding the respective rights of victims and offenders, on which the Supreme Court has been divided in recent years. We shall return to these issues subsequently.

Sentencing Options. Certain sentencing options have been developed in recent years for the benefit of the victim. The most notable is the use of compensation or restitution orders, whereby the offender must compensate the victim for the loss, suffering, or injury he or she has inflicted. Courts of common law have traditionally had the power to make such orders, but such powers were limited, and they were rarely exercised (Vennard, 1978; Lamborn, 1979). Criminal courts were reluctant to become involved in the quantification of losses, which they regarded as the function of civil courts. Moreover, this remedy was rarely sought by victims themselves (who have had no standing in the criminal court) or by prosecutors on their behalf. Finally, when issued, such orders might remain unenforced, since at best they would have the force of civil judgment debts, execution proceedings being left to the initiative of the individual beneficiary.

Concern for the victim's predicament has led to an expansion of the use of victim restitution (Harland, 1981). By 1988, all 50 states had restitution laws "that provide statutory reinforcement of states' common law authority" (NOVA, 1989:12). Moreover, this remedy has gained support as a sanction to be imposed upon the offender from two camps: persons disillusioned with offender rehabilitation who would rather emphasize the latter's debt to society in general and to the victim in particular;[4] and traditional rehabilitationists who regard the obligation to pay restitution itself as a rehabilitative measure for the offender. (This was a recurring theme of the National Symposia on Restitution; see Hudson and Galaway, 1977, 1980; Galaway and Hudson, 1978.) The result has been "a dramatic upsurge" in the use of restitution orders (ABA, 1981:17). Moreover, legislation has been introduced in many states and on the federal level to require the court to consider a restitution order in every case, or even to mandate a restitution order where the defendant is able to pay (ibid., 17–20; NOVA, 1989:13; Victim and Witness Protection Act of 1982, amending sec. 3580 of the U.S. Code). Restitution programs were also developed as a form of diversion, rendering the trial itself unnecessary. The objective here is similar, but in this case the process may, in obviating the need for a criminal trial, have additional objectives, calculated to bring benefits to all parties concerned.[5]

Other noncustodial alternatives may be of assistance to victims, notably community service orders, which may be directed to the victim's benefit rather than the community in general (Beha et al., 1977). Finally, another practice adopted in recent years has been to impose financial penalties or "surcharges" upon offenders, not for the benefit of their immediate victims but in order to finance victim-welfare programs, thereby lessening the need to resort to public funds for this purpose.

The Sentencing "Equation." Victim harm may be relevant at the sentencing stage not only in determining a disposition that will have immediate practical relevance (such as those considered under the previous heading) but also, in a symbolic sense, in determining what will be the "just" measure of punishment in the particular case.

Generally speaking, the definition of the offense under law reflects the gravity of the injury inflicted: murder is a more serious offense than aggravated battery, while a simple assault is less serious. However, from the second half of the 19th century onward, the prevailing view among criminologists was that a sentence should be individualized according to the needs of the offender, rather than "looking back" to the nature of the offense. Recently, the pendulum has swung again, toward a sentencing "tariff" based upon the gravity of the offense. Some would go further than the traditional legal categories and fix the sentence according to the precise degree of harm inflicted upon the victim (Wolfgang, 1982), resulting in a new form of individualization of the sentence but now individualized according to the victim's suffering. The trend in this direction is apparent in some of the emergent "sentencing guidelines" which specify the degree of victim harm among the aggravating circumstances that a court should consider in determining sentence, or among the grounds for deviating from the standardized norms (see chap. 3 of the federal sentencing guidelines; see also title 4 of the Crime Control Act of 1990).

The Parole Decision. Similar consideration may arise where a parole board retains the discretion—sometimes "guided" by published norms—to determine early release dates for prisoners. In addition to the consideration of the degree of harm inflicted on the victim, the board may also consider subsequent developments in the offender-victim relationship, including the adjustment of financial claims (e.g., the implementation of a restitution order) and future risks to the victim. A proposed variation of this, whether at the sentencing or at the parole stage, would be to strike a "bargain" with the offender whereby restitution was bartered for a reduction in time served (Hassin, 1979).

The President's Task Force on Victims of Crime recommended the abolition of parole, and this policy has been adopted by the federal and a number of state systems. Where preserved, however, it has been recommended that victim participation be permitted (Office of Justice Programs, 1986:34); many states have enacted appropriate legislation for this purpose (NOVA, 1989:12), and model legislation has been developed for both victim notification of and participation in parole hearings (NAAG/ABA:1986).

Victim Representation. It has been suggested that protection of the victims' interests requires the appointment of special advocates to plead their cause. Thus some states have experimented with the appointment of victim/witness coordinators or locally appointed advocates who would have the general function of assisting victims through the complexities of the criminal justice system (ABA, 1981:39).[6]

The question arises whether a victim advocate should not also have the right to represent the victim in the judicial proceedings themselves. So far this has generally been proposed only in a very narrow context, where the victim's conduct may itself be placed in question during the course of the proceedings (see the New York Legislature's proposal, ibid., 45). However, the question may legitimately be raised whether the victim should not have the right to be represented by counsel throughout all the stages of the criminal process—pretrial proceedings, plea bargaining, trial, sentencing, and parole—even though "both prosecutors and defense attorneys are likely to consider it as an unnecessary—and unwelcome—intrusion into the criminal justice process" (ibid., 44).

The personal participation of the victims in the trial might be expected to attract similar, or perhaps greater, criticism, yet the final report of the President's Task Force on Victims of Crime (1982) recommended that the victim be granted constitutional rights "to be present and to be heard at all critical stages of the judicial proceedings" (114), and a number of states have now adopted provisions of this nature.

Proposals Providing Alternatives to Traditional Criminal Justice Processes

Insofar as modification of traditional criminal justice procedures may not provide adequate solutions for the victim's needs, other approaches may be considered—namely, whether to replace or to supplement these procedures.

Private Prosecution. One way to ensure that the victim has a visible role in the criminal process is to enable him or her to prosecute the offender, rather than this function being fulfilled by the state's representative. The historic power of the private citizen to instigate a private prosecution is still maintained in a number of jurisdictions (McDonald, 1976a). Although controversial (Ward, 1972), it has strong historical roots (Emsley and Storch, 1993); indeed, it may be considered the "true" form of the adversary system (Sebba, 1982). It may be appropriate to consider how far a revival of this procedure would be consistent with the reemergence of the victim in the criminal process.

Civil Proceedings. The historic response to criticisms of the inadequacy of the criminal process to deal with the victim's needs was that this was a matter for the civil courts. Thus any reform of civil procedures that renders civil remedies more accessible to the victim must be considered in this context. A case in point is the growth of the small claims court. Another possibility is the adoption of the system available in some European countries whereby the victim may be "joined" as a civil party to the criminal process, such that both criminal and civil issues may be determined simultaneously. Various intermediary models of procedure may also be considered.[7]

Informal Modes of Dispute Settlement. In the light of the inaccessibility and unattractiveness of formal legal institutions of justice, it has become popular in recent times to develop alternative processes, such as mediation and arbitration (see also the discussion of "informalism" in the introduction). Generally, the emphasis is on reconciliation between the parties. These procedures are designed to bypass the established bureaucratic procedures and to resolve the dispute as informally as possible. It is claimed that whereas traditional legal processes, particularly the adversary system, are confined to dealing with a specified charge or claim, informal procedures may resolve the whole spectrum of problems existing between the parties of which the alleged wrongful act was merely a symptom. This type of approach inevitably gives rise to the merger of criminal and civil claims, such formal differentiation being foreign to the informal nature of the proceedings.

Unlike the first two proposals under the present heading—the revival or strengthening of private prosecution or of civil-law remedies—there has been extensive experimentation in recent years with informal modes of dispute resolution, and a vast literature has developed (Sander and Snyder, 1982; Sebba, forthcoming) that discusses the issues involved.

Amelioration of the Victim's Situation without Reference to the Criminal Process

Many reforms have been designed to improve the position of the victim of crime irrespective of the nature of the trial process (or its alternatives). Indeed, some of these programs may take effect even if the wrongdoer is never apprehended.

Criminal Injuries Compensation Boards. The establishment of state compensation boards has perhaps been the most widely heralded measure resulting from the recent revival of concern for the victim. Early victim advocates, notably Schafer ([1960] 1970), took the view that any remedies victims might seek from the offender were likely to be inadequate, and ultimately (or at least in the first instance) the burden of redress must fall upon the state. While the pioneering model for a victim compensation board was adopted in New Zealand in 1963 (as mentioned in the introduction), in recent years most of the states of the United States have adopted legislation of this type (see Bureau of Justice Statistics, 1984:5–8; NOVA, 1989:1–5), and Congress provided for federal support under the Victims of Crime Act, 1984. Unresolved issues remain, however, regarding the optimal scope of these programs and the criteria for admissibility, affecting such issues as minimum and maximum claims, the relationship between the parties, victim precipitation, and the types of losses to be covered. Moreover, there has been controversy regarding the very idea of state compensation (Meiners, 1978), as well as the appropriate mode of financing such programs (Thorvaldson and Krasnick, 1980). However, the tendency has been for continual expansion of these programs—partly in order to qualify for federal funding (NOVA, 1989:2; Office for Victims of Crime, 1994:26).

Crisis Intervention and Welfare Services. Services to the victim are, together with victim compensation, seen to be the main focus of victim-related reforms (de Liege, 1985; Roberts, 1990). In this analysis they will be discussed under the next heading, in the framework of "catch-all" remedies.

Insurance. It is well known that many property owners recoup the material losses suffered through crime, at least partially, by means of private insurance. One method of ameliorating the victim's situation would be to encourage this form of self-help, whether merely by the dissemination of information or by providing financial taxation incentives to property owners, insurance companies, employers, and so on. A federal insurance program has also been of assistance here (Lamborn, 1979). However, there has in recent years been a trend to limit the liability of insurance companies for compensation due from an insured tort-feasor on the grounds of an "insurance crisis" (NOVA, 1989:29).

Third-Party Liability. The fear of crime has resulted in an emphasis in recent years on crime prevention measures. While such measures are generally adopted for the purposes of self-protection, in some instances they may be necessary for the protection of others. There is now developing an area of litigation whereby persons victimized by crime bring claims for damage against individuals, corporations, or public bodies that are alleged to have been negligent in taking adequate measures to prevent the victimization (Carrington, 1977; Castillo et al., 1979; Carrington and Rapp, 1991). This may apply to landlords who have failed to secure premises, police departments that have provided inadequate protection, or psychiatric hospitals or parole boards that have released persons with a high risk of violence into the community, as well as to common carriers, employers, and educational institutions. A Victims Advocacy Institute was established primarily for the development of such remedies for crime victims.

A further extension of third-party liability would impose upon the "innocent bystander" a duty to provide assistance even where there was no special relationship with the offender.

Escrow. Following the notorious "Son-of-Sam" murders in New York, the defendant apparently capitalized on his notoriety by selling his story to the press. Most states have introduced "Son-of-Sam" or "notoriety-for-profit" laws to ensure that any such financial gains be attached for the benefit of the victims of the crime (Bureau of Justice Statistics, 1984:10; NOVA, 1989:16). Federal provisions were enacted for this purpose under the Victim and Witness Protection Act of 1982.

"Catch-All" Remedies

Victims' Bills of Rights. Some supporters of victim programs (such as NOVA) appeared to take the view that piecemeal achievements were unlikely to guarantee sufficient consideration for the victim. They proposed that a comprehensive "victim's bill of rights" be adopted. There is clearly an analogy here with the first ten amendments to the U.S. Constitution which are known collectively as the "Bill of Rights" and are seen to be protective mainly of the rights of the criminal suspect or defendant.

The rights incorporated in such a bill would normally overlap with the areas discussed under previous headings, some provisions dealing with victim treatment in the criminal process, others providing a guarantee of state compensation. In some respects, however, such bills would go further and provide for more symbolic and unspecific rights, such as the "right to dignity."

The Attorney General's Task Force on Violent Crime (1981), while supporting in principle the establishment of "Federal Standards for the Fair Treatment of Serious Crime," declined to use the nomenclature "victim's bill of rights," "out of concern that the public or the courts might construe [it] as the creation of a new cause of action." Their preferred objective was to establish a standard that "would serve as a model toward which all prosecutors' offices throughout the country could strive"—clearly a weaker principle than that advocated by NOVA. Such standards or guidelines have meanwhile been issued both by the attorney general and by the judiciary.

During the 1980s, however, most states enacted some form of bill of rights (NOVA, 1989:6–8). Unlike the original Bill of Rights, such enactments were mostly at the simple legislative level. However, in 1982 California's constitution was amended by a citizens' initiative to incorporate a victim's bill of rights. Rhode Island, Florida, and Michigan adopted constitutional amendments in 1986–88, and by the end of 1994, 16 more states had followed suit (National Victim Center, 1994).

In 1990 Congress passed the Victims' Rights and Restitution Act of 1990 (as part of the Crime Control Act), which incorporated a list of victim rights and provision for their implementation. The list includes the right to be treated with fairness and "respect for the victim's dignity and privacy"; the right to reasonable protection from the accused; the right to notification of court proceedings; the right in principle to be present at court proceedings; the right to confer with the government attorney; the right to restitution; and the right to information about conviction, sentence, and release of the offender. The erstwhile fears of the Attorney General's Task Force were met by an express provision that no cause of action would arise as the result of the failure to accord the rights specified.

It is interesting to note, however, that while the list of rights granted to victims under the federal system by the above legislation is not expressly referred to as a "bill of rights," the same enactment incorporates a section entitled "Sense of Congress with Respect to Victims of Crime," whereby individual states were encouraged to "make every effort to adopt the following goals of the Victims of Crime *Bill of Rights*" (emphasis added). Moreover, the list of rights which follows, while similar to that introduced into the federal system under the earlier section, is nevertheless wider in scope. In particular, it includes a "statutorily designated advisory role" for the victim with regard to both prosecutorial and early release decisions. It concludes with the sweeping exhortation that "the victim of crime should never be forced to endure again the emotional and physical consequences of the original crime."

Finally, it may be observed that the concept of a victim's bill of rights has derived support from the adoption of the UN Declaration of Basic Principles of Justice for the Victims of Crime and Abuse of Power, which may be perceived as endowing victim rights with an elevated, universalist, or quasi-constitutional status.

Victim/Witness Assistance. While a somewhat more specific concept than the previous heading, victim/witness assistance tends to be used as an all-embracing label that may entail a diffusion of programs or services, some directed at witnesses (including victims who are witnesses), others designed to assist victims per se. In this category reference may be made to the numerous crisis intervention programs (developed in particular for sexual assault victims).

Victim/witness programs have multiplied in recent years. A review published in 1980 identified 280 (Cronin and Bourque, 1980), but by 1990 there were an estimated 5,000 (Skogan et al., 1990). These programs are designed to keep victims and witnesses informed about the developments taking place in the cases in which they are involved, and to achieve such objectives as a reduction in waiting time, the prevention of intimidation by defendants, the provision of specially trained personnel to deal with victim/witness problems, and the obtaining of financial compensation for time spent in appearances before the police and the courts. Some provide crisis intervention and other assistance before the victim's involvement with official criminal justice agencies. (A brochure published by Victim Services in New York City—a pioneer in the field—lists 30 programs or services provided by the agency, with a budget of $19 million and 500 employees, in addition to volunteers.)

By 1988, provision had been made by 33 states for funding general victim or victim/witness services, and by 48 states for domestic violence services (NOVA, 1989:5); federal support for such programs was authorized by Congress under the Victims of Crime Act of 1984 and extended in 1988 and 1992 (Office for Victims of Crime, 1994:4).

The above attempt at a classification of the proposed remedies constitutes only a very preliminary stage in the task of conceptualizing and evaluating the contribution or potential contribution of these reforms. For a more meaningful evaluation to be undertaken, criteria must be developed whereby the innovations may be judged. An attempt to develop such criteria will be undertaken in part 2 of this study. However, evaluation of the innovative proposals is also dependent upon the fulfillment of an additional precondition, namely, some familiarity with the system prevailing before the initiation of the reforms, from the point of view of the victim's role in that system. Yet while "neglect of the victim" has become a universally accepted slogan, documentation has been surprisingly sparse. Thus the reformist literature—and legislation—has been hasty in proposing solutions to problems, the nature of which have been only superficially studied, with conclusions generally reached on an impressionistic basis. It will be the task of the next chapter to attempt to fill this gap in the literature.

2

The Victim's Traditional Role in the Criminal Justice System

As may be evident from the introduction, it has in recent years become accepted dogma, almost a truism, that the contemporary criminal justice system has dealt with the victim harshly and unfairly—at least before the current innovations. This view is reflected in the concept of "secondary victimization" (*Canadian Federal-Provincial Task Force*, 1983:60; Mawby and Walklate, 1994:33), a term designated to express the view that the initial victimization at the hands of the offender may be followed by further victimization on the part of society, particularly in the context of the functioning of the criminal justice system.[1]

This message has been delivered in a number of ways. Some writers have emphasized the phenomenology and the pathology of victimization: "The traumatic effects of a violent crime are multiplied by neglect, lack of immediate resources, and the failure of such support systems as the courts, the police, the legal profession" (Reiff, 1979:75). "In this state of heightened vulnerability, [the victims] must cope not only with their everyday lives but also with a whole new set of problems created by the victimization" (Bard and Sangrey, 1979:106). Sociolegal writers, on the other hand, have observed the "alienation" and the "distinctly secondary role" (Goldstein, 1982:516–19) played by the victim in the criminal justice process, and have noted the historical decline of the victim's role in this process (Schafer, 1968; McDonald, 1976b; Sebba, 1982; Joutsen, 1987: chap. 2). Finally, sociologists and political scientists have shown how the organizational and bureaucratic character of the criminal justice system inevitably leads to a sacrifice of—or at least the placing of a low priority on—the interests of the victim (Ziegenhagen, 1977; Hagan, 1980; Elias, 1986).[2] Moreover, the criticism is not necessarily limited to the institutions of criminal justice as such. Some writers have pointed to the limited role of extra-legal agencies, including mental health programs, in coming to the assistance of the victim (Salasin, 1981:15; Reynolds and Blyth, 1976; Friedman et al., 1982).

Accepted dogma, however, does not always correspond with empirical fact. Indeed, two of the earliest surveys endeavoring to investigate the role of the victim in the criminal justice system expressed strong reservations as to the accuracy of such generalizations about the victim's exclusion from, and dissatisfaction with, the system (Hall, 1975:981, n. 263; Knudten et al., 1976). It may also be asked whether disregard of the victim, insofar as it takes place, has been a universal phenomenon, or whether its incidence varies from jurisdiction to jurisdiction, in the way that "legal cultures" are said to vary (Ehrmann, 1976).

Another factor to consider is whether negative occurrences related to victims may be connected with particular types of offense. As noted above, much attention has been devoted by feminists to the plight of rape victims and battered women, but these may not necessarily be representative of crime victims generally. Indeed, one study (Smith, 1983) has focused upon possible differences in the treatment of victims of offenses committed by offenders who were known to them as compared with victims of offenses committed by strangers.

Until fairly recently, there have been very few empirical studies of the criminal justice system that examined the role of the victim. Most studies tended to focus on the police and to a lesser extent on the prosecution, the judicial sentencing function, and other criminal justice agencies. Thus, much of the more general criticism relating to the predicament of victims has been of an impressionistic nature, based upon anecdotes or individual cases. Fortunately, however, revival of interest in the victim has spawned a number of empirical studies from which a certain amount of hard data may be derived regarding interactions of criminal justice agencies with victims. Other research focuses on victim decision making, and in particular on the decision to complain to the police (see Gottfredson and Gottfredson, 1988: chap. 2; Greenberg and Ruback, 1992).

A number of these studies are associated with the Victim Services Agency and the Vera Foundation in New York (see, e.g., Davis, Russell, and Kunreuther, 1980; Connick and Davis, 1981; Friedman et al., 1982), while other relevant recent studies have been conducted by the Institute of Social Analysis (Smith, 1983) and INSLAW (Hernon and Forst, 1983). Earlier studies of relevance include those reported by Hall (1975), Knudten et al. (1976), and Ziegenhagen (1976). Some studies are confined to a particular type of victim, such as the victim of rape (Holmstrom and Burgess, 1978). Two of the most comprehensive studies have been conducted outside the United States but in closely comparable legal systems (Hagan, 1980, in Canada; Shapland et al., 1981, in England). Finally, some of the nonvictim-oriented research that has focused on the police, the courts, or other agencies has alluded directly or indirectly to victim-related factors, such as the relevance of the seriousness of the injury to the decision making of the agency in question (see below).

The present chapter endeavors to summarize the evidence emerging from this literature relating to the role of the victim in the criminal justice system. It will deal with the following topics: (1) the victim and the police, (2) the victim and the prosecution, (3) the victim and the trial, (4) the victim and the jury, (5) the victim and the sentencing judge, and (6) other stages in the criminal justice system. Additional sections will deal with traditional legal remedies available to overcome the limitations of the criminal justice system and will discuss the role of certain agencies operating outside the system. Regarding the victim's relationship with each of the main decision-making bodies in the criminal justice system (police, prosecution, court) particular attention will be paid to the following issues: (1) the nature and frequency of the victim's contact with that agency; the degree to which the agency takes into account (2) victim harm and (3) other victim characteristics; (4) the extent to which the victim's views are taken into consideration by that agency; and (5) the extent to which the victim is kept informed about its decisions.

It should be noted that this chapter is not directly concerned with victim attitudes toward the criminal justice system, which forms the subject matter of chapter 5. The purpose here is rather to present an objective descriptive analysis of the victim's role in the system. Further, as noted, the emphasis is on the victim's interaction with formal criminal justice agencies rather than on the preliminary decision as to the submission of a complaint. Finally, the analysis here relates to the victim's role in the "traditional" criminal justice system. This chapter does not attempt to assess the possible effect on the victim's role of various innovations that may be intended to ameliorate this role, which will be considered in part 3 of this study. It focuses on the system *as it operated prior to these innovations.* It may be noted that, in addition to the evaluation research specifically applied to existing criminal justice institutions, there has also developed a body of experimental research in social psychology that may also be relevant to our understanding of prevailing concepts of justice. Three theories of particular interest in the present context are (1) attribution theory, (2) the "just-world" theory, and (3) equity theory. An attempt to clarify these concepts will be made in the appendix. While other psychological approaches, particularly in the realm of *procedural* justice, will be considered subsequently, the three theories alluded to here appear to be particularly relevant to our understanding of certain aspects of the traditional decision-making processes in the criminal justice system—and in particular to perceptions of the victim (to be considered further in chap. 5). Some reference will consequently be made to these theories in the course of this chapter.

The Victim and the Police

Research findings indicate that in a very real sense the victims rather than the police are the "gatekeepers" of the criminal justice system, for most offenses would not be known about were it not for initiatives taken by victims. Thus, Black (1980), in his study of 5,713 incidents, found that "only 13% of the incidents came to police attention without the assistance of citizens" (88). The police, for the most part, tend to fulfill a "reactive" rather than a "proactive" function in dealing with crime. Hindelang and Gottfredson (1976) point out that since "decisions made at the earliest point in the system have the greatest potential for affecting the system . . . it seems more appropriate to conceive of the victim, rather than the police, as the initial decision maker" (76).

Since the police force is the criminal justice agency with which the victim will normally have the first—and often the only—contact,[3] its functioning and treatment of the victim may be expected to have particular importance. It is at this point that the victim transfers his "gatekeeping" function to the representatives of the state.

Contacts. The initial contact between victim and police is dependent on two decisions that must be made by the victim, before his or her initial contact with the system. First, there must have arisen a situation that the victim has defined as the commission of a crime (see Sparks, 1982:14; Burt, 1983). Second, the victim must have reached a decision to report the offense to the police.

While studies of the police (e.g., Piliavin and Briar, 1964; LaFave, 1965) have for many years shown how the police exercise discretion in reaching a decision whether to define a citizen's conduct as a criminal act by performing an arrest and instigating an investigation (McCabe and Sutcliffe, 1978), it has been clearly shown that victims, too, exercise a similar discretion. The automatic reporting of offenses is neither the legal norm—there is generally no sanction for nonreporting—nor the behavioral norm. For victim surveys have shown that the majority of acts defined as offenses are not reported by the victims to the police (Sparks, 1982:98; Greenberg and Ruback, 1992:8).

The reasons for nonreporting, and the degree to which these reasons are connected with attitudes to the criminal justice system in general or the police in particular, will be considered in chapter 5. In the context of this chapter the point of emphasis is the sudden metamorphosis in the victim's role. In conveying to the police the information regarding the commission of the offense, the victim concomitantly transfers to them the role of decision maker, or gatekeeper, who determines whether or not a criminal process may ensue. It is perhaps this metamorphosis that serves to highlight the limitations on the victim's role from this moment onward—as illustrated by the very fact that further contacts between the victim and the criminal justice agencies generally occur only on the initiative of these agencies.

While there appears to be no study dealing specifically and comprehensively with the initial contact between the victim and the police, some information is now available on the number of contacts that take place in the course of an investigation and the nature of these contacts.

The leading English survey notes that the police force is the agency with which the victims are likely to have the largest number of contacts. Notification of the offense is followed by the making of statements, participation in photographic and identification procedures, and so on (Shapland et al., 1985: chap. 3). However, Hernon and Forst (1983) reported on the basis of their American survey[4] that the modal number of contacts was only one or two for all crime types, although the estimated mean number of contacts ranged from 3.7 contacts for burglary to 9.5 for homicide[5] (the victim in this case being the family of the deceased). Moreover, in the sites surveyed in their study, the mean, but not the modal, number of contacts with prosecutors tended to be as great, and sometimes greater. Thus the preeminence of police over prosecutors in this respect noted by Shapland in England may not apply in the United States.

The purpose or content of these contacts as reported in the American study referred to were generally connected with the evidence or the facts of the case. These accounted for between 61% (police estimate) and 68% (victim estimate) of the conversation time spent, as compared with the 14%–15% of the conversation time that was devoted to "victim's problems and concerns," the remainder being concerned primarily with "court matters" (Hernon and Forst, 1983).

Relevance of Victim Harm. A large number of studies of police decision making have been published. Many of these were designed to determine the weighting, if any, attributable to such variables as race and socioeconomic status of the suspected offender. Such studies usually control for type or seriousness of offense, which are generally assumed to be significant. Offense seriousness, in turn, may be expected to reflect, or even be measured by, the amount of harm inflicted upon the victim, a topic to be considered below in the context of the sentence of the court.

At the same time, the weight to be attributed to offense seriousness in general, and to victim harm in particular, may depend on the orientation of the decision maker, as well as on the normative and bureaucratic framework within which he or she is operating. Thus when police adhere to a "law enforcement" philosophy (cf. Wilson, 1978), or when a "deterrent" approach seems appropriate in view of the characteristics of the suspect (Landau, 1978), victim harm may be expected to assume greater importance than when a welfare or "labeling" philosophy has been adopted.

The evidence available from studies specifically concerned with the effect of victim harm on criminal-justice decision making is, indeed, not unequivocal. Hernon and Forst (1983) found that 48% of the police officers interviewed in their study said that they did not consider victim harm in their decisions to arrest, but some expressed the view that it would affect the decision to investigate the case in the first place. Moreover, when considering a number of hypothetical cases ("scenarios"), police tended to regard the degree of physical injury suffered by the victim, indicated by his or her having been hospitalized for at least 10 days, as relevant to the likelihood that the case would be accepted for prosecution.[6] This applied both to knife assaults and to sexual assaults, but not to robbery. However, the fact that the victim needed psychological counseling or had suffered a property loss of at least $1,000, did not significantly affect their views.

A study by Bynum et al. (1982) of "official records of a medium-sized midwestern police department" indicated a direct correlation between the amount of property loss inflicted in the course of property offenses and the amount of investigative effort applied.[7] However, for personal offenses the degree of personal injury was not significantly correlated with this variable, nor were either of these measures of harm (property loss or personal injury) significant in the multivariate analysis. This led the authors to suggest that "the routine approach to processing cases may override any influence of victim characteristics." Similarly, a recent British study based on assault victims located at a hospital found "almost a random relationship between *seriousness*, as we defined it, and the reporting, investigation, and prosecution of assault" (Cretney and Davis, 1995: 130). Moreover, Black (1980) found that arrest rates were only moderately higher for felonies (58%) than for misdemeanors (44%) (90). He nevertheless concluded that "the probability of arrest is higher in legally serious crime situations than in those of a relatively minor nature" (103).

Finally, in a study of decision making by the Philadelphia police, Hohenstein (1969) found that the seriousness of the offense, as measured by the Sellin-Wolfgang scale, was one of the three most important factors determining whether the police decided to make an arrest.[8]

Relevance of Other Victim Characteristics. Some studies have indicated that police decision making—in particular the decision to arrest—is influenced not only by the sociodemographic characteristics and demeanor of the suspect (cf. Piliavin and Briar, 1964) but also by similar variables relating to the victim. Bynum et al. (1982), who were concerned not with arrests but with the intensity of the investigation, found some slight support for this hypothesis. For personal offenses, "victim-employment status" had a significant zero-order correlation with the dependent variable, but this disappeared in the multivariate analysis.[9] However, for burglary offenses the victim's income bracket emerged as a significant variable in the multivariate analysis. Race of the victim did not emerge as a significant variable in this study but has been found in some studies to be a relevant factor (Elias, 1986:143).

Gender and age of the victim are sometimes thought to be relevant variables in police decision making, perhaps on the basis of the just-world theory which renders "defenseless citizens," that is, females and the elderly, more deserving of police support (Bynum et al., 1982:303). In the latter study, however, the findings in this respect were generally neither consistent nor significant; but for personal offenses, cases in which victims were under 21 or over 45 were more likely to result in intensive investigation.

Somewhat mixed findings also emerged in this respect from the INSLAW study (Hernon and Forst, 1983). Police respondents considered that the sex of the victim would be relevant to the decision to prosecute only in the case of armed robbery, where the probability of prosecution was thought to be lower for female victims. Age of the victim was perceived as relevant in cases of robbery and sexual assault, but neither age nor sex were perceived as relevant to the prosecution decision in cases of burglary, assault with a knife, or homicide.[10]

Finally, many studies have indicated that the existence of a prior relationship between victim and suspect reduces the probability of a formal action on the part of the police (Reiss, 1971; Black, 1980).[11] LaFave (1965), whose study of arrest practices conducted on behalf of the American Bar Foundation was based upon a survey of practices in three states, observed that where the parties concerned "are in a continuing legitimate relationship with each other, such as neighbors, landlord and tenant or parties to a contract," the police generally feel that "such disputes are principally private in nature and that as long as the conduct is not serious, enforcement resources need not be diverted to it" (119). This attitude was adopted more forcefully where a "domestic dispute" was concerned. LaFave cited the Detroit police manual of 1955 exhorting the police to "recognize the sanctity of the home and endeavor diplomatically to quell the disturbance and create peace without making an arrest" (ibid., 121).

Police respondents in the INSLAW study also believed that in physical assault cases prosecution would be more likely where the parties were strangers. Further, where "nonstranger" cases were processed by the police, there was some indication that the type of offense may be downgraded.[12] However, the question of police response in nonstranger cases—and in particular domestic violence cases—has been the subject of considerable controversy in recent years owing to dissatisfaction on the part of feminist groups and their sympathizers with the effective "decriminalization" of domestic violence. Practices may have been changing in this area even before the widespread legislative reforms that have been adopted in recent years (Zalman, 1991).

Relevance of Victims' Views. The police force is generally perceived in the literature as a bureaucratic institution whose decision making will be influenced by institutional norms and requirements, exercised in accordance with professional judgment. This view does not seem to allow much scope for sensitivity to the views expressed by the complaining citizen (Elias, 1986:142). Data supporting this hypothesis are cited by Ziegenhagen (1977), who points out, drawing from the survey data collected by Ennis in 1967, that the police did not respond to 23% of calls on the part of citizens, and that in a quarter of the cases in which they did respond, the matter was not regarded by the police as a crime.

However, many studies of police decision making indicate that, even before the recent victim-related reforms, the victim's views have carried considerable weight in the process. Thus Black (1980:93) found that in cases in which the victim expressed a desire for an arrest, an arrest was made in 72% of the felony cases and 87% of the misdemeanors, whereas where the victim wished no arrest to be made the respective percentages were 9% and 14%.[13] The author differentiates between incidents where the police observed the offenses and other cases, and concludes: "Plainly the complainant's preference is a more powerful situational factor than evidence, although the two operate jointly" (ibid.). LaFave (1965) observes that "in many cases involving minor offenses, police feel that prosecution should be undertaken only if this is the desire of the victim" (49). Hohenstein (1969), in the study referred to above of police dispositions regarding juveniles in Philadelphia, concludes that "the attitude of the victim was the primary factor influencing the decision" (149; see also Lundman et al., 1978).

The findings of Hernon and Forst (1983) were less positive in this respect. While 58% of the victims reported at least some influence in the handling of their cases, 65% of the police respondents were of the opinion that the victim was "not involved at all." Forty-eight percent thought that he or she should be more involved. Moreover, "involvement" may be a very limited phenomenon, having been defined in this study as "nonbinding involvement—the victim is consulted and may express an opinion, but the decision maker is not required to follow the victim's wishes." Similarly, some ambiguity and mutuality in police-victim decision making were observed by Cretney and Davis (1995:chap. 4) in their British study.

Cases in which there was a prior relationship between the suspect and the victim present a special problem in this context. It has been noted that the police often view such cases as "private disputes" (LaFave, 1965; see also Parnas, 1967; Smith, 1983:4). This may lead to a reluctance on their part to process the complaint as a criminal case (McLeod, 1983:395–98). However, it may also lead the police to take special note of the victim's views when deciding how to proceed.[14] Police reluctance to proceed with these cases is based partly on their anticipation that the victim will subsequently change his or her mind and attempt to withdraw the complaint (LaFave, 1965:120).

Smith (1983) studied two samples of nonstranger violence, one resulting in court adjudication, the other in a mediation process. She found that while the police arrested the suspect in 49% and 27% of the respective samples, "between 81% and 94% of the complainants would have wanted an arrest to be carried out" (Smith, 1983:30). When compared with Black's data cited above, which indicates that victims' views were generally taken into account, these findings seemed to lend some support to the first of the two hypotheses posited here, namely, that there was a greater reluctance on the part of the police to accede to the victim's wishes in prior-relationship cases.

Victims' Information. One characteristic of the victim's relationship with the police, as with other criminal justice agencies, is the unidirectional flow of information. The victim is called upon to supply all the information in his or her possession, but the police have traditionally been under no duty to reciprocate, even to the extent of keeping the victim informed about the degree of progress made in the investigation, about whether or not the suspect has been arrested or released on bail, about the filing of charges, and so on. Thus the English study referred to above found that victims' knowledge about their cases was "both scanty and rather patchy" (Shapland et al., 1985:49). Similar findings emerged from the American study conducted by Hernon and Forst (1983).[15]

The Victim and the Prosecution

Although most prosecutions are generated as a result of an act perpetrated against an individual (or corporate) victim, the public prosecutor assumes the role of representative of society as a whole. Insofar as the prosecutor is concerned with the victim's interests, this derives either from his or her recognition that it was the victim's complaint which gave rise to the file being considered, or from more practical concerns regarding the victim's testimony, on which the possibility of a successful prosecution may rest. However, while "prosecutors have been in the forefront of the victims' rights movement, and many are sensitive to victims' interests" (Gittler, 1984:144), there may be institutional pressures militating against consideration of victims' interests on the part of prosecutors. The available data on the prosecution's relationship to the victim will now be reviewed.

Contacts. "Prosecutors work, over a period of time, with police officers, defense attorneys, and judges, and develop continuing relationships with such individuals. In contrast, the prosecutor's contact with any one victim is relatively brief and limited" (ibid.).

The modal response for the estimated number of contacts with the prosecutor for victims of robbery, burglary, and assault in the Hernon and Forst study was one or none.[16] The mean number of contacts, however, ranged from 2.3 to 3.0 for burglary to 10.9 to 11.1 for homicide (Hernon and Forst, 1983:24–27). These figures do not differ substantially from the estimated number of contacts with the police. As to the topic of conversation, "evidence, facts of the case" accounted here for between 51% (victim's estimate) to 55% (prosecutor's estimate) of the conversation time—somewhat less than for the police-victim contacts. However, the difference is accounted for by a greater attention to "court matters" (35% in the victim's estimate, 26% in the prosecutor's), while the proportion of the conversation time devoted to "victim's problems and concerns" was very similar here (13% in the victim's view, 17% in the prosecutor's) as compared with 14%–15% of the police-victim contacts.

Relevance of Victim Harm. The somewhat limited evidence available seems to indicate, surprisingly, that the amount of harm inflicted on the victim may not have played an important role in the decision to prosecute. Hernon and Forst (1983) found that prosecutors did not perceive the fact that the offense resulted in the loss of at least $1,000 worth of property, or that the victim needed psychological counseling, as relevant to the prosecution decision for any of the following five offenses considered: homicide, sexual assault, aggravated assault, robbery, and burglary. Moreover, the fact that the victim had to be hospitalized for at least 10 days affected only prosecutions for sexual assault. However, these negative findings (supported also by Fisher, 1984) may have been a function of the arbitrary choice of variables;[17] perhaps correlations between prosecution decision making and physical injury would have been significant. Further, the authors of this study found that there was a large amount of variance among respondents. This, in a relatively small sample, would tend to reduce the significance of the other variables.

Further evidence of the limited significance of victim harm in prosecutorial decision making was found in the study conducted by Stanko (1981–82). Her study, conducted in New York County's prosecutor's offices in 1975 and 1976, concluded that a critical factor in the screening decision with regard to serious felonies[18] was the prosecutor's prediction of the court (judge and jury) reaction to the victim's evidence—or what the author termed the victim's "stereotypical credibility" (see below). "The result may be that the victim's quest for justice is often determined more by stereotypes than by actual harm rendered against them by assailants" (238).

Relevance of Other Victim Characteristics. Hernon and Forst (1983) found that sex, age, and prior relationship were generally perceived by prosecutors as not relevant to the prosecution decision, with the exception that for knife assault, prosecution was more likely where the suspect was a stranger, and for sexual assault where the victim was over 65 years old. Stanko (1981–82), as noted, found that prosecutors were apparently influenced by factors that they believed would influence judges and juries (but perhaps were also consistent with their own philosophies, see p. 238): "A pleasant appearance, residence in a good neighborhood, a respectable job or occupation, lack of nervous mannerisms, and an ability to articulate clearly, are decided advantages. Inferences that a victim might be a prostitute or pimp, a homosexual, or an alcoholic, on the other hand, may seriously damage a victim's credibility" (230).

Similarly, Williams (1976), in her study of 5,042 alleged violent crimes brought before the District of Columbia prosecutors in 1973, hypothesized that prosecutors would be influenced by the extent to which the victim appeared to be an innocent and conforming citizen, taking note of such factors as the victim's contributory responsibility for the commission of the offense and his or her prior relationship with the suspect. The victim's employment and degree of cooperation were also hypothesized to influence the decision to prosecute. The author found that these hypotheses were partially validated, in particular that cases of "perceived provocation or participation were more likely to be 'no-papered' " (Williams, 1976:205). The author concluded that the prosecutor, more than the court, took victim characteristics into consideration in the decision-making process, "perhaps in anticipation of how the judge and jury will perceive the victim" (207). This might explain the findings of another researcher that the prosecution in South Carolina was less likely to seek the death penalty when the victim was black (Paternoster, 1984).

Smith (1983), in her study of nonstranger violence, reviewed the findings of the studies conducted in New York City by the Vera Institute and the Victim Services Agency, and concludes: "The findings of these studies suggest that prosecutors often believe (a) that, in general, complainants who know the defendant often make uncooperative witnesses, (b) that defendants in relationship cases should normally be prosecuted only if the complainant demands it, and (c) that defendants in relationship cases, when prosecuted, do not merit as severe a punishment as defendants convicted of victimizing a stranger" (4). Williams (1976) also found that "cases appeared to be dropped if they involved a family relationship and pursued if the victim and defendants were strangers" (206).

Relevance of Victims' Views. Since the prosecutor's initial "contact" with the victim is generally in the form of a file conveyed by the police, it might be anticipated that such depersonalization would limit the influence of the victim's views on the progress of the case. Moreover, since the prosecutor is concerned with processing large numbers of files with a maximum amount of efficiency in a minimum amount of time, his or her main reference groups for this purpose are inevitably defense counsel and the courts, with whom the processing must be negotiated.[19] Thus "there is simply little that compels prosecutors to seek and consider the opinions of complainants." Indeed, it is "functional to distance them from the decision making process" (Davis, Russell, and Kunreuther, 1980:58, 59).

Nor do ideological considerations necessarily weigh in favor of prosecutors' taking into account the views of victims. Prosecutors perform a public function and may not necessarily identify with the victims whose injuries led to the state's involvement. Indeed, English bar etiquette expressly prohibits contacts between prosecuting barrister and complaining witness before the giving of evidence (Shapland et al., 1985:68–69).[20] American prosecutors, while not subject to such restrictions, were reported to have taken steps to neutralize the potential impact of the victims' views on the court proceedings (McDonald, 1977). Moreover, they were thought to have been particularly suspicious of victims who appeared to be using the criminal justice system to be furthering their own "private disputes" in such matters as check forgery and domestic disputes (McDonald 1976a; and see Hall, 1975:950, n. 97). However, even before the recent developments in this area, the American Bar Association Standards specified that prosecutors should take into account victim attitudes and sentiments (McDonald, 1982).

Whether they were influenced by the American Bar Association Standards or not, the limited data available seem to indicate a somewhat higher level of victim input into the prosecutors' decision making than seems to have been generally thought (cf. Miller, 1969; Hall, 1975). The prosecutors themselves, at least, were of the opinion, according to the INSLAW study, that victims were involved in the criminal justice system, with 59% taking the view that the victim is "somewhat" involved, and 20% responding that he or she is involved "a great deal" (Hernon and Forst, 1983). Whether, when considering the victim's involvement in the criminal justice system, respondents had in mind the prosecution stages is an open question. Another study conducted by INSLAW (Buchner et al., 1983, 1984) found that while most prosecutors stated that their decisions were influenced by the victim's needs, at only one of three sites surveyed did they consult victims before negotiating a plea bargain in more than 50% of the cases. Similar unevenness was found in a survey conducted by Georgetown University of six jurisdictions in which 74% of prosecutors responded that the victim's views were taken into consideration before a plea bargain was concluded (McDonald, 1982). In a simulation study reported in the same paper, only 41% of the sample of prosecutors selected the "Victim Attitude" card before making a decision on a plea bargain. Moreover, among Elias's sample (1983) of 342 victims of violence in Brooklyn and Newark, only 12% indicated that they had been consulted by the prosecutor. Of these, approximately one-half felt that their views had been adopted (108).

The low consultation rate reported in Elias's study is consistent with the criticisms of victims' rights advocates, but not with the responses of prosecutors presented above. It may be that there are cases in which prosecutors feel that they have formed an impression of the victim's attitude, yet the victim feels he or she has not been consulted.

The degree of input on the part of the victim may be connected with the type of case. Thus McDonald (1976a) found that prosecutors frequently consult the victim in serious cases. Hall, on the other hand, found from his Tennessee survey that while in serious cases (such as homicide) "the adamant victim could overcome the prosecutor's reluctance to charge" (1975:948),[21] in nonserious cases it was the reluctant victim's desire not to prosecute that was likely to be honored by the prosecutor (951). Further, Davis et al. (1980) found that in nonstranger cases prosecutors were reluctant to proceed "without a clear expression of interest from the complainant" (see also Smith, 1983).

Victims' Information. The frequency of contacts between prosecutor and victim and the topics of these contacts do not indicate much attempt on the part of prosecutors to keep the victim informed. Kress (1976) alluded specifically to the prosecutor's "cavalier attitude" and failure to keep the victim informed (10). However, Connick and Davis (1981) noted, on the basis of a small-sample study in New York City, that where the victim and offender were personally acquainted, considerably more effort was taken in this respect; in 42% of these cases the victim received explanations as compared with only 11% of the stranger cases (16).

The Victim and the Trial

The problems encountered by victims in their capacity as witnesses in the criminal trial are by now widely recognized, as evidenced by the rapid growth of victim/witness programs and related legislation (see below, part

3). However, there have been only a few empirical studies concerned specifically with witness-related problems. Notable examples are Cannavale and Falcon's (1976) study of witness cooperation, and the Vera Foundation's study of the role of the complaining witness in an urban criminal court (Davis, Russell, and Kunreuther, 1980). Reference may also be made to a seminal article by Ash (1972). However, some of the studies referred to earlier that focus on the experiences and attitudes of victims in the criminal justice system, such as the Holmstrom and Burgess (1978) rape study, the study by Elias (1983) of victims of violent crimes, and the English study by Shapland et al. (1985), included sections dealing with this stage of the criminal process. Another pioneering study specifically differentiated between the experiences and attitudes of victim/witnesses and witnesses who had not been victims (Knudten et al., 1976). There has also been a small amount of research relating specifically to the courtroom experiences of victims, notably in Britain (see, e.g., McBarnet, 1976; and the recent in-depth study by Rock, 1993).

The generally neglectful attitude toward the victim at this stage of the criminal process was summarized by Davis et al. (1980) as follows: "No-one seems to have the time or the interest to find out what he wants, nor to make an effort to let him know what is happening, or why" (64). Citing the earlier work of Ash, the authors note that the result of this situation for the victim is an experience that is "dreary, time-wasting, depressing, confusing, frustrating, numbing and seemingly endless." (See also Shapland et al., 1985:62–63; McDonald, 1977.) Among the specific complaints alluded to by Davis et al. were *(a)* trial delays; *(b)* failure to keep victims informed; *(c)* inappropriate physical accommodation in the waiting room and the courtroom, often involving undue proximity to the defendant and his or her supporters; *(d)* victimization by the defendant and/or his or her supporters; *(e)* loss of time; *(f)* expenses not compensated for; *(g)* delay in returning property required as evidence, and damage to such property.

A different type of criticism relates to the nature of the adversary proceedings in the courtroom. Much of the literature on this topic has been connected with proceedings at rape trials and the cross-examination of women victims (Berger, 1977; Adler, 1987). The defense strategy of "blaming the victim" (Holmstrom and Burgess, 1978:212) is often considered a particularly oppressive characteristic of the adversary system. Moreover, the "degradation" inherent in the course of cross-examination, such as cutting into answers and using vilifying techniques (Shapland et al., 1985:65–66; Rock, 1993:34), is not restricted to rape victims (McBarnet, 1976:7). Prosecutorial management strategies may be even more unsettling

(Shapland et al., 1985:67). However, while most of the writers in the victim-oriented literature seem to be in agreement on the existence of these problems, it is not clear how far these techniques have a destructive effect on the victim/witness. Shapland's study found that "victims . . . expected some problem in being able to tell their story and in being able to convey their idea of their identity as victims. They took active steps to accomplish this, mostly to their own satisfaction" (ibid.). Moreover, McBarnet (1976:14) suggests that a "morally indignant and highly involved victim" may even adopt an active, aggressive role.

The lack of consideration for the victim/witness at this stage, as at other stages of the criminal justice system, seems to have stemmed primarily from a combination of two factors. The first factor, which will be considered further in chapter 12, is the absence of any legal or conceptual role for the victim at these stages. Although he or she is the prime mover in the process that has been set in motion, legally the victim's role in court has been merely that of a witness (Forer, 1980). The second factor derives from the bureaucratic needs and interests of the institutionalized agencies (judge, prosecutor, and defense counsel) which control the process. For if students of the court system such as Blumberg (1979) and Feeley (1979) have pointed out how the interests of the defendant, who has a recognized role in the process, tend to become submerged by bureaucratic considerations, how much more true is this of the victim, who until now has had no recognized role. In most cases there would be a "deal" (plea bargain), to which the victim would not be a party; in other cases, the indignity of the courtroom experience described above.

The Victim and the Jury

Theoretically, there is little opportunity for juries, in the course of their decision making, to take into consideration victim-related factors. For, unlike the other agencies reviewed in this chapter, the jury is not invested with discretionary powers. Except in the relatively rare—albeit significant—cases in which the jury has a sentencing function, its official function is to determine whether the legal requirements of the defendant's guilt have been established and to convict or acquit accordingly. In the majority of cases the conduct of the victim will not formally affect this verdict but will be relevant only as an aggravating or mitigating factor in determining the sentence. To this rule there are some exceptions: the most notable case in which victim conduct will be legally relevant to the verdict involves the issue of consent in rape. Consent, of course, would be a valid defense to many other charges, such as theft and trespass, but is rarely an issue in such cases. The concept of provocation has only limited recognition in criminal law, while "victim precipitation" and contributory negligence are generally considered irrelevant to issues of criminal responsibility (see Gobert, 1977; Wolfgang, 1985.)

However, the research conducted by Kalven and Zeisel (1966) and their colleagues—the so-called Chicago Jury Project—established that juries are not guided solely by the official legal norms. Where they feel that the conviction of a defendant would be unjust, even if the elements of the offense have been proven, they will register an acquittal. This is known as "jury equity." The victim's conduct could clearly provoke such a verdict, if the jury were to feel that he or she was in some way blameworthy and that consequently it would be unfair to lay all the responsibility at the defendant's door.

Possibilities of this nature have led social psychologists to formulate various hypotheses regarding jury decision making given certain victim characteristics. These hypotheses have been developed within the theoretical frameworks referred to earlier, in particular, attribution theory and the just-world theory. Since there seems to have been little opportunity to explore the hypotheses referred to in the course of actual jury deliberations at a trial, the experiments are generally conducted with student samples or with samples of citizens qualified for jury service.

While there is no place here for an in-depth analysis of the extensive literature in this area, fraught as it is with conflicting hypotheses and methodological problems (Luginbuhl and Frederick, 1978), brief mention will be made of some of the findings. The following summary is derived in part from the studies themselves, but mainly from the reviews by Seligman et al. (1977), Field (1978), Luginbuhl and Frederick (1978), and Koch and Bean (n.d.). Following the analysis in the previous sections, here, too, one may distinguish between findings related to the effects of *(a)* victim harm, *(b)* victim characteristics in general, and *(c)* victim-offender relationships. Contacts with the victim, taking into account the victim's desires, and keeping the victim informed do not seem to be relevant in the present context. It should be noted that the research summarized here relates almost exclusively to the offense of rape.

Victim Harm. Gold et al. (1978) found that victims were assigned less responsibility the more severe the crime ("sympathetic reaction pattern"). Field (1978) cites studies indicating the relevance of the degree of force used against the victim. Krulewitz and Nash (1979), on the other hand, hypothesized that rape victims would be held more responsible where the rape succeeded than where an attempt failed.

Victim Characteristics. A number of studies are cited in the reviews referring to the importance of the appearance of the victim (Field, 1978), and in particular his or her (usually her) attractiveness (Seligman et al., 1977; Field, 1978; Luginbuhl and Frederick, 1978) and dress (Field, 1978). Similarly, importance is also attached to the age of the victim (Field, 1978), marital status (Seligman et al., 1977; Field, 1978), social role (Seligman et al., 1977), and "respectability" (Luginbuhl and Frederick, 1978; Koch and Bean, n.d.). Finally, attention is paid in rape cases to the victim's prior sexual experience (Field, 1978) and previous rape history (Seligman et al., 1977). The hypotheses do not always operate in the expected direction. Thus, according to some studies, the more "respectable" victim of a sexual assault is perceived to be more at fault than the less "respectable" victim—perhaps because the observer, especially if female, identifies with the victim and wishes to protect herself from such an occurrence. Similarly, while physical attractiveness in a rape victim may be seen by some to provoke a rape and thereby increase the victim's responsibility, an alternative hypothesis holds that a less attractive victim is the more responsible, since she must have provoked the offender in some way (Seligman et al., 1977).

Victim-Offender Relationship. The victim's prior relationship with the offender is seen to affect the respondent's attitudes (Seligman et al., 1977; Luginbuhl and Frederick, 1978; Field, 1978). Other studies attribute importance to the degree of resistance displayed by the victim. The experimental nature of the research in this field and the lack of unanimity in the findings clearly limit the policy conclusions that may be drawn at this stage. However, they clearly suggest that victim characteristics may play a part in the decision-making processes of the criminal justice system beyond the role legally attributed to these characteristics, in particular with regard to decisions by lay persons. Moreover, these decisions appear generally to derogate in some way from the victim's recognized role—or nonrole—in the system, since it appears that decision makers may often be "judging" the victim, not just the defendant.[22] These issues clearly require further elucidation. Note should also be taken of the distinction made by Luginbuhl and Frederick (1978) between attributions by persons such as jurors who have been explicitly invested with the task of judgment (labeled by the authors as the "jury process model") and attributions made in a less structured situation (e.g., observing a criminal incident in the street, labeled the "naive observer model"). Attributions falling in the second category are also relevant to this study, but not in the context of jury decision making. The authors suggest that the failure to make this differentiation may have contributed to the conflicting nature of the research findings.

The Victim and the Sentencing Judge

Victim-Judge Contacts. Unlike in the case of the police and to some extent the prosecutor, the traditional criminal justice system does not provide for informal contacts between victims and the sentencing judge. The main opportunity for contact between these two parties would normally be during the course of the trial, when the victim testifies. However, this opportunity is limited to the minority of instances in which the case goes to trial, whereas the majority of cases terminate in a plea bargain. In these cases, insofar as the judge obtains information regarding the victim, it will generally be secondhand via the prosecutor or the probation officer's report (Hall, 1975:953), or occasionally at the rather brief pretrial proceedings, which will be considered below. Thus, judges are the least likely of all criminal justice agencies to have contact with victims, and the number of contacts they do have are fewer than for most other criminal justice officials (Hernon and Forst, 1983).[23] In her study of nonstranger violence, Smith (1983) found that "only 26% of the victims reported any interaction with the judge" (35).

Relevance of Victim Harm. Traditional concepts of criminal law have measured the seriousness of crime in terms of two main dimensions: the amount of harm inflicted, and the mental state of the perpetrator. Thus manslaughter is more serious than wounding because of the greater harm inflicted; murder is more serious than manslaughter because of a higher degree of intentionality or foreseeability.

The relevance of these concepts to the issue of sentence and punishment, as distinct from the issue of guilt, was seriously questioned by the positivist school of criminology with its concept of the individualization of punishment (Saleilles, 1911). According to this approach, the seriousness of the crime was relevant only to the issue of guilt, whereas the disposition was based entirely on characteristics related to the personality of the offender, in particular his or her potential for rehabilitation on the one hand, and dangerousness *(l'état dangereux)* on the other.[24] However, the older concepts, while they never disappeared from the courtroom, have recently been reaffirmed in the academic literature with the rise of the justice or just-deserts model of criminal justice (Fogel, 1975; von Hirsch,

1976), which has revived the view that punishment should be a function of the measure of harm inflicted by the offense and the degree of culpability of the offender (von Hirsch, 1976).[25] Moreover, while the perceived relevance of the offender's culpability—in the sense of his or her mental attitude to the criminal act—has been the subject of some controversy in the literature (see Sebba, 1984), the relevance of the degree of harm inflicted in determining the appropriateness of the punishment seems to be widely acknowledged.[26] Indeed, considerable thought has been devoted to the question of scientific methodology for developing measures to establish a scale of offense seriousness based upon the degree of harm inflicted, and, as noted, it has been suggested that such a scale should form the basis of sentencing policy (Wolfgang, 1976; and see below, chap. 6). It would thus be expected that the degree of victim harm would be reflected not only in legal categories laid down by statute but also in the actual dispositions ordered by the sentencing court.

How far have modern court practices—before the introduction of recent reforms such as "structured" sentencing and victim-impact statements— taken into consideration victim harm in determining the sentence? The examination of this issue is fraught with methodological difficulties. First, because of the virtually unlimited number of variables relating to offense, offender, victim, judge, and so on, which may theoretically affect the disposition, it is extremely difficult to obtain sufficiently accurate and complete data and a large enough sample to enable adequate control of these potentially relevant variables. Second, the degree of harm inflicted, the independent variable being considered here, is difficult to measure across different types of offense, since the nature of the harm inflicted may be qualitatively different; the use of psychophysical scaling (Sellin and Wolfgang, 1964, 1978) has been proposed as one of the more sophisticated methods of overcoming this problem. Third, the dependent variable is also problematic, since dispositions, too, may vary not only quantitatively but also qualitatively—prison, fine, probation, and so on (cf. Sebba, 1978). However, some attention has been devoted in recent years to the possibilities of unidimensionable scaling of this variable (see Erickson and Gibbs, 1979; Sebba and Nathan, 1984). Perhaps because of these methodological difficulties, the findings of the studies have not been unequivocal regarding the impact of victim harm.

Edward Green's analysis (1961) of a large sample of convictions in the Philadelphia criminal court in 1956 and 1957 attributed considerable importance to victim harm in the sentencing decision. After determining the probability of a penitentiary sentence for each type of offense, the author commented: "The above scale of offenses suggests that the criteria by which the judge weighs the relative gravity of different forms of criminal behavior consist of three interconnecting variables, *each an aspect of the offender-victim relationship*" (Green, 1961:39; emphasis added).

The three victim-related variables referred to by Green were "the specificity of the victim" (whether an individual, a business, or "the public"); "the degree of personal contact between the offender and the victim"; and "the degree of bodily injury." He considered that these three combined variables reflected a moral principle, which he called the "inviolability of personality"; and while he noted other variables which affected the severity of the sentence, inviolability of personality appeared to be "the paramount value . . . around which the reorganization of penal values is taking place."

There are certain limitations to this analysis. First, the classification of offenses was somewhat arbitrary; in particular, it is questionable whether "narcotics violations" should have been classified with offenses involving "personal contact between the offender and the victim" (40). Second, the dependent variable, as noted, related not to the duration of prison sentences but only to their probability of imposition. Third, the analysis dealt with a single independent variable rather than being multivariate. The main weakness, however, is that comparisons were exclusively among offense categories. It was shown that felonious assault was dealt with more severely than robbery because of the assumed greater seriousness of the injury inflicted by such offenses. But it was not shown that assaults involving greater harm were sentenced more severely than assaults inflicting lesser harm.

Hogarth (1971), in his study of the sentencing philosophy of Ontario magistrates, employed more sophisticated multivariate modes of analysis, such as discriminant function analysis, and found that the seriousness of crime, as measured by the Sellin-Wolfgang scaling system, which, as noted, lays emphasis on the amount of harm inflicted, was a predictor of both the type of sentence imposed and the duration of institutional sentences (347–49). However, when a sample of magistrates was asked to specify what information was relevant for the sentencing decision, only 29% responded that information on the "degree of personal injury or violence" was essential and 12% that the "amount of damage or loss to property" was essential. Of the sample, 42% and 59%, respectively, stated that this information was nonessential (232, 281). The magistrates attributed greater importance to information regarding the offender's culpability, in particular the degree of planning and premeditation involved in the commission of the offense, with

62% stating that this information was essential. The author commented that "most magistrates consider the 'moral quality' of the criminal act to be more important than the actual harm incurred by the victim" (233). It may also be noted in this context that Green (1961) in his elaboration of his degree-of-bodily-injury variable explained that "the severity of the sentences varies directly with the extent to which the criminal intent or the criminal act embodies the element of bodily harm" (41). Thus, the significance of victim harm for the sentencing court may be related more to the harm intended than the harm inflicted.

Some later studies dealt more specifically with the impact of degrees of victim harm on the sentencing decision. Most of these tended to detract somewhat from the hypothesis regarding the relevance of victim harm for this decision. Myers (1979), in her study of 205 dispositions following trial in Indiana, found that harm sustained was not a significant variable. This variable was measured by the type of harm inflicted: injury to the person, to property, to both, or to neither. The dependent variable was whether or not a prison sentence was imposed. Hernon and Forst (1983) found on the basis of their "scenario" cases[27] that the judges' responses on their sentencing decisions were affected by victim harm only in the case of knife assaults, and only in respect of one of the three indicators harm variables employed, namely, "10 days hospitalization."

Conklin (1972), on the other hand, in a study of robbery cases in Boston in which he used multiple regression analysis, found that the infliction of physical injury on the victim or the loss of more than $100 increased the probability that the offender would be bound over to a superior court, "where he was usually indicted and often sentenced to a state prison" (171). However, the author also found that robberies involving $100 or more were less likely to result in findings of guilt (168–69). Mention may also be made here of a study of the lower court in New Haven, Connecticut (Feeley, 1979:130–41), where regression analysis indicated that a more serious offense or the use of a weapon increased the probability of conviction but not the severity of the sentence (for which a scale was employed). However, "public order" offenses were sentenced less severely than other types of offense, providing some support for Green's thesis regarding the "inviolability of the victim," since public order offenses have no personal victim, whereas most, although not all, of the other types of offense have such victims.

There are certain cases in which there is irrefutable evidence that the court has taken note of victim harm, namely, where the disposition includes an order to the defendant to pay restitution to the victim, whether as a condition of probation or otherwise. As noted above, although this power has traditionally been vested in the court, until recently its use was somewhat circumscribed (McDonald, 1977). It seems that in the past neither prosecutor nor judge placed a high priority on determining the amount of loss inflicted upon the victim in a process that was concerned primarily with proving the offender's guilt. The recent attempts to revive and expand this remedy imply the placing of increased emphasis on victim harm (see chap. 7).

Perhaps too much significance should not be attributed to those studies that appeared to indicate that the degree of harm inflicted upon the victim was of only limited relevance to the severity of the sentence. As noted, there are a number of methodological problems complicating research in this area. It should also be taken into account that, at least in nontrial cases, the offense for which the sentence is being imposed is, as a result of plea bargaining, not that which the defendant was actually thought to have committed, and this may inhibit a genuine attempt to take victim harm into account. It has also been suggested that judges may have paid limited attention to the degree of victim harm on the assumption that this had been considered at the earlier stages of the criminal justice process, such as the prosecution decision or the probation officer's recommendation (Myers, 1979), although in this last study victim harm as such was not found to have affected these decisions either.

It certainly seems surprising, if, as some of these studies suggest, the degree of harm inflicted on the victim has been of only marginal relevance to the severity of the sentence. It is equally surprising how little information is available on this very fundamental matter, which touches on the root of the penal system. On the one hand, insofar as there is a trend toward the adoption of structured sentencing, based upon a "desert" philosophy (see below, chap. 7), it may be anticipated that victim harm will be reflected therein, although the *court's* discretion in this matter will be reduced. On the other hand, victim-impact statements are intended to enhance the court's sensitivity to victim harm at the sentencing stage.

Relevance of Other Victim Characteristics. Unlike victim harm, which is regarded as a legitimate factor in the determination of the severity of the punishment, other victim characteristics such as sociodemographic variables are not generally formally recognized as relevant to conviction or sentence, although certain forms of victim conduct, such as provocation, might be considered relevant (see, e.g., Dawson, 1969:91–92). However, attribution theory has been invoked to hypothesize that such variables might in fact have considerable significance, and some support has been found for such hypotheses both in the social psychological literature (see Denno and Cramer, 1976:217–19; Ziegenhagen, 1977:83–84) and in criminological and sociological studies.

Thus, while Hernon and Forst (1983) found the sex variable not to be significant, Myers (1979) found that a prison sentence was somewhat more likely where the victim was a woman ($0.1 > p > 0.05$; 1979, table 2). The victim's age, employment record, and criminal record were not found to be significant. Hernon and Forst (1983) found the victim's age to be significant only for homicide and sexual assault. Denno and Cramer (1976), who attempted specifically to test hypotheses derived from attribution theory, found victim characteristics such as age, ethnic identity, appearance, and attractiveness to have rather low correlations with the sentencing decision. There were slightly stronger associations between ethnic identity (Kendall's Tau, $B = 0.23$) and attractiveness (0.26) and "judge's reaction."[28] However, there has been considerable research indicating that defendants in capital cases are more likely to be sentenced to death when the victim is white (see, e.g., Carter, 1988:440), although the decisions in these cases are often those of juries rather than judges. Finally, Conklin (1972) found that robberies committed against a business were more likely to result in a finding of guilty, and following a finding of guilt, defendants in such cases were likely to be bound over to a superior court and consequently to receive a more severe sentence.

Victim conduct and victim-offender relationships, however, seem to be more strongly associated with disposition outcome. As noted earlier, Green (1961) found in his Philadelphia study that there were three critical variables, all of which he considered to be connected with victim-offender relationships; one of these—specificity of the victim—was also found to be significant in the study of Ontario magistrates conducted by Hogarth (1971:347, 349). Other studies have paid particular attention to the existence of a prior relationship. It is sometimes hypothesized that the sentence will be less severe where such a relationship existed. However, Hernon and Forst (1983) found support for this hypothesis only in respect of the judges' responses regarding homicide. Myers (1979:537) did not find this variable significant for judges; her finding for probation officers in this respect will be referred to below. "Alleged victim misconduct," on the other hand, did have a moderate association with the type of sentence imposed in the above study (significant at the 10% level). Similarly, Denno and Cramer (1976) found that victim provocation was "moderately related" to the defendant's sentence (Kendall's Tau, $B = 0.28$), and "strongly associated" ($B = 0.41$) with "judge's reaction."

Relevance of Victims' Views. Where a full trial takes place, the court may form some impression regarding the effects of the offense on the victim on the basis of the victim's own testimony. In other cases, some information in this respect may be conveyed indirectly by the prosecutor, or possibly by the probation officer, at the sentencing stage. However, before the introduction of "victim-impact statements" and "victim statements of opinion," which will be considered below in chapter 8, the system did not provide any clear opportunity for the victim's views to be made known to the court.

Bard and Sangrey (1979) observed, however, that "in some jurisdictions provision is made for victims to express their feelings to the judge after a conviction and before sentencing" (130). Moreover, the effort made by prosecutors in some cases to prevent the judge from observing the victim's attitude (McDonald, 1977) indicated that such attitudes were thought to have a meaningful effect upon the outcome. A study conducted in New York showed that victims were much more likely to have an opportunity to express their views on the disposition where they had a prior relationship with the offender. In 52% of the prior-relationship cases, the victims were consulted on this matter by the prosecutor, as compared with only 4% of the stranger cases ($p < 0.01$; see Davis et al., 1980: table 4.1). Moreover, in 21% of the prior-relationship cases, bench conferences were held in which the victim's wishes were considered, as compared with 3% of the stranger cases ($p < 0.1$). This supports the view that in prior-relationship cases the dispute has to a greater extent been perceived as the victim's rather than the state's alone.

Nevertheless, even in nonstranger cases, it would be unlikely that the victim would feel that his or her input had been decisive. Smith (1983), whose sample was confined to nonstranger violence, found that 66% of the 113 victims whose cases reached court felt they had had "little or no influence" (37–38).

Victims' Information. How far is the victim informed of the final outcome of the case, whether or not he or she was consulted hitherto on the course it should follow? Although lack of information was one of the recurring complaints referred to by the various studies, the data emerging from these studies have not been uniformly negative.

Hernon and Forst (1983) found that 78% of their sample knew the outcome of the case in which they were involved, and, where the outcome was a sentence by the court, 76% knew what this sentence was. Moreover, they found that these figures for the overall sample did not vary greatly across sites.

Connick and Davis (1981) reported on the results of two studies conducted in New York City. The first study, of victims whose cases were tried
in the Brooklyn Criminal Court, found that in 66% of the prior-relationship
cases, but in only 50% of the stranger cases, were victims aware of the
outcome. Moreover, the later study, of a sample of cases dealt with by the
Brooklyn Supreme Court, showed that in only 41% of the stranger cases was
the victim aware of the outcome. Hagan (1980) found that knowledge of the
outcome of a case was primarily a function of attendance in court. Overall,
49.5% were aware of the court's disposition.

The disparity between the findings of these studies may be partly connected with the relatively small size of the samples. However, while it
may be considered satisfactory to find samples where more than three out
of four victims were aware of the outcome of their cases (and some of the
remainder may have been indifferent), samples in which less than one-half
were so informed provide fuel for the critics of the system. Moreover, it
appears that some victims may even be unaware that the court has ordered
restitution in their favor (Hudson and Chesney, 1978:137).

Other Stages in the Criminal Justice System

In addition to the main stages of the criminal justice system discussed
above—police, prosecution, trial, and sentence—there are other decision-
making stages, also of concern to the victim. In respect to most of these,
however, little direct information on the victim's role has been available,
reflecting the absence of any role for the victim at these stages.

Perhaps the most important decision not included in the previous discussion is the bail hearing. In most cases, a suspect arrested for alleged
injury to the victim, having been taken into custody, will be released on
bail, although in recent years the concept of "preventive detention" has
increasingly gained recognition. Apart from general considerations of public safety and the risk of evasion of justice (which have to be balanced
against the presumption of innocence and the constitutional prohibition
on excessive bail), release on bail may present immediate danger to the
victim. A released suspect may seek vengeance against the victim for
having complained to the police, or may attempt to intimidate the victim
in order to prevent incriminating testimony in court; and the risk may be
aggravated where the parties are known to each other.

Until recently, however, the bail hearing has not been concerned with
the victim. According to the Nashville, Tennessee, survey conducted in

the 1970s, the victim was only rarely present, and although some prosecutors and judges thought he or she might influence the decision, the author concluded that "the victim's impact on this phase of the criminal proceeding is seemingly minimal" (Hall, 1975:946). Studies both in the United States and in Britain have indicated that ignorance as to whether the suspect has been released on bail is also an issue of serious concern (Elias, 1983:105; Shapland et al., 1985:52).

A related proceeding is the arraignment, at which the charges are formally read and the defendant's plea is heard. Elias (1986) noted that "more victims appear at this proceeding than the others," although in his own sample "less than one-half of the respondents questioned were present" (147, 104). The British survey, on the other hand, found that only 22% of respondents knew of any pretrial appearances (Shapland et al., 1985:56–57). As to their contribution to the proceedings, Elias found that the victims' role at the arraignment was limited, their main potential input being their ability to have charges dropped (1983:104).

Another important stage where victim-related variables may be relevant is the presentence report of the probation officer. Myers (1979) found a weak correlation ($0.1 < p < 0.05$) between victim gender and probation officers' recommendation. She also found—contrary to expectations—that probation officers were "more likely to recommend a prison sentence if the victim knew the defendant and had not engaged in conflict with him prior to the crime" (537). Myers thus took the view that probation officers were to some extent "individualizing" for the victim as well as for the offender. Similarly, it appeared from the INSLAW study (Hernon and Forst, 1983) that victims occasionally had contact with probation officers, who sometimes referred to the victim in the presentence report, a practice subsequently adopted in the "victim-impact statement" to be discussed in chapter 8.

Different views are expressed in the literature as to the consideration given to the victim's views in the presentence report (Gittler, 1984: n. 177). Historically, the probation officer's role was seen to focus on the offender and the offender's needs, and he or she could not be expected to protect the victim's interests, which may be in direct conflict with those of the offender. However, here again, as noted, new procedures are developing.

The final stage of the criminal process in which the victim has an interest relates to procedures resulting in the release of the offender from a penal institution, by way of parole or clemency. According to the Tennessee survey, a victim could appear personally before the Board of Pardons and Paroles to express an opinion regarding a parole release or clemency decision. However, there were few cases in which victims made their views known to the board either directly or through their influence on the opinions of judges or district attorneys. It appears that victim's views, when expressed, were taken into account but were given relatively little weight (Hall, 1975:963).

Recent reforms and guidelines aimed at improving the victim's position in the justice system (see especially chap. 8 below) have included parole and clemency procedures within their ambit. Moreover, added weight may now be attributed to victims' views at prerelease proceedings, owing to the risk of lawsuits based upon negligent release from institutions (see below, chap. 13).

Remedies for Nonrecognition and Civil Alternatives

Where the victim is aware of a decision made in the course of the criminal process and is dissatisfied with this decision it may be possible to adopt one of the following three courses: (1) to compel the criminal justice agency to alter its decision, (2) to prosecute or compromise the case, or (3) to file a civil claim.

Where a public agency acts wrongly, or refuses to act, it may be possible for an aggrieved citizen to obtain a writ of mandamus from the courts. However, there are two serious limitations to this remedy in the present context (Miller, 1969; Hall, 1975). First, the courts are reluctant to interfere with the exercise of discretion by a public official. Second, a petitioner must prove "standing," that is, that he or she is an interested party. Traditionally, courts have held that criminal justice is a matter concerning the community as a whole rather than any particular individual, including the victim (see, e.g., *Eacret v. Holmes*, 333 P. 2d. 741, 1958). Thus the same considerations that gave rise to the victim's grievance—the lack of any recognized role in the system—have also operated to prevent the victim's securing a judicial remedy for this grievance. However, a number of states have provided a statutory remedy in some cases, and one writer (Green, 1988) has proposed a model statute to enable aggrieved citizens to seek declaratory actions in order to bring about the instigation of prosecutions by the authorities.

Some states maintain the possibility of private prosecution; this enables a victim, through his or her attorney, to prosecute the alleged offender himself. However, the survival of this power has been severely criticized (Miller, 1969; Ward, 1972; Green, 1988; but see Note, 1955), and at the federal level it has been precluded by the Supreme Court (Green, 1988:495). Moreover, it has often been limited by the rule that "private prosecutors may participate only if the district attorney controls and manages the prosecution" (Hall, 1975:976).[29] Thus the private prosecution does not serve as a remedy where the district attorney refuses to prosecute.

Conversely, some states have "compromise" statutes, which provide for the dismissal of a case where the parties have reached a civil settlement, thus providing the victim with some power to *prevent* a prosecution. However, this power, too, is subject to limitations (Hall, 1975), and an agreement not to file a complaint may constitute the offense of compounding.

Most criminal offenses give rise to civil actions in tort—for assault, conversion, and so on. The institutional response to the victim's limited standing in the criminal justice system is to point to the availability of civil remedies. While there is indeed no normative obstacle in the way of this remedy, the practical obstacles have generally been almost insurmountable: (1) ignorance of the law on the part of the victim; (2) inability to pay legal fees, or the charging of legal fees out of proportion to the amount of the claim; (3) ineligibility for legal aid; (4) difficulty in locating the offender and proving the case; and (5) the offender's lack of means to pay. The possible expansion of these alternatives—the private prosecution and the civil suit—will be considered in chapter 12.

Agencies outside the Criminal Justice System

While the legal norm traditionally designates the criminal justice system as the official mechanism for dealing with victimization in society,[30] in practice other agencies, both formal and informal, may serve a similar function. Indeed, the same social institutions that are thought to fulfill a social control function (and thus to contain deviance; see, e.g., Landis, 1956) may also be of assistance to the victim. Victims may thus have recourse to medical, welfare, religious, or educational institutions, as well as to the more informal family, peer group, and network units.

Information regarding the use of these various mechanisms is rather sparse. Victimization surveys are usually concerned only with reporting to the police and not with the use of alternative agencies. However, a few of the in-depth studies of victim experiences (Holmstrom and Burgess, 1978; Shapland et al., 1985) have considered the role of hospitals in personal injury cases, and mental health professionals have discussed their role in the provision of assistance to victims (*Evaluation and Change*, 1980; Salasin, 1981).

A Victim Services Agency study (Friedman et al., 1982) has cast some light on the availability of informal support networks in New York City, as well as on the degree to which victims refer to other agencies. A somewhat similar study of domestic violence victims has been conducted in Britain (Smith, 1989), and a comprehensive Canadian report (*Canadian Federal-Provincial Task Force*, 1983) considered possible sources of support for the victim both inside and outside the criminal justice system.

Available data suggest that alternative agencies are of limited usefulness to victims (ibid., 70). Medical treatment is frequently depersonalized (Holmstrom and Burgess, 1978:2–31), and medical services may be subservient to legal and evidentiary needs (Shapland et al., 1981: chap. 3). As for mental health services, when "110 upper-level officials" responsible for mental health policy were interviewed, "the majority of respondents in most cases classified all types of services to victims as being a low priority or not a priority at all" (Rich, 1981:136). However, rape and domestic violence victims were given a higher priority than "other crime."

Knudten et al. (1976) identified more than 200 agencies functioning in Milwaukee in the 1970s which could provide a variety of services to victims ($N = 159$) and witnesses ($N = 56$), including counseling, financial, legal, and medical assistance. The widespread failure to take advantage of these services was explained in part by ignorance of their existence, but in part by the fact that "sizeable proportions of victims and witnesses either did not think they would benefit from such agencies, or simply did not want any help" (54).

Friedman et al. (1982) also reported on the limited resort by victims to community agencies, including special victim-assistance agencies with which the victims were often not familiar. However, victims did often resort to informal support systems. Victimizations involved an average of four other persons besides the victim, and the availability of such persons was found by the authors of the study to be critical in determining the victim's ability to cope with the experience. The expansion of victim-assistance programs, and the effectiveness of their contribution, will be considered in chapter 10.

Conclusions

In spite of the intensive activity generated by the need to reform the role of the victim in the criminal justice system, precise knowledge about his or her role in the preexisting system remains inadequate, rendering speculation as to the outcome of proposed reforms somewhat uncertain. The preceding discussion suggests that the information available on the operation of the system with regard to the victim may be summarized at three different levels: (1) the normative, (2) the pragmatic, and (3) the subliminal.

The Normative Level. According to the legal norms prevailing before the recent spate of victim-oriented legislation, the victim had virtually disappeared from the criminal justice system, which was guided almost exclusively by "public policy" interests, the relevant agencies acting in the name of the state or the people rather than of the victim. At such critical decision-making stages as arrest, bail, prosecution, verdict, sentence, parole, and clemency, the victim was not generally considered a relevant party. There were some exceptions to this—such as the citizen's arrest, certain archaic prosecution practices, and the ordering of restitution by the court—but these constituted the exception rather than the rule. Also, in some locations, prosecution authorities were exhorted in their instructions to take note of victim desires in certain types of cases. Finally, the degree of victim harm was, according to many legal analysts, one of the fundamental dimensions for determining the degree of the offender's culpability, but, apart from an element of doubt emerging from the empirical studies on whether this was in fact the case, such attention to victim harm was regarded primarily as a measure of the offender's injury to society, and any direct connection with the victim as a person was on a somewhat abstracted level.

The Pragmatic Level. In general, the actual role attributed to victims by criminal justice agencies has not differed substantially from their normative role: it has been very limited. These agencies, however, have been governed by other considerations than the official legal norms—partly ideological ones related to the individual philosophy of the decision maker, but mainly pragmatic ones related to the efficiency of the processes involved. These pragmatic considerations might operate in favor of or against the victim's interests. Thus, on the one hand, some prosecutors have given special weight to the views of victims in cases where they feared that the complainant might retract before the court hearing. They might, on the other hand, for the same reason, refuse to prosecute such cases in the first place. Moreover, some law enforcement officials would see certain cases as "really private matters," in spite of their being legally undifferentiated from any other criminal complaint. Further, many prosecutors have been concerned with how the case will be projected in the courtroom, resulting in certain "stereotypical" cases that would not be prosecuted for fear of anticipated failure to secure a conviction.

The Subliminal Level. Whether there are processes at work in the criminal justice system whereby cases, and victims, are stereotyped and then treated according to the stereotype is in essence an empirical issue. Social psychologists have attempted to study the validity of alternative approaches and hypotheses in this area, such as attribution theory, just-world theory, and equity theory. This research is still in its infancy, and the tentative findings are somewhat conflicting, as are some of the hypotheses themselves (see appendix). Nevertheless, the impression is created from these studies that processes of this nature do in fact operate and that the perception of the victim on the part of criminal justice personnel, especially in nonstranger cases or cases involving alleged victim precipitation, is not necessarily governed solely by rational and objective analysis of the relevant data. This results in deviations from the decision-making patterns indicated by both normative and pragmatic considerations.

The treatment of victims on all three levels described above—the normative, the pragmatic, and the subliminal—attests to the vulnerability of their standing in the traditional criminal justice system. The most notable deficiencies have been the failure to grant the victim any formal status in the decision-making process, or even to notify him or her of the decisions taken. How the victim perceives such treatment will be the topic of chapter 5; and how far the various innovations or proposed innovations are calculated to remedy the deficiencies in the system from the victim's standpoint will be the main focus of part 3 of this study.

Two final observations: First, there has been little evidence, at least before the most recent reforms, that agencies outside the criminal justice system have been capable of filling the void left by the criminal justice agencies with respect to caring for the victim, although many victims receive help from informal support systems. Second, in spite of the enormous quantity of research conducted on various aspects of the criminal justice system, our knowledge of the victim's role, on all the different levels considered above, is still—even after the recent wave of victim-related literature—rather limited, since research directed specifically at the focal issues as defined here has been comparatively sparse.

Part II

The Parameters of Justice

3

The Framework of Analysis

Having established in the preceding chapter that there is substantial truth in the rhetoric that points to the limited role of the victim in the criminal justice system and to certain disturbing features resulting therefrom, the question arises whether the remedies recently adopted or currently proposed (as described briefly in chap. 1) are appropriate, in both conceptual and practical terms, to rectify the problems described. It is not sufficient, however, merely to evaluate these remedies against the background of the various criticisms implied in the description of the victim's traditional role in the system. Rather, remedies must be developed in the light of a more comprehensive consideration of the victim's needs, while taking into account other characteristics that a system of justice might be expected to possess.

In this and the following chapters in this section, an attempt will be made both to assess the victim's needs more comprehensively and to identify the other qualities of an optimal justice system. Only then will it be possible to evaluate the specific proposals intended to ameliorate the victim's situation.

The first premise upon which the framework of analysis proposed here rests is that there are three parties whose needs must be met and whose interests must be protected by a system of justice. While the present study focuses primarily upon the victim, it would clearly be unreasonable to propose a scheme of justice designed to take account of the needs and interests of the victim while totally ignoring the needs and interests of the offender (or the suspected offender)—except under an extreme absolutist neo-Kantian philosophy whereby a transgressor were to sacrifice all his rights. Moreover, such a principle could not in any case be applied to a mere *suspect* or *accused* person. Similarly, in a democratic society, the interests of the public at large must be taken into account, both for pragmatic considerations and as a matter of principle. This need for a balance of interests has been only rarely referred to in the victim-oriented literature, which has tended to focus too narrowly upon the victim's needs. The main exception to this has been the concern expressed in some quarters (such as the American Civil Liberties Union) that certain victim-related reforms, especially those advocated by the political conservatives referred to in the introduction, might derogate from the rights of the defendant. Such criticism was expressed about the Californian Victims' Bill of Rights, which ostensibly deprived defendants of certain presumed advantages, such as the possibility of a plea bargain.[1] Nevertheless, the triadic approach presented here—consideration of the needs of victims, offenders, and public—seems rarely, in spite of its obviousness, to have been spelled out explicitly in the literature[2] (but cf. Ashworth, 1986).

This triadic approach is of course simplistic and raises some difficult issues. The first issue relates to the relative importance of the three categories which the justice system must take into account. Should each category be attributed equal weight? A "gut reaction" seems to dictate that the victim's interests should be worthy of greater consideration than the offender's, inasmuch as the latter has been labeled the wrongdoer. Surely, however, the framers of the U.S. Constitution—and in particular of its Amendments—had good reason for providing offenders (and suspected offenders), rather than victims, with guarantees. Could victim advocates justify a total reversal of this position?

Similarly, the degree of importance to be attributed to the public's interests may also be controversial. Some professional law enforcement or rehabilitationist personnel may see the public's interest as a somewhat secondary consideration, whereas persons with a more "populist" orientation would stress its importance. It is beyond the scope of the present study to explore further, let alone to determine, what should be the relative weight attributed to these three interest groups, or even to speculate about the degree of consensus that prevails in this respect.[3] Further consideration should be given to these questions on the levels both of empirical research and of theoretical analysis. For the purposes of the present study it will suffice to draw attention to the need to consider the different interests of the various parties.

A second major issue raised by the triadic approach presented here is the problem of defining the categories that have been identified, and in some instances of differentiating between them. Undoubtedly, the most difficult problem in this context is that of defining victimization. This is an issue with which much of the victimological literature has been concerned (see, e.g., Friedrichs, 1983; Elias, 1986:28–32; Fattah, 1991: chap. 4). One of the pioneers of victimology (Mendelsohn, 1974) took the view that the concern of victimology was not confined to victims of crime but included victims of other trauma and misfortune, such as road accidents and natural disasters. This view was conceptualized by Young-Rifai (1982a) to include various situations in which persons have "imbalances in their relationships or communication with their environments" (76). Moreover, psychological literature has drawn attention to the similarity between the traumatic effects of criminal and other forms of victimization (Janoff-Bulman and Frieze, 1983).

Others have adopted a more relativist perspective, arguing that victimization is a "social construct" (Quinney, 1974) or an "act of interpretive reality construction" (Holstein and Miller, 1990:107), and that perceptions of victimization are dependent on the social context and on the viewpoint of the observer. This point is well illustrated by the Goetz case: if youths coming from socioeconomically deprived or ethnically-historically deprived (Carter, 1988) backgrounds attempt to rob a white man of a few dollars and he shoots them, who is the victim? Even the norm-oriented legal system has a problem with this type of case, as well as in other areas of conflict between social or cultural groups, such as rape cases.

Conflicting values may, again, lead to definitions of victimization not recognized by the prevailing legal system. Radicals have long held that the criminal law and its implementation reflect the power structure in society. Laws against theft, poaching, and so on, are designed to protect prevailing inequalities (although the new "left realists" have perceived that they also protect the underprivileged), while much "true crime," involving economic oppression of the underprivileged, has not been formally penalized.

This approach, whereby victimization is not limited to cases of formal breaches of the criminal law, has been echoed, in a human rights context, in the UN Declaration of Basic Principles of Justice for Victims of Crime and Abuse of Power. This declaration, as its name implies, grants rights to victims of "abuse of power" and of other violations of international norms relating to human rights, even if such violations have not been criminalized by the country in which they took place (see sec. 18 of the declaration; Lamborn, 1988).

However, the present study will adopt a more conventional definition of victimization, partly because most of the literature—in particular the empirical literature—that is available for analysis is concerned with conventional victimization, but mainly because the innovative programs this study seeks to evaluate have also been developed for such cases, most of the programs having been adopted by legislative or law enforcement bodies guided by traditional concepts of crime and victimization.

Even within the conventional criminal justice definitions of victimization, however, there may be alternative criteria for determining whether such definitions have been fulfilled. As Burt (1983) has pointed out, the infliction of criminal harm does not in itself give rise to the attribution of victim status but is merely the first stage in this process. Additional stages are required for this to occur. The second stage is for the ostensible victim to perceive that a harm has been inflicted;[4] the third, that he or she should claim a victim role from the agents of social control and significant others; and the fourth, that the latter should concur with the appropriateness of ascribing this status in the instant case.[5] While many of the remedies for victimization considered in this study will in practice be operational only when all the above requirements are fulfilled, in principle the first and second stages are sufficient to bring the incident in question within its terms of reference. The study is concerned with the remedies available to a person who perceives him- or herself as a victim of a criminal offense.[6] Indeed, in a sense it may be said that the second stage alone is sufficient. A person who perceives him- or herself to be a victim of a criminal offense, even if this is not the case, should be entitled to the pursuit of appropriate remedies and should have access to certain procedures for this purpose, even if ultimately the claim of victimization will fail.

Miers (1980) has argued that the legal definition of victim is itself flexible and relative, since, for example, victim compensation boards may exclude certain types of victims, such as victims who contributed to the commission of the offense or who are related to the offender, thereby depriving them of their victim status for certain purposes. As Christie (1986) has pointed out, there are stereotypical traits that the "ideal" victim should possess to gain popular sympathy—and perhaps also material support—from society. Thus the infliction of a crime does not guarantee all the benefits of victim status. On the other hand, insofar as compensation may be awarded to a person victimized by a perpetrator who was not criminally responsible for his or her conduct, there may be a victim of crime without the existence of a criminal (Lamborn, 1968).

Other types of classification of victim are employed in the literature (see, e.g., Silverman, 1974; Landau and Freeman-Longo, 1990), some of which have important legal or sociological implications; these include classification according to type of offense, relationship with the offender, or previous victimization. Such classifications have no a priori bearing on the subject matter of the present study, with one exception. Victims of crime may be divided into *(a)* individuals, *(b)* corporations or other commercial entities, and *(c)* the community or state (Wolfgang and Singer, 1978).[7] These categories raise very different issues and may call for different solutions. Clearly, for example, the dynamics of informal dispute resolution between offender and victim would not be the same where the victim was a corporation or the state. In spite of the importance of these categories (especially the corporate victim: see Hagan, 1980) the present study will focus on the type of victimization with which most of the proposed remedies have been concerned, namely, personal victimization.[8]

In sociological terms there are also problems in differentiating between the main categories referred to—"victims," "offenders," and "public." On certain levels of analysis, victims and offenders are not discrete categories. First, they tend to come from the same populations (Singer, 1981; Fattah, 1991: chap. 5). Second, a relatively high proportion of individual victims are self-reported offenders (Singer, 1981) or have had contacts with law enforcement authorities as suspects or offenders (Ziegenhagen, 1976:270; Maxfield, 1984; Sampson and Lauritsen, 1990).[9] The causal connection here has been recognized by the federal Crime Control Act of 1990, section 251 of which provides for grants to "provide treatment to juvenile offenders who are victims of child abuse and neglect, and to their families so as to reduce the likelihood that such juvenile offenders will commit subsequent violations of the law." Third, in an individual case (e.g., a domestic dispute) it may be difficult to determine who is the offender and who is the victim. Fourth, for the radical, as indicated above, it may be the offender who is seen to be the victim of the criminal law (see Balkan et al., 1980; Friedrichs, 1983; and cf. *Victims of Crime*, 1985:9). However, while the problems are very real, they are bypassed by the law, which creates a notional dichotomization or ideal typology of victim on the one hand and offender on the other, with hardly any recognition of intermediary status (Gobert, 1977; Wolfgang, 1989); and subject to the previous comment regarding access to remedial procedures according to subjective definitions of victimization, it is the legal definitions that constitute the terms of reference for the present study.

There may be similar difficulties in differentiating in behavioristic terms between victims and "the public." Since crime is "extraordinarily common" (Skogan and Maxfield, 1981:13), many, perhaps all, of the "public" have been victimized in the past or will be in the future. Moreover, in any specific case of victimization there may be eyewitnesses who may suffer both from the experience itself and from the subsequent involvement with the legal system.[10] In addition, the immediate victim's support system creates further indirect victimization. Studies have shown that most victimizations result in some degree of suffering or inconvenience to a number of additional persons (Shapland et al., 1981:213; Salasin, 1981:26; Friedman et al., 1982; Riggs and Kilpatrick, 1990; Mawby and Walklate, 1994:43). Such indirect victims, with the exception of surviving family members in homicide cases or the families of minors or incapacitated persons, have not generally gained official recognition,[11] and clearly greater attention must be devoted to this issue.

Finally, like the victims, the offender population may also merge in some respects with the "general public." Self-report studies indicate that virtually the whole population commits offenses on occasion; attachment of the "offender" label must therefore depend upon the seriousness and the frequency of the criminal acts committed (as well as their discovery), rather than representing an absolute dichotomization between offenders and nonoffenders. Further, the "suspect" or "defendant" whose guilt has not been established has an intermediary status between "offender" and "public." It appears that the U.S. Supreme Court has attempted to differentiate in this respect between suspects whose innocence is fully presumed and whose constitutional rights must be guaranteed, and those who are found in compromising circumstances that tend to identify them as potential offenders (see O'Neill, 1984). Such differentiation, however, may be problematic both in principle and in practice. At any rate, no convincing grounds have yet been raised for its adoption when considering the victim's rights vis-à-vis those of the suspected offender.

Having established, at least for operational purposes, that there are three distinct interest groups that a justice system must take into consideration, the needs of these parties—and of the system as a whole—have to be ascertained. The identification of these needs entails the development of an additional dimension for inclusion in the theoretical framework of analysis. While the literature has enumerated a variety of problems encountered by crime victims (see, e.g., Salasin, 1981; Waller, 1982; Shapland et al., 1985; Skogan et al., 1990), it seems that the interests and concerns of victims, as well as of other parties, involved in the justice system may be translated into three levels of need at which the system will have to provide satisfaction: (1) coping needs, (2) perceived justice needs, and (3) fundamental principles of justice. A brief elaboration of these terms will follow.

Coping Needs

Many of the programs being developed are clearly designed to overcome the material discomforts and needs of the victim, and also to compensate him or her for the losses and injuries inflicted in the course of the crime, for the loss of time expended in the subsequent proceedings, and so on. Thus some reformers favor state compensation schemes over offender restitution, on the ground that the latter will prove inadequate to meet the victim's needs.

The coping needs of the victim are also taken here to include his or her immediate treatment needs, such as medical attention and counseling. The expression is thus used in a wide sense to include restoration of both the property and the person of the victim and to cover needs both objectively and subjectively defined. It also includes the victim's long-term needs, including immunity from further victimization. Thus a measure that is designed to bring the victim effective financial compensation, but that will result in a vengeful offender remaining at large, may ultimately prove to be counterproductive in terms of coping.

At the same time, while the victim's coping needs may be the dominant consideration, the offender's coping needs must also be taken into account, not in the sense that the system must necessarily provide for all such needs, but that it should not make excessive demands. The offender should not, for example, generally be deprived of all expectations of future earning capacity. This is partly out of concern for the public and the prevention of vengefulness, and partly because society has an intrinsic interest in facilitating the offender's ultimate rehabilitation.

Finally, in developing appropriate remedies for the victims, the public's coping needs, too, must be considered. On the one hand, the public has an interest in limiting the costs of any proposal for which taxpayers may have to bear the burden, victim compensation schemes being the obvious example.[12] On the other hand, the public has a coping interest of a different nature in any developments resulting either in the rehabilitation of the offender who has been apprehended or in the deterrence of this and other potential offenders, in order to reduce further victimization.

The public may also have psychological coping needs. Reports in the press (or via communication networks) of violent attacks upon innocent citizens may have a traumatic effect on the general public, in particular those sections of the public having a greater degree of vulnerability, real or perceived (cf. Skogan and Maxfield, 1981). The reaction of the justice system must take into account the need to mitigate this trauma and to assuage the fears created. The precise dimensions and extent of the coping needs of the parties, however, should not be a matter for speculation. Once the concept has been acknowledged, it is for empirical research to determine the nature and extent of these needs. The data currently available on this topic will be considered in the next chapter.

Perceived Justice Needs

In addition to the victim's need to cope with the material harm and emotional trauma inflicted by the victimizing act, it may be anticipated that if this act has been defined by the victim as having a criminal character, this will give rise to certain expectations on his or her part of the institutions of law enforcement and justice. Thus, even if the victim's essential material needs are met (e.g., by compensation from the state), if in his or her perception the wrongdoer has gone unpunished, the victim may yet remain dissatisfied. Further, it may not be sufficient that the outcome of the proceedings accord with objective standards of propriety and reasonableness. To cite the old adage, justice must also be "seen to be done." The procedures themselves must be designed to maximize the victim's perception that the measures taken are appropriate in the circumstances.

The above comments apply in substance to the offender also. While there may be no consensus that offender satisfaction is a sine qua non for the justice system, clearly a system under which the offender's sense of justice could be enhanced without cost to other interests would be preferable; it might also reduce his or her inclination to recidivate.

Last, the degree of public satisfaction with any adopted system must also be considered. If it is true that the current victim orientation in criminal justice derives partly from public concern with crime, it follows that any reforms introduced should be consistent with the general wishes of the public. This would apply not so much to the procedures followed in the course of the administration of justice, which would be of less concern to those not directly involved, but rather to the outcomes, that is, the ultimate fate of the offender and victim respectively, information about which is likely to be more widely disseminated.

Like coping needs, identifying the perceived justice needs of the parties is also a matter of empirical research. The complexity of this topic and the limited scope of the information currently available will emerge from the review of the available data in chapter 5.

Fundamental Principles of Justice

On a purely utilitarian approach to social change, it might be sufficient to confine one's concern to the coping and perceived justice needs of the relevant parties. Any change justified according to these criteria could be unequivocally advocated. On another view, there may be certain values or ideals inherent in a legal or social system, certain absolute principles, which may not be infringed; or there may be social goals that are desirable in themselves. This view is held by certain schools of moral, social, political, and legal philosophy and has been applied both to retributive justice, as illustrated by Kant, and to distributive justice, as reflected in the writings of John Rawls. Similarly, social philosophers have developed theories of justice based on recognition of prior *right*, on *desert*, and on *need* (Miller, 1976). Moreover, natural law and social contract theories, which had fallen victim to positivist thinking, have been given new impetus as a result of the Rawlsian debates. De facto recognition of fundamental rights is evidenced further by the fact that most nations have adopted written constitutions in which such rights are entrenched.

Unlike coping and perceived justice needs, fundamental principles of justice are sought on an abstract, ideological, rather than empirical, level.[13] The recognition of the relevance (or perceived relevance) of such fundamental principles adds a third tier to the present analysis. The interaction of the relevant parties and levels of need may be presented schematically as follows:

Parameters of Justice by Levels of Need and Relevant Parties

	Victim	Offender	Public
First Level: Coping Needs	Compensation Treatment Protection from further victimization	Inexcessive drain on resources Protection from vengeance	Reasonable drain on resources Protection from future victimization
Second Level: Perceived Justice Needs	Satisfaction with procedures and outcome	Satisfaction with procedures and outcome	Satisfaction with outcome
Third Level	Fundamental principles of justice complied with		

A detailed analysis of these three levels of need, with emphasis on the victim's perspective, will be presented in the three following chapters.

4

Coping Needs

As noted in the preceding chapter, the designation "coping needs" includes here financial, medical, and emotional needs, subcategories into which this chapter is divided.[1] This classification of needs is not absolute, however. "For most victims, physical, emotional and financial effects tended to occur together as part of a complex process" (Shapland et al., 1981:7). For example, while fear of crime has been classified as an emotional reaction, it may have, at least in part, a rational basis and may result in rational and practical consequences. The literature refers to the case of parents who, having fallen victim to a crime, were no longer willing to leave their children alone at home in the evening. In this example, while fear of crime may be classified as an emotional consequence, requiring a babysitter is a financial one.

Moreover, the nature of the impact is, to some extent, a function of the selection of response by the victim; some victims react at the "instrumental" level, by taking appropriate preventive action, while others experience anxiety or otherwise internalize their reaction, that is, at the "stress" level (Friedman et al., 1982:8). Thus, although presented here under the heading coping needs, the data accumulated relate rather to an elucidation of the *impact* of victimization than specifically to the needs following from it (cf. also Maguire and Corbett, 1987:76; Maguire, 1991:391).·Indeed, few of the impact studies, with the notable exception of Skogan et al. (1990) and the comprehensive study by Maguire and Corbett (1987), attempt specifically to determine victims' needs resulting therefrom.

Further, the topics dealt with in this chapter under the heading of coping needs may also merge with the "perceived justice needs" to be discussed in the next chapter. This is particularly true of the victim's emotional needs. Emotional consequences of victimization may be related to the victim's view of society and to the victim's allocation of responsibility for what has occurred. This point was emphasized by Symonds (1980), who claimed that the perception of inadequate support resulted in a "second injury." This, in turn, seems conceptually related to—although not identical with—the idea of "secondary victimization" alluded to by other sources[2] (see, e.g., Joutsen, 1987:54). This term refers to the victim's treatment at the hands of the justice system, the subjective aspect of which relates to the victim's "perceived justice needs."

Particularly relevant in this context is the rape victim's reportedly unhappy experience with the police and the justice system (see, e.g., Veronen et al., 1979), an instance where emotional consequences will interact with justice consequences. Again, psychotherapy, which appears to reflect an emotional need, and legal measures, which appear to reflect a justice need, may be alternative avenues of dealing with the same victimization symptoms, in particular the relief of anger (Waller, 1982:14).[3] Thus it may sometimes be hard to differentiate between emotional consequences and perceived justice needs.

The problem of classification was until recently outweighed by the problem of inadequate documentation. Despite the intensity of legislative and administrative policies designed to ameliorate the lot of the victims, relatively little was known about the effects of crime on them (Sparks, 1982:109; Skogan, 1987:136). The studies were fragmented, and the findings appeared to be widely inconsistent. Moreover, in many cases their conclusions reflected a political agenda (cf. Maguire, 1991:381). However, the two studies referred to above (Maguire and Corbett, 1987; Skogan et al., 1990), together with recent attempts to analyze systematically the literature on the impact of crime and the needs of the victim (Lurigio and Resick, 1990; Maguire, 1991; Mawby and Walklate, 1994: chap. 2), have to some extent clarified the confusion.

The available literature was classified by Waller (1982) into the following categories: victimization surveys; studies of the impact of particular types of crime (burglary, robbery, mugging, and rape); studies of particular types of victim (women, children, and the elderly); and surveys conducted by victim-assistance agencies or sponsored by local authorities in order to assess victim needs. Maguire and Corbett (1987) and Skogan et al. (1990), however, endeavor to integrate the second and fourth of these objectives. Note should also be taken of a group of researchers (e.g., Baril, 1984) who adopted a qualitative, "in-depth" approach in an attempt to empathize with the victim, in the belief that a more meaningful picture of the impact of victimization would be produced.

No attempt will be made here to document all the evidence available from the existing studies. It is proposed to mention only the most salient findings and to draw attention to some of the more problematic issues.

Financial Problems

A report, *The Economic Cost of Crime to Victims*, was published by the Bureau of Justice Studies on the basis of National Crime Survey data (Shenk and Klaus, 1984). This report showed that the total losses inflicted on victims of crime in the United States amounted in 1981 to $10.9 billion: $2.8 billion through "personal crimes" and $8.1 billion through "household crimes." The equivalent figures for 1990 were $4.6 billion and $14.6 billion, respectively (U.S. Dept. of Justice, 1992:148), but they underwent a modest decline between 1990 and 1992 (Klaus, 1994).

On the macro level, therefore, victim losses are of enormous magnitude. However, since the losses are distributed over a very high number of victimizations (33.6 million in 1992), the loss to each individual or household victimized was relatively modest: the median loss for "personal victimization" was $45 and for "household" victimization $65 (Shenk and Klaus, 1984:1). Apart from motor vehicle theft, for which the median loss was $1,500, the highest median loss for the offenses included in the 1981 analysis was $160 for burglary, $145 for rape, $85 for robbery, and $64 for assault. For larceny offenses the median was $40–$50. It was also noted that some 36% of the total losses reported were recovered or reimbursed (Shenk and Klaus, 5). However, the mean losses inflicted in the course of these offenses in 1992 was considerably higher: $3,990 for motor vehicle theft, $834 for burglary, $234 for rape, $555 for robbery, and $124 for assault. These differences may reflect the passage of time and the fact that means, unlike medians, are influenced by outlying responses—that is, a few very high losses will substantially inflate the figures produced (especially for burglary and robbery).

There is, of course, considerable variety in loss levels. Thus the minimum loss for the top quartile of burglary victims in the National Crime

Survey for 1981 was $645, and for rape victims it was $400 (Shenk and Klaus, 1984:3). Moreover, while "medical expenses contributed relatively little to the economic cost of crime to victims" (ibid., 4)—only about 2% of the total cost, for those victims of rape and robbery who incurred medical expenses (nearly one-half of the rape victims but less than 10% of the robbery victims)—these medical expenses were relatively high, with medians of $200 and $195, respectively (cf. also Klaus, 1994:2). By 1990, in 62.5% of crimes of violence in which the magnitude of medical expenses were known, these amounted to $250 or more (based on data in U.S. Dept. of Justice, 1992: table 84).

On the other hand, even the infliction of relatively high losses does not necessarily mean that the material aspect of the victimization was the most important for the victim. The study conducted in New York City for the Victim Services Agency (Friedman et al., 1982) found a relatively high incidence of material loss but a relatively low *salience*. "Property loss" was the problem most frequently referred to by respondents, 68% of the sample, but only 32% were designated by the researchers as having "financial loss" as their primary concern. Similarly, in a British study of burglary victims, only 28% of the victims named financial loss as the worst aspect of the offense, while 60% specified "intrusion upon privacy" or "emotional upset" (Maguire, 1991:395). Finally, a study of a sample of 323 victims in Pima County, Arizona, found that, when asked whether they had "enough resources to meet their daily living expenses"—that is, whether they could *cope*—the vast majority (83%–84%) replied affirmatively, both at the initial interview conducted shortly after the victimization and at the follow-up interview conducted four to six months later (Smith et al., 1984:27, 52–53).

Losses vary significantly, however, both in terms of amount and in terms of impact according to sociodemographic variables. The 1981 National Crime Survey study found that losses for blacks were higher than for whites for all categories of offense (Shenk and Klaus, 1984: table 8). Females incurred higher losses for crimes of personal violence, males for crimes of theft (ibid., table 7). The study indicated evidence of relatively greater losses being inflicted upon more vulnerable groups of the population—blacks and females. Further, for most personal crimes, the lower-income (less than $7,500) or middle-income ($7,500–$14,999) groups suffered as great or greater losses as compared with persons belonging to higher-income groups. Moreover, it should be noted that persons earning under $7,500 have the highest victimization rates for personal crimes, including robbery, and are the second highest category in respect to crimes of theft (U.S. Department of

Justice, 1992:33; the highest category was the *wealthiest*, with incomes of $50,000 or more). Thus while victimization losses (other than car theft) inflicted upon individuals are generally rather low, for some populations not only is the risk of victimization relatively high but the implications are substantial.

Medical Problems

The 6 million violent victimizations in 1990 (U.S. Dept. of Justice, 1992:16) resulted in 1.3 million victims receiving medical care (88); 10.4% of violent victimizations, and 31.0% of those involving injury, resulted in medical expenses being incurred (89). In 8.2% of violent victimizations— 24.2% of those involving injury—the victim received hospital care (91). In over 60% of these cases, treatment took place in the emergency room; in 7.5% hospitalization exceeded three days (91). Only 63.8% of injured victims had health insurance coverage or were eligible for public medical services (90), but this figure appears to have risen to 69% by 1992 (Klaus, 1994:2). Moreover, lower-income victims were more likely to sustain injury than higher-income victims (U.S. Dept of Justice, 1992:88).

The latter is only one of the variables affecting the probability of injury; cumulative data analyzed by the Bureau of Justice Statistics from 1979 to 1986 show that "white male central city residents under 25 and with family incomes of less than $10,000 had the highest average annual rate of injury from crime" (Harlow, 1989:5–6). Finally, nonstrangers were more likely to sustain injuries than strangers (U.S. Dept. of Justice, 1992:88), but a somewhat lower proportion of such injured victims were likely to need hospital treatment (91).

The survey conducted for the Canadian Federal-Provincial Task Force (1983) found that only 22% of the 1.6 million crimes included in the sample involved personal contact, but that these resulted in 50,500 nights in hospital and 405,700 days lost owing to some form of incapacitation (59). In Shapland's English sample of victims of offenses of violence more than 65% of the victims used medical services, but only a small number were detained in hospital (Shapland et al., 1985:102). Thus medical (other than psychological) problems, while generally confined to victims of crimes of violence, appear to be fairly serious for a substantial number of such victims. The financial costs involved were referred to in the previous section. How far crime victims are in need of specialized medical services, whether because of the nature or circumstances of the injury or because of the interaction with law enforcement personnel, is a question worthy of greater attention. Hitherto such special needs have been recognized primarily in connection with rape. Shapland et al. (1985:102–3), in their English study, concluded that much could be done to provide support for victims in this context.

Emotional Problems

Although emotional problems, as noted, seem to be more difficult to research than the previous topics, a growing literature is emerging. Some writers are quite unequivocal as to their findings. Thus, the survey conducted by the New York Victim Services Agency reached the following conclusions:

1. "The most common problems (affecting three-quarters of the sample) from which crime victims suffered, were psychological problems including fear, anxiety, nervousness, self-blame, anger, shame and difficulty sleeping."
2. "Emotional problems affected victims of property crime (burglary) as well as victims of violent or personal crimes (robbery and assault)."
3. "Although crime-related problems had declined in severity four months after the incidents, half the victims continued to have problems." (Friedman et al., 1982:5–6)

How far are these three conclusions supported by the other literature dealing with the emotional effects of victimization? Lists of reactions similar to those noted above—although varying in order of frequency or salience—appear in other victim studies. These include anger, shock, and confusion (Maguire, 1980:262, on the basis of a study of burglary victims in England), and "worry, fear, loss of confidence" for the same type of victim in the British Crime Survey (Hough, 1984: table 2). However, the Canadian burglary victims studied by Waller and Okihiro (1978:37) were most likely to specify surprise. Baril (1984) referred to "numbness, disbelief and fear" (see also Baril, 1980).[4] Smith et al. (1984:8) listed "fear, anxiety, vulnerability, disorientation, anger, revengeful, self-blame, embarrassment" as the victim's emotional problems, but they selected anxiety, fear, and stress as the emotions to be measured in their study. Smale (1984), in an intensive study of samples of victims of both violent and property crimes, found that "fright" and "fear of recurrence" were present for almost all victims, while between one-quarter and one-half experienced "the need to air feelings," "distrust of others," "sense of sharing responsibility," and "fear" (87). Another study referred to by Waller (1984) identified seven symptoms of "victim crisis," namely, "serious residual effects (!), memory loss, physical upset or nausea, confused state of shock, fear, crying or shaking, and nervousness" (98; see also the specific fears listed by rape victims in Veronen et al., 1979:157).

Even less consistency is found in the extensive literature analyzing the specific clinical syndromes associated with victimization and its emotional impact, pioneered in Bard and Sangrey (1979, 1980), *Evaluation and Change* (1980), and Salasin (1981) and reviewed in Lurigio and Resick (1990) and Maguire (1991). Some of these writers have traced a number of stages in the emotional reactions to victimization. Thus Bard and Sangrey (1979, 1980) referred to three stages: (1) the impact stage, (2) the recoil stage, and (3) the reorganization stage. However, the three stages described by Paap (1981) are different: (1) discovery, (2) "working the case," and (3) resignation; while Symonds (1980) describes four stages of response: (1) shock, disbelief, and denial; (2) "frozen fright"; (3) depression and hostility; and (4) integration with lifestyle. Other characteristic syndromes noted in the literature are guilt and self-blame (Friedman et al., 1982:2), helplessness (Symonds, 1980), and "idiocide," or the denial of status and stature (Weiss, 1980).

Despite inconsistencies, the clinical literature has granted recognition to Post-Traumatic Stress Disorder (PTSD), which is said to be applicable to crime victims—27.8% of one sample of female victims (Kilpatrick et al., 1987). This syndrome has been recognized by the American Psychiatric Association (Waller, 1982; Janoff-Bulman and Frieze, 1983) and the World Health Organization (cf. *Victims of Crime*, 1985).

Much of this clinical literature may be of doubtful general validity (see Maguire, 1991), as evidenced by the diverse patterns of emotional reaction indicated by the different theories. Friedman et al. (1982) cite the literature review conducted by Silver and Wortman, who concluded that there was "no evidence of stages of adjustment"; see also Young (1990:198) and Smith et al. (1984:5). Friedman and his colleagues endeavored to employ a more objective measure of emotional impact, the Affect Balance Scale, comprising four positive indicators (joy, contentment, vigor, and affection) and four negative measures (anxiety, depression, guilt, and hostility). A comparison between their New York sample of victims and a group of college students produced significant differences on all measures (Friedman et al., 1982:110), but these may have been due to differences between the samples. Smith et al. (1984), in their study of victims in Pima County, Arizona, employed scales designed to measure anxiety, fear, and stress. The mean score for the anxiety items was found even at the second interview to be substantially higher than the average for female college students, and to approximate the average score for "neuropsychiatric patients diagnosed as suffering from an 'anxiety reaction' " (39).

Lurigio (1987), too, found significant differences between victims and nonvictims on a number of measures of vulnerability and "a wide range of symptomology," including "uncontrollable urges to retaliate" (463); and Maguire and Corbett (1987:66–67) found that female victims of serious offenses were twice as likely to show symptoms of psychiatric disturbance as the general population three to six months after the crime. The findings as to the *prevalence* of emotional problems varies among the different studies. Knudten et al. (1976), in their Milwaukee study, found that only 20% of the victims in their sample, but 57% of the victims reaching the courts, suffered mentally or emotionally. Similarly, only 32% of the "complaining witnesses" in a Brooklyn sample referred to emotional difficulties. In the British Crime Survey, "Over half of the victimizations were said to have caused no practical problems, while two-thirds did not lead to any emotional upset" (Mayhew, 1984:5). However, it seems that more than one-half of burglary victims encountered some emotional problem (Hough, 1984: table 2); while 60% of all victim respondents in the 1988 survey reported that a family member showed *some* emotional reaction, generally anger (Mawby and Walklate, 1994:42). Finally, 75% of the New York City sample referred to above suffered from the emotional reactions specified (Friedman et al., 1982:86).

These differences in the findings have been attributed to methodological factors, such as the nature of the sample, the use of open or closed questions, and the mode of interviewing (traumatic and emotional effects, it is believed, are more likely to be referred to in personal interviews than in telephone interviews or survey questionnaires) (cf. Mayhew, 1984:18 n. 8; Maguire, 1991). Thus the range of British victims responding that they were "very much affected" by the offense varied from 12% in the British Crime Survey to 79% of those interviewed by victim-assistance personnel (Maguire, 1991:394).

The second conclusion of the Victim Services Agency study was the generality of emotional problems for all types of victimization, not only for victims of violence. There is support for this view elsewhere in the literature. While the earlier studies tended to concentrate on offenses of violence (especially rape; cf. Resick, 1990), studies of burglary victims reveal that they, too, suffer emotional reactions. Indeed, 65% of Maguire's burglary victims were still experiencing stressful reactions for up to 10 weeks after the incident (Maguire, 1980:264).

However, other studies indicate that the impact of property offenses is generally less than that of violent offenses (Maguire, 1991:395)—burglary being an exception, owing to its perceived intrusiveness into the victim's life. Thus the British survey conducted by Maguire and Corbett found that while 36%–40% of victims of reported robberies, serious assaults, and burglaries responded that they were "very much affected" by the offense, the corresponding figures for most thefts—as well as for minor assaults—were under 15% (ibid., 396; cf. Mawby and Walklate, 1991:42).

Similarly, care must be taken not to assume that the emotional trauma, where it occurs, is of uniform character, magnitude, and duration for all types of offense. It should not be anticipated that the impact of property offenses, even where traumatic, would have the same magnitude as rape or incest. Smale (1984) found that victims of violence were more likely to experience psychological problems, while victims of property offenses were more concerned with the probability of recurrence of the offense. Sales et al. (1984:131), who interviewed 127 victims at a rape crisis center, found that "the recovery process for assault victims lasts longer than the several months predicted by crisis theory," and advocated controlled comparisons of different populations of victims. It should be noted in this connection that some writers on crisis theory have hypothesized the generalizability of crisis or victimization pathologies, whereby not only would types of crime victim not necessarily be differentiated from one another, but crime victims would be undifferentiated from other forms of victimization and even from other "undesirable life events" (ibid.). This issue recalls the debate referred to in the preceding chapter on the issue of defining the term *victim*.

Similar confusion relates to the third point specified by the New York study, on the question of the duration of negative emotional effects. In their discussion of the literature, Friedman et al. (1982) refer to crisis reaction up to six weeks. They found that most problems designated as serious in the first interview were no longer so designated by the second interview, after four months (table 5.1; cf. also Smith et al., 1984). Moreover, the tendency for problems generally to disappear during this period applied to all categories of victim (Friedman et al., 1982: tables 5.2, 5.3). However, even after four months, differences between certain subgroups continued; for example, more problems were indicated by low-income victims (under $15,000 per year) and injured victims. Affective reaction scores improved during this period for seven out of eight items (ibid., 197–98).

Wide divergencies appear in other studies, particularly in relation to sexual assault (Maguire, 1981:400–402). Fear and anxiety among rape victims were measured by Kilpatrick et al. (1981) over a six-month period, over which a gradual decline was found. Sales et al. (1984), however, found that their sexual assault victims, while appearing to have recovered after six months in terms both of behavior and stress symptoms, subsequently experienced a relapse in the latter respect. Holmstrom and Burgess (1978) claimed that 26% of the rape victims in their study had not recovered after six years, and Silver et al. (1983) found that three-fourths of their sample of incest victims were still "searching to find some meaning" in the incest twenty years later (87).[5] It is evident that violent sexual offenses are more traumatic than other types of offense, but some other victims of violence "may suffer analogous problems" (Maguire, 1991:401). Shapland et al. (1985:99) found that psychological effects persisted among victims throughout a two-and-a-half-year follow-up but then declined (Shapland, 1986:220). Some writers claim that certain residual symptoms of victimization are never erased (Sales et al., 1984:120; see also Maguire and Corbett, 1987:64). Finally, Connick and Davis (1981) note that the emotional impact of the crime is more likely to be bounded in space and time when the offense was committed by a stranger; in other cases there is a greater probability of reminders after long intervals. This finding is not confirmed by the review of Lurigio and Resick (1990:56–57) in the context of sex offenses. This topic is worthy of further study, since it may have implications regarding the optimal modes of resolution of nonstranger conflicts.

Postcrime distress and recovery are also related to preexisting emotional problems and to sociodemographic variables (Lurigio and Resick, 1990:52–54; Maguire, 1991:197–98); thus most studies—but by no means all—indicate that more vulnerable groups, such as older victims, females, and those with lower incomes, are more adversely affected (ibid.).

Similarly, Lurigio and Resick (1990) point to the significance of *post-victimization* variables, based in the social psychological literature, in determining the degree of traumatization by the offense. They refer to behavioral self-blame, which will lead the victim to believe that he or she can avoid such traumas by behaving differently; this is part of a wider literature on attributions of causality or responsibility for the victimizing experience. (See, inter alia, vols. 39 (2) and 40 (1) of the *Journal of Social Issues*.) They also refer to "cognitive restructuring," whereby the experience is reinterpreted, for example, in comparison with the lot of other less fortunate persons.

According to another approach based in this literature, victimization problems derive primarily from the shattering of three types of generally shared assumptions. "The three assumptions are: 1) the belief in personal invulnerability; 2) the perception of the world as meaningful and comprehensible; 3) the view of ourselves in a positive light" (Janoff-Bulman and Frieze, 1983:3). This hypothesis, however, as well as the others referred to above, requires testing and validation no less than the more psychoanalytically oriented theories.

Somewhat more systematic information has been gathered on the subject of the *fear* of crime. It may be surmised that persons who have been victimized would live in greater fear of victimization than persons who had not had the experience. However, the survey data are somewhat ambiguous on this point. Garofalo (1977a) found that certain types of victims had greater fear levels but that there was no overall trend in this respect.[6] Some writers have even suggested that victimization may reduce fear, since the actual experience proves to be less traumatic than anticipated (cf. Skogan, 1985:2). Skogan and Maxfield, on the other hand, in their study of fear in Chicago, Philadelphia, and San Francisco in 1977, found that victims were between 30% and 60% more likely to indicate fear than nonvictims (1981:62); this finding was reaffirmed in a "panel" study conducted by Skogan (1986), in which samples drawn from Houston, Texas, and Newark, New Jersey, totaling 1,738 persons, were interviewed twice, with a 12-month interval between interviews.

The salience and intensity of fear, however, seem to emerge more unequivocally not only from the clinical literature reviewed above but also from smaller surveys of victim populations. The New York Victim Services Agency study found that "a major emotional response to crime was fear. More than 60 percent of victims reported feeling 'very much' or 'somewhat' less safe in their homes, and more than 40 percent felt less safe in their neighborhoods. After the crime, 60 percent of the 274 victims interviewed reported taking added precautions in their homes and 38 percent said they went out less at night. Twenty-four percent went out less during the day" (Friedman et al., 1982:71).

A degree of discrepancy between the picture emerging from some of the general survey data and that presented by the New York study may be explained partly in terms of the nature of the sample, and partly in terms of the *measure* of fear adopted. The surveys use a miscellany of such measures, none of which relate directly to the incident, since the same questions are designed for nonvictims. They therefore elicit the respondent's general attitude on the issue, rather than measuring whether any modification of this attitude took place consequent to the offense.[7] Further, personal *fear* is not always distinguished from a general *concern* about crime (Mayhew, 1984). Finally, New York City may not be a representative location for testing manifestations of fear; compare, for example, the more moderate impact noted by Smith et al. (1984) in Pima County, Arizona.

The effects of victimization on fear may vary by type of offense, but the findings are not uniform as to the types of offense arousing greater fear levels. Surprisingly, however, some American studies have associated increases in fear levels primarily with offenses involving an element of property loss (Garofalo, 1977a; Smith and Hill, 1991). It has, of course, been established that certain more vulnerable sections of the community, such as females and the elderly, are more likely to be fearful of crime (see, e.g., Skogan and Maxfield, 1981), but it does not follow that these groups are more strongly affected by victimization experiences in this respect.

Insofar as the experience of victimization results in increasing fear and the resultant spread of fear and suspicion in the community as a whole, this result would seem to negate the Durkheimian hypothesis that a crime leads to an increase in social solidarity (Conklin, 1972). Increase in mutual suspicion was suggested by the findings of a study conducted by Lejeune and Alex (1977); however, the survey reported by Smith et al. (1984) found that this phenomenon was only modest and did not reach pathological dimensions. Friedman et al. (1982) found that in 32% of the cases victimization was likely to affect adversely the victim's ability to relate to other people, but at the same time more than half the sample "felt better about people's willingness to help" as a result of sympathetic support systems or favorable police response" (205; and cf. Young, 1990:198), a finding that would tend to validate the Durkheimian thesis. This last finding may also be indicative of the importance of support networks, whether formal or informal. It has also been suggested that fear could be a useful and cost-effective learning experience giving rise to rational consequences such as the taking of proper precautions (Skogan, 1985:13).

Effects of Crime and Needs of Victims

As noted earlier, the literature reviewed in this chapter generally analyzes the "effects" of crime rather than attempting to define the needs of victims. This is partly owing to the arbitrary or subjective element in the definition of a "need"[8] as compared, for example, with a "problem" or an "inconvenience" (Maguire and Corbett, 1987:60–61). Maguire and Corbett also point out that many adverse effects of victimization do not necessarily give rise to a need, since the victim does not require any outside help in overcoming the problem (61). Skogan et al. (1990) found that most problems were overcome with the help of family and friends, so that assistance was not usually required from outside agencies.

Nevertheless, these studies did endeavor to assess the nature and extent both of "needs" and "unmet needs" (Skogan et al., 1990) and of "unresolved problems" (Maguire and Corbett, 1987). Thus Skogan et al. (1990) "asked about seventeen categories of assistance that victims might possibly need" (21). Most of the victims (of robbery, assault, and burglary) had either no needs (39%) or only one (20%) (22). The main clusters of need which victims had were counseling and advice (36%), household repair/security (22%), and financial or housing assistance (16%) (25), although, as the authors point out, the latter "needs" are related less to the victimization experience itself than to the prevention of future crime.

However, most needs were, as noted, met by family and friends or, to a lesser extent (see also chap. 10), by victim-assistance agencies. The *unmet* needs were mainly of a practical nature, particularly assistance in filing insurance claims (Skogan et al., 1990: fig. 5), specified by more than one-half of the sample. Maguire and Corbett (1987:77) calculated that some 30%–40% of victims of recorded offenses of burglary or violence in Britain are in need of support from a victim-assistance scheme; for other categories their assessments were much lower.

Conclusions

While the impact of victimization in terms of the financial and medical needs to which it gives rise may require further examination, the general picture in these respects is clear. Most victims have no medical needs following their victimization and will have suffered relatively modest financial losses. A minority of victims, however, may have serious problems either because of the greater injuries or losses they have incurred, or owing to their reduced ability—whether because of objective or subjective factors—to deal with these problems.

In relation to the emotional impact of victimization, the methodological issues are incomparably more complex and the findings inconsistent. However, there is evidence that the emotional problems accompanying victimization are the dominant ones, even for victims of property crimes. The New York survey cited above found that psychological problems dominated all others: "The impact of the crime . . . was first and foremost psychological. . . . Even when describing practical problems stemming from the crime—stolen property, disruption of daily routine, damaged property, medical complications, medical expenses, lost income, problems with employers—three-quarters of the victims described the impact of the crime in psychological terms" (Friedman et al., 1982:xvii). The authors noted in the concluding section of their report that they were "stunned at the general impact of a crime on the victim's psychological state, and at the alterations in daily life which were so often a part of the post-victimization experience" (266).

A similar conclusion was also reached by Smith et al. (1984). Moreover, Shapland (1984) refers to "the persistence and consistency of the prevalence of physical, social and psychological effects over time, compared to the low level and decrease over time of financial loss" (142). Maguire (1991:395–96), however, suggests that the more serious effects are confined to offenses of violence and burglary, owing to its intrusive element. For most offenses are probably trivial, and victims have trouble in recollecting them (Fattah, 1981).

The nature of the emotional problems identified appears also to depend to some extent on the perspective of the researcher; writers with a welfare orientation emphasize such "routine" effects as fear and anxiety, those adopting a more psychoanalytic orientation tend to identify traumatization on a deeper personality level. Social psychologists diagnose problems in terms of being a threat to the victim's assumptions about the world, including his or her attributions of responsibility to him- or herself and others.

Identification of the dominant problems encountered by victims and the diagnosis of their causes will tend to determine the optimal remedies proposed. Further, insofar as victims appear to be in need of assistance to overcome their problems, the question arises whether such assistance should be professional or voluntary, whether those providing assistance should be specialists in providing service to crime victims, or whether the answer lies in the strengthening of existing support networks. The identity of the helping agent may determine, inter alia, whether the victim adopts a "stress" or an "instrumental" reaction; a psychoanalyst may emphasize therapy, and a behaviorist may suggest instrumental reactions such as the purchase of a lock. The nature of the intervention may also influence the victim in his or her decision to seek a remedy from social services or within the criminal justice system, the main dichotomy around which the present study revolves (see esp. chap. 12).

It is clear from existing studies that insofar as victims continue to be handled by traditional law enforcement personnel, these should be required to display a greater sensitivity than in the past, and that, for example, "the collection of evidence should not override the provision of care and support that the victim needs during a period of crisis" (Shapland et al., 1981:65, and 1985:30). This principle has of course been recognized by policy documents (see, e.g., President's Task Force, 1982; ABA, 1983) and reflected in the subsequent legislative and administrative reforms. However, the American Psychological Association (1984) pointed out that while "to some extent these laws are likely to significantly aid victims and reducing [sic] the impact of the victimization experience," "it is also likely . . . that some of the provisions in these laws will have just the opposite effect" (142). Attention is implicitly drawn here to the need for evaluation of the reforms referred to.

The above warning on the part of the American Psychological Association also serves as a reminder of the oft-heard allegation of "secondary victimization," whereby the emotional impact of the victimization itself may be further aggravated by the victim's experience with the criminal justice system, or possibly even with other social agencies, such as the compensation board (see chap. 9). However, favorable experiences may be expected to reduce this trauma.

The question of what is a favorable or an unfavorable experience with the justice system cannot be assessed exclusively on the basis of the policies and attitudes adopted by that system as documented in chapter 2, or by the coping needs of the victim as documented in the present chapter. They are also a function of the victim's perceived needs and expectations from that system. This will be the topic of the next chapter.

5

Perceived Justice Needs

This chapter deals with the perceived justice needs of the main parties involved in the criminal justice system. Unlike the next chapter, which will be concerned with abstract concepts of justice, the issues to be considered here are essentially empirical ones. Perceived justice needs cannot be determined a priori, but only as the result of evidence obtained by means of surveys or research. However, as will become evident from the following discussion, most of the evidence regarding these needs is of a somewhat indirect nature. When considering perceived justice needs it seems appropriate to differentiate between what seem analytically to be two different questions: (1) What is known about people's fundamental attitudes, concepts, and sentiments regarding the institutions and functions of justice in society? (2) How far are people satisfied with the criminal justice system as it actually operates, or as it is perceived by them to operate, today?

Naturally, these two questions are interrelated, since it would be expected that the greater the extent to which the present system is attuned to people's fundamental concepts of justice, the higher the degree of satisfaction that will be expressed with this system. Conversely, satisfaction, or nonsatisfaction, with the prevailing criminal justice system may serve as an indicator, albeit indirect, of fundamental attitudes to justice. Partly for this reason, and partly because considerably more direct evidence is available on this topic, the degree of satisfaction with the current system will be examined first.

Data Sources

The sources of knowledge in this area derive both from surveys and from specific research projects. Thus, a number of public opinion surveys of the Harris-Gallup variety have dealt with questions related to criminal justice. Academic criminologists are familiar with the General Social Surveys conducted by the National Opinion Research Center; an analysis of public attitudes to crime and punishment deriving from these sources was published by Stinchcombe et al. (1980). Other surveys have been conducted on a localized basis in individual states, by state crime commissions and other local bodies. The proliferation of such studies was documented some years ago by the International Center for Comparative Criminology in Montreal, which located "well over 500 studies" published in the years 1967–76 alone (Baril, 1984:75). The scientific merit of these studies is, however, often limited. A recent comprehensive analysis of both the sources and the findings was conducted by Roberts (1992).

Another important source that has emerged in recent years is the victimization surveys, notably the National Crime Survey. These have provided data on certain aspects of the topic; in particular, some impression of the public's attitude to the police may be gleaned from responses by victims on the nonreporting of offenses committed against them, and the reasons for such nonreporting. One advantage of such surveys is that they enable comparisons to be made between the attitudes of victims and those of nonvictims. In general, however, information deriving from these surveys on the victims' attitudes to, and expectations from, the criminal justice system has been very limited. The British Crime Survey is notable for its attempt to explore these issues more widely; this orientation was also adopted by the European-based International Crime Survey launched in 1989.

In-depth research on attitudes to the criminal justice system, on the other hand, is rather sparse. A number of studies deal with specific issues, such as the problems encountered by rape victims (see esp. Holmstrom and Burgess, 1978) or racial differences in attitudes to the police (Jacob, 1971). There is no doubt that since the publication of the review by Mackay and Hagan (1978), which identified only four studies of victims' attitudes, this literature has been considerably enriched by a number of detailed studies, such as one conducted by Hagan (1980) in Canada, Shapland et al. (1985) in England, and the series of studies conducted by the Vera Institute of Justice and the Victim Services Agency in New York City (Davis, Russell, and Kunreuther, 1980; Davis, Tichane, and Connick, 1980; Connick and Davis, 1981; Friedman et al., 1982). Some studies of victims' attitudes have been carried out in the context of particular victim-oriented programs, the most notable example being Umbreit's study of the meaning of "fairness" in the context of offender-victim mediation (Umbreit, 1988) and some recent research on victim-impact statements (Davis and Smith, 1994b; Erez et al., 1994). Finally, the in-depth "qualitative" studies and the experimental literature should also be noted. However, while the cumulative contribution of these studies to the literature should not be underestimated, most of the research has limitations, whether geographical or methodological, such that our knowledge of victim attitudes and their implications is still somewhat rudimentary.

Studies of the defendant's attitude to the criminal justice system are probably fewer still in number (but see Casper, 1978; Casper et al., 1988), although more research has been conducted on *prisoners'* attitudes (see, e.g., such classics as Sykes and Messinger, 1960), perhaps because prisoners constitute, in the most literal sense, a "captive audience."

The above-mentioned studies are relevant not only to the question of the attitudes of the different parties to specific criminal justice agencies as they function today, but also to the wider question of fundamental concepts and attitudes regarding justice and its proper functioning. In this area experimental studies may be more appropriate than empirical ones, since the concern is with "basic" justice needs and "ideal" justice systems, unrelated to the practices prevailing in the "real world" (although even experimental situations will not be entirely uninfluenced by real-world considerations).

The experimental studies that are relevant in this context belong mostly to the areas of social psychology which were referred to in chapter 2, but in particular to equity theory. Whereas attribution theory and the just-world theory are concerned mainly with the reactions of third parties, and tend to focus on causality and blame rather than the appropriateness of the societal response, equity theory is more concerned with the interpretations and reactions of the parties to the victimization themselves. Another distinct but related area of research to have developed rapidly in recent years pertains to the perceived fairness of the *procedures* rather than the *outcomes* (cf. Lind and Tyler, 1988:10–12). The relevance of these areas of research will be demonstrated below.

Finally, the most significant attempt to orientate the experimental literature of social psychology to the predicament of the crime victim is found in the recent monograph by Greenberg and Ruback (1992), but the focus here is mainly on the dynamics of victim decision-making—and in particular the decision whether to report the crime—rather than on the broader issues of justice needs and perceptions with which this chapter is primarily concerned.

Methodological Issues

While a considerable amount of data are now available regarding people's feelings about the police and other criminal justice agencies, the validity of these data is questionable and their interpretation problematical. Research on attitudes is a highly complex area fraught with ambiguities (Robert, 1979; Skogan, 1981; Walker and Hough, 1988; Roberts, 1992; Durham, 1993).[1] Responses may depend not only on the sample selected but also on the phrasing of the question and the "set" within which it is presented. Terms and concepts prevailing in the criminal justice vocabulary may convey varying messages or images to different respondents (Robert, 1979; Baril, 1984). This problem can perhaps be reduced by conducting exploratory, qualitative research prior to the quantitative survey (Robert 1979:81). However, rejection of quantitative research in favor of qualitative (see, e.g., Baril, 1984) results in other disadvantages, such as the lack of representativeness and a risk of "analysis which smacks of psychoanalysis" (Robert, 1979:86).

Another general problem of attitude research is the difficulty in reaching conclusions regarding people's behavior on the basis of their verbal expressions. Attitude studies would be on firmer ground if in addition to the eliciting of responses to attitudinal questions, it were also possible to study the conduct of the research population giving expression to such attitudes. However, while such research may sometimes be feasible in relation to courts and the police,[2] it is extremely difficult to do this for the general public or for victims. These groups have few opportunities to give expression to their attitudes by means of specific and recorded conduct, other than their decision to report an offense and to "cooperate" with the criminal justice agencies. Even these decisions may be difficult to document, particularly on the "micro" level necessary for the measure of, or at least the elucidation of, their attitudes.

Mention must be made here of the pioneering attempt of Greenberg et al. (1982) to compare the results of adopting alternative methodological approaches to the study of victim behavior in relation to the reporting of a crime. Their main concern was the relative influence of victim characteristics and situational factors—and especially the conduct of third parties—on the decision to report. The authors compared the merits of (1) "archival analysis," that is, the study of police reports, (2) interviews with victims, (3) simulative studies (interviewing respondents), and (4) the experimental approach, whereby a "crime" was constructed and the conduct of the "victim" (as he or she believed him- or herself to be) was observed. Certain similarities as well as inconsistencies emerged, and the authors attempted to account for the latter. The overall impression created regarding the respective merits of the four methods was that *(a)* official records are lacking in the type of data required; *(b)* interviews create problems of reconstruction of the event; *(c)* simulated situations may be too remote from "real life"; and *(d)* experimentation seemed to produce both valid and relevant results. The authors, indeed, "placed more confidence in the experimental findings than in the simulation findings" (81). However, such research is complicated and expensive and may be difficult to apply to certain areas such as homicides. The authors in fact concluded that "no single methodology has a monopoly on virtue" (82).

Most of the surveys considered in this chapter are considerably less sophisticated and rely instead on verbal responses to questions in determining attitudes to the criminal justice system of the population surveyed. Moreover, they generally adopt somewhat simplistic criteria for the dependent variable. The most common measures of a positive attitude on the part of the respondent are whether he or she was "satisfied" with the functioning of the agency in question, or whether this agency was regarded as "fair," "just," or "effective." An obvious problem here is the subjective nature of the criteria. Differentiated responses may reflect the different experiences undergone by the respondents at the hands of the agency in question, or different notions of the standard ("justice," "fairness," etc.) according to which the agency is being measured.

Further, it may not be clear whether the agency is being evaluated by reference to some *ideal* standard perceived by the respondent to be the appropriate criterion, or whether the baseline according to which the respondents are measuring their perceptions of the agency in question are the *anticipated* standard of conduct that they expected from that agency. This last interpretation was adopted by Kelly (1982:14) in order to interpret her findings on the relatively favorable evaluation of the police by her sample of rape victims, who at the same time voiced considerable criticism of the police. Indeed, in a well-known article on attitudes to the police, one researcher operationalized the concept of injustice as "incongruence, or a gap between expectations and perceptions" (Jacob, 1971:69). The extent of this gap between expectations and perceptions may not, however, suffice as the sole measure of the respondents' feelings about the performance of the agency concerned, for, as Jacob points out, "the gap may be large but the person may feel injustice is not very salient to him" (70).

More common methodological issues which arise here, in particular in the context of victim attitudes, relate to the need for longitudinal studies for the purpose of measuring change and to the question of control and comparison groups. These issues are dealt with in the article by Mackay and Hagan (1978) referred to above and will be alluded to in the course of this chapter.

The research pertinent to the determination of fundamental concepts of justice,[3] as distinct from attitudes toward the operation of existing agencies, raises its own methodological problems. First, what are the fundamental questions pertaining to notions of justice which are raised, explicitly or implicitly, by the available studies, or which should be raised by any other studies which may be designed? Second, how much of the evidence emerging from the surveys and studies conducted can be seen to be pertinent to the more fundamental questions, rather than merely reflecting attitudes to the existing system?

On the first issue, one of the fundamental issues relevant to this study is the degree to which the relevant parties, in this case the victim and the public, are *punitive,* that is, to what degree of severity they feel that the perpetrators of an offense should be punished. While this question may be raised in the context of the same types of survey in which the evaluations of present-day criminal justice agencies are elicited, it is distinct in its implications, since it need not be logically related to the functioning of these agencies. It may instead be concerned with either of the following dichotomies: *(a)* punitiveness versus leniency, that is, how far respondents wish to impose relatively harsh, as opposed to relatively light, sanctions on offenders; and *(b)* punitiveness versus rehabilitation, that is, how far the sanctioning system favored would have a backward-looking orientation to the offense committed rather than a forward-looking orientation to changing the offender (cf. Walker and Hough, 1988).[4]

The second issue is more problematical. Not only in the survey data but even in the experimental data it may be difficult, when endeavoring to study "fundamental" justice needs, to control satisfactorily for respondents' attitudes toward the prevailing system. Perceptions of justice cannot be studied in a void. Even if respondents are not relating explicitly to the prevailing criminal justice practices, they may be influenced indirectly by them. Moreover, they are inevitably responding within the frame of reference of contemporary values and institutions. In indicating their expectations of a justice system, respondents may or may not be able to transcend some of the traditional principles or conventions upon which the present system is founded, but they are unlikely to be able to liberate themselves entirely from prevailing socioeconomic and political values and mores. Nevertheless, the distinction between attitudes to the present system and "fundamental" attitudes is useful in the context of the present study, which is based upon the somewhat optimistic premise that changes in the structure of the criminal justice system are negotiable, whereas changes in the socioeconomic and political systems are beyond its terms of reference.

The following sections of this chapter will review the data available on attitudes of the public in general, and of victims in particular, to the existing system. The more fundamental issues will be discussed subsequently.

Citizens' Attitudes toward Police

Surveys of citizens' attitudes to the police have consistently indicated a high degree of support for that body. The surveys conducted for the President's Commission on Law Enforcement and the Administration of Justice indicated considerable support for the police even among groups who were sympathetic to civil liberties and not in favor of wide police powers. One of these surveys "found that 91 percent of the respondents believed that their local police were doing an excellent (22 percent), good (45 percent), or fair (24 percent) job of enforcing the laws" (Ennis, 1967:53, cited in Garofalo, 1977b:11). Similarly, "35 percent felt that the police were respectful towards persons like themselves, and 88 percent felt that the police in their neighborhoods were honest" (Thomas and Hyman, 1977:309). Evaluations of data relating to 13 cities included in the National Crime Survey in 1972 and 1973 and in 1975 revealed that between 79% and 81% of respondents rated their local police "good" or "average." This, however, seems to indicate less enthusiasm than evidenced by the earlier surveys. Moreover, "fully two-thirds (68 percent) of the respondents felt that some improvement was needed in their local police."

Other studies tend to support the generally favorable image. Smith and Hawkins (1973) conducted a survey in Seattle "designed to assess respondents' views of the fairness of the police as a group," using five measures related primarily to the impartiality or selectivity of law enforcement. Seventy-two percent of the respondents were in the "most favorable" or "more favorable" categories. Thomas and Hyman (1977) whose study was based on 3,334 households in Virginia, concluded that "the vast majority of those in our sample described the police as effective, equitable in their treatment of citizens, and respectful" (316). Among 892 respondents in a British Columbia sample, 70% evaluated their local police as "good," and 22.6% as "very good" (Koenig, 1980:246). Later surveys in the United States and Canada indicated that 84% and 86%, respectively, of the population were satisfied with the police (Brillon, 1983:81). However, a survey conducted in 1991 on behalf of the National Victim Center found that only 64% of the public rated the functioning of the police as "excellent" or "fair" (Flanagan and Maguire, 1992:178).

Finally, while the 1988 British Crime Survey found that 85% of respondents rated police performance as "good" or "very good," this constituted a decline as compared with earlier surveys, a decline that was "consistent with the findings of independent polls" (Skogan, 1990:1, 2). Moreover, the 1989 International Crime Survey found that in most of the participating European countries (including Britain) the view that the police were doing a good job of controlling crime was nearer to 60%, while on average "16% did not feel capable of expressing an opinion" (Van Dijk et al., 1990:71). The evaluations of the non-European countries, including the United States and Canada, were higher.

Support for the police indicated by these studies was by no means uniform across all components of the population. Thus, Garofalo (1977a) found "very large differences between racial groups on evaluation of police performance in the 'impact cities' " (28). The proportion of whites who evaluated local police performance as good was more than twice the comparable proportion of African Americans (54% versus 25%; see also Garofalo, 1977b:13). Other studies, too, have drawn attention to differential perceptions of the police according to respondents' race (see Jacob, 1971, and the studies referred to therein; Ku, 1977; Thomas and Hyman, 1977:315, who found that "the majority of blacks in this sample are highly critical of the police"; Skogan, 1990:15). Age, too, is a variable that has been found to be related to attitudes toward the police: positive evaluations according to age group increased from 29% in the lowest age group (16–19) to 60% among the "65 or older" (Garofalo, 1977a:86, table 38; see also Garofalo, 1977b:15; Skogan, 1990:15; Van Dijk et al., 1990:72).

Victims' Attitudes toward Police

A number of studies have attempted to determine how far attitudes toward police are influenced by victimization experiences. It is sometimes hypothesized that the experience of being victimized would be found to result in a lower opinion of the police. This might follow either from the victim's feeling that the police had failed to provide protection, or as a result of negative experiences with the police as such. The validity of this hypothesis is directly relevant to the present research, both in order to determine whether persons with victimization experience represent a special constituency in the context of the public's attitudes to the criminal justice system, and, more specifically, to determine how far victims seem to have been satisfied with their experiences in the course of their encounters with this system.

The National Crime Survey data analyzed by Garofalo (1977a), being a victimization survey, was able to throw light on this topic. In general, it was found that there were "only small differences in evaluation of police performance" between victims, defined as persons who reported having been victimized during the previous twelve months, and nonvictims (29, table 38). Six percent fewer victims than nonvictims gave good ratings, and six percent more gave poor ratings. This trend was consistent for whites among the different age groups, but less consistent for blacks (table 42).

A number of other surveys have examined the differences between victims and nonvictims in attitudes toward police. An earlier analysis using the National Opinion Research Center data collected for the President's Commission in 1967 also found that victims of crime were less likely to express support for the police (Black, 1971, citing Black, 1970).[5] This finding was confirmed by Koenig (1980) and by the International Crime Survey (Van Dijk et al., 1990:72). Moreover, the decline in support for the police in Britain has been attributed to "mounting dissatisfaction among those who contacted the police," particularly crime victims (Skogan, 1990:24). However, as noted by Garofalo (1977b), "the evidence concerning the relationship between victimization and attitudes towards the police is somewhat conflicting" (21). Thus Parks (1976) listed a number of studies on the relationship between attitudes toward police and victimization experience, and concluded that "the consensus is that these relationships are weak or non-existent" (89), although he himself questioned the validity of this finding. Smith and Hawkins (1973), in their Seattle study referred to above, concluded that "there was no difference in attitudes about police fairness among victims and non-victims" (140). Similarly, Thomas and Hyman

(1977) concluded from their Virginia survey that "victimization per se is not a significant correlate of evaluations of police performance" (316). Moreover, Garofalo (1970:21) cited a number of other studies lending support to this proposition.

The inconsistencies between the surveys that found differences between the attitudes toward the police of victims and nonvictims and those that found no such differences may be partly explainable in terms of methodological problems in the operationalizing of satisfaction with the police (cf. Thomas and Hyman, 1977:311). Moreover, in the nonnational surveys local factors may be operating. There are other findings, however, emerging from some of the studies referred to which raise different types of explanations.

One type of explanation relates to the *degree* of victimization. Some studies indicate that attitudes toward the police are less favorable on the part of victims of more serious offenses. Thus, in Garofalo's analysis of the National Crime Data for 1982 and 1983, among white persons whose experience with victimization was with robbery or assault, between 16% and 22% evaluated police performance as poor, as compared with single-digit percentages for victims of other types of offense, and 6% for nonvictims (1977a:96, table 43).[6] Similarly, in his later analysis, Garofalo offered an explanation of the discrepancy in the findings between the different studies, namely, that "victimization is defined here only on the basis of personal crimes that involve contact between the victim and offender" (1977b:21).

Further support for the hypothesis that it is only relatively serious victimization that substantially affects attitudes toward the police is found in two additional measures adopted in Garofalo's second survey: (1) the number of victimizations experienced during the preceding 12 months, and (2) the seriousness of the victimizations "scored by a method derived from Sellin and Wolfgang (1964)" (ibid., 22; see also 57–58). Both measures were associated with respondents' ratings of police. With regard to the number of victimizations, the most negative rating was given by 12% of the nonvictimized respondents, 22% of the once-victimized, 27% of the twice-victimized, and 33% of those victimized on three or more occasions. Similarly, such ratings were given for 13% of the respondents whose victimization was so minor that it had a seriousness score of zero, 14% of respondents with a score of 1 to 2, 23% of respondents with a score of 3 to 5, and 33% of respondents with a score of 6 or more. Comparison between the nonvictimized and the victims with a low seriousness score is particularly significant here, since it suggests that a *minor* victimization, even in the case of "personal" crime, has little effect on attitudes toward the police.

These findings raise the possibility that the routine differentiations between victims and nonvictims adopted in the victimization surveys may not be adequate in the context of the present analysis of attitudes. Victimization as such may not be a meaningful event (cf. chap. 4, above). There is indeed some support for this hypothesis, there being some 35 to 40 million offenses committed in the United States every year (U.S. Dept. of Justice, 1992:3–4). The statistical probability of being victimized over a five- or ten-year period must therefore be extremely high. Paradoxically, however, Skogan and Maxfield (1981), writing when victimization rates were at their peak, took the view that "recent and personal experience with crime are relatively infrequent" (44; see also Sparks, 1982:95). It is thus quite plausible that only serious, or recent and serious, victimizations will give rise to any meaningful differentiation in attitudes between victims and nonvictims.

Finally, in the context of the seriousness hypothesis, mention must be made of a counterhypothesis. Poister and McDavid (1978), on the basis of a survey conducted in Harrisburg, Pennsylvania, found that victims of more serious offenses were *more* satisfied with the police than victims of less serious offenses. The explanation offered by the authors of this study was that the police were perceived to have invested greater efforts in dealing with the offenses, thereby giving rise to a higher level of satisfaction. This study, however, seems to run counter to the picture emerging from the studies and surveys reviewed above. It may, on the other hand, be consistent with the next hypothesis.

The second—and highly plausible—hypothesis that may be offered to explain the data is that attitudes toward the police depend neither upon the fact of victimization as such, nor upon the degree of victimization, but rather upon the nature of the respondent's experience in contacts with the police, whether as a result of victimization or otherwise. This was the finding of Smith and Hawkins (1973), who concluded that attitudes toward the police, as measured by "opinions on police fairness," were positively correlated with "degree of satisfaction with police action" and negatively correlated with "observing police officers 'do wrong' "—an experience claimed by 27% of the sample—and with previous arrest experience on the part of the respondent. In this context it is important to recall that many victims have had other experiences of contact with the police, whether as suspects or "consumers of police services" (Maxfield, 1984). Some British studies support the view that the more the contacts were urgent and crime related, the less likely the consumer was to be satisfied (Skogan, 1990:14).

Koenig (1980), in the Canadian study referred to above, concluded that "evaluation of local police appears much less favorable among those who have experienced or observed a police field practice perceived as improper and slightly less favorable among individuals who have experienced a punitive legal sanction or been victimized by some types of crime—particularly crimes against the person" (247). Parks (1976), reporting on a survey of some 4,000 respondents in the St. Louis area, found that evaluations on the part of respondents who were satisfied with the police response resembled those of the nonvictims, but those "who were dissatisfied with the police response after they were called were much more negative in their evaluations and perceptions" (98). Finally, Jacob (1971), in his Wisconsin study, found that "evaluations of actual police were most related to satisfaction with specific agencies and much less related to income, age, sex, or education of the respondent" (86). This was in addition to the race factor, which, as noted above, was found to be significant.

It thus seems to emerge that while race, and perhaps age, appear to have a generalized effect on attitudes to police, these attitudes are significantly affected by the personal experience of the respondent whether as victim, suspect, or observer. Moreover, it should be noted that this may also account for the "generalized effect" of race and age; for the categories holding the lower evaluations, that is, blacks and younger respondents, are more likely to have come into contact with the police not only in the capacity of victim but also as offenders or suspects (cf. Thomas and Hyman, 1977:316) and are thus more likely to have undergone negative experiences.

The survey data reviewed above, which suggest that attitudes toward the police may be a product not only of sociodemographic and cultural factors but also of particular experiences of victims and witnesses, have been supplemented in recent years by the surveys and in-depth studies, some conducted on a longitudinal basis, of victims and witnesses. These studies have begun to enrich our knowledge of victims' experiences at the different stages of their encounters with the criminal justice system, and their reactions to these experiences.

These studies generally report a high level of satisfaction with the police on the part of victims. Knudten et al. (1976), in a pioneering survey of 386 crime victims in Milwaukee County, reported that 41% of the sample stated that they were "very satisfied" with the police, while another 40% were "satisfied." In the study by Davis, Russell, and Kunreuther (1980), of 295 complaining witnesses in the Brooklyn Criminal Court, 86% of the sample expressed a favorable opinion of the arresting officer (table 5.1). Even in a sample of victims generally thought to suffer from discriminatory treatment on the part of the police, the general evaluation of the police was not unfavorable. Smith (1982), for her sample of nonstranger violence in Charlotte, Minneapolis, and Los Angeles, found that 74% of the victims whose cases reached the court were satisfied with the police, while 17% had "mixed feelings." In Kelly's (1982) sample of rape victims in Washington, D.C., 75.6% expressed satisfaction with patrol officers and 79.6% with detectives. Similarly, Baril (1984) in her in-depth study of small shopkeepers in Montreal, found that the police officer was "clearly the most respected and appreciated among the various agents of the legal system" (80).

One of the most detailed of these studies was that conducted by Shapland et al. (1985) in two English Midland cities, Coventry, and Northampton, in the course of which samples of victims of physical violence were interviewed at different stages of the criminal process.[7] At the first interview, 76% to 77% of the victims stated that they were either satisfied or very satisfied with the police at the first contact. Some of the relevant considerations on the part of these victims will be referred to below, but particular attention was devoted to the crucial but unresearched second stage of the process, the victim's experience in making a statement to the police (required from 93% of the sample). This usually occurred within 24 hours of the commission of the offense (71). A few respondents "were very unhappy about the statement being taken when they were shocked or in pain and knew that they did not do it well" (73). This was particularly true where the statement was taken in the hospital casualty ward. The preferred solution would have been to have made the statement in the victim's home (73). While most victims were satisfied that the statement recorded precisely reflected their own words, sometimes the victim "felt that the police had already decided what should be in the statement and he was just being asked to sign it" (75). Nevertheless, 42% were satisfied and 30% very satisfied with the way the statement was taken. This account is presented here in some detail—and in spite of the uncertainty of its applicability in other cultures—since it indicates a critical area of research on which there is little knowledge available.

Victims tended to be more dissatisfied with the police as the proceedings developed, such as when no suspect was apprehended (97–99), or when a suspect was released on bail or "cautioned," a form of diversion (100). However, this dissatisfaction arose not from these developments themselves—the police were credited with having done their best (99)—but from the failure to keep the victims informed (99, 111). Further, the decision not to prosecute or to plea-bargain, decisions that in England are often vested in the police, was often resented. Victims "often considered that the power to decide that the offender should not be prosecuted should rest with the victim, not the police, whatever their criteria might be" (105). Here again, however, it was the failure to inform that particularly upset the victims (106).

What were the qualities exhibited by the police of which victim-respondents either approved or disapproved? In the survey conducted by Knudten et al. (1976), 50% of the victims gave police officers an "excellent" rating and 23% a "good" rating for effort, and 42% "excellent" and 28% "good" for effectiveness. The lowest rating, "poor," was specified by fewer than 10% for both qualities. However, Goldsmith (1978) suggests that doubts about efficiency and technical competence may be a ground for dissatisfaction, and the reasons offered by large numbers of victims for their failure to report offenses committed against them lends strength to this hypothesis.

The importance of the manner displayed by police officers was emphasized in Shapland's English study, in which female sexual assault victims attributed greater significance to this quality than to the officer's sex (Shapland et al., 1985:74) and generally commented upon it favorably. Knudten et al. (1976) found that 60% of the victims rated the police as "excellent" and 26% as "good" on courteousness. Police activities that were sometimes commented upon unfavorably in these studies included delay in response time (Shapland et al., 1985:48);[8] failure to return the victim's property, taken by the police for evidentiary purposes, for several weeks after the final disposition (Davis, Russell, and Kunreuther, 1980:67); the failure to arrest the suspect (Smith, 1983:30); denial of the victim's request to see the statement to the police prior to his court appearance to give testimony (Shapland et al., 1985:88); and, above all, the failure to keep the victim informed about how the investigation was proceeding (Goldsmith, 1978:3; Shapland et al., 1985:92–93).

This last complaint seems to emerge as the critical factor in the relevant studies. As noted above, victims were less upset by results or decisions in the course of the investigation which might seem undesirable from the victim's point of view (nonapprehension, nonarrest, release on bail, reduction of charge, etc.) than by failure to inform them of these developments:[9] "This lack of information from the police caused considerable dissatisfaction amongst victims and a feeling of being let down after they themselves had cooperated with the police in the early stages of the case" (Shapland et al., 1985:130).

Owing to the probability that more and more of the sources of the dissatisfaction listed above are likely to emerge as the investigation and trial progress, it is perhaps not surprising that the degree of satisfaction felt toward the police seems to decline over time. This was found by Shapland et al. (1985:239), who interviewed the victims at four stages of the proceedings. While respondents observed that police officers were helpful and effective on the first contact (58), and the initial procedures generally were satisfactory (92–93), both degree of satisfaction and overall ratings of police subsequently declined (239).[10] Knudten et al. (1976), on the other hand, found that victims who reached the felony trial stage "were the group most likely to indicate satisfaction with the police and district attorney"; and in Kelly's survey of rape victims, many indicated that their opinions of the police—unlike their opinions of prosecutors—improved as a result of their experiences (Kelly, 1982:20). This may be consistent with the findings of Poister and McDavid (1978) that victims of more serious offenses were more satisfied with the police.

In conclusion, it appears that while levels of satisfaction with the police are generally high for both victims and nonvictims, there is some evidence that victims tend to be less satisfied than nonvictims. The absence of uniformity in the findings may be explained by many factors, including the lack of salience of the victimization experience for many respondents, the nature of the questions asked, geographical differences in police image and police practices, and so on. However, interviews with victim samples indicate various grounds for dissatisfaction, in particular the lack of information provided to the victim. Other grounds are evident from the review in chapter 2 of the evidence on police attitudes toward victim-related issues, including the relevance, or lack of relevance, of victim harm in police decision making, the context of police conversations with victims, and the degree of attention paid to the victim's views. It will be recalled that while some researchers claimed to have found that victim-related factors—including the victim's views—were regarded as important, ultimately the police assumed the role of protectors of the public rather than of the particular victim.

This, in turn, raises wider issues regarding police-community relations and the role of the police in society. While the police, indeed, are part of the state's law enforcement system, they also function on a community level and maintain a general interest in a favorable rapport with the public. Moreover, since they are virtually the only public agency to which citizens can turn at all times, they fulfill a wider and more flexible function than law enforcement alone (cf. Kalogeropoulos and Riviere, 1983). Insofar as they fulfill a service or public assistance function as well, they will not have discharged their perceived obligations to the complaining victim merely by processing the complaint according to accepted bureaucratic procedures.

Attitudes toward Prosecutors

As compared with the other main components of the criminal justice system, the police and the courts, the prosecutorial function is the least visible of the criminal justice agencies. Neither are the prosecutors physically in the public eye like the police,[11] nor are their decisions routinely reported in the media like those of the courts. For this reason there is little evidence available regarding the public's perceptions of the prosecutor. However, some of the studies focusing on victims' perceptions (Cannavale and Falcon, 1976; Knudten et al., 1976; Ziegenhagen, 1976; Connick and Davis, 1981; Kelly, 1982; Smith, 1983; Shapland et al., 1985) have considered their attitudes toward prosecutors.

Knudten et al. (1976) reported that 75% of the victims in their Milwaukee sample indicated "overall satisfaction" with district attorneys.[12] However, this was lower than the corresponding figure for their satisfaction with the police (81%). Moreover, only 27% were "very satisfied" with the district attorneys as compared with 41% for the police. Furthermore, when asked for specific ratings for effort, effectiveness, and courteousness, the district attorneys received fewer "excellent" ratings than the police on all three items (37%, 29%, and 55%, respectively, for the district attorneys, as compared with 50%, 42%, and 60%, respectively, for the police).[13]

In three respects there are striking similarities between the above findings and those of the smaller study of rape victims in Washington, D.C., conducted by Kelly (1982). First, Kelly, too, found that satisfaction expressed with regard to prosecutors, although fairly high (68.8%), was lower than that expressed toward police, as reported in the previous section. Second, here, too, specific ratings as to how the victims were treated (a measure that seems close to the "courteousness" rating in the Knudten study) indicated poorer evaluations of prosecutors, whom 59.4% of the victims perceived as having "treated them with understanding," as compared with the police, for whom the equivalent figures were 64.1% for patrol officers and 74.5% for detectives. Third, in both studies the specific ratings with regard to these specific qualities, for both police and prosecutors, were consistently lower than the overall satisfaction rates with these agencies. Kelly's explanation of the last phenomena is that "victims rated police and prosecutors highly because they expected to be treated so poorly."

The main criticisms of the prosecutors in the Kelly study seem to have been not so much a lack of courteousness as a lack of consideration for the victim's role in the proceedings: "Victims primarily objected to being excluded from their case" (1982:12). They were neither consulted about plea bargains nor informed of the outcome of the case (cf. above, chap. 2; see also Ziegenhagen, 1976:267). "The more frequently victims heard from the prosecutor and were consulted about the case, the more satisfied they were with services" (Kelly, 1982:18–19).[14] This neglect resulted in the related complaint that the prosecutor was not representing them; indeed nobody was. Thus, for example, victims, unlike defendants, were unable to obtain postponements of the hearings to suit their convenience. Similarly, in Cannavale and Falcon's (1976) study of witnesses in the D.C. Supreme Court, 36% of the respondents ($N = 880$) agreed that "prosecutors do not care about the victim in a case" (63, fig. 5–6). Moreover, for those of the witnesses who were victims, this percentage was even higher.

On the other hand, the victims in Kelly's sample who testified at trial "were more likely to be treated with understanding by the prosecutor, probably because the prosecutors were likely to spend more time preparing those individuals to testify" (Kelly, 1982:18). This is consistent with the findings of Knudten et al. (1976) that victims who reached the felony-trial stage tended to be more satisfied with both police (as noted above) and district attorneys. Apparently, disadvantages inherent in the additional "administrative runaround" involved, generally associated with increased dissatisfaction, were outweighed by the satisfaction of greater involvement in the criminal process (Knudten et al., 1976:119–21).

A related criticism directed at prosecutors in these studies relates to their perceived excessive sympathy for or leniency toward the defendant. Thus, in the Cannavale and Falcon witness study, while 56% of the sample apparently believed that the prosecutor *did* care about the victim[15]—the figure being slightly lower for witnesses who were victims—69% agreed with the statement that "prosecutors are interested in securing an honest and fair hearing for the accused" (1976:63, fig. 5–6); this figure was higher for witnesses who were victims (60). Similarly, victims in Shapland's British study complained that prosecutors did not protest defense tactics designed to cast doubt on the victim's testimony (1985:143).[16]

As a result of their negative experiences, 34% of Kelly's sample declared that their opinion of prosecutors had deteriorated, more than twice the percentage whose opinions had improved (1982:20)—the reverse of her findings with regard to police officers. Ziegenhagen, who conducted interviews with a small number of New York victims of personal crimes, also reported "a striking decline of satisfaction with the prosecutor's office and judges after victims had been exposed to criminal justice personnel" (1976:268).

Thus, in spite of the evidence presented in chapter 2 that some victim-related factors—and sometimes even the victim's views—were already being taken into account by prosecutors when the studies surveyed here were conducted, prosecutors nevertheless appear to evoke a somewhat negative image on the part of victims, more negative than that of the police. This may be partly because the prosecution lacks a tradition of community relations and is identified with an organizational structure of professionals for whom the individual citizen's interests appear remote. It is also probable that the negative aspects of court procedures and outcomes, to be considered in the following sections, "rub off" onto the prosecutors.

Formal norms adopted recently in many jurisdictions, such as those referred to in the introduction to this volume, are intended to enhance the victim's role, inter alia at the prosecution stage. The research reviewed above will require replication as these norms are implemented.

Attitudes toward the Courts

Direct contacts with the criminal courts on the part of the general public—indeed, even on the part of victims—are doubtless considerably fewer than their contacts with the police, and this may partly explain the paucity of academic literature on attitudes toward the courts.[17] With the exception of isolated questions in public opinion surveys relating to "harshness" (see below), the data available on attitudes toward the courts seem to be somewhat limited. This is surprising, not only because there is presumably somewhat greater exposure on the part of the public to the courts, which have a civil as well as a criminal function, than to prosecutors, but mainly because the courts are by democratic tradition the ultimate decision-making body in the justice system.

One of the few detailed analyses that I have found on the issue of public perception of the courts was the study of Turpen and Champagne (1978), based upon "approximately 4,300 interviews which were taken in ten major cities in the United States" (262). In this study, 6.5% of respondents held the view that the courts were always fair, 57.6% usually fair, 26.3% sometimes unfair, and 9.6% often unfair. The authors raised two methodological problems regarding their observations. First, the cities from which the respondents were selected were not necessarily representative, and thus they warn against "over-interpretation or over-generalization" (262). Second, it does not logically follow that "sometimes unfair" implies a lower rating than "usually fair," although this was the view considered more likely by the authors (after interviewing some students on this issue).

A more fundamental question, however, not dealt with adequately in the Turpen-Champagne study, relates to the meaning of "fairness." This is a highly subjective concept, which will depend on the social and penal philosophy of the individual respondent. The treatment of this issue in this study seems unsatisfactory. On the one hand, the authors state that "justice and fairness are not terms which lend themselves to precise definition, but most of us have some generalized notion of what they mean" (261–62). On the other hand, respondents were also asked to specify "the ways in which courts are unfair." These were grouped by the authors into "Procedures" (nine categories, including "unfair sentences", selected by 4.5% of those responding to this question), "Problems of Harshness and Leniency towards Some" (14.6% "too harsh," and 31.0% "too lenient"), "General Unfair" (14.7%), and "Other" (3.4%). This categorization blurs what seems to be the most fundamental differentiation in the context of perceived unfairness on the part of the courts, namely, whether the courts are seen to be at fault in some uniform or generalized way or whether they are thought to discriminate against certain classes of individuals. Some light is cast on this issue in another table presented by Turpen and Champagne (263, table 2) in which respondents were asked to specify the "group to whom courts are unfair." The authors were somewhat bewildered by the response "everyone" on the part of more than half of those responding (55.2%),[18] which seemed to them to "make little sense" except on the emotional level. However, if this table were cross-tabulated with the "perceptions of the ways in which courts were unfair" it might emerge that this response reflected the view that the courts were uniformly and consistently at fault in their level of sentencing, rather than guilty of any particular bias. Thus, if sentences are seen to be generally too lenient, this may be seen as a form of "unfairness" with regard to victims, although it is not clear whether victims were ever specifically alluded to in the study, but would not be discriminatory in the usual sense.[19]

Most of the surveys dealing with attitudes of the general public toward the courts lay emphasis on the generalized level of overall harshness versus overall leniency.[20] Stinchcombe et al. (1980) reviewed the responses to the question whether local courts dealt harshly enough with criminals, as reflected in the findings of various Gallup polls and the General Social Survey of the National Opinion Research Center during the years 1965 through 1978. (The findings of 12 polls were reviewed.) These indicated an almost perfectly monotonic increase in the proportion of respondents who expressed the view that the courts were "not harsh enough," rising from 48.9% in 1965 to 84.9% in 1978. By 1982 this figure had reached 86% (Flanagan et al., 1985), although subsequently there was a moderate decline: in 1989 83% were of this opinion (Flanagan and Maguire, 1992:203). This represents a very substantial increase over the years and hardly seems explicable in terms of the hypothesis suggested in Stinchcombe et al. (1980) of "a desire for the courts to return to their earlier level of punitiveness" (34).[21] Indeed, public support for harsher penalties by the courts in response to this type of question appears to be a universal phenomenon. "In fact, the question concerning sentencing severity generates a more consensual response than any other in criminal justice" (Roberts, 1992:147), even if the intensity of the response may be more moderate in other countries (cf. Pitsela, 1991:748).

At the same time, these findings should not necessarily be interpreted as an absolute measure of punitiveness, a topic that will be further discussed later in this chapter. One reason for this (others will be considered below) is that the supposedly punitive response may actually be a camouflage for other types of criticism, such as dissatisfaction with the degree of protection granted to defendants or with plea-bargaining practices. Thus, a series of studies by the Michigan Commission on Criminal Justice (1977) showed that the proportion of people who agreed that "courts have gone too far protecting people in trouble with the law" increased from 58% in 1973 to 78% in 1977; and a recent review of the literature suggests that this view continues to prevail (Roberts, 1992:140).

As to the perception of discrimination on the part of the courts toward different populations, the Turpen-Champagne study examined this issue too. As noted above, when asked to specify to whom the courts were unfair, more than half the respondents answered "everyone," indicating a reluctance to identify any form of discrimination. Social-class discrimination was specified by 22.8% of persons responding to this question, but this represented only about 6% of the total sample. The numbers specifying racial groups were smaller still. Perceptions on this may of course be culture bound: a British survey found that 82% of the public believed that "some groups were treated differently," mainly on the basis of socioeconomic factors (Shaw, 1982).

Further clarification of this issue may be derived by analyzing the relationship between respondent characteristics and their perception of the courts as fair or unfair. While race, age, and one of the social-class variables were statistically significant in the predicted direction, the contribution of these factors to the total variance was very small, the highest contribution being 1.2% for race (Turpen and Champagne, 1978:266–71). The authors concluded that "perceptions of judicial unfairness seem to represent a broad-based attitude in the population which is largely unrelated to those variables which are generally thought to explain alienation from the legal system" (267).[22] Again, the recent review of the literature by Roberts (1992) supports the view that "the perception of systemic inequity is most clearly associated with the courts" (141).

As noted, there is indeed evidence that the public feels greater dissatisfaction with the courts than with other components of the criminal justice system (Reynolds and Blyth, 1976). In a survey of 10,000 residents in Joliet and Peoria, respondents were asked to rank the various criminal justice agencies on a scale from 1 to 9, where 1 indicated "much too lenient" and 9 "much too harsh." "Local judges" received a median score of 2 in Joliet and 3 in Peoria, as compared with median scores of 3 for the "corrections system," 4 for the "local criminal justice system," and 5 for the "local police" (Ku, 1977:29; and cf. Roberts, 1992:139). These findings will be considered below.

How far do *victims* differ from the general public with respect to their attitudes to the courts? Fagan (1981: tables 2 and 3), who hypothesized that the experiences of victimization would reduce support for the courts, found no evidence to support this. The Turpen-Champagne study, too, included the experience of victimization among the variables for which the effect on perception of court unfairness was examined. As with other variables referred to above, the victimization experience was significantly associated with the perception of unfairness ($p < 0.001$) in this study, but here, too, the contribution to the variance was very slight ($r^2 = 0.005$). A study based upon an ABC News poll of 2,464 adult respondents also found a low correlation between "victimization experience" and negative perception of the criminal courts (Flanagan et al., 1985). These findings suggest that attitudes of victims may be substantially similar but slightly more critical than those of the general public, the difference deriving either from the failure of the criminal justice system to prevent the victimization or from the victim's personal experiences with the system. However, the account of the system's handling of victims presented in chapter 2 would lead one to anticipate substantially more critical attitudes on their part.[23] It should also be noted that in the matter of punitiveness, to be considered in greater detail below, victims do not in general seem to hold stronger views than nonvictims (Cullen et al., 1985; Brillon, 1988).

A somewhat more precise impression of the specific attitudes of victims can be obtained from the studies that focus exclusively on victims, and the remainder of this section will be concerned with the findings of these studies. It should be noted, however, that insofar as victim-related reforms might be expected to have changed victims' perceptions of the courts, such changes would not yet be evident in the studies reviewed here. Indeed, the purpose here is primarily to consider the victim's justice needs emerging from prereform evaluations of the system.

The degree of support expressed for the courts in the victim-oriented surveys has mostly been only moderate. For while Knudten et al. (1976) found that only 14% of their Milwaukee sample indicated dissatisfaction with the courts, in the study by Davis, Russell, and Kunreuther (1980) of complaining witnesses in the Brooklyn Criminal Court, only 72% of the sample had a favorable opinion of the judge. Further, only 65% of Hagan's (1980) Canadian sample ranked the judge's performance as good or very good, and only 63% of the sample interviewed by Smith (1983) expressed satisfaction with the judge, which represented only 53% of responding victims.[24] In the British sample (Shapland et al., 1985) 53% were satisfied, including 6% "very satisfied," with the way the courts had dealt with their case. Among 872 victims interviewed in the Portland, Oregon, area in 1974, only 45% expressed a favorable attitude toward the courts (Schneider et al., 1976:101). Other surveys of victims and witnesses reporting negative attitudes include Cook and Fischer (1976), Ashworth and Feldman-Summers (1978), Rentmeister (1979),[25] Hunter and Frey (1980), and Ziegenhagen (1976), who concluded, on the basis of a New York study, that "there appear to be few features of the victim-witness role that are satisfactory from the victims' viewpoint" (266).

Such generalizations may be of limited usefulness, however. A more informative picture may be obtained by attempting to locate specific areas of dissatisfaction. For this purpose, differentiation will be made between *(a)* attitudes toward court procedures, *(b)* perceptions of judges' character and attitudes, and *(c)* attitudes toward the court's decisions, in particular its final disposition. Finally, perceptions of the courts will be compared with those of the other criminal justice agencies considered hitherto.

Court Procedures

Holmstrom and Burgess (1978), who conducted a follow-up study of rape victims in the Boston area, observed, "Overwhelmingly, both adult and young victims found court an extremely stressful experience" (222). Particularly stressful were cross-examination by the defense lawyer, confrontation with the accused, and the public setting of the trial. In other studies, not confined to rape victims, the findings were somewhat less negative. Smith (1983), who interviewed victims of nonstranger violence in New York, found that "for a sizable minority of victims there clearly is room for improvement," yet she found it reassuring that "at least one half of the victims were satisfied with the system's response." Shapland, too, concluded that in spite of the considerable inconvenience and unpleasantness involved (see below), "the problems that being a witness does bring are not sufficient to outweigh the benefits of participation" (Shapland et al., 1985:159).[26]

What were the grounds of victims' dissatisfaction with court procedures? Smith (1983) noted that "court victims typically reported that they had little opportunity to participate in the process" (90). Heavy caseloads appeared to be a factor in preventing due consideration for the victim, particularly in large cities.[27] However, the reduced caseload of a higher court did not appear to guarantee a higher level of satisfaction. More specifically, victims in Smith's study complained about "long waiting periods, unnecessary trips, lack of interaction with officials, general neglect, and lack of consideration for their feelings" (1983:94). Shapland et al. (1985), whose monograph included a detailed account of the victim's role in court as a witness, made the following observations: "In general one has the impression of victims being isolated and confused at court, not knowing what they may be required to do or what they may do. They do not realise what is happening around them and in few cases is the trouble taken to explain it to them" (113).[28]

In the study by Cannavale and Falcon (1976), the witnesses were asked to specify their complaints. The main areas in which improvement was advocated were better protection (28%), better attitude toward witnesses (20%), speedier trials (20%), better pay for witnesses (15%), and better facilities (12%) (57). There was generally little difference between the figures for witnesses who were victims and for witnesses who were not victims, the greatest difference being on the "better attitude" item, specified by 22% of victims as compared with only 16% of nonvictims. This difference may perhaps be explained in terms of a greater sensitivity or greater expectations from the court on the part of witnesses who were also victims.

Perceptions of Judges

The perceptions of the personality and character of the judge were often less negative than those of the court process, but the findings nevertheless give ground for concern.[29] While 83% of the witnesses in the study by Cannavale and Falcon (1976) agreed with the statement that "judges are very intelligent," and 78% agreed that "judges are sincerely interested in the rights of citizens," a sizable minority (27%) agreed with the statement that "judges think they know everything and don't listen to what anyone else has to say" (64). It is thus perhaps surprising, in view of the questionable status of the victim in the criminal court, that three-fifths of the victims in Smith's small study "thought that the judge was concerned with their interests and were satisfied with the judge" (1983:90). However, this sample may be unrepresentative, since it comprised nonstranger cases, some of which were dealt with in a special domestic relations court, in which judges "specifically volunteered for this assignment" and were "especially careful, professional and courteous in their treatment of victims and their cases" (91). Finally, 75% of the victims in the Milwaukee sample studied by Knudten et al. (1976) rated the judges "excellent" or "good" in terms of courteousness, although this was lower than their ratings of police and district attorneys on this attribute.

Perhaps a more serious matter than the judges' perceived courteousness and consideration is the degree of fairness and impartiality attributed to them. The qualified enthusiasm for the judiciary in these respects on the part of the general population was noted above. The evidence from the special victim and victim/witness studies reviewed here is hardly more encouraging. In Ziegenhagen's (1976) New York City sample of victims of personal crime, "judges were more often described as impartial, while about equal numbers of victims perceived the judges' behavior as friendly or hostile" (267). However, Reynolds and Blyth (1976), who found in their Twin Cities study that courts were rated "low to average," reported that "respondents were clearly upset by what they considered to be biased, inconsistent decisions in the legal system" (339). Moreover, in the witness study by Cannavale and Falcon (1976), it was found that only 72% agreed with the statement that "judges *try* to be fair in all their court decisions" (emphasis added), while 20% were prepared to agree to the statement that "most judges will accept bribes." Finally, Shapland et al. (1985), in their English study, noted that "the impression that most victims have is that both magistrates and judges are very inconsistent" (236).

Attitudes toward Court Decisions

Victims' attitudes toward court decisions have been measured primarily by their views on the appropriateness of dispositions in terms of severity.

Such views may either be ascertained generally, that is, in relation to "punishments meted out by the courts," or specifically, in relation to the specific case in which the victim was involved. The latter are of particular importance, since there may be a discrepancy between generalized attitudes to the sentencing of offenders and the solutions perceived as appropriate in individual cases. Thus, in Shapland's English study, 28.7% and 26.1% of the respective samples[30] expressed the view that sentences in general should be greater, while a further 25.5% and 39.8% specified that violent offenders should receive heavier sentences (1985:238); yet when respondents were asked which sentence they considered to be appropriate to the defendant in their particular case, and their answers compared with the sentences imposed, it emerged that "the wishes of victims were very similar to how sentencers actually view such cases" (153; cf. Hough and Moxon, 1985; and below). At the same time, when victims were subsequently notified of the sentence actually imposed, 38% disapproved, mostly because they found it too lenient (155).[31]

Knudten et al. (1976) invited their Milwaukee victim respondents to rate the penalty imposed by the court as lenient, fair, or harsh. The number of respondents designating the penalty as "lenient" was generally greater than the combined figures of those who considered it "harsh" and those who perceived it as "fair" (tables 21–25). In Hagan's Canadian sample, too, 53% of the sample viewed the sentence imposed as "too easy" (Hagan, 1980:118). Davis, Russell, and Kunreuther (1980) found that 43% of their sample were dissatisfied with the outcome, 53% of them because of the leniency of the disposition.

Satisfaction with the disposition is not necessarily a function of the severity of the sentence alone. Smith (1983) noted that satisfaction on the part of her interviewees depended not only on the defendant receiving an "appropriate" or sufficiently severe sentence but also on the court's following their wishes. In this connection note should be taken of the finding of Davis, Russell, and Kunreuther (1980) that "most complainants upon entering the court had fairly specific ideas about what they wanted the court to do in their case" (23).[32] However, when Shapland et al. (1985) asked the victims in their British study "Who do you think should have a say in what the sentence should be?" very few proposed such a role for the victim, while "others said that they would not like to see victims having any say because they would be biased" (236). The discrepancy between this view and the one expressed in Smith's study may be due to a less developed consciousness of the victim role—or its inadequacy—in England; but it may also be a function of the sample in Smith's study, which was concerned mainly with nonstranger violence. Indeed, this may also partly explain the third factor found by Smith to affect the victim's satisfaction with the outcome, namely, whether he or she continued to be bothered by the defendant. Even apart from the victim's ability actually to influence the disposition, the fact of his or her being *consulted* by the prosecutor or judge has been found to be associated with satisfaction at the outcome (Davis, Russell, and Kunreuther, 1980:67).

The frustration of seeing the court impose an excessively lenient sentence (in the victim's perception), coupled with his or her apparent inability to have any meaningful say in the decision-making process, while leading to a low evaluation of the case outcome, does not necessarily "rub off" onto the judge (cf. the earlier observations on perceptions of court procedures as compared with judges' standing). Thus, Connick and Davis (1981) cited data collected in a small sample in the Brooklyn Criminal Court in which only 20% of the victims in the "stranger" subsample were satisfied with the case outcome, while 75% rated the judge fair and 76% were satisfied with the judge's handling of the case; the figures in prior-relationship cases were 24%, 64%, and 72%, respectively—a substantially similar pattern. In the Milwaukee sample, too, the prevailing view on the part of the victims that penalties were too light did not seem to have prevented their holding a generally favorable opinion of the courts.

Finally, there are other outcome variables that may affect victim satisfaction with the court, unrelated to the severity of sentence. Shapland et al. (1985:158) found that victims were significantly less satisfied where the charge was reduced during the passage through the courts or, not surprisingly, where the defendant was acquitted. On the other hand, in her nonstranger study Smith (1983:43) found identical satisfaction rates for convictions and acquittals.

Comparison with Other Agencies

Yet another measure of the degree of satisfaction with the courts is obtained by comparing victims' perceptions of the courts with their perceptions of other criminal justice agencies. Here, too, the picture that emerges is somewhat unfavorable to the courts. In the study by Davis, Russell, and Kunreuther (1980, table 5.1), the 72% of the sample who expressed a favorable opinion of the judge was lower than the corresponding figure for the arresting officer (86%) and the prosecutor (81%). In the study by Smith (1983), the 63% expressing satisfaction with the judge compares unfavorably with the 74% who were satisfied with the police, although the figure for the prosecutor in this study was lower (56%) than that for the judge. Knudten et al. (1976), who, as noted, found only 14% of the victims expressing dissatisfaction with the judges, also found that the percentages of "very satisfied" respondents (24%) or of "very satisfied" and "satisfied" combined (66%) were lower than the equivalent percentages for police (27% and 75%, respectively). Moreover, respondents' ratings of judges in terms of effort, effectiveness, and courteousness were lower than their ratings of the police on these items, and somewhat similar to those for prosecutors (but somewhat lower in terms of courteousness, and fractionally lower in terms of effort). Hagan (1980), in his Canadian study, also found that the percentage who ranked the judge's performance "good" or "very good" (65%) was substantially lower than for the police (85%) and slightly lower than for the prosecutor (68%).

These findings in relation to victims are consistent with attitudes expressed by the general public. Thus Roberts (1992:139) refers to a recent poll conducted in Colorado in which two-thirds of respondents gave positive ratings to the police but only one-third to judges, with prosecutors and public defenders somewhere in between. He comments that "it is clear that the public have more positive attitudes towards front-end components" of the criminal justice system. Data provided by a recent survey conducted by the National Victim Center would appear to confirm this hypothesis. Respondents were asked to rate various criminal justice agencies "in accomplishing their part of the criminal justice mission." Ratings of "excellent" or "good" amounted to 64% for the police, 48% for prosecutors, 45% for judges, 32% for prisons, and 22% for parole boards (Flanagan and Maguire, 1992:178).

The above findings are naturally a cause for concern. It may be that the unfavorable comparisons between perceptions of the courts and the police can be partly explained in terms of the greater personal contact the latter agency has with the public. Nevertheless, as noted earlier, the courts represent the pinnacle of the legal system, and have, since the English Bill of Rights and the writings of Montesquieu, if not earlier, been attributed a critical role in the preservation of democratic values. Thus, negative views expressed by the general public, such as "a strong tendency for the respondents to believe that courts tended to be unfair" (Turpen and Champagne, 1978:262), as well as the more specific criticisms on the part of persons experiencing the justice system, clearly present a serious problem.

However, certain issues that may contribute to the negative image of the courts may have to be better differentiated, at least insofar as the implications for victims are concerned. First, the perceptions of the functioning of

the courts and their procedures must be distinguished both from perceptions of the ultimate dispositions ordered by the court and from the perceived functioning of the judge. Dissatisfaction may not prevail to the same
extent with these different elements.[33] In particular, it should be noted that
the functioning of the court as a whole reflects not only on the judge but also
on the other parties concerned; thus Fagan (1981), in constructing his "support for the courts scale" included one item relating to charge reduction by
prosecuting attorneys, and another item relating to delaying tactics by *defense* attorneys.

Another issue in need of clarification is the degree to which victims'
unfavorable perceptions of the courts as compared with other criminal
justice agencies may be attributable to the location of the courts in the
victims' experience timewise. For it has sometimes been observed that the
victim becomes increasingly dissatisfied as he or she becomes "enmeshed"
in the system (cf. Knudten et al., 1976). On this hypothesis the victims'
dissatisfaction would accumulate by virtue of his or her expectations being
disappointed by all the agencies; and a more negative image of prosecutors
as compared with police, and of courts as compared with police and prosecutors, would not necessarily redound to the discredit of the courts themselves. Some indication of this is found in Hagan's study, in which victims
were interviewed both before and after the court hearing, and a slight
improvement was noted in the rating of the judges (Hagan, 1980:113).[34]
The identical finding was reported by Shapland et al. (1985:248).

However, the victim's apparent decline in confidence in the system as it
progresses may not be entirely connected to his or her direct personal
experience with that system for, as noted, a similar pattern was observed in
respect of the general public, who also appear to favor "front-end" agencies
(Roberts, 1992:139).

Noncooperation with the Criminal Justice System

One of the best indicators of attitudes toward the criminal justice system
may be the degree to which the public in general, and victims in particular,
are willing to cooperate with this system, particularly in terms of reporting
crimes and providing testimony. From the system's point of view, it is of
course critical to its functioning that members of the public will be actively willing to perform these tasks.[35] Moreover, one might surmise that
such cooperation would be perceived by members of the public to be obliga-
tory, both in order to seek justice where they themselves have been victim-

ized and by way of civic duty, in order to maintain the "rule of law" and to ensure that the criminal justice system can continue to function (see, e.g., Stuebing, 1984).

Although these principles may have been accepted dogma until recently, the victimization surveys conducted over the last few years have shown that the reality is very different. These surveys, which are considered to have a high level of validity, almost invariably indicate that most victimizations are not reported (Sparks, 1982). In 1990 only 37.7% of victimizations in the United States were reported by the victims, and only 34.7% of personal (as distinct from "household") crimes (U.S. Dept. of Justice, 1992); and the British figures for 1988 are almost identical, having been lower still some years earlier (Mayhew et al., 1989:16). Moreover, while less is known about this topic, observers of acts of victimization (bystanders) may also be reluctant to intervene and invoke law enforcement procedures (Shotland and Goodstein, 1984). Finally, apart from initial reporting, concern has been expressed by criminal justice agencies that, even where offenses are investigated or prosecuted, citizens are often unwilling to cooperate with the authorities. The key question that arises in the present context is the following: insofar as the above description of the "inhibitions" of the public with regard to activation of or cooperation with the criminal justice system is correct, do these inhibitions derive from negative attitudes toward and experiences of this system or from other causes?

There seem to be four types of data that can be helpful in determining whether such noncooperation with the criminal justice system derives from negative attitudes or experiences: (1) data on the grounds specified by victim/witnesses for not reporting an offense, (2) data on the correlates of nonreporting, (3) data on the degree of association between nonreporting and negative attitudes to the criminal justice system, and (4) data on the views expressed by victim/witnesses regarding their intention to cooperate with the criminal justice system in the future. The evidence on these four issues will be examined briefly.

Grounds for Nonreporting. In the course of victimization surveys, respondents are asked to specify the reasons why they have refrained from reporting offenses. Categories of response used by the National Crime Survey included "nothing could be done," "victimization not important enough," "police wouldn't want to be bothered," "it was a private matter," "fear of reprisal," and "victimization was reported to someone else." Most of these categories do not reflect upon the respondents' attitudes to the criminal justice system, but the categories "nothing could be done" and "police wouldn't want to be bothered," for all their ambiguity (Gottfredson and Gottfredson, 1988:23), do seem to suggest a degree of reservation regarding law enforcement agencies. Mayhew et al. (1989:24–25) note that "previous research has shown that what victims feel about the police has relatively limited significance in non-reporting" but found that the percentage of cases in which police-related factors were specified rose from 23% in the 1984 British Crime Survey to 32% in 1988 (table 4).[36]

The Correlates of Nonreporting. While there is strong evidence that the seriousness of the crime may be the main factor associated with the decision to report (Sparks, 1982:99; Mayhew et al., 1989:24; Van Dijk et al., 1990:68), there is also some indication that reporting patterns are lower for those groups who are known to hold more negative perceptions of the police. Thus, younger victims are less likely to report victimization, and to some extent this is true of African Americans (U.S. Dept. of Justice, 1992). Moreover, one study found that various categories among the more vulnerable sections of the public—female heads of households, persons lacking social support systems,[37] and persons with financial and other problems— were less likely to report victimizations (Biblarz et al., 1984); and the Canadian Urban Victimization Survey found that among crimes of violence, "many serious victimizations . . . went unreported . . . because the perceived danger or costs of reporting outweighed the advantages" (Solicitor General Canada, 1984:116). Analysis of the British Crime Survey data also indicated that "many incidents at the trivial end of the range are reported, and *many regarded as serious by their victims are not*" (Mayhew et al., 1989:29; emphasis added).

Nonreporting and Negative Attitudes. In addition to the above indirect evidence on the association between attitudes toward law enforcement authorities and nonreporting, there is also some direct evidence on this topic. Garofalo (1977), using National Crime Sample data, found that victims rating the police more highly were only marginally more likely to report a victimization; the reporting rate declined from 51%, for those giving the police the most positive rating, to 47% for those giving the police the most negative rating. The relationship became much more evident when seriousness of offense was controlled for, using the Sellin-Wolfgang scale: positive ratings of police were associated with reporting of offenses with low seriousness scores, but not for offenses with moderate or high seriousness scores. This is consistent with findings noted in the previous paragraph and indicates that attitudes to the authorities, while less important than the seriousness of the offense, may be a meaningful factor in reporting behavior.

This topic was examined in considerable detail in a study conducted by Schneider et al. (1976), who studied the association between attitudes to the criminal justice system and reporting trends, for a sample of approximately 900 victims of the Portland, Oregon, area. The results of multivariate analysis showed that for property offenses the seriousness of the crime and participation in the local antiburglary program were the strongest predictors, but trust in the police and the perceived quality of police-community relations also contributed to the probability of reporting.[38] For personal crimes, "understanding local issues" and seriousness were the best predictors, but "belief the police would catch the person," "belief that the police would recover property," and "belief that the courts would punish the offender" added further explanatory power, while "trust in police" was an alternative predicting variable. The authors further concluded that the attitudinal variables were more important for crimes against the person and for the less serious property crimes.

Insofar as a relationship has been established between nonreporting and negative attitudes toward the police, it would be anticipated that respondents with negative attitudes would lay greater emphasis on reasons connected with these attitudes when specifying why they did not report the offense. The analysis conducted by Garofalo indicates that such a pattern was barely perceptible in respect to the response that "police would not want to be bothered" (put forward by 13% of the cases in which reasons were given for nonreporting where respondents held a negative rating of the police, but by only 7% of respondents with a positive rating). However, the "nothing could be done" category of reason was unrelated to respondents' rating of police. Finally, it should be noted that while Garofalo's figures suggested a slight tendency for persons with high evaluations of the police to report victimizations with greater frequency than persons with low evaluations, the same figures also showed that persons failing to report had the same distribution of ratings as persons reporting. Garofalo concluded that the reporting experience did not have a negative effect on subsequent ratings of the police. This would suggest that, in contrast with the view expressed above, insofar as negative attitudes to the police are associated with prior victimization experience, these attitudes derive rather from the failure of the police to protect the victim by preventing the victimization than from negative experiences with the criminal justice system.

Declared Future Intentions. Some surveys have elicited views of victims or witnesses as to the likelihood of their cooperation with the criminal justice system in the event of a future victimization. This, too, may be regarded as a measure of the satisfaction felt by such persons with the treatment received in the current case.

Cannavale and Falcon (1976), in their review of the somewhat sparse literature on noncooperation with prosecutors, referred to a Milwaukee survey in which 40% of a sample of 240 witnesses indicated that they would be less cooperative in the future. The main reasons for noncooperation with prosecutors cited by witnesses were, according to this review, trial delay, loss of income, inappropriate physical accommodations, and witness intimidation (12–13). The picture emerging from the study conducted by the authors themselves was somewhat less pessimistic. In their own sample, based on 7,849 cases opened in Washington, D.C., in the first half of 1973, 81.2% of respondents stated that they "would be willing to serve as a witness in another case in the future" (140). This compared with 91.2% of the sample who stated that they agreed to serve as a witness in the case in which they were then involved (138),[39] indicating that for some their recent experience had been discouraging. Of the 9.9% who stated explicitly that they would not be willing to serve as a witness in the future—the remainder being unsure or giving conditional responses—the main category of reason offered was "waste of time, no justice" (149).

In the British study conducted by Shapland et al. (1985), the victim sample was asked during both their first and their final interviews whether they would be willing to report offenses in the future. The question was asked in relation to four hypothetical offenses, in both the two main research locations. Responses for three out of the four offenses varied from 75.7% to 100%,[40] and there was a tendency for positive responses to be lower on the second interview, although some individuals changed their minds in a positive direction. Among reasons specified for a negative change of mind were the trouble involved in reporting, lack of information received, retaliation, the sentence, the negative attitude of the police, and the probable failure to apprehend the offender. The authors' general conclusion was that "problems with the police are the main reason for victims deciding that they will not report a further offense" (253), although attitudes to the police were also the main consideration among those who changed in a positive direction.

Evidence of victims' general outlook, elicited by the New York study of "victims and helpers" (Friedman et al., 1982), may be indirectly relevant here. In that study there appeared to be a tendency for respondents to have a greater faith in other people where they perceived the police as having gone out of their way in reaction to the crime.[41] Ultimately, it seems that negative experiences with the criminal justice system as such may contribute only marginally to the level of noncooperation. Much nonreporting is based upon utilitarian considerations of efficacy, while some believe there is a moral duty to report (Smith and Maness, 1976; National Crime Victimization Survey, 1992: table 111). Among a group of rape victims, "even those who were dissatisfied with services and poorly treated, for the most part, were willing to cooperate and advise others to cooperate with law enforcement in the future. They too recognized the judicial process as the 'only game in town.' Not to play is to allow criminals to go free" (Kelly, 1982:29).

The fact that most victims are willing to cooperate in the future may be an indication that negative experiences with the criminal justice system are not of catastrophic dimensions. Yet, even if only a small minority develop an antagonism toward the system, this could have serious implications— first, because the addition of such "rebels" in a situation where already most offenses are not reported could lead to noncooperation on a large scale, and second, and more pertinent to the present topic, because it suggests that for some victims the experience is indeed a very negative one.

Punitiveness

The studies of the attitudes both of victims and of nonvictims reviewed above seem to indicate a general dissatisfaction with various aspects of the criminal justice system. One such aspect frequently mentioned is the perceived leniency of sentences meted out by the courts, which, as noted above, has been an almost universal finding on the part of public opinion polls. Should these findings be taken as conclusive proof of a high level of punitiveness per se, or do they merely reflect a degree of dissatisfaction with the functioning of the courts? Put another way, is other evidence available on the degree of punitiveness of the attitudes of the public and of victims, independent of their perceptions of the criminal justice system as it operates today?

Recent studies which have endeavored to elicit the public's views as to the appropriate penalties for particular offenses present a very different picture from that indicated by the opinion surveys referred to above. Thus, for example, the jurors in a study conducted by Diamond (1989) did not select harsher penalties than those selected by the judges, even though they shared the common view that "courts are too lenient." British Crime Survey data also indicated "a fair degree of congruence between the courts and the public." Roberts (1992), who reviewed a number of studies in this area, concluded that "the preponderance of evidence supports the view that the public are not harsher than the courts, or at least are not consistently harsher as the poll findings would suggest" (149).

Roberts (1992:150) refers to two studies in which contrary findings were noted. Blumstein and Cohen (1980), who recorded the views held by a sample of 603 Pennsylvania residents (out of 2,500 approached), found that the prison terms selected were longer than those normally served. Zimmerman et al. (1988), who used a national sample of 1,920 randomly selected American adults, found that prison sentences were both more likely to be selected and of longer duration than the prevailing practice in the state of New York, perceived by the authors to be "middle range" in relation to national variations. The findings of Blumstein and Cohen indicated, however, that while the sentences selected by respondents were longer than those actually served in practice, they did correspond to the sentences imposed by the courts (i.e., not allowing for early release). This suggests that the views expressed may in fact have reflected respondents' views of the prevailing norm indicated by court policy. Some speculation of this nature was also expressed by Zimmerman et al. (1988:131–32).

Even if the findings of these two studies cannot be entirely "explained away" in this manner, there is clearly a substantial discrepancy between the findings based on sentence selection and those of the polls referred to earlier. It seems that the ostensible dissatisfaction with the leniency of courts' sentencing cannot really be interpreted as an expression of punitiveness and a desire for harsh sentencing in specific cases. This dissatisfaction may reflect in part a general sense of frustration with the perceived increase in crime[42] and the apparent failure of law enforcement agencies to control it. It may also be based in part on ignorance of the realities of courts' sentencing practice (Roberts, 1992:112). There is also a gap between the policies supported by the public *in general* and the penalties preferred in individual cases. "Once the human details of an offense and offender are described, the average offender appears far less deviant, powerful and dangerous; severe punishment appears less justified" (Diamond, 1989:249; see also Thomson and Ragona, 1987:339–43).

Further, there is some evidence to the effect that victims of crime, in spite of the data presented in the preceding section regarding their dissatisfaction with the perceived leniency of the courts, are also not excessively punitive. Blumstein and Cohen (1980), in the study referred to above, compared the penalties assigned by different categories of respondent. While they noted a degree of association between sociodemographic characteristics and the degree of punitiveness of responses,[43] when they compared respondents who reported victimization experiences with nonvictims, they concluded, "Surprisingly, victimization experience has no effect on the sentences respondents assign" (243). The British Crime Surveys have also explored attitudes to punishment, and there, too, it emerged that victims were no more punitive than nonvictims (Hough and Moxon, 1985; see also Brillon, 1988).[44] A German study found that only 17.4% of victims favored harsh sentences, and even among victims of violent crime the figure was only 20.9% (Baurmann and Schadler, 1991:15).

Nor do the data emerging from the in-depth victim studies indicate a high level of punitiveness. Among a sample of felony victims in Ohio, 60% of those submitting a victim-impact statement suggested that the offender be incarcerated, but "these 'punitive' victims constitute[d] . . . only 33% of the total number of victims in the sample" (Erez and Tontodonato, 1990:456). Shapland et al. (1985), in their English study, asked victims during their initial interviews what sentences they would like to see imposed upon the offender. Although the sample related to offenses of violence, only 40% favored a custodial sentence: "Victims did not seem to be very punitive even at the early stage in the case." Moreover, these victims were not simply predicting what they anticipated the courts would do: "What they expected the courts to give was often very much lower" (151). Nonpunitive reactions were also recorded in some of the plea-bargaining and sentencing involvement experiments described in chapter 8 below. Finally, in a Dutch study that will be described in greater detail below, more than two-thirds of the sample considered the sentence imposed too lenient, but less than one-third would have sentenced the offender to more than one year's imprisonment (Smale and Spickenheuer, 1979:78–79).

Data of a somewhat different nature are found in the study of witnesses by Cannavale and Falcon (1976). In their sample, 42% agreed with the statement that "punishment for breaking the law is often too severe," while 70% agreed that "some acts are legally defined as crimes when they really should not be." This sample seemed more critical of injustices in the criminal justice system and the social structure generally than of the conduct of offenders and the need to be punitive.[45] This might be partly explained in terms of the similarity and overlap between victim/witnesses and offender populations, as noted in chapter 3.

Another reason for the apparently low emphasis on punishment on the part of both victims and the general public may be that the dependent variable being measured in these studies is often less related to the "punitiveness-versus-leniency" dichotomy (the "severity axis") considered hitherto and closer to the second meaning of punitiveness discussed in the introduction to this chapter, that is, punitiveness versus other sentencing objectives (the "penal philosophy axis"). Thus, recent studies (Thomson and Ragona, 1987; Cullen et al., 1988) show that the public maintains substantial support for rehabilitation and other utilitarian objectives of sentencing, although not necessarily to the exclusion of punitiveness in the first sense (cf. Penley, n.d.).

Support for utilitarian objectives, including rehabilitation, is found among victims too. Van Dijk and Steinmetz (1988) found that the victimization experience led to a greater emphasis on preventive rather than repressive sanctions. Victims interviewed in Shapland's study favored such sanctions as probation, community service, or some form of "treatment" (Shapland et al., 1985:151). Similarly, Chandler and Kassebaum (1979), in their Hawaii survey, found that victims placed considerable emphasis on rehabilitation of the offender. In the sample studied by Davis, Russell, and Kunreuther (1980), only 28% of the complainants clearly opted for punishment of the defendant as the principle outcome sought from the court, many others being more concerned with restitution or protection for themselves.[46] In Hagan's (1980) Canadian study, "punishment" was given a lower rating than other sentencing priorities both before and after the court experience, with "individual deterrence" and "reformation" being the most commonly cited objectives (109). Vennard (1976), on the basis of a small English survey, found that property crime victims were primarily concerned with compensation (restitution), although assault victims placed greater emphasis on retribution. Indeed, several researchers have found that the public is more inclined than the courts to opt for restitution (Roberts, 1992). A wide-ranging study conducted in Hamburg found that a majority of the public, unlike professional criminal justice personnel, favors alternative measures such as restitution, mediation, or private settlement for all but the most serious offenses (Boers and Sessar, 1991). Holmstrom and Burgess (1978), in their comprehensive study of rape victims in Boston, found that the majority of victims felt ambivalent about their assailant's conviction.[47] "Two themes emerged. One was that the victim felt sorry or bad about what happened. . . . A second theme was that the defendant really needed help, not the prison sentence that he received" (256).

Another question that arises in this context is the *salience* of the punitiveness instinct, insofar as it exists. Thus Kelly (1982), on the basis of interviews with 100 rape victims in the Washington, D.C., area, found that victims were interested in having their assailants convicted, but that the verdict explained only a small part of the victims' satisfaction. "These findings suggest that how victims are treated is more important than if offenders are punished" (19). Similarly, in the INSLAW study (Hernon and Forst, 1983), victims expressed somewhat punitive views, but they felt less strongly about the need for punitiveness than about the need to keep the victims informed. "In short, retribution is not the sole concern of victims" (Kelly, 1982:19).

Some other dimensions of punitiveness have been studied in two European studies that will be briefly referred to here. Smale and Spickenheuer (1979), in a small Dutch study of 100 victims, examined the relationship between the victim's need for retaliation (of which punitiveness was one of the indicators), his or her feeling of guilt at not having prevented the commission of the offense, and various offense-related and sociodemographic variables. The general lack of punitiveness found was referred to above. The need for retaliation among victims of violence was found to be associated with the seriousness of the injury and with the infliction of lasting physical effects. Surprisingly, however, property crime victims were more retaliative than violence victims. Other surprising results were the nonsignificant effects of acquaintance with the offender, knowledge of the sentence, and the payment of compensation. These negative findings may have resulted from the limited size of the sample. Note must also be taken of the lapse of time before the interview, "a good two years after their victimization had taken place" (76). Indeed, this study is notable primarily for its conceptualization and objectives, which are worthy of replication elsewhere.

The study conducted in Hamburg, which was referred to above, was much more comprehensive. Views were elicited from a large sample regarding the appropriateness of different types of sanction or informal methods of social control for a variety of offenses, modified experimentally in terms of the degree of injury inflicted and the harm intended. In addition to the general support for nonpunitive measures, respondents were specifically asked about the "needs and interests of victims" (Beurskens and Boers, 1985); here only 13.3% of 1,484 respondents specified "punishment," the preferred responses being restitution (32.9%), community service (26.3%), and apology (16.5%).[48]

Since the views of the victims did not differ very substantially from those of the nonvictims, the result is an apparent discrepancy between the relative nonpunitiveness expressed here as compared with the sanctions selected in vacuo, that is, unrelated to victim needs. This suggests that the low degree of punitiveness expressed here may reflect *justice* needs of the victim, as perceived by victims and nonvictims alike, rather than expressing society's perceived *coping* needs, such as social protection.

Defendants' Attitudes

Considering the vast literature that exists in the field of corrections generally, it is surprising how little of this deals specifically with offenders' perceptions of the system. Lawyers have traditionally been concerned with due process and penologists with the rehabilitation of the offender. It may be surmised that the attainment of both these objectives would be contingent upon the defendants' perceiving the procedures with which they were involved and the outcome as having been basically fair, even given that the ultimate purpose of these procedures is to explore the possibility of inflicting pain upon him or her.

The few studies available suggest that defendants' perceptions are not wholly negative. Casper (1978) reported on interviews conducted with 628 defendants charged with felonies in Phoenix, Baltimore, and Detroit after their court cases were concluded; 70% perceived the judge as being "unbiased and fair to both sides," 60% thought that the treatment generally was fair, and 53% even considered the sentence received "about right." Their perceptions of the prosecutors, on the other hand, were less favorable. Similarly, Krohn and Stratton (1980), on the basis of 153 interviews with prison inmates, found that 74% reported being fairly treated by the judge, although only 42% felt the sentence was fair. Nearly two-thirds thought they were fairly treated by the police (64%) and the prosecutor (62%). In both studies perceptions of public defenders were rather negative, while private attorneys were regarded somewhat more favorably in the second study and substantially more so in the first.

While no direct comparison can be made with the perceptions of victims described earlier, owing to differences in sampling and methodology, the general impression is that victims do not have substantially more favorable views of law enforcement personnel than defendants, in spite of the fact that law enforcement processes are supposedly designed, as noted, to inflict pain upon defendants (if found guilty) and to protect victims, or the community they represent. A further irony is that defendants are often least satisfied with the one agency purporting to assist them—the public defender. There may be, of course, a common explanation here: each party has high expectations from the agents who purport to be protecting their interests and are disappointed if their performance, as perceived by these parties, does not comply with these expectations.

A further point conveyed by some of the literature in this area, as well as in other areas considered in this study, is that perceptions of fairness may depend less upon the outcome of the proceedings than upon the procedures

followed (Casper, 1978:11; Tyler, 1984). In a reanalysis of the data collected
in the study by Casper referred to above, Casper et al. (1988) examined the
correlates of defendant satisfaction, as measured by evaluation of the severity of the sentence, whether defendants felt they were treated fairly, and
whether they had regrets as to how they handled their cases. These were
correlated with three independent variables: (1) severity of sentence; (2)
perceived "distributive justice," measured by the defendant's view of his
or her sentence as compared with what others receive for the same offense;
and (3) "procedural justice," as measured primarily by the defendant's
views of the personnel involved (judge, prosecutor, defense attorney).
While most of the correlations were significant, only procedural justice
was correlated with all outcome-satisfaction measures at the 0.1% level.
Moreover, since just over one-half of the defendants received custodial
sentences, the authors felt that they had successfully refuted the view
expressed by some earlier writers to the effect that procedural factors are
only of significance to defendants in relatively trivial cases.

Equity

Equity theory, as explained briefly in the appendix, purports to explain the
reactions of individuals confronted with a situation in which they "find
themselves participating in inequitable relationships" (cf. Austin et al.,
1976; Walster et al., 1976). Since the paradigm case of the creation of such a
relationship, as evidenced by the terminology of equity theorists, is an
injurious act involving a "harmdoer" and a "victim" (also referred to as
"exploiter" and "exploited"), it is evident that this theory is highly pertinent to the topic of this chapter.

The inequitable relationship is alleged by equity theorists to give rise to
two forms of distress: "retaliation distress" and "self-concept distress."
Such distress is alleviated by "restoring equity." As noted in chapter 2, this
may be achieved either by restoration of "actual equity," by means of such
practical measures as *retaliation* or *compensation*, or by "psychological
equity," whereby the new situation is rationalized to explain away the
inequity. These reactions are attributed both to the participants in the
inequitable relationships and to impartial observers.

The selection of the appropriate reaction to an inequity is generally
perceived by equity theorists to be based upon a cost-benefit analysis (Austin et al., 1976:168, 172). Thus, for a victim, compensation is the most
beneficial reaction: "If the victim secures compensation, he has restored

the relationship to equity" (Walster et al., 1976:24). If this is not feasible, retaliation may be sought as an alternative. This, too, "will cause the harmdoer (as well as the victim) to perceive that the relationship is again an equitable one" (ibid., 25). Only if neither of these methods of "restoration of actual equity" is practicable will resort be had to psychological equity, and the inequity will be rationalized. This may be achieved in various ways.[49] "Victims sometimes console themselves by imagining that their exploitation has brought compensating benefits. . . . Victims may also convince themselves that their exploiter actually deserves the enormous benefits he receives," much to the chagrin of reformers pursuing social justice (ibid.).

Equity theorists, and in particular those few who have concerned themselves with crime victims, tend to regard the present criminal justice system as insensitive to the implications of their theory (but cf. Longshore, 1979). While informal pressures are sometimes exerted upon defendants by law enforcement personnel to compensate the victim (Macaulay and Walster, 1971), restitution has not in modern times been a primary function of the criminal justice system. Moreover, retaliation on the part of the victim has hardly been encouraged, except insofar as it is implicit in retributive measures of justice imposed by courts in the name of the state. However, the prevalence of psychological equity, in which the victim is compelled to rationalize his suffering, emerges in much of the critical literature on the victim's predicament. Thus, whether explicitly or implicitly, equity theorists advocate reform of the system, and support is derived from their theories for some of the proposals to be considered subsequently. First, however, it will be necessary to examine more closely some of the assumptions and criticisms of the theory, in order to determine how far it should be recognized as a valid basis for the formulation of policy.

One assumption of equity theory which has been criticized is its purported *universality*. As noted earlier, it has been presented as a general theory of social behavior (Berkovitz and Walster, 1976:vi). It purports to apply in particular to the following areas: business relationships, exploitative relationships, helping relationships, and intimate relationships (Walster et al., 1976:7). It may be questioned whether a single theory may adequately explain these diverse situations. However, it seems plausible that inequity might be perceived as the focal issue in the second category, exploitative relationships, with which the present study is concerned; it is also partly concerned with helping relationships, in which as the result of the exploitative relationship a third party may be called upon to help the victim.

A related criticism questions the *exclusivity* of the theory. Can human behavior in any of these areas be explained solely by equity theory? This unidimensionality has been criticized: "Man does not live by equity alone" (Homans, 1976, citing Karl Weick). Kidd and Utne (1978), too, have criticized this unidimensionality and the assumption that other distinct norms of justice, such as equality and need, are encompassed by the equity norm (see also Folger, 1984:5; Umbreit, 1989:137). They have argued further that equity theory is too simplistic an explanation for human reactions unless it also takes account of *attribution* theory: "Variations in the perceived cause of inequity are crucially important in determining whether one is aware of an inequity at all, the means parties may choose to reduce inequity and restore justice, and the amount of distress generated by an acknowledged inequity" (Kidd and Utne, 1978:305). The variables (or "additional information") that Kidd and Utne perceive as being relevant to the degree of distress and the consequent mode of reaction to inequities are *(a)* locus of causation of the inequity; *(b)* the "stability" (i.e., duration and frequency) of the inequity; *(c)* the degree of intentionality—an intentional inequity being more distressful than an unintentional one; *(d)* the extent to which the inequitable behavior can be controlled; and *(e)* the sense of personal responsibility for the inequity (306–7). Another commentator, Homans (1976), has argued that equity theory has taken insufficient account of the power relationship between the parties. Some of these criticisms seem pertinent. In particular, it seems doubtful whether the selection of the mode of reaction—compensation, retaliation, or rationalization—would depend entirely on a cost-benefit analysis, irrespective of personality and social-structural considerations (cf. Brickman, 1977).

Another problematic aspect of equity theory is its attempt to apply identical principles to all parties to the inequitable situation. Not only does the theory posit that both harmdoer and victim will suffer distress from the inequitable relationship, but the forms of distress are subjected to the same classification—retaliation distress and self-concept distress—as are the modes of reaction adopted for the restoration of equity. While this makes for a neat and balanced theory, it seems doubtful whether the perception of an inequity *invariably* gives rise to distress or motivates an attempt to reduce the injustice (Greenberg, 1984; and see the discussion of offender's perceptions below). This somewhat simplistic approach is further aggravated by the application of a similar model to *observers* of the inequity, who are stated to undergo substantially the same reactions.[50]

While all these criticisms have a certain validity and derogate from the universal acceptability of equity theory as a guide to social relationships, the theory nevertheless appears to have substantial persuasiveness, in particular in relation to the focal area of the present study—crime victims. That a victim suffers distress, whether or not it can be dichotomized precisely in the above way, seems incontrovertible, and the availability of three main options by way of reaction—compensation, retaliation, or rationalization—also seems to ring true. There is, too, an element of plausibility in the order of priorities attributed by equity theorists to harmdoers and victims alike, namely, a preference for compensation, failing this, retaliation, and failing this, rationalization ("psychological equity"). However, is there any hard evidence that this is in practice how victims react? The question of evidence is critical. In the absence of such evidence it would hardly be justified to develop a policy of criminal justice that relies upon a theory that had yet to be validated. Moreover, the primacy of equity and compensation as the basis for justice in social relations has been questioned in the psychological literature itself.

Thus, Hogan and Emler (1981), who, with other writers, regard equity theory as "closely tied to the notion of distributive justice" (134), have argued that distributive justice is "an inappropriate analytical focus for understanding how the concept of justice functions at the level of the individual" (128). Among their criticisms of distributive justice are its emphasis on material goods and the assumption of familiarity, on the part of the decision maker or reacting individual, with all the relevant inputs and outputs. They question whether most people in fact believe in equity or in the existence of a relationship between merit and reward as hypothesized by the just-world theory described in chapter 2. On the other hand, the authors argue that a *retributive* concept of justice suffers from none of these weaknesses, and is "older, more primitive, more universal, and socially more significant" (131).[51] Does the empirical evidence lend support to this view that retribution is the preferred reaction to inequity?

In the previous section the available survey evidence and research on punitiveness was reviewed. However, the findings described were not directly related to the equity hypothesis, since no direct choice was presented between a compensatory solution and a retaliative, or retributive,[52] reaction. Nor does the equity theory literature abound in documentation of research that would test these alternative hypotheses. Moreover, this literature has tended to focus more on the harmdoer than on the victim. Finally, it has been more concerned with the primary dichotomy inherent in this theory—namely, the choice between restoring actual equity and restoring psychological equity—than with the secondary issue of whether the chosen form of actual equity is retaliation or compensation.

A notable exception, in spite of its limitations, is the research conducted by de Carufel (1981) in Canada. De Carufel examined two questions of direct relevance to the present study: (1) whether, given the creation of an inequity, victims placed priority on punishment for the harmdoer or on compensation for themselves, and (2) if compensation were important, whether it mattered if such compensation issued from the harmdoer or from a third party. The research involved an experiment in which, following an inequitable distribution of pay, four alternative solutions were adopted: (1) the harmdoer was compelled to compensate the victims (victim compensated, harmdoer "suffers"), (2) the harmdoer was fined an amount equivalent to his unfair gain (victim not compensated, harmdoer suffers), (3) the government compensated the victim (victim compensated, harmdoer does not suffer), and (4) the government censured the harmdoer, without ordering any material steps to rectify the inequity ("moral support," victim not compensated, harmdoer does not suffer). The degree of "satisfaction" and "fairness" of the outcome as perceived by the victims was measured on a nine-point scale.

The general validity of the findings of this study may be questioned, since not only was it experimental, but it was conducted with university students, and with small samples. Moreover, in spite of the terminology employed ("harmdoer" and "victim") there was no indication that any *criminal* conduct was involved, although the inequity created was apparently willful.[53] Nevertheless, the seeming uniqueness of the experiment and the plausibility of the findings warrant that careful note be paid to the results of this study. These results indicated that while both victim compensation and harmdoer's payment (termed in the research "suffering") significantly affected both outcome measures (the degree of victims' satisfaction and the perceived fairness of the solution), compensation was the more important, the differences between the mean satisfaction and fairness scores for victim compensated or not compensated being greater than those for payment or no payment by the harmdoer. Specifically, mean scores on the satisfaction scale followed this order: harmdoer paid compensation (7.7) > compensation by third party (4.4) > harmdoer fined (2.2) > moral support (1.7) (de Carufel, 1981:451).

The main finding, however, was that "subjects were very satisfied when the harmdoer suffered *in order to provide the compensation*." This finding suggests that victims may not be interested in retaliation or retribution as such but rather in compensation. Nevertheless, the compensation must be retributive, in the sense that it must issue from the wrongdoer. Receiving compensation from a third party "produced only moderate satisfaction."

The reduced level of satisfaction experienced by recipients of compensation from a third party is explained not only by the lack of any punishment being inflicted upon the harmdoer, and the inequity resulting from this gain, but also by a new inequity created by the third-party compensation. Thus while government compensation may have "eliminated to some extent the disadvantageous inequity" that arose initially, it "may have also created a simultaneous advantageous inequity with respect to the government's intervention on their (the victims') behalf." Thus, "subjects may have felt 'two inequities' pulling in opposite directions" (452–53).

In support of this last hypothesis, the author cited research indicating that recipients of aid generally[54] experience inequity in such circumstances, which is reduced if they have an opportunity to reciprocate. The hypothesis is further supported by a second experiment reported in the same article (de Carufel, 1981), where victims indicated higher levels of satisfaction and perceived fairness on being offered gratuitous compensation for a disadvantage suffered when they were granted an opportunity to reciprocate than if no such opportunity were offered.[55] De Carufel's studies appear to lend some credence to equity theory and to indicate its potential relevance to the issues under discussion.

In this context, mention should be made of two other studies (both doctoral dissertations) with a bearing on equity theory, which have the advantage of having been conducted with actual crime victims rather than experimentally. Hammer (1989), whose explicit objective was to test the validity of equity theory, examined the relationships among stress, perceived equity, and outcome of case for a sample of robbery victims. The author hypothesized that a more punitive response on the part of the criminal justice system would give rise to a greater perception of equity and to greater satisfaction on the part of the victim, as well as contributing to the victim's recovery. The findings produced a number of correlations in the expected direction and thus lend some support to the view that "harsher punishment of criminal offenders may help to restore a sense of equity to victims, and thus promote recovery" (95); but there were also some contrary findings, in particular in respect to female respondents. The author concluded that "the determinants of a victim's sense of equity and recovery from victimization appear to be more complex than a simple application of equity theory can explain, and further investigations are needed" (95–96). Hammer does not appear to have envisaged the possibility of the restoration of actual equity by the "primary" mechanism of a *compensatory* process; nor, indeed, were the alternative mechanisms of "psychological equity" examined.

The second study, by Umbreit (1988), focuses on the meaning of *fairness* in the perceptions of a sample of victims of juvenile burglars referred to a victim-offender mediation program. One of the research questions raised by the author was the validity of equity theory as compared with the more encompassing approach of Deutsch based upon the values of equality and need as well as equity (18; and cf. chap. 6 below). Content analysis revealed that while compensation for the victim—as posited by equity theory—played an important role in the victims' responses, the offenders' rehabilitation needs were perceived as being of even greater concern. These studies, together with de Carufel's, suggest that more research in this area would be fruitful both in the laboratory and in direct application to the criminal justice system.

Before concluding the discussion of the relevance of equity theory to the victims of crime, one further aspect of this topic must be mentioned. The literature considered above relates almost exclusively to *outcomes*, that is, to substantive aspects of the justice system. However, much of the research on the criminal justice system reviewed in the preceding sections has indicated that victims may be more concerned with the fairness of *procedures* than of outcomes. Some social psychologists have criticized the equity literature for ignoring this aspect of justice (see Folger, 1984; Tyler, 1984), and a body of research has developed on the perceived fairness and on the preferences of the parties in relation to different procedures of justice (Lind and Tyler, 1988). This has resulted in a debate over the relative significance of procedures as compared with outcomes in determining perceived fairness (Landis and Goodstein, 1986; Casper et al., 1988). This literature, too, supports the view that for victims in particular procedures are important in determining perceptions of fairness (Heinz, 1985; Umbreit, 1988:109). It will therefore be particularly relevant in the context of the discussions of procedural issues in chapters 8 and 11.

Since it was established in chapter 3 of this study that victims' needs could not be considered without taking into account the needs of defendants and the public, a brief discussion will follow regarding the applicability of equity theory to these categories.

Offenders ("Harmdoers")

Equity theory, as noted, is said to apply to the participants in an inequitable relationship. This includes not only the victim but also the harmdoer. Indeed, as noted, more attention has been devoted in the equity literature to the reactions of the harmdoer than to those of the victim. Harmdoers, too, are said to suffer both retaliative distress and self-concept distress and to react by restoration of actual equity, or, as an alternative, psychological equity (see, e.g., Walster et al., 1976; Utne and Hatfield, 1978). How far the two forms of distress are universally experienced by criminal offenders may be questionable. Adherents to subcultural theories of crime may doubt this, although the "shared-values" approach of Sykes and Matza (1957) would support it. It may also be doubted whether the psychopath experiences such distress.

More relevant to the present discussion is the question whether the harmdoer favors the relief of distress through the actual restoration of equity by the payment of compensation; the alternate method of actual equity, the equivalent of retaliation by the victim, would be to seek self-inflicted punishment (Walster et al., 1976:10), a theory supported by some adherents to the psychoanalytical approach. While "studies verify the fact that harmdoers do commonly compensate their victims" (ibid.), such experimental findings may not be valid for real-life offenders. Techniques for restoring psychological equity, for example, by derogation of the victim, have been documented both in the experimental and the criminological literature (see Walster et al., 1976:10–11; Sykes and Matza, 1957; and Landau, 1977). The proposition that this type of solution is adopted only because the offender lacks any appropriate avenue for the restoration of actual equity seems doubtful but is worthy of empirical verification. The extent to which offenders are disposed to compensate their victims is of course critical in the context of the development of restitutionary remedies in criminal justice, to which further attention will be devoted subsequently.

Nonparticipants

Equity theorists hold that "impartial observers should react to injustice in much the same way that participants do, with one qualification: observers should react less passionately than do participants" (Utne and Hatfield, 1978:77). While it seems plausible that observers may be upset by a manifestation of inequity, the mechanisms involved are less clear. Do they, too, share the retaliation distress and self-concept distress attributed to the participants? This aspect of the theory seems to be less well documented in the literature. However, there is said to be "strong evidence that participants and impartial observers react to injustice in much the same way" (ibid.).

It seems doubtful whether the dynamics involved in the selection of the mode of restoration of equity are identical for participants and for nonparticipants. In most cases nonparticipants do not have the same facility for restoration of actual equity as do participants. It is perhaps for this reason that the emphasis in the literature dealing with nonparticipants has been on restoration of psychological equity. This literature has tended to merge with that dealing with attribution theory and, more especially, the just-world theory. Thus the bystander reacts to an apparent inequity by attributing to the victim characteristics that would justify the inequity. This type of analysis is also applied to law enforcement personnel such as jurors, when they attribute blame to the victim and acquit the defendant; although here they apparently possess the alternative option of restoring actual equity by convicting the defendant.

Yet another category of nonparticipant in the inequitable act is the general public. Accounts of crimes presented in the media or conveyed informally may give rise to distress from which may follow either a desire for actual equity or a rationalization. Of greater interest here are the reactions that follow accounts of criminal proceedings and their outcome. In some cases, the legal reaction may be perceived as being either too lenient or too harsh, and an inequity may be perceived. As noted earlier in this study, the criminal justice system has to seek solutions that are acceptable to society at large, as well as to the parties involved.

Conclusion

Equity theory, if valid, provides overwhelming arguments for the adoption of an equity model in the criminal justice system. First, it suggests that the parties, including nonparticipants, in fact prefer that the wrongdoer pay compensation to the victim rather than that the former should be punished, compensation being the optimal mode of restoring actual equity. Second, it suggests that the victim suffers from the failure to have equity restored to a greater extent than was otherwise evident on the basis of the literature reviewed earlier. The view that the trauma of victimization is further aggravated by secondary victimization by the criminal justice system has already been noted. Equity theory, however, suggests that non-compensation in itself may lead to a derogation of the victim by others. Lerner et al. (1976) report a study by Lincoln and Levinger that indicates that "innocent and uncompensated suffering often produces lower evaluation of the victim" (140); the popular concept of a "loser" seems to illustrate this. The end result is thus *tertiary* victimization.

It is therefore not surprising that some adherents to equity theory have advocated that its tenets be adopted by the criminal justice system. This view is found primarily in the literature on restitution, which will be considered below. A more comprehensive approach has been put forward by Brickman (1977). He has argued that the principal aim of the criminal justice system should be to compensate the victim for his or her loss and suffering and (in addition) to compensate society for the costs involved in the administration of criminal justice. Since the amount of compensation paid by offenders would thus exceed their gains, a deterrent effect would also be present. This view may conflict with the principle insisted upon elsewhere in the equity literature that adequate compensation must precisely balance the harm done. Excessive compensation would merely create a new inequity (Walster et al., 1976:14), just as insufficient compensation would not fulfill the requirements of actual equity and thus be unattractive to the harmdoer. Brickman further argues that by paying compensation, the offender's self-image—and the community's perception of him or her—would be enhanced, thus contributing to the offender's *rehabilitation*.

The desirability of adopting a restitutionary model of justice follows from equity theory only so far as this theory has been shown to be valid. As noted, many aspects of the theory are still inadequately researched, and the relevant experimental findings derived from selected samples are not necessarily applicable to "real-life" offenders and victims. Indeed, in view of the obvious relevance of the theory for criminal justice, it is surprising how underresearched this topic is. The study referred to in the previous section by Smale and Spickenheuer and the dissertations by Umbreit and Hammer are significant in endeavoring to explore some of these issues with a relevant population.

A model of justice based on equity theory, if the theory were valid, would take account of the psychological needs of the parties. However, such a model may not necessarily be consistent with certain principles regarded by legal philosophers as fundamental. Such principles will be discussed in the next chapter.

6

Fundamental Principles of Justice

The two preceding chapters considered the coping needs of victims and their perceived justice needs, on the basis of the empirical evidence available on these topics. In order to develop the optimal justice system, is it sufficient to take account only of these coping and justice needs of the victim—as well as those of the other relevant parties (offender and society)—or are there some overriding principles with which a justice system must comply in order to be worthy of the name? Such principles, if they exist, would not be derived from empirical observation but would rather be deduced on the basis of philosophical or jurisprudential analysis. It is with the question of the existence and identification of such principles that this chapter is concerned.

The topic may be divided into three distinct questions. First, does the philosophical-jurisprudential literature suggest that recognition should be given to certain fundamental principles of justice which will be applicable to the criminal justice system in general and to the role of the victim in particular? Second, do prevailing systems of law, including the U.S. Constitution and international law conventions relating to human rights, subscribe to any such principles? This question is independent of the preceding one: on the one hand, accepted principles of jurisprudence may have been ignored by the policy makers responsible for drafting constitutional documents; on the other hand, such documents may have adopted principles not necessarily supported by the jurisprudential literature as universal or fundamental.[1] Third, irrespective of the degree to which jurisprudential analysis or constitutional documents have hitherto recognized as fundamental certain principles that may have a bearing on the justice system and the victim, does it seem appropriate to adopt such principles today? The review of victims' needs in the preceding chapters did appear to indicate that victims have basic needs which have not been adequately taken into account by the traditional legal system. However, the degree to which these needs can be translated into definable rights or principles will partly depend upon the evaluation of current victim-oriented reforms to be considered below, while the merits of the recognition of constitutional rights for victims will be discussed in chapter 10. The present chapter will therefore focus on the first two questions specified above.

Fundamental Principles of Justice in Jurisprudential Theory

Jurisprudential literature is familiar with the historic controversy between the "natural" and the "positivist" theories of law. The former represents the view that the legal system must reflect certain accepted fundamental principles of morality generally seen to derive from divine or supernatural sources. The development of this view is associated in particular with the ancient Greek philosophers and St. Thomas Aquinas (Lloyd and Freeman, 1985: chap. 3), and in modern times it has been associated primarily with Catholic scholars. The positivist school of jurisprudence, the origins of which are identified with Bentham and Austin, holds that the law has no necessary content, being the product of autonomous and secular forces of legislation.

While the concept of "natural law" as such has tended to hold a limited appeal in modern jurisprudential writing,[2] many philosophers have taken the view that the law must necessarily reflect certain moral or political ideals—what has been somewhat disparagingly termed "metaphysical absolutes" (McDougal et al., 1980:68), or, more sympathetically, a "deontological" approach. Emphasis on moral content is found in particular in the German "idealist" school of the nineteenth century, associated with Kant, with his concept of the "categorical imperative." Moreover, while positivist thinking has generally dominated modern Anglo-American jurisprudence, nonpositivist approaches have increasingly come to the fore in the last decades. One factor here may have been the phenomenon of the moral excesses perpetrated within the framework of the legal system under the Nazi regime, which led jurists—in particular Lon Fuller and H. L. A. Hart—to debate whether such pernicious norms could properly be termed "law." Even Hart himself, who in the context of the aforementioned controversy fell firmly in the positivist camp, took the view that the law had a "minimum content" (see Lloyd and Freeman, 1985: chaps. 6, 3).

Another contemporary legal philosopher has endeavored to present a more comprehensive reformulation of natural law theory in secular terms. In his *Natural Law and Natural Rights* J. Finnis (1980) sought to identify the "basic forms of human good"[3] and the "basic requirements of practical reasonableness" which enable us to differentiate between "ways of acting that are morally right or morally wrong," thus arriving at "a set of general moral standards."[4]

A greater threat to positivist thinking, however, has come from social contract theories. Historically associated with Hobbes, Locke, and Rousseau, such theories resemble the natural law approach in that they hypothesize that the nature of social institutions and social relationships is predetermined. This approach has been criticized not only because its historical basis is doubtful, but also because "however the contract was envisaged, anyone could write his own ideas into its terms" (Heath, 1963:6). Nevertheless, it is in the social contract tradition that there has emerged one of the most articulate and stimulating theories of modern idealist jurisprudential literature, that of John Rawls (1971). In his *Theory of Justice* Rawls (1971) deduces two fundamental postulates of justice which rational persons "in the original position"—that is, when determining the future institutions of the society they were creating, and in ignorance of the role in society which they themselves were destined to fulfill—would adopt in order to ensure the fairness of the principles to be evolved (12). These principles are concerned with the distribution of liberties and of social and economic inequalities in society.[5] This theory will be relevant to some of the topics to be considered in this study, such as the justice of adopting a public compensation scheme for victims.

Apart from the mainstream natural law and social contract theories, innumerable idealist political ideologies of all colors—extremes ranging from individualism to totalitarianism—have been held by different schools and writers to provide the necessary basis for the legal system (Friedman, 1967). Notable among them is Marxist analysis, which, although positivist in some respects (see McDougal et al., 1980:78; but cf. 76), and in spite of the ambivalence among Marxist thinkers regarding the role of law—destined ultimately to "wither away" with the state itself[6]—has had specific implications for the content of the legal system. "By reiterating the crucial role of the sharing of material values (especially wealth, well-being and skill), Marxists have defined an indispensable agenda for the enlargement of human rights everywhere" (ibid., 77).

Reference may also be made here to the "Republican Theory of Criminal Justice" recently developed by Braithwaite and Pettit (1990). While initially rejecting deontological approaches in favor of a pragmatic approach to criminal justice, the authors are led to adhere to a concept of social philosophy[7] that they trace historically from ancient Rome through Montesquieu. The basis of the republican idea is "negative liberty," or the "minimization or elimination of interference by others" (57); this is closely linked to a concept called "dominion," which is conditioned upon three premises, resembling in the style of their formulation the postulates of John Rawls.[8] This theory, according to the authors' analysis, has wide-ranging implications for the criminal justice system and gives rise to four presumptions in this area (chap. 6): (1) parsimony in the use of resources, (2) checking of power by means of the recognition of rights, (3) reprobation or disapproval as the primary reaction of the community to criminality, but also (4) *reintegration* "for those citizens who have had their dominion invaded by crime or punishment" (91). The relevance of this for the victim is emphasized.

There thus emerges a dichotomy not specifically between legal positivism and natural law but between legal positivism and the various idealist approaches, including natural law, all of which perceive the character of the legal system to be predetermined by some "higher-order" characteristic attaching to human society as a whole. In principle, legal positivism[9] imposes no such constraints.

However, the above dichotomy, too, is insufficient for the purposes of the present analysis. So-called positivists, while in principle repudiating a priori theories of the character of human society,[10] have frequently had strongly held views as to the proper objectives of social action. The most notable example is Jeremy Bentham, who evaluated all public measures in terms of their "utility" or their "tendency to augment the happiness of the community" (Bentham, 1948:3). Other positivist approaches that have advocated specific agendas for social action are the social engineering school of Roscoe Pound, which posited the need for legal reforms based upon empirical study of the facts, and the social defense school in criminology, which gave priority to the need to rehabilitate and control the offender.

Similarly, the political scientists McDougal, Lasswell, and Chen (1980), while rejecting a priori theories of human rights, have developed a complex agenda for social and political action in this area.

It will therefore be more useful for present purposes to consider the applicability of such "fundamental principles of justice" not according to their a priori or theoretical foundations, the analysis of which would be beyond our scope here, but according to the nature of the principles and the area of their applicability. Thus classifications that differentiate between civil and criminal law, between retributive and distributive justice, and between substantive and adjective law are relevant in the present context, insofar as they involve various principles governing the relationships between offender and victim, offender and society, and society and victim. While there seems to be no classification in which the categories do not overlap to some extent, it seems that the fundamental principles to be considered here can be conveniently classified according to their focus upon (1) reaction to wrongdoing, (2) reaction to victimization, or (3) structure and procedure.

Reaction to Wrongdoing. This label would apply to the retributive approach, which advocates a reaction to wrongdoing based on the deserts of the offender. It also applies to the school of social defense, which holds to a more crime-preventive philosophy. These approaches are concerned with determining the proper societal reaction to the offender under criminal law. Since, however, wrongdoing also raises legal issues between the wrongdoer and the person wronged, traditionally an area governed by the civil law, tort philosophy will also be relevant, in particular the controversy regarding the *corrective* function of tort law. Moreover, considerations of distributive justice have also been perceived as directly relevant to penal philosophy (Sadurski, 1985, 1991).

Reaction to Victimization. This heading is concerned with philosophies that may be applied in developing remedies designed to assist victims. Naturally, there is some overlap with the previous heading, since victims may be assisted by corrective policies applied to the wrongdoer, at least in the framework of tort law, and possibly even by retributive policies (see below). However, the emphasis under "reaction to victimization" is instead upon how society as a whole should use the assets at its disposal—that is, questions of distributive justice. Here the jurisprudential literature dealing with social contract merges with the broader literature of social philosophy in which discussion is devoted to the identification and elaboration of the fundamental guiding principles for the distribution of goods—

principles such as equality, right, desert, and need. As noted, such principles clearly have relevance for society's treatment of the victim (cf. Mawby, 1988).

Structure and Procedure. The literature both of political science and of jurisprudence has raised some norms of political or legal organization to the level of fundamental principles. This applies, for example, to the principle of legality, the separation of powers, and "due process of law"; indeed, the U.S. Constitution is sometimes said to be concerned mainly with processes. Some of the principles involved govern the structures and the interrelationships of political institutions, while others determine the way the laws will be applied in individual cases. Such principles, too, will be relevant in determining optimal solutions for administering justice among victims, offenders, and society.

All the ideologies referred to may be criticized either on the basis of some alternative ideology or on pragmatic or *utilitarian* grounds. A utilitarian approach would argue that each specific issue must be examined on its merits, and the optimal solution determined on the basis of the calculus of happiness thereby achieved or on some other "cosequentialist" criterion (cf. Primoratz, 1989:9). As noted above, utilitarian principles may also be employed to test various policies or principles in the justice area. However, in the present study, utilitarian criteria will tend to coincide with the other criteria to be applied to these policies, namely, those which have been adopted in the two preceding chapters, "coping needs" and "perceived justice needs." Insofar as these needs are met to an optimal degree, utilitarian criteria will be substantially satisfied, and there will thus be no need to invoke utilitarianism as the basis for independent "fundamental principles" of justice.

The above-mentioned principles will serve as a backdrop in the course of the analysis of the innovative victim-oriented programs in subsequent chapters, where some of the underlying issues, and in particular their application, will be further pursued. However, a brief discussion of some of the concepts referred to may be appropriate here, in particular retribution and social defense, and the main alternative guiding principles of distributive justice.

Retributivism

The principle of talionic retributivism ("an eye for an eye, and a tooth for a tooth"), common to the Bible and other early codes such as Hammurabi's Babylonian Code and the Roman XII Tables, has often been regarded as part of the natural order of mankind, that is, as part of "natural law." It is, for example, often cited as an argument for the death penalty. However, scholars have interpreted the above-mentioned provisions in different ways (cf. Kaufmann, 1977). Thus Maimonides regarded the talion not as a mandatory sanction but as a maximum penalty for the offense, designed to prevent extreme and disproportionate measures of vengeance on the part of the victim. Moreover, at the time these codes prevailed it seems that financial accommodation between the parties was in fact the dominant method for the resolution of legal disputes.[11] In the Kantian version of retributivism, on the other hand, there was no doubt about its mandatory character as society's proper reaction to the commission of a crime.[12] This doctrine is significant in the present context not so much for what it ordains in terms of society's punishment of the offender but rather in that it seems to preclude other, and especially more conciliatory, approaches to sanctioning which might have significant implications for the role of the victim.

Support for retributivist doctrines fell into decline with the rise of utilitarianism and the adoption of "forward-looking" objectives of punishment such as rehabilitation and incapacitation, as well as the more "classical" objective of deterrence. However, these objectives have in turn been criticized as insufficient justifications for punishment. Empirical research has cast doubt on the efficacy of both deterrence and rehabilitation (Blumstein et al., 1978; Martinson, 1974), while the individualized decision-making processes associated with the latter have been criticized for their arbitrariness (American Friends' Service Committee, 1971). The efficacy of long-term imprisonment as a means of incapacitation has also been doubted by some researchers (Van Dine et al., 1977), and selective incapacitation is regarded by many criminologists as both unjust and difficult to implement (see, e.g., Monahan, 1981). Thus one of the strongest motivations for the revival of retribution as the objective of punishment has been "the really insuperable difficulties that attend any alternative to it" (Hospers, 1977:195). This type of argument also forms the basis of the contemporary just-deserts position, as formulated in the report of the Committee for the Study of Incarceration "Doing Justice" (von Hirsch, 1976); although it is arguable that this somewhat negative reasoning cannot be considered to have raised retribution to the level of a "fundamental principle."

At the same time, adherence to retributivism on the basis of its putatively superior merits continues. In a well-known exposition of this view, Mabbott argues that "it is manifestly unjust to deprive a person of his liberty as a consequence of committing a criminal act for any reason other than the fact that he committed the crime—in short, that he 'deserved' the punishment" (Wilson, 1977:111). Finnis (1980) quotes a line of argument reminiscent of Kant when arguing that the offender by his act "gains a certain sort of advantage over those who have restrained themselves," and that "punishment rectifies the disturbed pattern of distribution of advantages and disadvantages throughout a community by depriving the convicted criminal of his freedom of choice, proportionately to the degree with which he had exercised his freedom, his personality, in the unlawful act" (263). Even the Hegelian idea of the "right to be punished" has been echoed in recent times by Morris and Gardiner (1981).

Other writers, including Hart and Rawls, have favored a "mixed" philosophy of punishment, incorporating both retributivist and nonretributivist elements (cf. Primoratz, 1989: chap. 6). In *Punishment and Responsibility*, Hart (1968: chaps. 1, 9) differentiated the "general justifying aim" of punishment and the "principles of distribution," according to which the responsibility and punishment of the individual would be determined. He placed greater importance on retribution in distribution, which he saw as guaranteeing that only a guilty person will be punished. Similarly, in "Two Concepts of Rules," Rawls suggested that the legislature might base criminal law legislation on utilitarian ideas, while the courts would apply retributivist criteria (see Cederblom, 1977).[13]

Retributive theories posit that the offender should be punished to a degree considered equivalent to the harm inflicted on society as a result of the offense.[14] Although the harm is generally inflicted upon a specific victim, this aspect is not generally emphasized in the theoretical literature, as distinct from the "applied" literature to be discussed in the next chapter. Similarly, such theories have generally failed to incorporate any role to be played by the victim. Vengeance on the part of the victim is perceived by classical retribution theory to be the antithesis of legal punishment (cf. Primoratz, 1989:70–71). The positive analysis of victim hate articulated by Murphy (1990), albeit as a subsidiary factor in retributive punishment, is cited as something of an anomaly in this literature; and the possibility of a role for the victim, if considered, is generally rejected (Cederblom, 1977).

This rejection by retributivists of a role for the victim is somewhat paradoxical, since, as noted, the societies from which the retributive approach was derived appear to have placed the main emphasis in their sanctioning system on compensation for the victim. Thus, biblical laws enjoined the thief or trespasser to repay the owner a multiple value of the property stolen. Further, etymologically the word retributive means "to pay back," and it is by no means clear that the original connotation was paying one's debt to society rather than to the victim.

Be that as it may, tentative consideration has been given in recent years to the restoration to the victim of a role in the retributive scheme of things, whether on a purely conceptual level or in terms of practical policies (Sebba, 1982). One form this reorientation has taken is the so-called restitutionary theory of justice. Thus, Barnett (1977, 1980) has argued that crime is an offense by one individual against another, and "justice consists in the culpable offender making good the loss he has caused" (Barnett, 1977:287). In a similar vein, Barnett and Hagel (1977), adopting a concept of individual rights from Dworkin,[15] attribute to the criminal justice system the function of enforcing the victim's moral rights and enabling the victim "to rectify the ambivalence created by the criminal act" (17). It seems that the Barnett and Hagel scheme of justice (cf. also Rothbard, 1977; Gittler, 1984) does not preclude various characteristics of a retributive system as generally understood, including the imposition of penal sanctions on the defendant, but in this case, too, the victim would play a more active role. However, Barnett and Hagel unequivocally assert that one generally accepted characteristic of a retributive system of justice—the exemption from or mitigation of accountability where the perpetrator's mental health is in question—has no place under their concept, for it would have the effect of depriving the victim of his or her rights. Perhaps the restitutionary theory, to be considered further in the next chapter, might appropriately be described as "quasi-retributivist."[16]

Social Defense

Social defense is a twentieth-century school of penal philosophy (and penal policy) that lays emphasis on the treatment and control of offenders. The treatment orientation points to the roots of this movement in the positivist school of criminology, of which it is an offshoot.[17] While its correctional objectives bestowed upon this school a utilitarian character, social defense adopted the value-laden objective of ameliorating the situation of "both society and the citizens" (Ancel, 1985:18).

The variety of meanings attributed to the term are described in Marc Ancel's account of this movement. Ancel argued that the identification of social defense with mere repression, and the charge that individual rights were sacrificed by this approach, were unfounded or were true only of some of the earlier advocates of social defense, such as Adolph Prins (ibid., 52). Nevertheless, even if adherents of this movement are correct in perceiving treatment of the offender as serving the offender's interests, a view that has been questioned by liberal and radical critics in recent years, a greater emphasis is clearly placed by this school on the main objective, the protection of society. One of the key concepts of the social defense school is the "safety measure," which must be applied to individuals "in proportion to their individual capacity for doing harm" (Ancel, 1965:15). This leads to the other key concept, the notion of "dangerousness," and the need to focus safety measures on *(a)* habitual, and *(b)* abnormal offenders (ibid.). Moreover, social protection should be sought, according to this approach, not only by treatment but also by prevention (17–18). While the limits of state intervention in order to further these objectives may be imprecise,[18] social defense is clearly a doctrine that gives priority to what are seen to be societal needs and interests. Insofar as the individual offender's interests are taken into consideration, they are evaluated somewhat paternalistically: the experts will determine the offender's treatment needs.

This emphasis on societal interests in dealing with offenders has implications for the present study. The espousal of social defense doctrines might tend to inhibit an orientation of the criminal justice system toward the victim.

Distributive Justice

Classification of the alternative criteria upon which distributive justice may be based varies somewhat in the literature. The main dichotomy is sometimes seen to be between justice according to *desert* and justice on the basis of *equality*, a dichotomy that dates to Aristotle (see Walster and Walster, 1975). Sometimes *need*—a concept close to but distinct from equality (Miller, 1976:147)—is seen to be the main alternative to desert. To need and desert, Miller, in a leading text on social justice (1976), adds a third category, justice based on *rights*.[19] This seems to be the least satisfactory of Miller's terms, since "right" is not so much a criterion or parameter of justice but a tool to describe the legal situation after a particular criterion or normative standard has been adopted or is seen to be inherent. Thus if "desert" or "need" be adopted as the appropriate criterion for justice, they, too, would give rise to rights. Miller's rights category would thus be better described as "tradition" or "status" as the basis of rights. However, it may also be useful to adopt such a term to describe any residual theory that rejects a priori principles for the distribution of goods in society, such as need or desert (see also Galston, 1980). Thus, for example, defense of rights could describe Nozick's rejection of various normative principles for the distribution of property (see Nozick, 1974).

Another writer often cited in the social psychology literature is Deutsch (1975), who proposed the following three criteria for social justice: equity, need, and equality. Equity is related to the concept of desert, both of which are seen to predominate in societies whose primary concern is economic productivity.[20]

These alternative criteria for social justice are not viewed by their proponents as competing values in all societies at all times. Rather, a particular culture with a particular economic orientation will be dominated by a particular conception of social justice. Thus Miller's rights criterion (which he associates with the philosophy of David Hume) is identified with conservative hierarchical societies—such as feudalism—in which the respect for traditional rights is the dominant motif. His desert criterion (illustrated by reference to the writings of Herbert Spencer) is identified with the competitive market economy—such as Western industrialized states—in which individualism and merit are rewarded. His need criterion (associated with the views of Peter Kropotkin) is identified with communalism and "social solidarity" as the guiding principle. Similarly, Deutsch (1975), as noted, identifies equity with an emphasis on economic productivity, equality with an emphasis on "enjoyable social relations," and need with an emphasis on "the fostering of personal development and personal welfare" (143). In view of the relativity of the criteria to their socioeconomic setting, it may be argued that these are not objective or "fundamental" principles of justice but rather a description of the subjective views of the members of the particular group, and therefore pertain to the analysis of perceived justice needs, the topic of the previous chapter. However, the classifications and the analyses referred to are not, even in the case of the social psychologist, based upon empirical research but are instead inductive. Moreover, the values are thought to be "fundamental" to the societies concerned.

Fundamental Principles of Justice under the Constitution

A constitution is the mechanism whereby rights and principles that are perceived to be fundamental in the society in question are granted superior legal status in that society and are thereby ostensibly rendered both normatively binding upon its lawmakers as well as its citizens and immune from routine and casual revision.[21] How far does the U.S. Constitution incorporate any of the principles considered above, or any other rights affecting crime victims?

The U.S. Constitution does not relate directly to crime victims. However, it concerns itself extensively with the criminal justice system. The Bill of Rights, ratified in 1791, perpetuated a number of characteristics of the common-law system of criminal justice which were thought to protect the citizen from arbitrary incrimination on the part of the government. Thus, the right to silence, the right to a jury trial, the right to counsel, the right to the confrontation of witness, and the right to "due process" are incorporated in these provisions, which applied originally only to the federal government but were subsequently extended to the individual states by virtue of the Fourteenth Amendment, as interpreted by the Supreme Court. In effect, these provisions guaranteed a perpetuation of the so-called adversary system, apparently foreclosing the possibility of alternate and possibly less formal procedures, in particular in criminal cases.[22] The procedural characteristics of the system were thus elevated to the status of fundamental rights. Further, the reference to "excessive fines" and to "cruel and unusual punishments" in the Eighth Amendment seems to imply, perhaps somewhat paradoxically, that the prevailing system of criminal sanctions is retributive—or at least punitive—in character. For if this were not the case, there would be no need for the imposition of such limitations on the severity of the sanction.

It has been suggested, however, that another amendment to the U.S. Constitution has direct relevance to the victim. In an article written at the behest of the American Bar Association's Criminal Justice Section, Richard Aynes (1984) argued that the Fourteenth Amendment, which mandates the "equal protection of laws," should in effect be interpreted as a charter guaranteeing a number of rights to crime victims. He argued that "protection of laws" implied a "positive duty to supply protection," and that it "seems that there is a consensus that there is an affirmative duty upon government to protect those under its jurisdiction" (55). Aynes also sees the government's duty to protect its citizens as the corollary of the citizens' duty not to violate the law (66), and as consistent with the purposes of government as laid down in the Declaration of Independence (79).[23] Aynes notes historical precedents whereby public authorities—the sheriff, or the municipality—were held to be absolutely liable for the misconduct of their charges or inhabitants, in effect rendering them "insurers" against damage inflicted upon those to whom a duty is owed (110ff.). However, he balks at insisting that the contemporary government's duty to protect its citizens should result in such "insurance" but rather seeks recognition for two more modest rights: (1) for the citizen's right to compel the law enforcement authorities to perform their duty (cf. also Willing, 1982), and (2) for the recognition of tortious liability for damages for failure in the performance of this duty. Thus the government would be liable to the victim if it failed to take into account the victim's interests at one of the decision-making stages. It would follow that two of the major obstacles to such suits under contemporary law—lack of "standing"[24] for the victim in the criminal justice process and sovereign immunity of the state for suits by its citizens—would be implicitly removed.[25] Finally, Aynes sees the recognition of these rights as stepping-stones toward the ultimate recognition of a more comprehensive right, the "right not to be a victim" (116).

While Aynes's thesis is in many ways persuasive, its basic premises are legally questionable. First, as pointed out by O'Neill (1984), both the federal and the state constitutions are more concerned with imposing restraints upon governmental activity than with imposing obligations: "They rarely require that government promote goals" (368). Moreover, the issue under discussion here was specifically addressed by Judge Posner in a federal case (cited in O'Neill, 1984:368–69):

> There is no constitutional right to be protected by the state against being murdered by criminals or madmen. It is monstrous if the state fails to protect its residents against such predators but it does not violate the due process clause of the Fourteenth Amendment or, we suppose, any other provision of the Constitution. The Constitution is a charter of negative liberties; it tells the state to let people alone; it does not require the federal government or the state to provide services, even so elementary a service as maintaining law and order.

Further, the Fourteenth Amendment refers to *equal* protection, not *absolute* protection. It was essentially a provision enacted to contend with discrimination. Its history, as Aynes himself recounts, is closely identified with the aftermath of the Civil War and the desire to compel the erstwhile rebellious states to grant equal civil rights to their black citizens. Moreover, while other types of legislative classification (i.e., those unconnected with racial categories) have also been subjected to the test of the Fourteenth Amendment, they have generally been held not to be discriminatory if the purposes of the classification were shown to be "rational" (Mason et al., 1983:612).

The applicability of the equal protection clause was expanded considerably in the 1960s, when the Supreme Court began to identify certain "fundamental rights," such as the right to travel, or "suspect categories," such as race or nationality, to which restrictions could not be applied other than for "compelling state interest" (Mason et al., 1983; Feeley and Krislov, 1990). Thus, designation of crime victims as a category from whom rights were to be excluded might give rise to judicial intervention under the Fourteenth Amendment,[26] but this is a far cry from the absolute duty of protection suggested by Aynes. The emphasis in the Fourteenth Amendment is on equality of consideration rather than on the extent of the protection itself.

However, Aynes may be on stronger ground in his operative conclusions, where, as noted, he refrains from insisting upon absolute protection but merely argues that law enforcement personnel should have a universal duty to investigate and be liable in tort for the failure to exercise reasonable judgment in making decisions in which victims may have an interest. For if it can be shown that law enforcement personnel in practice investigate most cases, and take some account of victims' interests, then the failure to follow this practice in certain individual cases might amount to discrimination. While most cases referred to in the literature in which the courts have been asked to invoke the equal protection clause involve discrimination by legislation against *classes* of citizens, the wording of the Fourteenth Amendment prohibits the states from denying to "*any person* within its jurisdiction the equal protection of the laws" (emphasis added). This would clearly cover the discriminatory exercise of administrative discretion under law, and not just the enactment of discriminatory law.

Thus, while it may be problematic to invoke the Fourteenth Amendment in favor of a governmental duty of *absolute* enforcement of the law, there are stronger grounds for arguing that this provision prohibits discriminatory enforcement of the criminal law. This view has recently received support—unrelated to claims based on the U.S. Constitution—from the republican theory of justice of Braithwaite and Pettit (1990), which recognizes "the right of a victim to have the authorities apply the same criteria as with other victims in determining how far to investigate the offence, whether to prosecute, whether to convict and how to sentence" (77).

As a matter of practice, the courts have, as noted, shown great reluctance to interfere with the discretion of law enforcement authorities, whether for fear of the infringement of the separation-of-powers doctrine, out of reluctance to interfere with discretionary powers, or because of a lack of standing on the part of petitioners (Welling, 1987:94–105; Green,

1988:492–93).[27] Welling, Green, and other writers have, accordingly, proposed new modes for enhancing the victim's status vis-à-vis law enforcement authorities, which will be considered in subsequent chapters.

However, insofar as one seeks to base the remedies on "equal protection," a larger and more fundamental issue not directly considered by Aynes must be dealt with. This is the question whether the prevailing criminal law and criminal processes are in fact designed to protect *victims*, such that the conclusion may be reached that it is indeed the victim who has the right to the "equal protection" of these laws and processes. This question may be subdivided into two further questions. First, is the criminal law concerned with protection? The social defense school would indeed attribute considerable importance to this objective. On the other hand, under a retributivist view, whether Kantian or following the just-deserts school, punishment is not essentially concerned with protection, or indeed any other forward-looking function, but is exclusively *backward* looking. Without entering here into an exhaustive discussion on the philosophy of punishment, it seems that the protection of society is accepted as at least one of the purposes of punishment. Moreover, there are certain stages of the criminal process, notably bail and parole hearings, where protection of the public is one of the main considerations.

The second and more problematical question is whether the protective purpose of the criminal law is directed at the victim rather than at society in general. The problem here is that even if the victim has some recognized special interest in the criminal process (as to which, as we have seen, there is considerable ambivalence), this seems to be primarily a *retributive* interest. The protective interest—that is, the prevention of future criminality by the same offender—is not the interest exclusively of the victim but of prospective future victims, the public as a whole.[28] It could then of course be argued that any citizen, including the victim, had a Fourteenth Amendment interest in protection from the offender. In this case, however, it cannot be said that there is any inequality in the way law may be applied in a particular case in which the government refrains from taking action, since the victim is (in theory) being placed at risk from the offender "equally" with other members of the public.[29]

Similar problems arise with the ultimate goals that Aynes would strive to achieve, namely, recognition of "the right not to be a victim." This slogan is fraught with ambiguity. If it means that every citizen has an enforceable right to prevent his or her own victimization, it is mere casuistry, for by definition offenders do not recognize this right and its implementation is impracticable. If it means that it should be recognized that acts of victimization are not protected by law, it is simply a truism. Criminal victimization is, by definition, prohibited by law. Moreover, a potential victim is even permitted to take what would otherwise be unlawful measures to counteract such victimization (the right to self-defense). If, however, bearing in mind that rights have correlative duties, the question being addressed is *whose right* is the corollary of the potential offender's duty not to victimize, this is of focal importance for this study. Are violations of prohibitions under the criminal code in fact offenses against the victim? While practically this is so—the injury is inflicted upon the victim's person or property—legal convention appears to regard the offense as committed against the state, as evidenced by the mechanisms of law enforcement, including the Bill of Rights, and by the tort-crime dichotomy.[30] On this analysis, it is not the citizen who has a right not to be a victim; it is the state that has a right not to have its citizens victimized. However, as indicated earlier, it is this approach—one that places all the emphasis in criminal justice on the state, to the exclusion of the victim—that has been the cause of much disaffection with the present system. Recognition of the "right not to be a victim" in this sense would require a radical rethinking of the criminal process, which again may not be consistent with the present Constitution.[31] This theme will be resumed in chapter 12.

The President's Task Force on Victims of Crime (1982), while making no far-reaching claims regarding the constitutional rights of the victim under the present law, suggested that a radical change be brought about by means of constitutional amendment (114–15); and other proposals have been made of a similar hue (Lamborn, 1987). These proposed amendments deal primarily with the status of the victim from the procedural point of view, and their implications will be considered in chapter 8, which deals with procedural reforms.

Welfare Rights. The discussion of need as a basis of distributive justice (cf. Sadurski, 1985: chap. 6) might lead to recognition of a general right to welfare. Included in this right might be the entitlement of victims to compensation or services from the state (although there might be a problem in justifying a preference for victims over other needy categories; see below, chap. 9). While there is an extensive literature dealing with the philosophical arguments in favor of or against the recognition of such a legal right (see, e.g., Plant et al., 1980; Mawby, 1988), and support for such recognition has been based upon the interpretation of Rawls's principles of fairness (Michelman, [1975?]), attempts to argue that such a right currently exists under the U.S. Constitution by virtue of the Fourteenth Amendment (Michelman, 1969), or that it is a "fundamental right" and therefore deserving of special scrutiny (Feeley and Krislov, 1990:813), do not seem to have gained much support from the Supreme Court (Rice, 1979:39).

Fundamental Principles of Justice in International Law

The development of international law has been concerned primarily with the relationships among states. Developments in the twentieth century have increasingly focused attention on the rights of (minority) *groups*, while since World War II there has also developed a body of human rights law whereby certain basic rights appertaining to *individuals* are recognized in international law (see, e.g., Shaw, 1991: chap. 6). These rights impose obligations upon individual states regarding the treatment meted out to their citizens, in some cases granting remedies to the individuals concerned—again, an innovation from the point of view of international law. Obligations of this nature are specified, inter alia, in the Universal Declaration on Human Rights; the International Covenants on Economic, Social, and Cultural Rights and on Civil and Political Rights; the American Declaration of the Rights and Duties of Man; and the European Convention on Human Rights. Not all these documents impose binding obligations on the signatory states (Brownlee, 1971:106), and even when so binding, the norms outwardly adhered to are not necessarily incorporated into the domestic law of these states. Nevertheless, the adoption of such documents on the international plane does point to the existence of certain fundamental principles, which have been agreed to in substance among a majority of the states in the United Nations or in the region concerned.

What rights of crime victims can be inferred from these documents? Article 3 of the Universal Declaration of Human Rights, adopted by the General Assembly of the United Nations in 1948, declares, "Everyone has the right to life, liberty, and security of the person." This is echoed in article 1 of the American Declaration of the Rights and Duties of Man. This clearly indicates that the Utopian-sounding principle specified by Aynes as the ultimate objective of victim sympathizers—recognition of "the right not to be a victim"—has in fact already gained recognition.[32] Here too, however, the question arises as to the practical ramifications of the recognition of this right.

It may be that affirmation of the right to life, liberty, and the security of the person—property being generally dealt with under separate provisions—implies an obligation on the part of the state to protect its citizens from infringements of such violations. The reason this is not explicit is that the primary intention of such provisions is to protect individuals not from abuses perpetuated by other citizens but rather from abuses emanating from the state itself. This is further borne out by other provisions of these documents specifying a right to the protection of the law. The Universal Declaration of Human Rights specifies the right to such protection against "arbitrary interference with . . . privacy, family, home or correspondence" and "attacks upon . . . honor and reputation."[33] Here, again, the emphasis is upon the prevention of governmental abuses of citizens rather than acts of victimization by other citizens. Naturally, the same applies to the extensive body of international law prohibiting torture (Rodley, 1987).

Further, as in the case of the U.S. Constitution, the extensive references to criminal processes in these charters of human rights focus upon the rights of offenders and suspected offenders, rather than those of victims. Such provisions, insofar as they impinge upon victims, may be considered as limiting rather than enhancing their protection. Even the prohibition on torture, as implied by the name of the leading international document—"Convention against Torture and Other Cruel, Inhuman or Degrading Treatment or Punishment"—belongs analytically to the struggle for the protection of the rights of offenders, or of persons so perceived by the state, even though it also takes the significant step of rendering torture a criminal offense (art. 4) and designating the recipient a victim (art. 5).

It may also be noted that some international legal documents, such as the International Covenant on Economic, Social, and Cultural Rights of 1966 and the European Social Charter of 1961 have recognized general rights to medical and—in the second case—welfare services, which are in principle applicable to crime victims; but no such category is specifically alluded to in these documents. Article 8 of the European Convention for the Protection of Human Rights and Fundamental Freedoms specifies the right to "respect for private life," and this provision was held by the European Court of Human Rights, in the *Case of X and Y versus the Netherlands,* in 1983, to obligate the state to provide protection under the criminal law against sexual abuse (Berger, 1992:282). Under a Dutch law considered by the court, only the victim could file a complaint, so that in the case of an assault committed against a handicapped girl, no prosecution took place. Her father was thus successful in his claim for compensation. This case seems to be a landmark in its recognition of victims' rights but seems to have attracted little attention in this literature.

Another major breakthrough in this area occurred in 1985, when, after intensive activity on the part of victim advocates, the Seventh United

Nations Congress on the Prevention of Crime and Treatment of Offenders adopted the "Declaration of Basic Principles of Justice for Victims of Crime and Abuse of Power," which was in turn adopted by the UN General Assembly. The declaration deals with two focal areas: *(a)* "Victims of Crime" and *(b)* "Victims of Abuse of Power." The first category relates to the conventional definition of crime victims, and the declaration lays down norms providing for (1) access to justice and fair treatment, (2) restitution, (3) compensation, and (4) assistance. These were the areas on which victim advocates, hailing mainly from Western democracies, had been focusing and continue to do so. The standards incorporated in the declaration in these areas will be relevant when considering the mainstream victim-oriented remedies.

However, "some States, primarily from the developing world, indicated strong concern about abuse of political power exemplified by the conduct of some transnational corporations, matters not effectively regulated by national criminal law" (Lamborn, 1988:108). With this in mind, part *B* of the declaration was added to cover "Victims of Abuse of Power." The definition of victims here, as noted in chapter 3, is wide and includes individuals and collectivities who have suffered harm "through acts or omissions that do not yet constitute violations of national criminal laws but of internationally recognised norms relating to human rights" (sec. 18). Although the operational sections of the declaration dealing with this category of victim are somewhat inconsistent in their terminology (cf. Lamborn, 1988:112–13), the main purport of the declaration in respect of this category of victim is to encourage the enactment of legislation criminalizing the conduct involved, the provision of material and other remedies (secs. 19, 21), and the negotiation of international treaties (sec. 20).

As might indeed be anticipated in the light of its title, the declaration is concerned almost exclusively with victims. Being aware that victim-related principles are liable to have implications for offenders too, the General Assembly resolution adopting the declaration specified that measures taken to promote the interest of victims should be "without prejudice to the rights of suspects and offenders" (sec. 2). However, one of the policies that states are encouraged to adopt under the resolution is "to establish and strengthen the means of detecting, prosecuting and sentencing those guilty of crime" (sec. 4(d)); but the emphasis here is perhaps on comprehensiveness, rather than on toughness, in law enforcement, and is doubtless intended to reflect the secondary objective specified in this section, namely, "to curtail victimization." At the same time, another policy encouraged by the same section is "to prohibit practices and procedures conducive to abuse, such as secret places of detention and incommunicado detention" (sec. 4(g)). This clause does not seem to be intended to improve the lot of persons suspected of "traditional" offenses but is presumably aimed at the victims of abuse of power covered by the second part of the declaration. However, a committee charged with the task of considering modes of implementing the declaration, which listed a number of international standards the violations of which should be considered to be covered by the heading "victims of abuse of power," included the Standard Minimum Rules for the Treatment of Prisoners (see Bassiouni, 1988:78). Thus under this part of the declaration, the borderline between victims and offenders is necessarily blurred. Finally it should be noted that while declarations of this nature are not generally considered under international law to be of legally binding force,[34] "a declaration which may appear hortatory may, as practice develops, come to embody the law" (Asamoah, 1966:245).

Conclusions

In this chapter the question was raised whether there are fundamental principles of justice that need to be taken into account when formulating a policy toward victims. Such principles were sought both in the jurisprudential-philosophical literature and in constitutional documents. While certain concepts and expressions such as "fairness" and "equality" appear to be widely regarded as basic to the idea of justice, attempts to find a universally acceptable principle or standard by which any legal system can be tested, while often stimulating fruitful debate, have proved problematical. There appear to be a number of reasons for this. First, most theories are based upon inadequate premises. Either they have some metaphysical or speculative foundation—such as divine inspiration or social contract—whose concept and content are inevitably open to speculation, or they are based on the writer's sometimes highly personal views on the characteristics of mankind which a legal system must take into account. Second, the nature of any theory and the priority of values on which it is based will be related to the political, moral, social, or political philosophy of its author and will be culturally determined (cf. Miller, 1976; Diamond, 1981). Third, even within the framework of a given approach, there may be competing principles of justice, rather than a single formula against which all policies may be tested (Miller, 1976:361). Thus, while some of the principles expounded in the jurisprudential literature (such as Rawls's theory of justice, or utilitarianism) may have relevance to victim-oriented policies, and their

implications will be considered in the ensuing discussion, they should not
be regarded as absolute.

Principles incorporated in constitutional and international charters do
ex hypothesi have the status of fundamental legal principles. But existing
provisions of the U.S. Constitution do not appear to have direct bearing on
the status of the victim in the justice system in spite of the valiant attempt
of Professor Aynes to show the relevance of the Fourteenth Amendment in
this respect. Note should be taken, however, of the proposals to amend the
U.S. Constitution, as well as some amendments effected in state constitutions (see below, chap. 10). Moreover, an exhortation to respect victim
rights is now enshrined in an international document that imposes, upon
UN members, at least a moral obligation. Additional documents may apply on the basis of regional affiliation, notably to members of the Council
of Europe (cf. Tsitsoura, 1984).

It may also be appropriate to recognize new fundamental principles,
which will address themselves to the role of the victim, and to incorporate
such principles into the Constitution. Such proposals might be based on
the analysis of victim-related problems in the current literature. However,
the failure of abstract thinkers to develop universally acceptable theories
from which to derive these principles leaves open the possibility that they
might alternatively derive from empirical studies such as those surveyed
in the two preceding chapters. If a particular view as to the requirements of
justice for victims were both widely and strongly (i.e., saliently) held by
relevant sectors of the public, this might be a consideration for adopting
these views at the level of a fundamental or constitutional principle.[35]

Part III

Evaluation of Victim-Oriented Reforms

7

Reforming the Objectives of Sanctioning Policy: The Desert Model of Sentencing and Restitution

In this part of the study the main reforms described briefly in chapter 1 will be considered in the light of the requirements of the system as reviewed in chapters 4 through 6. Attention will thus be paid to the degree to which the reforms and proposals appear to be calculated to address *(a)* the coping needs and *(b)* the perceived justice needs of the relevant parties (and in particular of the victim), and to take account of *(c)* fundamental principles of justice adhered to by some of the dominant theories. As far as possible, differentiation will be made between the a priori merits of the proposals in question, that is, the degree to which they appear to have a potential for meeting the needs described, and the actual effectiveness of the measures specified, where such proposals have already been adopted and insofar as evaluative data are available.

In this and the chapters that follow in this section, the discussion will relate primarily to questions of principle and matters giving rise to controversy. No attempt will be made to consider in detail the innumerable practical and administrative problems that arise at the implementation stage of such detailed proposals as those of the Proposed Model Legislation (NAAG/ABA, 1986). Further, the report of the President's Task Force (1982) deals with such matters as police training and procedures for the speedy return of victims' property held by the police for evidentiary purposes. These issues are of the utmost importance, but their analysis in detail goes beyond the scope of this study. In a general way, however, such issues may be clarified by the analysis of the victim's role in the criminal process, and of victim-assistance programs.

This chapter will focus on substantive reforms in the criminal justice system which have a direct bearing on the victim's situation. The main reforms addressed will be desert sentencing and restitution. While the importance of the last topic in the present context is obvious, desert sentencing, while not ostensibly concerned with victims, also appears to be of the greatest relevance.

The Desert Model of Sentencing

How far are recent developments in sentencing philosophy calculated to affect the way in which the victim is considered at the sentencing stage? As noted in chapter 2, victim-related factors have traditionally been reflected in sentencing practice, in which victim harm has generally constituted one of the main components—if not the exclusive determinant—of the seriousness of the offense and the punishment therefor. This has applied both to the formal legislative norms and to court practices as revealed by empirical studies. However, the weight given to the seriousness of the offense in the sentencing decision was diminished under the influence of the principle of individualization of punishment, whereby factors relating to the personality and circumstances of the offender, rather than the seriousness of the offense, were to determine the outcome. The sentencing "tariff" could be modified or rejected in favor of an individualized sentence (Thomas, 1967). Similarly, under the system of indeterminate sentencing, individual circumstances might determine the release decision of the parole board.

The principle of individualization, which was mainly a reflection of the rehabilitationist philosophy, has been eroded in recent years in favor of the neoretributivist just-deserts philosophy, which posits that the seriousness of the crime and the culpability of the offender should be the exclusive measures for determining the severity of the sanctions (von Hirsch, 1976). Partly under the influence of these views, both Congress and many state legislatures have enacted laws that would reduce or even eliminate the discretionary powers of both the courts and parole boards to individualize sentences (see, e.g., the Comprehensive Crime Control Act of 1984), notably by making provision for the publication of sentencing guidelines and other modes of structured sentencing (Ashworth, 1992a). It is true that these laws often purport to take into account a variety of sentencing objectives,[1] including general deterrence and incapacitation, and that their enactment was influenced by a number of the ideological-political forces referred to in the introductory chapter to this book, and in particular by the "law-and-order" ideology. However, it seems that the just-deserts philosophy constituted the main intellectual force behind this revolution. Moreover, the principle of *proportionality*, which appears to reflect primarily a desert philosophy, has recently been adopted as the basis of sentencing policy in Britain and other countries (von Hirsch and Ashworth, 1992:83; see also U.S. Sentencing Commission, 1987:1.2).

While the standard criminological literature and some specialist monographs (e.g., Cullen and Gilbert, 1982) deal extensively with the demise of the rehabilitationist philosophy and the rise of the justice or desert model, almost no consideration has been given to the *victimological* implications of this revolution. The development of the victim and the just-deserts movements have been coincident in time, and in one significant respect at least share a common goal, namely, the deemphasis of the personality of the offender as the focus of the criminal justice system. There has nevertheless been scant analysis of the relationship between the theoretical underpinnings of the two movements. More particularly, little attention has been paid, until recently (cf. Cavadino and Dignan, 1993), to the implications of the development of a desert model of justice for the status of the victim, whether in symbolic or in practical terms.

The replacement of an individualization or rehabilitationist mode of justice by a deserts model will now be considered in terms of the three levels of analysis adopted in this study: coping needs, perceived justice needs, and fundamental principles of justice. Since the just-deserts model has been advocated on ideological rather than pragmatic or empirical grounds, it will be appropriate in the first place to consider this model from the point of view of the principles of justice involved, with special reference to the victim.

Fundamental Principles of Justice

It would be beyond the scope of this study to engage in a detailed critique of the desert model of justice in the light of various theories of retributive and distributive justice. The reader is referred to the general literature on this topic, and in particular to the extensive writings of Andrew von Hirsch in defense of the theory, and, among its critics, to Cullen and Gilbert (1982) and Braithwaite and Pettit (1990; see also Pettit and Braithwaite, 1993). The present analysis will focus instead on aspects of the theory and its implementation that lay emphasis on victim-related factors in determining the penalty to be imposed upon the offender.

On a retributivist or desert view, the severity of the sanction is in principle to be determined by the seriousness of the offense and should be proportional to it. What are the components of offense seriousness, and how is their relative magnitude to be determined? While desert theorists have yet to adopt an agreed answer to this last question (von Hirsch, 1985; Ashworth, 1992a), the proposed solutions are inevitably related to victim harm. Thus Sellin and Wolfgang (1978) suggested that the seriousness of delinquent acts could be assessed in terms of the amount of injury, theft, or damage inflicted upon the victim, and that the relative seriousness of specific types and degrees of harm could be measured empirically on the basis of respondent perceptions. Such measures could, it was suggested, be incorporated in a sanctioning scheme (Wolfgang, 1976; Nevarez-Muniz, 1984) which would result in a retributive sentencing tariff based exclusively upon the degree of harm inflicted upon the victim.

Another view, referred to by von Hirsch (1985:65–66), holds that since the public may have insufficient knowledge of the harm actually inflicted by various types of offense, data deriving from victimization studies should be used. Von Hirsch himself expressed a preference for developing a scale of "interests" adapted from Feinberg (1984), whereby personal safety and livelihood interests were the most serious, various other interests being graded lower on the scale. More recently, von Hirsch and Jareborg (1991) have developed a scale based on the degree to which the offense constitutes an invasion of what they call the "living standard."

While all these scales tend to focus on the injury to the victim as the point of departure for determining the appropriate sentence,[2] the leading statement of the just-deserts position asserted that the seriousness of crime be measured by *two* components: harm and culpability (von Hirsch, 1976). The degree of culpability was to be measured by such characteristics as the type of mens rea and the degree of moral turpitude involved in the commission of the offense. The addition of this component of seriousness would tend to dilute the victim-oriented component of offense seriousness;[3] it would also accommodate with greater facility the punishment of attempts and of victimless crimes. Conversely, it might result in reducing the seriousness level where the victim's conduct was perceived to have contributed to the commission of the offense.

The principle of culpability may have a limiting or negating effect on the harms for which punishment is due. In particular, harmful results of the crime that were unforeseen by the offender seem in principle to be excluded from the ambit of the calculation of offense seriousness—certainly harms that were *unforeseeable* (cf. Sebba, 1994). The Federal Sentencing Guidelines (sec. 1B1.3) originally defined the injury that is to be taken into account in sentencing as "harm which is caused intentionally, recklessly or by criminal negligence" (U.S. Sentencing Commission, 1987:1.15), but this provision was subsequently amended so that relevant conduct now includes "all harm that resulted from the acts and omissions specified" (U.S. Sentencing Commission, 1994:16). This topic, which has been somewhat neglected in the just-deserts literature (but see Singer, 1979:26–27), has become of focal interest in the light of recent Supreme Court cases to be discussed below.

Culpability may, perhaps more frequently, be an aggravating circumstance, as in cases where the offense is committed with "deliberate cruelty" or "callousness," illustrations of what Singer (1979) terms "*unnecessary injury*" (85, emphasis added). In some cases, such as the sentence increase for "vulnerable victims" (Federal Sentencing Guidelines, sec. 3A1.1), the rationale could arguably be based on either aggravated harm or aggravated culpability.[4]

Other victim-related characteristics may be more difficult to classify under the headings of either harm or culpability in the context of desert sentencing, and their relevance to desert sentencing is therefore in question. How far should the sentence be affected by the attributes or "moral worth" of the individual victim?[5] This was one of the issues raised in the recent Supreme Court cases *Booth v. Maryland* (1987 55 LW 4836), *South Carolina v. Gathers* (1989 490 US 805), and *Payne v. Tennessee* (1991 115 L Ed 2d 720), all of which involved the admissibility of victim-related evidence at the sentencing stage of capital murder trials. (These will be considered again in the framework of the discussion of victim-impact statements.) In the first of these cases it was held that evidence of the personal characteristics of the victims was inadmissible. Justice Powell was "troubled by the implication that defendants whose victims were assets to their community are more deserving of punishment than those whose victims are perceived to be less worthy" (4838 n. 8). The inadmissibility of such evidence was affirmed in *Gathers*, but in *Payne* a differently constituted court overruled the earlier cases and held evidence of the victim's attributes to be admissible. However, Chief Justice Rehnquist denied that the purpose was to differentiate the sentence according to the "worthiness" of the victim, but rather "to show instead each victim's 'uniqueness as a human being' " (734). Not only is the potential here for differential sentencing in conflict with democratic values, but it also leads away from the declared objectives of desert-based and structured sentencing—that is, uniformity (see, e.g., U.S. Sentencing Commission, 1987:1.2).

Another issue that arose in these cases was related to the admissibility of evidence of the emotional impact of the crime on victims and their families. In *Booth*, a majority of the Court "reject[ed] the contention that the presence or absence of emotional distress of the victim's family . . . are proper sentencing considerations in a capital case." In *Payne* the majority overruled the earlier cases on this point too, and held that evidence of the impact of the crime on the family was admissible. Moreover, it imposed no clear limitations on this principle in terms of the type of harm that would be relevant, its remoteness, or the culpability of the offender with regard to that harm. In his dissenting opinion in *Booth*, Justice White took the extreme view that an offender could be held "accountable . . . for the full extent of the harm he caused." Chief Justice Rehnquist, in delivering the majority opinion in *Payne*, was less specific, but Justice Souter seemed to favor a broad concept of accountability based upon the principle that "every defendant knows . . . that the person to be killed probably has close associates, survivors, who will suffer harms and deprivations from the victim's death." These formulations appear to go beyond the principles generally adhered to by desert theorists.

The issues raised above are concerned with the effect on the sentence of victim-related factors connected with the commission of the offense. Some of the recent legislation or guidelines specify as mitigating factors benefits conveyed to the victim by the offender *after* the commission of the offense (e.g., restoration of property, payment of compensation, etc.). To a just-deserts purist, "these factors are highly incompatible with a deserts concept—that the focus on sentencing must be exclusively, or virtually exclusively, upon the crime, not upon the criminal's later reaction to the crime" (Singer, 1979:90). A fortiori, the amelioration of the victim's situation by outside parties, for example, by an award under a state compensation plan, would not be relevant as a mitigating circumstance.

It will be recalled that desert-based sentencing was advocated in large measure to counter the disparities that prevailed under the previous system, in which one of the main objectives was to achieve individualization of the sentence based on the needs of the offender. It is something of a paradox that, to echo a visionary paper delivered by Marvin Wolfgang

(1982) at the Third International Symposium of Victimology in 1979, the developments described above appear to be leading to the "individualization of the victim." This must surely be the probable effect of taking account of the victim's personal and moral attributes, or the emotional impact of the offense on the victim's family, in determining offense seriousness. Wolfgang argued: "This victim individualization not only does not violate the model of just deserts, it may indeed enhance it, enrich it by providing greater precision in the proportionality of the severity of sanctions to the gravity of victimizations" (57). Von Hirsch (1985:79), too, appears to tread this path when he engages in discussion as to whether the seriousness of a broken finger inflicted in the course of a crime would be affected by the fact that the victim was a concert pianist.[6] Elsewhere, von Hirsch and Jareborg (1991:5 n. 14) suggest a differentiation between "cases of special harm resulting from vulnerabilities shared by significant numbers of persons" and "cases of special harm that are more idiosyncratic to particular individuals"; presumably their intention is to exclude the second category from the sentencing equation, or to modify its significance. Moreover, they would presumably only take into account "culpable" harm, that is, harm that was foreseen, or at least foreseeable. Even so, the very analysis is strongly suggestive of Wolfgang's thesis.

Desert theory purports to relate the punishment to the wrong inflicted by the offender upon the *community*. Yet the developments in "proportionate" sentencing described above, which are in a large measure consistent with desert theory, clearly allocate a very central role, at least on the symbolic level, to the *victim*.

Coping Needs

Neither the traditional rehabilitation-individualization model nor the justice model of sentencing speaks directly to the issue of the victim's coping needs. Under the rehabilitation model, the victim would not normally benefit materially except in those cases in which the offender was placed on probation with a condition of the payment of restitution. Sentencing under the deserts model also does not purport to bring any benefit to the victim, except under the restitutionary justice version, where restitutionary payment rather than imprisonment is perceived as the measure of desert. However, many advocates of restitution, following the pioneering writings of Eglash (1958) and Schafer (1976), specifically base their advocacy of this approach upon rehabilitationist goals rather than desert (see below).

Recent legislation enacted to encourage the payment of restitution by offenders remains ambiguous in respect of its underlying philosophy. On the one hand, restitution is advocated as a general policy, to be considered by the court in all cases, thereby implying that it is not a rehabilitative measure to be applied according to individualized considerations. On the other hand, such provisions are not to be enforced universally, as a desert philosophy might imply. At most, an obligation is imposed upon the courts to consider a restitution order. Moreover, such legislation has not generally been incorporated in desert-oriented sentencing reforms but has been enacted independently. Thus the deserts model as such does not appear to contribute directly to the resolution of the victim's coping needs.

Perceived Justice Needs

The replacement of the rehabilitation model by the desert or justice model in current academic and political thinking has taken the form of a sort of "moral crusade."[7] It seems to have been assumed, especially by the law-and-order lobby, that the public in general, and victims in particular, would ardently support the move toward determinate and proportionate sentencing. Moreover, both liberals and radicals emphasized the unfairness of indeterminate sentences, which gave rise to apparently arbitrary decisions regarding the term of imprisonment to be served by an offender under the rehabilitationist system. Yet firm data regarding the views and perceptions of the relevant parties in this respect are somewhat rudimentary; moreover, while they do provide some support for the prevailing ideology, this support is not unequivocal.

Much of the evidence and related discussion of these topics derives from the scaling literature that was inspired by the seminal work of Sellin and Wolfgang (1978) referred to above on the "measurement of delinquency." Their original study, conducted with selected samples, showed that respondents to a questionnaire were able to make meaningful quantitative differentiations between the relative seriousness of different types and degrees of victimization. This approach enables a precise calculation of the weightings attributed by respondents to the various physical components of the offense and its outcome, such as the seriousness of the injury inflicted, the use of intimidation, the commission of a sexual assault, the breaking into of premises, and the monetary value of the loss inflicted.

This psychophysical scaling approach to offense seriousness was subsequently replicated on general populations, notably in a survey conducted in the Baltimore area (Rossi et al., 1975) and in a cross-national study linked to the National Crime Survey (Klaus and Kalish, 1984; Wolfgang et al., 1985). The original study emphasized only physical harm and took no account of the offender's culpability as determined by the mental element. This, too, was shown to affect perceived offense seriousness (Sebba, 1980) and was partially taken into account in the subsequent studies referred to.

As noted earlier, these two elements, the harm inflicted on the victim and the culpability of the offender, are the components of offense seriousness to have gained recognition under the just-deserts philosophy. There is thus a general consistency between this philosophy and public perceptions of criminal responsibility and punishment as measured by the psychophysical studies, although the degree to which the two dimensions are integrated in the public perception may vary (Warr, 1989), and there is considerable evidence (Shachar, 1987) that the public includes in its seriousness evaluation "fortuitous" harms, unforeseen by the perpetrator, the relevance of which to desert is, as noted above, problematical. The nationwide replication study referred to also found that victim vulnerability affected perceived-seriousness scores;[8] as noted above, this, too, is generally accepted as a legitimate element for consideration under the just-deserts doctrine. Further, one study (Riedel, 1975) concluded that the surrounding circumstances and background of the offender were not perceived as relevant to respondents' estimation of offense seriousness—again, a finding generally seen as consistent with the just-deserts approach. However, both Riedel's findings and the exclusion of personal circumstances from desert sentencing principles have been disputed (see Parton et al., 1991:75; Ashworth, 1992b:116–17).

Further, most of these studies have noted a general consistency among different population groups in estimating the seriousness of offenses, thus providing support for the "consensus," as opposed to the "conflict," view of legal norms.[9] Such consistency is a precondition of the adaptation of a just-deserts model, for the fixed tariff of punishment, the adoption of which is implicit in the model, would have to be acceptable to society as a whole.

A unique study in this respect was conducted by Hamilton and Rytina (1980), who asked respondents (a quota sample of 391 residents of the Boston area) (a) to assess the seriousness of a number of offenses, (b) to assess the severity of various penalties, and (c) to select an appropriate punishment for particular offenses. This enabled the researchers to ascertain how far the penalty selected for an offense was proportional to the seriousness of that offense, thereby providing a test of whether individuals applied standards of proportionality in selecting sanctions, as dictated by just-deserts philosophy. A strong correlation was found between the two measures. "The general theoretical question—whether the norm of just deserts is used by individual respondents in organizing their cognitions and associated judgements—appears to have been answered with a resounding, if monotonic 'yes' " (1130). Moreover, when between-individual correlations were examined, the data suggested "a high level of consensus on the norm of just deserts." However, lower-income and black respondents were found to adhere less strongly to the just-deserts principle and to deviate from the group norms, thereby lending support to the conflict hypothesis.

Some support for the main findings of the above study is found in the research conducted by Blumstein and Cohen (1980) referred to in chapter 5. A sample of residents in Allegheny County, Pennsylvania, were asked to select the appropriate sanctions for 23 different offenses.[10] Various measures of severity (selection of prison sentence, mean sentence length) were correlated with the results of the two best-known scales of offense seriousness, those of Sellin and Wolfgang (1978) and of Rossi et al. (1975). Correlations varied from 0.73 to 0.97. The authors concluded that "the sentences of our survey respondents are largely consistent with the principle of just deserts as it relates sentence severity to offense seriousness" (Blumstein and Cohen, 1980:236).

The implications of the psychophysical studies are mostly rather indirect. With the notable exception of Hamilton and Rytina, most of the psychophysical research has been concerned exclusively with the determinants of offense seriousness, without express application to the sanctioning system.[11] Thus, respondents might have been considering measures of seriousness for a different purpose, such as the measure of harm caused to society;[12] indeed, the scales were originally devised by Sellin and Wolfgang as a basis for criminal statistics rather than punishment. By the same token, respondents might, even if oriented toward a sanctioning system, take cognizance of other factors, such as the offender's background, even though they perceive such factors as irrelevant to offense seriousness as such. Moreover, some of the conclusions derived from the analysis of psychophysical data may be partly a function of the formulation of the hypotheses selected and the methods adopted for testing them (Sebba, 1980:126).

There are indeed some research findings that raise doubts about the degree to which the public favors the deserts model, at least in its pure form. One of the psychophysical replications found that respondents attributed seriousness weighting to harm inflicted even if such harm were unintended and unforeseen by the perpetrator of the injurious act (Sebba, 1980). This, of course, is in conflict with the "culpability" element in the desert paradigm. Further, a review of the findings of the psychological literature (Miller and Vidmar, 1981) noted the importance of the *motivation* attributed to the perpetrator, as well as his or her conduct before and after the offense, factors that are considered irrelevant to desert sentencing. There seems to be a discrepancy here between moral culpability, to which these factors would be relevant, and legal culpability, to which they are not. The appropriate response or remedy for perceived injustices as posited by equity theory may correspond rather to moral criteria of culpability than to the legal criteria specified by the desert model. In principle, the need to restore equity, with its implication of balance and equivalence—whether this restoration is achieved by a compensatory or a retaliatory process— has much in common with the concept of just deserts.[13] However, the solutions to various dilemmas raised in these two areas of literature (cf. Utne and Hatfield, 1978) may differ—equity solutions being determined empirically, just-deserts solutions inductively. Thus, equity theorists have noted, on the basis of survey and observational data, that where the harmdoer has also suffered, this suffering reduces the inequity and would thus result in a mitigation of the punishment (Austin et al., 1976:189).[14] This is in conflict with pure just-deserts theory (Singer, 1979).

A corollary of harmdoer's suffering is the reduction of the victim's sufferings. It was noted earlier that *post factum* restitution by the offender is not regarded as a mitigating factor by pure desert theory. Under equity theory such payment would constitute a contribution to the restoration of equity. A reduction in victim suffering brought about by an outside body, such as a state welfare service, would a fortiori not be considered a mitigating factor under desert principles. Indeed, even equity theory seems equivocal on this point. Yet a small study conducted by Cohn (1974) showed that the provision of such a service to the victim had the effect of mitigating the need to punish the offender in the perception of the respondents.

A more serious challenge to the view that the public unequivocally adopts a deserts view of sanctioning is found in surveys in which respondents were asked to identify with alternative sentencing philosophies. In a survey of 1,248 members of the general public, Forst and Wellford (1981:806) found that while just deserts ("to punish the offender in direct proportion to the seriousness of his crime") was seen to be "extremely important" or "very important" by the majority of the respondents, an almost identical proportion (72%) placed rehabilitation ("to reform the offender through treatment and correction measures to convert him into a useful and productive citizen") in the same categories. In another survey in which 1,121 responses were elicited from Washington State residents (Riley and Rose, 1980), 97.8% thought rehabilitation should be the goal of the correction system, and 73.4% took the view that this goal had a high, or the highest, priority. This compared with the corresponding figures of 91.4% and 45% for the goal of punishment (350). However, while punitiveness here referred to a fixed sentencing system and rehabilitation indicated indeterminate sentencing, the former appears to have had negative connotations (e.g., "the use of traditional prisons") not emphasized by most just-deserts advocates and was associated by the researchers with conservatism. Moreover, in a third survey reported by Cullen and Gilbert (1982:259)—themselves severe critics of the deserts approach and advocates of rehabilitation—a larger proportion of the public appears to have supported deserts rather than rehabilitation as a sentencing philosophy. More recently, however, Cullen et al. (1988) reported findings indicating continued support for rehabilitation, while support for punishment reflected its utilitarian rather than its desert aspects.

Thus it may be premature to conclude unequivocally that the public favor a desert model of justice. While the principle of proportionality seems generally acceptable, the available findings "do not tell us about the relative strengths of just deserts as a norm or about people's willingness to use alternative principles of justice" (Hamilton and Rytina, 1980:1141).[15] Further, the support expressed in many of the studies for both punishment-desert and rehabilitation raises questions as to how these terms are interpreted by the public (cf. Penley, n.d.; and see above, chap. 5).

The preceding discussion relates to the degree to which public attitudes appear to favor a desert model of justice. As to victims, there seems to be no specific evidence in the literature; we do not know, for example, how far victims would regard unforeseen or "subjective" harm as justifying punishment. It has been noted in chapter 5, however, that victims do not seem to be more punitive than other citizens and frequently cite other priorities rather than punishment. The extent of the victim's preference for restitution and other "victim-oriented" measures will be considered subsequently.

A number of studies have been conducted with criminal justice personnel,[16] who, it appears, lay considerable emphasis on rehabilitation. Forst and Wellford (1981) found that, unlike the general public, all categories of criminal justice personnel included in their study—judges, prosecutors, defense counsel, and probation officers—were more likely to attribute importance to rehabilitation than to just deserts (see also Berk and Rossi,

1977). This may, as noted, reflect an institutional interest on the part of the respondents who participated in the study.

Last, but by no means least, it is essential to ascertain the views of *defendants* in this matter. While it has often been assumed that offenders are profoundly distressed by the apparent inequities and arbitrariness reflected by discretionary and indeterminate prison sentences, there has been little systematic study of offender perceptions, and such evidence as is available does not seem to support this assumption. Thus, in the study conducted by Forst and Wellford (1981), only 37% of the 550 federal prisoners interviewed regarded just deserts as a "very important" or "extremely important" goal of sentencing, as compared with 65% who favored rehabilitation. In another study conducted by Shelly and Sparks (1980) employing psychophysical techniques, in which mean scores for offense seriousness were plotted against the penalties allocated for these offenses, the results did not reflect support for proportionality. Moreover, some respondents advocated greater individualization in sentencing as well as greater consistency.

The literature reviewed above suggests that the public may share some general perceptions of offense seriousness and culpability upon which a proportional sentencing system as envisaged by the just-deserts model may be based. However, a number of special populations may be less inclined to accept this model, including ethnic minorities (Hamilton and Rytina, 1980), criminal justice personnel (Forst and Wellford, 1981), and prisoners (Shelly and Sparks, 1980; Forst and Wellford, 1981). Further, general attitudes at the macro level may be replaced by a different approach when specific applications are called for (Cohn, 1974). Finally, as regards the attitudes of victims on this question, little is known.

Conclusion

In view of the close connection between the development of the just-deserts and the victim movements, in terms of both temporal proximity and, to some extent, common politico-ideological antecedents, it is surprising how little attention has been paid to examining the merits and demerits of the desert model in relation to the victims of crime. It emerges from the preceding survey that the fundamental concepts of justice underlying the desert model are to a degree victim oriented, in that they tend to lay emphasis on victim harm; but inasmuch as the element of culpability plays a prominent role, this may reduce the victim orientation, since it removes the emphasis from the suffering of the victim to the moral turpitude of the offender. Moreover, the coping needs of the victim are largely ignored under this model, except by the small school of advocates of the restitutionary theory.

It also emerges that while the desert model may be consistent with the sense of justice felt by the public in general and victims in particular, this topic has hardly been explored. Since both the just-deserts and the victim movements seem to have developed to a considerable extent as the result of what was thought to be dissatisfaction by the public and by victims with the former system, it is surprising that there has been little attempt to determine the extent to which this supposed dissatisfaction has been reduced by the new sentencing models.

Restitution

The history of restitution in the criminal courts is in effect the history of the role of the victim. The larger role played by the victim in early justice systems reflected the main function of such systems—to arrange for the resolution of the conflict between the two adversaries. Similarly, the decline of the role of the victim referred to in the opening chapters of this book reflects the decline in the use of restitution as the main disposition in the criminal trial, insofar as trials could be labeled "criminal" under early systems, the criminal-civil dichotomy being then less developed (Schafer, 1968). The function of the criminal trial became more punitive. Monetary remedies for the victim became the objective of civil legal processes, to be used only rarely in criminal cases.[17] Similarly, views expressed by such pioneers as Tallack and Garofalo to the effect that the criminal justice system should pay greater attention to the victim's needs usually included a proposal to require offenders to make restitution to the victim (Schafer, 1968:23–24; Garofalo, 1975; and see Smith, 1975), at least until the relatively recent development of the concept of *state* compensation.[18]

At the same time, it is clear that the advocacy of restitution has had a broader base than this concern for the welfare of the victim, and that its popularity in the literature cannot be attributed exclusively to this movement. Part of the attractiveness of the idea of offender restitution derives from its multifaceted appeal, or, less charitably, its "chameleon" quality (Shapiro, 1990). As pointed out by Hudson and Galaway (1978), restitution may be supported as being consistent with most of the generally accepted objectives of criminal justice. Indeed, restitution programs have mostly laid greater emphasis upon the benefits to be derived by the offender than those to be bestowed upon the victim (Hudson et al., 1980). Theoretical writers, too, have often emphasized this aspect (Eglash, 1958).

Restitution may therefore be regarded in part as an offshoot of the rehabilitation movement; indeed, it was advocated by some of the pioneers of the positivist school of criminology (Weitekamp, 1991), in which this movement has its roots. It may also have derived support from labeling theory, for restitution may advance the labeling objective of a *minimal* form of intervention with the offender, thus, in the labeling view, causing a minimum of harm (see, e.g., Schur, 1973). Rehabilitation and labeling were popular approaches in the 1960s and 1970s; and restitution, as well as diversion and community service, may be regarded as a product of these philosophies, subsequently interacting with the victim movement. Additionally, as noted in chapter 6, there are conceptual links between restitution and retribution or desert, while some writers have found support for restitution in other aims of criminal justice, including deterrence (Tittle, 1978).[19]

Restitution programs were common even before the contemporary victim movement took root. The Minnesota Restitution Center, one of the most active institutions in this area, was founded in 1972. Restitution programming "mushroomed in the '70s" (Hudson et al., 1980:16), and most states passed or amended legislation during this period to facilitate or encourage its use (ABA, 1981; Bureau of Justice Statistics, 1984). By the mid-1980s there were several hundred restitution programs (Smith et al., 1989). These developments were accompanied by a massive literature on this topic;[20] by 1980, Hudson et al. (1980) identified 336 related publications, most having appeared in the preceding decade.

Restitution has received further impetus in recent years from federal governmental and legislative activity. The Victim and Witness Protection Act of 1982 amended title 18 of the U.S. Code to grant federal courts a general power to order restitution, rather than solely as a condition of probation (Slavin and Sorin, 1984:508). Moreover, a court refraining from making such an order, or even ordering only partial restitution, was obliged under this legislation "to state on the record the reasons therefor" (sec. 3579(a)(2); now sec. 3663). The expansion of court-ordered restitution was recommended by the President's Task Force on Victims of Crime (1982) and by the American Bar Association's Guidelines for the Fair Treatment of Crime Victims and Witnesses in 1983. By 1988, restitution laws had been adopted by all 50 states (NOVA, 1989), and in some cases entrenched in their constitutions (Hillenbrand, 1990:194), while model restitution provisions have been incorporated in the Uniform Victims of Crime Act, 1992. Provision for restitution is also laid down in the UN Declaration of Basic Principles of Justice for Victims of Crime and Abuse of Power. Finally, a right to restitution is listed among the victim's rights recognized by Congress under the Victims' Rights and Restitution Act of 1990 (sec. 502), while another section (sec. 506) advocates that states adopt the same goal in their victims of crime bills of rights.

It would seem from this review that the principle of restitution has today won universal acceptance, its earlier support on the part of certain offender rehabilitationists now being supplemented by a broad front of victim advocates. However, in spite of—or perhaps because of—the fact that restitution to the victim has been advocated from so many quarters,[21] and despite the explosion of programs and literary activity in this area, a large number of major issues, both conceptual and empirical, remain unclarified.

The uncertainties regarding restitution derive partly from confusion in the terminology and in defining the subject matter, in at least three areas. First, some of the literature deals simultaneously with *restitution* on the part of the offender and *compensation* schemes administered by the state (see, e.g., Newton, 1976). Moreover, this differentiated terminology is not universally accepted; in England the term *compensation* may refer to restitution by the offender (see, e.g., Vennard, 1978; Harland, 1980).

Second, while the term *restitution* generally refers only to monetary payments by the offender to the victim, it is sometimes taken to include other forms of reparation, such as service to the victim and, more commonly, service to the community (Hudson et al., 1980.) Third, a restitution order may take the simple form of a sanction imposed by the court at the sentencing stage in lieu of or in addition to any other sanction (see, e.g., the Victim and Witness Protection Act of 1982), or it may be part of an elaborate program or "project" involving special personnel, negotiations between the parties, a formal contractual agreement, and the supervision of its implementation. Such programs may be adopted at various stages of the criminal process. As indicated below, in these programs the emphasis tends to be placed on the rehabilitation of the offender, whereas a simple restitution order seems to be oriented primarily to meeting the victim's needs, whether material (coping) or justice needs.

It is doubtless partly owing to these areas of confusion that much of the research in this area is methodologically faulted, and that such an expansive literature has produced so few firm data about the effects and implications of restitution. This literature will nevertheless be analyzed here for the light it can cast on the issues being examined in this study.

Coping Needs

Determining the ability of restitution programs to achieve their objectives is highly problematical. Hudson et al. (1980:168), in their National Assessment of Adult Restitution Programs, noted that restitution programs were assumed to bring various benefits to victims (financial redress, involvement in the process, satisfaction), to offenders (rehabilitation, reduced intrusiveness into their lifestyle), and to the criminal justice system or the public (reduction of costs, increased credibility of the system). They were attributed a large number of outputs or outcomes; the authors listed no less than 68 (52), employing at least nine measures of benefit (175). These objectives inevitably conflict. Moreover, "rationales linking restitution activities to victim, offender or system benefits . . . tend to be implicit, and poorly developed" (173).

The lack of clear formulation of goals (see also Weitekamp, 1991) is only one of the obstacles in the evaluation of the achievements of the use of restitution. Another is the great variety of situations in which restitution is used: as a form of pretrial diversion, as a condition of probation, as an independent sentencing sanction, as a sentencing sanction in combination with other sanctions, and as a condition of parole. McGillis, on the basis of a national survey, differentiated between four main program models: (1) those organized by prosecutors as part of victim/witness programs, (2) restitution within victim-offender reconciliation programs,[22] (3) restitution-employment programs, and (4) routine probation supervision (Karmen, 1990:284). Similarly, a juridical analysis conducted in Germany (Mueller-Dietz, 1991:201–4) differentiated procedural, enforcement, and substantive orientations to restitution. These variations complicate the evaluation of the effects of various program components and the generalizability of any conclusions. The problem is further compounded by the need to differentiate between adult and juvenile restitution programs, between financial and "service" restitution, and between restitution to the victim and restitution to the community.

What is even more critical, while a number of reports on restitution programs purport to be evaluative, the employment of rigorous evaluation methodology has been almost nonexistent. Of 31 evaluations of restitution "projects" or "programs"[23] reviewed by Hudson and his colleagues (1990), only four employed experimental design, while the large majority used no controls of any kind (53; see also Hudson and Galaway, 1980). Even in 1989 the same writers took the view that "shortcomings in the evaluations done, along with the weak research designs used, means that we have learned only a modest amount about restitution programs, in spite of millions of dollars having been spent" (Hudson and Galaway, 1989:5). Smith et al. (1989), in reporting in the same year on their study of restitution enforcement, also noted "the paucity of empirical research on these issues" (see also Harland and Rosen, 1990). Moreover, while a number of publications have purported to evaluate restitution programs, no American studies seem to be available of the routine use by courts of the power to order restitution, or of the implementation and efficacy of such orders in these cases, although some British findings will be referred to below.

The main question under the present heading in the context of this study is how much the victim stands to gain materially from restitution orders—if used systematically and implemented effectively. Harland (1981) analyzed the potential for restitution on the basis of the National Crime Survey data for 1974 and concluded that "relatively few victimizations are so costly, even in terms of gross loss, as to negate the possibility of a restitutive disposition."

Ongoing data from the same source would seem to confirm this conclusion. In 1990, 50.2% of personal crimes, of which there were 14 million, involved losses of under $100, 68.6% under $250; since 9.5% involved no or unknown losses, only 21.9% involved losses known to be $250 or more, of which nearly half were under $500. For household crimes, of which there were over 14 million in 1990, values were somewhat higher: 37.9% of the losses were under $100, 32.5% were of $250 or more; moreover 36% of completed burglaries had a value of $500 or more, as did, not surprisingly, 90.3% of completed car thefts. Naturally, the figures now are higher than in 1974, but the general pattern has remained constant (*National Crime Victimization Survey Report*, 1992:94–95).

Even assuming this conclusion to be correct,[24] there remain a number of obstacles to the feasibility of restitution by the offender. These obstacles possess varying degrees of surmountability. The most insurmountable relates to the fact that only a minority of offenders are apprehended and brought to justice—the well-known "funneling" or "shrinkage" effect (see Karmen, 1990:288)—whereby there is a fallout of cases at various points in the criminal process. Even if restitution were to be introduced at an early stage of the proceedings, this would be of no avail in the majority of property victimizations in which the offender is never apprehended. Offenders processed through "alternative systems," such as mental health, would also be exempted (Harland, 1982).

Further, even among apprehended offenders, not all would be able to afford restitution. The figures presented by Harland (1981) included some victimizations where the losses were relatively large, and this problem would be considerably aggravated if offenses against the person were included. Moreover, while little is known about the distribution of income among offenders generally, Harland attempted to explore this issue by reference to the findings of a survey of the income of jail inmates during the 12 months prior to their incarceration (in 1972), where it was found that "more than half had incomes of less than $3,000" (19); in 1978 the median income was $3,714 (Slavin and Sorin, 1984:569). Even assuming that offenders' incomes have substantially increased since then, they might find restitution payments problematical. This problem could of course be resolved in the case of offenders sentenced to imprisonment by ensuring that they earn a minimum wage and that a proportion of this be earmarked for the victim. Indeed, Kathleen Smith (1975) proposed that the very duration of the prison term be determined by the payment of restitution to the victim. Currently, however, "restitution and a term of imprisonment are irreconcilable because prison wages are very low" (Slavin and Sorin, 1984:570). The alternative possibility of some form of service to the victim might be even more problematic. Restitution has been said to be particularly appropriate for white-collar crime, especially where committed by corporations, whose ability to pay is evident (Goldstein, 1982); but its selective usage, while other offenders received more punitive sentences, would be perceived as discriminatory.

Problems also arise in respect to the method adopted for determining the amount of loss. Since restitution assessments are not the main concern of criminal—as opposed to civil—proceedings, the method of estimating the loss may be somewhat haphazard.[25] Victims often claim that the amount of restitution awarded does not cover their actual losses, let alone compensate for pain and suffering (Hudson and Chesney, 1978:135; Bonta et al., 1983; Vennard, 1976; Smith et al., 1989:113), although discrepancies tend to emerge between the assessments made by victims, offenders, and courts (Hudson and Chesney, 1978). This problem will have been aggravated by the 1990 Supreme Court case of *Hughey v. U.S.* (109 L Ed 2d 408), to be considered below, which held that an award of restitution must be limited to the loss caused by the specific conduct that was the basis of the crime for which the offender was convicted.

The reluctance of criminal justice personnel, such as prosecutors and judges, to concern themselves with the assessment of restitution (see below) is also a limiting factor. This has probably been the main reason for the restricted use of restitution orders in the past, and their confinement to property cases involving liquidated damages. Indeed, the difficulties involved in grafting a civil or quasi-civil remedy onto current procedures in the criminal courts (cf. Klein, 1978), are seen as one of the main obstacles to the integration of the restitutive remedy into the contemporary system. Such problems led, according to Molumby (1984), to the "demise of restitution" in the state of Iowa, one of the pioneering states in the recent history of restitution legislation (Hudson et al., 1980:15).

This unwillingness on the part of criminal courts to become involved with financial assessments of harm should have been overcome by two types of measure introduced as part of the reforming legislation: first, by the introduction of victim-impact statements—introduced at the federal level together with the restitution legislation, under the Victim and Witness Protection Act of 1982—which were designed to ensure that the court would have the relevant information regarding the extent of the harm inflicted upon the victim; and second, by the mandatory or quasi-mandatory formulation of the restitution provisions themselves.

However, provisions such as the federal ones, although mandatory in spirit, leave room for maneuver (Roy, 1990). The revised section 3579 (d) to title 18 of the U.S. Code specifies that "the court shall impose an order of restitution to the extent that such order is as fair as possible to the victim *and the imposition of such order will not unduly complicate or prolong the sentencing process"* (emphasis added). Qualifications of this nature may appeal to the traditional judicial reluctance to enter into restitution calculations. Similarly, on the equivalent quasi-mandatory provision adopted in England in 1988, whereby magistrates must give reasons for not making an award, Marshall (1990) comments that "it may have little effect because most magistrates have quite plausible reasons for not doing so (not enough information, poor defendant, victim implicated in precipitating crime, size of loss disputed, etc.)" (86). Nevertheless, some increase in the use of compensation orders has been observed since the new legislation came into force (Moxon et al., 1992; Ashworth, 1992b:251).

Information relating to the success of the reforms in this respect in the United States is only partial (see Harland and Rosen, 1990). A survey of judges conducted by Smith and Hillenbrand (1989) found that "all respondents said they usually order the defendants to make restitution to the victim when the crime results in financial losses which the defendant is in the position to pay" (66). There are two qualifications here: "usually," and the evaluation of the defendant's means. Moreover, the respondents represented those 36 states in which victims' legislation was perceived to be more developed (6). Karmen (1990), on the other hand, concluded that, in spite of the wave of legislation, "the implementation of restitution remained the exception rather than the rule in most jurisdictions" (282). Figures for the U.S. Sentencing Commission guideline cases—to which the above-cited provisions apply—show that in 1992 restitution was ordered in only 17.1% of the cases (Maguire et al., 1993:525); and while in the Brooklyn criminal court the use of restitution orders increased tenfold in the 1980s (Davis et al., 1992:748), Weitekamp (1991:429) has produced some evidence indicating that the use of restitution may have been more extensive, at least in certain jurisdictions, *before* the rise of the victim movement and its accompanying legislative reforms.

A related problem is that of enforcement of the orders. Some researchers have found that restitution orders are not always implemented. Hudson and Galaway (1980:191) reported two studies, one conducted in Minnesota and one in England, which found that "one fourth of those ordered to pay restitution failed to satisfy the order"; moreover "the larger the amount ordered, the less frequently it was completed." Another study by Brown (1983), based upon a sample of 448 offenders ordered to pay restitution, found that only 44% had made all the payments due according to the schedule determined in the restitution order, while 18% had made no payment whatsoever (Brown, 1983:148–49). A more recent study by the American Bar Association (Smith et al., 1989) is not much more encouraging. At the four sites selected for in-depth study, the rates of "full payment" varied from 61% in New York City, where the program operated under the auspices of the Victim Services Agency, to 25% in Montgomery, Alabama. Conversely, the rates for "paid none" varied from 22% (Salt Lake City) to 62% (Montgomery), while the average amount collected varied from 67% to 10% (86).

The above study included an in-depth analysis of the factors associated with successful compliance, such as the avoidance of excessively high awards, community ties on the part of the offender, and continuing efforts on the part of the program administrators to secure compliance (Smith et al., 1989: chap. 5). Some practical implications may be drawn, as also from the study by Lurigio and Davis (1990) indicating the positive results following the use of "threatening" letters sent to liable defendants, clarifying their obligations. It does not appear, however, that any simple remedy has emerged from these studies which could radically improve the situation.

One of the traditional weaknesses of the compensation order was that enforcement was generally left to the victim, who was not always even aware that the order had been made (Hudson and Chesney, 1978:137); moreover, probation officers, when charged with this task, did not place a high priority on enforcement of restitution orders (Shapiro, 1990). The Victim and Witness Protection Act of 1982 did not entirely overcome this problem. For while it provided that the order could be enforced either by the state or by the victim, the mode of enforcement was to be "in the same manner as a judgement in civil action" (sec. 3579(h), now 3663 of the U.S. Code). A similar policy was adopted in the Uniform Victims of Crime Act, 1992 (sec. 403), and by NOVA (1989:13). It was partly for this reason that Slavin and Sorin (1984:573), following an exhaustive analysis of the provisions of the act, concluded that restitution "may be an illusion." This pessimistic conclusion seems to be confirmed on the state level by the research of Smith et al. (1989), who concluded that "the victim gets short shrift in the restitution process" (113).

Consideration should be given to granting "equal status" to compensation orders for the benefit of victims and the state's equivalent sanction, the fine. In Britain compensation orders are enforced in a similar way to fines (Newburn, 1988: chap. 7), and compliance rates appear to be higher. In Israel, not only are compensation orders enforceable as fines, but any sum collected is regarded in the first instance as compensation.[26] For cases in which restitution orders are combined with terms of imprisonment, the garnishment of prisoner earnings has been considered both in the United States[27] and elsewhere (Joutsen, 1987:237). Finally, in Britain the possibility has been raised that restitution that the offender has been ordered to pay should, in the first instance, be available from public funds (Newburn, 1988:47; Moxon et al., 1992:31).

In principle, the use of restitution as a sanction is thought to bring some objective gains not only to the victim but also to the offender. It will be recalled that restitution programs were developed with an emphasis on the offender, and it is to the offender that most of the variables used in evaluating these programs relate: "Offender measures far outnumber measures used for victims" (Hudson et al., 1980:49; see also 50–51). Since those words were written, restitution provisions have been expanded, generally as part of explicitly *victim*-oriented legislation; yet even recently Smith et al. (1989) observed: "Restitution has been motivated by offender-oriented concerns for rehabilitation or punishment, and that seems to remain the case today" (113). This particular "offender-gain," namely, rehabilitation, can perhaps be regarded above all as a societal gain, and will be considered below.

However, insofar as restitution is designed to replace other sanctions—and in particular, imprisonment—this may be regarded unequivocally as a gain for the offender, in that it will be less punitive and will involve a lesser degree of intervention with his or her freedom. The evidence available so far, however, suggests that restitution is not widely used as a replacement for imprisonment, but rather for minor offenders for whom a custodial sentence would not in any case be anticipated:

> One of the most consistently reported findings in the body of evaluation work is that restitution projects and programs established for the purpose of diverting offenders from custodial confinement generally do not fulfil this mission. The study done on Tasmania by Barnes; the most recent evaluation of the British Community Service Program; the Georgia Restitution Shelter Study; and studies done on the project in Alberta, British Columbia, all present information showing that only a relatively small proportion of persons admitted would have been incarcerated in the absence of the program. This apparent inability of diversion projects to substantially divert from more severe penalties and to actually increase the degree of social control exercised over offenders raises disturbing questions. What about the case of an offender who, in the absence of the program, would not have been imprisoned, fails to complete the restitution order, and is subsequently imprisoned? Instead of helping to reduce rates of imprisonment as intended, the project is likely to increase the number under custodial confinement. (Hudson and Galaway, 1980:190)

We have here an illustration of the well-documented phenomenon of "net-widening" (see, e.g., Austin and Krisberg, 1981). Weitekamp (1991), who confirms this pattern, suggests, on the basis of the experience of a Philadelphia court, that restitution could in fact be used, with favorable results, for hard-core offenders. However, in view of the prevailing views of criminal justice personnel to be considered below, it seems that only a radical revision of the system, such as the abolition of imprisonment as a sanction for many crimes of at least middle-range seriousness, could ensure that the desired effect would be achieved.

Another problem for the offender is the possibility of discrimination against the poor defendant. Reference is made in the literature to the possible "servitude" of the poor offender enslaved for life in order to pay off his debt. Indeed, it has been suggested (Klein, 1978) that it was just such inhumanity that accompanied the early restitutionary phase of legal history and that led to the evolution of the modern retributive system. The issue is not so clear-cut, however. If, for example, offenders were all obliged to pay restitution out of prison earnings, there would be no discrimination in favor of the wealthy. This, however, would only be applicable where a prison sentence was justified in the first place.

Finally, consideration must be given to the objective gains and losses to society as a whole which would accompany the more extensive adoption of restitution. Theoretically, there would be a large financial saving. The costs of administering a restitution program are considerably less than those of running a prison; it has been argued that even a residential restitution program is cheaper than incarceration (Lawrence, 1990). Further, restitution by the offender theoretically obviates the state's need to compensate the victim.

However, these benefits are, for the present at least, more apparent than real. As noted, there is no evidence that the use of restitution has resulted in a reduction in incarceration rates; and while some progress *may* have been made regarding its function in compensating the victim, it is by no means clear that this burden would otherwise have been borne by the state. It should be noted in this context that while restitution orders tend to be used more for property offenses (Newburn, 1988:18)—although there is considerable variation by location (Smith et al., 1989:78)—*state* compensation, to be considered in chapter 9, is generally reserved for offenses of violence; thus public funds, as distinct from insurance, are not generally saved by the use of restitution orders as currently practiced.

The other potential form of societal benefit might be a reduction in recidivism, if restitution orders were either to have an absolutely rehabilitative effect, or to be more beneficial—or less harmful—in this respect than the sanction they replaced.[28] Since the publication of the research review conducted by Martinson et al. (1975), criminologists do not generally anticipate that any one type of intervention will achieve uniformly better results in terms of recidivism than other types. A particular form of intervention may be beneficial for some offenders and detrimental to others (Van Voorhis, 1983).

Data regarding the effectiveness of restitution in this respect are limited. As noted above, the overwhelming majority of "evaluations" of such programs have lacked the necessary design and controls for any conclusions to be drawn. Moreover, such evidence as is available is somewhat inconclusive. In a quasi-experimental study in a western metropolitan area in the United States in which probationers who were obligated to pay restitution were compared with a second group who were not so obligated, it was concluded that no rehabilitative consequence could be observed (Miller, 1981). An evaluation conducted at the Minnesota Restitution Center found that more controls than experimentals were returned to prison for new offenses, but more experimentals than controls were returned for parole violations. The explanation of closer parole supervision of the experimentals was offered for this phenomenon. The overall outcome was that more experimentals than controls were returned to prison (Hudson and Chesney, 1978:139–41). More recently, Lawrence (1990:215) reported a similar finding with regard to a residential restitution program in Texas. Failure rates were higher than for parolees, again attributed to more intensive supervision of the former. Weitekamp (1991:436, 443), too, found that failure rates in his Philadelphia sample were high owing to the difficulties in meeting restitution requirements but that recidivism rates were lower than for prisoners; however, the samples do not appear to have been matched (433). As noted, however, inconclusive findings may conceal an interaction between type of offender and type of intervention: Van Voorhis (1985) has indicated that the ability to comply with a restitution order depends primarily upon the offender's ability to assume responsibility and thus upon his or her moral development. This implies that the use of restitution orders for offenders selected according to the appropriate criteria would be more successful. However, this would involve the need to employ diagnostic techniques in sentencing and would raise issues of equality of justice.

More systematically positive findings have been recorded for juvenile restitution programs. Both Schneider (1986) and Rowley (1990) found that juvenile restitution diversion programs were generally more successful than control groups adjudicated by traditional processes. Ervin and Schneider (1990) explored various hypotheses that might explain the relative success of a number of restitution programs as compared with control dispositions; their tentative conclusion was that the success of restitution was attributable to the opportunity it provided to participants to be *rewarded* by successful completion of the program. The apparent success of certain juvenile restitution programs can hardly be generalized with regard to the indiscriminate use of restitution as a sanction for adults, in particular in view of the rather limited findings of the adult-related evaluations. At the same time, insofar as the use of restitution may be desirable on the basis of other criteria, equivalence of outcome in this respect may be a consideration in its favor.

Perceived Justice Needs

Equity theory would seem to suggest that if the offender is ordered to pay full restitution to the victim, this should be perceived by the observers of the inequity—including the parties themselves—as the most favored mechanism for the restoration of equity. Is information available on the attitudes of the parties to restitution proceedings, so that the validity of the equity hypothesis in this respect can be tested?

Victim Attitudes. In the course of their National Assessment of Adult Restitution Programs, Hudson and his colleagues conducted an attitude survey among samples involved in 19 of the projects in the National Assessment. The results were reported by Hudson et al. (1980, chap. 9) and Novack et al. (1980). Questionnaires were mailed to offenders and victims, of whom 194 offenders and 152 victims responded, representing response rates of 30%–34% for offenders and 43%–46% for victims.[29] Conclusions based on the overall results of this study must be treated with caution, not only because of the modest response rate, but also because a number of projects were involved, having varied characteristics, and decisions regarding restitution were taken at different stages. Further, some projects involved community service rather than monetary restitution, while others involved both in combination—although some of the detailed presentations of findings differentiated between these types of programs.

In cases where monetary restitution was awarded, only 44% of the victims expressed satisfaction with the "overall treatment of the offender," while 56% were dissatisfied (Hudson et al., 1980:184). However, where restitution was combined with community service, 84% of victims were satisfied. The location of the decision in the criminal process seems also to have been a critical factor here.[30] Where the decision was part of a pretrial diversion scheme, 82% of the victims expressed satisfaction, as compared with only 43% where the restitution order was made as a condition of probation or at the incarceration stage—generally linked to a parole release (185). This may be partly explained by the contacts between victims and program staff which took place in the diversion programs (184). Other possible explanations might be an increase in expectations as the case proceeded through the system, or more effective implementation of the payments in the diversion programs.[31]

Similarly, while 60% of the victims (overall) thought that the offender's monetary restitution requirements were fair, this increased to 79% where restitution was determined at the pretrial phase, as opposed to 47% and 56% at the probation and incarceration phases, respectively (185). In almost all the other cases the victim thought that the requirements were too lenient.

Somewhat more favorable among the earlier surveys was that conducted by Davis et al. (1980), who reported that 67% of a New York sample, based on two courts, considered the amount to be fair; also favorable was that conducted by Kigin and Novack (1980), who reported that 78% of the victims in a Minnesota juvenile restitution program said the type of restitution was fair, 74% said that the amount was fair, and 76% were satisfied with the restitution outcome.

However, the more recent and comprehensive study conducted by Smith et al. (1989) indicates the persistence of problems affecting victim satisfaction. In particular, there appears to be a gap between the perceptions of the program administrators in this respect and the victims themselves. For while 73% of the program directors interviewed (N = 75) believed that victims were either "very satisfied" or "somewhat satisfied" (35), among the (approx. 200) victims interviewed at the four selected sites (see above), only 56% were satisfied with the amount awarded and 33% with the amount received, while 78% "believed that the restitution program or the court could have done more to collect their restitution" (105–7).

The researchers developed a satisfaction scale based on three measures of satisfaction—with the size of the award, the speed of payment, and the amount of money received. Using a regression model, which explained more than half the variance, they found that the main predictors of victim satisfaction were *(a)* the proportion of the award paid by the offender, *(b)* whether the award covered their losses, and *(c)* whether they were kept informed during the process. The last factor appears to be the most meaningful in the context of the model, being independent of the input measures. These findings, and especially the last, may be linked to those of a small survey conducted a few years ago in a British magistrates' court. There, too, the findings were mixed, and victims were dissatisfied especially when the amounts were not paid in full or did not cover the losses, or where payment was delayed. As to the last category, however, "What they were most upset about was the lack of communication or information from the court about the delay" (Newburn, 1988:38). These studies may illustrate the phenomenon noted by Shapiro (1990:76) whereby restitution—and other provisions designed to assist victims—may raise victim expectations while exacerbating their sense of powerlessness within the criminal justice system.

However, in order to assess the potential for the expansion of restitutionary sanctions, it is important to separate questions relating to victims' satisfaction with these sanctions, based on their own experiences, from the question of their acceptance of restitution as a sanction in principle, and in particular their perceptions of the relative merit of restitution as compared with other sanctions.

Respondents in the National Assessment survey were asked to identify the fairest sanctions for the crime victimization in which they were

involved (Hudson et al., 1980:186–87); 61% of the victims selected monetary restitution, 10% selected other forms of restitution, 6% selected probation, and 23% selected incarceration. While this seems to indicate that
restitution is indeed the sanction most favored by victims, two qualifications must be added: the sanction selected here may have been influenced
by the experience of the victim in the instance cited; and a supplementary
question, in which victims were invited to select a combination of sanctions, revealed that only 12% of victims favored restitution as the sole
sanction,[32] others favoring its combination with some other sanction.

Similarly, few victims interviewed in the British Crime Survey selected
compensation (i.e., restitution) as the sole sanction—only 7% of burglary
victims, and 4% of car theft victims, while "a further third of victims of
both burglary and car theft wanted compensation and some other punishment" (Hough and Moxon, 1985:168–69). These results are consistent
with the finding noted above regarding the higher level of satisfaction
where restitution was combined with community service. A German survey, however, based on a large sample of the citizens of Hamburg, found
that restitution was acceptable by most respondents, for most offenses, as
the *sole* sanction, and that having had a victimization experience was not
significant in this respect (Boers and Sessar, 1991); but for 18 of the 38
offenses included in the study, a majority favored some combination of
punishment and restitution (130–31).[33]

Offender Attitudes. Hudson et al. (1980:184–85) reported that approximately one-half of the offenders indicated that they were either "very
satisfied" (16%) or "satisfied" (33%) with their overall treatment in the
restitution programs surveyed. Again, the satisfaction rate was considerably higher (35% + 52% = 87%) where restitution was combined with
community service;[34] and for offenders, too, the satisfaction was higher
when restitution was part of a pretrial diversion program (82% satisfied)
than when it was coupled with probation or incarceration or parole—in
both those cases only 43% of offenders were satisfied.

The percentage of offenders in the above survey who thought the monetary payments were fair was almost identical for offenders as for victims:
79% when restitution took place at the pretrial stage, 48% when it was a
condition of probation, and 60% when coupled with incarceration or parole. However, unlike the victims, the offenders in almost all the other
cases, that is, those who did not view the restitution requirements as fair,
were of the opinion that they were too harsh, rather than too lenient (see
Hudson et al., 1980:185; Novack et al., 1980:67). Moreover, in contrast to
the above findings, in the New York City program (Davis et al., 1980:45), in

which restitution was ordered at the sentencing stage, "only 38% felt that the amount was fair," approximately half the satisfaction rate of the victims. Regrettably, the more recent evaluations of restitution referred to above appear to have neglected to study the offenders' perceptions.

Equity theory would hypothesize maximal offender satisfaction where the offender was ordered to pay restitution to the victim, conditional on the restitution being accurately assessed and the offender being able to pay. It should be recalled that both equity theory and restitution programs were developed with a focus on the offender (or "harmdoer") rather than on the victim. In this respect the findings reported above are not altogether encouraging, and it seems that either equity theory itself or its applicability in the present context and in the present circumstances has less than complete validity. In particular, it has been suggested by Harland (1981) that an offender may not be satisfied that an inequity is being remedied by the payment of restitution if his or her income is appreciably lower than that of the offender, as the available data suggest might often be the case:[35] "Notwithstanding the crime loss, the victim is still the more prosperous. Restitution could then become, in the offender's eyes, simply another source of unjust enrichment of the wealthy at the expense of the poor" (20). Moreover, the ability to take responsibility for the harm inflicted and its repair may require a level of maturity or moral development that may not be possessed by all offenders (Heide, 1983; Van Voorhis, 1983).

These doubts are apparently confirmed by the question asked by Hudson et al. (1980:187) regarding offenders' preferred sanctions. Only 29% selected monetary restitution, while 37% preferred community service, and 28% selected probation. One can only speculate as to the preference for community service over monetary restitution. Perhaps, in spite of the apparently greater intrusion of privacy involved, the requirements of community service were seen to be less onerous. Of more interest in the context of the present study is the possibility that the offender feels that his or her debt is owed to the community at large rather than to the individual victim. A clear-cut option to test this hypothesis would have been to provide the option of a fine payable to the state as an alternative to restitution payable to the victim.

Societal Attitudes. Data on the acceptability of restitution as a sanction on the part of the general community are relatively sparse. Two studies conducted by Gandy and colleagues related to this topic. The first (Gandy, 1978) focused on groups holding some special relationship to criminal or welfare proceedings: police, social work students, members of a women's community service organization, and probation and parole officers.[36]

Gandy compared support for what Eglash (1958) conceived as "creative restitution" with that for other penal objectives. Creative restitution was defined as "a process in which an offender, under supervision, is helped to find some way to make amends to those he has hurt by his offense" (119). Three forms of creative restitution were specified: monetary payments to the victim, service to the victim, and service to the general community. On an 11-point Likert scale ranging from "strongly agree" to "strongly disagree," creative restitution scored overall much higher than all other objectives of the penal system.[37] This was true for each category of respondent (122). Creative restitution was found to be positively correlated with a rehabilitation philosophy, and negatively correlated with other sanctioning objectives (124). It was, however, viewed as inappropriate for offenses against the person. Among the three forms of restitution specified, "monetary payments and service to the general community were considered to have somewhat greater potential than service to the victim." The author concluded that "the vast majority of the respondents were interested in the concept of restitution" (124). The second study related to a wider population in a southern city in the United States; this, too, found that "there was considerable support for the use of restitution sanctions" (Gandy and Galaway, 1980:98). Evidence for this deriving from more recent studies is reviewed in Galaway (1988).

Two studies conducted outside the United States have the advantage of having elicited views from wider samples and having offered respondents more clear-cut alternatives.[38] Galaway (1984, 1988) conducted a survey in New Zealand to determine how far the public would agree to the use of restitution as an alternative to imprisonment, in the wake of a recommendation of the New Zealand Penal Policy Review Committee. A questionnaire with descriptions of six property offenses was distributed to two population samples, inviting them to select the appropriate sanction.[39] The choice of sanction varied between the two samples. While both samples were offered the choice between imprisonment and a list of noncustodial sanctions—fine, probation, community service, and nonresidential periodic detention—the experimental version included the option of restitution while the control version did not. The analysis showed that fewer respondents in the experimental group selected imprisonment, and the differences were statistically significant for five out of the six offenses. The author concluded that restitution was an acceptable alternative to imprisonment for a substantial number of cases. The strength of this study is in the size and randomness of the samples,[40] and its application to the use of restitution orders in general, rather than to a particular type of program, as reported in much of the United States–based research.

The study conducted in Hamburg by Sessar and his colleagues has already been referred to. This survey was based on a random sample of 4,400 residents (the response rate was 44%), with additional subsamples representing various special population groups. This survey adopted a more victim-focused orientation. Respondents were asked to designate the most important need or interest of the victim after the commission of a theft or an assault. The distribution of the responses ($N = 572$) for the six options offered was as follows: restitution 33.7%, community service with payment being passed on to the victim 27.8%, an apology 15.9%, punishment 13.5%, victim assistance 10.0%, and personal service by the offenders 0.3% (Sessar, 1984:16). When theft victimization was differentiated from assault victimization, nearly one-half of the respondents (48.3%) selected restitution as the first priority for theft victims, and nearly one in five (19.2%) for assault victims. Further, when asked to choose, following conviction for theft, between payment of a fine to the state, payment of restitution to the victim, or one-half to each, 75% of respondents favored full restitution, 9.5% the fine, and 15.4% the compromise (19).

In the main part of the study, respondents were presented with 38 offense descriptions and invited to choose between five different approaches to social control. These were (1) private agreement on restitution or reconciliation outside the criminal justice system, (2) restitution or reconciliation achieved through an official mediator, (3) restitution as part of the criminal justice system, (4) punishment that would be waived or reduced if restitution were paid, and (5) punishment that would not be waived even if restitution were paid to the victim (Boers and Sessar, 1991:130).

> The results are extraordinary. Restitution instead of punishment is accepted for most of the hypothetical criminal incidents, not merely in addition to the criminal process but also instead of it, that is, within the framework of private settlement and reconciliation. Taken over 38 cases, the frequency of the responses to the five proposals is as follows: 23.9% for private agreement; 18.5% for private agreement with the help of a mediator; 17.4% for private agreement initiated by the criminal justice system; 18.8% for punishment to be mitigated or abolished in the event of successful restitution; 21.4% for punishment without consideration of restitution. (ibid.)

A detailed analysis reveals that for 18 of the 38 offenses a majority favored responses (4) or (5), that is, punishment, at least in the first instance (ibid., fig. 7.1). Nevertheless, the findings do indicate a high level of acceptance of restitution as a penal sanction. Thus, while restitution is not generally advocated as a universal remedy, it seems to be perceived by some as preferable to punishment even for the most serious offenses.[41] However, when research on the lines of the Hamburg study was replicated in Hungary (Arnold and Korinek, 1991), support for restitution was found to be less general. It is hoped that such research will also be replicated in common-law countries.

In view of some of the difficulties encountered by victims in the course of restitution proceedings, it may also be pertinent to study the attitudes of criminal justice personnel and related professions. The favorable attitudes on the part of various correctional personnel and related groups described in Gandy's study have already been noted. Gandy (1978) also reported a study in which attitudes to restitution were elicited from 250 members of the legal community in South Carolina.[42] Over 80% expressed support for the concept of restitution, indicating that "the legal community would help implement and support a program of creative restitution if it existed in South Carolina" (126). Monetary restitution was the favored form, while "creative restitution" generally was substantially more highly preferred than state compensation. Similarly, Hudson and Galaway (1978), who reviewed the restitution and community-service-related research, concluded that "the nonevaluative studies dealing with attitudes toward the use of financial restitution or community service show quite clearly that such sanctions are endorsed by criminal justice officials and lay citizens" (191).

However, Klein (1978) has pointed to the complications facing the criminal court in administering restitution orders. Indeed, as noted above, it has been suggested that difficulties of this nature resulted in the demise of restitution in the state of Iowa (Molumby, 1984). Similarly, an INSLAW study (Hernon and Forst, 1983:81 n. 11) found that because of the practical problems involved in the composition and enforcement of restitution orders, criminal justice personnel preferred the use of state compensation schemes—the reverse of the findings reported by Gandy. Canadian prosecutors were also found to consider restitution inappropriate for the criminal courts (Stuebing, 1984). A more recent study by Bae in Minnesota also reported that criminal justice officials "were much less likely to accept restitution as an alternative punishment to imprisonment for property offenders than was the public" (Roberts, 1992:152). The Hamburg study found that prosecutors were consistently and substantially less in favor of the restitution-based responses than the public, while the judges fell between the two (Boers and Sessar, 1991: table 7.1).

One explanation for these apparently conflicting findings may lie in the dichotomy between the two concepts of restitution alluded to above. Gandy and Hudson and his colleagues were considering restitution programs created primarily in order to rehabilitate the offender and involving a contractual agreement between the parties, with supervision by designated members of the program. These programs—whether for pretrial diversion, whether linked to probation orders, or whether postincarceration—function in effect as alternatives to regular criminal justice processes and tend to reduce the load on these processes. Such programs are in principle likely to appeal to criminal justice personnel, particularly if they concentrate upon the relatively minor cases, thus posing no threat to the prevailing system. On the other hand, the widespread use of restitution orders by the criminal courts, whether instead of or in addition to conventional sanctions, imposes a heavy burden of investigation and administration, particularly if the courts assume the burden of enforcement of these orders. Such a development is consequently less welcome and, as indicated earlier, may be encountering some implicit resistance. However, this is not to argue against a development that appears to have considerable support among the community at large and—in spite of reservations—among the parties to the offense.

Fundamental Principles of Justice

Most of the arguments raised in favor of restitution have a utilitarian character. Indeed, this must potentially be the optimal sanction in terms of Benthamite utilitarianism, maximizing the benefit of the victim, while minimizing the suffering of the offender and the cost to the state. It has also been found by Braithwaite and Pettit (1990:127) to be consistent with their "republican theory" of justice, in that it complies with their criteria of reprobation and reintegration and, it would seem, with their criterion of parsimony.

It would also be difficult to fault this objective on the grounds of inconsistency with "fundamental principles of justice" as elaborated in the previous chapter. Can there be anything offensive in the two basic components of the restitutive idea: that the offender will make some kind of practical repayment for the wrong committed, proportional to the extent of the damage inflicted; and that this payment should redound to the benefit of the victim of the harm inflicted? Objections to such an approach would seem to have to rely on somewhat extreme attitudes. Thus, a Marxist or radical might place full responsibility for the harm inflicted on the socioeconomic structure and exempt the offender from any personal obligation to make amends.[43] From a very different standpoint, a Kantian might argue that punishment must be perceived to be such, and must therefore possess purely negative and repressive attributes (cf. also von Hirsch, 1976:121).

However, retributivists have expressed other reservations with regard to the restitutive approach. Ashworth (1986:95–96) points to the emphasis in restitution on the loss inflicted and the exclusion of the mental element, that is, culpability, in determining its quantum. Moreover, retributivists have tended to deemphasize victim-related aspects of retribution and hence to be somewhat ambivalent regarding the role of restitution. Thus Sadurski (1985), in "Giving Desert Its Due" says, "Punishment is distinct and independent of restitution; restitution is a matter of the losses of the victim, punishment is a matter of illegitimate benefits of the offender. Hence, punishment restores the equilibrium of benefits and burdens by imposing an additional burden upon the criminal without necessarily bringing any benefits to the victim" (243). Inclusion of the word "necessarily," however, appears to leave the door slightly ajar for the possibility of restitution in Sadurski's concept of retribution. Thus Duff (1986) observes that "it is true that the idea of compensation is quite distinct from that of punishment . . . but the same activity—making a financial payment, or providing material assistance—could serve both purposes" (284). Conversely, a recent analysis of Zedner (1994) found reparation—of which, as noted, restitution is a form—to be not inconsistent with retribution, although she concludes that reparative remedies could be more effectively developed if pursued as an independent goal.

Barnett (1977, 1980), in his "restitutionary" theory of justice, differentiated this from retribution. On the other hand, McAnany (1978) has compared the restitutive and retributive approaches and noted the similarity in conceptual underpinnings: emphasis on justice, blame and responsibility, a backward-looking orientation, and the equalization of offenders.[44] Moreover, there is nothing sacred in the measure of retribution being calculated in terms of the duration of prison sentences. In an earlier day, retribution was achieved by a variety of other sanctions, both corporal and financial (Schafer, 1970). Retributive or "punitive" restitution might operate on principles distinct from those on which civil compensation was based (Shapland, 1984; Thorvaldson, 1990).

For example, the level of payment might in certain circumstances be *higher* than the loss inflicted.[45] Alternatively, an additional punitive component might be payable to the victim to compensate for the indignity and the injustice (cf. Thorvaldson, 1990:27), or to the state to cover costs and in consideration of the infringement of norms designed to protect the public as a whole, or in consideration of the "symbolic gravity" of the crime (Shapland, 1984:146). In some instances, however, a penal orientation may have a limiting effect, as illustrated by the reluctance of the English courts to order the paying of compensation from family assets unrelated to the offense (Ashworth, 1992b:251), or by the 1990 decision of the U.S. Supreme Court in *Hughey* (109 L Ed 2d 408) to limit restitution to the offense of conviction. Paradoxically, the application of an offender orientation may result in greater flexibility; restitution ordered under the Federal Probation Act is unrestricted by the offense of conviction, for in the interests of rehabilitation it is considered desirable that the offender should take full responsibility for his or her *acts* (Hillenbrand, 1990:199).

A more serious problem of justice and desert is raised by the differential ability of offenders to pay restitution. This may result in variations in the level of the burden inflicted being determined not by the seriousness of the offense but by the personal circumstances of the offender. In extreme cases, such circumstances might lead to the offender's incarceration in default of payment. The same problem, of course, applies today to the fine as a penal sanction. In the case of the fine, however, the problem can be resolved by such techniques as the Swedish "day-fine" system (see Newton, 1976; Morris and Tonry, 1990:143ff.). This is problematical in the context of restitution (*pace* Wright, 1982:253), since in the case of restitution it is insufficient that justice be done to the offender in terms of equal *suffering*. Justice must also be done to the victims in terms of equal *benefits*, that is, proportional to the loss inflicted.

Some type of solution to this problem could be developed if restitution were indeed to have an unequivocally punitive character. If the restitution payments could be made only from earnings from prison labor or community service, the punishment would then be standardized for offenders of differing income groups. This would be inappropriate, however, for minor offenses where no prison term were contemplated or in a system where restitution were to substitute for imprisonment, as is widely advocated by reformers. At the same time, even if restitution in certain cases proved to place a heavier burden on less affluent offenders, this would be at worst no different from the current situation regarding the civil liability of wrongdoers. However, it should not result in their incarceration: this principle has been recognized by the U.S. Supreme Court (see below).

The preceding discussion has focused on the reservations, or potential reservations, of retributivists in relation to the restitutive orientation. Mention should be made here of two recent approaches, both very favorable to a restitutive or, more broadly, "restorative" orientation, based upon a mixture of retributivism and utilitarianism.[46] Cavadino and Dignan (1993) propose an individualized restorative sanction, which would provide for alternative sanctions and would lay emphasis on negotiated settlements, but would operate within the limits set by a proportionate or desert sentencing. Wright (1982: chap. 10) advocates that an assessment of the appropriate sanction level be determined—possibly in terms of a numerical score—for each offender, according to his or her due, but the offender's individual "package," whereby he or she "makes amends" to the victim and society, would vary with the circumstances. These proposals provide enterprising and humane solutions, combining individualized justice with desert. They are not likely, of course, to satisfy "pure" desert advocates. Moreover, in addition to the problems of their implementation, they do not necessarily ensure full restitution to the victims—this being merely one of a number of alternative sanctions in both approaches.

Finally, objection in principle to a restitutionary policy may be voiced by *social defense* advocates. This philosophy, it will be recalled, places emphasis on the protection of society, preferably by means of rehabilitating the offender. While restitution is seen by many of its supporters to have rehabilitative potential, it is often advocated as a substitute for institutional treatment. Societal control would thus be reduced, and "career criminals" and "dangerous" offenders might be free to repeat their acts. A policy of "punitive restitution" would operate to some degree as a constraint on such offenders, for example, if they were obliged to pay restitution through prison earnings; but the restraint would be limited according to the dictates of the desert principle—that is, commensurate with the harm inflicted rather than the harm predicted. Ironically, however, restitution as practiced today is, as noted earlier, more closely linked to the rehabilitationist ethos than to the victim movement (see, e.g., Hillenbrand, 1990) and may even reflect social defense philosophy more than it reflects the "restitutionary" theory of punishment.

Constitutional Issues

Restitution proposals and practices raise a number of constitutional issues (Edelhertz et al., 1975; Note, 1984; Upson, 1987). For instance, restitution programs have been criticized for lack of due process. Where damages are sought in a civil action, the defendant is entitled to a jury trial, the right to cross-examine witnesses, and the protection of the rules of evidence. These rights are absent where restitution is awarded at the sentencing stage of a criminal trial (Slavin and Sorin, 1984:534). However, in the 1984 *Welden* and *Satterfield* cases (see Upson, 1987), the appeal court upheld the validity of the federal restitution provisions, emphasizing that a criminal, not a civil, sanction was involved. On the other hand, as noted above, in the case of *Hughey* in 1990 the U.S. Supreme Court held that the restitution order was limited to the offense of conviction. This ruling might in fact redound against the interests of defendants, since the prosecution— and certainly the victim—would have an interest in all charges being pursued, in order not to prejudice restitution rights.

Also, where the indigence of the defendant results in imprisonment for defaulting on restitution payments, there is the possibility of attack under the equal protection and due process provisions of the Fifth and Fourteenth Amendments, or the cruel and unusual punishment provision under the Eighth Amendment (Upson, 1987). In *Bearden v. Georgia* (1983 461 U.S. 660), the court indeed held it to be "fundamentally unfair" to punish a person for lack of financial resources.

Another constitutional argument that might be invoked in this context would be the possibility that a relationship of servitude be created. This could presumably be defended under the exception to the Thirteenth Amendment, which exempts the prohibition on slavery in the case of "punishment for crime whereof the party shall have been duly convicted." But if incarceration or some other form of service were extended beyond a period that could reasonably be justified as punishment, this provision might be invoked.

However, the right of the victim to restitution is now guaranteed under the constitutions of certain states (Hillenbrand, 1990:194). Further, the procedural right of the victim to be heard, as enshrined in certain state constitutions (NOVA, 1989:9) and proposed on the federal level (President's Task Force, 1982), might also indirectly enhance the victim's substantive rights. Finally, as noted earlier, the victim's right to restitution has been recognized on the international plane under the UN Declaration of Basic Principles of Justice for Victims of Crime and Abuse of Power. Insofar as the victim's "right to redress" (Gittler, 1984:139) is implemented, careful attention should be given to the question whether such implementation can be consistent with the exhortation of the Federal Guidelines for the Treatment of Crime Victims and Witnesses to the effect that restitution should not be awarded in derogation of defendants' rights.

Subject to this proviso, there would seem to be a strong argument for the proposition that, in cases where the state is successful in investigating a crime and chooses to take action against the offender, the victim should be granted a recognized substantive interest in this proceeding. Recognition of such a right would seem to be generally consistent with coping needs, perceived justice needs, and fundamental principles of justice.

8

Reforming Trial Procedures: Victim Participation

Philosophers of law have observed that procedural reform frequently gives rise to the more significant changes in substantive law.[1] In the present context, too, it is possible that enhancing the victim's role might affect the outcome of the criminal justice process, for example, by giving rise to an increase in the use of restitution. Procedural reforms, however, may be a worthy objective in their own right. As was shown in chapter 5, one of the main complaints on the part of victims was the lack of information and the fact that they were not encouraged to feel a part of the proceedings. Particular reference may be made in the present context to Umbreit's small study of burglary victims (1989), where he found that "nearly all victims expressed the need to be involved in the criminal justice system," whether actively or passively (110), and to the large German survey reported by Kilchling (1991:53–54), in which a majority of both victims and nonvictims believed that the victim's role at both the investigation and trial stages should go beyond that of mere witness. Thus, irrespective of any effect on case outcomes, there may be some value in reforming procedures for their own sake, in the anticipation that this may lead to greater satisfaction on the part of the parties concerned.

In chapters 1 and 2, the criminal justice process was reviewed on a stage-by-stage basis (arrest, bail, plea bargain, trial, sentence, parole), and it would be possible to adopt a similar perspective for the purpose of considering procedural reform. However, a more useful approach seems to be to classify the topics to be discussed by considering the victim's role in the criminal justice system as envisaged by the reform in question. The critical variable in this respect seems to be the degree of *victim participation* in the criminal process.

Victim participation could be treated as a continuous variable,[2] but it can more conveniently be dealt with as a categorical one. Three main types of victim participation will be analyzed here: (1) indirect participation, (2) vicarious participation, and (3) personal participation. A fourth category, (4) personal confrontation, will be considered only briefly in the present chapter, since it pertains less to the reform of the present criminal justice system than to the creation of alternatives (see below, chap. 11). These terms will be clarified in the course of the analysis.

Since the discussion here will focus on issues of principle relating to the victim's role in the criminal process, emphasis will be placed on the more formal stages of the proceedings, that is, those of a judicial or quasi-judicial nature, rather than on the more administrative aspects, such as the apprehension and investigation functions of the police. These are also areas in which some of the more interesting experimentation and evaluation have been conducted in recent years. However, much of the following analysis will also have implications for the less visible decision-making processes.

Indirect Participation

Indirect participation refers to techniques whereby criminal justice personnel are supplied with information concerning the victim which they may be expected to take into account in the decision-making process. Thus, the victim's "participation" is mediated by the traditional role players in the criminal justice system. The victim has access in some way to one of these role players but does not participate directly in the decision-making process. Another, purely passive, form of participation takes place when criminal justice agencies inform the victim of the developments taking place in the wake of their complaint.

Chapter 2 examined how far the various agencies took into account victim-related information under traditional practices, differentiating in particular between the attention that was paid, on the one hand, to objective information regarding the victim's circumstances and the extent of the victimization and, on the other hand, to the views expressed by the victim regarding his or her expectations from the system. The police in deciding whether to make an arrest or pursue an investigation, the prosecution in deciding whether to prosecute, the court in making a bail determination and when imposing sentence might all be expected to take into account at least the objective information relating to the victim. However, opportunities for conveying both factual and attitudinal information have in the past been somewhat limited. One of the main purposes of the reforms has been to increase the flow of such information, as well as to require that information be conveyed by criminal justice personnel to victims regarding the decision-making processes.

The President's Task Force (1982) emphasized the importance of conveying attitudinal information relating to the victim and placed the main responsibility for this task upon the prosecutor: "Prosecutors have an obligation to bring to the attention of the court the view of victims of violent crimes on bail decisions, continuancies, plea bargains, dismissals, sentencing and restitution. They should establish procedures to make sure that such victims are given the opportunity to make their views of these matters known" (65). The duty placed upon the police in this respect was more limited and focused mainly on the need to investigate reports of intimidation (57).

The prosecutor's duty under the President's Task Force recommendation was limited to bringing information to the attention of the court. The American Bar Association's guidelines, on the other hand, obligate the prosecutors themselves to take note of the victim's views before the prosecutors' own decision making: "Victims or their representatives in serious cases should have the opportunity to consult with the prosecutor prior to dismissal of the case or filing of a proposed plea negotiation with the court, and should be advised of this opportunity as soon as feasible" (ABA, 1983:16). The federal Victim and Witness Protection Act of 1982 directed the attorney general to issue guidelines for the treatment of victims by prosecutors in cases of serious crime which would mandate consulting with the victim or family about their views before decisions relating to the dismissal of the case, pretrial release, plea negotiations, and pretrial diversion. The guidelines that were issued mandated consultation at five additional stages, namely, the decision not to seek an indictment, continuancies, proceeding against the accused as a juvenile, restitution, and sentencing in general (cf. Goldstein, 1984:230–32). Moreover, the federal Victims' Rights and Restitution Act of 1990 bestows upon the victim "the right to confer with attorney for the Government in the case" (sec. 502(b)(5)). The right to confer with the prosecution has now been incorporated in the constitutions of Michigan and certain other states (NOVA, 1989:9; National Victim Center, 1994).

Some legislation makes specific reference to the prosecution decision making to which the victim's views may be thought to be relevant. Thus the Victims' Rights and Restitution Act, while nonspecific as to the right granted at the federal level, is more explicit in relation to the goals the states are encouraged to adopt: "Victims of crime should have a statutorily designated advisory role in decisions involving prosecutorial discretion, such as the decision to plea-bargain" (sec. 506(3); see also the ABA *Guidelines for the Fair Treatment of Crime Victims and Witnesses*, 1983:16).

By 1988, 24 states had granted victims some status with regard to plea-bargaining decisions (NOVA, 1989:12). Such provisions take a variety of forms (Polito, 1990:251–53), including physical presence at the hearing, to be considered below under "direct participation." These procedural rights are not accompanied by substantive rights to control the outcome of prosecutors' decisions. However, the possibilities of challenging prosecution inaction through judicial review have been explored by Green (1988), while Wainstein (1988) has argued in favor of court-ordered prosecution at the instigation of a victim threatened with further victimization. Finally, Kennard (1989) would grant the victim a veto over any proposed plea bargain.

An even more popular institution developed in recent years for the purpose of increasing victim input into the criminal justice system has been the *victim-impact statement*. This is a statement that is made available to the sentencing judge and incorporates information regarding the nature of the harm inflicted upon the victim. This would include, under section 3 of the federal Victim and Witness Protection Act of 1982, "information concerning any harm, including financial, social, psychological and physical harm, done to or loss suffered by any victim of the offense."[3] The emphasis here is on the first of the two elements referred to earlier, that is, objective information; presentation of the victim's views may be included, but for this purpose an alternative vehicle may be available, namely, a Victim Statement of Opinion (NOVA, 1989:10).

The main techniques for implementing such provisions, as reviewed in a national survey conducted by McCleod (n.d.), are (1) incorporation in the probation officer's presentence report, (2) submission of a separate report by a probation officer or prosecutor, and (3) an oral presentation by the victim at the sentencing hearing, which for the purposes of the present analysis may be better classified as "personal participation." Two further categories mentioned by McCleod relate to parole proceedings. Hillen-brand and Smith (1989:45), in their survey of the impact of victims' rights legislation, differentiated further between statements submitted by victims, which were in narrative style, and the use of standard forms; clearly the former has a greater potential for psychological impact. By 1988 legislation providing for victim-impact statements had been enacted in nearly all states (NOVA, 1989:10), as well as in Canada (Giliberti, 1991) and Australia (Sumner, 1987, 1994; Ashworth, 1993).

Finally, in addition to the above provisions for increasing victim input into criminal justice decision making, most guidelines and legislation place heavy emphasis on "passive" participation, namely, the duty to inform the victim of developments in the case (see, e.g., ABA, 1983; NOVA, 1989:13–15; Victims' Rights and Restitution Act of 1990, sec. 502(b)(3) and (7); Uniform Victims of Crime Act, 1992).

What are the implications of the reforms outlined above in terms of the parameters of justice as designated by the present study? Law journal articles have appeared in support of (Eikenberry, 1987; Polito, 1990) or in opposition to (Henderson, 1985; Dolliver, 1987) the recognition of enhanced procedural rights for victims, while a plethora of comments have appeared in the wake of the leading Supreme Court cases *Booth v. Maryland* (1987) and *Payne v. Tennessee* (1991), referred to in the preceding chapter. Empirical evaluations have been sparser, but particular note should be taken of studies of the implementation (McCleod, n.d.) and the effects (Davis et al., 1990; Davis and Smith, 1994a, 1994b; Erez et al., 1994) of victim-impact statements, and of the work of Erez and her colleagues, incorporating both empirical evaluations (Erez and Tontodonato, 1990, 1992) and integrated overviews of the issues (Erez, 1990, 1991, 1994). The evidence emerging from these and other sources will now be considered.

Coping Needs

The practical needs of the victim are not affected by procedural changes as such. However, the availability of victim-related information to the decision-making bodies may influence the substantive outcome of the case. Indeed, one of the declared objectives of victim-impact statements has been to increase the probability that the court will make a restitution order.[4] This does indeed seem a possible outcome. The courts in the past have been reluctant to order restitution partly because of the need to enter into precise assessments of the losses incurred. The additional information on this matter which might be available in a victim-impact statement, or as a result of victim-prosecutor contacts, might provide an incentive to make such an order. Further, a cumulative or interactive effect might be produced by the combination of these procedures and the provisions discussed in the preceding chapter mandating the consideration of restitution orders on the part of the courts. Moreover, the exemption granted to the federal courts under the Victim and Witness Protection Act of 1982 from the obligation to make a restitution order where such an order is liable unduly to "complicate or prolong the sentencing process" may be more difficult to invoke where a comprehensive assessment of the amount of damage inflicted upon the victim is filed with the court. Finally, the complaint that the amount designated in the restitution order generally falls short of the victim's true losses—and in particular of the victim's assessment of those losses—should also be partly met by the new procedures.

Empirical evidence regarding the effect of victim-impact statements on restitution is mixed. The nationwide survey conducted by Hillenbrand and Smith (1989:123, 125) found that financial information in the victim-impact statements was thought by criminal justice officials to be "most useful" and to affect both the likelihood and the amount of a restitution award. However, their New York-based survey of victims found that 54% were of the opinion that these statements had no effect on restitution awards.

One precondition for the effectiveness of these procedures is that they will be implemented. In Hillenbrand and Smith's survey only 27% of the victims reported having made victim-impact statements, and similarly low rates are described in most of the surveys reported;[5] but compare the studies by Erez and Tontodonato (1990) and Walsh (1992), both conducted in Ohio, where participation rates were considerably higher. The generally low rates may be explained in part by the fact that prosecutors may perceive these statements as superfluous, inappropriate, burdensome to the victim, or adding to their burden of discovery to the defense (Henley et al., 1994). Kennard (1989) claims that "since over ninety per cent of all criminal cases end in a negotiated plea, most victims never have the opportunity to present a statement" (430). While it may not be true that there is no opportunity for a statement in these cases (cf. Erez and Tontodonato, 1990), the effect of the statements may be substantially reduced (Villmoare and Neto, 1987:62).

Offenders are not directly involved in these procedures. However, the fact that the disposition of the case is modified as a result of such procedural reforms will of course be of direct concern to the offender. An additional input of victim-related information may result in the refusal of bail or its being set at a higher level, a custodial sentence instead of probation, a longer term of imprisonment than would otherwise have been imposed, a restitution order, or the refusal of parole or clemency.

Even if these outcomes were to cause additional hardship to the offender, the availability of more—and more accurate—information to the decision-making agencies could hardly be faulted on this ground, unless the offender were denied the opportunity to dispute the accuracy of such information. Thus, if a victim-impact statement were filed with the court as a confidential document, whether as part of the probation officer's presentence report or otherwise, this may result in denying the defendant an opportunity to contest the accuracy of the information, since constitutionally protected adversary rights have not been held to apply to such documents.[6] Moreover, although the majority opinion of the Supreme Court in *Booth v. Maryland* found that the admission of evidence of this nature could have an inflammatory effect on the jury, this decision was effectively overturned in *Payne v. Tennessee* (see chap. 7 above; Sebba, 1994).

It is not altogether clear, however, that additional victim input will necessarily redound to the offender's disadvantage (cf. Rubel, 1986:236, 249; Erez, 1990:25). A study by Erez and Tontodonato (1990) of 500 felony cases processed in Ohio found that, employing multivariate analysis, the submission of a victim-impact statement influenced the likelihood of incarceration ($p < 10\%$), but not the length of the prison term. However, the apparently positive effect on type of disposition should be treated with caution, both because of the significance level and because there may have been differences not controlled for between cases in which victim-impact statements were submitted and those in which they were not. Thus Davis et al. (1990), in a New York City study using an experimental design, found "no evidence that using victim-impact statements puts defendants in jeopardy and/or results in harsher sentences" (6; see also Davis and Smith, 1994b). Similarly, a detailed analysis of the effects of the introduction of the victim-impact statement in South Australia also found no indication that sentences became more severe (Erez et al., 1994). (In a study of *parole* proceedings, however, victim testimony was found to be the main predictor of parole refusal; see Bernat et al., 1994.)

Four types of explanation are offered in the course of these studies as to why the statements appear to have had almost no effect on sentencing severity: (1) Implementation problems—for example, statements are often not taken or may be perfunctory. (2) Criminal justice officials have this type of information even without the statements. (3) "Officials have established ways of making decisions which do not call for explicit information about the impact of crime on victims" (Davis and Smith, 1994a: 467–68). That is to say, the "established ways" are resistant to innovations. (4) The effects of victim-impact statements may indeed exist but they are concealed. As a result of victim-impact statements, sentence severity more closely reflects the harm inflicted by the offense, that is, they increase proportionately in sentencing (ibid., 457, referring also to Erez and Tontodonato, 1990). However, since in cases where the harm is serious this will result in enhanced severity, but in cases where harm is moderate the result will be *less* severity, the overall results appear to indicate an absence of any effect. This hypothesis, however, has yet to be substantiated.

The study by Walsh (1992:301) focusing on the effects of victims' sentence recommendations in sexual assault cases in Ohio found that this variable did not significantly affect the sentence outcome. Moreover, offenders for whom the victims recommended imprisonment (the majority) were almost as likely to receive probation as imprisonment (299). However, when nonrecommendation cases were included in the analysis, it emerged that these cases attracted harsher sentences than those in which recommendations were submitted. Walsh concluded that it was "likely that some of the sex offenders granted probation would have been imprisoned were it not for the probation recommendations they received from their victims" (304). Moreover, while Walsh's sexual assault victims tended to be punitive in their orientation, Henderson and Gitchoff (1981) reported that communication with victims by a private agency preparing presentence reports on behalf of the defense resulted in an almost total abandonment of retributive views. Other studies indicating the nonpunitiveness of victims were alluded to in chapter 5.

Finally, some additional cost to the public must inevitably be incurred by providing that extra information be collected by the criminal justice agencies. A system whereby the probation officer has to obtain information from the victim in a sense doubles his or her clientele: data must be gathered from or about the victim as well as the offender. Even where victim-impact statements are filed directly by the victim, some administrative costs will be involved. However, the costs of such measures have generally been estimated to be slight (ABA, 1981:47). Naturally, if the reformed procedures result in changes in the ultimate disposition, this could produce indirect costs such as those of detention or incarceration.

Again, however, this surely cannot be an argument against increasing the information made available to criminal justice agencies.

Perceived Justice Needs

The analysis of available data on victims' attitudes to the justice system presented in chapter 5 indicated that procedural reform might, in the victim's perception, be more important than substantive legal change. Victims seemed more distressed by prevailing procedures, including the lack of information conveyed to them by the criminal justice agencies and their lack of recognition as a party to the process, than by the dispositional outcomes. The indicators were that a greater involvement with the system may lead to a reduction in the level of discontent.

Some evidence of victim satisfaction in the "post-reform" era is beginning to emerge. A recent Dutch study (Wemmers, 1995:338) attributed generally positive results to the passive involvement of victims in the system, insofar as this took place. Among the 359 victims interviewed by Hillenbrand and Smith (1989) in the United States, nearly two-thirds said they were kept informed of the police investigation (129). "Good information about case status" was the second most satisfying factor about the way the case was handled, but "lack of information *re* case progress" was the second *least* satisfying factor (146–47)! When asked specifically about various categories of information, "very satisfied" responses varied from 21% to 34%, while "not satisfied" varied from 33% to 43% (142).

When, on the other hand, the victims were asked to relate to the opportunity they had had to "have a say" in the charging and sentencing decisions, dissatisfaction levels were higher still—49% and 54%, respectively (ibid.). Further, Erez and Tontodonato in Ohio (1992), Davis and Smith in New York (1994b), and Erez et al. in South Australia (1994) all found that the submission of victim-impact statements (VIS) did not increase the level of victims' satisfaction. The first of these studies found that "those who had completed a VIS with the expectation that it would have an impact but who felt that it had no true effect on the outcome were more likely to believe the sentence was too lenient" (403). The failure to meet expectations was also observed in the South Australian study and in a Canadian evaluation (Giliberti, 1991:713). It should be noted that in the New York City study (Davis and Smith, 1994b) a special effort was made to ensure that the victim understood the purpose of the victim-impact statement, but that this failed to enhance their feelings of involvement. (Indeed, many remained unaware that such a statement had been prepared.)

While further research is clearly required on all aspects of victim participation, two are particularly worthy of attention. The first is the mode of
submission of the statement. Is more satisfaction obtained when the statement is prepared by the victim in person rather than through an intermediary, and is the "narrative" style (McCleod, n.d.) more satisfying than the
completion of a standard form? Second, is it more satisfying to liaise with
probation officers or with prosecutors for this purpose? On the one hand,
probation officers may be more skilled in dealing with human problems (cf.
Villmoare and Neto, 1987:63). On the other hand, probation officers are
traditionally identified with the offender's interests, while the prosecutor,
it would seem, can more easily be perceived as being on "the victim's
side."

Such research may help to identify sources of satisfaction or dissatisfaction related to victim participation in criminal justice procedures. Meanwhile, various hypotheses on this topic emerge from the above data. As
noted, one reason for the apparently low level of victim satisfaction, as
indicated by Erez and Tontodonato, may be unwarrantedly high expectations. Another explanation may be problems relating to implementation,
some of which were alluded to earlier. Thus Polito (1990) supports a constitutional amendment on the subject of victims' procedural rights in order to
ensure that adequate remedies will be available for their enforcement.

A third possibility is that, in spite of the impression deriving from the
research surveyed in chapter 5, the enhancement of the victim's procedural
status may not be sufficient, unless the outcome, too, is perceived as
satisfactory. In the survey conducted by Hillenbrand and Smith (1989),
while many procedural matters were alluded to by victim respondents,
"treatment of defendant" was nevertheless the main factor specified in the
determination of both the victim's satisfaction and his or her dissatisfaction (146–47; cf. Giliberti, 1991:703; Erez et al., 1994:58).

Finally, satisfaction may be limited owing to the fact that the victim's
participation in the procedures considered in this section has generally
been *indirect*. The emphasis in these procedures is on activities conducted
by criminal justice personnel rather than by the victim. Considerations of
bureaucratic convenience may further derogate from victim involvement.
For example, it has been suggested that the probation officer might obtain
the information necessary for the victim-impact statement from the police
file (ABA, 1981:47). This would relieve the probation officer of the need to
locate the victim, and thus abort any possible result in terms of enhancing
the latter's personal involvement. A reform of this type in Australia,
whereby courts rely on police summaries for victim information, has given

rise to the phenomenon of "victims of efficiency" (Douglas et al., 1994). There may rather be a need for procedures involving a more active role for the victim, and these will be considered below.

The *defendant*'s perception of the procedural reforms considered here are somewhat speculative. The positive effects attributed by some writers to outcomes—notably restitution—that emphasize the offender's responsibility toward the victim have already been noted. The same should apply to procedures in which this responsibility is emphasized. However, insofar as the victim-related material is considered in confidential presentence documents, this could encourage resentment toward the victim rather than contribute to an enhanced sense of responsibility.

A delicate topic to which little thought or attention seems to have been devoted—at least in the academic literature—is the effect of the dual role of the probation officer. As noted above, the probation officer, whose presentence report has hitherto focused upon the offender, has generally been perceived as being sympathetic to the offender's interests; for the probation officer's institutional role has been to draw attention to the individual offender's needs and circumstances. This role of the probation officer at the presentence stage may have been important, too, as the background to his or her additional role in some cases: the supervision of those offenders who were subsequently placed on probation. To confer on the probation officer the novel task of providing the court with information regarding the nature of the harm inflicted upon the victim—and sometimes also the latter's views on the disposition—is surely to revolutionize this role. This change might radically alter the offender's perspective of the balance of power in the sentencing court, as well as of the nature of probation as a correctional outcome.

The issue of *public* perceptions seems not to be a major issue in the present context. The public is not generally a witness to the criminal justice proceedings. It may become acquainted with the outcome of the case, generally on a sporadic basis, through the media and personal contacts; but it is less concerned with procedures. However, the issue of whether the public believes that criminal justice personnel should be equipped with more information regarding victim harm and victim attitudes is a researchable one. It may be surmised that the public would be sympathetic to procedural changes directed to that objective, except for sections of the public identifying with offenders rather than with victims.

It is not clear that the professional public, however, is entirely sympathetic to such reforms (cf. Goldstein, 1984:242ff.). It is true that some of the documents cited above have been produced by professional representative bodies of judges and lawyers, and that justice-related and legally qualified personnel undoubtedly have had a dominant input in creating the legislation so far enacted. However, a study conducted by INSLAW (Hernon and Forst, 1983) found that only 56% of the judges interviewed favored victim-impact statements. On the other hand, they were favored by 71% of the prosecutors and 66% of the police and were viewed as effective by most of the criminal justice officials whose responses were recorded by Hillenbrand and Smith (1989).

Fundamental Principles of Justice

By most criteria the availability of more information related to victim harm, measured objectively, is calculated to improve the level of justice meted out by the courts. This applies particularly if sentencing policy is related to desert, but it may also be compatible with other sentencing objectives. However, if the sentence, or the decision to charge, to refuse bail, to deny parole, and so on, were to be based upon the suffering and deprivations of the individual victim and his or her family—and evidence of this type was held in the recent Supreme Court case of *Payne v. Tennessee* to be admissible in sentencing—this might be problematic even in the context of desert theory. As noted in chapter 7, von Hirsch's concept of just desert, following that of most traditional retributivists, is based upon harm and culpability, and the latter implies that the offender should only be punished for harms that were foreseen, or at least foreseeable. This would not necessarily include the full range of victim suffering (cf. Sebba, 1994).

Some support for this harm-oriented approach is found in Murphy (1988) and in Talbert (1988), who designates it "social retribution"—as compared with "moral retribution," which lays emphasis on the personal responsibility of the perpetrator. Moreover, a degree of support may also be derived from public perceptions, which, as noted earlier, attribute seriousness even to unforeseen harm. However, it seems doubtful whether such a sentencing policy can be justified in terms of classical retributivism. Nor is it necessarily consistent with social defense, since the infliction of greater harm, and in particular unintended harm, in an individual case, is not necessarily an indication of future dangerousness. It is equally doubtful whether this type of victim contribution to sentencing can further other sentencing aims, such as rehabilitation, as suggested by Talbert (1988).

Moreover, the Court in *Payne* has gone further, and declared that the *attributes*—that is, moral character—of the victim may also be taken into account, thereby recalling the concept of "individualization of the victim" envisaged by Wolfgang (1982) and aggravating the aforementioned problem of justification in the context of sentencing policy. Further, the question of the admissibility of the victim's opinion of the offender and of the appropriate sentence, which may be conveyed either through a victim-impact statement or a "victim statement of opinion," whether written or oral, was left open. These issues raise, in increasing order of magnitude, the questions of fairness, due process, and equality in sentencing.

It may be observed in this context that the UN Declaration of Basic Principles of Justice for Victims of Crime and Abuse of Power specifies the following: "6. The responsiveness of judicial and administrative processes to the needs of victims should be facilitated by: . . . *(b)* Allowing the views and concerns of victims to be presented and considered at appropriate stages of the proceedings where their personal interests are affected, without prejudice to the accused and consistent with the relevant national criminal justice system." It is questionable whether victim views and concerns can be presented at the sentencing stage, either directly or indirectly, "without prejudice to the accused." The Supreme Court cases considered in the present and the preceding chapters, in which "victim concerns" were voiced before the jury and the defendants were sentenced to death, would not seem to conform to this formula. The phraseology of the Florida and Kansas constitutional amendments, purporting to balance enhanced victim involvement in the process by a proviso that would negate interference with the rights of the accused, may also be problematic. These issues arise even more acutely in the context of *direct* victim participation, which will be considered below.

Vicarious Participation: Victim Advocacy

The preceding section dealt with the degree to which various criminal justice agencies or personnel succeed in taking account of victims' needs and desires. Under the present heading a more radical alternative will be considered, that specially appointed persons be charged with promoting these needs and desires. This in theory would mean that the victim's own representative would assume a role in the criminal justice system on his or her behalf,[7] a vicarious mode of participation by the victim.[8] Such representatives are sometimes referred to as "victim advocates." However, care must be taken to distinguish victim advocacy in this sense from the broader usage sometimes adopted, which includes almost any activity conducted to improve the welfare of victims (cf. Elias, 1986: chap. 7).

Even in the narrower sense, the term "victim advocacy" has not yet developed a very specific connotation, which in turn reflects the relative infancy of the concept. Certain dichotomies may be usefully invoked to elucidate the different possibilities. The victim advocate *(a)* may or may not be an advocate in the sense of a legally qualified attorney; *(b)* may or may not possess legally recognized status in the criminal justice system; *(c)* may be concerned with a particular stage of the process, such as the sentencing decision, or may be invested with a more generalized role; *(d)* may be concerned exclusively with the victim's interests as they are affected by the criminal proceedings, or may have wider concerns on the victim's behalf. As to the last point, the present analysis will focus on victim advocacy in the course of the criminal process, rather than broaden the discussion to other aspects of victim assistance which will be considered in chapter 10.

As a result of recent reforms, traditional criminal justice personnel, such as prosecutors and probation officers, may have responsibility for the presentation of the victim's views before the court; but this does not render them "victim advocates." However, these agencies may appoint special persons to fulfill victim-related functions. Thus McCleod (n.d.:23–24) notes that many prosecutors' offices have victim-service units, which play an active role in assisting victims to submit victim-impact statements. In this context she employs the term "victim advocates." The federal Victims' Rights and Restitution Act also requires criminal justice agencies to designate officials who will be responsible for "identifying the victims of crime and performing . . . services" (sec. 503(b)), but the emphasis here is on the provision of information to victims rather than on active promotion of their interests.[9] However, the constitutional amendment adopted by the state of Washington specifies that where "the victim is deceased, incompetent, a minor, or otherwise unavailable, the prosecuting attorney may identify a representative to appear to exercise the victim's rights" (Eikenberry, 1989:31).

Since the concept of victim advocacy in the above sense is still in its infancy, few data are available to evaluate the potential contribution of this institution to the criminal justice system. Dubow and Becker (1976) described two "grassroots" attempts by communities in the Chicago area to pursue victims' interests in the criminal justice system. In one case, the citizens themselves (the Early Ardmore Group) monitored the measures taken in the courts against a neighborhood gang that was causing considerable anxiety on the part of local residents. In the other case (the Hyde Park Project), lawyers were appointed for a similar purpose, and the program involved "reaching out" to victims to enable them to have their interests protected.

Davis, Tichane, and Connick (1980) issued a detailed account of the first year's experience of the Victim Involvement Project in the Brooklyn Criminal Court. This was a project in which paralegal workers, with previous experience in a victim/witness-assistance scheme, were attached to the court in order to represent the interests of victims. It was hypothesized that such a scheme would be successful in promoting victim interests for the following reasons: *(a)* the staff were paraprofessionals and thus "understood the concerns of court officials"; *(b)* they were permanently located in the courtroom and would thus develop a rapport with these officials, particularly prosecutors; and *(c)* they would be in the possession of information on the victim which would be useful to prosecutors and would thus have something "to offer in exchange" for their own petitions on the victim's behalf (20–21).

Another project of relevance to the present topic is the Victim Impact Demonstration Project administered at the Brooklyn Supreme Court and evaluated by the Victim Services Agency (Fisher, 1984). One special characteristic of this project was the fact that the task of preparation of the victim-impact statements was neither imposed upon existing criminal justice personnel nor left to the victim but was requested from specially appointed professional counselors. The other special characteristic was that the statement was prepared close to the initiation of the complaint rather than before the sentencing decision. It was hypothesized that this would encourage the establishment of a closer link between the victim and the prosecutor, providing information that might affect prosecutorial decision making as well as judicial dispositions.

The most obvious form of victim advocacy, however, seems to have been almost totally neglected in the empirical literature and barely mentioned in the Anglo-American legal literature (but cf. Fleming, 1978; Hillenbrand, 1989). This is the possibility that the victim will be represented by an attorney during the course of the criminal process. The literature bewailing the "disappearance" of the victim as a party to the penal process has generally overlooked the provisions retained in a number of states for the participation in this process by the victim's attorney, whether for the purpose of conducting a private prosecution or in order to assist the public prosecutor (see Note, 1955; McDonald, 1976a; Goldstein, 1982; Gittler, 1984; Davis, 1989).

While the concept of the private prosecutor has wider implications, both for the criminal process as a whole and for the victim's role in that process, and will consequently be discussed in chapter 12, more pertinent in the present context is the second alternative, the appointment of an attorney who has not assumed the prosecution role. Such an attorney has no direct control over the course of the proceedings; his or her sole function is that of victim advocate, to ensure that the victim's interests are made known and taken into account by those invested with decision-making powers. This role is recognized under German law in the person of the *Nebenklage*, the "auxiliary" or "subsidiary" prosecutor. This term refers to the victim but in practice generally means the victim's attorney; indeed, legal aid may be available for this purpose (Bohlander, 1992:413–14). This institution has been comprehensively evaluated (Schulz, 1982), and its scope has recently been extended by legislation (Kaiser, 1991).

In spite of the historical and comparative materials on this institution on the one hand, and its intrinsic interest on the other, scant consideration has been devoted to this concept in the recent victim-oriented proposals. The main compendia of reform descriptions and proposals (e.g., NAAG/ABA, 1986; NOVA, 1989) seem to ignore this possibility. However, the American Bar Association legislative review (ABA, 1981) devoted a chapter—albeit very short—to the topic "Counsel for the Victim." The legislative proposals reviewed there limited the idea of appointing counsel to cases in which the victim's reputation, whether moral or legal, was likely to come into question during the course of the proceedings; thus the objective of these proposals seems to be the *protection* of the victim rather than the pursuance of the victim's rights and remedies. Nevertheless, the procedural implications of such a narrow role can be generalized; and indeed the discussion of the merits of such a proposal in the ABA publication suggests the possibility of a wider application of the concept of victim's counsel (44).

The same concept seems to be hinted at, although not explicitly advocated, by the "Findings and Purposes" section of the federal Victim and Witness Protection Act of 1982, which in sec. 2(a)(5) states: "While the defendant is provided with counsel who can explain both the criminal justice process and the rights of the defendant, the victim or witness has no counterpart." A lack of balance and the existence of an injustice are indicated here, the apposite remedy for which may seem obvious, although, in retrospect, it does not appear to have been in the minds of the policy makers.[10]

Nevertheless, there is one area in which victim advocacy by private attorneys does appear to have developed within the framework of the recent reforms. In many jurisdictions, victims today have the right of "allocution," that is, to present their views in person at the sentencing hearing. This institution will be discussed under the heading of "direct participation." In most of these jurisdictions, if the victim does not wish to exercise this right in person, another person may appear on his or her behalf. "Survey research has shown that attorneys, followed by family members, are the most frequently authorized persons to speak for victims" (McCleod, n.d.:25). This development is surely worthy of further investigation and evaluation. Finally, a more modest right to the *presence* in court of "an advocate or other support person of the victim's choice" has been provided by the recent constitutional amendment in Illinois (see art. 1, sec. 8.1 of the constitution). In spite of the limited scope of this provision, its constitutional status is worthy of note.

There follows a discussion of the merits and demerits of the victim advocacy proposals according to the criteria adopted in this study, insofar as this is possible in the light of the limited material available.

Coping Needs

The potential for victim advocacy to contribute to the victim's coping needs depends upon the advocate's ability to influence the decision-making processes of the criminal justice system. However, the advocate's role may also require that he or she advise the victim about remedies that are not an integral part of these processes, such as the filing of applications to state compensation schemes and the instigation of civil suits against the defendant or third parties.

Relatively little information is available on the contribution of the advocacy role (as defined above) as distinct from the more diffuse "victim-assistance" role (which will be discussed in chap. 10). Evaluations of some of the modest schemes referred to above point to marginal but not unequivocal achievements. With regard to the Chicago experiments described by Dubow and Becker, no evaluative research is referred to. However, the authors mention limitations on the ability of the citizens in the Early Ardmore Group and the lawyer in the Hyde Park Project to pursue their desires in the courtroom, owing to lack of legal standing. Generally, the Hyde Park lawyer seems to have actively pressured criminal justice personnel, so that some results might have been anticipated. At the same time it appears that since he was appointed by a community organization—the South East Chicago Commission—he felt he had a community responsibility that might not always accord with the interests of individual victims.

The Victim Involvement Project in the Brooklyn Criminal Court was accompanied by a comprehensive attempt at evaluation. Since evaluation was undertaken of a variety of outcome variables, both objective and subjective, a number of samples were studied, thereby somewhat complicating the research design (Davis, Tichane, and Connick, 1980: chap. 2). One of the limitations on the advocate's role here was, again, a lack of legal standing before the court and the need to communicate through the prosecutor (20–21). Thus, the Victim Involvement Project "faced the same obstacles that victims themselves faced in trying to be heard" (18). However, the program staff were also only moderately successful in securing the attendance of the victim in court, which they regarded as important for the pursuance of their claims (21). Nevertheless, they were apparently instrumental in alleviating the problems associated with court appearance, such as obtaining court excusals (ibid., chap. 3). Finally, some outcome differences were found by the researchers, apparently as a result of the activities of the Victim Involvement Project staff. Thus, the use of restitution orders by the court, although disappointingly small, was significantly greater for the experimental sample than for the controls (ibid., 50, table 4.1a).

In the other New York City project referred to here, in which counselors prepared victim-impact statements for use by prosecutors and judges, a complication arose with the design when it emerged that the prosecutors did not in fact refer all of the experimental sample to counselors so that statements could be prepared (Fisher, 1984:7). Consequently, in the analysis the experimental group was divided into two according to whether such statements had indeed been filed. The preliminary analysis revealed a potential for coping benefits among the experimental group who met with the counselors to file victim-impact statements, in that 53% of this group reported having been informed of special services for victims, as compared with only 19%–20% of the other groups (ibid., 8–9, table 3). However, the size of the first group was rather small ($N = 39$). Moreover, it emerged that no greater use was made of this information in terms of referral to these services on the part of the victims.

The potential advantage of a legally qualified attorney as compared with the personnel involved in the above-mentioned experiments lies both in his or her forensic and advocacy skills and in the greater probability that permission would be granted to address the court as occasion arises. No systematic data are available on the functioning of the victim's attorney in the U.S. jurisdictions where this practice is followed.[11] However, McDonald (1976a), on the basis of informal investigations, concluded that these advocates—where they were not actually prosecuting—had two types of roles: a "kibbitzing" role, whereby they attempted to provoke the decision-making authorities into rulings that would satisfy their clients;

and a reconnoitering role, whereby they assessed the evidence in order to determine whether it would justify the initiation of a civil suit against the defendant for the recovery of damages. Naturally, this role is calculated to improve the victim's material position. However, it is doubtful whether there are many cases in which a victim could afford legal representation at both a criminal and a civil trial, and in which the defendant would have sufficient means to render such litigation profitable.

Somewhat more systematic information is available regarding the German *Nebenklage* or auxiliary prosecutor. Data for 1979 showed a varied use of this institution in different types of courts, amounting to between 3.7% and 10.2% of the cases (Schulz, 1982, appendix A). Moreover, its use may have increased following the adoption of liberalizing amendments to the law in 1986 (cf. Kaiser 1991); it seems that Kaiser's 1989 survey found that auxiliary prosecutors participated in approximately 23% of the cases (fig. 16) and that it had become popular with attorneys as a result of the relatively high fees (561). A recent Polish survey (Bienkowska and Erez, 1991) found that 36% of victims participated as private prosecutors, but since many of these acted on their own behalf, without legal representation, the findings of this study will be dealt with under the next heading.

Anticipated benefits to the victim from this system include, apart from exercising a degree of control over the proceedings and thus presumably enhancing satisfaction (see below), a higher probability of a restitution award from the criminal court and of obtaining information that will be of assistance in a subsequent civil suit (Schulz, 1982:172ff.). The introduction of any form of victim advocacy must also take cost into account. The type of programs described in the American literature require the appointment of full-time professional personnel, while the appointment of privately appointed attorneys would presumably involve even greater cost, whether to the state or to the individual victim. In the latter case, victim advocacy would become a remedy exclusively for the socioeconomic elite.[12]

As for the *defendant*'s coping needs, in addition to the factors referred to under the previous heading, representation of the victim in criminal proceedings by an attorney increases the importance of competent representation on behalf of the defense and is likely to hamper negotiations regarding verdict and disposition (cf. Davis, Tichane, and Connick, 1980: 68). In the context of the *Nebenklage* proceeding, it has been claimed that this is burdensome for the defendant, both in the way it affects the chances of rehabilitation and in the risk of a higher burden of costs (Roxin, 1983:393). In terms of the practical effects on the *public*, the main consideration is likely to be the cost involved—mainly of the legal representation, if this were at the public expense, but also of possibly more protracted proceedings.

Perceived Justice Needs

The evaluation of the Victim Involvement Project (VIP) found that "two-thirds of those who reported talking to a VIP representative believed that the VIP person was looking out for their interests" (Davis, Tichane, and Connick, 1980:60). This indicates that the staff was relatively, but not completely, successful in conveying the image of victim advocates. Moreover, it appears that these victims were no more likely than others to feel that they had any influence on the disposition of the case, probably because they "did not perceive VIP as a central element in the decision-making process" (61). Satisfaction was associated with type of disposition, and they appeared to regard contacts with prosecutors as more important for this purpose (63–64). On the other hand, victims who received an explanation of the proceedings in court were more likely to state that they had been well treated, and such explanations were more frequent where there had been contact with the VIP staff, although in some cases the explanation had been forthcoming from the prosecutor.

In the Victim Impact experiment it was anticipated that "giving victims a chance to express the effect of the crime on them would increase their feeling of involvement in the court process and their sense of fair treatment by court officials" (Fisher, 1984:11). There was no evidence, however, that this was achieved. There were only small differences between the experimental group for whom the impact statements were prepared and the control sample in respect to how well they felt they were treated, how well they were informed, and whether they had had a chance to express their views "to people in court" (ibid., table 5).[13]

This last finding is particularly disappointing: only 33% of those who met with program staff felt that they had "very much" had a chance to express their views to "people in court," although a further 43% responded "to some extent." This may be because the staff were not fully identified by the victims as court personnel. It may also be that where no victim-impact statements were prepared by the staff, prosecutors took more care to elicit the victims' views; for among the "experimental group" who had *not* been involved in victim-impact statements (see above), a higher proportion selected the "very much" response.

However, there is some evidence that indicates that representation by an attorney is perceived as being beneficial to victims in the course of criminal proceedings. Villmoare and Neto (1987:50), in a study of victim participation in sentencing, which will be considered below, found that legal representation increased the victim's involvement in the process. Kaiser (1991, fig. 9) found that 64.3% of his victim sample designated attorneys as the preferred choice to be responsible for their interests.

Fundamental Principles of Justice

Programs in which victims are assisted in conveying information about their views to criminal justice personnel cannot be considered a threat to prevailing concepts of justice, except insofar as the use of such information infringes upon due process or other concepts as discussed under the preceding subheading. On the other hand, the introduction of an advocate with an active role in the judicial proceedings on the *Nebenklage* model raises a question of the balance of forces in adversary proceedings and the possible creation of a third party to these proceedings. This will be further considered below.

Conclusions

The existence of a victim advocate, whose exclusive function is to further victim interests, seems in principle to have a greater potential than placing reliance upon existing criminal justice personnel, who inevitably have other tasks or different priorities. The limited research available suggests that such a role might produce at least some practical and perceptual benefits.

There are two interrelated dangers in such a system, however. The first danger is that, if a new agency is involved, it may become institutionalized as part of the criminal justice system with resulting negative repercussions. A new program "may become used by the system in pursuit of the system's objectives, and in the process the program may lose sight of its original goals" (Dill, cited in Davis, Tichane, and Connick, 1980:85). Indications of this phenomenon emerged both in the Chicago Hyde Park experiment (Dubow and Becker, 1976), where the advocate felt he was representing the interests of victims as a class, and in the Victim Involvement Project, where for the staff to maintain their role in court entailed their "acceptance of existing norms concerning appropriate dispositions in different types of cases and traditional methods of operation" (Davis,

Tichane, and Connick, 1980:77). The authors recalled Eisenstein and Jacob's account of the functioning of the criminal justice system, in which judge, prosecutor, and defense counsel share common goals of maintaining group cohesion and reducing uncertainty (23–24). The victim advocate may also be coopted into this system.[14]

The second danger is that such personnel may in some respects constitute a *barrier* to contact with the criminal justice system rather than a link with that system. The staff of the Victim Involvement Project were not seen as an integral part of the court process (ibid., 81–82). Thus, the "victim's sense of involvement was related to the extent and quality of interaction with judges and prosecutors (whom victims correctly recognized as the big decision-makers) but not with VIP staff" (ibid.). The authors concluded that "direct contact between victims and prosecutors seems necessary for victims to feel part of the process" (ibid.). This apparently was also the feeling of some of the prosecutors interviewed in the study (ibid., 67), in spite of the advantage for them in terms of convenience in dealing with program professionals.

These problems would probably be mitigated if the victim advocate were a qualified attorney, such as under the German *Nebenklage* system, rather than a paraprofessional, and if such an attorney had legal standing before the court to argue on the victim's behalf. The problems would be mitigated even further if the victim were represented by his or her own personal attorney rather than a public official (see Weigend 1986:13–15).

However, apart from the cost involved in such a system, whether to the victim or to the state, and the possible implications of creating a "third party" in the system, it is not clear that such representation would necessarily be preferable to the victim's own personal participation. Thibaut and Walker (1975) conducted experiments indicating that persons involved in a conflict prefer procedures that maximize their power of control. They cite evidence consistent with this theme which shows that persons experienced greater satisfaction in the role of spokesperson as compared with the role of "constituent" or client.[15] This, of course, may be counterbalanced by a lower level of efficacy and articulation on the part of the client who pleads his or her own case. Thus the research does not serve to suggest, in the authors' view, that "in a legal setting a client may wish to exchange roles with his attorney but rather to illustrate again an apparent need on the part of individuals to have as much involvement as possible in decisions affecting their outcomes."[16] The possibility that the victim will personally be an active participant in the criminal justice process is the topic of the next subsection.

Personal Participation

For some supporters of victim rights, the appointment of an agency to represent the victim's interests is insufficient. They insist on granting the victim a personal role in the criminal process. Moreover, such advocates of active victim participation can invoke both the psychological theories referred to in the previous section and research indicating the frustration felt by victims with their limited traditional role in the criminal justice process (e.g., Shapland et al., 1985). In response to such demands, many states now allow victims to present an oral statement at the sentencing hearing or "allocution" (NOVA, 1989:10). As argued in the President's Task Force report: "When the court hears, as it may, from the defendant, his lawyer, his family and friends, his minister, and others, simple fairness dictates that the person who has borne the brunt of the defendant's crime be allowed to speak" (1982:77). Although this argument was put forward in support of allocution, the report went much further in supporting the victim's right to participate in the criminal process. It proposed an addition to the Sixth Amendment of the U.S. Constitution to the effect that "the victim, in every criminal prosecution shall have the right to be present and to be heard at all critical stages of judicial proceedings" (114).

A constitutional amendment in this vein was adopted by Florida in 1988, specifying as follows: "Victims of crime or their lawful representatives, including the next of kin in homicide cases, are entitled to the right to be informed, to be present, and to be heard, when relevant, at all crucial stages of criminal proceedings, to the extent that these rights do not interfere with the constitutional rights of the accused" (NOVA, 1989:9). This provision is wider than the Task Force recommendation in that it applies not just to "judicial proceedings" but to "all crucial stages of criminal proceedings." However, it is narrower in that it has two provisos: *(a)* relevance, and *(b)* noninterference with the rights of the accused (cf. the clause in the UN Declaration cited above).

Other states have also provided for direct victim participation, whether by statute or by constitutional amendment. One objective of these reforms is to guarantee the victim the right to *attend* the trial, from which the victim, as a witness, was traditionally excluded under the "rule of sequestration," a source of considerable frustration among victims (Kelly, 1980:180). Other provisions allowed for a more active contribution, whether at sentencing, as noted above, at plea-bargaining proceedings, or at parole hearings (NOVA, 1989:9–12, 18–19).

One commentator has suggested, in the course of an analysis of the plea-bargaining provisions, that such "rights" may be of dubious value without enforcement provisions (Welling, 1987:340–45), although the courts may be more inclined to intervene in individual cases following the incorporation of such rights in constitutional provisions—as reflected in the recent Arizona parole case referred to below in chapters 10 and 12. As yet there seems to have been relatively little empirical evaluation of most of these provisions. An empirical study of the allocution rights granted under the Victims' Bill of Rights adopted in California in 1982 was conducted by Villmoare and Neto (1987), while some general data are included in the surveys already referred to by McCleod (n.d.) and Hillenbrand and Smith (1989). Further, evidence of the effect of direct victim participation in informal proceedings is available from the studies of mediation and restitution programs to be discussed in chapter 11. Finally, detailed findings are available from some earlier pioneering experimentation with the participation of victims in plea-bargaining negotiations.

The experiments on victim participation in plea-bargaining followed a proposal put forward several years ago by Norval Morris (1974) in recognition of the fact that the character of criminal justice was in effect being determined in secret deals between prosecutors and defense counsel, in the absence of some of the key parties to the criminal proceedings—for offenders, victims, and generally also judges were not included. Moreover, it has been argued that recent sentencing developments have rendered the victim's interest in the plea-bargaining process even more acute, both because sentencing guidelines have reduced the judge's discretion and enhanced the importance of the charging decision, and, more particularly, because the 1990 Supreme Court decision in *Hughey* has limited the measure of restitution which may be ordered to the harm inflicted by the offense of conviction (Starkweather, 1992:861).

One advantage of the experiments conducted to explore Morris's proposal was that the expansion of the negotiation proceedings to include these parties resulted in an increased similarity to the trial itself, at least in terms of dramatis personae. Another advantage was that the experiments were accompanied by comprehensive evaluation programs. The first experiment with the "pretrial settlement conference" was conducted in Dade County, Florida, in 1977 and was evaluated by the University of Chicago (see Kerstetter and Heinz, 1979; Heinz and Kerstetter, 1979; Heinz and Kerstetter, 1980). For the second experiment, this time called a "structured plea negotiation," three sites possessing different characteristics were selected (Wayne County, Michigan; Jefferson County, Kentucky; and Pinellas County, Florida) in order to increase the generalizability of the findings. The evaluation of this experiment was conducted by INSLAW (Buchner et al., 1983). The following discussion of the coping and perceived-justice effects of victim participation will rely heavily upon these research evaluations.

Coping Needs

A precondition for the amelioration of the victim's situation as a result of the introduction of a novel procedure is that the procedure be complied with, at least in substance. In the case of the plea-bargaining experiments, no gains could be anticipated unless the victim's participation in the process—at the very least his or her physical presence—were actually achieved. Thus there was some disappointment in the first experiment, where of the 378 cases included in the experimental group only about one-third actually participated in the conference. In the second experiment the participation rates were lower still, varying between 17% and 26% over the three sites (Buchner et al., 1983:3:17). However, the researchers established that this apparently lower participation rate derived partly from communication failures and partly from uncertainty as to the identity of the victim. They concluded that of those notified some 50% actually attended the conference. Moreover, in this second experiment the main variable associated with the decision to participate was the seriousness of the offense.[17] Thus there seemed to be no ground for the concern that victim participation would fail for extraneous reasons such as fear of the offender or the alienation of minority groups. However, economic factors seemed also to play a part, and difficulty in taking time off work was a frequently cited ground for nonparticipation. Problems of communicating with the victim in order to secure his or her presence at court also seemed likely to prove to be an endemic problem.

In cases where the victim was in attendance, the potential for an effect on the outcome of the case derived either from his or her interventions or from the mere presence at the conference of the victim or the other parties invited as part of the experiment.[18] Both of the researches indicated that the contributions of the victim and the defendant to the proceedings were modest in quantitative terms; they left most of the speaking to the professional personnel. Nevertheless, most victims made some contribution.[19] Moreover, a content analysis in one of the studies suggested a shift in focus of the exchanges in the experimental proceedings, in that relatively more time was devoted to issues of concern to the "lay" parties, such as the facts of the case, than to the legal issues, which were of more concern to the professionals (Kerstetter and Heinz, 1979:49; Buchner et al., 1983:2:34).

As to the outcome of the proceedings, generally speaking this was not radically affected by the experimental situation, whether in terms of the nature of the disposition or its severity. Thus the evaluation of the first project concluded that "the conference process . . . did not result in any major changes in the kinds of decisions that were reached" (Kerstetter and Heinz, 1979:108).[20] There was evidence that in one courtroom less use was made of incarceration (106), while in another there was an increase in restitution orders (104); but the authors took the view that "the trend in the findings that the conference may have resulted in more lenient sentencing is too fragmentary to be conclusive" (108). Similarly, in the second experiment, while "it was feared that victim presence would inhibit prosecutors from negotiating," it was found that "in none of the three sites was victim presence related to the type of agreement reached at the conference" (Buchner et al., 1983:2:15).

There are both methodological and substantive reasons for not regarding "outcome effects" as the determining criteria for the present purpose. Methodologically, since many of the conferences to which the victims were invited were in fact held without the victim, comparison with control groups cannot be considered decisive in measuring the effect of the victim's presence. Moreover, the earlier experiment was further complicated by the fact that although allocation of cases to the experimental "conference" procedure was conducted on a random basis, in a number of these cases no conferences were held for a variety of reasons (Kerstetter and Heinz, 1979:19, 32–33).

Substantively, while it might be expected that the presence of the victim would lead to a greater inclination to consider restitution orders, aggregate case outcomes cannot be considered the main criterion for determining the value to the victim of participation in the proceedings. There are two reasons for this. First, victims' wishes are not monolithic: some may be more punitive than the prosecutor, and some less so. Thus, the expression of victim wishes, even if taken into consideration in the individual decision-making process, will not necessarily be reflected in aggregate distributions of outcome. Second, the main product anticipated is not to be sought so much in the practical results of the case as in the victim's perceptions that they have a role to play in the system. Thus the real test of the success of these experiments is to be found in the attitudinal data to be considered below.

The findings of the victim allocution study conducted by Villmoare and Neto (1987) were at least as negative in terms of the variables considered above, and perhaps more so. The authors estimated that no more than 3% of eligible victims exercised their right to allocution (52). This may be explained partly by lack of information: out of a sample of 171 victims interviewed, 56% were not aware of their right to allocution. Both lack of knowledge and failure to exercise their rights may have been partly attributable to the lack of significance attributed to the right by criminal justice officials, and particularly judges, many of whom reported that the victims' views were already known through the victim-impact statement. On the other hand, the prosecutors surveyed by Hillenbrand and Smith (1989:45) viewed *oral* victim statements as more effective than other types, although judges did not share this perception (69). Many of the victims in the allocution study seem to have shared the judges' view that their appearance would not have much effect on the outcome, while others were deterred by emotional or practical problems (42–43).

As to the *defendant*'s coping effects, it is possible that the participation of additional parties could result in the exercise of coercive pressure at a plea-bargaining negotiation, giving rise to a less favorable outcome. However, it is generally felt that plea bargains as such are likely to result in lighter sentences (see Buchner et al., 1983: chap. 6); while, as noted, the effect of victim participation in the experiments described here did not appear to render sentences harsher (see also Welling, 1987:311). In this respect the findings are generally consistent with those relating to indirect victim participation.

Finally, Buchner et al. found that the program they evaluated had the effect of increasing the judge's involvement in the negotiations and consequently the judge's acceptance of the idea of the "sentence differential" (i.e., the guilty plea as a mitigating factor).

As to costs to society, the conferences did not seem to be unduly burdensome. The mean time spent on each conference was 10 minutes in the first experiment (Kerstetter and Heinz, 1979:62) and 7 to 9 minutes in the second (Buchner et al., 1983:32). The latter study noted that the disposal time was faster for the experimental group, while the former assessed the costs involved as being no different from those of the regular procedures. As to California's system of allocution, "the effect of the workload on the system has been minimal" (Villmoare and Neto, 1987:59).

Moreover, the plea-bargaining experiments were accepted by the judges— enthusiastically by some (Buchner et al., 1983:3:43). The reservations expressed by other legal practitioners, both prosecutors and defense (3:46), may be explained in terms of institutional interests; but fears of disruption of the proceedings or intransigence on the part of victims proved unfounded.

Perceived Justice Needs

The first of the plea-bargaining studies adopted four criteria for determining whether the experimental procedures affected attitudes. The first criterion was whether the victim felt that he or she had *knowledge of the disposition*. It was found that "the victims in the test group were somewhat more likely to feel they knew the disposition than the control victims" (Kerstetter and Heinz, 1979:111), but the difference was not significant. The authors concluded that knowledge of the disposition was a function of whether the victim or the police officer attended the proceedings, but it could not be concluded that the nature of the proceeding was a factor determining the degree of cognitive involvement.

The second criterion was *satisfaction with the disposition*. A combined measure was constructed based upon satisfaction with the process and its perceived fairness. It was found that in all groups victims, defendants, and police were all relatively satisfied with the process. Insofar as there was variance, this was not attributable to the experimental procedure. There was greater variance among the controls than between the controls and the experimentals. Moreover, variation in satisfaction could not even be attributed to attendance at the conference (this applied to defendants also) but rather to individual courtroom differences (115–16).

The third criterion was *satisfaction with the process*. Here again the ratings were generally positive. For the victims, however, there was "some evidence that the conference procedure contributed to the overall positive evaluation of the way the courts processed cases" (117). This seemed to indicate the importance of the experimental procedure. However, not only were there some courtroom variations here but, surprisingly, the difference between victims who attended the conference and those who did not was not significant, although "those who attended were generally more positive than those who did not" (119). The authors commented: "One explanation for this anomaly, assuming more than statistical noise is operating, may be that the increased satisfaction comes not from participation in the conference, but in the consultative process which included notifying victims of the conference opportunity. Thus receiving information about the availability of the conference may be the key to the test effects" (119).

The fourth criterion was *general attitude to the criminal justice system*. Here, neither the experimental procedures nor the decision to attend had a significant effect on either victim or defendant views (120–21).[21]

Similar, although not identical, questions were asked of the victims in the second experiment. In two of the three sites, victims participating in the experiment were more likely to know the outcome of the case than the controls (Buchner et al., 1983:3:29, table 3.12). In the third site almost all knew the outcome irrespective of the program, since they were routinely informed by the prosecutor. Substantial percentages were dissatisfied with the outcome in all sites; in one site the percentage was 63%, in the others 29% and 28%. However, while both experimentals and controls were generally satisfied when the defendant was sentenced to imprisonment, the experimentals were more satisfied when the outcome was probation ($p <$ .06). This suggests that victim involvement might result in greater understanding for a seemingly lenient sentence.

The responses regarding satisfaction with the experimental procedure were somewhat disappointing in this study. While many were satisfied with the experimental procedure immediately after the conference took place (57%–80%), the numbers declined (53%–63%) at the second interview six to eight weeks later, by which time appreciable minorities (28%–40%) expressed dissatisfaction (ibid., table 3.10). Regrettably, no comparative figures are available on this point. Moreover, only a minority felt that their view of the court system had improved as a result of the conference; and while 60%–64% thought that the conference was a better method than a trial for handling a criminal case, and a large majority thought that it was either important or very important to attend the conference (73%–94%), these last figures declined after six to eight weeks. More significantly, substantial proportions (22%–50%) felt that the victim had no influence during the conference (ibid., tables 3.10, 3.15).

General views on the criminal justice system were elicited from victims subjected to the experimental and regular procedures regarding such issues as the punitiveness of the courts and the fairness of judges. Generally, only minorities agreed that "the court system cares about the victim's needs," but the minorities were somewhat larger among the experimental groups (ibid., table 3.16). Similarly, the proportions of experimentals who expressed a willingness to cooperate with the system in the future tended to be higher, but not significantly so (table 3.14). However, experimentals were appreciably more favorably disposed toward plea-bargaining (table 3.37).

The *defendants'* views of the plea-bargaining process bore some resemblance to those of the victims. Large majorities took the view immediately after the conference that attendance was very important and that the bargain was very fair and were satisfied with the procedure; again, the proportions declined after six to eight weeks (ibid., table 3.21). Defendants were generally satisfied with the conference when an agreement was reached (table 3.22). Satisfaction levels were also related to the final sentence imposed (table 3.23). Defendants in the experimental group were more likely to agree with the statement that "the court system cares about victim's needs," although only a minority of defendants agreed with this statement. The evaluators concluded that "greater respect for victims among defendants could be a by-product of the SPN [structured plea negotiation] experience" (ibid., 3:62).

In the California allocution study, 54% of the victims who exercised this right felt different after making their statement to the judge, mostly in a positive sense, but a substantial minority felt angry or helpless. Moreover, less than half felt that their involvement affected the sentence (Villmoare and Neto, 1987:44). This was not their dominant consideration in exercising their allocution right, however (43).

The researchers developed a satisfaction index, based on the victim's satisfaction with law enforcement and with the district attorney and on his or her opinion of the judge (ibid., 49). Satisfaction on this scale did not correlate with victim participation, but this was explained partly by the fact that the offenses in such cases were often of a more traumatic nature; it was also noted that victims sometimes elected to participate at sentencing because they were dissatisfied with the other criminal justice agencies (49–50). Moreover, the satisfaction index was positively correlated with the researchers' criminal justice involvement index, which reflected the victims' *(a)* interaction with the district attorney, *(b)* court activity, and *(c)* knowledge of allocution rights. The results should be treated with caution, as the number of respondents who actually participated was rather small.

Finally, reference may be made here to the Polish study, based on a sample of 1,496 returned questionnaires, conducted by Bienkowska and Erez (1991). Under the Polish criminal justice system, "victims who participate as subsidiary or private prosecutors can make statements concerning the penalty for the accused" (221). As noted earlier, 36% participated as subsidiary or auxiliary prosecutors, while another 22% were private prosecutors. Only 12% of these, however, exercised the above right. Moreover, "only 15% of the victims who made a statement about the sentence felt satisfied after making it," while "72% stated they did not think in reality their statement had any effect on the penalty" (222).

Psychological research and surveys of victims gave rise to rather high expectations from the direct participation of the victim in the system, at least in terms of victim satisfaction. The evaluations discussed above indicate that these expectations have not been met. This seems to have been due mainly to the perceptions of the participant victims that their presence was largely symbolic and that they were able to make no meaningful contribution to the outcome, given the entrenched interests of traditional criminal justice personnel. In this respect the potential for meaningful participation and consequent satisfaction may be greater in the context of informal modes of dispute resolution to be discussed in chapter 11.

However, it may also be observed that ability to play an active role in the forensic drama may in part be a function of personality, and that, in spite of the greater anticipated benefits from direct participation, some victims obtain greater satisfaction in an *indirect* role. To cite Villmoare and Neto (1987): "An informal or face-to-face interview or conversation with a generally sympathetic probation officer appears to be, for many victims, a more comfortable and emotionally satisfying experience than a recitation in open court" (63).

Fundamental Principles of Justice

In principle there is considerable appeal in the idea that the victim should have the right to appear in person at all the relevant stages of the criminal process, a process initiated as a consequence of his or her victimization. There is also some appeal in raising this right to the level of a constitutional amendment, as has occurred in Florida and been proposed on the federal level and by NOVA (Lamborn, 1987), as well as being incorporated in the UN Declaration. This might have the effect of enhancing both its symbolic and its practical significance (Polito, 1990) in spite of objections in principle to this type of constitutional amendment (Dolliver, 1987). Proposals of this nature raise fundamental issues relating to the nature of the prevailing criminal justice system, and the possibilities of creating an additional party to the proceedings. These issues will be considered in chapter 12.

Perhaps even more challenging are the questions raised by proposals of this nature regarding the relationship between procedural and substantive reforms. It may be that procedural reforms of this nature—as indeed indicated by most of the empirical evaluations—do little to change substantive outcomes, whether owing to the inflexibility of criminal justice personnel, to the inhibitions of victims, or to normative structural limitations, in particular fixed sentencing provisions (Hall, 1991:262). Insofar as this is the case, the evidence suggests that victims will remain dissatisfied.

If, on the other hand, victim participation *were* to influence offender dispositions, or even bail and charging decisions, additional issues would be involved, in particular the equality of treatment required both by desert philosophy and by constitutional principles. Deviance from the norm may occur in a mitigating direction, since victim participation may result in lighter sentences, and in particular in an emphasis on restitution. This seems to be acceptable in terms of the constitutional protection of the defendant but is of course rejected by desert theorists.

Clearly, deviance in the opposite direction is a cause for greater concern. As indicated in the context of indirect participation, evidence of victim attributes or the impact of a murder on survivors, held to be constitutionally admissible in the 1991 Supreme Court case *Payne v. Tennessee*, discussed above, must inevitably have a potential to give rise to harsher sentences, this surely being the main reason prosecutors invoke such evidence. The admission of *direct* testimony, as occurred in *Payne*, in which a grandmother testified as to the impact on the surviving child of the murder of his mother and baby sister, probably has an even greater potential for emotional arousal of the decision makers—in this case the jury. This potential may be further aggravated where the oral testimony includes an expression of the victim's sentiments regarding the offender and a recommended sentence. Although the Supreme Court in *Payne* refrained from ruling on the admissibility of such statements, they are recognized under many legislative provisions, some of which have been considered above.

Since the principle of victim participation in the proceedings is nevertheless a positive one, the formulations of the UN Declaration and the Florida and Kansas Constitutions, to the effect that the victim's right to be heard is guaranteed only insofar as it does not "prejudice" or "interfere with" the rights of the defendant, has a strong attraction. On a broad interpretation of defendant prejudice, however, the proviso might tend to negate the victim's participatory rights altogether. While an appropriate "balance" is often called for (e.g., Polito, 1990:269), it is difficult to predict where the point of gravity will lie in the case of a constitutional amendment; developments in Florida and Kansas should be followed carefully. However, in view of the apparent difficulties in integrating victim and offender rights within the prevailing adversary model, consideration should be given to alternatives. This will be the subject of chapter 12.

Personal Confrontation

In the context of some of the procedures described in this and the preceding chapter, references are occasionally made in the literature to direct contacts between the victim and the offender. Such contacts occurred, albeit only rarely, in some of the restitution programs reviewed by Hudson et al. (1980:79), in the plea-bargaining experiments (Heinz and Kerstetter, 1979:172), and particularly in the victim-offender reconciliation programs (Galaway, 1985).

A notable aspect of the literature on this topic is the account presented of attitudes toward such encounters. While the potential for victim-offender communication is still largely an unknown quantity, and reservations have been expressed by criminal justice personnel (Hofrichter, 1980:108), both offenders and victims seem to be favorably disposed. Thus Novack et al. (1980:64–65) reported that 57% of the victims and 90% of the offenders in their study stated that they would have liked to have met with the other party to determine restitution agreements (see also Bussman, 1985). Moreover, while victims may have strong initial reservations regarding such encounters (Smale and Spickenhauer, 1979; Hofrichter, 1980:113–14), those who have actually experienced them seem more enthusiastic. In one study reported by Hudson and Galaway (1980:188), all twelve victim participants, as well as 85% of the offender participants, expressed the view that they would want to meet the other party if they were in the same situation again (cf. also Bonta et al., 1983).

"Confrontation" in the present context refers to a moderately structured proceeding in which justice personnel are involved. Since the proceeding is designed to produce a specific result, such as a plea, or a restitution arrangement, what takes place is in fact a form of negotiation. At the same time, such proceedings are clearly less structured than a conventional formal judicial proceeding. Hofrichter (1980:111), in considering victim involvement in restitution, defined negotiation as a "non-judicial but judicially approved system"; this seems to apply also to victim-offender reconciliation projects (Galaway, 1985). Thus while restitution programs and plea-bargain conferences may be adjuncts to the criminal justice system proper, it does not follow that procedures followed in these frameworks are appropriate for the criminal *trial*. Confrontation or negotiation between offender and victim must rather be regarded as supplements or *alternatives* to the criminal justice system, and will consequently be dealt with more extensively in chapter 11 below.

Following an impressionistic survey of a cross-section of restitution programs, generally confined to property offenses, Hofrichter (1980) drew a conclusion, partially supported by the foregoing analysis in this chapter, that "it is good for the victim, good for the system and good for justice if victims are restored to a participatory role in the adjudication of criminal offenses." Victims appear to derive some satisfaction from participation in the process, and offenders also seem to accept victim participation. Moreover, it is thought that "the more knowledge the offender has of the victim and the effects of the offense, the less the offender will be able to use 'justification techniques' " (Hudson and Galaway, 1980). Hence there is an assumed gain in terms of rehabilitation. However, justice, if based on desert or social defense, may be threatened by negotiated criminal justice. This theme will be resumed in chapters 11 and 12.

9

Remedies Unrelated to the Criminal Process: State Compensation and Escrow

State Compensation

This chapter will consider remedies designed to ameliorate the victim's predicament that do not directly impinge upon the criminal justice procedures. The attraction of such remedies is that they can exist alongside the present system and do not involve "rocking the boat," with all the problems following therefrom as described in the preceding chapter. On the other hand, they raise other problematic issues. Further, in some instances they, too, may ultimately have indirect implications for traditional criminal justice procedures. The main remedy to be considered under the present heading is the state-administered victim compensation scheme.

Criminal Injury Compensation Schemes

Since the possibilities of recourse against the offender are generally viewed as being limited, in particular because of low apprehension rates and lack of resources at the offender's disposal, public compensation schemes are frequently cited as the chief remedy for victim losses. The state compensation scheme is an institution that has developed with an astonishing rapidity, with some of the characteristics of a moral crusade.[1] While the concept has ancient roots, and was advocated in the nineteenth century by both utilitarians and criminologists of the positivist school (Joutsen, 1987:253), its revival in recent times seems to date from an article published in 1957 by the British penal reformer Margery Fry.

The first modern scheme was introduced in New Zealand in 1963 and 1964, followed by Great Britain in 1964 and California in 1965. Other jurisdictions followed with something of a snowball effect (see the graphs of the adoption of this remedy in U.S. jurisdictions in Ramker and Meagher, 1982:68) and McGillis and Smith (1983:8). By 1982 over 60 jurisdictions in the world had such programs, while the United States had 33 (McGillis and Smith, 1983:2, 7).

The President's Task Force on Victims of Crime (1982) affirmed the importance of such schemes and proposed that federal legislation—which had been considered by Congress in every session since 1965[2]—should be adopted in order to subsidize the states in this matter. In 1984 such legislation was finally enacted in the form of the Victims of Crime Act, or VOCA, and funding began in 1986. VOCA funding provided further impetus to state legislators, and by the end of 1991 all states with the exception of Maine, as well as the District of Columbia and the Virgin Islands, had adopted state compensation programs. Maine was considering—and subsequently adopted—such legislation (Parent et al., 1992:iv, 1).

On the international level, provisions relating to state compensation were incorporated into the UN Declaration of Basic Principles of Justice for Victims of Crime and Abuse of Power, while in 1983 the Council of Europe adopted the European Convention on the Compensation of Victims of Violent Crimes (Tsitsoura, 1984; Willis, 1984; Bassiouni, 1988). This topic has also been popular in the professional literature. During the years of rapid development, academic writers focused on legal issues regarding the scope and implementation of such schemes and philosophical discussions as to their justification.[3] Subsequently, there were a number of attempts to conduct comprehensive reviews of such programs.[4]

Empirical studies of this institution have been relatively few. As the programs developed, some macrostudies were conducted to examine the question of the costs to society of such programs (Garofalo and Sutton, 1977; Garofalo and McDermott, 1979; Jones, 1979). Relatively little attention has been devoted to studying the impact of compensation programs, beyond some macrostudies by Doerner et al. (1976) and the study of the implementation and impact of the New York and New Jersey programs conducted by Elias (1983b).[5]

In view of the large public expenditure involved in the administering of these programs, it is surprising that these issues have not been more extensively researched. This point was noted by McGillis and Smith (1983), whose research was commissioned following a recommendation of the Attorney General's Task Force on Violent Crime (1981) that "a relatively inexpensive study" be conducted on this topic: "In a critical area of public policy, ignorance can potentially be far more expensive than research" (25–26).

There follows an analysis of the available data regarding victim compensation from the point of view of the parameters adopted in this study.

Coping Needs

Victims. The early years of victim compensation programs presented an excellent illustration of the gap between the rhetoric and the reality of social reforms. For while establishment of such programs was accompanied by considerable polemics concerning the plight of victims and the need to assist them, the available information regarding their outcome suggests that their actual contribution to victims' welfare was paltry. The proportion of crime victims who actually received compensation under such schemes was estimated at less than 1%. There are indications, however, that some improvement may subsequently have taken place.

The very limited benefits of the programs seem to have been related to three underlying factors: (1) the desire to expend only limited public funds, (2) the legislators' image of the "deserving" victim, and (3) a lack of realism in the formulation of legislative policy, that is, the gap between norms and actuality.

As the figures presented below will indicate, compensating victims of crime at the public expense is potentially costly. Federal subsidies only became available in 1986, in the wake of VOCA. Yet even in 1989 "almost half the program directors said that existing funding for program administration was inadequate" (Parent et al., 1992:14). In order to save public funds, and thus establish a program that will appear beneficial without excessive demands on the taxpayer, benefits under the compensation scheme have been limited in the scope of their coverage. This resulted, in the first instance, in the restriction of the programs to crimes of violence. Indeed, even property damage resulting from violence, such as broken locks or spectacles, is rarely included (McGillis and Smith, 1983:87;

NOVA, 1989:1; Parent et al., 1989:5), and where it is included, it is subject to very low maximum awards (Parent et al., 1992:30). Compensation is provided mainly for medical treatment, including counseling, loss of income, and funeral expenses (22).

Few of the programs allow recovery for pain and suffering, which accounts for 51% of the awards in a jurisdiction that does allow such claims, namely, Hawaii; and see the British scheme (Home Office, 1993:2–3). Some programs require that victims prove financial hardship before their claims will be considered (McGillis and Smith, 1983:70; Parent et al., 1992:23). Finally, almost all programs incorporate a maximum limitation in the amount that may be awarded to the individual claimant (between $5,000 and $50,000, but most frequently $10,000), and many specify a minimum, generally $100 (Parent et al., 1992:29–30). It has been estimated that this last type of requirement has the effect of excluding large numbers of otherwise eligible victims, including many categories of the neediest victims, such as the elderly and the disabled (Garofalo and Sutton, 1977:39, 77).

Some limitations, however, were removed in most states in order to comply with VOCA funding conditions, which were tightened up further in 1988 (Parent et al., 1992:2–3). Thus, for example, VOCA required the removal of residency qualifications and inclusion of the victims of drunk driving offenses under the compensation program.

Since the intention of the legislators was to assist "deserving" or "innocent" victims, various provisions are included in the relevant legislation which are designed to exclude the "undeserving." Conversely, the programs generally cover losses suffered by "Good Samaritans" in the course of providing assistance to victims or in the pursuance of law enforcement.

In this context, which victims are considered to be "undeserving"? "Contributory misconduct" to the commission of the offense causing the injury seems to be a universal ground for denying or reducing compensation both in the United States and in Europe (McGillis and Smith, 1983:64, 71; Parent et al., 1992:23; Joutsen, 1987:265; Miers, 1990:82ff.; Greer, 1994:359ff.). A more problematic ground is the character, status, or lifestyle of the victim, for example, being a prisoner,[6] having a criminal record, or being unemployed (!)—"presumably because they could not have suffered any loss of earnings" (McGillis and Smith, 1983:66). This ground for exclusion may tend to interact with the previous one, as illustrated by an extract from a policy statement issued by the British compensation board, cited by Miers (1990): "In particular the Board will look critically at any provocative, annoying or loutish behaviour which can be seen to be attributable to the applicant's own over-indulgence in alcohol or the misuse of drugs" (86). However, its policy in this respect seems subsequently to have been modified (Greer, 1994:363). In non-common-law countries there is said to be less emphasis on lifestyle as a qualifying, or rather disqualifying, factor (Van Dijk, 1985:3; Joutsen, 1987:265); but Kirchhoff (1983–84) notes the rejection by the German Compensation Board of "twilight zone" cases involving, for example, violence in the context of beer drinking and homosexuality.

Third, "unworthiness" or "innocence" may also derive from the victim's ongoing relationship with the offender: having a blood relationship, a sexual relationship, or belonging to the same household. These exceptions, which were also calculated to prevent fraudulent claims as well as to exclude the possibility that the *offender* might benefit from the compensation payment ("unjust enrichment"), were calculated to exclude large numbers of victims, since much crime, especially that of personal injury, is committed within "criminal" subcultures, among nonstrangers, or in situations of developing interpersonal conflict. These limitations, however, have been reduced in the United States as a result of the federal funding provisions, which now require compensation to be paid in domestic violence cases, which were excluded under the "household" and "family" rules. Similarly, there has been an attempt to narrow down the "unjust enrichment" exception (Parent et al., 1992:21–22).

Finally, "unworthiness" may be related to the victim's conduct after the offense was committed, for example, whether the victim reported the offense to the police and how speedily application was made for an award. This type of requirement is generally classified by the literature under the separate heading of "cooperation with the authorities" (Miers, 1990:72; Parent et al., 1992:25).

A compensation scheme is of little value to victims who are unaware of its existence. A Louis Harris survey conducted in New York found that only 35% of the victims questioned knew of the existence of the scheme (Bucuvalas, 1984:36–39; cf. also Friedman et al., 1982:55). A general lack of awareness is thought to be true of other jurisdictions also (Ramker and Meagher, 1982:76; McCormack, 1991:334, 336), although program directors perceive some improvement in this area (Parent et al., 1992:12).

One method adopted by some schemes to overcome this problem is to impose an obligation on law enforcement personnel to notify victims of their rights—including the possibility of applying for compensation. This came to be known as the "reverse Miranda" (McGillis and Smith, 1983:93; Doerner, 1977:108). However, a survey conducted by Rich and Stenzel

(1980) found that few of the schemes had endorsed the obligation to inform victims; moreover, such provisions had mixed results (McGillis and Smith, 1983:93). Further, even an informed victim may not have the know-how or the resources for filing a claim, or even convenient geographical access, since most of the programs are centralized (cf. McCormack, 1991:336–38). A decision to seek legal advice will not necessarily resolve the problem, since the compensation tribunals are ambivalent in their attitude to the participation of attorneys and the fee allowed—sometimes limited to between 2% and 15% of the award—may be insufficient to attract an attorney's services (Friedman et al., 1982:169; McGillis and Smith, 1983:84–85; Parent et al., 1992:32).

These inhibiting factors, combined with lack of information on the one hand, and familiarity with program eligibility restrictions on the other, have undoubtedly contributed to low application rates on the part of victims. A survey conducted by Doerner (1977) indicated that the rate of claims filed in California, Maryland, Massachusetts, and New York during the years 1967 through 1975 varied from 0.25% to 2.97% of the violent crimes known to the police. The Louis Harris survey conducted in New York found that among the victims who had heard of the Compensation Board (35% of the sample) only 7% filed a claim—representing 2% of the sample. Of those suffering injuries, 10% filed a claim (Bucuvalas, 1984:37). Similarly, Elias (1984:110), on the basis of his study of compensation claims in Brooklyn, New York, and Newark, New Jersey, estimated that "less than 1% of all violent crime victims (who constituted about 20% of all crime victims) applied for compensation" (cf. also Hudson, 1984:43). More recently, McCormack (1991:329) reported that 8.5% of *recorded* victims of violent crime in New Jersey in 1987 applied for compensation. In a national survey he found that application rates varied widely among the states "from a high of 31 percent (in Colorado) to a low of 1.2 percent (in Illinois and Louisiana)" and that the national average was 6% (330, 334).

Further, the studies conducted by Elias and others found that compensation boards only made awards in about one-third of the cases in which applications were made. However, McCormack (1991:330–36) reported a national average of 65.7%—again, with considerable variation by state, from 31% for New Jersey to 100% for Washington. The national figure was a slight improvement on the 60% noted by McGillis and Smith (1983:100–103).

The cumulative effect of restrictive criteria for eligibility, poor dissemination of information, difficulties or inhibitions in the making of applications, and the rejection of claims results in the tiny proportion of victims of violent crime who actually receive compensation from the boards. Where application rates did not exceed 2% and success rates were one in three, less than 1% of such victims were compensated. McCormack's more recent national survey estimated that nationwide 3.8% of victims of reported violent crime received compensation—a rate that would be reduced by half if unreported crime were to be taken into account (McCormack, 1991:330, 333). Similarly, Parent et al. (1992) estimate that claims were filed in less than 2% of the estimated 5.7 million violent crime victimizations that occurred in the United States in 1987 and that 70% of these were allowed (32, 16). Even allowing for some further improvement since the data for these studies were collected in the late 1980s, the outcome is not encouraging for victims.

It seems probable that the overwhelming majority of the uncompensated victims do not in fact qualify under current eligibility requirements. Some 90% of crimes of violence do not result in the need for medical treatment (Garofalo and McDermott, 1979:446); approximately one-half fail to report the offense (although proportionately few of these are involved in serious offenses); many do not meet the minimum loss requirement; and some are not "innocent." Moreover, Parent et al. (1992:6, 16) estimate that a large proportion of the remainder are covered by private medical insurance, thereby rendering them ineligible for compensation.

Parent et al. (1992) estimate that between 168,000 and 336,000 victims per year are eligible, depending upon the precise eligibility criteria applied. Since the programs surveyed reported making 65,000 awards in their last fiscal year, the authors concluded that the programs may be reaching between 20% and 50% of potentially eligible victims, and that "the proportion of eligible crime victims served by compensation programs is higher than it is generally believed to be" (6). Even if this is true, most victims may still be ineligible because their losses are of the wrong type, their injuries are insufficient, or they are insufficiently "innocent" or cooperative with the police, and so on.

Studies conducted in other countries also indicate only a moderate level of success with compensation awards. Canadian studies (Statistics Division, 1984; Stuebing, 1984) found that the vast majority of the public were unaware of the existence of a compensation board. Indeed, only 13% of victims who had received medical treatment and who were thus prima facie candidates for awards knew they could file claims. Moreover, fewer than one-third of those who had this knowledge—3.8% of all the treated victims—actually filed claims.

The British Criminal Injuries Compensation Board cited a 19% application rate in its early years (Vennard, 1978). Sophisticated attempts in more recent years to assess the eligible population have produced estimates of the proportion applying as being between 26% (Newburn, 1989:13) to nearer two-thirds (Miers, 1990:34), of whom 65% are successful in obtaining awards. In Germany, on the other hand, Villmow (1986:423, 428) found that only 6% of victims of violent acts made applications and that "benefits were denied in 63% of the cases." These figures, based on data collected in the late 1970s, strongly resemble those of the early American studies. Another German scholar found that "many victims apply, but the law gives almost nothing" (Kirchhoff, 1983–84:29), while a Dutch study concluded that "less than one per cent of all victims of violent crimes are reached by the fund" (Van Dijk, 1985:6).

Apart from the low probability of receiving an award, the delay involved in applying to the compensation tribunal and in obtaining the award may also be a problem. In many cases, the victim may be in need of immediate funds to deal with the victimization trauma. Some schemes recognize this need and grant emergency awards. Delay may in itself be a cause of victim hardship, in addition to the bureaucratic complications of systems "plagued with red tape and huge backlogs" (Cronin and Borque, 1980:100). Most of the American schemes, however, now make provision for emergency awards. Finally, even those applicants who are successful may receive less than the sum requested, owing to maximum limits, financial need requirements, disputed evaluations, and so on.

These findings hardly suggest that victim compensation schemes—at least as they function today—are a universal panacea for meeting the victim's material needs. Victim compensation "gives too little, too late, to too few of the crime victims" (Van Dijk, 1984:84). They lend credence to the view expressed by Elias (1983a) that victim compensation schemes are in fact symbolic gestures on the part of the political establishment. The existence of such schemes tends to conceal the fact that most victims still lack an adequate remedy. The legislation providing for federal subsidies in the United States has encouraged expansion of the schemes, as well as requiring removal of some of the eligibility restrictions. Others, however, remain. VOCA (sec. 1403(a)(1)) specified that property damage would not be covered by the federal grant. Moreover, this grant only covers a maximum of 40% of the cost of the scheme, or rather of the state's expenditure on compensation payments two years earlier; the remaining 60% of the funding, as well as administrative costs, will still have to be raised by the state. Hence the reluctance of many program administrations to promote their services (Parent et al., 1992:14).

Offenders. Public compensation of the victim does not in itself directly involve the offender. Advocates of restitution, however, might argue that such provisions would have a negative effect on offender rehabilitation. The offender's belief that the state will compensate the victim would tend to negate his or her personal responsibility for the harm inflicted and to operate as a "neutralization technique." Moreover, this would result in encouraging crime, and therefore also be harmful to society as a whole.

However, compensation programs may have more direct consequences for the offender. The state generally assumes a right of subrogation whereby the benefit of any civil suit or restitution claim brought against the offender becomes vested in the state or the compensation board (Teson, 1982:562–63; Parent et al., 1992:30; and see sec. 317 of the Uniform Victims of Crime Act, 1992). Thus it may be argued that the function of state compensation is to ensure that financial assistance be available to the victim, but not to relieve the offender of his or her liability.

There is thus a potential threat to the offender's resources similar to that discussed under the topic of restitution. However, this potential is limited by the fact that claims will relate exclusively to injury compensation and will arise only where a specified minimum loss has been incurred. Hence the liability of offenders to compensate may be limited, as indicated by the low amounts in fact recovered through subrogation.[7]

Apart from the possibility of the offender's covering the cost of compensating the victim on the *individual* level, an increasingly popular solution to the problem of cost is for offenders to carry the burden *collectively*, by means of the levying of an indemnity on all offenders—or on all offenders falling into particular categories—in addition to the penal sanction imposed by the court. Unlike the somewhat cumbersome, and in many cases probably fruitless, remedy of instigating civil suits against individual offenders, the collective levy is a much more realistic approach in practical terms, as evidenced by the fact that the majority of the compensation programs currently obtain a large part of their funding in this way (Parent et al., 1992:38). The justice of this solution will be discussed below. In terms of offender resources, however, the strain is relatively marginal, since the burden is shared among offenders as a whole, rather than devolving on the individual perpetrator. The indemnity usually takes the form of a fixed fee or percentage of the fine imposed.

Society. Before their instigation, there was considerable speculation regarding the cost of victim compensation programs. This speculation developed into more specific assessments during the late 1970s, when Congress was considering proposals whereby the federal government would pay 25%

or 50% of the cost of all state compensation. It is revealing to review these assessments with the hindsight of familiarity with the contemporary costs of the programs.

Garofalo and Sutton (1977) used data from the 1974 National Crime Survey to estimate the numbers and extent of injuries for which claims could be filed under a compensation scheme. They concluded that the maximum cost of a program, if all those eligible applied and in the absence of minimum-loss criteria, would be approximately $261.1 million, while the incorporation of such criteria might reduce the cost to $174.3 million or $143.6 million, depending upon the criterion adopted (37). In another study by Garofalo and McDermott (1979), using National Crime Survey data for 1974 through 1976, other eligibility criteria were added— exclusion of victims who were related to the offender, and the requirement that the crime must have been reported to the police. The costs of the various combinations were estimated to vary from $276.6 million (no eligibility criteria) to $194.7 million (all criteria apply). Jones (1979), using both FBI and National Crime Survey data, arrived at a maximum cost of $248.4 million. In spite of the methodological problems involved in making such assessments, the similarity of these assessments indicates a high level of reliability, although Meiners (1978), an opponent of victim compensation, estimated its cost as $400 million and predicted that this would rise to $1 billion.[8]

By contrast, Jones (1979:138), on learning of the low utilization experience of the New York compensation board, "adjusted" his estimate to only $48 million; he therefore concluded that a federal bill under which a 25% subsidy was being proposed would cost the federal government considerably less than the $30 million it was planned to allocate for this purpose.

In retrospect it appears that Jones's revised estimate was probably the closest, if somewhat too conservative. This can be explained in terms of the particularly low utilization rates in New York when Jones obtained his data, as compared with prevailing practices nationwide. Data presented by McGillis and Smith (1983) regarding the operating costs of 28 state compensation boards in 1981 indicated a total cost, that is, including overheads, of approximately $57 million. At the end of the 1980s, the 41 programs responding in the survey by Parent et al. (1992:36) paid out a total of $125.6 million, over 30% in California.[9] Given inflation, these figures may not be substantially higher than Jones's. The point is of importance, since his original estimate—as well as those of the other researchers—was five times higher, an indication of the extent to which victims' needs are unmet, and to which costs to the public are being "saved."

In addition to the costs of the compensation awards themselves, the administrative costs of the programs must be taken into account. These amount on average to 16.1% of the award totals but vary considerably by state, from 2.7% for Missouri, to 31.4% for Wyoming.[10] The costs of these programs do not necessarily fall upon the general public. Data collected by Parent et al. (1992:38) at the end of the 1980s found that while a dozen states financed an average of 83% of the budget out of general revenue, a majority of the states covered most of the budget out of fines and penalties levied on offenders. On average, 15% of the budgets were at this time covered by federal subsidies under VOCA, a percentage that was expected to increase as more states complied with federal requirements. This federal budget—the Crime Victims Fund—is also paid for primarily from fines, as well as special assessments of between $25 and $50 per offense (2).

It is difficult to draw conclusions about whether any public program is or is not "excessively costly." It has been observed that the cost of a compensation program is not unduly heavy as compared with other federally funded programs. The same is true if its costs are compared with other heads of criminal justice expenditure. Moreover, it seems somewhat bizarre to save public funds by administering a program that will fail to reach most of the people for whom it is nominally intended, although, as noted above, perhaps this was the intention of the policy makers. Further, some expansion of the program may be relatively low in cost. It was once calculated that by removing the minimum award requirement, the number of potential beneficiaries could be nearly tripled with only a 12% increase in costs being incurred (Garofalo and McDermott, 1979:456–57). On the other hand, if the programs were to be rendered comprehensive and to be fully utilized, costs would—on the basis of the early estimates—rise considerably. It was once estimated that extension of the programs to property offenses would cost 7% of the gross national product![11]

In addition to direct economic cost, other types of social costs and benefits are envisaged as the result of the implementation of compensation schemes. One anticipated benefit is a greater willingness to report crimes and to cooperate with the criminal justice system, thereby increasing the efficiency of law enforcement. However, a series of analyses conducted by Doerner and his colleagues in both the United States and Canada (see, e.g., Doerner et al., 1980) did not produce any conclusive evidence that the introduction of compensation programs gave rise to higher reporting rates. This is not surprising in the light of the lack of awareness of the programs and the low rate of successful claims. In such circumstances, any positive feedback would surely be slight. Nor do attitudinal surveys suggest that victims having contact with compensation tribunals express any greater readiness to cooperate with law enforcement authorities in the future (see below).

Meiners hypothesized that the availability of state compensation would act as an *incentive* to the commission of crime. This economic analysis is supported by the "neutralization technique" argument raised above, to the effect that offenders can rationalize that their conduct does not inflict a direct loss on their selected victims. However, while this attitude is commonly attributed to housebreakers, it seems less plausible in the context of crimes of violence.

Perceived Justice Needs

When the function of the New York State Crime Victims Compensation Board was explained to them, 93% of the victims interviewed in the Louis Harris survey expressed their approval (Bucuvalas, 1984:43, 45). The sentiment behind this statistic may simply have been that something should be done to help victims. Respondents did not have to choose between alternative remedies for the victim. Thus 94% favored "making convicted criminals help pay part of the cost of compensation and services for victims," and 95% favored offender restitution (47).

By contrast, the specific attitudes of victims to the compensation boards were much more negative. First, a generally poor image seems to be indicated by the fact that even among those who knew about the boards many did not bother to apply (37–38). Moreover, other studies have shown that those who have had experience with compensation claims express negative views. Elias (1984) found that "80% of those who did recover were not satisfied with their award. Three quarters of all applicants said they would not apply for compensation again. Almost one in five ruled out a future claim because, although they had received an award from their first application, they considered it insufficient" (111).

Satisfaction has thus been found to be related to the victim's experience with the compensation board, and in particular to the outcome of the claim. The study by Doerner and Lab (1980) found that claimants who received compensation from the Florida Crimes Compensation Commission in 1977 were more likely to be satisfied with the commission and to declare their intention to cooperate with it in the future than claimants whose claims were rejected. Elias, too, found that "some claimants (those receiving adequate rewards) had more positive awards than did non-claimants generally" (111). However, "so overwhelmingly negative were most claimants (those receiving an inadequate or no award) that the victims who did not encounter the compensation board at all (nonclaimants) actually had significantly more positive attitudes and a greater willingness to cooperate than did those who had such contact (claimants)—a result precisely opposite from that expected by compensation's proponents" (ibid.). For similar reasons a Dutch study also found that "the Fund on balance tends to generate more negative than positive feelings amongst its applicants" (Van Dijk, 1985:15).

Thus, the effect of the encounter with the compensation boards on the part of the relatively few victims who do have contact with them is far from being wholly positive. Moreover, even for those victims who receive awards and develop favorable views of the board, this does not generate any "spin-off" benefit resulting in such victims having a better opinion of the criminal justice system generally than other victims, or in having a greater disposition to report offenses in the future (Doerner et al. 1976; Doerner and Lab, 1980; Shapland 1984:140; Van Dijk, 1985:15).

Most of the victims in the Louis Harris survey cited above, who expressed support for the New York compensation board, had not had personal experience with the board. At the same time, most respondents supported expansion of the program, even if this meant extra cost to the state; indeed a majority even favored its extension to victims of property crime (Bucuvalas, 1984:47). The question arises whether liberalization of the programs would reduce the apparently high level of dissatisfaction expressed today on the part of the persons encountering the compensation boards, or whether it would have the opposite effect. This would depend partly on the extent to which claimants had accurate information and realistic assessments of the anticipated decisions of the boards. It would also depend on the nature of the liberalization of the board's policy. Elias (1984), for example, found that New Jersey claimants were more satisfied than New York claimants, and he attributed this to the fact that claims were recognized in New Jersey as of right, rather than *ex gratia* (112).

Similarly, the effect of other program variables, including procedural variables, should be monitored to determine how each is related to victim satisfaction. Shapland et al. (1985) argue that the interest shown by the compensation board, and its recognition of the victimization—where this in fact occurs—may be more important to the victim than the award itself. Per contra it has been suggested that one source of *negative* reactions of victims to the compensation experience may be that the state representative appears in an adversary relationship vis-à-vis the victim (Grabovsky, 1985).

This, in turn, leads to the final point: the true adversary, if there is to be one, is surely thought to be the offender. Hence it is from the offender that the victim expects payment. This is supported by the small survey conducted by Van Dijk (1985:11). Payment deriving from another source (the state) may give rise to dissatisfaction. Such a hypothesis would be consistent with equity theory, to be considered below.

As to *offenders*, little information is available regarding their attitudes toward victim compensation. On one view they might be expected to approve of such programs, which, as suggested above, might even be seen as providing a rationalization for their continued offending. Equity theory, however, hypothesizes the contrary. Indeed, it hypothesizes that both participants and observers of the inequity created by the criminal offense should be dissatisfied. For not only has the initial inequity between harmdoer and victim not been remedied, but a new inequity has been created. The state, which was not the cause of the initial inequity, has undertaken to incur a loss in order to compensate the victim. This gives rise to a further inequity, and the distress created by the original inequity—to all parties concerned—is thereby compounded, or at least replaced by a new inequity. Some support for this hypothesis is found in the experimental research conducted by de Carufel (1981) described in chapter 5.

The situation is further complicated in the context of the American compensation schemes by virtue of the fact that much of the compensation funds derives not from the collectivity of taxpayers but from offenders, albeit not the specific offender who caused the particular inequity. This is clearly a topic worthy of further investigation.

Similarly, the general public might also be expected to support victim compensation schemes, and some evidence has been found to this effect (St. Louis, 1976). On the one hand, the public is thought to identify with the victim. On the other, the schemes are relatively inexpensive, since most victims do not benefit from them. Indeed, these are the very reasons for which some writers believe victim compensation schemes to have been adopted so enthusiastically by politicians.[12] The fact that most programs are at least partially funded by fees levied on offenders would be calculated to strengthen public support even further, as would provisions whereby the state could seek reimbursement of the payment from the offender.[13]

Nevertheless, objections might be forthcoming from conservative monetarists who object to any form of public expense or state interventionism that might be associated with welfare, and who might expect the victim to rely either on recourse to the offender or on private insurance. The majority of a sample of jurists also objected to the principle of imposing a duty on the state to compensate victims and expressed a preference for offender restitution (Gandy, 1978).

Finally, if equity theorists are correct, state compensation creates a problem of perceived inequity for all who "observe" it, because these payments, when forthcoming, are made by the wrong party—the state rather than the harmdoer. The inadequacy of the payments might be another source of perceived inequity, and this would be consistent with the findings referred to above; however, in accordance with equity theory it is also possible that victims who received less than full compensation might attribute this to their own "unworthiness," leading to restoration of psychological rather than actual equity (see above, chap. 5). Both extensive surveys and in-depth research are required to explore these issues further.

Fundamental Principles of Justice

The literature on victim compensation, especially the earlier writings, has devoted considerable attention to the question of the rationale behind the concept.[14] Does the state have a duty to compensate the crime victim? If so, what is the source of this duty? If not, why should crime victims receive preferential treatment over other categories of victims? Why should compensation be paid to victims of violent crimes but not to victims of property crimes?

If a pragmatic or utilitarian response is given to these questions—for example, if victim compensation schemes are justified in terms of cost-benefit analysis—the question of fundamental principles of justice does not arise. The value of the schemes must from this perspective be tested solely by empirical evaluation of their relative costs and benefits, which were considered above. Other "pragmatic" objectives that have been tested empirically are crime reduction and the prevention of the alienation of victims (Carrow, 1980a:6–7). On another view, the search for an agreed rationale is likely to be fruitless, compensation schemes having been established not as a result of the force of theoretical arguments for their adoption, nor in the wake of scientific research, but simply to meet political needs (Miers, 1978; Greer, 1994:397).

Nevertheless, a brief attempt will be made here to consider some of the arguments raised in support of victim compensation schemes, insofar as they raise issues of justice. The most frequently cited rationales are the state's duty to protect its citizens, the social welfare theory, and the "shared risk" theory, whereby taxation is seen as a mechanism for social insurance against crime (Lamborn, 1973b:462–64; Carrow, 1980a:5–6; Merrill, 1981:268–69). Most of these arguments are derived, albeit not always explicitly, from the literature of social philosophy dealing with the relationship between the citizen and the state, and with the justificational bases for the distribution of goods among categories of citizens according to various criteria. These are very different issues from those that arose when justice-related criteria were discussed in previous chapters, where the focus was on the appropriateness of various sanctions from the perspective of the competing philosophies of punishment; indeed, insofar as jurisprudential issues have been raised in the present context, they have been related instead to *civil law*.

However, although this point has been generally ignored in the literature, victim compensation schemes may also raise certain criminal justice issues, as well as the social justice issues of which there has been a greater awareness. In other words, victim compensation may have a bearing not only on *distributive* justice but also on *retributive* justice.

Distributive Justice. Various principles of distributive justice were considered earlier in chapter 6. The three alternatives posited by Miller (1976)—right, desert, and needs—appear to represent alternative principles upon which compensation schemes might be based. However, in view of the special role played by the state in criminal justice, it may be appropriate first to consider the rationale for state compensation deriving from social contract theory.

One frequently mentioned justification for state compensation schemes is the state's failure to fulfill its undertaking to enforce the law and prevent citizen victimization, an area in which the state has assumed a virtual monopoly (Lamborn, 1973b:462), perhaps by virtue of a social contract (Merrill, 1981:268). This monopoly is said to give rise to an implicit obligation on the part of the state to protect all citizens and to pay compensation if it fails in this obligation. This argument may have been weakened by the rapid development of private security in recent years, which seems to imply a perceived dilution of the state's duty to protect, and thus also to compensate on failure to do so! Historically, however, when the local parish was responsible for the maintenance of order, ratepayers would be liable for the compensation of victims, a tradition that survives in Ireland for certain property offenses (Greer and Mitchell, 1982: chap. 10).

Most authors do not discuss the applicability of the social contract in depth—perhaps because of its clearly fictitious nature—but merely note that it has not been generally accepted, as indicated by the failure of most states to recognize victim compensation as a *right*. Aynes, whose thesis regarding the right not to be a victim was discussed in chapter 6, did not insist upon the social contract theory in justification of his argument. Moreover, the social contract theory was invoked indirectly by Meiners (1978) as a basis for the case *against* victim compensation. Meiners applied the principles of justice posited by Rawls, which themselves derive from a variation of social contract theory, to the issue of victim compensation and concluded that the use of public funds for victim compensation was in conflict with these principles. Meiners argued as follows: "Random victimization is similar to natural disasters that none could have been reasonably expected to foresee or prevent. . . . Most random disasters result in relatively small costs which can be borne by the victim. Individuals can either bear the full costs of the misfortune at the time of occurrence or spread the cost over time by purchasing insurance" (68). Meiners therefore argued that citizens "in the original position," that is, about to form a social contract or constitution, would not have opted for state responsibility for random disasters resulting in small costs, with which he classifies criminal victimization, but only for very costly tragedies which "few individuals can afford" (68). The ability of even the most unfortunate to afford some form of self-assistance follows in his view from the application of Rawls's difference principle of income distribution (69).[15]

There are a number of difficulties with Meiners's analysis, such as determining what persons in the original position would see as a "small" and what as a "costly" tragedy. Since many victimizations are costly at least from the point of view of the individual victim, if not objectively so (see chap. 4), this might lead to precisely the opposite conclusion from that reached by Meiners—that citizens would see themselves as greatly benefiting from a compensation scheme at relatively low public cost.[16]

Another argument put forward by Meiners, apparently as a part of his Rawlsian analysis, is that victimization is not in fact entirely random but depends partly on personal preferences for risk taking, which affect the probability of victimization (68–69). The implication here is that parties to the social contract would not have anticipated paying compensation for injuries that could have been avoided. It is true that victimization is not random. However, its distribution is related to variables such as age, sex, ethnic group (Skogan and Maxfield, 1981), and lifestyle (Hindelang, 1982; Fattah, 1991: chap. 12), variables that are not, or are only partly (in the case of lifestyle), under the victims' or potential victims' control. Moreover, it is questionable how far citizens should be obligated to inhibit their daily activities in order to prevent victimization. It has also been argued that the avoidance of locations perceived as dangerous in fact *increases* the probability of crimes being committed in these areas (Wilson and Kelling, 1982), since the dilution of the population present renders those remaining even more vulnerable.

Even if we accept the conclusion that Rawls's principles do not justify recognition of the victim's right to compensation from the state, the basis for this conclusion is not the social contract approach as such but the particular terms of this contract as envisaged by Rawls. While Rawls's second principle is concerned with reconciling equality and need as a basis of justice—neither of which would seem to exclude state compensation—his first principle is concerned with preserving a maximum amount of liberty. This may tend to operate as a conservative, limiting principle when applied to the distribution of goods in society. Perhaps this discussion on the applicability of the Rawlsian thesis to victim compensation merely illustrates the difficulties of basing particular rights on a social contract approach.

More specific recognition of victims' rights was developed by Aynes (1984) based on the Fourteenth Amendment. Indeed, if a right to absolute state protection could be read into this provision, it would clearly follow that the state had a correlative duty to protect the citizen from victimization, and if it failed in the performance of this duty, to pay compensation. As indicated in chapter 6, however, this interpretation of the Fourteenth Amendment is problematic. In practice, states are naturally reluctant to recognize the existence of such a duty "because if there were such a duty it would be impossible to confine it to personal injury as opposed to damage to property" (Greer and Mitchell, 1982:325).

The rejection of the "rights" approach to victim compensation is reflected in the principle adopted in many jurisdictions having such schemes, that all payments are to be *ex gratia*, at the discretion of the tribunal empowered to make the award. Indeed, in England the scheme has always been administered on a nonstatutory basis, and when a statute was finally enacted in 1988, it was not implemented (Miers, 1990:16–17; Home Office, 1993:7). Moreover, even under those schemes in which the victim's claim is recognized as of right, many categories of victim are excluded from its benefits. Were the victims seen to have an absolute right to compensation, there would be no grounds for adopting eligibility criteria, except perhaps those which were intended to ensure the validity of the claim.

The *desert* criterion of justice seems to be closest to that in fact adopted by compensation schemes. As noted above, compensation is paid only to victims who are seen to be "deserving" according to various moral or ethical criteria. Thus victims may be excluded from the programs if they are thought to have contributed in some way to the commission of the offense, if they are morally or legally "tainted," or if they have failed to cooperate with law enforcement agencies. "Desert" is of course referred to here in a positive sense, as a basis for reward, as contrasted with the negative desert, which refers to the principle on the basis of which punishment is due (cf. Miller, 1976:87). Operationally, the principles upon which the victim's (distributional) desert is established and measured are the inverse of those upon which the offender's (retributional) desert is determined under the justice model, namely, the seriousness of the injury inflicted, for which here, too, the application of psychophysical scales have been suggested (Wolfgang, 1975); and the "nonculpability" of the victim (cf. von Hirsch, 1976).

Politicians and the promoters of victim-oriented programs hold to an image of the "ideal" victim whom they want to assist, and be perceived to be assisting. This image, however, is somewhat remote from the reality, especially where crimes of violence against the person are concerned. Victims are likely to belong to the same subculture as the offender (see above, chap. 3). The fact that ideal victims may account for only a relatively small part of the actual victim population is, of course, an advantage economically for the promoters of these programs, insofar as their funding has to be supported largely out of public resources (i.e., their constituents' taxes). As indicated earlier, because of the relatively small number of claimants, the programs are relatively inexpensive.

However, serious doubts arise as to whether the desert approach can be justified. The starting point for all rationales of victim compensation is not that the victim is a worthy citizen,[17] but that he or she has been the object of a criminal offense. Although the concept of distribution based upon principles of desert may be a dominant force in contemporary political thinking, there seems to be no logical justification in superimposing such a principle on compensation schemes in order to restrict their application, for the rationale for these schemes does not derive from this principle. One may also recall in this context the feminist complaint before the reform of rape laws that the rules of evidence applied to rape trials made it seem that it was the female victim who was on trial, since the proceedings focused on her alleged proclivity to consensual sexual intercourse, both in the instant case and on previous occasions (Berger, 1977). Thus, the "worthiness" of the victim became the dominant issue in the criminal trial. A similar trend is evident in the present context.

Need is in principle the most "progressive" criterion for social justice. It is closely identified with the principles of the welfare state and the provision of benefits to the socially disadvantaged, principles that have gained support in both the legal and social work literature. The need criterion is indeed invoked by some compensation tribunals, but only in a negative sense. Some jurisdictions apply a "needs test," restricting compensation awards to the needy, although in the United States this requirement is becoming relatively less common (Parent et al., 1992:23). Such provisions have been criticized not only because of their limiting function but also because the means test is perceived as stigmatic. Moreover, as noted, the need principle has an exclusively negative function here, for it does not allow for an award to be made to a needy person not fulfilling the other requirements laid down by the scheme's provisions.

Need as a positive criterion would be an attractive principle upon which to base a compensation scheme. According to such a criterion, all persons who had suffered loss as the result of victimization and who were in need of compensation could receive it. However, there would be many practical objections to such a scheme, in particular the breadth of its application (depending on the definition of need) and the administrative complications involved in the widespread application of means tests, as well as the objection to such tests referred to above.

Moreover, the needs approach also raises a problem of principle. If the criterion for assistance to the disadvantaged is need, why should special privileges be granted to persons whose disadvantage stems from a criminal offense rather than from other causes (cf. Miers, 1978)? This is the problem of "horizontal equity," which arises whenever a particular category of victim is selected for favorable treatment (cf. Fleming, 1982, in the context of drug injury compensation plans). Harris et al. (1984), in the course of a comprehensive analysis of various compensation options available in Britain in the wake of different types of injury, concluded that "the future policy-maker should plan to phase out all existing compensation systems which favour accident victims (or any category of them) over illness victims" and "the abolition of every compensation scheme which is based on a particular category of causation" (327–28).[18] Thus, not only is a needs or "consequence" approach entirely remote from the philosophy of the prevailing system (cf. Miers, 1990:330), it may be inconsistent with the very existence of crime compensation schemes.

Retributive Justice. Since victim compensation schemes are a mechanism whereby public funds are allocated to a particular category of individuals, they are generally thought to raise questions primarily of distributive justice. Compensation programs may, however, also involve latent issues of retributive justice. This possibility arises both on the basis of philosophical considerations and because of the practicalities of current compensation schemes.

As to the philosophical considerations, it is suggested that the term *retribution* may be concerned not only with the infliction of sanctions on the offender but also with the *restitutio in integrum* of the victim. The relationship between court-ordered restitution orders and retributive theory has been discussed elsewhere in this volume. The connection between restitution and retribution was seen to rest in part upon an analysis of the early history of criminal justice, which was once essentially a mechanism for the payment of compensation by the offender to the victim, generally on the basis of a tariff. The suggestion that restitution could be seen as retributive was also based upon the idea that retribution means that while the offender must pay for his or her sins, such payment need not take the form of a corporal or other punishment enacted by the state, but could also be a monetary payment to the victim.

This argument may be developed further. The term *retribution* derived from Latin literally means "paying back." This concept has two components: the duty of the offender to repay, and the right of the victim to be paid. The development of the criminal justice system has been such that all the emphasis has been placed upon the first component. The state has assumed the victim's erstwhile role as prosecuting party in order to ensure that the offender indeed fulfills his or her obligation and repays his or her debt, albeit not to the originally designated beneficiary. There now appears to be an awareness that the second component—the victim's right to *restitutio in integrum*—has been unjustly forgotten. If, in recognition of this right the state, rather than forgoing its role as the agency that exacts justice from the offender, elects to continue in this role but also to pay the victim his or her due, could this not be construed as merely completing the retributive process?

The adoption of this view would have implications for the determination of the conceptual basis upon which compensation programs rest. Clearly, the above analysis would lead to the adoption of the "rights" approach. If the state were seen as a kind of intermediary for the performance of justice vis-à-vis the offender on the one hand and the victim on the other, there would be no ground for the incorporation of eligibility requirements based upon desert or need.

This concept of the role of compensation programs leads directly to the second part of this analysis, based upon the structure of current compensation schemes. As noted earlier, recognition of the principle that the state has some responsibility toward victims was not accompanied by a concomitant opening of the public coffers. The reverse was true: methods were sought for financing these schemes without draining public revenues. The most attractive solution, and one that has been widely adopted in the United States, was to transfer the financial burden to the offender. Indeed, this is undoubtedly seen to be a matter of ideology and justice rather than mere economy or administrative convenience. Offenders were the cause of victimization and should be made to pay. This approach undoubtedly lies behind the provision incorporated in many of the schemes for the subrogation to the state of the victim's remedies against the offender; this type of provision is primarily a matter of ideology, since, as noted above, the potential for substantial revenue by this mechanism seems to be limited. Such provisions tend to place the compensation program within a retribution-restitution framework. For if the state is to pay compensation to the victim and then to exact it from the offender, this is directly analogous to the restitution process of the criminal court. Rather than the judge ordering the offender to pay reparation to the victim, another state agency achieves the same result by a more circuitous route. On this analysis, compensation payments by the state possess the same degree of retributiveness as restitution orders (cf. chap. 7).

The other type of funding provision is much more important in practice but much more problematical from the point of view of the current analysis. As noted above, most state compensation schemes in the United States are funded, at least in part, by levies on certain categories of offenders. On the surface this, too, appears to be an expression of retributive principles: offenders are being made to pay for the harm inflicted upon victims.

However, this extension of the retribution principle is objectionable in many ways.[19] Offenders convicted of public order offenses or attempts, or of other charges involving no harm or almost no harm to a victim, are compelled to pay for the harm inflicted by other offenders. This may be seen as a form of collective punishment and may be criticized on a number of grounds of principle.

First, criminal law generally confines vicarious responsibility, the rationale for which is difficult to identify (Fletcher, 1978), to certain limited categories. Second, to place all offenders in a single category for the purpose of collective responsibility contradicts the trend of modern criminology to regard criminality as a relative concept rather than a characteristic that dichotomizes the population into "them" and "us" (or in this case, the liable and the exempt). Third, collective punishments that have been exacted in the past, whether in tribal society or in times of military occupation, have been condemned by international and human rights lawyers. Fourth, to adopt a Rawlsian analysis, it is doubtful whether persons "in the original position" would have wished to undertake responsibility for the harm inflicted as a result of offenses committed by others. If this is retribution, it is a far cry from the concept of desert as countenanced by advocates of the justice model of punishment.

On the other hand, these objections do not in principle apply to the financing of compensation schemes out of payments of fines (but see Thorvaldson and Krasnick, 1980). On the contrary, it seems wrong that the state, through the mechanism of the fine, should assume the victim's role in exacting retribution and should pocket the proceeds. Fine money should be available first and foremost for the benefit of victims. Of course, this differentiation between fines and special levies could be circumvented simply by increasing fines, so that additional funds were made available to finance victim compensation without any loss to other public revenues. However, while it is true that the level of fines is arbitrary and does not usually purport to be based upon scientific measures of offense seriousness, to raise fines beyond the level that seemed otherwise appropriate expressly for the purpose of assisting victims in general seems wrong in principle.

Conclusion

It seems that victim compensation schemes are based primarily on a desert model of (distributive) justice, or at best a rights model with desert as a limiting principle. Programs operating on this model, because of their eligibility criteria, their failure to disseminate information effectively, and other reasons considered above, benefit relatively few victims and have not been very favorably perceived. Moreover, their basic rationale is hard to defend. Both "rights" (unqualified by desert) and "need" are easier to defend as criteria for awarding compensation, but both would be costly; the first because all crime victims would have to be compensated in full, and the second because, apart from administrative complexity and costliness, it raises the issue of equality with victims of other types of misfortune.

Reimbursement of state expenditure by individual offenders is justifiable on the same general grounds as direct restitution payments. However, this does not apply to the imposition of a collective burden on entire categories of offenders.

Escrow

Another remedy unrelated to the criminal justice system that has been introduced in recent years is the establishment of escrow funds, by virtue of "Son-of-Sam" laws. Such laws are designed to prevent offenders from capitalizing on their offenses by selling their story to the media, following the example of the perpetrator of the Son-of-Sam murders in New York. The laws provide that monies paid under such contracts may be attached by the state and held in escrow for the benefit of victims who may subsequently succeed in bringing civil suits against the offender. In the absence of such suits, the monies may be paid into a Crime Victim Fund, to finance victim assistance or state compensation schemes, or may be returned to the offender. Under some laws, a percentage of the money may be made available for defense counsels' fees. Such laws have now been passed by most states (NOVA, 1989:16), and by Congress under the Victims of Crime Act of 1984.

On the face of it, such legislation—although it has encountered constitutional obstacles—seems to be of a generally positive character from the point of view of the criteria of the present study. If assets accruing to the defendant are held in escrow to meet future claims by the victim, this is merely a technique for enhancing the victim's chance of a successful suit under prevailing civil-law provisions. No substantial change in the sanctioning of defendants or the rights of victims is involved. In principle the justice of escrow provisions has thus to be measured according to the justice of allowing victims to bring a civil suit. Victim compensation by means of a civil suit, to be discussed in chapter 12, would appear to be a generally desirable objective from the point of view of the coping needs of the parties, perceptions of justice, and, with certain reservations, fundamental principles of justice.

Nevertheless two observations may be made regarding such legislation that cast serious doubt on its value. The first criticism is the rareness of the phenomenon. While acts of victimization are recorded in millions per annum, and of serious victimization in at least hundreds of thousands, the number of cases giving rise to the establishment of escrow funds is counted in single digits. The coping benefit of such legislation from the point of view of crime victims is thus minute. The phenomenon described in relation to victim compensation—namely, the adoption of legislation for political ends rather than as a solution to real problems—appears to apply here in an even more extreme form. The wave of Son-of-Sam or "notoriety-for-profit" statutes adopted in recent years may genuinely assuage the moral indignation of some sections of the electorate that offenders are capitalizing on their crimes, but it will do little to assist crime victims.

The second observation derives from the conceptual analysis employed in this study. Escrow is discussed in the present chapter as a remedy unconnected with the criminal justice system. In this respect it resembles public compensation schemes, which indeed are often responsible for administering the relevant funds (NOVA, 1989:16). However, as will emerge from the subsequent analysis of alternative models of justice, the underlying approach of the two remedies is radically different. Compensation schemes place responsibility for assisting the victim on the state; escrow is essentially an adjunct to a civil-law action instigated by the victim against the offender and is thus consistent with the approach that favors settlement of the conflict between the parties directly involved. Greater consideration should be devoted to the question of which of these two approaches is the more desirable. Further, if the facilitation of civil actions by victims against offenders is recognized as a desirable objective, why is such facilitation limited to those extremely rare cases in which offenders benefit from media contracts? Why not undertake more comprehensive reforms that would facilitate civil suits in general?

Not only have these laws been little used, they have now been dealt a further blow by the Supreme Court, which, in the 1991 case of *Simon & Schuster v. Members of the New York State Crime Victims Board* (50 CrL 2019) held that the New York Son-of-Sam law—which, it will be recalled, was the first such law to be enacted—was inconsistent with the First Amendment of the Constitution. While the objective of depriving offenders of the profits deriving from their offenses was deemed to be a worthy one, the law was too widely drafted, since *(a)* the reference to the crime committed might be relatively marginal to the work in question, and *(b)* there was no requirement that the "offender" should have been convicted of, or even charged with, the offense.[20] This "remedy," therefore, is of more interest for the theoretical issues it raises than for its practical implications.

10

"Catch-All" Remedies: Victim/ Witness Assistance and Victims' Bills of Rights

The two remedies dealt with in this chapter, victim/witness-assistance programs and victims' bills of rights, are not in fact specific reforms but comprehensive terms that effectively include or overlap with the reforms and proposals considered in the preceding chapters. The main difference between these two topics is that the first concept, victim/witness assistance, emphasizes services provided to victims from the point of view of the service provider, while the bill-of-rights concept focuses rather on the victim's perspective of the services to which he or she may be entitled, as well as on the victim's role in the criminal process vis-à-vis the offender. However, both terms are lacking in precision and may overlap. A publication of the Bureau of Justice Statistics (1983) classified "recognition of the rights of victims and witnesses" under the heading "Victim and Witness Assistance." Nevertheless, the difference in perspective referred to here, as well as differences of substance in the focal areas of concern, renders the separate treatment of each topic desirable.

Victim/Witness Assistance

The victim/witness-assistance program is perhaps the most popular expression of the victim movement. It appears to have received its initial impetus when the LEAA funded eight such programs in 1974 (Finn and Lee, 1983:v),[1] although according to Roberts (1990:44–45) the first such program was established in 1969. The American Bar Association also developed a Victim/Witness Assistance Project (see Lynch, 1976; ABA, 1981:5), and other organizations such as NOVA and Aurora became active in this field. Growth of such programs was slowed by the decline of federal budgets for this purpose at the end of the 1970s, but their support by local agencies ultimately provided them with greater security (Finn and Lee, 1983).

Moreover, there was a renewal of federal activity in this sphere. The Victim and Witness Protection Act of 1982 provided for the development of guidelines to be issued by the Department of Justice to ensure that law enforcement personnel became sensitized to the service needs of victims. Many specific proposals were incorporated in the President's Task Force on Victims of Crime of 1982, while the Victims of Crime Act of 1984 provided for federal funding to the chief executive of each state for the financial support of eligible crime victim assistance programs; thus "by 1986 the funding and stability of victim service and witness assistance programs had increased dramatically" (Roberts, 1990:46). In 1989 the Victims of Crime Act provided $43 million for distribution to local victim-service programs (NOVA, 1989:6). Moreover, states have devised numerous methods for raising revenue for this purpose, including penalties imposed on convicted offenders or fine surcharges, tax concessions, and alcohol taxes; and funds for programs assisting victims of domestic violence may be raised from charges on certificates of marriage, divorce, births, and deaths (ibid., 5–6).

Roberts (1990:42) refers to "over 600" programs serving crime victims in 1987. However, Davis and Henley (1990:157) and Young (1990:182) refer to between 5,000 and 6,000 programs! In Britain, too, victim-support programs increased rapidly during the 1980s (Maguire and Corbett, 1987:10), although state funding has been very limited, heavy reliance being laid on volunteer activity (Mawby and Gill, 1987; Rock, 1990). Some other European countries also have burgeoning victim-assistance movements (see *Guidelines for Victim Support in Europe*, 1989), and a number of the provisions of the UN Declaration of Basic Principles of Justice for Victims of Crime and Abuse of Power of 1985 relate to victim assistance (see secs. 14–17).

While victim/witness-assistance programs may differ considerably both in content and in priorities, a study conducted for the National Institute of Justice identified a "common set of assumptions" that was shared by 280 projects identified by the authors (Cronin and Bourque, 1981:7). These were

That victims and witnesses have been badly treated by the criminal justice system as well as by the criminal.

That projects based in local agencies or organizations can help to ameliorate this situation.

That the criminal justice system as well as individual victims and witnesses will benefit from the effort.

The specific purposes of the projects were also threefold:

To ameliorate the effects of criminal victimization by the offender or by the criminal justice system.

To envisage and facilitate the participation of victim and witnesses in the criminal justice system.

To improve the criminal justice process through more effective and efficient victim/witness utilization.

The specific content of the programs, as noted, may vary; one review identified six main areas of victim/witness assistance: (1) emergency services, (2) counseling, (3) advocacy and support services, (4) claims assistance, (5) court-related services, (6) system-wide services (Finn and Lee, 1983:8; within each area a number of specific services were listed, totaling 31). NOVA adopted an eightfold classification based upon the chronological order according to which the service would be provided: (1) emergency response, (2) victim stabilization, (3) resource mobilization, (4) representation of victim's views following arrest, (5) assisting victim prior to court appearance and (6) at court appearance, (7) presentence services, and (8) postsentence services (NOVA, n.d.; Young, 1982).[2]

The President's Task Force on Victims identified sixteen services that a model victim/witness-assistance unit should provide.[3] Other classifications appear in the earlier reviews by Rosenblum and Blew (1979) and in Dussich (1981), Schneider and Schneider (1981), Ziegenhagen and Benyi (1981), and Viano (1979:53ff.); some of these classifications focus on functional categorization of the services, others on differences in the underlying philosophies. The Victims of Crime Act of 1984 defined "services to victims of crime" as including the following four services: (1) crisis intervention services (defined as "counselling to provide emotional support in crises arising from the occurrence of crime"); (2) emergency services—transportation to court, short-term child care services, and temporary housing and security measures; (3) assistance in participating in criminal justice proceedings; and (4) payment of costs for a "forensic medical examination of a crime victim."[4]

Roberts (1990:31) presented some survey data indicating the frequency with which various services were provided by different programs. He found that some 60%–70% of the programs (a) explained the court process, (b) made referrals to other agencies, (c) provided court escorts, (d) helped the victim file claims to the compensation board, (e) educated the public, (f) advocated with an employer on behalf of the victim, and (g) provided transportation to court. However, this list does not include crisis counseling, which according to Roberts is the focal activity of some programs.

Since the various programs may provide any combination of these and other services, the development of a useful typology is problematical. One meaningful classification would be by the identity of the sponsoring agency, generally police, prosecution, or community-based organization (see Cronin and Bourque, 1980:14–15; Roberts, 1990:120–21). However, Cronin and Bourque (1980, 1981), who conducted a mail survey of 227 programs, developed a useful classification of their own, which appeared to be applicable to the universe of programs, namely, a division into those focusing on the victim as victim (the "victim model"), those emphasizing the needs of witnesses (the "witness model"), and those which attempted to combine the functions (the "victim-witness model").[5] The force of this classification was enhanced by an analysis (Weigend, 1982) of the rationales for, and implications of, the establishment of such programs, in which it was cogently argued that an orientation toward victims and an orientation toward witnesses are not merely different but actually inconsistent and conflicting: "The victim-program must seek to implement the client's wishes. . . . It should not be located in or have close ties to any law enforcement agency" (Weigend, 1982:8–9).

In spite of the proliferation of victim/witness-assistance programs, the boundless energy and relatively generous funding that have been invested in their development and maintenance, and the current official federal policy of renewed encouragement to the programs, hard data on their effectiveness have been relatively sparse (cf. Skogan et al., 1991:98). Some of the earlier publications provided useful summaries of the basic concepts of such programs (Viano, 1978; Young, 1982). There have also been at least five more comprehensive attempts to consider the way in which such programs actually function,[6] and some of these have incorporated some tentative evaluations. Only during the last few years have some more methodologically rigorous evaluations of the effectiveness of programs been undertaken, but on a selected and localized basis.

The more comprehensive analyses take one of two forms: an in-depth study of a number of selected programs, or a more general survey of the field. Thus Rosenblum and Blew (1979) presented an overall review of four of the better-known pioneering programs (in Brooklyn, N.Y., Milwaukee County, Wis., Multnomah County, Oreg., and Pima County, Ariz.), each of which had been independently evaluated by a research institute. Cronin and Bourque (1980, 1981), on the other hand, contacted 227 programs, of which 20 were visited and studied in greater depth by the authors and their colleagues. Their evaluation of the programs was based upon the evidence of written records made available to them. Much of the evaluative material in these records was problematical, however, since it was not the fruit of methodologically rigorous research (Cronin and Bourque, 1980:89ff). Similarly, Rosenblum and Blew (1979) differentiated between evaluation of (1) the program design, (2) delivery of services, and (3) the impact of the programs, and found the third level of evaluation the most problematic (59ff).[7]

The third overview was conducted by Finn and Lee (1983). This survey reviewed the available literature, contacted a number of programs, and visited six. This analysis, however, was concerned with the operational rather than the evaluative aspects of victim/witness-assistance programs.

In 1985 Roberts (1990) conducted a National Survey of Victim Service and Assistance Programs. Of 312 programs contacted, comprehensive information on the functioning of the programs was supplied by 184. In addition to the descriptive aspects of the study, it incorporated self-evaluation by program staff of their "strengths, problems and needed changes" (ibid., chap. 5). However, there was no direct evaluation of the impact of the services on the clients.

The last available overview was conducted in 1989 by Skogan et al. (1990, 1991). This involved an in-depth study of four programs (in Evanston, Ill., Rochester, N.Y., Pima County, Ariz., and Fayette County, Ky.). The emphasis here was on determining the needs of victims and assessing, on the basis of interviews with 470 victims, the extent to which these needs had been met by the programs.

As noted, some more localized studies have been designed more specifically to evaluate program impact. The dearth of evaluative data noted by Cronin and Bourque resulted in the sponsoring of an evaluative study of one specific program—in Pima County, Arizona—undertaken by the Institute for Social Analysis (Smith et al., 1984; Smith and Cook, 1984; Cook et al., 1987). The focus of this study was on the effects of crisis intervention (see, e.g., the literature review in Smith et al., 1984: chap. 1); but in addition to the sample of victims receiving crisis intervention services, an additional sample provided with "delayed services"—including counseling, assistance in applying for protection orders, social service referrals, and court services (Smith et al., 1984:22–23)—was also studied. Both samples were compared with a control group. Regrettably, allocation to the three groups was not randomized, such that "differences in victim adjustment which are detected among the comparison groups are not clearly attributable to the presence or absence of service" (10).

Other evaluations have been conducted in recent years by Skogan and Wycoff (1987), of a program whereby police in Houston contacted victims to offer assistance; and by Davis (1987), of an experiment conducted by the New York Victim Services Agency, whereby groups of victims were assigned to three different types of intervention, two psychological ("crisis intervention with supportive counseling" and "crisis intervention with cognitive restructuring") and one material. In both studies, experimental procedures were adopted and comparisons were made with groups who did not benefit from the interventions.

Mention should also be made here of the multilevel study of British victim-support schemes by Maguire and Corbett (1987). This study analyzed survey data received in relation to 177 of the 193 schemes listed in 1984 (11), but also included questionnaire data from the British Crime Survey and in-depth interviews with victims in selected districts. An evaluation study has also been conducted in the Netherlands (Steinmetz, 1988).

In the following pages an attempt will be made to consider the potential contribution of the programs from the point of view of the parameters of the present analysis, relying primarily on data emerging from the above-mentioned studies. Emphasis is placed here on programs involving the provision of material or therapeutic assistance, generally by specially appointed persons (including volunteers), rather than on guidelines or training courses directed at criminal justice personnel fulfilling their normal function (cf. Rosenbaum, 1987). Nor is the present analysis concerned with institutions specifically dealt with in other chapters, such as state compensation.

Coping Needs

The first precondition for an effective service is accessibility. However, Davis and Henley (1990) noted that, while little information is available on this, "the scant evidence that does exist suggests that service programs reach only a small fraction of persons victimized by crime"; while Maguire (1989:129) has estimated that in Britain, with the most extensive victim-support system in Europe, less than 5% of victims of *reported* crimes are reached, and probably no more than 1% of all crime victims. This applies even where an "outreach" policy is adopted, although this may not always be possible for reasons of confidentiality (Bureau of Justice Statistics, 1983). Where reliance is placed on victim initiative, the lack of knowledge regarding the existence of the programs (Friedman et al., 1982:12; Shapland et al., 1981:219) will be a barrier. On the other hand, there is evidence that victims who seek assistance, or those selected by the programs for this purpose, are likely to be among the more serious cases (Maguire and Corbett, 1987:215; Davis and Henley, 1990:167). Another limiting factor in this context may be a tendency for the schemes "to deal almost exclusively with one-off, stranger-to-stranger offences" (Corbett and Maguire, 1988:33).

However, even for those who are exposed to the programs, the evidence of their usefulness is far from unequivocal. Cronin and Bourque (1980), in the course of their comprehensive analysis of the benefits of victim-assistance programs, found that victims were generally favorably disposed toward the programs, but that it was difficult to find hard data that would identify specific benefits (see 93ff.; this part of their review related specifically to programs on the "victim model"). This conclusion has been largely supported by subsequent studies. Skogan et al. (1990) conducted a comprehensive study of the relationship between victim services and victim needs in four locations; the victims in their sample, half of whom had been in contact with a victim-assistance program, received some assistance with most of their problems—but generally not from the programs but from other sources (fig. 5). Of those requesting services in the survey by Hillenbrand and Smith (1989), of 359 victims, a majority reported receiving the service for most items (145). Again, the service was presumably not always arranged by victim-assistance personnel—for example, a relatively high proportion requested, and were granted, police protection. On the other hand, victim/witness staff based in prosecutors' offices are presumably helpful in supplying information regarding the criminal proceedings (Hillenbrand and Smith, 1989:164).

With respect to *financial benefits* to the victim, Cronin and Bourque found the evidence to be "sketchy." "It appears, for example, that projects can increase the quantity and quality of state victim compensation claims filed, but the claims review, approval, and disbursement process is out of project hands" (Cronin and Bourque, 1980:100). One benefit, however, that these authors found to be clearly established was the saving of time for witnesses, whose contacts with the criminal justice system, and in particular the courts, were better coordinated (Cronin and Bourque, 1981:40).

There is evidence in the literature that victims may take precautions to *prevent further victimization*, but there is no clear basis for attributing this to victim-assistance programs (ibid.; Skogan and Wycoff, 1987); indeed, programs frequently do not cater to the security needs of victims (Skogan et al., 1990). Victims are also thought to have benefited in recent years from a greater sensitization that has developed on the part of the police to their needs, but this, too, cannot unequivocally be attributed to the existence of the programs (Cronin and Bourque, 1981:98; and cf. Rosenbaum, 1987).

As to the contribution of such programs to the victim's ability to overcome *emotional and behavioral* problems, Salasin (1981:16) emphasized the lack of knowledge in this area and the inadequacy of traditional evaluation techniques (cf. also Rich, 1981:141), while another author has noted "the difficulties involved in providing a clear conceptual definition of effectual coping" (Wortman, 1983:215). Nevertheless, the evaluation projects have attempted to assess the programs in this respect. Thus Cronin and Bourque (1980) found that there was "almost no evidence about the success of victim projects in reducing emotional trauma" (99).

The Pima County evaluation studied this issue in considerable depth, adopting a number of output measures (anxiety, fear, stress, behavioral functioning, and nervousness). Fear levels remained constant for all three groups—those receiving crisis intervention, those provided with "delayed services," and controls—from the time of the critical interview until the follow-up interview some months later. The anxiety level, which dropped for all categories, dropped most steeply for the crisis-intervention sample ($p < 0.001$), while the mean stress levels dropped more for both treatment groups than for the controls ($p < 0.001$) (Smith et al., 1984:35–40). It cannot necessarily be concluded that the greater reduction in anxiety and stress was attributable to the treatment, since, as noted, allocation to the groups was not random but was probably related to the perceived needs of the victims. Nevertheless, the fact that the anxiety level for the crisis-intervention group actually dropped below that of the other categories by the second interview (albeit very slightly) indicated the probability of a program contribution.

The British study by Maguire and Corbett (1987) focused mainly on victims who had received assistance from victim-support personnel, but they also matched a small subsample (N = 26) with victims who had not received such support. They concluded that "there are signs . . . that a visit from a VSS volunteer may have some effect in reducing anger and, in particular, in altering attitudes towards the offender" (170); respondents were less punitive and more likely to agree to mediation.

The results of the quasi-experimental American studies referred to above were largely negative. In the study by Davis (1987), which compared the effects of two methods of crisis intervention with material assistance, as well as with a control group, no significant differences were found among the groups on various psychological measures applied over the first three months after victimization. Skogan and Wycoff (1987), who compared a sample offered assistance by police officers with a control group, found differences on various measures, including fear of crime and satisfaction with the police and the neighborhood, to be only minor, and mostly not in the expected direction. Similar types of experiments conducted in the Netherlands also produced largely negative results (Steinmetz, 1989).

Many programs have been limited to particular types of victims, notably victims of rape. Coates and Winston (1983) conducted a review of rape crisis centers. Of 63 centers responding, "92.5% reported that the groups had been an overall success." However, they noted that evaluation studies—including their own—were methodologically inadequate (e.g., absence of comparison groups), so that while it was generally observed that "support groups do ease feelings of deviance for most of their members, we still lack firm support for this conclusion" (183).

Various explanations are offered for these rather negative results. First, even an experimental design may not fully control for higher levels of need or traumatization among the experimental group (Steinmetz, 1989). Second, it may be difficult to measure the contribution of a usually very limited counseling program (involving perhaps one or two meetings). Third, a much longer period of counseling may be required for the more traumatized cases (Davis, 1987); while in Britain, where visits generally take place the day after the incident, the support will be absent during the period of relapse (Maguire, 1989:137). Fourth, it has also been observed that while the emphasis in these programs is generally upon psychological counseling, the greater need may actually be for material assistance, which many of the programs fail to provide (Davis and Henley, 1990:165–66). Skogan et al. (1990), in their study of the relationship between victim services and victim needs, found that many of the most frequently cited needs, particularly related to security and filing insurance, were not met by the programs and concluded that "there was not a very good match between victims' needs and victim services" (45). In Britain the reverse problem has been noted (Maguire, 1989:137), that is, victim-support volunteers focus on practical assistance where emotional support is needed. Finally, victims receiving assistance may have more contacts with the criminal justice system, giving rise to negative effects as a result of "secondary victimization" (Steinmetz, 1989).

The largely negative findings noted here may be partially balanced by at least some positive data relating to expressed satisfaction, which will be considered below. Nevertheless, the findings must give rise to concern in view of the high expectations accompanying the establishment of the programs; they also indicate the need for further research.

The coping needs of society may be considered here under the headings of *(a)* cost and *(b)* the contribution of the programs to the functioning of the criminal justice system. Much of the literature on victim/witness-assistance programs is of a practical nature and is concerned with budgeting and funding (cf. Roberts, 1990). Precise cost-benefit analysis, however, is a different matter. Rosenblum and Blew (1979), after considering this issue, concluded that "it is impossible precisely to assess the savings, if any, which accrue from them" (65). But Cronin and Bourque (1980) reported detailed calculations on the cost of various aspects of the programs, such as cost per client assisted, cost per contact, and cost per capita, per annum, for the population in the jurisdiction served. These varied according to the nature of the program. While estimates per capita of population served varied only between 13 and 23 cents, the median cost per client (in the sites visited for which data were available) varied between $7 for the "witness model" and $48 for the "victim model" (Cronin and Bourque, 1980:55, 77, 80). Smith et al. (1984:24) reported that the average cost per client for the Pima County program, which also handled disputes of a noncriminal nature, was $55; although for crisis intervention it was only about $34, since the crisis unit was manned mainly by volunteers. (The Victims of Crime Act of 1984 requires that volunteers be utilized as a condition of eligibility for federal funding.)

The authors compared these figures with the costs of other components of the criminal justice system such as trial or mediation, estimated at $100 to $200, and probation, estimated at between $450 and $1200. This is somewhat misleading, in that the cost of the programs is cumulative with these costs rather than alternative. Perhaps the point intended to be made, however, is that the cost of providing such assistance to the victim is relatively modest, particularly when compared with the amounts expended on the offender. On the other hand, Lowenburg (1981) reported on an earlier evaluation of the same program conducted by the Stanford Research Institute which concluded that there was a slight net saving: "Overall, the program produced $127,122 in annual measurable social benefits compared with an annual operation cost of $121,560" (409).

But even if the costs are moderate, the financial benefits to the system may not be substantial. Saving results primarily from the fact that closer contacts with victims or witnesses may result in fewer continuances and less waste of police time. Moreover, victim/witness programs may be performing tasks otherwise undertaken by the police. On this latter point, Cronin and Bourque (1980:116–17) concluded that police time was, indeed, saved, freeing police officers for other tasks.

It has also been generally anticipated that enhanced cooperation would bring about not only financial savings but also an increased probability of securing a conviction in the current case (cf. Karmen, 1990:180–81) and a greater readiness to cooperate in the future—for example, by the reporting of offenses. Insofar as such cooperation is calculated to render law enforcement more effective, this, too, would have implications for financial costs.

Considerations of this type have been instrumental in the establishment and encouragement of witness-oriented programs by law enforcement authorities. Analysis of the available evidence by Cronin and Bourque (1980:104–12, 120–21) showed that the programs did produce modest increments—about 10% to 15%—in witness appearance. However, these findings are not uniform (Karmen, 1990:181). Moreover, there was no evidence of either an increase in conviction rates or a greater inclination on the part of clients to cooperate with the criminal justice system in the future (Cronin and Bourque, 1980:91–92; cf. Davis, 1983:240). These findings will be considered further in the ensuing discussion relating to measures of satisfaction with the programs.

Perceived Justice Needs

There does not appear to be much specific evidence regarding the effect of victim/witness schemes on perceptions of the justice system, although there is certainly some evidence of consumer satisfaction with individual services. Referring to the "victim model," Cronin and Bourque commented: "It appears that a majority of project clients do like the services offered and will report that they have been helpful. Thus if we take the client opinion at face value, the victim is helped by victim model projects" (1980:99). The same applied also to the "witness model" (115). Rosenblum and Blew (1979) referred to one program survey that reported that "99 percent indicated they would contact the program again if they had similar problems" (54). Similarly, in the Pima County study, 89% of victims in the crisis-intervention sample stated that the program helped, as did 86% of those receiving "delayed services" (Smith et al., 1984); and high rates of "consumer satisfaction" were also noted by Maguire and Corbett (1987:154–55).

Further, the INSLAW study referred to in chapter 2 reported that a victim program increased the probability that the victim would be familiar with the outcome of the case and less likely to report that he or she had not been kept informed (Hernon and Forst, 1983:33–35); these are issues that were described earlier as being critical factors in causing victim dissatisfaction.

Not all the evidence is quite as unequivocal, however. The INSLAW study found that only 67% of the sample were satisfied with the victim-service staff, which was no higher than the level of satisfaction with prosecutors and rather lower than the rate of satisfaction with police officers (Hernon and Forst, 1984:46). Moreover, in the Pima County evaluation, in spite of the positive results reported above, 49% of the sample receiving crisis intervention and 75% of those receiving "delayed services" felt that they were in need of more assistance, as compared with only 44% of those who had received no services, whose need should have been greatest (Smith et al., 1984:67).[8] No more than 10%–11% of the samples interviewed designated the program as being their most helpful source of support; family, friends, or even the police were named in this connection more frequently than the victim-assistance program (68–69).

Further, Cronin and Bourque (1980), in spite of their specific findings relating to victims' reported reactions, commented that "the evidence for increases in victim or witness satisfaction associated with either project type also is relatively weak" (92). And while expressing general satisfaction with services provided, "clients apparently are not markedly more satisfied with the system, more 'willing' to cooperate, or more likely to report crime" (Cronin and Bourque, 1981:30). Similar findings were also reported by Rosenblum and Blew (1979:62–63). Finally, some of the earlier surveys even raised doubts about the general degree of satisfaction with the programs (Britton et al., 1976; Hunter and Frey, 1980).

It may be that the limited proven effectiveness of victim/witness-assistance programs is simply due to the methodological difficulties of showing significant objective or even attitudinal changes. Davis and Henley (1990) cited the Pima County evaluation as follows: "The authors concluded that 'despite the victims' feelings that the program helped them considerably, the measures of emotional trauma did not indicate any substantial effects' " (168). It seems from this citation that the authors of the evaluation did not attribute significance to "the victims' feelings that the program helped them considerably," in the light of the negative results of the psychological tests. Maguire (1989), however, explicitly regards victim satisfaction as insufficient as an objective for victim support: "VSS [Victim Support Schemes] should not be satisfied simply because their clients are satisfied" (138).

It may also be that programs are in need of modification. Greater attention should perhaps be paid to Weigend's argument on the need to focus either on victim or on witness needs, to prevent conflicting objectives (cf. also Karmen, 1990:181). Similarly, a researcher associated with the Victim Services Agency in New York, which conducted some of the earlier surveys, concluded that "victim/witness programs had little success in increasing cooperation because they perpetuated the treatment of victims as nothing more than witnesses for the prosecution" (Davis, 1983:297).

However, it is also possible that victim/witness-assistance programs are capable of providing a kind of "process" satisfaction at the time the service is provided, but not of influencing victims' long-term perceptions of the criminal justice system, or even of the programs themselves. It may be that the citizen has an operational dichotomy between, on the one hand, his or her expectations from "the system," represented in this case mainly by the police (Shapland et al., 1981:215), and, on the other hand, informal support networks that may be perceived as the mediating agency for eliciting justice from the offender (ibid., 213; Friedman et al., 1982:65). This dichotomy may leave no clear role for victim-assistance programs. Possible support for this view may be derived from the Hamburg survey, which found that relatively few respondents—and fewer victims than nonvictims—specified "victim assistance" as the most important need or interest of victims of an assault or theft; see Sessar (1984: table 1), Beurskens and Boers (1985: table 2).

In any case it seems that in spite of the considerable expenditure of funds (especially in the U.S.), and of human resources (particularly where services are largely volunteer-run, as in Britain), the potential contribution of victim/witness-assistance programs is not yet entirely clear; further research is required, and greater attention must be paid to conceptual issues (cf. Mawby and Gill, 1987), such as the structure and personnel of the programs, the optimal balance between counseling services and material assistance, the optimal timing of the intervention, the degree to which special programs and services should be developed for victims alone or for victims and witnesses (cf. Knudten et al., 1976; Denton, 1979), and, if for victims only, whether programs should specialize further according to the type of victim[9] (see ABA, 1981: chap. 3) or type of service.

Fundamental Principles of Justice

The justice considerations related to victim-assistance programs are in some respects similar to those arising in the context of victim compensation. These programs do not constitute an integral part of the criminal justice system, and the retributive aspects related specifically to righting the wrong inflicted do not arise here; but the question of priorities in the allocation of public resources—and in particular the question whether crime victims merit priority over other types of victims in competing for these resources—seems to be identical. Moreover, the possibility of drawing upon the offender's assets by way of fines or penalties in order to finance victim-assistance programs also arises here. Indeed, the Victims of Crime Act of 1984 adopts the identical funding mechanism for both compensation schemes and victim assistance.

Since victim assistance is not generally governed by statute, it is less closely linked to the concept of *rights*. Victim assistance is not specifically referred to as a right under the Victims' Rights and Restitution Act of 1990, at either the federal or the state level. However, the act does require that a "responsible official . . . inform a victim of public and private programs that are available to provide counseling, treatment, and other support for the victim" (sec. 503(c)(1)). Moreover, the Victims of Crime Act of 1984 requires state compensation boards to compensate for mental health counseling (cf. NOVA, 1989:21–22). Insofar as these boards are governed by *desert* in their concept of the "worthy victim" (see chap. 8, above), limitations deriving therefrom will apply to the funding of counseling too.

It is an interesting question whether victim-assistance programs are also governed by desert considerations. In Britain, where victim support sometimes involves a "filtering" process, stereotypic views as to which victims are worthy of assistance may be introduced where the filtering is implemented by criminal justice officials (Maguire and Corbett, 1987:87, 99–100), introducing an element of desert in what is otherwise perceived as a *needs*-based system (Mawby and Gill, 1987:131). Mawby (1988), however, is critical of need as a criterion for assistance, in part because of the difficulty of establishing objective measures of need, while survey evidence indicates that subjective perceptions are very fluid (131–32). Thus Mawby and Gill (1987) favor a rights orientation that, in addition to information and compensation, would include "the right to specialist advice and support," including "mandatory automatic referral with . . . the onus on victims to refuse" (231).

British victim advocates tend to have reservations regarding a rights orientation, which is identified with "antioffender" overtones associated with the U.S. victim movement (Mawby, 1988:130) and is also seen as potentially derogating from the emphasis on voluntary services (Reeves, 1988), although this emphasis is not necessarily perceived as precluding the advocacy of equal access to these services (ibid.)! As indicated above, however, the rights rhetoric reflected in the incorporation of victim assistance in legislative enactments does not necessarily entail the bestowal of *enforceable* rights. There seems to be a strong case for providing all crime victims with a right of access to victim assistance agencies. It is much more problematical to define specific services that could be claimed as of right, particularly under a system operated largely by volunteers, which Mawby and Gill appear to support.

Another justice-related issue worthy of consideration is the nature of the relationship of the assistance program to the community (cf. Elias, 1986), and the extent to which there is a genuine contribution here to community justice (to be discussed in chap. 11). This, in turn, together with the question of the relationship of victim-assistance programs to established criminal justice agencies, will have implications for the type and extent of social control exercised by these programs and their ability to adopt nonestablishment positions on victim-related policies.

Conclusion

A review of the available evidence on the treatment of the victim in the criminal justice system (see above, chaps. 2, 4, and 5) showed that both the objective (coping) and the subjective (perceived) needs of crime victims are unmet by the traditional model of the criminal justice system. It has therefore been regarded as self-evident that what Biderman (1981:28) called the "burgeoning victim assistance industry" would meet these needs, and this appears to have been the assumption behind the federal legislation designed to fund victim/witness-assistance programs.

However, rather little is as yet known regarding Cronin and Bourque's third (and main) hypothesis relating to these programs, to the effect that "the criminal justice system as well as individual victims and witnesses will benefit from the effort." While on some level services are clearly being provided to some individual victims—usually generating a positive response—the overall benefits both to victims and to the criminal justice system may be marginal and not worthwhile in cost-benefit terms. Further, the plethora of models and objectives of such programs make it likely that some will be more beneficial than others, but the one study located that attempted to evaluate alternative approaches (Smith et al., 1984) found no significant differences between them. There is a similar lack of knowledge on such issues as the need for specialized services for crime victims and for programs oriented to special categories of victims (children, rape victims, etc.), the feasibility of combining victim with witness assistance (cf. Weigend's thesis referred to above), and the problem of a diffusion of agencies which may be operating simultaneously (cf. Shapland, 1983:236).

Further, while the need of victims for support, and in particular emotional support, has been established by the research reviewed in chapter 4, it appears that the programs do not always place their emphasis on the areas of greatest need. Moreover, it may be that organized initiatives, whether professional or voluntary, cannot substitute for informal support networks (Friedman et al., 1982; cf. Skogan et al., 1990).

The need for more research in this area was most clearly articulated by Cronin and Bourque (1980) in their review of the available evidence. These authors listed many of the issues on which such research might focus (appendix D). Smith et al. (1984) were generally more optimistic—an optimism perhaps not altogether justified by their own findings; but they, too, pointed to the need for paying greater attention to the long-term needs of victims, and for further research (105–6). Similarly, the UN review, while also expressing considerable optimism, observed that "the absence of a theoretical framework and of scientific evaluation of most of the services offered prevents accurate assessments of their efficacy, despite the appreciation expressed by victims" (*Victims of Crime*, 1985:43–44). More recent researches have improved this situation only marginally. The Victims of Crime Act of 1984 requires that programs funded by federal subsidy demonstrate "a record of providing effective services" (sec. 1404 (b)(1)(B)(1)). This requirement necessitates a more comprehensive debate on the meaning of "effectiveness" and of the criteria for its measurement, as well as the implementation of evaluations in order to determine whether these criteria are being met.

Finally, the orientation in the United States (unlike Britain) toward the provision of victim services on a rights basis—a trend given further impetus by the "bills of rights," to be dealt with in the next section—necessitates further conceptual thinking *(a)* as regards the relative merits of *victim-*

oriented programs as compared with *witness*-oriented programs, and *(b)* as to the relationship between the provision of victim assistance by the state on the one hand, and the enhanced role of the victim in the criminal justice system on the other, an issue that will be discussed further in chapter 12.

Victims' Bills of Rights

The concept of a victims' bill of rights is one of the more recent of the victim-oriented innovations discussed in this work. One of its earliest proponents appears to have been Reiff (1979) in his book *The Invisible Victim*, in which a chapter was devoted to his proposal for a "bill of rights for victims." As with many other of the victim-related proposals, it quickly became popular. A Victims' Bill of Rights was enacted by the state of Wisconsin in 1980, and by 1988, 45 states had adopted such bills (NOVA, 1989:7). Many states have recently passed constitutional amendments guaranteeing victims' rights (cf. National Victim Center, 1994; Lamborn, 1995), and in some cases, such as Arizona, the term "victims' bill of rights" has been expressly adopted. At the federal level, the Victims' Rights and Restitution Act of 1990 articulated a list of victim rights applicable to the federal jurisdiction and exhorted all states to adopt the "goals of the Victims of Crime Bills of Rights" (cf. above, chap. 1). At the international level, similar concepts have been incorporated in the UN Declaration of Basic Principles of Justice for the Victims of Crime and Abuse of Power, while the British Home Office has published a "Victim's Charter."

What are the rights of the victim envisaged by such proposals? Naturally these vary from list to list. NOVA (n.d.) proposed seven main "rights for victims and witnesses": (1) a right to be treated with dignity and compassion, (2) a right to protection from intimidation and harm, (3) a right to be informed concerning the criminal justice process, (4) a right to counsel, (5) a right to reparations, (6) a right to preservation of property and employment, and (7) a right to due process in criminal court proceedings (4–5). Each of these rights was subdivided into a number of more specific rights, numbering 29 in all.[10] The UN declaration has four main components: access to justice and fair treatment, restitution, compensation, and assistance. Reiff's list comprised nine items (Reiff, 1979:114), while state legislation appears to focus mainly upon criminal justice proceedings and practical problems related to these (NOVA, 1989:6–7).

How do the rights differ from the services to victims discussed in the previous pages in the context of victim/witness-assistance programs? First, as noted in the introduction to this chapter, the perspective is different, for whereas victim-assistance debates tend to focus on the structure of the agencies concerned and the nature of the services they offer, the bill-of-rights rhetoric relates more explicitly to the victim. By the same token, the ideology is different, since the term *right* suggests an absolute duty on the part of the state to respect and protect the right, whereas victim-assistance programs tend to use the language of "need" (see above).

Third, the concept of a victims' bill of rights is more comprehensive than that of victim services, since it includes items such as compensation and restitution which are not generally an integral part of victim/witness-assistance programs, although such programs may assist in the claiming of such remedies. Indeed, the victim-rights concept is sometimes even taken to include issues that relate primarily to the enforcement of law and sanctions vis-à-vis the offender, and only indirectly (if at all) to the victim, such as the insanity defense and plea bargaining (see, e.g., the California Bill of Rights; McCoy, 1987:50–51).

NOVA (n.d.:12–13) attempted to integrate the concepts of rights and assistance by presenting a chart of "the victim rights system" in which the various services that may be offered to victims are considered on a stage-by-stage basis. Indeed, these were the very stages proposed by Marlene Young (the executive director of NOVA) in her analysis of victim assistance considered earlier (Young, 1982a). It is evident, however, that these eight stages, representing the chronological order of experiences of victim/witnesses from the commission of the crime to the termination of the criminal proceedings, differ both literally and analytically from the seven *rights* identified by NOVA as described in the previous section. Indeed, since this chart includes the various forms of assistance that "family and friends" are invited to provide the victim, it seems difficult to reconcile the services specified therein with the concept of victim rights, except perhaps in a vague moral sense.

The issue of victims' rights is thus distinct from victim/witness assistance and is deserving of independent attention. At the same time, many of the specific proposals designated as victims' rights have been considered under other specific headings: victim/witness assistance, restitution, compensation, victim involvement in the criminal process, and so on. For this reason it will not be necessary in this section to consider most of the rights themselves from the particular perspective of this study—that is, their capacity to meet the coping needs and perceived justice needs of the parties, and to comply with fundamental principles of justice. However, insofar as their designation as "rights," or as components of "bills of rights," may raise issues that have not been dealt with adequately in earlier chapters, these will be dealt with briefly below.

Coping Needs

In principle it may seem that the designation of certain legislative measures as a victims' bill of rights would not in itself bring any special benefits to the victim, beyond those incorporated in legislation dealing with these same topics—victim compensation, victim-impact statements, and so on—but not so designated. At the same time, there may be certain advantages from the point of view of the victim's interests in such designation. The main advantage of such designation would seem to be the probability that a number of victim-oriented provisions will be adopted within a short time. The adoption of legislation is a complex procedure, and the likelihood that a number of different bills, sponsored by different legislators on different occasions, would all be adopted would surely be small. A package of proposals, however, may not be substantially more difficult to legislate than a bill dealing with a single topic,[11] or, as in the case of California, may be a means whereby a popular initiative may bypass legislative obstacles (McCoy, 1987:16–17). Moreover, the addition of the attractive nomenclature "victims' bill of rights" may actually enhance the chances of the proposals' adoption by the appropriate body.

In theory a more substantive benefit might follow from such designation. It has been seen that certain benefits offered to victims are granted on a partial or discretionary basis: compensation schemes have eligibility requirements and are frequently *ex gratia*; victim/witness-assistance programs may be localized or selective in their target populations. The classification of such benefits as victim rights suggests the recognition of a general legal basis for the pursuance of such benefits, with a corresponding duty upon the government to provide them; this will apply a fortiori if the bill of rights is incorporated into the constitution, as has in effect now occurred in an increasing number of states. Thus the benefits would be offered not only to persons perceived as "suitable" or "worthy" victims based upon a desert-oriented philosophy, but to all victims qua victims.

However, it seems doubtful whether this has been the result of the legislative technique whereby victims' bills of rights have been adopted. This issue could be clarified further by means of a close analysis of certain types of legislation, such as the introduction of victim-compensation schemes, comparing legislation adopted independently with legislation enacted as part of a victims' bill of rights, in order to determine whether the latter technique results in a legally more advantageous status being granted to the victim, whether as a result of more positively formulated wording incorporated in such provisions, or of the courts' applying principles of interpretation more favorable to victims.

While no specific study of this nature appears to have been conducted, some more generalized findings are available on the impact of this type of legislation. Clark (1986) attempted to evaluate the implementation of New York State's Bill of Rights, "known as the Fair Treatment Standards for Victims," enacted in 1984. Agencies reported being in compliance with many of the standards, except where lack of funding prevented this.

In the course of a more comprehensive study, Hillenbrand and Smith (1989) hypothesized that "practitioners in states with specific legislated rights would be more likely to extend those rights to victims than practitioners in other states" (162). However, they found that "with few exceptions, the contents of the legislation reviewed in the study made no significant difference in the frequency prosecutors, probation officials, judges, and victim-witness personnel reported they informed or notified victims, consulted with them, considered their views, or provided them services" (163). It might be argued that this finding is actually favorable to victims' bills of rights. *All* the states in their survey had *some* victim-related legislation, which varied only "in the specific rights encompassed and in the features of those rights" (162). It may be that such legislation has a "halo effect," producing benefits in related areas not specified in the legislation of the particular state.

It may also be that victims' rights legislation is a necessary but not sufficient condition for the provision of the intended benefits. The authors of the above study found that "prosecutors with funds to implement victims rights said they provided certain rights in a number of specific areas more often than prosecutors without such funds" (163; see also 164–65). This confirms the findings of the New York study referred to above.

Apart from the specific benefits generally included in victims' bills of rights, this concept is also sometimes seen to include far-reaching forms of protection, as reflected in the bill of rights advocated for the states under the 1990 legislation, to the effect that "victims of crime should be treated with compassion, respect and dignity throughout the criminal justice process" (sec. 506(1)), and the more categorical right granted under section 502(b)(1) "to be treated with fairness and with respect for the victim's dignity and privacy."[12] The operationalization of such rights would clearly bring benefits to victims beyond those specified under other headings.

However, apart from the question whether rights such as dignity and respect should be exclusive to crime victims, it is also unclear how such rights could be enforced. Indeed, as noted in chapter 1, federal authorities initially avoided the rights terminology in favor of "standards" in order to prevent this issue arising. Subsequent legislation overcame the enforcement issue by means of the insertion of exemption clauses. Thus section 502 of the Victims' Rights and Restitution Act of 1990 includes a clause specifying that "this section does not create a cause of action or defense in favor of any person arising out of the failure to accord to a victim the rights enumerated" (cf. also NOVA, 1989:6–7). On the other hand, it has been suggested that the courts may nevertheless retain the formal power to enforce such provisions (Goldstein, 1984), in which case the question of the degree of dignity with which a victim is treated—or even the amount of compassion shown—might be justiciable. The Texas constitutional amendment of 1989, which grants the victim "the right to be treated with fairness and respect for the victim's dignity and privacy throughout the criminal justice process" (art. 1, sec. 30(a)(1)), provides the victim with "standing to enforce the rights enumerated in this section" (sec. 30(e)).

As to the effects of victims' rights legislation on *defendants*, these will not generally differ from the implications of the specific proposals incorporated therein, as considered elsewhere in this study, except insofar as the rights may have been incorporated into the state's constitution; for example, the "right to receive prompt restitution from the person or persons convicted" under sec. 2.1.8 of the Arizona Constitution. Indeed, the victim's right under this same constitutional amendment to be present at the parole hearing has resulted in the revocation of parole where the victim was not properly notified of this right (*State ex rel. Hance v. Arizona Bd. of Pardons and Parole*, 150 Ariz. Adv. Rep. 42, 1993).

Mention has also been made of the extension of the concept of victims' rights to include matters pertaining directly to the prosecution and punishment of offenders, as occurred in the case of the citizens' initiative in California. Thus, attempts to abolish or limit the insanity defense or plea bargaining, or to erode the exclusionary rule, have clear implications—generally detrimental—for defendants, and have resulted in objections from the American Civil Liberties Union (cf. Meador, 1982), as well as constitutional challenges (McCoy, 1987:49).

Perceived Justice Needs

No empirical evidence is available to me on the perceived significance of victim-oriented reforms being designated as "rights," or being incorporated in a victims' bill of rights. It seems reasonable to suppose that such designation is welcomed by victims, as well as by the public at large. Indeed, this is undoubtedly one of the attractions of such legislation: the legislators are seen to be providing a remedy for a need with which most of their constituents can identify. Moreover, it may be perceived as having the moral equivalence of the Bill of Rights incorporated in the U.S. Constitution. Since the Bill of Rights is seen as protecting offenders and suspected offenders, the use of this terminology creates an aura of balance, and hence of perceived justice. The British government's Victim's Charter also uses an emotive term, with associations dating back to the Magna Carta!

However, as noted earlier—particularly in the context of victim compensation—there may be a substantial gap between the stated objectives of this type of legislation and its practical results. The gap is likely to be further camouflaged by attaching a popular slogan to such legislation, although if victim rights were to be effectively and comprehensively recognized by such legislation, at considerable financial cost to the taxpayer, popular attitudes might prove to be more equivocal.

Finally, the question of the *defendant's* perspective of victim rights as a concept—as distinct from specific measures that have been considered elsewhere—is one of which little is known and which requires research.

Fundamental Principles of Justice

Various justice-related issues that arise in connection with the different proposals incorporated in victims' bills of rights have been discussed in this book in the context of these proposals, while the more general issues of fundamental rights, and of victims' rights vis-à-vis the state, are discussed in chapters 6 and 12.

Advocates of victims' bills of rights have, in particular, sought some general overall principle of victim rights which should serve as a basis for their recognition. NOVA's basis for its advocacy of victim rights is rather nebulous.[13] Reiff argues more persuasively that "every criminal act involves a breach of law and a person wronged. The duty and obligation of the criminal justice system is to rectify both these acts, not to ignore the person wronged and deal exclusively with the breach of law" (Reiff, 1979:112).[14] The purpose of his proposed bill of rights is "to make the victim whole again,"[15] to guarantee that "he or she will be restored to whatever condition of life existed before the criminal act" (ibid.). While this principle appears to have a certain cohesiveness, it shares some of the weaknesses of the NOVA rationale in that it ignores the justice issues— although these are dealt with by Reiff in his discussion—and is ultimately unworkable. A victim can rarely in fact be restored to his or her "previous condition of life," so that the issue becomes one of compensation. Since it leaves open the question of who is to compensate and even how the compensation is to be calculated, it does not appear to provide an adequate foundation for a universal principle of victim rights.

The problem becomes more acute when it is proposed to elevate victim rights to a constitutional principle, or to a precept of international law. The attempt by Aynes (1984) to recognize the existence of such a right today under the Fourteenth Amendment was discussed in chapter 6 and was shown to be problematic. Hence victim advocates have supported an amendment to the constitution for this purpose. The amendment to the U.S. Constitution proposed by the President's Task Force on Victims in 1982 related exclusively to victim participation in the decision-making stages of the criminal justice system and was therefore considered in chapter 8. As noted above, however, a number of states have adopted constitutional amendments of a more comprehensive nature, including the right to be treated with respect and dignity—in Rhode Island even with "sensitivity"—by criminal justice officials (see NOVA, 1989:9; National Victim Center, 1994).

The provision of explicit guarantees under the Constitution is surely the ultimate expression of concern for crime victims. However, it raises more acutely a number of questions related to the role of the victim which have been referred to elsewhere in this book, such as whether the Constitution is an appropriate mechanism for guaranteeing rights vis-à-vis other individuals (as opposed to the government), and whether guaranteeing victims' rights is necessarily at the expense of the offender, and, if so, how the two bills of rights can be reconciled. It also raises the question of the justifiability of granting victims priority over other needy or injured categories, but on this issue victim advocates may now cite the UN declaration in their support.

11

Informal Modes of Dispute Resolution

In recent years there has developed a strong movement in favor of the replacement—or, more usually, the supplementing—of traditional adjudicatory modes of justice by informal modes of dispute resolution. Unlike most of the proposals under discussion in this study, the "alternatives" or "informal-justice" movement has not been orientated primarily toward the victim. In this respect it bears a similarity to the restitution movement discussed in chapter 7, which may be considered its stepsister.

In another respect the "informal-alternatives" movement, as it will be termed here, has more in common with the just-deserts movement, in that both movements have taken the form of a broadly based crusade in favor of a major change of orientation in the justice system. The irony is that while these two movements were almost precisely contemporaneous in development,[1] they have been almost directly conflicting in objectives, the one advocating greater normative precision and formalism, and the other the reverse.[2] Moreover, while it is true that the informal-alternatives movement, unlike the just-deserts movement, is concerned primarily with *civil* justice, it is sometimes specifically applied to criminal justice, too, and indeed to a large degree purports to abolish this distinction. For this reason the topic is undoubtedly relevant to the subject matter of the present study.

274

What are the forces behind the move toward informalism? One of the most powerful of these forces has surely been the professional legal establishment, or at least significant sections of it. In 1976 leading jurists (including Chief Justice Warren Burger) convened the National Conference on the Causes of Popular Dissatisfaction with the Administration of Justice. The conference was held in commemoration of the address delivered by Roscoe Pound to the American Bar Association seventy years earlier entitled "The Causes of Popular Dissatisfaction with Administration of Justice," with a view to reviving this theme and drawing policy implications from it.[3] It was felt that the legal system had become overburdened to the detriment of the functioning of the courts and all parties concerned. At the conference Frank Sander presented a seminal paper entitled "Varieties of Dispute Processing," in which he proposed "a flexible and diverse panoply of dispute resolution processing" (Sander, 1976:130), including the use of arbitration and mediation techniques in appropriate cases.[4] The Department of Justice and the American Bar Association followed through with programs to develop alternatives to conventional adjudication methods (Bell, 1978; Erickson, 1978a, 1978b).

If the legal establishment was interested primarily in relieving the regular system of an oppressive caseload, some supporters of informal alternatives have emphasized the needs of the public, or that section of the public for whom the regular system was too remote, whether because of its cost or its technicality: the "neglect of the plaintiff"—or potential plaintiff—is the direct civil-law equivalent of the "neglect of the victim." This perception of "unmet needs" (cf. Curran, 1977:260–61) led to the "access-to-justice" movement, which generated a not inconsiderable literature (see, e.g., Cappelletti and Garth, 1978).

However, many advocates of informal alternatives have not regarded these alternatives exclusively as second-best substitutes for the "real thing." The more radical or romantic advocates have viewed informal proceedings as a desirable end in themselves, a more humane, "warmer way of disputing" (Smith, 1978), or a means of establishing "socialized courts" (Harrington, 1982). This appears to have been true of Griffiths (1970), who advocated a judicial proceeding that would resemble the settlement of a family argument; of Danzig (1973), whose detailed proposal for the reorganization of the criminal justice system in urban areas stimulated much of the literature on this topic; and of Christie (1977), whose well-known essay "Conflicts as Property" advocated the replacement of prevailing systems of adjudication in criminal cases by an informal, decentralized, and deprofessionalized proceeding. Moreover, the last two writers also adhered to a neighborhood or community orientation for the justice system. According to this approach, not only should dispute-resolution proceedings treat the views of the individual parties concerned with greater respect, but the resolution of the dispute should also be recognized as being the concern of the immediate social environment in which the disputants reside, rather than of a distant, impersonal, and monolithic state. Support for this approach may also be found in the "republican theory" of Braithwaite and Pettit (1990; see esp. 121–22).

Another version of the radical romantics may perhaps more accurately be described as the "religious romantics" (cf. Sebba, forthcoming). Some of the pioneers of informal alternatives, and in particular of the victim-offender reconciliation projects (VORPs), were associated with the Menno-nites and the Quakers (Peachey, 1989; Marshall and Merry, 1990). These "alternative" advocates tend to emphasize the need for the offender to acknowledge responsibility and to seek an informal "restorative" proce-dure (Zehr, 1990), generally operating *within* the criminal justice system, whether in substitution for or in addition to the regular proceedings. This approach will often lay emphasis on meetings or confrontations (cf. chap. 8) between offenders and victims, although not necessarily between offend-ers and their *own* victims (cf. Launay and Murray, 1989).

The above approaches reflect the three main declared objectives of infor-malism: (1) reduction of judicial overload, (2) access to justice, and (3) a "superior process" (cf. Johnson, 1980). Another group, consisting of some criminal justice specialists, has seen informalism as bringing specific bene-fits to the parties to the criminal act—offenders and their victims. Particu-lar emphasis has been placed here on the offenders. Informalism may in this context be seen as an integral part of the rehabilitation and labeling philosophy, more specifically, as an integral part of the concept of *di-version*. Most diversion programs require an informal hearing involving police or probation officers, as well as quasi-judicial personnel, often pur-porting to represent the community. Of particular relevance in the present context are those proceedings in which the victim also participates; restitu-tion programs, in particular, which also may be classified as an informal alternative, are clearly calculated to benefit the victim. Relatively few studies, however, have considered the informal-alternative movement spe-cifically from the victimological point of view (but see Sheleff, 1977), although there has been a greater emphasis on this approach in recent publications, particularly in Britain (see Wright and Galaway, 1989; Wright, 1991; and Davis, 1992). Finally, in addition to the supposed bene-fits to the machinery of justice and to the parties involved, it has also been suggested that informal justice—in particular community-based justice—can be a vehicle for social change (cf. Warhaftig, 1981).

Further support for the various arguments in favor of informal alternatives has derived from a large body of literature,[5] much of it pointing to the existence and apparent success of informal dispute mechanisms in a variety of settings over space and time. The main focus has been upon anthropological studies of primitive societies (see, e.g., Felstiner and Drew, 1978; Nader and Todd, 1978; Meschievitz and Galanter, 1982), famous illustrations being "The Cheyenne Way" (Llewellyn and Hoebel, 1941), and the Kpelle Moot in Liberia (see Aaronson et al., 1977:5); but studies have also been reported of comrades' courts in socialist societies (Naumova, 1983) and specialist administrative tribunals in Western industrialized societies (Blegvad, 1983). Moreover, in addition to a wide-ranging academic literature on conflict resolution in various contexts of human activity, such as divorce mediation, labor negotiations, and international relations, specialist journals have emerged on the resolution of legal conflicts.[6]

The result of the various pressures in favor of alternative dispute resolution—"the unusual alliance that makes up the ADR" (Singer, 1990:7)—has not been confined to generating literature. It has also resulted in the adoption of specific programs. A number of experimental programs were established during the 1970s (see Cook et al., 1980:5–6), notably those connected with the Dorchester Urban Court, the so-called Neighborhood Justice Centers, and the Brooklyn Dispute Resolution Center;[7] the latter were established and evaluated at the behest of the National Institute of Justice. In 1980 Congress adopted a Dispute Resolution Act, which was intended to provide further encouragement to new programs in their field, but the necessary funds were never appropriated—a fact seen by one critic as "an appropriate symbol of the futile effort to establish 'justice without law,' by law" (Auerbach, 1983:137). However, there has been considerable legislative activity on the part of the states (see Freedman, 1982), and at least 350 Neighborhood Justice centers have been established (Singer, 1990:8).

Among bodies established to promote informal alternatives, mention may be made of the Special Committee on Alternative Means of Dispute Resolution of the American Bar Association (now the Section on Dispute Resolution), the National Institute for Dispute Resolution, and the Institute for Mediation and Conflict Resolution. Following a clearinghouse for "grassroots" programs, a Dispute Resolution Clearinghouse was established in conjunction with the National Criminal Justice Reference Service (Warhaftig, 1982). Informal alternatives have also been developed in other countries, such as Canada, which pioneered VORP (Peachey, 1989),

Britain (Marshall and Merry, 1990), and France (Bonafe-Schmitt, 1989), and have been encouraged by legislation in the Germanic countries (Dunkel and Rossner, 1989). In New Zealand the Family Group Conference, in which the victim is invited to participate, has become, by statute, the chief mechanism for the processing of juveniles charged with offenses (Morris and Maxwell, 1993). Finally, article 7 of the UN Declaration of Basic Principles of Justice for Victims of Crime and Abuse of Power specifies that "informal mechanisms for the resolution of disputes, including mediation, arbitration and customary justice or indigenous practices, should be utilized where appropriate to facilitate conciliation and redress for victims."

Is this flurry of activity an indication that the arguments of the reformers were received with universal approval and that their goals are now being implemented? Such a conclusion would be premature. Most of the arguments put forward by the proponents of informal alternatives have been challenged, notably by Felstiner (1974, 1975), Abel and his associates (1982a: vol. 1), and Tomasic (1982). It has been questioned whether informal proceedings are really preferable to formal ones for the parties involved, and whether the notions of "community" and "neighborhood" are not merely a myth. It has also been doubted whether such programs really provide "access to justice," and if they do, whether this is necessarily desirable. Moreover, some radicals regard these programs as an obstacle to, rather than a promoter of, social change. Even the benefits to the official system in terms of reduced caseloads have been questioned. Indeed Tomasic (1982) listed eighteen assumptions upon which in his view the informal-alternatives movement was based, most of which he shows to be largely unproven (see also Felstiner, 1984; Merry, 1989).

While some of these criticisms are ideological, others are empirically testable. Some evaluations of the still largely experimental programs are now available,[8] and it is possible to determine with somewhat greater precision the strengths and weaknesses of these projects and of the arguments invoked in their support and to their denigration. Before analyzing the evidence emerging from these studies, however, some consideration must be given to the issue of definition.

Definition of Subject Matter

Some of the doubt regarding the merit of informal modes of dispute resolution may derive from confusion or uncertainty over the subject matter involved. Proposals for change may focus upon the identity of the adjudicator, the character of the norm invoked, or the nature of the procedure (Aaronson et al., 1977:viii–ix). The emphasis may be either on civil or on criminal disputes. If the latter, divergence from the traditional criminal process may occur at a number of points (ibid.). The informal proceeding may from that point substitute for the formal one, or may be *additional* to it. It may be intended to handle all disputes, or may be limited according to the type of the dispute or the relationship of the parties. The technique of adjudication may be in the nature of arbitration or mediation. It may be coercive or noncoercive. It may or may not have a "community" orientation.

The ultimate objective of the alternative processes may also vary. Coates (1990) lists "six goals," Marshall (1988) identifies twelve "frequently cited aims," and Merry (1982:181) refers to "a wide range of conflicting and contradictory political goals and interests." Programs may be intended primarily to reduce the caseload in the existing system, to provide a forum for disputants who were previously without one, to improve upon existing procedures by conveying to disputants an enhanced perception of the justice of the process or of the outcome, or to resolve underlying conflicts between the disputants. The different possible permutations of these objectives, and of the procedures involved to secure their achievement, render evaluation—and even discussion of the issues—somewhat problematical.

There seem to be four key characteristics of the "alternatives" movement which give expression to most of the prevailing objectives and expectations of this movement. These are as follows: (1) deprofessionalization of the procedure—the proceeding is not to be directed by a professional judge, nor are lawyers to be employed (but cf. Abel, 1982a:4, 9; Tomasic, 1982:232–33); (2) informality of proceedings—the traditional adversary process is to be inapplicable, as are the concepts of due process and the rules of evidence; (3) outcome by consent—the parties are voluntarily to arrive at an agreed decision with the assistance of a mediator; and (4) a local or community-based forum. In principle, these characteristics are shared by the so-called Neighborhood Justice Centers, which have often been regarded as the flagships of the movement toward informalism. The third characteristic is not always fully applicable to programs operating on the VORP model, since formal conviction and sentencing procedures may take place in addition to the mediation proceedings (cf., e.g., Marshall and Merry, 1990:8).

The following discussion will relate primarily to programs complying with these characteristics—including VORP-type programs, in view of their importance in the context of victim-oriented innovations. The merits and demerits of these programs will be considered employing the analytical scheme adopted throughout this study, differentiating between coping needs, perceived justice needs, and principles of justice.

Coping Needs

Victims. In order for mediation proceedings to be beneficial to the parties concerned, the first precondition is that the proceedings should actually take place. However, in a substantial proportion of the cases referred to the mediation agency this was not the case. The overall picture for the three Neighborhood Justice Centers in this respect, based upon 3,947 referrals between March 1978 and May 1979, was that 48.7% of the dispositions were classified as "cases unresolved, no hearing," while a further 16.5% were resolved without a hearing (Cook et al., 1980:25, table 3.1). The most common reasons cited were "the respondent's refusal to participate in mediation or the inability of the NJC to contact the respondent due to inadequate information"; other reasons included the complainant's withdrawal (ibid., 24). In the Dorchester study, the failure to hold the hearing, which occurred in approximately one-third of the cases, was attributed almost equally to complainants (16%) and respondents (14%) (Felstiner and Williams, 1980:22). At the Brooklyn Dispute Resolution Center, too, where mediation was limited to felony cases in which there was a prior relationship between the parties, a substantial proportion of the parties did not appear, although they had agreed in principle to do so (Davis, Tichane, and Grayson, n.d.:15, 95). Among 2,372 cases referred to five Florida mediation programs in 1978, "the total no-show rate was 27.6%, and 68.8% of those were respondent no-shows" (Bridenback et al., 1980:10, and table 5). An evaluation of VORP in Indiana and Ohio found that half of the possible meetings occurred (Coates and Gehm, 1989:257), but the number of cases in this type of program in which at least one meeting takes place was somewhat higher (ibid.; Marshall and Merry, 1990:107–8). Nonparticipation here was more likely on the victim's part (Marshall and Merry, 1990:108, 113). The variables associated with nonparticipation are still relatively unexplored (ibid.).

The second precondition for a beneficial outcome is that the parties should in fact have been able to reach an agreement. One of the characteristics of mediation, by contrast with arbitration, is that the consent of both parties is required. In 6.3% of the cases referred to the Neighborhood Justice Centers—about 18% of those in which mediation sessions actually took place—no resolution was reached at the hearings (Cook et al.,

1980:25, table 3.1). In the Dorchester program, this was true of 10.6% of the cases mediated (Felstiner and Williams, 1980:22, table 18). The Florida evaluation reported a failure to reach agreement in 19.3% of the cases (Bridenback et al., 1980:26, fig. 2). In the Brooklyn Dispute Resolution Center, there appear to have been almost no such cases.[9] Similarly, the VORP evaluation found that in 98% of the cases in which face-to-face meetings occurred agreements were reached (Coates and Gehm, 1989:257). Marshall and Merry (1990:118, 121) also report very high rates of agreement for mediated cases, but lower rates for cases that were indirectly *negotiated.*

In the light of traditional models of adjudication, in which the judge imposes the ultimate solution upon the two warring adversaries, the rate of agreement reported here seems strikingly high. It may be that reluctant parties are filtered out at the "no-show" stage, and those who actually appear for the sessions are only the positively motivated. Moreover, respondents who have been referred by criminal justice agencies in lieu of trial may be motivated by the latent threat of formal criminal proceedings if the mediation fails (see in this respect the findings of Marshall and Merry, 1990:118). This would not apply, however, to victim-complainants, who are apparently free to accept or reject any proposal for an agreed outcome. It may be, however, that subtle pressures are exerted by the mediator, or possibly even by the defendant. Alternatively, it may be that complainants are so pleased to participate in a proceeding in which their views are elicited that their demands are modest. These possibilities may be further tested by examining the nature of the agreements and the expressed views of the parties (see below).

It is also pertinent to consider the variables affecting the probability of an agreement taking place. Thus, it has been found that cases referred under threat of prosecution are more likely to result in agreement between the parties (Garofalo and Connelly, 1980:435, 582). Second, it has been found that conflicts related to property are more difficult to resolve than cases involving violence (ibid., 583–84). Similarly, in cases where the parties had an intimate relationship, an agreement was more likely to be reached. These last variables may be interrelated (ibid., 1980:584).

The next issue to consider is how far the agreements reached were beneficial to the victim-complainants. Surprisingly little attention has been devoted to analysis of the content of the agreements. Cook et al. (1980:90, table 5.1) classified the agreements reached at the Neighborhood Justice Centers into 25 categories, the largest of which were monetary restitution, "no contact between parties," and "no verbal abuse or harassment." The evaluation of the Honolulu center's program, in which most of the disputes were civil in character, classified 38% of the agreements as being concerned with restitution, 16% with establishment of child support or visitations, and 8% with "specified behavior, communication or contact"; the remaining categories were smaller still (Berger, 1982:2). The Florida study, in which the disputes evaluated were mostly referred by law enforcement agencies and were thus presumably criminal in character, differentiated between the undertakings of *respondents* and *complainants.* Respondents undertook mainly "disengagement" (25.5%), "alteration of past behavior" (24.3%), or payment/restitution of money/property (18.0%); other categories each represented less than 6% of the sample. On the other hand, 35.2% of complainants undertook no obligation, 19.9% "disengagement," 13.9% to "establish cooperative relationships," 8.7% "alteration of past behavior," and 6.3% not to pursue prosecution (Bridenback et al., 1980:12–13). While the categories used in these studies appear to be discrete, the Brooklyn evaluation ($N = 144$) allowed for concurrent characteristics. The most frequent characteristics observed in agreements in this study were "end harassment" (95%), establishing methods for handling future problems (35%), limited interaction between the parties (24%), behavioral restrictions (36%), restitution (20%), "express provision that the relationship be ended" (21%), and "express provision that the relationship be continued" (13%) (Davis, Tichane, and Grayson, n.d.:47).

Coates and Gehm (1989:257), however, found that 87% of the VORP agreements they studied included an element of restitution; and Marshall and Merry (1990:116) claim that the domination of restitution is a characteristic of the American programs, whereas in British programs the outcome is often merely an apology, which also appears to have a high priority in France (Bonafe-Schmitt, 1989:191).

The distribution of outcomes indicated here calls for a number of comments. Many of the agreements appear to deal with the interpersonal relations between the disputants, the category with which the programs purport mainly to be concerned. However, an agreement to *sever* the relationship ("disengagement") appears to be one of the most popular modes of resolving the dispute on this level. While this may be the most practical solution in an urban environment, it seems a far cry from the vision of reconciliation between the parties in a community setting; nor, indeed, was this option available in the primitive societies from which some advocates of informalism drew their inspiration. Thus, while agreements may have been reached relatively frequently in interpersonal dispute cases (see above), the "resolution" of these cases is often a somewhat negative phenomenon.

At the same time, victim-complainants may be perceived to have gained from these proceedings, in that however slight the direct benefits may appear, they are more than those generally emerging from a regular criminal trial, to which victims are not even a party, although they may be awarded restitution. Moreover, it is probable that many of the cases, if handled by routine criminal justice processes, would never even reach the trial stage.

On the other hand, unlike the criminal trial, at mediation proceedings victim-complainants may themselves be subjected to control measures.[10] A substantial proportion of agreements incorporated undertakings on the part of the victim-complainants, illustrations of which were presented above. While undertakings of this nature may be beneficial to the relationship between the parties and to social tranquility, the incurring of such obligations by the victim-complainant must, from a legal or a civil-libertarian point of view, be considered a loss or a burden. An analogy may be made here with the imposition of a rehabilitative measure on the offender in a criminal case.

To what extent does the emergence of an agreement indicate that the problem has been resolved? In general, there has been insufficient monitoring both of the degree of compliance with any agreement that is reached and of the effects of the agreement on the disputing relationship. In some of the evaluation studies, however, disputants were questioned on these issues; and sometimes disputants were questioned again on the matter some time later, as in the Brooklyn evaluation, where respondents were approached at two time intervals after the conclusion of the mediation hearing.

The Florida evaluation found that 75.1% of complainants and 82.8% of respondents declared that the problem was resolved or "partially resolved" (Bridenback et al., 1980: table 18; see also Felstiner and Williams, 1980:27, tables 30.5, 30.3; Coates and Gehm, 1989:257). The Final Evaluation Report of the Neighborhood Justice Centers Field Test found that 79% of the complainants and 87% of the respondents stated that *they* had kept all terms of the agreement, while 69% and 67% respectively stated that *the other party* had kept all terms of the agreement. Moreover, 72% of complainants and 78% of respondents stated that there were no more problems with the other party (Cook et al., 1980:49, table 4.2). The Brooklyn evaluation found that by the second evaluation, two and a half years after the cases were disposed, "only a small number of disputants were still experiencing interpersonal problems. . . . Fewer than 8% of the complainants and 7% of the defendants reported that they still had problems with the other disputants" (Connick and Davis, 1981:31). This was partly attributed, however, to a lessening of contacts between the parties.

The significance of the findings reported above depends to a large extent on what would have been expected in the wake of regular formal processes, an issue rarely addressed and not, of course, known to the disputants in the informal programs (Felstiner and Williams, 1980:26). With this in mind, both the Neighborhood Justice Centers and the Brooklyn evaluations compared mediation samples with control groups that were processed by the courts. The former found that 70% of complainants passing through the regular system reported that the dispute was resolved, a number not substantially different from the experimental sample (Cook et al., 1980:99–100). In the Brooklyn study, however, significantly fewer complainants passing through the court perceived the defendant's behavior as having improved (Davis, Tichane, and Grayson, n.d.:61).

Somewhat more disturbing are the findings regarding the relative degree of successful resolution according to the types of dispute involved. It has generally been found that interpersonal disputes—although having a better prognosis than property disputes in terms of the probability of a mediation agreement—are less likely to hold in the long run, as contacts between the parties are resumed. By contrast, in property disputes, where agreement is reached, it is more likely to be maintained (Garofalo and Connelly, 1980:592–95).[11]

Felstiner and Williams (1982) developed a somewhat different classification, according to "dispute level." Level 1 refers to the "one-shot dispute," with no underlying interpersonal problems. Level 2 denotes cases of "escalating misunderstanding," and level 3 occurs where there are "underlying emotional and/or behavioral problems" (126). Employing this classification, they confirmed the finding that "the higher the level of dispute the more it is likely to be settled at mediation" but "the more likely it is that an agreement will break down" (128). The authors note that although the informality of the proceedings and the mediator's technique may be calculated to produce discussion of the underlying problems, the mediators then proceed to deal with the "overlying" material, that is, the concrete issues referred to mediation. "Mediation is not psychotherapy and that is what many of the disputes that come to mediation require, if any form of social intervention would be helpful" (147). In this respect, the claims of mediation advocates, namely, the resolution of underlying conflicts, may be unrealistic (see also Marshall and Merry, 1990:151).

The final matter to be considered under victims' coping needs is that of "access to justice." This term is generally applied to civil claimants but may also be adapted to criminal complainants. Their potential gain in access by virtue of the establishment of informal mechanisms of dispute resolution may take three forms. First, as already noted, cases dealt with by such procedures rather than in criminal proceedings result in the victim's active participation and in an outcome for which the victim's consent is required, whereas the victim's contribution to the criminal process is nugatory. On the other hand, the victim may have lost the supposed benefit of the imposition of a formal criminal sanction on the defendant, while at the same time being exposed to a possible measure of control which would not have been the case had the defendant been prosecuted in a conventional proceeding.

Second, if the matter were dealt with by the routine agencies of criminal law enforcement rather than an informal alternative, there would be a high probability that no action would have been taken against the defendant. In the Brooklyn Dispute Resolution Center program, cases deemed appropriate for mediation were randomly assigned either to the experimental (mediation) or to the control (court) procedures (Davis, Tichane, and Grayson, n.d.:14). It was found that "70 percent of control cases were either dismissed outright or adjourned in contemplation of dismissal" (52). The Neighborhood Justice Centers evaluation conducted "court comparison studies" (Cook et al., 1980:125); here, too, it was found that a substantial proportion of the comparison cases did not in fact reach the trial stage (77). The Dorchester evaluation reached a similar conclusion (Felstiner and Williams, 1982:133). It also emerged from these studies that where defendants did reach the courts, sentences were mostly light. Thus, compared with cases which would have been closed by the prosecution authorities, victim-complainants make a net gain in access to justice by virtue of the informal proceedings, except inasmuch as this proceeding exposes them, too, to a possible control measure.

The concept of access, however—and this is the third and main point—is really intended to apply to matters that would not otherwise have been dealt with in any alternative proceeding. The advocates of informal alternatives motivated by the "access to justice" consideration assumed that the cases to be dealt with by such procedures would be instigated directly by the victim-complainant, or referred by a community agency. In such cases there would be a net gain in terms of access, if it is assumed that these cases would not have reached any alternative forum. However, it has been questioned whether there are, as often assumed, large numbers of grievances "out there" vainly awaiting a resolution mechanism, or whether the grievances that exist are in fact amenable to resolution in a mediation procedure between individuals (see e.g., Buckle and Thomas-Buckle, 1982). It has also been asserted by radical critics that grieved citizens would do better not to have their disputes resolved on an individual basis but to seek class-oriented remedies (see Abel, 1982b:280–89; and see below). Whatever the merit of these arguments, it is certainly true that the overwhelming majority of disputes—particularly disputes of a criminal character—which have been dealt with by the programs under consideration here were referred by criminal justice agencies that were already investigating the complaints in question. It is also the case that programs such as those in Los Angeles (Venice) and San Francisco, which endeavored to rely upon the spontaneous initiative of aggrieved citizens, had considerable difficulty in attracting clientele (Tomasic, 1982:229–30), and the San Francisco program has consequently modified its approach (Singer, 1990:122; Shonholz, 1993:230). Thus, the potential of such programs for the expansion of dispute processing, at least in the framework of the present social structure, must be questioned.

Offenders. Defendants appear to gain in a number of ways from informal modes of dispute resolution. First, in a sense they are simply being provided with an additional option, since as their participation is ostensibly voluntary, they may elect either to pursue this course or to opt out and be processed in the regular criminal (or possibly civil) justice system.

Second, mediated agreements, as illustrated above, are less oppressive than traditional penal sanctions; in particular, the possibility of a custodial sanction does not arise. Indeed, it appears that this characteristic of informal alternatives is uppermost in the minds of defendants-respondents (see below).

Third, the fact that the victim-complainant, too, may be subjected to some restrictive undertakings as part of the agreement ultimately reached may be seen as a further gain for the respondent, not only in the "zero-sum game" sense, whereby your opponent's loss is your gain, but also insofar as a respondent's genuinely held grievances vis-à-vis the complainant may be dealt with in the framework of this agreement.

Fourth, as respondents are ostensibly being offered here a quasi-therapeutic program designed to improve their interpersonal relationships and to prevent their becoming involved in further conflict, the potential benefits may be perceived not only in therapeutic terms but also in the prevention of future involvement with the criminal justice system.

However, forceful arguments can be put forward for the contrary view. First, participation on the part of the defendant may not be genuinely voluntary, since when expressing consent to the mediation proceedings the defendant will generally be aware that a criminal trial would entail the risk of a more serious outcome. Indeed, even after the mediation proceedings are under way, it is not unusual for the mediator to "remind" the respondent of the possible consequences in the event that no mutual agreement be reached (Tomasic, 1982:226).

Further, there is some evidence that respondents, while undergoing a reduced sanctioning risk by agreeing to mediation proceedings, are in fact exposing themselves to enhanced measures of social control. The explanation for this lies in the fact that mediation proceedings do not generally deal with serious crime but rather with minor disputes, in particular those involving family members and neighbors, which the regular criminal justice system would have neither the time nor the patience to process. As noted above, control groups constructed in the Neighborhood Justice Centers, the Brooklyn Dispute Resolution Center, and the Dorchester Mediation project found that many or most of such cases dealt with by conventional means would have been dismissed; and this applied even to the Brooklyn program, which dealt with felonies. Moreover, these studies also found that among those cases which did reach the courts, the probability of a custodial sentence was extremely slight (Davis, Tichane, and Grayson, n.d.:52; Cook et al., 1980:77). Thus it may be that the true effect of the mediation alternative is to "widen the net" of legal control (cf. Austin and Krisberg, 1981; Cohen, 1979) exercised upon offenders or respondents dealt with by such procedures. Moreover, in the event of a defendant rejecting the mediation option, the possibility arises that if subsequently sentenced in a criminal court, evidence of refusal of a mediation offer may aggravate the sentence, on the analogy of a not-guilty plea.

The implications of the informal processes for subsequent formal ones are particularly relevant in VORP-type programs, in which the mediation process is not generally intended to supplant the formal procedure, so that a subsequent formal sentence may be the norm. Coates and Gehm (1989) compared a VORP sample with a matched sample that was dealt with by conventional procedures only. They found that the incarceration rate was about 20% for each sample, but that the mean duration of the incarceration was substantially less for VORP offenders (258–59). However, they did not dismiss the possibility that the mediation process involved an "additional cost to the offender" (259). Marshall and Merry (1990:131ff.) also invested considerable effort in endeavoring to assess the impact of mediation on the outcome that would have been probable without it. They found some indication of a reduction in custodial sentences and an increase in restitution, but in particular a move from fines to community sentences.

This suggests somewhat mixed results in terms of net widening. They also noted that "a poor outcome to the intervention can have a negative impact on sentence" (141).

Third, the "help" provided to the respondent toward his or her rehabilitation has not been established by the evaluation research. As indicated below, the data on recidivism rates on the part of disputants who have participated in mediation proceedings as compared with comparison groups are not uniformly in favor of the former category.

Finally, while this point has been insufficiently studied in the evaluation literature, there is a clear danger that such proceedings import second-class justice. Respondent-defendants participating in informal proceedings are deprived of due process guarantees such as the right to silence, the right to counsel, the right to cross-examine witnesses, and the right to a jury trial. A respondent who is legally innocent may hesitate to reject the offer of a mediation proceeding because of the risk of a punitive sanction that may result from formal proceedings, but may thereby sacrifice the constitutional protections that would lead to a total exoneration. This issue will be further considered below.

Society. A number of possible advantages are thought to accrue to the criminal justice system as a result of the establishment of alternative modes of dispute resolution. The first of these may be defined in terms of cost-benefit analysis. Alternative forms of dispute resolution have been encouraged by official agencies as providing an inexpensive form of justice for persons or disputes for which the conventional system was ineffective or unnecessary, thereby releasing resources that could be devoted by that system to the cases it retained. The experience so far accumulated suggests that this objective has encountered two obstacles. First, the analysis conducted in some depth by Felstiner and Williams (1982:144) of the cost of informal processing in Dorchester concluded that "mediated costs are 1 to 3 times the amount of court cases saved."[12] This is explained by the fact that most of these cases would not have involved costly correctional treatment had they been processed by the criminal justice system but either would have been dismissed or would have resulted in probation, most of the costs being incurred in the probation cases (145).

Second, the alternative programs have not succeeded in releasing substantial resources within the conventional system, since the numbers handled by these programs are insignificant as compared with the caseloads incurred by the conventional system. It could be argued that both types of saving would increase as the programs are expanded and more—and more serious—cases are diverted into the alternative programs, but this may never occur, for professional criminal justice personnel, the main source of referrals to the programs, are unlikely to forgo cases they perceive as constituting their essential diet.[13]

It might be anticipated that if the underlying causes of the parties' grievances have been resolved, they—and in particular the alleged offender—would not constitute a further danger either to each other or to the general public. The critical evaluation of the Brooklyn Dispute Resolution Center found that continued hostility between the parties was infrequent during the four-month follow-up period: the police were called in only 12% of the cases, and an arrest made in only 4%. However, these relatively low figures could not be attributed to the mediation proceeding, since the figures were almost identical for the control group (Davis, Tichane, and Grayson, n.d.:62). Further, while arrests for violent acts *against the other party* were assessed at only 7%–10% of the cases during the two-and-a-half-year follow-up of the mediation sample, 31% of the defendants were arrested at least once during this period, indicating that they remained a threat to the public if not necessarily to the original complainant (Connick and Davis, 1981:33–34). Moreover, Felstiner and Williams (1980:44–45) found that general recidivism rates were no lower among their mediation sample than among the control sample; if anything, the opposite tendency was observed. Marshall and Merry (1990:193–97) formed the impression that some of the British VORC-type schemes led to a degree of "behavioral improvement" in terms of criminality but noted mainly the dearth of hard data in this respect both in North America and in Britain. It may also be noted that the Brooklyn study found no recognizable gain arising from the program in terms of cooperation by victims with law enforcement authorities (Davis, Chytilo, and Schraga, 1980).

It will be recalled that some advocates of alternative modes of dispute resolution anticipated more far-reaching societal benefits beyond those related directly to crime and criminal justice, such as enhancing community solidarity, bringing about social change, or reducing the general level of social or interpersonal tension. The first and most specific of these objectives has proved to be problematical (see, e.g., Nelken, 1985),[14] particularly in the context of the urban metropolis. As noted above, dispute resolution centers that have attempted to develop from "the community" rather than relying upon professional agencies—generally pertaining to the criminal justice system—for referrals, have achieved only moderate success. Moreover, mediators do not seem to be necessarily identified with a specifically community role. Communities of the type in which prestigious figures are the natural candidates for the role of mediator exist in traditional, particularly rural, societies and may even survive urban development in such societies (Naim, 1983). However, the concept does not fit well with Western industrialized societies (see, e.g., Harrell-Bond and Smith, 1983). Indeed, the ethnic mediation systems once prevalent among certain groups in such societies have undergone a decline (Doo, 1973). Finally, the issues affecting a community, in the sense of a local geographic unit, are frequently not of such a nature that they can be resolved by an internal mediation procedure between individuals, since they may involve public agencies and bureaucracies, in many cases having ramifications beyond the locality (Buckle and Thomas-Buckle, 1982; Kidder, 1981).

The idea that informal justice alternatives might constitute a vehicle for social change is identified primarily with the grassroots concept of community dispute resolution, whereby the proceedings would be initiated directly from the community and could accommodate disputes affecting groups or classes of citizens (Warhaftig, 1981; Merry, 1982:188–89). However, the prevailing models—with the possible exception of the San Francisco Community Boards (see Merry and Milner, 1993)—are seen by many radicals as serving as primarily an "overflow" for the criminal justice system, and thus as a means of expanding state mechanisms of social control. At the same time, insofar as they handle "original" grievances raised directly by citizens, the prevailing mode of resolving disputes on an individual basis is perceived as a means of ensuring the atomization and control of such disputes and of inhibiting the development of group momentum toward changes in the socioeconomic structure (cf. Abel, 1982b). Which of the functions discussed here—promotion of social change or neutralization of social conflict—is the preferable objective is naturally an ideological question.

The more amorphous idea that the existence of local institutions readily available for the resolution of conflicts might contribute to the general reduction of interpersonal tensions is perhaps less controversial. However, it has been argued that it may be counterproductive to encourage citizens to define problems as grievances requiring resolution. Our knowledge of the processes involved is at present still somewhat rudimentary. Seminal theoretical analysis has been published on the theory of dispute resolution (Abel, 1973) as well as pioneering research on the processes whereby an experience becomes labeled as injurious ("naming"), injury is attributed to the fault of another ("blaming") and thus becomes a grievance, and the grievance is referred to some agency in the pursuit of a remedy ("claiming") (see Felstiner et al. 1980–81; and in the context of victim decision making, Burt 1983). It has been suggested that it may be preferable not to encourage this "transformation" process and that the very existence of dispute-resolution mechanisms may encourage perceptions of victimization (Vidmar, 1981; cf. Quinney, 1974). Alternatively, it may be preferable for perceived grievances to be forgotten (Felstiner, 1974) or to be handled on a one-to-one basis without third-party intervention (cf. Sander, 1976; Cain, 1983). Finally, it has been argued that whereas the mediation ethos regards conflict as a pathological phenomenon requiring therapeutic intervention, conflict is in fact "an integral part of social relations" (Felstiner and Williams, 1982:120, citing the German sociologist Richard Rosellen). These arguments are all worthy of consideration and exploration without necessarily negating the positive potential of informal alternatives, if not for resolving innumerable unrecognized conflicts, then at least for disputes that are currently so recognized.

Perceived Justice Needs

In a number of evaluation studies, victim-complainants were interviewed about their attitudes to the mediation proceedings and outcome. Reactions were generally favorable (Marshall and Merry, 1990:145). Cook et al. (1980) found that among their Neighborhood Justice center sample 84% of the complainants were satisfied with the process and 88% with the mediator. High rates of satisfaction with the process and/or the mediator were also recorded in the Florida study (Bridenback et al., 1980: table 19), in the Brooklyn Mediation proceedings (complainants, 94% of whom appreciated the opportunity to tell their story), and among Dorchester interviewees (both complainants and respondents). A significant minority (about a quarter) of a sample of victims who participated in the New Zealand Family Group conferences said they felt worse as a consequence (Morris et al., 1993:312–13), but the situation at such conferences bears greater similarity to the plea negotiation proceedings described in chapter 8 than to the other procedures described here, in that the victim is one of several parties present. In particular, many victims were intimidated in the face of the defendant's family. Other studies indicating a desire on the part of victims to have an opportunity to meet with the offender were cited in chapter 8.

As to the *outcome* of the proceedings, 73% of the Brooklyn sample expressed satisfaction (Davis, Tichane, and Grayson, n.d.:51), 78.3% of the Dorchester participants (including defendants) were "glad that they used mediation" (Felstiner and Williams, 1980), and 88% of the complainants using Neighborhood Justice Centers were satisfied with their experiences

(Cook et al., 1980:48). These attitudes may in fact be a response to the process itself rather than the specific outcome, which may be of lesser importance (Garofalo and Connelly, 1980:587).

More notably, Davis, Tichane, and Grayson (n.d.) found that in all areas—opportunity to tell their story, the fairness of the judge or mediator, the fairness of the outcome, and satisfaction with the outcome—complainants referred to the Brooklyn mediation proceedings expressed more favorable views than the control group who were referred to traditional procedures (50–51; Davis, 1982).[15] Most complainants participating in the Neighborhood Justice Center proceedings (72%) would wish to bring a further problem to that forum, as compared with 16% who expressed a preference for the courts. Similarly, 65% of the Dorchester interviewees, including respondents, *preferred* mediation, as compared with only 11.7% who preferred the courts. Davis, Tichane, and Grayson (n.d.) found that "complainants in both the experimental and the control groups preferred mediation by a two-to-one majority" (53); and Cook et al. (1980) also found that all satisfaction indices favored the Neighborhood Justice Center over the regular courts (99–100). Marshall and Merry (1990) found in their evaluation of British VORP-type reparation projects that "victims who met their offender in mediation were more satisfied with the sentence passed on the offender than the control group victims" (165–66). They concluded, "Mediation clearly affects victims' punitiveness towards their offenders, and leads them to be more satisfied with less severe sentencing" (166). However, nearly one-half of the victims attending the New Zealand Family Group conferences were dissatisfied with the outcome, even though the outcome was supposedly conditional on their agreement (Morris et al., 1993:314–15). Finally, 97% (!) of the victims who participated in the Indiana VORP program indicated that they would choose to do it again (Coates, 1990:129–30). Marshall and Merry's observation appears to have been applicable here, too, for "in some cases victims complained that their client was punished too much by having to do VORP and some jail time" (130).

In contrast with these generally favorable findings in regard to perceptions of the mediation programs, mention must be made of Sally Merry's ethnographic study of the use of informal proceedings among working-class communities in New England. According to Merry (1990): "People go to court in these three neighborhoods out of a search for an impersonal moral authority with the power to enforce its rules" (83). They tended to be dissatisfied with officials who "endeavoring to provide what they consider justice, convert these problems from legal to moral or therapeutic discourse" (179). These reservations, which are linked also to the issue of social justice considered below, suggest the need to take into account possible variations in the justice needs of different sectors of the population.

Like their victim-complainant counterparts, defendant-respondents, too, have been found by most studies to hold very positive views regarding mediation proceedings. Respondent ratings in the Neighborhood Justice Center evaluation were almost identical to complainant ratings regarding satisfaction with the process (81%) and with the mediator (88%), the choice of a Neighborhood Justice Center (73%) rather than a court (12%) for the handling of a future problem, and overall satisfaction with the experience (88%). In the Florida study, too, 82.5% of the respondents expressed satisfaction with the process (Bridenback et al., 1980). Among the Brooklyn samples, defendants were more likely to feel that they had an opportunity to tell their story in the mediation process (90%) than in the court process (44%; p < .01). They were also more likely to believe that the outcome was fair (p < .05). Satisfaction with outcome was marginally, but not significantly, greater, while the fairness of the mediator or judge was rated almost equally high by both samples. Overall, the authors found that "over nine out of ten defendants in both the experimental and the control groups indicated that, in a similar circumstance, they would rather have their case handled in mediation than in court" (Davis, Tichane, and Grayson, n.d.:56). Evaluations of VORP-type programs, in both the United States and Britain, also found that offenders' views were favorable (Coates, 1990:130; Marshall and Merry, 1990:166).

It may be surmised that the victim-complainant's preference for mediation proceedings derives primarily from the very fact of his or her involvement in these proceedings, in contrast with the traditional criminal process to which the victim is not a party. On the other hand, as noted earlier, a perceived advantage to the defendant is that in truly alternative proceedings there is no risk of the imposition of a severe sanction, while in VORP-type proceedings there may be an expectation—and even a perception—of a subsequently reduced sentence. The defendant may also derive satisfaction from the fact that the complainant-victim may be under pressure to reach a compromise agreement and to make certain undertakings, with the possible implication that he or she, too, may be partly responsible for the events giving rise to the dispute and the resulting proceedings.

While these evaluations seem to support a genuine preference by the parties for an informal proceeding, they cannot be interpreted as an all-embracing rejection of the established judicial structure in favor of the resolution of disputes at the community level. For, as previously indicated, most of the informal proceedings reviewed above take place in the margin of the official system and under the general control of that system (Tomasic, 1982:231). At the same time, they undoubtedly indicate some perceived merit in these processes.

Apart from the direct evidence of participant satisfaction with informal proceedings, two areas of experimental evidence may be relevant to parties' perceptions of mediation proceedings. With regard to the proceedings themselves, the experiments conducted by Thibaut and Walker indicated that potential disputants generally favored adversary proceedings (rather than "inquisitorial" proceedings on the European model) because of the greater control this gave them. This would seem to favor mediation, since even though such proceedings are not *formally* adversarial, the parties actively participate and the outcome is notionally in their control. However, the authors found that where there was a high degree of conflict of interest between the parties, there was a need for a decision on the part of a third party empowered to apply objective norms (Thibaut and Walker, 1975:20; 1978).

With regard to the *outcome* of the proceedings, equity theory posits that benefits to the contending parties are anticipated in proportion to their respective inputs. A mediated settlement reached with the agreement of both parties may be assumed to constitute an optimal disposition for the parties concerned (cf. Coates and Penrod, 1980–81). This conclusion is consistent with the European survey evidence referred to below. Umbreit (1988:136–38), in his study of mediation involving burglary victims, found that equity theory was supported by the increased level of distress felt by victims as a result of the victimization and the perceived fairness of being compensated ("restoring equity"). However, the emphasis placed by the victims on the need to rehabilitate the offenders (juveniles) was seen by Umbreit as recognition of the principle of *need*. This principle may be expected to play a prominent role in the context of an exchange relationship and is thus particularly relevant to mediation.

As to *public* perceptions of informalism, little direct evidence seems to be available from research conducted in the United States, although a survey conducted in Minnesota found that 82% of respondents would consider a mediation proceeding if a nonviolent property crime were committed against them by a juvenile or young adult (Umbreit, 1994:11–12). European surveys focusing on civil disputes have indicated a preference for informal over formal justice, on both a procedural and a substantive level. Thus a Bulgarian survey (Naumova, 1983) found that, from the procedural point of view, peasant respondents preferred "flexibility" (61%–66% of the samples) to the formality of "law" (34%–39%), while from the substantive point of view, respondents preferred "compromise" (71%–79%) to "justice" (21%–29%).[16] Similar surveys conducted in other European countries, including industrialized areas in western Europe, have reached very similar conclusions (Kurczewski, 1983:239 n. 6). However, a study conducted in the Soviet Republic of Georgia (Yakovlev, 1985:48) found a preference among respondents for "law" and "justice"; this suggests that expressed preferences should be seen in the context of the system prevailing at the location of the survey and the degree to which it is accepted.

A more formalistic orientation might be anticipated in respect of conduct traditionally regarded as criminal. A priori it seems that at least two areas of concern might emerge: first, that mediation proceedings do not allow for punitive, and in particular for incapacitative, sanctions; and second, that disparities in sanction are likely to be arrived at for similar cases. Moreover, the failure to stigmatize offenders by means of degradation ceremonies (cf. Garfinkel, 1956) might, too, be a cause of dissatisfaction for those for whom the "denunciatory" function of the criminal law is believed to be important (Walker, 1969:19), although stigmatization is not necessarily excluded by informalism (see the "reintegrative shaming" process advocated by Braithwaite 1989).

However, in addition to the Minnesota survey referred to above, a survey conducted in Hamburg in 1984–85, referred to in chapter 7, found that across 38 types of offense, 42.4% of respondents took the view that "victim and offender should privately agree on restitution or reconciliation (with the help of a third person if needed)" or that "victim and offender should agree on restitution or reconciliation mediated by an officially appointed person" (Boers and Sessar, 1991:130; the figures were 23.9% and 18.5% for the respective responses). Other responses favored invocation of the criminal justice system, but these included a further 17.4% favoring an agreement on restitution between victim and offender initiated by the official system. Informal processes were less popular for serious offenses; they were also less popular with judges and prosecutors than with the public.

Another large German survey conducted more recently (Kilchling, 1991) was somewhat less supportive. Out-of-court mediation was supported by 42.1% of victim respondents, but only 31.4% of nonvictims (55). Moreover, a third of the supporters of mediation specified that it should not entail direct contact with the offender. Further, a large majority rejected the "expropriation thesis," which was intended to reflect Christie's criticism of a state-sponsored justice system, in that they denied that it was the victim's task to negotiate with the offender.

Fundamental Principles of Justice

The adoption of informal modes of dispute resolution to replace traditional procedures, in particular traditional procedures of criminal justice, raises a number of issues pertaining to the fundamental issues of justice. Issues of *substantive* justice arise with regard to *(a)* departure from the traditional objectives of criminal justice, *(b)* departure from principles applicable in civil justice, and *(c)* the relationship between individual and social justice. Last, but by no means least, consideration must be given to *(d)* the implications of procedures that appear totally to abandon established principles of due process.

Traditional Objectives of Criminal Justice. Informal alternatives are clearly inconsistent with principles of retribution, which require that the offender be punished according to his or her deserts. It will be recalled that for Kant this principle was a "categorical imperative." Similarly, the contemporary just-deserts movement has advocated standardized sanctions based upon the seriousness of the offense, assessed according to the degree of harm inflicted and the culpability of the offender. While it is not clear that this school insists upon the principle of universal enforcement of the law, following the so-called principle of legality, it does emphasize uniformity of punishment once the law has been invoked; and it is clearly inconsistent with the desert concept that the nature of the sanction to be imposed upon the offender should be a topic to be freely determined by the parties involved in a mediation proceeding. Like cases would attract differing sanctions; indeed in some cases no sanction would be imposed, if this accorded with the complainant's wishes. Even the restitutive theory of retribution, considered in chapter 7, whereby retribution may take the form of financial indemnification, would not be satisfied here, for mediation proceedings do not necessarily result in restitution, and where they do, such restitution is not necessarily proportional to the harm inflicted.

Nor are other traditional criminal justice objectives met by mediation proceedings. *Social defense* is not attained, since dangerous offenders are unlikely to be confined as a consequence of such proceedings; nor is there any emphasis on *deterrence* either of the individual offender or of the public. A negotiated outcome may be consistent with *rehabilitation*, but there is no explicit attempt to determine mediated agreements according to this criterion. Mediation is thus unique in its radical departure from the formal objectives of the traditional criminal justice system. However, since *(a)* it is generally reserved for relatively minor cases, *(b)* it is in some cases combined with an additional formal proceeding, and *(c)* it is perceived by some to incorporate a substantial element of control over the disputing parties, and in particular the offender, the informal system is seen in practice to be quite compatible with traditional penal objectives. It may also be argued that the traditional utilitarian aims of punishment should defer to a "greater good," namely, the satisfaction of the parties involved.

Principles Applicable in Civil Justice. In some respects informal alternatives resemble civil suits, for in civil suits, too, the course of the proceedings is in principle determined by the parties involved rather than by the state. In regular civil proceedings, however, the *outcome* may be determined by the court according to accepted norms laid down in legislation and precedent. Tort cases—probably the most relevant in the present context—follow established principles of liability, and remedies are designed to achieve defined, albeit controversial, objectives (see chap. 12). Since the outcome of informal proceedings ostensibly depends upon the wishes of the parties, the formalized application of such principles will be absent. At the same time, as noted above, insofar as the parties themselves make judgments about the equitability of the distribution of goods between them, as described in equity theory, the consensual outcome should ensure an optimal level of interpersonal or "corrective" justice.

Individual and Social Justice. The resolution of disputes between individuals in the course of an official proceeding is generally perceived ipso facto as achieving justice between those parties. Where such resolution is arrived at voluntarily by the parties rather than being imposed according to extraneously determined norms, the quality of justice is thought by some to be enhanced (see, e.g., Christie 1977). As noted earlier, however, some radicals see informal alternatives as having the potential for obtaining more far-reaching social change; but others have criticized such proceedings for "atomizing" social conflict and neutralizing the pressure for such change. The analysis by Galanter (1974) of the introduction of reforms in legal systems suggests that such reforms rarely operate to the advantage of the less powerful (the "have-nots"), and few writers regard informal alternatives as a mechanism for redistribution of power in society (L.R. Singer, 1979:575), which may rather require the application of formal normative principles.[17] The desirability or otherwise of altering the power structure in society is of course a question of political ideology which must be taken into account in the present context.

Procedural Issues. The constitutional issues pertaining to informal alternative procedures have received relatively little attention (but see Aaronson et al. 1977:36; Cook et al. 1980:102). However, one law review article (Rice, 1979) specifically addressed this issue, focusing on the implication of the "equal protection" and "due process" clauses of the Constitution. Rice's article dealt with a number of mediation and arbitration alternatives to criminal prosecution which were investigated by the author.

The equal protection issue arises insofar as informal alternatives may be offered in some, but not all, criminal cases. It appears from Rice's analysis that such "screening" is likely to be acceptable so long as it is not based on clearly discriminatory criteria such as race or national origin of the defendant, and so long as the criteria employed "bear some rational relationship to a legitimate state purpose" (Rice, 1979:40).

The due process requirement would seem to be more problematical in the present context. However, Rice noted that "the state must provide due process protections only where its action threatens a constitutionally protected liberty or property interest" (46) and concluded that this does not apply to the informal alternatives, since "if, as is the case in most programs, the agreement is not judicially enforceable, no interest is jeopardized by participation in the programs" (50). According to Rice, the defendant is always free to reject the proposed settlement and will have lost nothing if then subjected to the regular criminal process. However, this ignores the possibility that the defendant may feel pressured to accept the settlement or may subsequently be penalized, whether by the prosecutor or the court, if he or she rejects it.

Rice also took the view that there was no right to counsel under the Sixth Amendment in such a proceeding, since it was not criminal in character, nor could it be considered a "critical stage" of the prosecution. Moreover, the author invoked the analogies of probation and parole revocation where the Supreme Court held "that the presence of counsel would actually be undesirable because it would significantly alter the nature of the proceedings" (65). While this is undoubtedly true, and the presence of advocates would clearly derogate from the informality of the proceedings and their conciliatory character, the possibility of respondent-defendants being pressured into agreements they might have been able to avoid seems to be a real one. It should be noted in this context that Rice found that the exclusionary rule, whereby unconstitutionally obtained evidence was rendered inadmissible, did not apply to informal alternatives, since the proceedings were too remote from the conduct of the police for the application of the rule to have a deterrent effect (29 n. 35).

Despite Rice's reassurances, the points referred to under the above headings raise acute questions of principle regarding the propriety of informal alternatives from the point of view of traditionally espoused standards of justice. One factor accounting for the relative lack of debate on these issues may be the view that traditional "formal" justice has in practice become informalized (*vide* the practice of plea bargaining), while the "informal alternatives" have themselves become formalized (Sarat, 1988)! Nevertheless, it would seem arguable that *(a)* these alternatives are not consistent with traditional constitutional principles, but *(b)* they reflect ideals—such as access to a conciliatory rather than a punitive forum, or to a "community" rather than a state institution for the resolution of disputes—that may themselves be worthy of recognition, perhaps even at a constitutional level.[18]

Be that as it may, the ideological doubts raised in this context are probably not of such magnitude that they should present an obstacle to the development of this type of remedy, insofar as it appears to be desirable in the interests of the coping and justice needs of the parties. In the latter respect, there is at least some evidence indicating that the parties' justice needs may be enhanced by this type of procedure. Greater doubts arise with regard to the ability of the informal dispute resolution to meet the parties' coping needs, particularly in view of the marginal use made of such procedures in the contemporary criminal justice system. They would, however, have greater merit if incorporated as an integral part of the prevailing system—a possibility that will be considered in the next chapter.

Part IV

Integration: Past, Present, and Future Remedies

12

Models of Justice

The purpose of this chapter is to consider the innovations and proposals discussed earlier in this study within a wider conceptual framework. As noted, discussion of justice reforms affecting victims has been characterized by a paucity of such conceptual analyses. While it is true that theoretical models may tend to have an abstract character that renders their direct applicability somewhat problematic (Verin, 1980:768), they nevertheless provide a useful framework for the analysis of practical as well as theoretical issues. Moreover, the adoption of this approach will not only enable the relationship between the various proposals considered earlier to be placed in perspective but will also provide a framework for the consideration of other possible approaches, such as the use of civil-law and private prosecutions; these alternatives were not discussed in earlier chapters of this study, for the focus was rather on proposals that have been the object of recent experimentation in the context of the victim's role in the justice system. Further, a conceptual analysis can provide a useful basis for the consideration of possible long-term reforms in the justice system.

Much of the literature dealing with conceptual models of justice has either been limited to abstract principles (such as those discussed in chap. 6 above) or has been concerned with models regulating the relationship between the state and the *defendant* (e.g., Packer, 1964, 1968; Goldstein, 1974; Griffiths, 1970; Herrmann, 1978; King, 1981; see also Damaska,

1986). On the other hand, models that relate to *victims* have tended to be limited in scope, focusing either on forms of dispute processing (Sander, 1976; Thibaut and Walker, 1978) or on types of services from which victims might benefit (Mawby, n.d.)[1] and the ideologies of the agencies concerned (Mawby and Gill, 1987, esp. chaps. 6 and 7).

However, somewhat more comprehensive models have been developed by Ziegenhagen (1977), Sebba (1982), Van Dijk (1984, 1988), and Cavadino and Dignan (1993). Van Dijk (1984) distinguished between "the care or social welfare ideology, the rehabilitation ideology, the retribution or reparation ideology and the abolitionist or anti-criminal justice ideology" (6). Van Dijk's "care" ideology includes state compensation schemes and crisis centers; his "rehabilitation" ideology includes "restitution programs as part of probation and some mediation programs"; his "retribution" ideology includes just deserts and restitution; and his "abolitionist" approach includes the use of civil-law and informal social control mechanisms.

While these ideologies may also be seen to have relevance to the present analysis, its structure has reflected instead the dichotomous conceptualization that I developed in an earlier article (Sebba, 1982). It was suggested there that a review of the issues and the various proposed remedies indicated that in considering the respective role of the victim, the offender, and the state, there were basically two approaches—an "adversary-retribution model" and a "social defense–welfare model":

> The first model emphasizes the role of the victim both at the trial and sentencing stages of the penal process. It suggests, in the first place, adhesion to the basic structure of the common-law trial, i.e., a confrontation between aggriever and aggrieved, and in the second place a determination of sentence which would 'fit the crime'—wherein the injury to the victim is the main component. At the same time, differences between civil and criminal proceedings would be minimized. In this model the state plays a somewhat subsidiary role as overseer and enforcer—acting primarily on behalf of the victim. The second model, on the other hand, essentially eliminates the victim-offender confrontation. Instead, the state plays a critical and mediating role vis-à-vis each party, endeavoring so far as possible to control the threat to society represented by the offender, whether by incapacitation or rehabilitation, and simultaneously to cater to the needs of the victim. . . . The key to the dynamics of these two models is in the following: under the adversary-retribution model the state provides the machinery for the victim himself to achieve the desired objectives, whether prosecution or compensation-restitution; under the social defense-welfare model the state would not only stand in the shoes of the

victim in prosecuting the offender, but would also stand in the shoes of the offender in compensating the victim. (231–33)

These two models can effectively accommodate all the proposals discussed in this study—informal alternatives being classified as a derivative of the adversary-retribution model (ibid., p. 236)—with the possible exception of third-party responsibility, which will be dealt with in the next chapter. Subdivisions of the models, or at least of the adversary-retribution model, will be elaborated below.

Ziegenhagen's conceptualization, although purporting to relate exclusively to the victim, is generally consistent with the preceding dichotomy. Ziegenhagen (1977: chap. 5) distinguished between the "managerial approach: the inefficient victim" and the "participation approach: victim as decision maker." Under the managerial approach the victim is a recipient of services, while under the participation approach the victim would fulfill an active role in the criminal justice process.[2] A somewhat similar dichotomy is also found in Black (1973) in the course of his discussion on the mobilization of law, where he distinguishes between the "entrepreneurial" model, in which the initiative for legal action is left to the citizen, and the "social-welfare" model, whereby the government determines the well-being of the citizen.

Cavadino and Dignan (1993) propose a sixfold typology that is intended to represent "forms of accommodation between retribution and reparative/victim-oriented responses to crime" (fig. 1). These include the "conventional" (traditional) model, the diversion model, the "victim allocution" model (a strong version of Ziegenhagen's participation approach), the "separatist model" (similar to the managerial approach), and two reparative models—the "court-led hybrid model" and the "integrated 'restorative justice' model"—which bear a resemblance to the integrative proposals presented at the end of the present chapter.

My earlier article (Sebba, 1982) briefly considered the relative merits of the adversary-retribution model and the social defense–welfare model. It was observed that "the unlimited resources and expertise available to the modern state should guarantee an advantage to the social defense–welfare model, whereby the state is directly responsible both for the correction and rehabilitation of the defendant and for the welfare of the victim." Nevertheless, the adversary-retribution model was seen to be on the ascendancy. Part of the explanation for this undoubtedly lies in the fact that the "unlimited resources" are in fact only potentially available to the modern state and are in practice rationed by economic stringencies. Further, there is considerable resistance to state-sponsored "expertise," as reflected in the antiprofessionalization movement (see, e.g., Cohen, 1983).

The more detailed analysis conducted in the present study appears to confirm the ascendancy of the adversary-retribution model. While the coping needs of victims are potentially more comprehensively met by state agencies rather than by individual offenders, the evaluation of their services—in particular state compensation schemes—has shown them to be rather ineffective in this respect. On the other hand, the study of perceived justice needs of victims appears to indicate the need for an adversary or quasi-adversary proceeding to meet these needs; and this may apply to the offender too. Finally, the dominant ideology in regard to principles of justice appears to have veered in the direction of retribution or restitution, rather than rehabilitation or social control, which is a goal consistent with the adversary-retribution model rather than its alternative.

For this reason, much of the remainder of this chapter will be devoted to a consideration of the various forms such a model may take. The following variables will be taken into account: *(a)* the role of the victim in the process, *(b)* the civil-criminal dichotomy, and, briefly, *(c)* the formal-informal dichotomy, the subject of the previous chapter. After consideration of the relationships among these variables, and their relevance to the development of an adversary-retribution model, the possibility will be examined of integrating this model with some elements of the social defense–welfare model.

The Role of the Victim in the Criminal Process

Various developments and experiments designed to enhance the victim's role in the penal process were discussed in chapter 8 above. This direction of reform was found to be generally worthy of encouragement, particularly when considered against the background of the present system as described in chapter 2 and of the assessment of the victim's perceived justice needs in chapter 5. The emphasis in chapter 8 was on the potential inherent in various modes of participation for meeting the needs of the parties involved in the process. In the present section, a more formal legal typology of the nature of victim participation will be considered.

Formally, there seem to be three directions in which the enhancement of the victim's role may develop. One radical option would be to restore to the victim his or her historical role in the criminal justice system as the prosecutor—the original adversary facing the defendant. There has been some limited discussion in the literature of the desirability or otherwise of maintaining the "private prosecution" in those U.S. jurisdictions where its existence has been preserved (see McDonald, 1976a; Note, 1955; Ward, 1972; Gittler, 1984:150–51; Meier, 1992), as well as in Canada (Law Reform Commission of Canada, 1986), Europe (Joutsen, 1987), and in particular Britain (Lidstone et al., 1980; Philips, 1981; Hetherington, 1989).

Yet while support for the continued existence of this option has been voiced (see below), and it has even been suggested that some expansion of this institution might be considered (McDonald, 1976a; Goldstein, 1982; Gittler, 1984), there has been, to my knowledge, no comprehensive proposal for its adoption as an overall solution, that is, the return of the prosecutorial power from the state to the individual victim,[3] or rather to the individual citizen, for historically the power to prosecute was not confined to the victim. Moreover, it has been suggested by Green (1988), on the basis of recent case law, and in particular the Supreme Court case of *Young v. United States ex rel. Vuitton et Fils* (107 S.Ct. 2124, 1987)—in which a private attorney was appointed "special prosecutor" to prosecute for contempt for violations of an injunction in a trademark case—that private prosecutions may today be unconstitutional under American law. Citing this and other cases, Green (1988) takes the view that private prosecutor statutes "compromise a criminal defendant's due process right to be prosecuted by a disinterested prosecutor" (495).

Nevertheless, the absence of any significant discussion, even at an academic level, of the revival of private prosecutions seems surprising, in view of the plethora of innovative solutions being propounded generally on the victim's behalf; for this is a remedy that not only is supported by historical tradition (Steinberg, 1984; Law Reform Commission of Canada, 1986: Appendix) but also would give expression par excellence to such current ideals as retribution (or desert) and the involvement of the victim in the justice system. Indeed, it would provide a means of returning to the victim his or her conflict (cf. Christie, 1977).

Moreover, if coupled with an emphasis on restitutionary justice—again, consistent with historical precedent (see chap. 7)—such a system could contribute to the alleviation of the victim's coping needs, in particular if the restitutional order were to have the force of a penal sanction, backed by state enforcement. Objections based upon the reluctance to rely upon the initiative of the individual citizen in instigating proceedings have not prevented the advocacy of other solutions of a civil or an informal nature, discussed elsewhere in this study, which share the same disadvantage (if such it is). It may be surmised that the reasons why this solution has not been more generally advocated are primarily the following:

1. Victims would prosecute out of vindictive motives; this has been the type of criticism leading the courts to restrict the use of private prosecutions (cf. Green, 1988:495). However, as noted in chapter 5, victims are not necessarily vindictive, nor prosecutors disinterested (Gittler, 1984:153–54; Goldstein, 1982:555). Moreover, a judicial process seems the proper outlet for vindictiveness (Boudreaux, 1989), in particular as the court would be the ultimate arbiter of both guilt and punishment.[4] Due process under the adversary system could continue, but with a change in the identity of the adversary.

2. The "public interest" would not be taken into consideration, in particular for the purpose of refraining from prosecution in "hard" cases where it would be desired to avoid the infliction of stigma on the defendant. This, however, ignores the victim's interest. Moreover, stigma can be reduced by judicial techniques such as probation without conviction. Alternatively, the decision to prosecute might be subjected to some form of control. In England, the Royal Commission on Criminal Procedure suggested that private prosecutions should be permitted where the Crown prosecutor declined to prosecute, if leave were granted by a magistrate's court (Philips, 1981:161); however, such judicial control of prosecution in the United States might be perceived as a breach of the separation of powers (Gittler, 1984:161 n. 135; Green, 1988:496).[5]

3. There would be a danger of "compounding," that is, accepting payment in consideration for nonprosecution (cf. Gittler, 1984:155). However, this may be regarded as unacceptable only insofar as private prosecution is seen to reflect a public interest. Moreover, if prosecution were indeed to be perceived as a private interest, perhaps compounding would cease to be an offense. Indeed, provision for mediation proceedings, either in lieu of or integrated with the criminal prosecution (see below) would in effect institutionalize the practice of compounding. Such practices would come to replace the plea bargain, which dominates the current system.

4. It is assumed that the cost of private prosecution would deter victims from invoking this process (cf. ibid., 130). This would depend upon the victim's access to investigatory services and upon the need for, and access to, legal representation. A British study found that in prosecutions conducted by private individuals little use was made of the services of advocates; among a sample of 392 cases, 90% were conducted by private individuals (Lidstone et al., 1980:101). There is also some basis in the research findings

referred to earlier for believing that prosecution without the use of counsel might be preferred by at least some victim-disputants. On the other hand, to prevent the inequality that would arise assuming that the *defendant's* right to counsel were retained, counsel would have to be made available to the victim-prosecutor.[6] This is seen to render such proceedings prohibitively costly (Gittler, 1984:154) where such prosecutions would be *supplementary* to public prosecutions taking place today.

This argument would not apply, however, if private prosecutions were to *replace* public prosecutions. Prosecuting victim advocates might have to be paid out of public funds. The question would arise whether such advocates would be personal attorneys appointed by the victim, whether they might be "class" advocates, or whether there would be a system equivalent to the public defender, namely, a system of public prosecutors. The wheel would appear to have turned full circle! However, such public prosecutors would legally be appearing on behalf of the victim rather than the state. If such a system seems not very different from the idea of maintaining the present system of public prosecution, while merely prevailing upon the official agencies to be more amenable to victim needs, this also indicates that the proposal for private prosecution may be less unthinkable than it seems at first glance.

5. The victim might not wish to prosecute, or there might be no specific victim, and the public might be threatened by having a dangerous offender at large. In response to this, a supplementary role might be preserved for the public prosecutor in such cases, in addition to those cases in which the state was the victim.[7]

It should be noted in this context that the private prosecution has survived, although only as an alternative to public prosecutions, in a large number of both common-law and civil-law jurisdictions. As to the former, the proposal on the part of the British Royal Commission on Criminal Procedure to limit the availability of private prosecution was not incorporated into the legislation establishing the "Crown Prosecution" system in 1985, for the view prevailed that private prosecution was, to cite one of the Law Lords, "an important constitutional safeguard and right of the ordinary citizen" (Hetherington, 1989:86, 153ff.).[8] Similarly, the Law Reform Commission of Canada (1986), which conducted a detailed review of private prosecution in historical context, concluded that "it is our belief that a criminal justice system that makes full provision for private prosecution of criminal and quasi-criminal offenses has advantages over one that does not. In any system of law, particularly one dealing with crimes, it is of fundamental importance to involve the citizen positively" (3).

Finally, Joutsen (1987:183ff.), in his review of European practices in this area, noted the existence of private prosecutions in many countries. In Finland, in particular, "the right of prosecution is always held by the complainant," who may act quite independently of the state prosecutor (187). Joutsen proffers the view that it is "almost always" preferable from the point of view of the complainant to have the offense prosecuted by the public prosecutor, on grounds of expertise, cost, and convenience, but he does not cite empirical evidence on this point.

It is strange that while American jurisdictions have adopted a number of novel and radical victim-related reforms and remedies in recent years, there has been almost no consideration of a remedy that has obstinately survived—albeit not widely used—in so many other jurisdictions. Indeed, as noted, the scope of this remedy in the United States may even be contracting, a process doubtless encouraged by the Supreme Court decision referred to above with respect to the defendant's right to a disinterested prosecutor. It is not altogether clear, however, that the revival of private prosecution would constitute a greater threat to the defendant than some of the victim-related reforms that have been adopted. Moreover, some of the punitive but notionally civil remedies currently gaining force on the American legal scene, which will be discussed below, bear a strong resemblance to private prosecution.

It is thus somewhat surprising that more thought has not been devoted to the consideration of this institution, as well as to its evaluation in the jurisdictions in which it has survived and the development of experimental programs in other jurisdictions. There may be then a firmer basis for considering the expansion of this remedy whether generally or for certain categories of victims.[9]

The least extreme of the three directions of reform would be to strengthen the victim's passive (or indirect) role in the criminal justice system, that is, by recognizing his or her interest in this system and the need for various agencies to take account of this interest. Such a trend is reflected in some of the reforms discussed in chapters 8 and 10, such as the American Bar Association's Guidelines, the federal Victims' Rights and Restitution Act of 1990, and the various victims' bills of rights. Moreover, as noted in chapter 7, the adoption of a "just-deserts" philosophy may in itself be seen as a reflection of this approach.

Support for this approach has been forthcoming from the U.S. Supreme Court in recent years. While its most dramatic expression can be seen in *Payne v. Tennessee*, in which the relevance of victim-related information at the sentencing stage was recognized, the view that "courts may not ignore the concerns of victims" dates back to the Burger Court (in particular to Chief Justice Burger himself).[10] Thus, for example, the Court refused to order a new trial in a rape case—sought on the ground that the defense had had insufficient time to prepare—where this would be likely to prove excessively traumatic for the victim (O'Neill, 1984:379–80).[11]

If the duty not to ignore the rights of the victim pertains not only to the courts but also to other state criminal justice agencies, recognition of this duty could lead to an enforceable right exercisable against the police and the prosecution—as well as against the prisons, the parole board, and the pardoning authority—when decisions are taken regarding the suspect-defendant's arrest, bail, prosecution, and release. This would require the recognition of the victim's "standing" before the courts so that victims could petition for an injunction against these agencies to prevent the implementation of a decision to which they were opposed, or for *mandamus* in the case of the state's refusal to act in accordance with their wishes.

Petitions to interfere with an agency decision have been notoriously difficult to pursue in the U.S. courts (Gittler, 1984:152, 162), and in *Linda R. S. v. Richard D.*, the Supreme Court held that "a private citizen lacks a judicially" cognizable interest in the prosecution or non-prosecution of another" (cf. Goldstein, 1982; Aynes, 1984; Gittler, 1984).[12] Nevertheless, the possible use of such remedies has been discussed in the recent literature (Green, 1988; Wainstein, 1988), and they are already available in other jurisdictions (Sebba, 1982:221; Gittler, 1984:180). Moreover, victims have specifically been granted standing under the recent Texas constitutional amendment to enforce rights conferred under that same amendment (see art. 1, sec. 30(e)).[13] Other possible remedies are appeals to a higher prosecuting authority (Sebba, 1982:221; Joutsen, 1987:185) or directly to the grand jury (Gittler, 1984:162). Pursuance of this approach would give the victim an indirect role in the penal process in ensuring that the state, having usurped the victim's erstwhile role as protagonist, was now discharging its duty as surrogate prosecutor.

There remains a possible intermediary role for the victim, between the extremes of private prosecution on the one hand and mere recognition as an indirect or vicariously interested party on the other. The victim could be given an active role in the system, not as a replacement for the representatives of the state law enforcement agencies, but in addition to these representatives. Developments in this direction were discussed above, in the context of plea bargaining and "allocution." Such a role could be played by the victim either in person or through an attorney. Thus, it may be recalled that, according to the German *Nebenklage* procedure, the victim has the right to be represented by his or her own advocate in the course of the criminal trial,[14] and similar practices are admitted in a number of U.S. jurisdictions (see above, chap. 8).

Some contributors to the academic debate have pointed out that granting status to the victim in the criminal process need not result in the conferral of total parity with the other parties, namely, the state and the defendant. Goldstein (1982) cited arguments to the effect that a "party's rights need not be unitary" and suggested that the victim's right to participate might arise only at certain stages of the process, "after conviction, on issues connected with restitution and sentencing, and before conviction, in hearings on dismissals, charge reductions, and guilty pleas" (553, 557).

Similarly, Gittler has noted that "there can be different types of parties with varying attributes, playing different roles in terms of the nature and extent of their participation in a proceeding. Thus, the characterization of the victim as a party would not necessarily mean that the victim would have the same or comparable rights to the state or the defendant at all stages of the proceedings" (Gittler, 1984:177). In an earlier version of her paper, Gittler suggested the concept of "quasi-party" and invoked various civil-law analogies, including the role of *amicus curiae*. On the other hand, Thorvaldson (1983) argued that the victim's interest in a criminal case could not be conceptually distinguished from the interests of the community.

The proposals to grant the victim quasi-party status are essentially consistent with the amendment recently adopted to a number of state constitutions (notably Florida and New Mexico) and the proposed amendment to the federal Constitution (President's Task Force, 1982:114) granting the victim the right to be heard at all "critical" stages of the proceedings. As indicated in chapter 8, this solution seems potentially consistent with the furtherance of victims' perceived justice and possibly also coping needs, although research findings so far available indicate only modest success.

One further issue that must be considered in this context is that of the rights of the defendant. As noted earlier, the California Bill of Rights ("Proposition 8") for the victim was opposed by civil libertarians as a threat to the constitutional rights of the defendant. However, in spite of the nominal concern for victims on the part of the proponents of that reform, the controversy focused instead on the traditional balance between government and defendant.[15] How far the enhancement of specifically victim-oriented rights might affect the defendant has received little attention, although an attempt to speculate on this has been made in the course of the present study.

Weigend (1982), in his illuminating article on victim/witness programs, asserts that criminal justice is a "zero-sum game" and that "no one can gain except on someone else's loss" (15), a concept that has been applied previously to the traditional parties in the system, the state and the defendant (cf., e.g., Hogarth, 1974). If Weigend is right, it may be impractical merely to attach to victims' rights legislation a proviso guaranteeing the preservation of defendants' rights, the formula adopted in constitutional amendments in Florida and Kansas (see chap. 8). Rather, priorities will have to be established and value judgments made regarding the respective rights and interests of victims and defendants.

While the available literature does not seem to have dealt directly with these issues, some of the relevant questions have been raised indirectly. Thus the restitution provisions of the Victim and Witness Protection Act of 1982 were initially held to be in violation of the due process clause of the Fifth Amendment (Gittler, 1984:176 n. 183)—that is, the constitutional rights of the defendant restricted the implementation of a measure designed to benefit the victim. (On appeal, however, the provisions of the act were upheld; see chap. 7.)

Reference was made earlier to Chief Justice Warren Burger's refusal to order a retrial in a rape case owing to the suffering that this would inflict upon the victim. Similarly, in *Maryland v. Craig* (497 U.S. 836 1991), the Supreme Court allowed the use of video testimony in order to protect a small child from having to face his alleged attacker in open court. In these cases the defendant's rights appear clearly to have been sacrificed to the victim's interests. In the cases dealing with victim-related evidence in capital cases, the justices of the Supreme Court were conscious of the need to determine where the balance between defendants' and victims' interests lay (cf. Sebba, 1994). The pendulum moved dramatically between the 1987 case of *Booth v. Maryland*, in which evidence of this nature was held to be inadmissible at the sentencing stage, to the 1991 case of *Payne v. Tennessee*, in which it was held to be admissible.

The more active the role conferred upon the victim, the more such issues are likely to arise, and only Solomonic solutions will prevent the occasional clash of interests and the need to establish priorities.

Criminal Law versus Civil Law

While a prolific literature has emerged on the use of informal alternatives to the criminal justice system, and some writers have referred to the adoption of a more "civilized" process—that is, a process that would bear a greater resemblance to the civil law (see below)—relatively little emphasis has been given in the victim-related literature on the availability to the victim of conventional civil remedies vis-à-vis the offender in respect of the wrong inflicted. While reviews of remedies available to victims may refer to the possibility of civil actions for damages (Stark and Goldstein, 1985) and may consider their advantages and disadvantages (Karmen, 1990:296–99; cf. O'Brien, 1992), most of the discussion of civil remedies has focused instead on the development of preventive measures, in particular "protection orders," intended to protect the victim from further injury (see, e.g., Finn and Colson, 1990), especially in relation to domestic violence and the prevention of the intimidation of witnesses (ABA, 1981). The development of civil actions for damages, on the other hand, has focused mainly on suits against "third parties," which will be considered in the next chapter.

The paucity of serious discussion of civil remedies is even more surprising than the neglect of private prosecution discussed above, for the civil remedy, unlike the private prosecution, is not a historic relic that has fallen into desuetude but the official legal remedy currently available in principle to almost all victims. Most crimes have their equivalent in the law of torts: most offenses against the person constitute the tort of assault, trespass, or negligence (cf. Greer, 1991:145), while thefts and frauds may be grounds for the tort of conversion. Thus the victim may sue the offender in a civil suit for damages—on the face of it the obvious mechanism for remedying the injustice inflicted by the offender.

Indeed, the availability of the civil-law remedy has been the traditional response of jurists when faced with criticism of the neglect of the victim in the criminal law. Moreover, in a civil suit the victim is the instigator of the proceedings, so that the conflict remains his or hers (cf. Nils Christie's critique referred to in chap. 11). At least in the context of the small claims court, the victim-plaintiff may retain some control (cf. Karmen, 1990:298), thereby creating a greater potential for personal satisfaction in accordance with Thibault and Walker's theory of procedural justice discussed in chapter 5. The question therefore arises, why is this remedy not generally perceived to be the solution to the victim's problems? Can its current limitations be overcome, rendering it a viable alternative to the other reforms considered in this study? Further, if the civil action is to provide a remedy for the victim, should it be more closely linked to the criminal process, or should it supersede this process altogether? These questions will now be considered, taking into account as far as possible the three main issues that have constituted the framework of analysis for this study: the coping needs of the parties, their perceived justice needs, and fundamental principles of justice.

Current Civil Remedies

While data regarding tort litigation practices in general are not well documented (Saks, 1992), there seems to be particularly little specific information available on the degree to which crime victims avail themselves of tort remedies against offenders. For evidence of the limited use of these remedies, the American literature has generally relied upon a small Canadian survey conducted in 1969 (see, e.g., Gittler 1984:138 n. 72). The Canadian study cited found that among a sample of 167 victims of serious crimes of violence in the Toronto area in 1966 only 14.9% even considered suing the offender for damages, only 5.4% actually consulted a lawyer for this purpose, 4.8% attempted to obtain compensation, and only 1.8% (3 of the 167) in fact succeeded in doing so (Linden, 1975). The impression of limited recourse to tort remedies is indirectly confirmed by some other studies, such as the low priority given to legal advice—presumably a precondition for a tort suit—in the New York study of victims' reactions to crime (Friedman et al., 1982:169). Similarly, the British study by Shapland et al. (1985) found that only 4% of their sample even knew about the possibility of a civil action, a finding similar to that of previous studies (124, 125).

The limited potential for bringing a successful tort suit may be evident to most crime victims and may go far to explain their limited use of this remedy: the perpetrator of the harmful act may not have been identified, the cost of bringing the suit may be prohibitive, and the defendant may lack assets (cf. Mueller and Cooper, 1974:85, 87; Karmen, 1990:298–99).[16] Further, the imposition of a prison sentence will do little to enhance the offender's ability to pay.[17] Finally, execution of judgment is left to the initiative of the plaintiff-victim, so that even where feasible it may be troublesome and expensive.[18] This may explain why penal reformers have tended to favor solutions involving recourse to the criminal court rather than advocate the enhancement of the victim's civil remedy (Harland, 1982).

However, it should be noted that law reformers have devoted considerable energy in modern times to democratizing the legal system, in the sense of endeavoring to render legal remedies available to wider sections of the population—based partly on surveys of "legal needs" (Curran, 1977)—in order to improve "access to justice." This process is seen to have passed through three stages (Cappelletti and Garth, 1978): first, the institution of legal aid schemes; second, the development of new forms of procedure, such as class and representative actions; third, a broader and more comprehensive approach, involving new, alternative mechanisms of dispute resolution, such as small claims courts, consumer tribunals, mediation proceedings, and so on. This approach also includes new substantive remedies, such as no-fault compensation in the case of accidents.

The last-mentioned reform has clearly had great impact,[19] but it is a departure from the traditional tortious action—and traditional tort philosophy (England, 1993: chap. 7)—in that it involves insurance, whether private or national. It has an equivalent in the context of crime victims in the form of the compensation schemes discussed above in chapter 9, although in some cases a tort action against the offender may have greater potential than a claim from the compensation board (Greer, 1991:145). On the other hand, much of the litigation in the courts and tribunals referred to is of a contractual rather than a tortious nature and thus not relevant to the crime victim. Further, insofar as the trends described are dependent on legal aid, "access to justice" may be expected to be affected by prevailing governmental policies, such as the degree of support for the Legal Services Corporation.

Calabresi (1979) reviewed some developments that were specifically calculated to democratize tort litigation, in particular the contingent fee and the possibility of claiming damages for "pain and suffering"—especially before a jury—which rendered tort suits potentially more remunerative (177–83). However, these developments also made the whole procedure more complex and costly and gave rise to pressure for reform, including reforms designed to limit the liability of defendants (NOVA, 1989:29). Moreover, the potential benefits may still not be great enough to render litigation accessible to the average crime victim, for whom the harm inflicted is limited. Finally, the reforms did little to overcome some of the problems referred to above, such as that of enforcing the judgment against a defendant with limited assets.

Thus, the present availability of traditional tort remedies for the crime victim, although unlimited in principle, seems to be limited in practice. Various modifications of this remedy will be considered below, including the possibility of tort litigation as an adjunct to the criminal process. However, the phenomenon of an independent legal remedy (viz., the tort action) that exists in theory but rarely in practice should in itself be an object of further study and consideration. Persons opposed to tampering with the criminal process for the victim's benefit have a special obligation to develop this existing alternative remedy. For these reasons, further research on the availability of the tort remedy seems essential.

Linkage of Civil and Criminal Remedies

One method of increasing the availability of civil-law remedies would be to strengthen their link with the criminal justice system, thereby both alleviating the burden imposed upon the victim who instigates proceedings and reducing the costs to be incurred. There appear to be three possible levels at which such linkage may take place.

The most tenuous type of linkage between the civil action and the criminal trial is reflected in some reforms carried out in the Israeli system a few years ago (Sebba, 1982). First, the former common-law rule applying to most American jurisdictions (Covey, 1975:220, 229), whereby findings of the criminal court could not be relied upon in the civil court but had to be proved ab initio by the plaintiff, was abolished. (An amendment proposed to the federal Criminal Code would have gone further and enabled a criminal conviction to trigger a civil class action; Goldstein, 1982:542–43.) Second, the judge who tried the criminal case could be requested to hear the civil claim immediately following the termination of the criminal trial.[20] This would be expected to increase efficiency and to reduce delays. Such reforms do not directly affect the criminal trial but are designed to reduce the victim's burden in the related civil claim. However, the instigation of parallel criminal and civil proceedings might be oppressive vis-à-vis defendants (McDade and O'Donnell, 1992).

The second level of linkage relates to the possibility of ancillary remedies of a civil nature being administered by the criminal court judge. Many states have provisions for criminal courts to issue protection orders to prevent the intimidation of witnesses (NOVA, 1989:15), and civil protection orders in domestic violence cases are sometimes combined with the hearing of the criminal charge (Finn and Colson, 1990:30–31). In Britain it has recently been proposed that the police be vested with power in such cases to seek civil remedies on behalf of victims (House of Commons, 1993:xxxviii). However, while this type of proceeding enables the victim to receive certain forms of assistance from the court, it is not tantamount to a civil claim for compensation.

The third and most extreme level of linkage is the possibility that the victim would be given standing at the criminal trial as a civil party. This differs from the consideration of quasi-party status above, which referred to the victim's standing as a party to the criminal proceedings as such.

Reference here is to the practice recognized under many legal systems in continental Europe whereby the victim has official recognition as a *partie civile*, or under the so-called adhesion process. Under this system, the civil claim is effectively integrated into the criminal trial.

Such integration is by no means a simple matter, and many aspects remain disputed among Continental jurists, as reflected by the diverse practices prevailing in different jurisdictions (cf. Joutsen, 1987:192–96). Spinellis (1986) argues that the term *adhesion* generally implies a more limited form of participation, as illustrated by the German system, compared with the concept of "civil party" as applied in France, Italy, and Greece. There are also varying approaches on the question of whether only the victim or other person suffering damage may instigate the action or whether the state may do this on his or her behalf, and whether the victim bringing such an action is still a "witness" for the purpose of the criminal trial or whether he or she becomes a party (Kobe, 1976).

Nevertheless, the value in principle of having such a proceeding was supported by a majority of the participants at the Eleventh International Congress on Penal Law who debated this topic in 1974, while "admitting however that this process may have certain disadvantages" (Resolutions of the Congress, 31). Surprisingly, "It was recommended, however, that the adhesion process should be restricted to a decision on whether the claim was justified, when the decision as to the amount of compensation would be left to the appropriate civil court or to a subsequent special criminal procedure" (32). While the technical difficulties of assessing compensation (restitution) in the course of a criminal trial have already been noted, the idea of a second judicial proceeding for this purpose would seem to defeat one of the main objectives of an integrated proceeding, namely, obviating the need for duplication.

European countries that have adopted this system, which is also prevalent in South America (Mueller, 1977:76), seem to have had mixed experiences. It has been particularly popular in the Nordic and (former) socialist countries (Joutsen, 1987:196). Indeed, in the Democratic Republic of Germany "the presentation of a civil claim [was] *an integral part of criminal proceedings*" (emphasis added).

The Federal Republic, on the other hand, used this system only rarely and reluctantly (Harland, 1982). Legislative reforms were introduced in that country in 1976 and 1986 in order to remove restrictions and encourage its wider use (Kaiser, 1991:546–49). However, a survey conducted by Kaiser (1991) revealed that it was perceived as a "foreign body" in the system by criminal justice professionals (575) and that its use, unlike that of the *Nebenklage* or subsidiary prosecutor, remained rare (561). The author concluded that "the attempt of a renaissance of the adhesive procedure has failed" (563). In contrast, a detailed study of the practice of the Austrian courts revealed that whereas only a single case of subsidiary prosecution emerged in a sample of 624, the injured person participated as a civil party in more than one-half of the cases—particularly, but by no means exclusively, in cases of property offenses (Kraintz, 1991:645, 665). The research found, however, that these civil parties only rarely exercised active participatory rights, such as the questioning of witnesses, apparently because this was not encouraged by the presiding judge (ibid., 655, 666).

In France, too, the civil party is a more popular institution than its German equivalent. One survey found that it was used by one-third of the victims (Sabatie, 1985). However, its relative popularity in France was sometimes attributed to motives of vengeance and extortion (Bouzat and Pinatel, 1970: 2:929). A 1931 law therefore limited the victim's right to set in motion the criminal trial for this purpose, and the Court of Cassation held that it should be seen as a right of an exceptional nature to be asserted only within the strict limits provided by the code of criminal procedure (ibid., 930). Amending legislation of 1983 has encouraged use of this remedy by alleviating the burden imposed upon the victim of paying costs into court when instigating his or her civil action (Verin, 1984); it also provided that a valid defense to a criminal charge may not necessarily relieve the accused of a duty to compensate the victim under the accompanying civil action (Merigeau, 1991).

These procedures appear to have considerable attractiveness in the context of the present study. The victim is granted standing at the trial, but only as a civil party.[21] Thus, the traditional balance between state and accused in terms of the criminal law is preserved. The victim is in a position to pursue his or her material interests while at the same time potentially deriving some satisfaction from involvement in the process. In this respect Spinellis (1986) notes that in many cases it is this involvement and the "moral recognition" of the victims' status that is the driving motivation, as indicated by the fact that they are often satisfied with "nonmaterial" damages (413–14).

It may be that the special characteristics of the adversary process, including the accused's right to silence, and the different rules in criminal and civil cases regarding burden of proof render the incorporation of such a procedure in countries with a common-law tradition such as the United States problematic (cf. Mueller, 1977:82); such considerations may explain the somewhat dismissive approach to the fusion of civil and criminal remedies by common-law commentators (Joutsen, 1987:195). However, in view of the benefits deriving therefrom, and in the light of the observation by Joutsen (ibid.) that the "imbedded distinction between torts and crimes" is "not necessarily understood by the complainants themselves" in common-law countries, it would seem that there was room for further consideration of the European "combined" models considered above, if not of an integrated model.

An Integrated Model: "Civilizing" the Criminal Process or "Penalizing" the Civil?

Not only does the subject matter of tort law overlap with that of criminal law, historically the two areas of the law were hardly capable of differentiation.[22] Nevertheless, the dichotomization of the law in this respect has been taken for granted in modern times, and the call for unification was in the past heard only very sporadically.[23]

Lamborn (1968) noted three main characteristics differentiating criminal from civil law: the identity of the enforcer (the state in criminal law, the private citizen in civil law), the identity of the beneficiary (the public vs. the plaintiff), and the nature of the sanction (punishment vs. compensation). To these may be added other traditional distinctions: emphasis on the moral turpitude of the perpetrator in criminal law (vs. emphasis on the harm caused in civil law) and differences in the rules of evidence as well as the procedural rights of the parties (cf. Mann, 1992:1813). However, many of the distinctions are not absolute but are instead matters of emphasis (cf. Epstein, 1977). Further, it is clear that the change in orientation that the victim movement has sought to introduce, such as an enhanced role for the victim in the criminal process and an emphasis on restitution in the sanctioning system, would confer on this process a greater resemblance to the civil action than has been the case in modern times. Other writers have emphasized the humane aspects of "civilizing" the criminal justice system—a concept suggested in 1976 on both sides of the Atlantic by Gilbert Cantor (Wright, 1991:41) and Louk Hulsman (Wright, 1982:249), respectively.

Conversely, tort litigation in the United States has been characterized by the development of the use of punitive damages, an institution that, while dating back several decades (Grube, 1993), has recently been forced into the limelight. This is owing perhaps less to the extent of its use (Galanter, 1991:769) than to the occasional dramatic example, such as the

Ford Pinto case, in which the jury awarded $125 million—subsequently reduced by the court—and to the passions that such damages arouse among legal theorists (see, e.g., England, 1993: chap. 11). Potential defendants, and in particular insurance interests, have endeavored to promote "tort reform" in order to reduce potential liability.

The use of punitive damages in traditional tort cases on the part of the courts has been accompanied by other related developments under statute. First, administrative agencies have increasingly been empowered both to impose punitive financial sanctions and to prosecute in civil judicial proceedings (Mann, 1992:1849–51). Second, under certain statutes, notably the False Claims Act, private citizens have been encouraged to instigate proceedings in the name of the government (so-called *ex tam* actions). Successful prosecution in a civil court will lead to multiple damages, a share of which is guaranteed to the plaintiff. Although such plaintiffs are referred to as "private attorneys general" (ibid., 1800), the action here, unlike that in a private prosecution, is civil in character and is brought for financial profit rather than vindication. Thus it resembles the historic "penal action" (Kenny, 1952). Third, under the provisions of the Racketeer Influence and Corrupt Organizations Act (RICO), "Congress converted entire sections of the federal criminal code into civil wrongs" (Mann, 1992:1848), enabling injured parties to sue for treble damages ("Civil RICO"). This development is the most pertinent in the present context, since the suit is brought by the victim and the penalty related to the harm inflicted.

The above types of proceedings, although civil in procedural terms, are at the same time unashamedly punitive in orientation and have been so designated by the U.S. Supreme Court (see, e.g., *U.S. v. Halper,* 104 L Ed 2d 487). Indeed, they often involve sanctions heavier than a criminal court would be empowered to impose following conviction. They may thus be considered the converse of the idea of "civilizing" the criminal process. These convergent (or intersecting) trends raise the question of the desirability of a merger of criminal and civil processes into an integrated system, whether this be perceived as "civilizing" the criminal justice system, as proposed in the ideological literature referred to above, or as "penalizing" the civil courts, in the spirit of the developments described by Mann. The implications of such a merger will be considered here from the point of view of the criteria adopted in this study.

As to the victim's coping needs, inevitably a system designed primarily to determine the amount of harm inflicted on the victim-plaintiff rather than the degree of moral turpitude of the perpetrator, and to impose upon the defendant an obligation to compensate rather than a purely punitive sanction, would in principle be more beneficial to the victim than the prevailing criminal justice system.[24] This would apply with even greater force if an enlarged "penal" compensation—or punitive damages—were available. Moreover, the chances of a successful prosecution would be enhanced if the burden of proof was that applicable in civil cases, and if defendants were not able to benefit from the constitutional guarantees designed to protect criminal suspects, such as the right to silence.[25] In this respect, even a "middleground jurisprudence" (Mann, 1992), that is, the adoption of standards between the criminal and the civil, would be beneficial from the victim's point of view.

The main disadvantage for the victim—in some respects resembling those mentioned in the context of private prosecutions—would be that in a purely civil matter between private parties the state does not conduct the investigation and organize the witnesses, nor does it take steps to ensure the execution of the court's order. A study of a small-claims court (O'Barr and Conley, 1988) found that plaintiffs generally assumed that this type of service was provided. These problems could be overcome if the instigator of the "integrated" process could have the benefit of the assistance of some of the investigative and enforcement agencies currently identified exclusively with the criminal process. On the other hand, with respect to "discovery" of documents, civil actions are advantageous (Mann, 1992:1855–58). Moreover, if an element of "informalism" were introduced (see below), formal problems of access to information would be further reduced.

The victim would also be deprived of the protection derived in some cases from having the offender incarcerated. To some extent this could be achieved by civil means, such as protection orders enforced by the threat of imprisonment for contempt of court in the event of noncompliance. However, since incarceration is generally intended to protect the public at large rather than the individual victim, it will be more appropriate to consider this issue under the heading of societal needs.

The *defendant* would gain from this system because there would not generally be a risk of incarceration. It is true that the baseline for liability might be broadened, since, if the criteria were those of civil law, liability would be incurred even in the absence of *mens rea*, although proof of mental element may result in an upgrading of the punitive sanction (ibid., 1801 n. 22). On the other hand, even under criminal law, responsibility is sometimes incurred without *mens rea*, while, conversely, some torts require proof of intent. As indicated above, the burden of proof would be lighter, although for civil actions of a punitive character some jurisdictions require

" 'clear and convincing evidence', a standard which lies halfway towards the criminal one of 'beyond reasonable doubt' " (England, 1993:149). Similarly, new standards would be developed—on the lines of the "middleground jurisprudence" described by Mann—in relation to both evidentiary issues and constitutional protections.

With respect to civil actions instigated by victims, the degree of protection provided by the U.S. Constitution may be limited, since the Constitution is seen essentially as an instrument to control state power rather than the claims of individual citizens (Dolliver, 1987:91; see also above, chap. 6). This was the reasoning behind the Court's decision in *Browning-Ferris v. Kelco Disposal* (1989, 106 L Ed 219), a case in which a jury awarded the plaintiff company $6 million in punitive damages—117 times more than the actual damages suffered by the plaintiff (243)—for an antitrust violation. A majority of the court held that the prohibition on "excessive fines" under the Eighth Amendment was confined to actions—including civil suits—that were initiated by the government, or in which the government had an interest; in other words, this prohibition was not seen to be applicable in *citizen*-initiated actions.[26]

Finally, what of the needs of society as a whole? While tort law has laid greater emphasis on the interests of the individual plaintiff and criminal law on the public interest, this dichotomization is not absolute (Blum-West and Carter, 1983:548–49; England, 1993:147). Some of the traditional functions of criminal law, such as deterrence and even retribution, are attributed to tort law (cf. Cane, 1987). Tort law appears to lack the rehabilitative and incapacitative orientations generally attributed to the criminal law, and a special solution not covered by traditional tort concepts may be necessary for the "dangerous" wrongdoer (civil commitment?). Similarly, a solution would have to be found for offenses lacking an individual victim, either government-initiated tort actions or "relator" actions on the model described above. Some attention was given to these issues in the preceding chapter in the context of informal alternatives, and they will be considered again in the framework of the proposed model presented at the end of this chapter.

As to financial considerations, the recent popularity of punitive civil proceedings is assumed to give rise to a saving in costs expended on the public prosecution agencies, in particular where private initiatives are concerned (Mann, 1992:1868). In addition, the emphasis on pecuniary sanctions rather than incarcerating institutions—insofar as these have been replaced (see below)—must surely result in a financial saving to the public purse. Finally, a system of punitive damages may result in a direct financial benefit to state revenues (or to a designated fund, possibly for the benefit of victims). A number of writers and legal systems have determined that damages ordered for punitive purposes should be payable, at least in part, to the state (cf. Grube, 1993).

What would be the consequences of adopting such a system from the point of view of the perceptions of the relevant parties? Evidence on this is inevitably of an indirect nature. However, it emerged from the studies of victims' attitudes that their main interest seemed to be a sense of participation in the process and the prospect of some material benefit (restitution). Both these subjective needs would be enhanced by the adoption of a civil or quasi-civil process. Moreover, the objective of meeting the claimant's perceived justice needs in this respect is recognized by some of the jurisprudential writing on tort law, in which considerable attention is paid to the "satisfaction" or even "vindication" function of the tort remedy (Cane, 1987:486), to which is attributed—at least in some legal systems—"the specific objective of assuaging the aggrieved party's violated sense of justice" (Tunc, n.d.:10). This appears to refer not only to the actual financial satisfaction represented by a successful claim but also to the psychological feeling of well-being that would follow such success. Thus, tort-based compensation has generally been found consistent with perceptions of equity (Harris et al., 1984:140ff.), while Walker (1982) observes that "civil justice or therapy may be better alternatives for relief of anger than state-controlled penal justice" (14).

Finally, insofar as civil remedies are more suited to conflicts of a "private" nature, it should be noted that many conflicts formally defined as criminal are in fact perceived by victims as being more amenable to private remedies. Thus Reynolds and Blyth (1976), in their survey of residents of Minneapolis–St. Paul, found that a majority of victims (63%) perceived "private treatment" as being the more appropriate for "interpersonal" conflicts, while substantial minorities elected for this solution for serious crimes (30%), crimes of medium seriousness (44%), and minor infractions (38%). In the Hamburg survey conducted by Sessar (1984), 51.6% of respondents favored "private assessment outside criminal justice system"[27] for property crimes (for some offenses the figure exceeded 85%), and 36.5% for violent crimes; and these figures were somewhat higher for respondents with victimization experience than for those without. Moreover, a majority of victims in the United States do not find it appropriate to report the offense to the police (U.S. Department of Justice, 1992:102), particularly in respect to "personal offenses."

The defendant might also be expected to appreciate the justice of incurring the obligation to repay the victim for the damage inflicted. Such an obligation would be consistent with equity theory, as noted in the context of restitutionary remedies; indeed, according to this theory, the sense of equilibrium should be shared by the victim and the observers. The use of punitive financial sanctions, however, might be problematical from this point of view unless these can somehow be rationalized in compensatory or equitable terms (see below).

There is also some indication that the general public, in spite of its presumed punitiveness, would not be entirely averse to the settlement of disputes along more "civil" lines. The Hamburg survey, as noted, showed wide support for "private assessment"; and mention was made earlier of evidence that the public is less punitive where the victims receive some attention (Cohn, 1974), as would be the case if they were to obtain restitution from the offender in a civil action. It is also well documented that law enforcement agencies see certain interpersonal disputes as having a private character (see chap. 2) and therefore more amenable to civil procedures.

Finally, are there fundamental principles of justice requiring the maintenance of a differentiation between the criminal- and civil-law systems? Although criminal law is traditionally seen as inflicting punishment on intentional wrongdoers, while tort law merely requires the payment of compensation for harm inflicted, we have seen from the foregoing discussion that this is a simplification. As noted, tort theorists attribute to the civil law objectives similar to those identified with criminal law (see also Williams, 1951), while one writer has particularly emphasized the penal aspects of this branch of the law (Stoll, 1970).

Further, the dichotomization between a criminal law based upon an ideology of societal retribution contrasted with a civil law concerned rather with a pragmatic reallocation of goods between private parties is clearly complicated by the conflicting schools of thought connected with each of these propositions. On the one hand, the schools of criminology that have predominated over the past two centuries[28] have emphasized the utilitarian functions of the criminal law, even to the extent of the virtual elimination of concepts of guilt and responsibility (Wootton, 1959; Gramatica, 1963), or of imposing responsibility for unintended harm, sometimes even in the absence of negligence (strict liability). Only recently has the retributive philosophy reemerged (see chap. 6). Further, some writers now analyze criminal, like civil, law in terms of its economic function; indeed, it is perceived by some members of this school as an alternative to the civil where problems of detection or insolvency might render civil liability inadequate (Posner, 1986).

On the other hand, tort theorists have been similarly divided into different schools regarding the function of this branch of the law. White's historical survey of tort philosophy (White, 1980) distinguishes a number of competing theories. Historically, the main debate was over the degree to which liability in tort was to be based on fault and moral principles, or whether liability might be "strict" and based on a utilitarian rationale.[29]

A new approach to tort philosophy, developed in German scholarship of the 1940s (Englard, 1993:11) and identified with much of the literature of the 1950s and 1960s (White, 1980), regards the main function of tort as the spreading of losses among different components of society and thus as a vehicle for administering distributive justice on a macro level rather than merely corrective justice, that is, between the parties concerned. (This is a distinction deriving from Aristotle; cf. Englard, 1993:11.) According to this approach, tort law is perceived as "public law in disguise" (White, 1980:218). By way of illustration, the principle of mutual social responsibility led many tort theorists to advocate no-fault insurance.

Contemporary approaches to tort, however, tend to emphasize—or reemphasize—the corrective function of tort law. The corrective approach may be based either on an economic, utilitarian rationale (Posner) or on equity and morality (Fletcher). At the same time, the writings of Calabresi and Epstein, respectively, indicate that neither the utilitarian nor the equitable rationale necessarily excludes the possible relevance of distributive or "public" considerations (Englard, 1993:14); and a similar conclusion has been reached on the basis of a "communitarian" analysis (Harris, 1989).

There are a number of key issues here that directly parallel the criminal-law debates. Some of these controversies have been marginal in criminal-law polemics. Thus ideological support for strict liability or utilitarian considerations as a basis for criminal responsibility tend to be comparatively rare (in spite of the pervasiveness of the former phenomenon). On the other hand, utilitarianism versus moral responsibility as the main criterion for dispositions has been a focal issue in criminal law too. Similarly, analysis of punishment in terms of distributive justice has fewer supporters in penal as compared with tort philosophy (but see Sadurski, 1985). Nevertheless, *(a)* restitutive sentencing bears a strong resemblance to corrective justice in tort, although arguably it has a different orientation (Thorvaldson, 1990), *(b)* the "admonitory conception of tort law" (White, 1980:239; Veitch and Miers, 1975; and cf. Englard, 1993:153) corresponds directly to the revival of retribution in the criminal law, and *(c)* provision for punitive damages may render the objectives of civil actions almost indistinguishable from those of criminal prosecutions. Even the widely held view that "tort law prices, while criminal law prohibits" (Coffee, 1991) is disputed by at least one noted tort theorist, Ernest Weinrib, who posits that a tort, as its etymology implies, "is a wrong, not a permissible act that an award of tort damages retrospectively prices or licences" (England, 1993:56).

Finally, reference may be made to the increasing emphasis on the *public* function of civil law. Here the issue is not limited to the above-mentioned controversies regarding the functions of tort law. There is an increasing perception that civil law generally is not confined in its effects to the disputing parties but fulfills a general social function. Thus Jolowicz (1983) observes that the class action is "much more than a means of securing redress for large numbers of small claimants; it provides a way of depriving the defendant of what are seen and described as his 'ill-gotten gains' and of deterring people from similar conduct in the future" (172). Such considerations have led to the view that "the non-criminal as well as the criminal law should be upheld and vindicated in the courts regardless of the wishes of those who are immediately affected by its breach" (ibid.). Some of these trends suggest that the move toward "privatization" (or "civilization") of the criminal law may be accompanied by a parallel, but reverse, move toward the "publicization" of the civil law, in addition to its "penalization." This, in turn, suggests a narrowing of the differential between the two areas.

A few years ago, Freiberg and Malley (1984) argued that the expansion of the use of "civil penalties" in a number of areas resulted in a "hybridization" that "tends to weaken or collapse the civil-criminal dichotomy" (390). This analysis has now been further fueled by the additional trends and ideologies noted above, namely, the desire to "civilize" the criminal law in general, the increasing "publicization" of the civil law, and the underlying comparability of tort and criminal-law philosophies. There is clearly a growing need to rethink the traditional dichotomy between criminal and civil law. This will have wide implications for theory and research, as well as in practical terms—not least in the context of victim-related remedies.

Informalism

The fragility of the crime-tort distinction is further illustrated by the movement in favor of informal alternatives considered in the preceding chapter. Most of the programs reviewed under that heading deal indiscriminately with both criminal and civil matters; the predominant type of conflict falling within the purview of the programs is primarily a function of the source of referral: criminal justice agencies refer primarily criminal conflicts, while community agencies are more likely to refer civil conflicts.

The reason why informal programs can effectively ignore the criminal-civil distinction without raising controversial issues is that the more technical procedural and evidentiary aspects of this distinction—relating to right to counsel, protection from self-incrimination, burden of proof, and so on—are dispensed with in the framework of these proceedings. Nevertheless, the fact remains that such programs effectively produce a merger of the two areas of law, criminal incidents being dealt with in an essentially civil fashion, resulting in a "corrective," rather than a retributive, type of disposition between the two adversaries. This at least suggests that the concept of "merger" as such is neither totally an anathema to justice officials nor totally impractical in terms of implementation.

Varieties of Dispute Processing?

The adversary-retribution model referred to at the beginning of this chapter can accommodate any of the procedural patterns alluded to above: a criminal process dominated by the victim (private prosecutions); a dual system, with both criminal and civil parties; a merged procedure largely civil in character; or an informal mediation procedure. The question arises, first, whether it is desirable that the justice system select the optimal procedure from among these possibilities and adopt it as a uniform solution, or whether it is preferable to maintain a variety of models from which a choice may be made in each case, as suggested in the well-known article echoed in the heading to this section (Sander, 1976).

Second, if there is to be a variety of procedures operating concurrently, is the selection of the procedure to be adopted in the particular case to be determined by the injured party, as advocated by some writers,[30] or by state officials, or is it to be predetermined according to the nature of the conflict? While inevitably some discretion as to the action to be adopted will always be available to the victim, who has the option of "lumping it" or of dealing directly with the wrongdoer (Felstiner, 1974; Sander, 1976), in principle it may be unfair to the defendant that the victim should have the option of selecting a more punitive or a more compensatory mode of procedure, provided that he or she is provided with at least one effective remedy. Moreover, the availability of both civil and criminal remedies, while intended to "shrink" the criminal law "next to an expanding arena of punitive civil sanctions" (Mann, 1992:1802), may in practice lead to "net-widening" (cf. Freiberg and Malley, 1984:380; Coffee, 1992); it may also discriminate against the economically disadvantaged, for whom civil sanctions would be perceived as less appropriate (Galanter, 1991:775). A unitary and substantially restitutional approach, on the other hand, whether labeled criminal or civil, would seem to cater optimally to the victim's needs, while the need for an additional and more punitive intervention would be determined by such factors as the degree of harm inflicted or the potential threat represented by the offender.

Another criterion sometimes suggested is the nature of the relationship between the parties, but the adoption of this criterion would be more controversial. While research suggests that conflicts between family and nonstrangers differ from other conflicts in their character and their amenability to resolution, there is a risk of "downgrading" the significance of nonstranger crime, as was the practice in the past, whereas the prevailing trend is rather to regard offenses committed against family members as equally or even more serious than other cases.

The fundamental problem in this context seems to be that of reconciling two conflicting trends that have been referred to at various stages in this study. One trend is toward more formalized justice, as reflected in the just-deserts model, which seeks to replace the arbitrariness that characterized the rehabilitation model of justice with the introduction of objective standards, uniformity, and thus, by implication, a greater fairness in both procedures and sanctions. The other trend is the move toward informality, destigmatization, and reconciliation. The first approach would result in standardization of outcomes according to objective criteria; the second would result in variations in outcome according to the determination of the parties involved. The simultaneous adoption of these two inconsistent approaches may be seen as a form of "trade-off" whereby the more serious cases are destined to receive the standardized treatment, and the minor cases are relegated to mediation proceedings (cf. chap. 11).

However, there is an element common to these two approaches, namely, a focus on the relationship between the offender and the victim—hence the inclusion of both under the adversary-retribution model. Under the first approach, a standardized equation is sought, based on a tariff reflecting "objective" criteria of justice (see above, chap. 7), while under the second model, the equation is to be determined ad hoc by the parties involved. The question is, can these two approaches somehow be combined? Here, again, the civil-law model can be of assistance, for under civil law the maximum

liability of the wrongdoer is determined by law, but any settlement negotiated between the parties, whether before or during the judicial proceeding, is
acceptable to the court; indeed it is encouraged. Thus, by analogy it has been
argued that a sentencing tariff would not be required where a sanction can be
determined by voluntary agreement (Wright, 1982:258). The tariff, which
under a "civilized" system would involve a financial penalty directly related to the injury inflicted—although on the analogy of the punitive civil
model it might be a multiple thereof—would thus become a maximum
sanction held in reserve. This would be reminiscent of the XII Tables of
ancient Rome, according to which the "talionic" punishment was due only
if the parties did not reach an agreement *(ni cum eo pacit)*, and of contemporary plea-bargaining practices.

The dynamics of integrating a formal system and an informal one must
also be considered, such as the question of whether they would be combined in the same forum, or whether, as in the case with the German
Schiedsmann, there would be an obligation to attempt to achieve an informal resolution to the conflict before one forum, with failure resulting in
referral to a more formal proceeding (Dunkel and Rossner, 1989:155–56).[31]
Other problems of such an integrated system have already been referred to,
such as the issue of procedural guarantees and society's need for protection
from "dangerous" persons (see also below).

If the combination of an informal and a formal system raises problems
mainly in the context of dynamics and procedure, the integration of civil
and criminal law raises issues of a more substantial nature. Clearly, the
nature of the remedy that the court would ultimately apply, in the absence
of a mediated settlement, would be primarily restitutional, but what
would be its determining criteria? Would there be an objective tariff, related exclusively to the injurious conduct and the harm inflicted, on the
model of desert sentencing and the guidelines? Would there be individualization of the tariff to take account of the perpetrator's circumstances,
following the traditional model of rehabilitative sanctioning? Or would
the tariff be individualized to take account of the needs of the victim, in
accordance with the practice followed in civil actions, where the specific
losses suffered by the plaintiff, including pain and suffering, form the basis
of determining the compensation award?

Clearly, sanctioning tariffs of the type falling within the just-deserts
approach could in principle be adapted to a restitutionary model of justice
(see chap. 7). As has been pointed out, the original form of tariff sentencing
was a scale of financial compensation determined by the damage inflicted.
In the case of intentionally inflicted harms, a somewhat inflated rate of

compensation might be applicable, on the model of punitive damages (or criminal restitution; cf. Thorvaldson, 1990), both by way of recompense for the indignity caused to the victim and for deterrence purposes. It will be recalled that these functions were seen to be consistent with both criminal and civil sanctions. This approach could also provide a solution for serious incidents in which the damage ultimately inflicted was slight (e.g., in the case of a failed attempt).

A more troublesome issue is that of differential ability to pay. A purely pecuniary sanctioning system favors the wealthy—as indeed do prevailing civil systems (cf. Galanter, 1974; 1991:775). A poor harmdoer under a civil or quasi-civil system might be compelled to undergo some form of custodial or noncustodial labor in order to discharge his debt (cf. Tallack, 1900; Ashworth, 1986:95). Some contemporary writers have considered this problem, essentially one of reconciling retributive and distributive justice. Thus Ashworth (1983), in the context of penal sanctions, suggests that the wealthy be singled out for custodial sentences, to compensate for the lack of impact upon such offenders of purely pecuniary penalties. Wright (1982), whose concluding chapter "Making Amends" lays greater emphasis on restitutionary justice, suggests that the sanction should take account of both the seriousness of the act and the harmdoer's ability to pay. A classic solution here would thus be an adaptation of the "day fine" or "unit fine" system, which takes both these elements into account.

The problem here is that such a system would result in an indigent wrongdoer making only a relatively small payment to the victim. This result would thus be quite inconsistent with the third possibility referred to above—individualization of the sanction according to the victim's loss and suffering. On the other hand, while this last type of individualization may not necessarily be inconsistent with an "objective" tariff, whereby the victim's loss and suffering are viewed as the measure of the harmfulness of the act, it would clearly conflict with individualization based upon the wrongdoer's circumstances. This predicament exposes a deficiency in the adversary-retribution model which may require supplementing by its alternative, the social defense–welfare model.

The Role of the Social Defense–Welfare Model

The foregoing analysis was based upon the hypothesis that the adversary-retribution model, besides being more in tune with prevailing philosophical attitudes, had the greater potential for meeting the needs of the victim as reviewed in this study, as well as those of the other relevant sectors of the community, including offenders or "wrongdoers." However, it is equally evident that this model cannot deal adequately with all the needs that arise from victimization. First, there are needs that are unconnected with the retributive or "corrective" (in the civil justice sense) process. "Welfare" is a wider concept than "retribution" and may encompass such services as crisis intervention and other forms of service that by their very nature are not available from the adversary. This may even include services related to the legal process, such as those provided within victim/witness-assistance programs. Second, the wrongdoer may not always be identified or located (apprehended) and thus may be unavailable as a source of retributive justice. Third, there may be a need for emergency or interim assistance before satisfaction may be obtained from the wrongdoer. Fourth, it might be argued that retributive justice cannot be implemented in a fully satisfactory manner as long as the system within which it operates is characterized by imbalances in terms of distributive and social justice. Finally the adversary-retribution model as described above does not allow for the possible need for special measures of social protection which may be considered necessary, beyond the restraints on the wrongdoer which may be imposed for the purpose of meeting the needs of the victim.[32]

Many of these measures, such as victim compensation from state funds, are dealt with elsewhere in this study. The emphasis here will be on possible mechanisms whereby the social defense–welfare model might optimally converge with the adversary-retribution model. Thus possible modes of combining state compensation and offender restitution were alluded to in chapter 7. Similarly, as noted, excessive punitive damages awarded in tort cases may be payable into a tort victims' relief fund (Grube, 1993:854, esp. n. 81). Under these systems, some victims would be (or are) compensated directly by the wrongdoer by means of adversary proceedings, while in other cases compensation is paid by state agencies with a welfare orientation, but partly out of monies provided by wrongdoers in adversary proceedings. A more general structure for integrating the two models within the current criminal justice system, or its quasi-civil replacement, will now be considered.[33]

First, neighborhood legal-aid agencies would assist the victim in pursuing retributive remedies vis-à-vis the wrongdoers but would also direct the victim to the various support agencies. A second critical stage for the victim should be the preliminary court hearing—the equivalent of the contemporary bail hearing—which would have an expanded function. It may already be used today to issue protection orders for the victim's benefit (Finn and

Colson, 1990). It should also provide an opportunity for a more comprehensive, although interim, review of the situation regarding both the offender and the victim. The judge should ensure that both parties are aware of their rights and of the options open to them. The victim should be made aware not only of available options regarding the offender—the modes of proceeding available, legal aid, and so on—but also of welfare options, such as application for an interim award from the compensation board. Indeed, perhaps the judge would be empowered to order such an award.

Moreover, interim access to the court on the victim's part need not necessarily be dependent on a bail hearing, or even on the offender being apprehended. Such access might be granted as of right so that the court could review the action taken by the law enforcement authorities to apprehend the offender or instigate proceedings—insofar as they retain this role—as well as to ensure that the victim has been granted access to the welfare services to which he or she is entitled.

A similar review, mutatis mutandis, would take place as part of the trial, sentencing, or dispositional process (cf. Sebba, 1994) or at the termination of the civil, quasi-civil, or informal alternative. Here again, where the restitution payment was reduced because of the wrongdoer's inability to pay, the court might have the power to order compensation for the victim out of public funds, in order to prevent the victim's falling into the "compensation trap" (Newburn, 1988:47, citing Miers). The state would be empowered to request supplementary remedies vis-à-vis the wrongdoer, insofar as these were required for protection of the public. The court would thus serve as guarantor both of the adversary-retributive interaction between victim and offender or wrongdoer and of the welfare and social defense interactions between the state on the one hand and both victim and offender on the other.

A Model Solution

In the course of the preceding pages, possible trends were reviewed in relation to the respective roles of criminal and civil law and procedures, of formalism and informalism, of the relevant parties—victim, offender, and state—and of the two models within which they interact (adversary-retribution and social defense–welfare). A hazardous attempt will now be made to present an optimal integrated solution, based upon the foregoing analysis and against the background of the needs of the parties and the justice considerations reviewed in this volume. It does not specifically take into account current U.S. constitutional requirements, but, as noted in chapter 11, these have not prevented the development of informal alternatives to the justice system and thus may not constitute an obstacle to other victim-oriented (but also offender-oriented) reforms.

Injuries giving rise to a cause of action would continue to be of two types, on the civil-criminal analogy. The terminology, however, would preferably be toned down; injuries with the required mental element would be termed "wrongs" and would be perceived to have a public dimension, while for civil breaches a morally neutral term would be employed. For this purpose some "intentional" torts—in particular those deemed worthy of punitive damages—would be classified with the wrongs, while some technical offenses might undergo the reverse reclassification. In principle, all actions would be brought by the injured party in a local or "community" court (echoes here of Danzig's seminal article cited in the preceding chapter!). Proceedings would be relatively informal, but a private attorney could be employed. A public attorney would be available to assist or represent the injured party in complex cases.

If the cause of action involved no wrong, the defendant would be liable to pay compensation in accordance with the harm inflicted or to comply with other remedies generally available. But if the injury were accompanied by *mens rea* and thus designated a wrong, the perpetrator would be liable in principle for, say, double damages. One-half of the additional amount would be payable, together with the basic assessment, to the victim, by way of recognition of the wrong inflicted; the additional amount (25% of the total sum) would be paid into a victim fund administered by the state.[34] It is hoped that the twofold penalty, as well as signifying the wrongfulness of the conduct, would also serve as a deterrent, while the emphasis on restoration of the victim's personality would minimize the perception of inequity in psychological terms. For offenses in respect of which the financial loss, if any, was not a true measure of the harm inflicted or threatened—for example, sexual harassment or attempted assault—a penalty tariff would be developed.

Since the additional damages would have a punitive character, these would be scaled down in the light of the financial situation of the defendant. Alternatively, they might be translated into alternative sanctions, such as community service; compare the concept suggested by Wright (1982:283), whereby a standardized sentencing score could be compiled by means of individualized sanctioning "packages" comprising varying elements.[35] In cases where the defendant was unable to pay, the victim would receive compensation (at least in respect of the harm inflicted) from the victim fund, which could subsequently recover from the wrongdoer. Assessment of compensation in cases of wrongs would be based on culpable, that is, foreseen, harm. In the light of the emphasis here on the role of the victim, contributory fault (on civil-law principles) might be taken into account here, but without prejudice to the share claimable by the state.

While the instigator of the proceedings would generally be the victim, the state would, or could, be represented at all "relevant" or "critical" stages—to adopt by analogy the terminology of the victims' rights constitutional amendments—as a subsidiary party. The interest of the state would be twofold: (1) to protect its interest in the punitive damages payable to the victim fund, and (2) to consider any additional action vis-à-vis the wrongdoer which might seem appropriate, in the interests of public safety (see below). The state would have independent standing in the community court, that is, the right to instigate a proceeding, only in respect of wrongs committed against the community as a whole, for example, causing damage to the environment.

Proceedings in the community court would, as noted, be somewhat informal, to ensure maximum involvement of the victim and perhaps to encourage consensual solutions; mediation of interpersonal disputes would be either an integral part of the proceedings or would be available "in the shadow of the court" (cf. Mnookin and Kornhauser, 1979). In recognition of the low priority placed in such a setting on formal legal rights, an appeal would be possible to a more formal court. (It may be recalled that most of the studies reviewed in the preceding chapter suggested that informalism was a popular mode of dispute processing, but that in one study it was found that participant-complainants favored a rights discourse.) Analogy may be made here to the Sheriff's Court in Scotland, which has a supervisory role with regard to the informal operation of the juvenile panels (cf. Morris, 1978:67–69). Moreover, if the state were to retain its claim to 25% of the full sanction, this would ensure that the sanction would incorporate a "retributive minimum" (cf. Cavadino and Dignan, 1993).

This higher court would have two additional functions. First, where the state representative in the community court formed the opinion that further action was required to restrain the wrongdoer, application could be made to the higher court for an appropriate order, possibly involving deprivation of liberty. Second, for serious offenses, such as rape or murder, the higher court would have trial jurisdiction (involving juries where appropriate). In these cases victims (and survivors) would prosecute through their attorneys, while the state, too, would be represented. In such cases, however, the state would have an independent right to prosecute if the victim refrained from doing so.

Finally, victims would have access to the community court on a continuing basis, in particular at the complaint and at the post-trial stages, to ensure both the enforcement of claims against the wrongdoer, and the recognition of entitlements from the state, for example, access to legal or counseling services, or a payment from the victim fund.

It may be noted that the emphasis in this proposal on the involvement of the victim and possible interaction between the parties, together with its lack of emphasis on offender (or "wrongdoer") characteristics, differentiates it from traditional rehabilitation or social defense models. On the other hand its restorative and informalist orientation distinguishes it from the just-deserts model; it is closer in spirit to Braithwaite and Pettit's "republican" theory (see chap. 6). Its potential for the optimal accommodation of the coping and justice needs of the parties would naturally have to be tested by experimentation and evaluation.

13

Third- (Fourth-?) Party Responsibility: A Third Model?

In the previous chapter it was shown how the various proposals and developments for ameliorating the situation of the victim can be dichotomized according to which of the two alternative models of justice they reflect— the adversary-retribution model or the social defense–welfare model. There are, however, two developments not yet considered in this study which do not fit easily into either of these models.[1]

The first of these proposals, *third-party liability*, has received considerable attention from some sections of the victim-rights movement. The term "third-party liability" refers to the attempts that have been made by, or on behalf of, victims to develop civil-law remedies vis-à-vis persons or organizations that failed to prevent the victimization. Such litigation has been brought against hotels, landlords, employers, and educational institutions for providing inadequate security against predators, and against psychiatrists and criminal justice officials who released from custody persons who subsequently committed crimes (Carrington and Rapp, 1991). Law enforcement officials have also been sued for failure to prevent the victimization by unapprehended criminals (Englard, 1993: chap. 13). Moreover, organizations have been established to assist in developing the legal remedies upon which such litigation rests (see Carrington and Nicholson 1984).

Although the attempt to establish a "new tort" of this nature (Carrington, 1978) has not been entirely successful, in some cases a duty of care has been recognized. Thus, in the much-cited *Tarasoff* case (1974–76), psychotherapists were held to be under a duty (in spite of the principle of professional confidentiality) to warn a patient's intended victim, while in other cases landlords have been held liable in negligence for environmental conditions that facilitated robbery, rape, and so on (England, 1993). Similarly, various provisions of the American Law Institute's Second Restatement of the Law of Torts modified the historic principle of the absence of responsibility for the wrongful acts of third persons (Carrington and Rapp, 1991: sec. 1.02(3)(b)). Under section 315 of the restatement, a duty to control the actions of third parties may arise where the defendant has a "special relationship" either with the injured party or with the person inflicting the harm, and section 448 specifically creates liability for a third party's tortious or criminal behavior if the "actor at the time of his negligent conduct realized or should have realized the likelihood that such a situation might be created and that a third person might avail himself of the opportunity to commit such a tort or crime" (American Law Institute, 1965:122, 480).

Litigation against law enforcement authorities has generally been unsuccessful, perhaps owing to an unwillingness to impose too many restraints on police discretion. In the English *Dorset Yacht* case ([1970] A.C.1004), the government was held to be liable in principle for the damage to a yacht caused by escaping Borstal (reformatory) inmates only insofar as it could have been foreseen that the youths would be likely to steal the plaintiffs' boat to escape from the island where they were working. The absence of any *general* liability was reiterated in a subsequent claim directed against the police for their failure to protect a victim of the "Yorkshire Ripper" (*Hill v. Chief Constable of West Yorkshire*, [1989] A.C.53). The decision of the House of Lords in this case was based both on public policy and on the absence of any special characteristics of the victim rendering her a probable target. On this point England (1993:195 n. 58) refers to a Canadian case in which the police were held to be liable to a victim of a serial rapist who was in a high risk category in terms of location and personal characteristics. In some American cases, parole or probation officers have been held liable for the failure to protect victims (Sluder and del Carmen, 1990).

The second proposal involves the imposition of a *general duty to assist victims*, in particular by intervention to prevent the victimization or, minimally, by the requirement of prompt reporting (Geis, 1991:300). Such a duty of assistance, popularly called "Good Samaritanism," exists under many legal systems (Takooshian and Stravitz, 1984).[2] It has been generally absent from common-law systems, except insofar as the Good Samaritan rule in tort imposes a duty of care upon persons who voluntarily undertake to assist (American Jurisprudence 2d, 1989: vol. 57A, sec. 208). The Second Restatement of the Law of Torts (American Law Institute, 1965) again imposes a "duty to aid or protect" given a "special relationship" between the parties (sec. 314A) and in certain other circumstances (secs. 321–25). A more broadly based duty has been imposed under pioneering legislation enacted in some states, notably Vermont (Takooshian and Stravitz, 1984; Grey, 1983; Geis, 1991), while Massachusetts and Rhode Island require prompt reporting by bystanders, limited in the latter jurisdiction to sexual assaults (Geis, 1991:300).

This issue has been generally ignored by victimologists but has been the subject of a specialized literature on the "innocent bystander" (see, e.g., Sheleff 1978). The topic received particular attention in the wake of the notorious case of Kitty Genovese in 1964, when 38 persons witnessed a brutal murder during a period of 45 minutes without taking any action (Shotland, 1984). A somewhat similar situation occurred in a Massachusetts rape case, resulting in the reporting requirements referred to above.

The common feature of these two proposals is that they impose responsibility upon a party other than the victim or the perpetrator of the injurious act, hence the reference in legal terminology to third parties. However, in the present study it has been shown that there are already two candidates for such responsibility vis-à-vis the victim, namely, the offender and the state. And in the context of criminal proceedings, the established parties are the defendant and the state, and the victim is a potential third party. Thus, from the point of view of this study, the additional party to be involved under the above schemes is in effect a *fourth* party—hence the title of the present chapter.

Each of the two proposals just mentioned involves complex issues of jurisprudence and philosophy. The emerging legal literature on third-party liability raises questions about the nature of the duty of care involved, the causal relationship between the breach of the duty and the harm resulting, and the immunities that may be claimed by public servants or professional personnel when the allegedly negligent act fell within their official duties (see, generally, Carrington and Rapp 1991; Englard 1993). Thus, for example, one writer (Schoenholz, 1980) has suggested that the liability of institutions releasing dangerous persons be strict, thereby obviating the need to prove negligence, on the analogy of the similar duty laid down in the famous *Rylands v. Fletcher* rule with

regard to dangerous substances. Similarly, the question of a general duty
of assistance or "rescue" raises such issues as the legal enforcement of
morality, the role of causation in tort law, and the appropriateness of a
criminal law as compared with a tortious norm (see Grey 1983: chap. 4;
Weinrib 1980; Woozley 1983; Menlowe, 1993).

Rather than attempt to deal with these challenging issues, the following
brief discussion will concentrate on two aspects: (1) the possible implications of the above remedies from the point of view of the parameters of
justice identified in the present study, and (2) the relationship of the two
remedies to one another and to the two models of justice discussed in
chapter 12.

Coping Needs

There appears to be considerable potential in both the remedies referred to.
As to third-party liability, if the various measures advocated by law enforcement officials and insurance companies for crime prevention are considered, it emerges that there are large numbers of crimes where better
lighting facilities (by house owners, institutions, municipalities, etc.),
more secure locks, more patrols, better communication facilities for alerting help, and so on, might have contributed to prevention of the offense or
mitigation of its consequences. Thus, while the amount of successful litigation of this type has probably been modest hitherto, if the standards required from potential defendants in such cases were raised, the burden of
proof upon plaintiffs lowered, and more legal aid provided, there would
seem to be considerable potential for such suits. Moreover, an evaluation
of "Tarasoff warnings"—the scope of which were subsequently narrowed
by legislation—concluded that these, too, were effective in reducing acts
of victimization (Fulton, 1991).

Similarly, while no research is known to me on the number of offenses
committed in the presence or in the hearing of bystanders (co-offenders
are, of course, a common phenomenon), it is possible that the imposition
of a duty to assist may also have considerable potential. However, some
authorities take the view that the imposition of such a duty could be
counterproductive, since persons in the vicinity would deny any knowledge of the danger (Shotland, 1984). Moreover, the limitations on the
power of legal norms to alter behavior patterns are well known (see, e.g.,
Cotterrell 1992: chap. 2).

Further, by comparison with suits against offenders, civil actions of the
first type against third parties are more likely to result in practical benefits,

since the persons or institutions involved are much less likely to be indi-gent; indeed, this type of reasoning may have influenced the recognition of liability in such cases (England, 1993). But this may be less true of the second type of case (the failure to intervene), and whether victims would benefit financially from the establishment of such a duty would depend on whether the duty to assist were defined in tort or criminal law (cf. Grey, 1983:198). However, if, in spite of the pessimistic prognosis referred to above, greater readiness to intervene were to result, the immediate benefit would be a reduction of victimization.[3] It might be argued, however, that a system based upon rewards is preferable to one based upon obligations and that the principle behind the Good Samaritan compensation laws (see chap. 9) should be extended beyond compensation for injury suffered in assisting law enforcement agencies to the payment of reward for philan-thropic acts. This would be consistent with psychological concepts of posi-tive feedback (see also Beccaria, 1880).

One point should be made here that might qualify the benefits to vic-tims offered by the types of development being discussed. Insofar as strin-gent standards are applied to the liability of third parties for the failure to prevent the victimization, it would be consistent to apply such standards to the victim as well. The concept of victim contribution to the offense (see chap. 4), for all the controversy attached, suggests that if strict stan-dards were applied, the victim, too, might in many cases have been held to have been able to prevent the commission of the offense or to mitigate its consequences. If this could be shown, surely the victim would have to bear the loss, or at least part of it, rather than the third party?

What would be the coping effects of the implementation of these forms of third-party responsibility upon the other parties considered in this study? Naturally, the general public—as opposed to those sections of it upon whom responsibility would be placed for failure to prevent or miti-gate the victimization—would be the direct beneficiaries of the transfer of responsibility to those individuals, for the need for compensation out of public funds would be obviated. Indirectly, offenders would also benefit from this "sharing" of the burden. On the other hand, they could be harmed by two phenomena that might emerge: (1) a reluctance to release potentially dangerous persons from penal or mental health institutions, to avoid the risk of third-party liability of the first type referred to above; (2) a trend toward violent intervention by bystanders and vigilantes, seek-ing to prevent the taint of passive responsibility, a phenomenon that might also endanger innocent citizens mistakenly suspected of commit-ting a crime.[4]

Perceived Justice Needs

While no survey data is known to me regarding attitudes to third-party liability, some tentative studies have been conducted regarding the imposition of a duty on bystanders. Thus Takooshian and Stravitz (1984) reported that while an earlier survey by Zeisel found that 75% of Americans felt that the offer of assistance should be a matter of the bystander's own conscience rather than a legal obligation, later surveys conducted by the authors showed that views had changed and this had become a minority view. However, from perusal of their data (6) it appears that a greater variety of responses were offered to respondents in the later surveys, and respondents in fact opted mainly for positive incentives, including "reward-[ing] involved bystanders" and "print[ing] names of involved ones in the press," rather than for the imposition of a legal obligation.

Some comparative data are available from a study conducted in the Netherlands. Here observers' reactions to bicycle thefts were recorded on the basis of (a) hypothetical questions, (b) questions regarding respondents' own past conduct, and (c) an experiment whereby such a theft was "staged." While a large majority in the first category (78%) opted for intervention, whether by "addressing the thief" or by "alerting the police," rather fewer in the second category (45%) reported actually having done so, while 93% of the experimental group in fact took no action (Van Dijk et al., 1983). This suggests that support for the norm may be at a rather superficial level. Nevertheless, the authors of both the above studies express some optimism about the potential for the encouragement of such a norm—if not by use of threats, then perhaps by incentives.[5]

On the other hand, the evidence deriving from equity theory, discussed in previous chapters, suggests that this type of solution might be problematic. None of the parties concerned—victims, offenders, members of the general public, or the third parties or bystanders incurring the liability—would gain satisfaction from compensation issuing from a source other than the primary cause of the harm. How far such a distribution of the loss among parties contributing only indirectly to its creation would be perceived to be preferable to the absence of any remedy whatsoever (i.e., leaving the victim to suffer the full loss) is an issue for research.

The fundamental *principles of justice* involved are too far-reaching to allow for a full analysis here and will only be considered insofar as they relate to the discussion on models of justice. The special feature common to the two proposals considered here—whose common element does not seem to have been widely recognized in the literature[6]—is that they do not seem fully consistent either with the adversary-retribution model, which relies upon the victim's initiative against the offender as the primary mechanism for justice, or with the social defense–welfare model, which perceives the state as the primary agency of support for the victim as well as for the control of the offender. Here the burden is imposed not upon the state, which represents society as a whole, but upon certain individual members of the public who were in a position to prevent the victimization or to assist the victim. The philosophical basis for such an obligation (as distinct from its economic rationale) is not, as in the case of the social defense–welfare model, that the victim is entitled to welfare on the basis of need, or that the state has failed in its duty to protect the victim through the official law enforcement agencies; rather it seems to be that individual citizens are seen to have a duty of mutual protection, prevention, and assistance (cf. the judgment cited in Carrington and Rapp, 1991:1–9).

On one level, this philosophy appears to be an extension of the social defense–welfare model. Social responsibility for acts of victimization and their consequences is so developed that an obligation is imposed upon each individual to prevent such acts or to mitigate their consequences. On the other hand, there is also an antibureaucratic, antistate element here.[7] The message conveyed is that control of the offender and protection of the victim are not matters for anonymous state agencies but for individuals in proximity to the parties to the conflict. This could be perceived as an extension of the self-help principle, of a return to community responsibility referred to in chapter 11 (cf. esp. Nelken, forthcoming), of the recently developed "communitarian" philosophy (cf. Mapel, 1989: chap. 7), or of the abolitionist school mentioned in chapter 12.

Clearly, these proposals require considerably more extensive analysis on all levels: in respect of the actual benefits they are likely to produce for victims and their implications for other parties involved, in respect of the perceived justice of these solutions, and in respect of their underlying philosophical premises. The preceding discussion was intended merely to emphasize the unique features of these proposals, as well as what seems to be a conceptual interrelationship between them; to point to the need to supplement the dichotomy presented in the preceding chapter with the consideration of a "third model"; and to indicate the importance of further study of the issues involved.

14

Final Reflections

The history of penal reform suggests that while pioneering enthusiasm may in itself produce positive results in the short run—and this in itself is an unproven hypothesis—this force alone is insufficient to sustain such reforms. Thus while Bishop Ridley's first Bridewell, Crofton's "progressive stage" and parole system, and Zebulon Brockway's reformatory were believed in their day to be successful, these institutions became institutionalized failures (see Howard, 1929; Rothman, 1971). The individualized model of rehabilitation on which the criminal justice system was based for a century was eventually seen to rest on "unfounded assumptions" (American Friends Service Committee, 1971), and research on this system led to the purported finding that in the context of the treatment of offenders "nothing works" (Martinson, 1974). Nor have "simple solutions" been found to succeed in relation to judicial structures and processes (Feeley, 1983). Is the current victim movement destined to share the fate of these earlier reform ideologies?

In the preceding pages a detailed analysis was presented of the many novel institutional reforms introduced in recent years to meet the needs of crime victims, perceived to have been the "forgotten figures" of the criminal justice system. The analysis has for the most part indicated that most of these reforms either appear to have a limited potential for satisfying victims' needs and expectations, or have been designed or implemented in such a manner as to limit their contribution in practice. Although the book is based upon a very different analytical approach, the title of Robert Elias's recent monograph, *Victims Still*, may indeed reflect the progress that has been made in this area, in spite of a degree of satisfaction expressed with many of the programs reviewed in the course of the preceding pages.

However, it would be premature at this juncture to draw the conclusion that "nothing works" for victims either. Rather, it will be more constructive to attempt to identify some of the main problems that have emerged either explicitly or implicitly during the course of the analysis, problems to which insufficient attention may have been paid, whether in the context of the reforms themselves or in the literature of advocacy or evaluation.

The first point to note is that the vast outpouring of victim-oriented materials and proposals in recent years has tended to be too particularistic. The focus on the material needs of the parties may ignore their emotional needs and usually ignores their justice needs. The focus on one particular remedy (for example, state compensation schemes) may result in a neglect to consider its relationship and consistency with another remedy (for example, restitution by the offender). There has been a failure to develop remedies within an overall conceptual framework taking into account the relationship between victims, offenders, and the general public. Similarly, conceptualization of the possible role and responsibility of additional proximate parties has been lacking. There has also been an insufficient attempt to integrate the different disciplines that have contributed to the victim-related literature, namely, social and political philosophy; jurisprudence; the empirical orientation of criminology, victimology, and sociology; and the experimental orientation of social psychology. Fragmentation in all these areas has contributed to the fact that the adoption of victim-oriented measures has tended to outpace our understanding, conceptualization, and evaluation of the issues involved.

The second point relates to the delimitation of the subject matter. This topic has, first of all, an "inward-looking" aspect, namely, in respect of the definition of victims and their typology. Here the question arises whether remedies are to be confined to "ideal-type" victims or to be extended to the large numbers who do not conform with this image; and similar questions arise with respect to indirect victims. As to the "outward-looking" aspect, questions arise regarding the priority of crime victims as compared with other claimants on societal resources and how far victims differ from other claimants in the nature and the extent of their needs.

The study conducted by the Victim Services Agency in New York (Friedman et al., 1982) indicates that the dominant factor determining the victim's ability to cope with the effects of victimization is the strength of his or her social network. This, in turn, suggests that remedies focusing specifically on the needs of crime victims may have a relatively limited potential, since the problem lies rather with the underlying social structure.

The disparity between victim needs and victim services noted by some writers suggests a possible failure to be guided by research on the issue of needs or a commitment to a particular type of professional service, irrespective of the victim's actual priorities. The disparity alluded to is usually that between *material* needs, such as locks for the doors, and *psychological* needs, such as counseling, both of which have been classified here as "coping needs." More neglected still is the question of the relationship between psychological variables relating to trauma, anger, and so on, and the *justice* needs of the victims, which are usually studied in the framework of surveys or laboratory experiments, notably on equity theory. In this context, reference should be made to the work of Greenberg and Ruback (1992), who endeavored to study—employing a variety of methodologies—the connection between emotional reactions of victims and their justice-related needs and decisions. Such integrative research is as yet in its infancy.

Another core issue to which social psychologists are making a notable contribution is the relative importance to victims and other relevant parties of *procedural* as opposed to *substantive* justice. If the contribution of Tyler and others, concerned primarily with the offender, has been to show that perceptions of procedural justice are no less important than the perceived justice of the outcome, research focusing on the victim, such as that by Shapland and others, seems to indicate that procedural justice—as measured particularly by the degree of information imparted to the victim and the extent of the victim's involvement—might be the only relevant concern; in other words, as long as victims were granted "voice" (Aquino et al., 1992), that is, the opportunity for some input into the decision-making process, the actual outcome of the case may be relatively insignificant. Later research suggests that the outcome, too, may be of importance to many victims and indeed that the involvement may in itself sometimes raise certain expectations as to outcome.

The main variable associated with outcome is, of course, *punitiveness*. On this issue—as on many others—methodology seems to be of the essence, for while polls persistently support the demand for harsh sentences, more sophisticated studies alluding to particular cases present a different picture. Victim-focused studies tend also to conclude that most victims, while, as noted, not necessarily indifferent to the outcome of the case, are not particularly punitive. There is also some indication that victim-oriented remedies, such as restitution, may serve as a substitute for punishment. This, in turn, raises questions regarding the appropriate functions and ideologies to be attributed to the justice system, and the relative support on the part of the public for noncriminal or victim-oriented alternatives. On this topic it seems, surprisingly, that comprehensive studies such as those conducted in Germany, indicating an openness on the part of the public to more flexible, and in particular victim-oriented, models, have yet to be carried out in the United States (but see Umbreit, 1994).

The last-mentioned topics are also pertinent to the issues considered in chapter 12. A focal area is that of the optimal form of adversary proceeding for the parties involved: a traditional criminal proceeding, granting the victim a "quasi status," casting the victim in the role of prosecutor, or replacement of the criminal process by a civil or informal one. In this context the potential for changing the system, based upon the evidence of the needs and the perceptions of the parties, seems to be more far-reaching than the reforms actually contemplated. The present trend in the United States seems to favor granting the victim substantial rights in the course of a government-dominated proceeding, whether or not these rights are actually intended to be exercised! This trend is evidenced, inter alia, by the spate of legislative reforms, and in particular by the recent constitutional amendments granting such rights, mainly of a passive nature but sometimes providing the opportunity to cast the victim in a more active role.

While reform legislation, including the amendments to state constitutions, reflects the desire not only to enhance the victim's role in the criminal-justice process but also to promote welfarist remedies, such as state compensation and victim assistance programs, it seems that this last orientation is less in keeping with prevailing American social, political, and economic philosophy. Research findings suggest that both these welfarist remedies are relatively more developed and better funded in Britain, with its stronger welfarist tradition, in spite of the recent domination of the political right in that country. It is also no coincidence that American programs—in keeping with a more rights-oriented philosophy and a more monetarist economy—are financed to a considerable extent by levies and penalties imposed upon offenders, thereby mitigating the strain on the public purse. Thus the potential for change in the United States seems to be along the offender-victim axis rather than the state-victim axis, and this is more naturally achieved in the course of criminal justice proceedings (or their alternatives) than by funneling funds from offenders to victims via public agencies engaged in victim assistance. An alternative direction more in keeping with prevailing ideologies is that of private solutions, including the development of third-party suits discussed in chapter 13, insurance, and the use of private law enforcement agencies.

The positive side of developing the offender-victim axis is that it provides some potential for increasing victim participation and thereby increasing victim satisfaction; but, as noted, the participation envisaged seems to be limited in scope, substantially remaining within the prevailing model of justice. The recent wave of constitutional amendments may provide a testing ground for the future direction of victim-related reforms. While they provide a potential for a more integrated and victim-oriented criminal justice system, there are two major "ifs" here. The first relates to the degree to which there is a readiness for change on the part of the institutionalized bureaucracies and work cultures of the criminal justice system. Enhancing the victim's role in the system requires that existing agents show a willingness to accommodate undisciplined nonprofessionals in a game hitherto played by established rules. On a more radical level, if alternative victim-oriented processes are to emerge, the established agencies must be willing—or forced—to be shunted aside altogether.

The second "if" relates to the nature of the dominant forces and ideologies involved in the victim-oriented reforms. Insofar as victim-related reform is merely a camouflage for tough law-and-order-oriented policies, as appears to have occurred, for example, in California (McCoy, 1993), the role of the victim is likely to be marginalized. The indications of the evaluations and experiments discussed in earlier chapters are that the trend of a genuinely victim-oriented system would be *less* punitive, not more. The future may thus depend on the political orientation of the reformists, on the sophistication of victim advocates, and on the latter's commitment to the genuine interests of their constituency.[1] It could go either way.

Appendix

The Contribution of
Social Psychology

In recent years there has emerged a developing literature in the field of social psychology relating to the criminal justice system in general and to the perceptions of victimization in particular. This literature focuses primarily on three concepts.

A. Attribution Theory. "Attribution theory has characterized people as 'intuitive psychologists' who logically (and often illogically) utilize various principles and causal schemata in order to attribute causal explanations for social behavior" (Borgida and White, 1978:342). This theory, associated in particular with F. Heider and developed by E. E. Jones and K. Davis, and H. H. Kelley (see McGillis, 1978), has frequently been applied in the criminal justice area. Thus, for example, "the admission of prior sexual history evidence in a rape case may enhance the likelihood that jurors attribute personal responsibility to the victim for the sexual assault" (Borgida and White, 1978:342).

A variation of this theory having special reference to victims is that of "defensive attribution" (Walster, 1966). Walster originally proposed that when hearing about an accident in which severe damage occurred, observers would act to protect themselves by assigning the person involved in the

349

mishap a high level of responsibility, thereby attempting to avoid the occurrence of that accident to themselves in the future, "It won't happen to me; I'll be more careful" (see Gold et al., 1978). This reaction is anticipated in particular where the observer feels some degree of affinity, either personal or situational, with the victim.

B. "Just-World" Theory. This theory was formulated by M.J. Lerner in a series of studies (see, e.g., Godfrey and Lowe, 1975) in which he argued that people have a need to believe that the world is fundamentally just. Thus, when people observe what appears to be an injustice they tend to interpret the situation in a way that will reduce or eliminate the injustice, for example, by attributing blame or responsibility to the victim. There is a clear similarity here with the previous theory, but the two theories may lead to differing hypotheses. "In contrast to just world theory (Lerner, 1970:277), attribution theory would predict that victims who have good motives would not be devalued when they are observed to suffer injustly" (Godfrey and Lowe, 1975:945). Such differences have led some researchers to regard the theories as alternative or conflicting (Godfrey and Lowe, 1975; Gold et al., 1978).

C. Equity Theory. This theory, developed by Walster, Berscheid, and Walster (1976) from earlier work by G. C. Homans and J. S. Adams, purports to be a general theory of social behavior (Berkovitz and Walster, 1976) based on four fundamental propositions:

> Proposition I: Individuals will try to maximize their outcomes (where outcomes equal rewards minus costs). . . . Proposition IIA: Groups can maximize collective reward by evolving accepted systems for "equitably" apportioning rewards and costs among members. . . . Proposition IIB: Groups will generally reward members who treat others equitably and generally punish (increase the costs for) members who treat others inequitably. . . . Proposition III: When individuals find themselves participating in inequitable relationships, they become distressed. The more inequitable the relationship, the more distress individuals feel. . . . Proposition IV: Individuals who discover they are in an inequitable relationship attempt to eliminate their distress by restoring equity. The greater the inequity that exists, the more distress they feel, and the harder they try to restore equity. (Walster et al., 1976:2–6)

The fourth proposition is followed by an elucidation of particular relevance in the present context: "There are two ways that a participant can restore equity to an inequitable relationship: He can restore actual equity to the relationship, or he can restore psychological equity" (ibid., 6). The first is achieved by taking some appropriate action to restore the equity, for example, by retaliation or compensation. Psychological equity, on the other hand, is achieved by various mechanisms of rationalization, such as derogation of the victim, denial of responsibility for the act, or minimization of the victim's suffering (Macaulay and Walster, 1971).

The literature on these different theories has, as indicated, for the most part developed independently. Although the emphasis in the first two theories is somewhat different from that of equity theory—attribution and just-world theories focus on the interpretations of behavior by third parties, while equity theory focuses on reactions to behavior by the harmdoer—there is nevertheless a clear connection between them.[1] Both equity and the just-world theories hypothesize that the situation will be interpreted to reduce or to eliminate the injustice ("inequity") only where there is no possibility of actually remedying the situation,[2] and that the "interpretations" frequently involve attributions. Moreover, all three theories provide explanations of how the victim's character or conduct may be devalued by the parties concerned.[3]

Research in these areas may be of relevance to the present study in a number of ways. First, since the research investigates people's feelings about victimization and injustice, it will be directly relevant to the discussion in chapter 5 on "subjective justice needs," where the needs and attitudes of victims, as well as offenders and the public, are considered. It may also be helpful when considering how far various innovations in the criminal justice system, such as schemes for compensation and restitution, are likely to meet these needs. Further, since the research also investigates how decision makers react to victimization and apparent injustices, it is of relevance in the context of the review of prior research incorporated in chapter 2, insofar as it may indicate the nature of the decisions that are likely to be reached under the present system, if the theories are valid.

However, since most of the studies in these areas are of an experimental nature, their usefulness in a discussion of the actual operation of the criminal justice system is limited. Nevertheless, it will be observed that some of the empirical (nonexperimental) studies of the criminal justice system referred to in this volume have used these theories as a framework for their research. Moreover, even the experimental studies may be helpful in the understanding of areas in which little "hard data" are available—in particular the functioning of juries, where the sample populations used in the studies are also likely to have a greater validity.

Finally, it should be observed that both the theoretical and the experimental literature in this field is becoming increasingly sophisticated, and the generalized hypotheses offered formerly are being subjected to qualifications (see, e.g., Tornblom, 1992), some of which are referred to elsewhere in this volume. In particular, there is a need to integrate the above-mentioned literature, which deals primarily with distributive justice, with the emergent literature on procedural justice considered in chapters 5 and 8.

Notes

Introduction

1. Additional microanalyses of particular jurisdictions will be referred to below.

2. A bibliography issued in Japan in connection with the Fourth International Symposium of Victimology in 1982 listed some 950 authors in English in this field, many of whom had produced several publications. Lists of German and Japanese authors appeared separately. Other anthologies are referred to in the United States survey prepared for the 1985 Milan Congress (*Victims of Crime*, 1985:4). See also the literature reviewed below relating to victims and the criminal justice system.

3. Some European surveys, which were developed considerably later than their American counterpart, have been more ambitious in this respect; see Hough and Mayhew (1983), Hough and Moxon (1985), Van Dijk et al. (1990), Van Dijk and Mayhew (1992).

4. Cf. the assertion in the literature on crime surveys that "victimization is a rare event" (see below).

5. A scientific, but not entirely successful, attempt to account for the apparently increasing punitiveness of the American population in terms of these factors was made by Stinchcombe et al. (1980).

6. The "law-and-order" issue was first placed on the national political agenda by presidential candidate Barry Goldwater in 1964 (Cronin et al., 1981).

7. See Rock (1986:221). For some general reflections on the problems of "victim talk," see Minow (1993).

8. See Christie (1977).

Chapter 1

1. The more widely discussed proposals were considered by the President's Task Force on Victims of Crime (1982). The degree of implementation of the Task

Force's recommendations was considered in a special report ("Four Years Later") by the Office of Justice Programs (1986; see also NAAG/ABA, 1986). For surveys of victim-related legislation, see ABA (1981), Bureau of Justice Statistics (1984), and the Legislative Directories prepared by NOVA for the U.S. Department of Justice.

2. For the convenience of the analysis, part 3 will not follow the fourfold classification presented here with absolute precision. Additional distinctions will be made between substantive and procedural remedies, between formal and informal procedures, and between novel and existing or historic remedies, such as civil suits and private prosecutions. Discussion of the latter category will be deferred to part 4.

3. The ABA report specified here: "(1) a list of specific economic losses; (2) identification of physical or psychological injuries and their seriousness; and (3) changes in the victim's work or family status resulting from the offense" (ABA, 1981:46). See also sec. 103 of the Proposed Model Legislation (NAAG/ABA, 1986); and see generally below, chap. 8.

4. Restitution orders are generally advocated as part of a noncustodial disposition. However, it is also sometimes suggested that prison earnings could be attached for the victim's benefit.

5. Cf. below, chap. 11.

6. The ABA report refers to the person who performs this function as an "ombudsman." However, the role of an ombudsman is generally to investigate complaints in cases of alleged malfeasance (or nonfeasance), rather than acting routinely in all cases.

7. Another form of civil proceeding that will not be considered in detail in the present study (but will be referred to briefly in chap. 12) is the administrative proceeding. In recent times the expansion of government regulations has given rise to new areas of infractions of a criminal or quasi-criminal nature in such fields as environmental protection and antitrust, as well as taxation. These infractions are frequently dealt with by administrative agencies. In some cases there may be specific personal or corporate victims, and their situation must be considered in the context of victim remedies.

Chapter 2

1. The term *secondary victimization*, however, has different meanings; see below, chap. 3.

2. This approach is consistent with the analysis of the bureaucratic character of the criminal justice system performed by earlier writers such as Blumberg (1979) and Feeley (1979).

3. A Canadian survey (Stuebing, 1984) found that for 94% of victims the only contact was with the police.

4. This study was designed "to learn how practitioners use information about

victim harm in their decision making and what effect practitioners' action have on victims' perceptions of the criminal justice system" (Hernon and Forst, 1983:5). Interviews were conducted with 389 victims, 112 police officers, 101 prosecutors, and 48 judges at eight different locations in the United States, and their views were elicited regarding their typical decisions in hypothetical ("scenario") cases falling within five offense types. These were supplemented by a small number of interviews related to real cases.

5. The figures cited here are based upon victims' estimates. The police estimates were sometimes somewhat different, but not substantially so.

6. However, these responses seem to relate primarily to the police evaluation of how the prosecutors will act, since the study notes that it is the prosecutors who actually do the screening.

7. The dependent variable was "an ordinal variable with the categories of (1) reviewing expert only, (2) making a few telephone calls, and (3) conducting more extensive investigation" (Bynum et al., 1982:307).

8. The most important variable was the victim's attitude (see below). The third important variable was the previous record of the offender.

9. This was probably due to the lack of linearity. For while the zero-order correlation indicated that for unemployed victims there was a very low probability that an intensive investigation would follow the complaint, for "marginally employed" the probability was relatively high (see Bynum et al., 1982, table 3).

10. In Hohenstein's study (1969) of police decision making with regard to juveniles, "the age and sex of both offender and victim were useless in the predictive typology" (149).

11. "The probability of arrest is highest when the citizen adversaries have the most distant social relation to one another, that is, when they are strangers" (Black, 1980:94–95). Oppenlander (1982) found a relatively high arrest rate in domestic dispute cases, but the absolute rate was low (9%), and the injuries were found to be more serious in such cases.

12. See Smith (1983:2), citing a Vera Institute study attributing this approach mainly to judges and prosecutors, but to a lesser extent also to police officers.

13. The numbers on which these percentages are based were small, owing to the many cases in which the complainant expressed no preference as to the arrest of the suspect.

14. However, Smith and Klein (1984) found that this was true only of neighborhoods with a relatively high socioeconomic status.

15. The authors found that 16% of their sample received no information about the progress of their case, and a further 5% learned about it only as a result of inquiries they themselves initiated. In that study, victims and criminal justice personnel were asked "Who keeps the victims most informed?" While 51.4% of the police respondents selected the police, only 25% of the victims gave this response. Nevertheless, among the different categories of criminal justice personnel interviewed, "the police responses came closest to corresponding to victim responses" (Hernon and Forst, 1983:32).

16. Similarly, in a sample of cases involving nonstranger violence, "approxi-

mately half of the victims who came to court (51%) reported that the prosecutor spoke with them" (Smith, 1983:33).

17. The selection of the 10-day hospitalization criterion might have been appropriate for rape, where there is a reluctance to risk prosecution in the absence of a strong case, but too serious a criterion to serve as a cut-off point for other offenses. As noted above in the text, however, the police perceived the hospitalization criterion as relevant to knife assaults too.

18. The study was limited to cases of robbery, rape, and assault. The author surmised that "victim credibility is less important in cases slated for disposition in the lower courts, since most of these cases will be resolved through plea bargaining" (Stanko, 1981–82:229).

19. Cf. the conclusions reached by Heumann (1978) and Feeley (1979) that prosecution decision making, and in particular plea bargaining, is influenced by professional norms rather than overcrowded court dockets.

20. The Royal Commission on Criminal Justice (1993:79) expressed concern at the lack of consideration for victims and other witnesses under the prevailing system, noting that "the victim's views may be insufficiently taken into account"; and a majority recommended abolition of the Bar's Code of Conduct in this respect.

21. The weight given to the victim's wishes varied among prosecutors. Thus one district attorney "while expressing concern for the victim's feelings, stated that he does not honor a victim's request to prosecute vigorously in either serious or petty cases because he considers it his duty to exercise independent professional judgement on the merits of each case" (Hall, 1975:949).

22. As to the relevance of *defendant* characteristics in this literature, see Field (1978).

23. However, the authors noted that contacts with probation officers were about equal in number to those with judges. Contacts with both judges and probation officers may be expected to have increased with the introduction of victim-impact statements; see below chap. 8.

24. The concept of *l'état dangereux* was developed by the school of social defense, an offshoot of positivism (cf. Ancel, 1965).

25. See also chap. 6, below.

26. However, there remains a question whether unforeseen harm, which is unrelated to the perpetrator's mental state, should be perceived as a component of offense seriousness; see Schulhofer (1974), Sebba (1980).

27. See above, n. 4.

28. The method of measurement here was somewhat unclear: "Ratings were based primarily on the judges' own in-court utterances and facial cues" (Denno and Cramer, 1976:220).

29. This is a major departure from the English tradition whereby all prosecutions were formally brought by private individuals; see Sebba (1982), Damaska (1985).

30. This may change as certain official agencies are established specifically to assist the victim, the most notable example to date being the criminal justice compensation boards.

Chapter 3

1. See also the discussion of whether the criminal justice system is a "zero-sum game," whereby the victim can gain only at the expense of the defendant (see below, chap. 12).

2. In the context of imagining a Rawlsian-type social contract (see chap. 6), Sterba (1980) has suggested that there are *four* interested parties whose views must be taken into consideration: criminals, victims, the public, and law enforcement personnel. However, while practical politics may render this a prudent policy, it seems undesirable in principle to place a category having a vested interest in the status quo on the level of the three other categories referred to here. An optimal protection of the interests of these three categories may require a radical revision of the current law enforcement structure, which its a priori protection would prevent. For a modified version of the triadic approach, see Marx (1983).

3. Thus, for example, supporters of "private" justice would tend to remove the public from the categorization of relevant parties (see below, chaps. 11 and 12).

4. Popular definitions of criminal victimization, particularly regarding rape, frequently differ from the legal definitions; see Klemmack and Klemmack (1976), Williams (1984). This, again, may be explained by the designation of victimization as a social construct; see LaFree (1989:66).

5. A somewhat similar analysis is found in Greenberg et al. (1982). Cf. also the analysis of the development of civil legal disputes by Felstiner et al. (1980–81) as a three-stage process consisting of "naming," "blaming," and "claiming" (see below, chap. 12; see also Coates and Penrod, 1980–81).

6. Cf. Hulsman (1985:12): "The most fundamental right of a victim is that his definition and his expressed needs are taken as a starting point for the consideration of an intervention in the public sphere." This concept should perhaps be extended to include a person who would perceive him- or herself as victim if supplied with elementary information. It might be argued that victim-oriented policies should seek, inter alia, to render victimized persons aware of their status. However, not all writers agree with this conflict-consciousness-raising approach: see below, chap. 11.

7. The classification is derived from Sellin and Wolfgang (1978). The authors named category (a) "primary victimization," category (b) "secondary victimization," and category (c) "tertiary victimization." The term *secondary victimization*, however, is used in at least two other senses. It may refer to the additional suffering inflicted on the victim by the law enforcement authorities or to the stress and inconvenience caused to the victim's support group.

8. A further category to be excluded from the study will be the so-called victimless crime, e.g., drug abuse, where the offender is the main victim. Wolfgang and Singer (1978:384) refer also to "mutual victimization."

9. Similarly, Cannavale and Falcon (1976) found that 27% of a sample of 919 witnesses had at one time been defendants, a finding which was "perhaps indicative of a 'community' of individuals who are periodically involved in criminal justice proceedings" (61). The "interchangeable roles of victim and victimizer" have recently been reflected upon by Fattah (1994).

10. A somewhat extreme position was adopted in the research conducted by Flanagan et al. (1985), wherein a "victimization experience" was defined as personally knowing someone in the neighborhood who was victimized.

11. However, some legislation, not confined to homicide cases, grants certain rights to "family members"; see the Massachusetts statute cited in Waller (1988:63).

12. However, the burden of these schemes is increasingly being placed on offenders; see below, chap. 9.

13. However, there may be an interaction between so-called abstract and empirical analysis; see below, chap. 6.

Chapter 4

1. Other classifications may be found in Knudten et al. (1976), Reiff (1979), Salasin (1981), Waller (1982), *Canadian Federal-Provincial Task Force* (1983), and Smith et al. (1984).

2. The concepts are not identical, since Symonds uses the term *secondary injury* in a psychoanalytical sense, in which the rejection seems to be felt by the victim at rather a low level of consciousness, whereas the other literature referred to here relates to more conscious and specific tribulations suffered by the victim.

3. However, in the same author's study of the impact of burglary it was found that "the emotional reactions experienced by a person immediately after victimization are not related to immediate retributive feelings" (Waller and Okihiro, 1978:39).

4. For victims of armed robbery, Baril and Morissette (1985) found that loss of confidence in other people and increased fear of another robbery were the most common effects, experienced by more than 70% of victims.

5. There could have been an element of self-selection here. Victims made themselves known to the researchers by answering advertisements. It is possible that there were victims who did not come forward as they had erased the experience from their memories (cf. Silver et al., 1983:84).

6. However, 31% of victims indicated a motivation to move, as compared with only 18% of nonvictims.

7. "Our survey question does not ever ask about 'crime' at all, but rather about feelings of safety while walking alone in the nearby community" (Skogan and Maxfield, 1981:55).

8. For a discussion of the alternative meanings of "need" in this context, see Mawby (1988:131–33).

Chapter 5

1. Some of the problems of attitudinal research pertinent to criminal justice were discussed by Hogarth (1971), in the course of his research on the attitudes of

magistrates. A considerable part of this research was devoted to the development of appropriate instruments for this purpose.

2. Thus Hogarth's study of Canadian magistrates incorporated both a survey of their attitudes and an analysis of their decisions (Hogarth, 1971). Green (1961), on the other hand, executed the reverse of the "jump" referred to here, in drawing conclusions about judicial attitudes on the basis of their decisions.

3. Reference here is to the empirical determination of "fundamental concepts" held by the relevant populations with which this study is concerned, rather than to the "fundamental principles" of justice, derived from abstract analysis, which will be discussed in the next chapter.

4. The terminology is problematic, because the currently popular just-deserts theory of punishment (von Hirsch, 1976) is backward looking but claims to be nonpunitive (in the first sense).

5. They were also more likely to favor civil liberties. However, both these findings may derive from the fact that the populations with relatively high probability of being victims also have a relatively high probability of being offenders; see chap. 3.

6. For African Americans, too, the assaultive categories were associated with higher percentages of poor ratings (Garofalo, 1977a:97).

7. A sample of rape victims in Birmingham was added in order to augment the size of the sample for this offense.

8. Dissatisfaction was expressed by only 13% of the respondents when the police arrived within 10 minutes of being called, rising to 78% where the police took over 30 minutes. "Although people's expectations obviously vary, it would appear that victims expected the police to arrive in about five to ten minutes" (Shapland et al., 1985:48).

9, However, the findings of Hagan, discussed below, cast some doubt upon this hypothesis.

10. Mean satisfaction scores (graded on a 1 to 5 scale, where 1 = "very satisfied" and 5 = "very unsatisfied") increased from 1.97 for Coventry and 1.77 for Northampton after the first contact, to 2.60 and 2.37, respectively, after the final interviews.

11. The 1982 British Crime Survey found that 82% of one of the subsamples had had contact with the police during the 18 months before the survey (Maxfield, 1984).

12. Connick and Davis (1981: table 6) reported on a small New York study with equally high ratings.

13. If the "good" ratings are combined with the "excellent," there were no substantial differences between police and district attorneys in respect of their ratings for effort and courteousness, but district attorneys remained lower in terms of effectiveness (61% as compared with 70% for the police).

14. However, Smith found that the frequency of conversation between victim and prosecutor did not in itself affect the degree of satisfaction. The author concluded that there was an additional precondition for this relationship, namely, that "the victim believed these conversations reflected an interest in their case" (Smith, 1983:35).

15. The figure is obtained by subtracting from the total (100%) the 36% who agreed that prosecutors did not care about the victim, and the 8% "don't know's."

16. Victims did not blame the defense attorney, for the latter was simply perceived to be fulfilling his function (Shapland et al., 1985:143).

17. This paucity of studies was reflected in a review of previous research in this area (Flanagan et al., 1985:68–70).

18. The number responding was a little less than the total responding "sometimes unfair" or "often unfair" to the first question, but there is no indication whether the question was directed exclusively at these groups or whether it was also put to those whose response was "usually fair."

19. A third possibility might be the view that the courts were inconsistent but not discriminatory, merely haphazard and unpredictable.

20. Qualities such as leniency and fairness are used here as a measure of attitudes toward the courts. Some studies, however, treat these qualities as *independent* variables which are hypothesized as factors likely to influence "support for the courts," the latter being measured by other indicators; see Fagan (1981) and the literature reviewed therein.

21. The authors' view that the level of punitiveness of the courts had decreased was based on a crude measure, comparing average time served in prisons with average arrest rates. Apart from the intrinsic limitations of this measure, it would be necessary for a breakdown analysis by areas to support the hypothesis cited.

22. Account must be taken here of the methodological limitations of this study, in particular in relation to the dependent variable (see above).

23. Flanagan et al. (1985:76) also favor the second of the two possible explanations for the more critical attitudes held by victims, namely, that they are the result of contacts with the system. However, the measure adopted in their study as an indicator of "victimization experience" included personally knowing someone in the neighborhood who was victimized, an "experience" that would not necessarily result in contact with the criminal justice system.

24. In effect the percentage was lower still; for 17 victims "felt unable to give a rating, mainly because they had never been informed of the progress of their case through the courts and so had little idea of what the court had actually done" (Smith, 1983:157).

25. In the course of a survey conducted in different locations in Brevard County, Florida, the authors found that "almost one-third of the respondents in the cities were unhappy with the results of complaint processing, although in Melbourne about two-thirds were dissatisfied."

26. Hagan also found that victims expressed very positive views about the fairness of the court procedures; but the significance of this finding may be suspect in the present context, since the question seems to have addressed the court's perceived fairness in relation to the *defendant* (Hagan, 1980:117).

27. "Picture the difference between victims who sat for brief moments in small Minneapolis courtrooms, carpeted on the floor and walls for improved acoustics, in which cases are considered for several minutes, as opposed to Los Angeles victims who sat for long periods in large courtrooms where numerous prosecutors and defense attorneys mingled in front of the rail while two or more cases were being presented and considered in rapid succession. Is it any wonder that Minneapolis victims more frequently stated that they understood the proceedings and were satisfied with their overall treatment?" (Smith, 1983:92).

28. Cf. also the findings of three Canadian studies: Brillon (1983); Stuebing (1984:19–21), and Baril (1984). Baril found that her sample frequently described the court procedure in theatrical terms, particularly in the sense that the "show" was scripted in advance.

29. "It may be that complainants were lenient in their ratings because they tended to blame 'the system' for lack of responsiveness rather than individual officials" (Davis, Russell, and Kunreuther, 1980:65). In Hagan's study procedures were rated more favorably than judges; but see n. 26 above.

30. The first figure refers to the Coventry sample, the second to Northampton. In a separate question dealing with prison sentences, the numbers advocating a greater use of prison were smaller (Shapland et al., 1981:238).

31. Similarly, Hagan (1982) in his Canadian study found that attendance in court rendered the victim less likely to perceive the sentence as too light, but knowledge of the disposition increased the probability that it would be regarded as too lenient.

32. The outcomes sought by the sample respondents appear in table 2.5 of their report. Dissatisfaction with the ultimate outcome was expressed by 43% of the sample (Davis, Russell, and Kunreuther, 1980:65).

33. Thus some studies have recorded "diffuse support" for the courts (Flanagan et al., 1985:67–68).

34. The difference between the positive ratings of police and judges was reduced from approximately 30 percentage points before the court hearing to 20 percentage points after the hearing. Perceptions of prosecutors and defense attorneys also improved slightly. But Kelly (1982) found that the perception of police tended to improve as a result of the case, while that of the courts (alternatively designated "prosecutors") tended to decline. However, in Kelly's study *(a)* the sample was confined to rape victims, *(b)* the changes in perception were attributed retrospectively, and *(c)* the reference point for the changes seems to have been before the offense took place rather than before the court hearings, as in Hagan's study.

35. On the "reactive" character of law enforcement, see chap. 2 above. However, the extent to which witness noncooperation will handicap the prosecution's ability to secure a conviction has been questioned (Davis, 1983).

36. See also the results of the 1989 International Crime Survey (Van Dijk et al., 1990:69); and cf. Kidd and Chayet (1984).

37. The importance of social influence on victim decision making has recently been analyzed by Greenberg and Ruback (1992).

38. However, "belief that courts would punish" did not contribute, while for "belief that the police would catch the person," the correlation was in the wrong direction.

39. The prosecutors, however, regarded a much higher percentage of the witnesses as uncooperative; see Cannavale and Falcon (1976:24–26). The reasons for the discrepancy are considered in chapter 6 of that study.

40. These three offenses were "an offense similar to the present one," a burglary, and an aggravated assault (Shapland et al., 1981:250–51). The fourth offense— being punched at a party—was considered worthy of reporting to the police by less than one-half of the sample.

41. Friedman et al. (1982:206). Of those who perceived the police as having gone

out of their way, 62% expressed the belief that people were "willing to help more," as compared with only 33% of those who perceived the police as "not helpful." However, these categories were rather small; most of the sample thought the police "just did their job" (of these, 51% believed people were "willing to help more"), and the tendency noted was significant only at the 0.1 level.

42. However, Stinchcombe et al. (1980) concluded that the steep increase in dissatisfaction with the leniency of the courts could not be explained in terms of increased fear of crime.

43. Men were more punitive than women, and African Americans more than whites. Income, too, affected the penalty selected, the highest and lowest income brackets being more punitive than the middle range; but this variation was found to interact with the sex and race variables; see Blumstein and Cohen (1980).

44. However, Wolfgang et al. (1985:74–75) found that victims attributed higher seriousness scores to offenses as compared with nonvictims. But Chandler and Kassebaum (1979), in a nonrepresentative survey conducted in Hawaii, found that victimized respondents were less punitive than nonvictimized respondents. Cf. also the findings of Stinchcombe et al. (1980) referred to earlier; and see Sessar (1984).

45. Thus, 30% agreed that "only poor people get arrested and sent to prison," and 67% that "if you have a lot of money and get caught committing a crime, you will probably get off free" (Cannavale and Falcon, 1976:65–66). Moreover, 82% agreed that "there would be less crime if there were not so much poverty and prejudice in our society." On the other hand, 97% of the sample agreed that "citizens should take more interest in what can be done to control crime in our society."

46. Davis, Russell, and Kunreuther (1980: table 2.5). The distribution of "outcomes sought" differed significantly between complainants who were previously acquainted with the offender and strangers.

47. There was also considerable ambivalence regarding the earlier decision to press charges. Only 41% were unequivocally in favor. The main reasons given in favor of pressing charges were protection of others, outrage, and punishment. The main reasons against were avoiding the ordeal of court, fear of revenge, and avoiding sending the defendant to jail.

48. Responses were differentiated according to the nature of the offense described (theft or assault) and the victimization experience of the respondent. Victims were somewhat more punitive than nonvictims for assault (21.8% as compared with 16.6%) and slightly less punitive for theft (6.9% as compared with 8.9%).

49. There is an analogy here with the "neutralization techniques" of delinquents as hypothesized by Sykes and Matza (see Walster et al., 1976:9).

50. There is an analogy here to the framework of analysis adopted in the present study, in which all parties—victims, offenders, and the public—are attributed with both coping needs and subjective justice needs. The nature of these needs, however, is recognized as being different for the different parties.

51. A more detailed social psychological analysis of retribution appears in the same volume as Hogan and Emler's essay (Miller and Vidmar, 1981); this analysis, however, makes no comparison with equity and restitutional theories but only with the behaviorist orientations in punishment.

52. For the purposes of the present discussion these terms are used interchange-

ably. Nevertheless, there is generally a difference of emphasis between them, "retaliation" connoting a somewhat more physical and immediate reaction on the part of the injured party, "retribution" implying a more abstract reaction, not necessarily undertaken by the same individual.

53. Cf. the definition of *harmdoer* as "one who commits an act which causes his partner's relative outcome to fall short of his own" (Walster et al., 1976:8). While the term implies a value judgment, the definition is in fact morally neutral.

54. It appears that some of this research deals with the provision of aid on an international level.

55. De Carufel (1981:456, table 2). However, where the compensating body was seen to have been responsible for the initial inequity, the suggestion of reciprocation for the subsequent "compensation" lowered the levels of satisfaction and perceived fairness.

Chapter 6

1. "The human rights demanded and protected within any given community are a function of many cultural and environmental variables unique to that community" (McDougal et al., 1980:71).

2. At the same time, "principles of natural justice" have been widely applied by common-law courts when reviewing administrative and quasi-judicial functions; see, e.g., de Smith (1980).

3. These are life, knowledge, play, aesthetic experience, sociability, practical reasonableness, and religion (Finnis, 1980:86–90). Cf. Rawls's list of "social primary goods": liberty and opportunity, income and wealth, and the bases of self-respect (Rawls, 1971:303).

4. Another leading critic of the positivist approach is Ronald Dworkin, who has laid emphasis on the primacy of individual rights, thereby echoing the natural-rights concept of the natural lawyers. "Individuals have rights when, for some reason, a collective goal is not a sufficient justification for imposing some loss or injury upon them" (Dworkin, 1977:xi). The elevated nature of these rights in Dworkin's view is clear from their derivation from extralegal sources, in particular from moral and political philosophy (see esp. ibid., chap. 4).

5. See Rawls (1971):

First Principle.
Each person is to have an equal right to the most extensive total system of equal basic liberties compatible with a similar system of liberty for all.
Second Principle.
Social and economic inequalities are to be arranged so that they are both *(a)* to the greatest benefit of the least advantaged, consistent with the just savings principle, and *(b)* attached to offices and positions open to all under conditions of fair equality of opportunity. (302)

6. See Lloyd and Freeman (1985: chap. 11).

7. The authors found that this theory complied with three desiderata that

should characterize the "target" of a criminal justice system: (1) that it be relatively uncontroversial, (2) that it should generate a stable allocation of accepted
rights, and (3) that it should provide a "satiable goal" (Braithwaite and Pettit,
1990: chap. 4).

8. See Braithwaite and Pettit (1990):

A person enjoys full dominion, we say, if and only if:
1. she enjoys no less a prospect of liberty than is available to other citizens.
2. it is common knowledge among citizens that this condition obtains, so that she
and nearly everyone else knows that she enjoys the prospect mentioned, she and
nearly everyone else knows that the others generally know this too, and so on.
3. she enjoys no less a prospect of liberty than the best that is compatible with the
same prospect for all citizens. (64–65)

9. The term *positivism* itself is a source of confusion. Legal positivism is
generally seen to have originated with Bentham and Austin in the early nineteenth
century. Social scientists, however, reserve the term positivism for the empirical
school, inventors of the discipline of sociology, founded by Auguste Comte and his
contemporaries later in that century. Further, penal philosophy tends to identify
Bentham (with Beccaria) as a leader of the classical school, against which the positivists rebelled. But see Mannheim (1973:24).

10. However, it should be noted that the positivist school of the social (and
natural) sciences was decidedly deterministic in its attitude to social change.

11. Thus the XII Tables in fact specified the talionic penalty only where the two
parties could not reach agreement (Jolowicz, 1939:174). The contemporary differentiation between civil and criminal sanctions was less clear at that time.

12. One may cite here Kant's well-known dictum that "even if civil society
were to dissolve with the full agreement of all its members . . . the last murderer
still confined to prison would first have to be executed in order that everybody
received what his deeds deserved" (cited in Kaufmann, 1977:223).

13. In *A Theory of Justice* Rawls is concerned with the principles of distributive
rather than retributive justice. However, Sterba (1980: chap. 3) has applied these
principles to retributive justice and has found that they result in a deterrence
principle of punishment, coupled with retributive principles of responsibility and
due process principles of procedure.

14. On the almost insuperable problems involved in determining this equivalence—perceived by many as the Achilles' heel of the retributivist approach—see
Pincoffs (1977). See also below, chap. 7.

15. See above, n. 4.

16. Cf. Barnett's concept of "punitive restitution" (Barnett, 1977:288).

17. Marc Ancel, one of the leading advocates of this philosophy, insisted that
"social defense is not a positivist doctrine" but "an indirect consequence, twice
removed so to speak, of that doctrine" (Ancel, 1965:46).

18. Thus "prevention" may justify pre-delictual measures. Indeed, the extreme
wing of the social defense school identified with Gramatica would adopt interven-
tionist policies, uninhibited by the formal norms of the criminal law—including
the notion of responsibility. This view was rejected by the "new social defense"
(Ancel, 1965:120–22).

19. Miller (1976:48) finds that Rawls's two principles of justice cannot be easily reconciled with these three main objectives of social justice, since Rawls's principles are not "strictly distributive."

20. Deutsch (1975:144) states, however, that while equity usually means "to each according to his contribution," his neo-equity analysis leads to the formula "from each according to his ability, to each according to his need." This would seem to merge equity with a socialist or welfarist orientation, with which the need criterion is generally identified.

21. However, constitutional principles are not necessarily absolute and may be subject to "balancing" (Berger, 1992; Stein, 1992).

22. The implications of this in terms of the feasibility of adopting mediation procedures are not necessarily negative; see below.

23. Aynes also found a basis for this duty in natural law and social contract theory, but expressed a preference for reliance upon the more explicit Fourteenth Amendment. See also below, on the support for this view emanating from the "republican theory."

24. Under this doctrine, a person will only be permitted to argue a claim before the courts if he or she is acknowledged to have a material interest in the subject matter of the litigation. Victims have generally not had such an interest in the criminal process acknowledged; but see the recent amendment to the Texas Constitution (art. 2, sec. 30(e)), conferring upon the victim standing to exercise his or her rights under the said amendment.

25. The immunity granted to states under the Eleventh Amendment, was, in Aynes's view, implicitly revoked by the Fourteenth Amendment, insofar as required for the effective implementation of the latter.

26. Conversely, designation of crime victims for favorable treatment might in certain circumstances be perceived as discriminatory; cf. the invocation of the Fourteenth Amendment in regard to policies of "affirmative action" (Mason et al., 1983:615).

27. However, some common-law jurisdictions have recognized a legal duty on the part of the police to protect victims in certain circumstances, the breach of which can give rise to an action in tort; see below, chap. 13.

28. Cf. Willing (1982), who argued that "standing" to pursue the right to law enforcement should be granted only to states, and not individuals.

29. Of course, in many cases the victim in the instant case will have a higher probability of being the future victim too. This is particularly true of domestic disputes.

30. See, e.g., Jeffery (1969); and see chap. 12 in this study. Compare, however, the restitutionary approach of Barnett, referred to above. According to his view, the offender's debt is not to society but to the victim (Barnett, 1977:288). However, the author does not consider the constitutional aspects of the issue.

31. The solution could of course be developed outside the criminal process in tort law; see n. 27, above.

32. See also the "duty to obey the law" laid down in art. 33 of the American Declaration of the Rights and Duties of Man (Brownlee, 1971:394), one of the few such documents to specify duties as well as rights.

33. Cf. also art. 5 of the American Declaration of the Rights and Duties of Man.

34. Some UN declarations purport to reformulate existing principles of international law and are thus perceived as articulations of binding norms; others are mere exhortations to member states to adopt the principles specified therein (Asamoah, 1966).

35. This approach raises the problem of which section of the public would have to hold the view in question: the general public? victims? offenders? all of these? For while democracies attach value to majority opinions per se, one of the functions of a constitution is to protect minority interests.

Chapter 7

1. See U.S. Sentencing Commission (1987:1.3–1.4). See also Singer (1979:95), who found many of the determinate sentencing provisions to be inconsistent with a desert approach. A more consistent attempt to incorporate a desert philosophy is found in the Minnesota Sentencing Guidelines, described by von Hirsch (1982) as a "landmark in this country's history of sentencing reform" (215).

2. See, e.g., sec. 2A2.2 of the federal guidelines on the offense of assault, which specify the addition of two points for "bodily injury," four for "serious bodily injury," and six for "permanent or life-threatening bodily injury" (U.S. Sentencing Commission, 1994:39).

3. This component of seriousness was also recognized in the national study designed by Wolfgang and his colleagues to determine public perceptions of seriousness (Wolfgang et al., 1985), in which some variants of *mens rea* were incorporated into the offense definitions.

4. The commentary on this section noted that "this adjustment applies to all offenses where the victim's vulnerability played any part in the defendant's decision to commit the offense" (U.S. Sentencing Commission, 1987:3.1). This emphasis on the decision rather than the outcome indicates that the main consideration for the additional severity in this case was in fact culpability rather than harm. (A slight modification of the commentary since 1987 does not affect this analysis.)

5. This may be distinguished from the victim's *official* status. There seems to be a consensus that it is legitimate to specify more severe penalties for injuries inflicted upon such persons as heads of state or police officers.

6. Such discussions are reminiscent of the controversies regarding the implementation of the talionic principle in ancient law (Cohn, 1977).

7. Moral overtones are evident in one of the earliest and most influential books which led to these developments, published by a Quaker group (American Friends' Service Committee, 1971); the tenacity of Andrew von Hirsch in his articulation and defense of the theory may also be pertinent in this context.

8. "The more vulnerable or weaker the victim is viewed as compared to the offender, the greater the severity of the act even though the physical injury is stated in the stimulus as invariant." The type of victim upon whom a loss was inflicted (individual, institution, etc.) appeared to be of minimal significance (Wolfgang et al.,

1985:30, 29). The same conclusion was drawn by another researcher in respect of the relative social status of offender and victim (White, 1975).

9. See, e.g., Rossi et al. (1975). For a methodological critique of the analyses upon which this conclusion is based, see Miller and Vidmar (1981:164), who cite findings in the psychological literature which indicate the existence of differences based both on cultural and on personality characteristics.

10. Since the response rate was only 24% (603 out of 2,500 households), the authors caution that the responses "may represent the views of those citizens most concerned about the problems of prison sentencing" (Blumstein and Cohen, 1980:230).

11. However, a few studies have been concerned with the relative severity of different sanctions, without relating these to specific offenses. See, e.g., Sebba (1978), Buchner (1979), Erickson and Gibbs (1979), Sebba and Nathan (1984).

12. Hamilton and Rytina (1980), however, found "support for what appears to have been an underlying assumption of previous researchers, that assessments of crime seriousness have something to do with punishment judgments as well" (1140).

13. Cf. Hogan and Emler (1981), who *contrasted* the equity model, with its emphasis on compensation, with retribution, which is the basis of just-deserts theory. Yet desert is clearly related to the second alternative of equity theory (where compensation is not feasible), namely, retaliation. Naturally, the third alternative of restoring *psychological* equity would be quite inconsistent with the just-deserts model.

14. The authors note that the experimental data on this point is inconclusive.

15. These authors in fact found that certain variables related to the offender, such as race and sex, "accounted for very small proportions of the variation in either crime seriousness judgements or punishment assignments," suggesting "little inclination among the respondents towards individualized punishment." They nevertheless cautioned that "a study explicitly designed to pit alternative versions of justice against one another could arrive at quite different outcomes" (Hamilton and Rytina, 1980:1121 n. 5).

16. As noted in chap. 3, law enforcement personnel are not regarded as a separate constituency in this study. However, insofar as reforms may be advocated within the structure of the present system, their support may be critical.

17. This situation prevailed until relatively recently. The Canadian Law Reform Commission cited a survey (covering the period 1967–72) that found that restitution was ordered in only 6 out of 6,294 cases (Klein, 1978:388).

18. Cf. below, chap. 9; for historical surveys of the use of restitution, see Jacob (1970), Laster (1970), Schafer (1970), Edelhertz et al. (1975), Hudson et al. (1980: chap. 1), and Gittler (1984).

19. The claim that restitution serves various objectives of criminal justice is also made by legal writers who seek to emphasize the criminal rather than the civil character of restitution; see, e.g., Note (1984).

20. A major contribution to this literature has derived from the "Minnesota School." Burt Galaway and Joe Hudson organized a series of symposia, a number of which resulted in publications; see Hudson and Galaway (1977), Galaway and Hudson (1978), Hudson and Galaway (1980). See also Hudson and Galaway (1975) for a reader incorporating some earlier "classics" in this area, and more recently Galaway and Hudson (1990). A notable contributor to the legal literature on this topic has been

Harland (esp. 1982); see also the earlier contribution of Edelhertz et al. (1975); and see the proposal for a "restitutionary court" (*Victims of Crime*, 1985:34).

21. "Dimly perceivable, in the eyes of a few, is the possibility that many of the direct dollar costs of crime can be transferred from the taxpayer and the victim, to the offender" (Edelhertz et al., 1975:i). If dim in 1975, such perceptions are now floodlit!

22. These will be considered below, in chap. 11.

23. The authors distinguish between a "single *project* operating within a relatively small geographical area" and a "more extensive *program* containing a diversity of restitution projects" (Hudson et al., 1980:44, emphasis added). A further 12 publications were classified as assessments of "opinions or attitudes about a restitution sanction" rather than evaluations.

24. A similar conclusion on the part of the Canadian Law Reform Commission was questioned by Klein (1978:404). Moreover, the data collected by Smith et al. (1989) suggests that the level of restitution-order awards tends to be higher than indicated by the above figures. The average awards made by the courts in 1987 in the four areas studied were $349 (New York City), $416 (Minneapolis), $3,352 (Salt Lake City), and $860 (Montgomery, Ala.) (see Smith et al., 1989:81). The Salt Lake City figure was partly explained by "a few awards exceeding $20,000" (ibid., 80). Similarly, the awards made by *federal* courts may be higher still. The mean payment ordered in U.S. Sentencing Commission Guidelines cases in 1992 was $52,059, and the median $2,716, but these included both restitution awards and fines. Moreover, the character of federal crimes tends to differ from "street crimes" (Maguire et al., 1993:525).

25. A variety of methods for estimating loss were identified in the 1974 National Crime Survey data by Harland (1981:12). These included original cost, replacement cost, personal estimate of cash value, insurance report, and police estimate. The British Home Office provides guidelines to the criminal courts based on the tariff of the Criminal Injuries Compensation Board, which in turn is based upon the levels of damages awarded in civil cases (Moxon et al., 1992: appendix A). Weitekamp (1993) has suggested the employment of psychophysical scaling in determining award levels.

26. See sec. 77(c) of the Penal Law, 1977 (as amended). For a similar provision in Scotland, see Joutsen (1987:237).

27. See the Uniform Victims of Crime Act, sec. 404.

28. It has been argued that "increased burdens of restitution may be the impetus for further crimes by the offender" (ABA, 1981:18). This would not apply, however, if restitution orders were used as a substitute for fines, or if payments were to come from prison earnings.

29. There appears to be a discrepancy in the method of calculation in the two publications reporting this survey.

30. The connection between these two factors—type of order and location in the process—is indicated in table 5.1 on p. 79 of this survey (Hudson et al., 1980), which reveals that of the four pretrial diversion projects included in this review, three involved both monetary restitution and community service, while one involved only community service; i.e., none was restricted to monetary restitution alone.

31. Some English studies, however, noted the victim's satisfaction at a court decision to award restitution, apparently signifying official recognition of the wrong done to them (Villmow, 1984:11).

32. But it is not clear whether restitution as a sole sanction was presented as a legitimate option. The report states that the respondents were "asked to identify a combination" (Hudson et al., 1980:187).

33. This calculation is based on response categories 4 and 5. While these responses do not necessarily indicate support for restitution, such support is implicit.

34. The satisfaction rate where community service was the sole order was 73%, i.e., between the rates for monetary restitution alone and monetary restitution combined with community service.

35. In the 1974 National Crime Survey data reviewed by Harland (1981), it emerged that among the cases in which a theft loss was reported, more than one-half of the victim's annual family income amounted to $10,000 or more. This was considerably in excess of the estimate for prisoners referred to above.

36. For this purpose, 705 individuals were approached, 427 of whom responded. The geographical location and sampling method were not specified in the publication referred to here.

37. The other objectives specified were retribution, deterrence, social defense, and "impact of imprisonment." These terms were not clarified in the publication referred to here.

38. In Gandy's study, agreement with the restitutional aim did not apparently preclude agreement with other aims.

39. A pilot study determined that for all offenses included in the questionnaire there was a reasonably high probability that respondents would select a custodial sentence.

40. The samples numbered 1,200 each and were drawn from the electoral roll. Response rates were 80% for the experimental group and 76% for the control group.

41. Restitution was more likely to be favored by respondents who were less fearful of crime. However, victimization experience, as noted above, did not generally affect support for restitution. Females were more supportive than males.

42. Comprising 57 judges, 51 solicitors, and 142 practicing attorneys. The study is attributed to a master's thesis by R. S. Bluestein.

43. See the related point made by Harland (above) with reference to the economic inequality between the parties. From another point of view, however, radicals might favor direct resolution of conflicts between offender and victim, eliminating the role of state, and this would encourage the use of restitution; see Thorvaldson (1983).

44. However, the author also notes some problems—both conceptual and practical—in equating the two approaches. He also notes that "restoration of the moral order is not a commercial transaction" (McAnany, 1978:26). See also the view that "some people feel insulted and compromised by a suggestion that money from an offender will put right the hurt and distress they have experienced" (Reeves, 1985:53) and that "there is simply no amount of money that will rectify certain wrongs" (Pilon, 1978:352).

45. Utah law allows for a restitution order for up to double the victim's pecuniary damages (Bureau of Justice Statistics, 1984:9). This type of restitution, as noted, raises theoretical objections in terms of equity theory.

46. Cf. the "mixed" theories referred to in chap. 6. However, it should be noted that while Cavadino and Dignan explicitly argue in favor of a mixed theory, Wright (1982:244, 262) purports to reject retribution but refers instead to "natural consequences."

Chapter 8

1. Sir Henry Maine's famous dictum about substantive law being "secreted in the interstices of procedure" is often cited in this respect. However, it is difficult to make a clear-cut differentiation between substantive law and procedure; see, e.g., Paton (1951: chap. 23). The nature of penal sanctions is clearly a substantive topic, yet it is frequently dealt with in the context of procedural analyses of the court's function.

2. The degrees of participation have not generally been recognized by the relevant policy documents; see, e.g., the somewhat vague and imprecise presentation of this concept by the National Conference of the Judiciary (1983:10).

3. Under the Sentencing Reform Act of 1987 the emotive character of the terminology was modified; the word "harm" was replaced by "impact," "victim" by "individual" (Hellerstein, 1989:405).

4. See Bureau of Justice Statistics (1984:12). Restitution was not specified as an objective by the American Bar Association (ABA, 1981). The Victim and Witness Protection Act, 1982, amended the Federal Rules of Criminal Procedure so that the presentence report would include information on victim harm and—in a separate subsection—"other information that may aid the court in sentencing, including the restitution needs of any victim of the offense." Thus, the requirement of the description of victim harm is not directly linked to the requirement of restitution needs.

5. See Hudson (1984:53), Henley et al. (1994), and the analysis in Hall (1991: 241–43); but see McCleod (n.d.).

6. See *Williams v. New York*, 337 U.S. 241, 245–46 (1949). Cf. the stricter approach emerging in Britain in this respect (Ashworth, 1993:507). See also the discussion in the previous chapter on the application of due process to restitution orders.

7. Weigend defines the victim advocate as a "friend in court" whose role is "to inform the victim about the criminal process and to represent his interests vis à vis law enforcement and defense personnel" (Weigend, 1986:166).

8. In legal analysis, a party with "standing" before the court may be represented by a lawyer. This is not regarded as "vicarious" participation, since notionally it is the party who is participating in the proceeding rather than the lawyer. From a social science perspective, however, the distinction between personal and vicarious participation is important. The legal approach will be adopted only in chap. 12, where the analysis is more jurisprudential.

9. However, the responsible official is also expected to assist the victim in contacting agencies which provide services and relief, as well as arranging for protection from suspects; see sec. 503(c)(1)(D) and (c)(2).

10. The operational part of the formulation here laid emphasis on the *informational* aspect of advocacy, and as noted, this, together with the *protection* aspect, set the tone in the subsequent federal legislation.

11. The usefulness of lawyers to battered wives has been emphasized in a study conducted by Bowker (1984). This study is concerned with multifaceted legal services, however, and not specifically criminal prosecutions.

12. However, it seems that the *Nebenklage* procedure is used by a cross-section of the population. In the data reported by Schulz (1982), at least 39% of the *Nebenklager* were workers.

13. The comparison may have been confounded by differences between the samples, owing to the selection procedure adopted among the experimental sample (see above). Those among the experimental sample for whom no victim-impact statements were prepared appeared to have been significantly less satisfied on two of these measures.

14. This too, however, might reflect an alteration of the "existing exchange relationships" (Davis, Tichane, and Connick, 1980:24) and thus bring some practical benefits to the victim. This is indicated indirectly by the dissatisfaction expressed by the defense attorneys with the role of the victim's representatives, who were sometimes an obstacle in concluding a negotiated outcome (ibid., p. 68).

15. Thibaut and Walker (1975:84). An earlier experiment conducted by Thibaut and Gruder in 1969 found that "in negotiation research involving bargaining between dyads composed of spokesmen and constituents . . . constituents who are not able to bargain directly with the opposing dyad wish to occupy the more active spokesman's role, whereas most spokesmen are unwilling to change roles with their constituents" (ibid). See also the reservations regarding the significance of this research by Hayden and Anderson (1979).

16. A description of victim advocacy in the context of sexual assault offers a psychoanalytical explanation for the thesis that the advocate's role should be limited: "The victim must control the situation. The victim's self-esteem is at stake. To take decision-making power away from the victims places them in a situation similar to that of the attack, a time when control was taken from them" (Spaulding, 1980:199). The idea that the victim rather than the advocate should play the dominant role seems to be reflected in German law. A German Constitutional Court decision of 1974 accorded witnesses, including victims, "the right to legal assistance of his own choosing and the right to dismiss the counsel he has chosen from the trial" (Ercman, 1985).

17. See Buchner et al. (1983). Such a relationship, however, was not found in the first experiment (Kerstetter and Heinz, 1979).

18. In both experiments, victim and defendant were invited, as well as prosecutor, defense attorney, and judge. In the Dade County experiment, police officers, too, were invited.

19. In the earlier project, 87% of the victims present made at least one contribution, but only 25% made five or more (Heinz and Kerstetter, 1980:175). In the later project, victims, when present, spoke for about 9%–10% of the time (Buchner et al., 1983:21–32).

20. This included the effect on the chances of a settlement as opposed to a trial (see chap. 7). Comparisons in this study were complicated by the fact that the

research was designed to compare the experimental and the regular plea-bargaining procedures, and also conference and nonconference cases.

21. There was some evidence of more favorable defendant attitudes in the experimental groups, but there was more variation within groups than between groups (Kerstetter and Heinz, 1979:120).

Chapter 9

1. The title given to one analysis of this development, "The Diffusion of Victim Compensation Laws" (see Doerner, 1979; Doerner and Silverman, 1980), conjures up the memory of the sex psychopath laws, the precipitous and irrational adoption of which were so perceptively analyzed by Sutherland (1950) in an article with a similar title. In fact, however, the authors seem to have been influenced by a concept borrowed from the study of political innovation (Doerner, 1979:121–24). Closer to the Sutherland approach is the analysis of Miers (1978, 1983).

2. McGillis and Smith (1983:31ff.). In 1978 bills were passed by both the Senate and the House of Representatives, but the compromise bill adopted by the conference committee was rejected by the House (ibid., 32).

3. See, e.g., Lamborn (1971, 1973a, 1973b), Edelhertz and Geis (1974), Drapkin and Viano (1974–75), Miers (1978, 1990), Meiners (1978), American Bar Association (1981), Merrill (1981), and Rich and Stenzel (1980).

4. See Carrow (1980a), Ramker and Meagher (1982), McGillis and Smith (1983), McCormack (1991), Parent et al. (1992), Greer (1994).

5. See also the studies reviewed therein (Elias, 1983b:34–38); and see Doerner and Lab (1980), Shapland et al. (1985), Villmow (1986), Newburn (1988).

6. In the case of New Mexico, such a provision was designed to exclude claims by victims of the prison riots in 1980.

7. Despite the fact that subrogation claims may be brought against insurance companies as well as offenders, they amount to less than 1% of total program revenues (Parent et al., 1992:30).

8. To the figure of $400 million, "Meiners added 10 percent for administrative costs, raising the total to $440 million. Meiners then adjusted this to $500 million to account for an increase in the crime rate and an increase in hospitalization costs. Meiners then doubled the $500 million to account for what he called the 'subsidy effect' " (Austern, 1980). The "subsidy effect" is a reflection of the increase in state expenditure that would result from the grant of a federal subsidy.

9. According to the Home Office (1993:2), the British Compensation Board pays out approximately 150 million pounds sterling per annum, for a population a quarter of the size; but in their estimate the total paid out by the United States in 1991 was somewhat *higher* than the British equivalent.

10. There is no clear relationship between relative administration costs and population size. New York had the second highest relative expenditure on administration costs (25.6%), while Texas had the second lowest (5.1%).

11. McGillis and Smith (1983:40). This assessment was put forward by Gerhard Mueller in 1965.

12. "Many of those supporting, and even some of those sponsoring, compensation schemes, later voted against the appropriations to fund the programs, or for extremely meager funding and very extensive and restrictive eligibility requirements" (Elias, 1983:214).

13. A Texas survey found that respondents' first choice was for a compensation fund supported by fines paid by offenders. This applied both to respondents who had been victimized and to those who had not (St. Louis, 1976:27).

14. See the references cited in n. 3 above. See also Chappell and Sutton (1974), Brooks (1976), Carrow (1980a), Elias (1983b:24–26).

15. This would seem to lead to the conclusion that public compensation schemes should be adopted, but with a high minimum eligibility requirement—to cater for "costly" tragedies only.

16. However, it may be recalled that Meiners himself believed that the programs would result in enormous public costs, benefiting not merely victims but also bureaucracies and lawyers.

17. This rationale may have influenced the establishment of compensation for "Good Samaritans." Indeed, the logic of this recognition might lead to the bestowing of additional rewards for such citizens, rather than merely compensating them for their loss.

18. This being a needs-oriented approach, some reliance on means-testing is inevitable under their scheme (Harris et al., 1984:338).

19. For different views on this, see Thorvaldson and Krasnick (1980) and McGillis and Smith (1983:121).

20. Justice O'Connor "listed numerous authors from St. Augustine to Jesse Jackson whose works would be covered by such a statute" (50 CrL 2019).

Chapter 10

1. Early developments are reviewed in Newton (1976b), Dussich (1981), Mawby and Gill (1987), and Roberts (1990).

2. The need for the last five stages only arises where law enforcement agencies have succeeded in apprehending and prosecuting the offender. The NOVA table classifying their eight stages labels them as "victim rights" or "victim and witness rights," but it is clear from the separate sevenfold classification of victim rights (see below) that the above classification is essentially a classification of services rather than rights.

3. "(1) Assist every victim who reports a crime, whether or not an arrest is made . . . (2) Respond to the scene of the crime to make crisis counselling available . . . (3) Provide 24-hour telephone hotline service to victims and witnesses for assistance, particularly if threats or intimidation occur . . . (4) Make emergency monetary aid available to help needy victims make their homes secure, replace such things as glasses and hearing aids, and buy food and other necessities . . . (5) Refer victims to appropriate social service and victim compensation programs and assist in filling out forms for compensation . . . (6) Educate the public about the

operation of the criminal justice system and the way it treats victims . . . (7) Assist in prompt return of victim's property . . . (8) Notify the victim of progress of the investigation, the defendant's arrest, subsequent bail determination and status of the case as it proceeds through the system . . . (9) Assist victims in making appropriate input on the following: bail determinations, continuances, plea bargaining, dismissals, sentencing, restitution and parole hearings . . . (10) Consult with victims and witnesses to facilitate the setting of convenient hearing dates . . . (11) Implement a victim/witness on-call system . . . (12) Intercede with the employers or creditors of victims and witnesses . . . (13) Assist the elderly and handicapped in arranging transportation to and from court . . . (14) Provide a translator service . . . (15) Coordinate efforts to ensure that victims have a secure place to wait before testifying . . . (16) Provide counselling or companionship during court appearances when appropriate" (President's Task Force, 1982:121–25).

4. Victims of Crime Act of 1984, sec. 1404 (d)(2) and (4). "Services to victims of federal crime" are defined much more widely, to include training of law enforcement personnel in the delivery of services, dissemination of information regarding services, and the payment of salaries to victim service personnel.

5. Cf. also the somewhat similar differentiation by Roberts (1990) between "victim service programs," which emphasize crisis counseling, and victim/witness-assistance programs, which have endeavored to "alleviate the stress and trauma of victims and witnesses who testified in court" (30–32). Cf. also the typologies referred to in Cronin and Bourque (1980:25).

6. The INSLAW study (Hernon and Forst, 1984) referred to in chap. 2 also includes some useful information on some aspects of the content of victim assistance, such as the number of contacts with personnel and the topics discussed.

7. Thus Cronin and Bourque (1980) found that "on-site observation of operating projects and field data collection, while extremely useful in detailing project process, yielded little evidence on outcome and impacts. On-site experience did, however, sensitize us to methodological weaknesses in the existing studies and provided some strong hunches about the likelihood of discovering 'success' on various measures" (89).

8. It may be that the "control group" might have been the least needful a priori (see above).

9. The Victims of Crime Act of 1984 allocates funding priority for "assistance to victims of sexual assault, spousal abuse, or child abuse" (sec. 1404 (a)(2)(A)). It is possible, however, that in contradiction with the stereotypes, potential candidates for victim assistance may often be young males (Shapland et al., 1984:223), who suffer the highest rates of victimization.

10. The rationale of the classification is not entirely clear. The "right to counsel" includes some rights that do not appear to involve any counsel or counseling, even in the broad sense of that term used by NOVA in this context; and "the right to participate in the criminal justice process" would seem to belong instead to right no. 7, "due process."

11. The state of Oklahoma took a middle path. Seven separate bills dealing with different victim-related measures were proposed simultaneously and were known collectively as the Victim's Bill of Rights. Five of these were adopted (see Turpen, 1981).

12. See also sec. 4 of the UN Draft Declaration of Basic Principles of Justice, which declares that "victims should be treated with compassion and respect for their dignity." Such expressions, which are now incorporated in some of the victim-oriented constitutional amendments (see, e.g., the amendments adopted in Texas in 1989 and in Arizona in 1990), appear to have originated in the earlier NOVA proposal referred to above.

13. Under the heading "Why Victim Rights?" is the following: "Recognition of the rights of victims and witnesses to be free from needless harm is the recognition of the human right to compassion, dignity, and justice" (NOVA, n.d.:3). This states both too little and too much. Too little, since NOVA's own list of rights goes beyond the issue of "needless harm"; it is clearly also concerned with issues of justice per se. Too much, since the "recognition of the human right to compassion, dignity, and justice" could be the basis of innumerable laws in a limitless number of areas.

14. The first sentence in this quotation is, of course, not quite accurate; some crimes are committed against the state or an organization, or are victimless.

15. This expression also occurs in some of the earlier literature; see, e.g., MacNamara and Sullivan (1974). See also Normandeau (1983:27).

Chapter 11

1. It seems that 1976 was a critical year for both developments. It was the year in which the National Conference on the Causes of Popular Dissatisfaction with the Administration of Justice was held (see below) and in which von Hirsch (1976) and his associates published *Doing Justice*.

2. See, on this paradox, de Sousa Santos (1982:256). It is, of course, possible to reconcile these conflicting developments by means of some kind of bifurcational or "trade-off" model; cf. Cohen (1979). Further, a "restitutive" or "reparative" paradigm may be linked indirectly to both the desert model and informalism; see below and Zedner (1994).

3. In fact, there has been a continuing advocacy of informal alternatives to conventional adjudication dating back to Pound's address and even before. This has been expressed in such developments as the establishment of municipal courts, domestic relations courts, and small-claims courts (Harrington, 1982). Similarly, advocacy of conciliation techniques by elements among the judiciary has also been a continuing tradition (Galanter, 1984–85).

4. The criteria for determining the appropriate forum would be (1) the nature of the dispute, (2) the relationship between the disputants, (3) the amount in dispute, (4) the cost of the proceedings, and (5) the speed with which the proceedings would be held (Sander, 1976:118–26).

5. See, e.g., Sander and Snyder (1982), a "selected bibliography" listing several hundred books and articles in this area.

6. See, e.g., the *Journal of Dispute Resolution*, published by the Missouri Law Review, in conjunction with the Center for the Study of Dispute Resolution (from

1984) and the *Negotiation Journal* ("On the Process of Dispute Settlement"), launched in 1985.

7. The Dorchester Urban Court, in addition to its "mediation component," comprised a "victim component," in effect a victim/witness-assistance program, and a "disposition component," which involved the development of presentence investigation reports. Together, these programs were intended "to build a structure for active community participation in the criminal process" (Snyder, 1978:749). The Brooklyn Dispute Resolution Center Program was established in 1977 by the Institute for Mediation and Conflict Resolution in conjunction with the Victim/Witness Assistance Project of the Institute of Justice (see Davis, Tichane, and Grayson, n.d.:7).

8. Among these are the evaluations of the NIJ-sponsored Neighborhood Justice centers (Cook et al., 1980; Roehl and Cook, 1982), of the Dorchester Urban Court (Felstiner and Williams, 1980 and 1982), of the Brooklyn Dispute Resolution Center (Davis, Tichane, and Grayson, n.d.; Davis, n.d.; Connick and Davis, 1981; Davis, 1982), of the Colorado Springs Neighborhood Justice Center (Jones and Gebhard, 1980), of the Neighborhood Justice Center of Honolulu (Berger, 1982), and of a number of citizen dispute-settlement programs in Florida (Bridenback et al., 1980). Findings of the earlier studies were summarized by Garofalo and Connelly (1980), while helpful analytical surveys are found in Merry (1982) and Tomasic (1982). More recent evaluations have focused on VORP or VORP-type programs; for analyses of these, see Coates and Gehm (1989) and Marshall and Merry (1990), surveying the American and British findings, respectively.

9. The authors of the evaluation report that in 56% of the 259 cases scheduled for mediation (i.e., 145 cases), mediation proceedings in fact took place (Davis, Tichane, and Grayson, n.d.:95). They report mediation agreements in 144 cases (47).

10. In rare instances a *complainant* in a criminal trial may be required to enter into a recognizance to keep the peace; see sec. 73 of Israel's Penal Law, 1977.

11. In a German survey, respondents who had been victimized perceived mediation as useful in particular for the "reduction of hostile feelings" (as well as for restitution), but this view was expressed more often in connection with cases of assault than with cases of theft (Beurskens and Boers, 1985: table 3).

12. See, however, McGillis and Mullen (1977:77–80) and Cook et al. (1980:99–102), who cite some earlier and more positive findings of Felstiner and his associates and conclude that "the cost of the mechanism might well be competitive with those of the courts."

13. Thus the preamble to the Dispute Resolution Act indicated that this legislation was designed to assist the establishment of informal mechanisms to deal with minor disputes. The German survey reported below indicated that criminal justice personnel were generally more reserved than the general public about the use of informal proceedings. However, there are some references in the literature to the use of conciliation procedures for serious cases, particular in the context of VORP-type programs (see, e.g., Umbreit, 1989). Further, the New York legislature in 1986 specified that felonies could be referred to the Community Dispute Resolution Centers (see *World Arbitration and Mediation Report*, 1992:288), but the indications are that this option is used sparingly.

14. Nelken (1985) pointed out the confusion surrounding the proposed role of the community in the justice system: "Communities can be agents, locus or benefi-

ciaries of crime control"; see also the title of a related article, "If Community Is the Answer, What Is the Question?" (Nelken, forthcoming). At the same time, the "community" rhetoric reflects some real needs and derives from a number of seminal writers on sociological theory, such as Toennies and Simmel (see Alper and Nichols, 1981: chap. 1). See also Warhaftig (1982), Yngvesson, 1993.

15. However, *(a)* not all those cases referred to mediation were actually mediated, *(b)* only one of the three differences was significant at the 5% level (the other three were significant at the 10% level), and *(c)* the differences had—in a very small sample—almost disappeared two and a half years later (Connick and Davis, 1981:35).

16. *Flexibility* was defined as "dispute settlement leading to satisfaction of both sides, even if that is not strictly in accordance with the legal rules." *Law* was defined as "dispute settlement strictly according to legal rules, even if not all interested parties are satisfied." *Compromise* was defined as "elaboration of a mutual agreement, according to the principle that everybody partially compromises his claims." Finally, *justice* was defined as "full satisfaction of the just claims of one of the sides, even though the other party is dissatisfied" (Naumova, 1983:177). The range of percentages derives from the fact that the sample comprised three subsamples (each numbering 800 respondents), representing different degrees of urbanization.

17. It has thus been pointed out that major normative changes such as that brought about by the Supreme Court case of *Brown v. Board of Education* would be unlikely to be achieved by informal negotiation. Further, it has been found that individuals who feel substantially deprived in terms of status recognition see a greater potential in formal rather than informal proceedings (Kulcsar, 1983). "Compromise may be ill-suited to the vindication of legally protected rights, and compromise may be impossible when a dispute involves several strongly held, but inconsistent, community values" (Note, 1979). See also Felstiner and Williams (1978), Felstiner and Drew (1978:30).

18. As noted, provision for informal modes of dispute resolution was incorporated into the Declaration of Basic Principles of Justice for Victims of Crime and Abuse of Power, which was adopted by the United Nations in 1985 (art. 7). However, the formulation of that article ("informal mechanisms for the resolution of disputes, including mediation, arbitration and customary justice or indigenous practices, should be utilized *where appropriate* to facilitate conciliation and redress for victims" [emphasis added]) does not indicate the recognition of a right. The ACLU publication on victims' rights (Stark and Goldstein, 1985) has a chapter entitled "The Right to Resolve Disputes outside the Traditional Justice System," but while guidance was offered as to the optional use of the various mechanisms available, the only right specified was that of the parties to settle their conflict between themselves.

Chapter 12

1. Mawby classified the sources of victim assistance as *(a)* statute (e.g., criminal justice agencies), *(b)* the private sector (e.g., insurance), *(c)* family and community, and *(d)* voluntary organizations.

2. In a later article, Ziegenhagen and Benyi (1981) consider how far the various victim-oriented programs fulfill the following four functions: (1) normative detection, i.e., identifying the deviant conduct; (2) normative definition, i.e., labeling conduct as criminal or otherwise; (3) response designation, i.e., determining the nature of the response, and (4) response execution, i.e., playing a role in the implementation of this response. Attribution of these functions to the victim is generally more consistent with the adversary-retribution model than its alternative.

3. Thus, Gittler (1984) observes that "it is possible to envisage a criminal justice system in which private prosecutions would be revived and the victim would be able to initiate a criminal action without the authorization or approval of the public prosecutor" and believes that "the impact of allowing victim-initiated private prosecutions would be beneficial" (151, 152); but what is envisaged here is ultimately a reserve power, to "serve as a useful safeguard and safety valve if the prosecutor was unwilling to take action" (154). The Helsinki Institute Seminar went somewhat further and passed the following recommendation: "The victim should be given more independence and legal guarantees in the initiation and conduct of the criminal process. Possibilities should be studied of transferring more offenses from public prosecution to private prosecution or, alternatively, of subjecting public prosecution to the consent of the victim" (Joutsen, 1984:12, recommendation no. 12). More radical proposals advocated by European writers such as Hulsman support the total abolition of the penal system. In this case, however, any disputational powers conferred upon the victim would not be prosecutorial in the criminal sense.

4. McDonald (1976b), in considering private prosecution practices in southern states, cited a source who observed that the main contribution of private prosecutors was to prevent plea bargaining. A generalization of this phenomenon "would bring the courts to their knees" (35). It is natural that victim advocates might object to a plea bargain between defendant and public prosecutor from which they were excluded. This would not necessarily apply, however, if the victim or the victim's advocate were the sole prosecutor, or indeed if he or she were involved in the plea bargain as a third party (see chap. 8).

5. Goldstein (1982) suggested control by the public prosecutor, who "would probably develop criteria for the classes of cases he would allow routinely to be brought by private parties, as well as those he would take over or move to dismiss" (560). This solution, which would have some similarity to the English position (Hetherington, 1989), is open to the objection that bureaucratic considerations might influence the public prosecutor's policies.

6. In the British study referred to, 89% of the defendants were, like the prosecutors, unrepresented (Lidstone et al., 1980). The Royal Commission recommended that where a magistrate's court had granted leave to file a private prosecution, legal aid would be available. In Israel an amendment was adopted to empower the court to *require* the private prosecutor to appoint an attorney—without provision for legal aid—where it appears to the court that the prosecutor is unable to handle the matter, or does so in a vexatious manner (sec. 73 of the Criminal Procedure Law [Consolidated Version], 1982).

7. A similar question was considered in the context of informal alternatives, namely, whether even the most serious offenses may be the subject of compromise between the parties.

8. In practice this right has been exercised mainly in cases of shoplifting and common assault (Hetherington, 1989:155).

9. Cf. the second schedule to Israel's Criminal Procedure Law (Consolidated Version), 1982, which lists the offenses for which private prosecutions may be instigated.

10. This was seen as part of a general trend by the court to differentiate between "good" and "bad" citizens, the victims generally being identified with the former. "Arguably linked to the growing interest both in 'victims' rights' and the rights of law-abiding citizens in general, the new 'good citizen/bad citizen' dichotomy has had a profound effect on the types of criminal case the Court has recently accepted for review" (O'Neill, 1984:364).

11. However, the chief justice seems to have been somewhat ambivalent on this point, for he also asserted that "inconvenience and embarrassment to witnesses cannot justify failing to enforce constitutional rights of an accused" (O'Neill, 1984:379).

12. 410 U.S. 614 (1973), at 619.

13. See above, chap. 10. These rights include "the right to confer with a representative of the prosecutor's office" but not to veto the prosecutor's decision. Moreover, the section expressly provides that the victim "does not have the standing to participate as a party in a criminal proceeding." In a recent case following from Arizona's constitutional amendment (see chap. 10), the petition to vacate the parole decision for failure to provide notice to the victim was brought by "the State of Arizona, asserting the rights of the crime victim." The court cited a statute which provided that "at the request of the victim, the prosecutor may assert any right to which the victim is entitled" (*State ex rel. Hance v. Arizona Bd. of Pardons and Parole*, 150 Ariz. Adv. Rep. 42, 1993).

14. It should be noted that these procedures generally allow for the "subsidiary" prosecutor to continue in his or her own right should the public prosecutor withdraw; see Marek (1985), Krapac and Loncarevic (1985). Damaska (1985), however, noted that the accommodation of additional parties is easier in the so-called inquisitorial system, in which the proceedings are dominated by the judge, than under the adversary system, where the traditional roles of the parties have a greater significance.

15. Cf. the alternative dichotomy discerned by O'Neill (1984) in his analysis of some Supreme Court judgments whereby "gains for criminals result in losses for the *law-abiding*" (372, emphasis added).

16. O'Brien (1992), however, refers to the "myth of uncollectability" and points out that courts are increasingly holding insurance companies liable for wrongful conduct committed by insured persons (8).

17. This may not be applicable in jurisdictions where prison earnings are realistic. The idea that prisoners' earnings should be specifically earmarked for compensation of the victim has appeared in a number of codes and has a history dating back to Ferri, Garofalo, and even Herbert Spencer; see Silving (1975).

18. However, tort litigation itself has a relatively high probability of succeeding; see Miller (1983).

19. Thus Professor Palmer wrote of the New Zealand accident compensation law: "A lot of people who received nothing under the old (tort) system are being compensated and compensated quickly" (cited in Cappelletti and Garth, 1978:119).

20. Cf. Israel's Courts' Law (Consolidated Version), 1984, sec. 77.

21. This notionally civil character, however, is affected by the penal character of the proceeding "pour prendre un caractère mixte, mi-penal, mi-civil" (Bouzat and Pinatel, 1970:930). Cf. also the Resolutions of the Eleventh International Congress on Penal Law (1974): "The adhesion process must necessarily be a mixed structure of civil and criminal procedure elements" (31).

22. See Sebba (1982:225–26). Even in modern times it has proved difficult to provide an unequivocal differentiation between the two areas; see Kenny's famous essay "What Is a Crime?" (Kenny, 1952; cf. Winfield, 1931). For a critique of the arguments invoked in favor of differentiation, see Epstein (1977). See also Shuman (1970), Hadden (1971), Ashworth (1986).

23. See Holmes (1964); cf. Hall (1943), Epstein (1977).

24. Maidment (1983) has suggested (in the context of the issue of domestic violence) that the effectiveness of the remedy may depend less on its designation as civil or criminal and more on pragmatic considerations, but that ultimately the efficacy of both types of remedy are limited by the underlying societal attitude to the form of victimization in question.

25. For a discussion of other differences in the two types of procedures from which the victim would benefit—although emphasizing the disadvantages to the defendant—see Freiberg and O'Malley (1984).

26. Even Justice O'Connor's vigorous dissenting opinion, which sought to apply the Eighth Amendment in this case, was based, inter alia, on the government's potential to "abuse its power by allowing civil juries to impose ruinous punitive damages as a way of furthering the purposes of the criminal law" (*Browning-Ferris v. Kelco Disposal,* 1989, 106 L Ed 219, p. 253). Two of the majority justices observed that the Fourteenth Amendment might apply in such cases to constrain excessive damages between private parties as an abuse of due process.

27. This term did not apply specifically to civil procedures but to various nonpenal solutions, including mediation; see Sessar (1984:19).

28. Not only was the positivist school utilitarian, but so was the classical school, which preceded it. It will be recalled that Beccaria laid emphasis on deterrence as the aim of the criminal law.

29. The fault vs. strict liability controversy is distinguished from the morality-utility controversy; see England (1993: chaps. 1 and 3).

30. The importance of vesting this discretion in the victim is emphasized by Maidment (1983), in her consideration of remedies for domestic violence in Britain. See also recommendation no. 19 of the Helsinki Seminar (Joutsen, 1984): "The victim should have the opportunity of proceeding according to different options, in accordance with his or her own needs."

31. It has been argued that the option of private prosecution in Germany and Poland is effectively a mechanism for reconciliation, since only 3%–8% of the cases in fact proceed to conviction (Marek, 1985).

32. Even Christie (1977), generally opposed to any formal judicial processing (see above, chap. 12), seems to allow for this possibility. Similarly, Wright (1982) provides for various measures of restraint that the court would be empowered to impose in serious cases, including supervision of the wrongdoer. These are ostensibly directed at protecting the victim but seem to have a wider protective purpose vis-à-vis society as a whole.

33. In this context it may be noted that the tension between the two models—an interparty, individual responsibility model, as opposed to a state responsibility, welfare model—has its direct parallel in the civil-law literature on the respective roles of tort and insurance (esp. public insurance) in compensating personal injuries (see, e.g., Harris et al., 1984).

34. The reservations expressed in chap. 9 regarding the levy of penalties on offenders in order to compensate victims of other offenders do not apply, or at least not to the same extent, in the instant case. Here the assessment of punitive damages is determined as a matter of principle, as an appropriate sanction for the wrongdoing, and not for the purpose of meeting a particular social or economic need.

35. See also Robinson's proposal for sanctions of equal "punitive bite," incorporated in the "hybrid approach" of Cavadino and Dignan (1993).

Chapter 13

1. One of the proposals was referred briefly to in chap. 1. The other does not generally receive mention in the victim movement literature.

2. This expression properly refers to the acts of bystanders who take action by reason of good citizenship or conscience. It seems less applicable to provisions for the imposition of a legal obligation, or even the specification of rewards, whereby the action would cease to be purely altruistic. Conversely, Geis (1991) refers to the laws which penalize the failure to assist as "Bad Samaritan" laws!

3. Mention may be made in this context of the alleged reluctance of physicians to intervene in cases of injury, for fear of negligence suits. A legal, as opposed to mere ethical, obligation to intervene might act as a counterweight to such inhibitions.

4. For example, the victim of a bag snatch, on pursuing the perpetrator, might find him- or herself attacked.

5. Van Dijk et al. (1984:10) expressly draw this conclusion. In the American study, this conclusion emerged from the data.

6. Some legal texts, however, deal with both issues in close proximity, as part of the law of negligence; see, e.g., the Restatement of the Law of Torts referred to above.

7. This is illustrated by the strong support for recognition of such a moral duty by the anarchist William Godwin. However, he was not in favor of enforcement of duties by legal compulsion; see Weinrib (1980:264–65).

Chapter 14

1. An interesting debate on the role of victim advocates and the extent to which victim-oriented reform may be consistent with "reintegrative" social policies has

recently been published in the *Law and Society Review*, in the wake of an analysis of Washington State's legislation on violent sex offenders (see Scheingold et al. 1994; Braithwaite and Pettit 1994).

Appendix

1. Berkowitz and Walster (1976) include in their volume on equity theory a contribution from Lerner and his colleagues on the "just-world" theory. It appears from their preface, however, that they regard attribution theory as pertaining to a different branch of psychology. Other writers have criticized equity theory for paying inadequate attention to attribution theory (Kidd and Utne, 1978).

2. See the above distinction between actual and psychological equity. For the application of this to the just-world theory, see Godfrey and Lowe (1975:944).

3. Koch and Bean (n.d.) in fact note six explanations in the literature for this phenomenon. However, there is at least one approach that would hypothesize sympathy for the victim: see Gold et al. (1978), citing studies conducted by D. Aderman.

Bibliography

Aaronson, D.E., Hoff, B.H., Jaszi, P., Kittrie, N.N., and Saari, D. 1977. *The New Justice: Alternatives for Conventional Adjudication*. Washington, D.C.: U.S. Department of Justice.

Abel, R.L. 1973. "A Comparative Theory of Dispute Organizations in Society." *Law and Society Review* 8:217–47.

———, ed. 1982a. *The Politics of Informal Justice*. 2 vols. New York: Academic Press.

———. 1982b. "The Contradictions of Informal Justice." In Abel, ed., *The Politics of Informal Justice*, 1:267–320.

Adler, Z. 1987. *Rape on Trial*. London: Routledge & Kegan Paul.

Alper, B.S., and Nichols, L.T. 1981. *Beyond the Courtroom*. Lexington, Mass.: Lexington Books.

American Bar Association (ABA). 1981. *Victim/Witness Legislation: Considerations for Policymakers*. Washington, D.C.: American Bar Association.

———. 1983. *Guidelines for Fair Treatment of Crime Victims and Witnesses*. Washington, D.C.: American Bar Association.

American Friends' Service Committee. 1971. *Struggle for Justice*. New York: Hill & Wang.

American Law Institute. 1965. *Restatement of the Law—Second: Torts 2d*. St. Paul, Minn.: American Law Institute Publishers.

American Psychological Association. 1984. *Task Force on the Victims of Crime and Violence*. Washington, D.C.

Amir, M. 1971. *Patterns of Forcible Rape*. Chicago: University of Chicago Press.

Ancel, M. 1965. *Social Defence*. London: Routledge & Kegan Paul.

Aquino, K., Steisel, V., and Kaye, A. 1992. "The Effects of Resource Distribution, Voice, and Decision Framing under Provision of Public Goods." *Journal of Conflict Resolution* 36:665–87.

Arnold, H.R., and Koriner, L. 1991. "Victimization, Attitudes towards Crime and Related Issues: Comparative Results from Hungary." In Kaiser, G., et al., eds., *Victims and Criminal Justice*, 51:99–121.

383

Asamoah, O.Y. 1966. *The Legal Significance of the Declarations of the General Assembly of the United Nations*. The Hague: Nijhoff.

Ash, M. 1972. "On Witnesses: A Radical Critique of Criminal Law Procedures." *Notre Dame Lawyer* 48:386–425.

Ashworth, A. 1983. *Sentencing and Penal Policy*. London: Weidenfeld & Nicolson.

———. 1986. "Punishment and Compensation: Victims, Offenders and the State." *Oxford J. of Legal Studies* 6:86–122.

———. 1992a. "Proportionality in the Philosophy of Punishment." In Tonry, M., ed., *Crime and Justice: A Review of Research*, 16:181–241. Chicago: University of Chicago Press.

———. 1992b. *Sentencing and Criminal Justice*. London: Weidenfeld & Nicolson.

———. 1993. "Victim Impact Statements and Sentencing." *Criminal Law Review*, 498–509.

Ashworth, C.D., and Feldman-Summers, S. 1978. "Perceptions of the Effectiveness of the Criminal Justice System." *Criminal Justice and Behavior* 5:227–40.

Atiyah, P.S. 1980. *Accidents, Compensation and the Law*. London: Weidenfeld & Nicolson.

Attorney General's Task Force on Violent Crime. 1981. *Attorney General's Task Force on Violent Crime: Final Report*. Washington, D.C.: U.S. Department of Justice.

Auerbach, J.S. 1983. *Justice without Law?* New York: Oxford University Press.

Austern, D. 1980. "Crime Victim Compensation Programs: The Issue of Costs." *Victimology: An International Journal* 5:68–71.

Austin, J., and Krisberg, B. 1981. "Wider, Stronger and Different Nets: The Dialectics of Criminal Justice Reform." *J. of Research in Crime and Delinquency* 18:165–96.

Austin W., Walster, E., and Utne, M.K. 1976. "Equity and the Law: The Effect of a Harmdoer's 'Suffering in the Act' on Liking and Assigned Punishment." In Berkowitz, L., and Walster, E., eds., *Equity Theory*, 163–90.

Aynes, R.L. 1984. "Constitutional Considerations: Government Responsibility and the Right Not to Be a Victim." *Pepperdine Law Review* 11:63–116.

Balkan, S., Berger, R.J., and Schmidt, J. 1980. *Crime and Deviance in America*. Belmont, Calif.: Wadsworth.

Bard, M., and Sangrey, D. 1979. *The Crime Victim's Book*. New York: Basic Books.

———. 1980. "Things Fall Apart: Victims in Crisis." *Evaluation and Change*, 28–35.

Baril, M. 1980. "Ils n'ont plus la liberté: Reactions à la victimisation et ses consequences." *Criminologie* 13 (1): 94–103.

———. 1984. "The Victim's Perceptions of Crime and the Criminal Justice System: A Recent Study of Small Shopkeepers in Montreal." In Block, R., ed., *Victimization and Fear of Crime: World Perspectives*, 75–86. Washington, D.C.: U.S. Department of Justice.

Baril, M., and Morisette, A. 1985. "Du cote des victimes, une autre perspective sur le vol à main armée." *Criminologie* 18:117–33.

Barnett, R.E. 1977. "Restitution: A New Paradigm of Criminal Justice." In Barnett and Hagel, eds., *Assessing the Criminal: Restitution, Retribution and the Legal Process*, 349–83. Cambridge, Mass.: Ballinger.

———. 1980. "The Justice of Retribution." *American J. of Jurisprudence* 25:117–32.

Barnett, R.E., and Hagel, J. 1977. "Assessing the Criminal: Restitution, Retribution and the Legal Process." In Barnett, R.E., and Hagel, J., eds., *Assessing the Criminal: Restitution, Retribution and the Legal Process*, 1–31. Cambridge, Mass.: Ballinger.

Bassiouni, M.C. 1985. "The Protection of 'Collective Victims' in International Law." *New York Law School Human Rights Annual* 2:239–59.

———. 1988. *International Protection of Victims*. AIDP. n.p.: Erès.

Baurmann, M.C., and Schadler, W. 1991. "Victims of Reported Crime—Their Expectations, Needs, and Perspectives: An Inquiry of Crime Victims Concerning Victim Protection, Victim Support, and Mediation." In Kaiser, G., et al., eds., *Victims and Criminal Justice*, 52(1):3–27.

Beccaria, C. 1880. *Crimes and Punishments*. 1764. Ed. J.A. Farrer. London: Chatto & Windus.

Beha, J., Carlson, K., and Rosenblum, R.H. 1977. *Sentencing to Community Service*. Washington, D.C.: U.S. Department of Justice.

Bell, G.B. 1978. "The Pound Conference Follow-Up: A Response from the United States Department of Justice." *Federal Rules Decisions* 76:320–36.

Ben-David, S., and Kirchhoff, G.F., eds. 1992. *International Faces of Victimology*. Mönchengladbach, Ger.: WSV Publishing.

Bentham, J. 1948. *An Introduction to the Principles of Moral and Legislation*. New York: Hafner.

Berger, K. 1982. *Neighborhood Justice Center of Honolulu*. Reston, Va.: Institute for Social Analysis.

Berger, M. 1992. "The Deconstitutionalization of the Confrontation Clause: A Proposal for a Prosecutorial Restraint Model." *Minnesota Law Review* 76:557–613.

Berger, V. 1977. "Man's Trial, Woman's Tribulation: Rape Cases in the Courtroom." *Columbia Law Review* 77:1–103.

———. 1992. *Case Law of the European Court of Human Rights*. Vol. 2. Dublin: Round Hall Press.

Berk, R.A., and Rossi, R.H. 1977. *Prison Reform and State Elites*. Cambridge, Mass.: Ballinger.

Berkowitz, L., and Walster, E., eds. 1976. *Equity Theory: Toward a General Theory of Social Interaction*. New York: Academic Press.

Bernat, F.P., Parsonage, W.H., and Helfgott, J. 1994. "Victim Impact Laws and the Parole Process in the United States: Balancing Victim and Inmate Rights and Interests." *International Review of Victimology* 3:121–40.

Beurskens, A., and Boers, K. 1985. "Attitudes of Victims and Nonvictims towards Restitution, Crime and Punishment: Tables." Paper presented at the 5th International Symposium on Victimology, Zagreb, Yugoslavia, August.

Biblarz, A., Barnowe, J.T., and Biblarz, D.N. 1984. "To Tell or Not to Tell: Differences between Victims Who Report Crimes and Victims Who Do Not." *Victimology: An International Journal* 9:153–58.

Biderman, A.D. 1981. "Sources of Data for Victimology." *J. of Criminal Law and Criminology* 72:789–817.

Bienkowska E., and Erez, E. 1991. "Victims in the Polish Criminal Justice System: Law and Reality." *J. of Comparative and Applied Criminal Justice* 15:217–25.

Black, D. 1973. "The Mobilization of Law." Reprinted as chap. 2 of *The Manners and Customs of the Police.*

———. 1980. *The Manners and Customs of the Police.* New York: Academic Press.

Blegvad, B.-M. 1983. "Accessibility and Dispute Treatment: The Case of the Consumer in Denmark." In Cain, M., and Kulcsar, K., eds., *Disputes and the Law,* 203–22.

Blumberg, A.S. 1979. *Criminal Justice: Issues and Ironies.* 2nd ed. New York: New Viewpoints.

Blumberg, M. 1979. "Injury to Victims of Personal Crimes: Nature and Extent." In Parsonage, W.H., ed., *Perspectives on Victimology.* Beverly Hills, Calif.: Sage Publications.

Blumstein, A., and Cohen, J. 1980. "Sentencing of Convicted Offenders: An Analysis of the Public's View." *Law and Society Review* 14 (Winter): 223–61.

Blumstein, A., Cohen, J., and Nagin, D. 1978. *Deterrence and Incapacitation: Estimating the Effects of Criminal Sanctions on Crime Rates.* Washington, D.C.: National Academy of Sciences.

Blum-West, S., and Carter, T.J. 1983. "Bringing White-Collar Back in: An Examination of Crimes and Torts." *Social Problems* 30:545–54.

Boers, K., and Sessar, K. 1991. "Do People Really Want Punishment? On the Relationship between Acceptance of Restitution, Needs for Punishment, and Fear of Crime." In Sessar, K., and Kerner, H-J., eds., *Developments in Crime and Crime Control Research,* chap. 7. New York: Springer-Verlag.

Bohlander, M. 1992. "Legal Advice in Criminal Proceedings in the Federal Republic of Germany." *Criminal Law Forum* 3:401–18.

Bonafe-Schmitt, J-P. 1989. "Alternatives to the Judicial Model." In Wright, M., and Galaway, B., eds., *Mediation and Criminal Justice,* 178–94.

Bonta, J.L., Boyle, J., Motiuk, L.S., and Sonnichsen, P. 1983. "Restitution in Correctional Half-Way Houses: Victim Satisfaction, Attitudes and Recidivism." *Canadian J. of Criminology* 25:277–93.

Borgida, E., and White, P. 1978. "Social Perception of Rape Victims." *Law and Human Behavior* 2:339–51.

Boudreaux, P. 1989. "Booth v. Maryland and the Individual Vengeance Rationale for Criminal Punishment." *J. of Criminal Law & Criminology* 80:177–96.

Bouzat, P., and Pinatel, J. 1970. *Traité de droit penal et de criminologie.* Vol. 2. Paris: Libraire Dalloz.

Bowker, L.H. 1984. "An Evaluation of the Services Rendered to One Thousand Battered Wives by Legal Professionals." Paper presented at the Annual Meeting of the American Society of Criminology, Cincinnati.

Braithwaite, J. 1989. *Crime, Shame, and Reintegration.* Cambridge, Mass.: Cambridge University Press.

Braithwaite, J., and Pettit, P. 1990. *Not Just Deserts.* Oxford: Oxford University Press.

———. 1994. "Comment—Republican Criminology and Victim Advocacy." *Law and Society Review* 28:765–76.

Brickman, P. 1977. "Crime and Punishment in Sports and Society." *J. of Social Issues* 33:140–63.

Bridenback, M.L., Bales, W.D., and Blanchard, J.B. 1980. *The Citizen Dispute Settle-*

ment Process in Florida: A Comprehensive Assessment. Washington, D.C.: U.S. Department of Justice.

Brillon, Y. 1983. "Les attitudes de la population à l'égard du systeme penal: Une perception negative de la justice criminelle." *Revue internationale de criminologie et de police technique* 36:76–88.

―――. 1988. "Punitiveness, Status and Ideology in Three Canadian Provinces." In Walker, N., and Hough, M., eds., *Public Attitudes to Sentencing,* 84–110. Aldershot: Gower.

Britton, B.K., Baron, R.S., Sanders, A.K., and Fox, S.S. 1976. *Assessment of the Victim Project.* Des Moines: Iowa Crime Commission.

Brooks, J. 1976. "The Case for Creating Compensation Programs to Aid Victims of Violent Crimes." *Tulsa Law J.* 11:447–503.

Brown, E.J. 1983. *The Correlates and Consequences of the Payment of Restitution.* Ann Arbor, Mich.: University Microfilms.

Brownell, The. Hon. H. 1976. *The Forgotten Victims of Crime.* New York: Association of the Bar of the City of New York.

Brownlee, I., ed. 1971. *Basic Documents on Human Rights.* Oxford: Clarendon Press.

Brownmiller, S. 1975. *Against Our Will: Men, Women and Rape.* New York: Simon & Schuster.

Bruinsma, G.J.N., and Fiselier, J.P.S. 1982. "The Poverty of Victimology." In Schneider, H-J., ed., *The Victim in International Perspective,* 87–95.

Buchner, D. 1979. "Scale of Sentence Severity." *J. of Criminal Law and Criminology* 70:182–87.

Buchner, D., Clark, T.F., Hausner, J., Hernon, J.C., Wish, E.D., and Zielinski, C.M. 1983. *Evaluation of the Structured Plea Negotiation Project, Draft of Final Report.* March 13.

―――. 1984. *Evaluation of the Structured Plea Negotiation Project: Executive Summary.* Washington, D.C.: INSLAW.

Buckle, L.G., and Thomas-Buckle, S.R. 1982. "Doing unto Others: Dispute and Dispute Processing in an Urban American Neighborhood." In Tomasic, R., and Feeley, M.M., eds., *Neighborhood Justice,* 78–90.

Bucuvalas, M.J. 1984. *Victims of Crime.* New York: Garland.

Bureau of Justice Statistics. 1981. *Victims of Crime.* Washington, D.C.: U.S. Department of Justice.

―――. 1983. *Victim and Witness Assistance.* Washington, D.C.: U.S. Department of Justice.

―――. 1984. *Victim/Witness Legislation: An Overview.* Washington, D.C.: U.S. Department of Justice.

Burt, M.R. 1983. "A Conceptual Framework for Victimological Research." *Victimology: An International Journal* 8 (3–4):261-69.

Bussmann, K.D. 1985. "Chances for Reconciliation with the Offender, or the Concept 'Mediation in lieu of Punishment.' " Paper presented at the 5th International Symposium on Victimology, Zagreb, Yugoslavia, August.

Bynum, T.S., Cordner, G.W., and Greene, J.R. 1982. "Victim and Offender Characteristics: Impact on Police Investigative Decision-Making." *Criminology* 20:301–18.

Cain, A. 1983. "Where Are the Disputes? A Study of a First Instance Civil Court in the U.K." In Cain and Kulcsar, K., eds., *Disputes and the Law,* 119–33.

Cain, M., and Kulcsar, K., eds. 1983. *Disputes and the Law.* Budapest: Akademiai Kiado.

Calabresi, G. 1979. "Access to Justice and Substantive Law Reform: Legal Aid for the Lower Middle Class." In Cappelletti, M., ed., *Access to Justice,* 3:169–90.

Canadian Federal-Provincial Task Force on Justice for Victims of Crime. 1983. *Canadian Federal-Provincial Task Force on Justice for Victims of Crime Report.* Ottawa: Solicitor General of Canada.

Cane, P. 1987. *Atiyah's Accidents, Compensation and the Law.* 4th ed. London: Weidenfeld & Nicolson.

Cannavale, F.J., and Falcon, W.D. 1976. *Witness Cooperation.* Lexington, Mass.: Lexington Books.

Cappelletti, M., ed. 1978–79. *Access to Justice.* 4 vols. Milan: Sijthoff & Noordhoff.

Cappelletti, M., and Garth, B. 1978. "Access to Justice: The Worldwide Movement to Make Rights Effective. A General Report." In Cappelletti, ed., *Access to Justice,* 1:3–124.

Carrington, F.G. 1975. *The Victims.* New Rochelle, N.Y.: Arlington House.

———. 1977. "Victim Rights Litigation: A Wave of the Future." *University of Richmond Law Review* 11:443–70.

———. 1978. "Victim's Rights: A New Tort." *Trial,* 39–41.

Carrington, F.G., and Nicholson, G. 1984. "The Victims' Movement: An Idea Whose Time Has Come." *Pepperdine Law Review* 11:1–13.

Carrington, F.G., and Rapp, J.A. 1991. *Victims' Rights: Law and Litigation.* New York: Bender.

Carrow, D.M. 1980a. *Crime Victim Compensation Program Model.* Washington, D.C.: U.S. Department of Justice.

———. 1980b. *Crime Victim Compensation: Policy Briefs.* Washington, D.C.: U.S. Department of Justice.

Carter, S.L. 1988. "When Victims Happen to Be Black." *Yale Law J.* 97:420–47.

Casper, J.D. 1978. *Criminal Courts: The Defendant's Perspective: Executive Summary.* Washington, D.C.: U.S. Department of Justice.

Casper, J.D., and Brereton, D. 1984. "Evaluating Criminal Justice Reforms." *Law and Society Review* 18:121–44.

Casper, J.D., Tyler, T., and Fisher, B. 1988. "Procedural Justice in Felony Cases." *Law and Society Review* 22:483–505.

Castillo, R., Dressler, T.W., Foglia, R., and Faber, M.J. 1979. "The Use of Civil Liability to Aid Crime Victims." *J. of Criminal Law and Criminology* 70:57–62.

Cavadino, M., and Dignan, J. 1993. "Reparation, Retribution and Rights." Paper presented at the British Criminology Conference, Cardiff.

Cederblom, J.R. 1977. Introduction to Cederblom and Blizek, W.L., eds., *Justice and Punishment.* Cambridge, Mass.: Ballinger.

Chandler, D.B., and Kassebaum, G. 1979. "A Suburban Community Responds to Crime: Victimization and Support for Punishment." *Sociological Symposium* 25:119–37.

Chapman, J.R., and Gates, M., eds. 1978. *The Victimization of Women*. Beverly Hills, Calif.: Sage Publications.

Chappell, D., and Sutton, L.P. 1974. "Evaluating the Effectiveness of Programs to Compensate the Victims of Crime." In Drapkin, I., and Viano, E., eds., *Victimology: A New Focus*, 2:207–20.

Christie, N. 1977. "Conflicts as Property." *British J. of Criminology* 17:1–15.

———. 1986. "The Ideal Victim." In Fattah, E.A., ed., *From Crime Policy to Victim Policy*, 17–30.

Coates, D., and Penrod, S. 1980–81. "Social Psychology and the Emergence of Disputes." *Law and Society* 15:655–80.

Coates, D., and Winston, T. 1983. "Counteracting the Deviance of Depression: Peer Support Groups for Victims." *J. of Social Issues* 39:169–94.

Coates, R.B. 1990. "Victim-Offender Reconciliation Programs in North America: An Assessment." In Galaway, B., and Hudson, J., eds., *Criminal Justice, Restitution and Reconciliation*, 125–34.

Coates, R.B., and Gehm, J. 1989. "An Empirical Assessment." In Wright, W., and Galaway, B., eds., *Mediation and Criminal Justice*, 251–63.

Coffee, J.C. 1991. "Does 'Unlawful' Mean 'Criminal'? Reflections on the Disappearing Tort/Crime Distinction in Criminal Law." *Boston University Law Review* 71:193–246.

———. 1992. "Paradigms Lost: The Blurring of the Criminal Law and Civil Law Models—and What Can be Done about It." *Yale Law J.* 101:1875–1893.

Cohen, S. 1979. "The Punitive City: Notes on the Dispersal of Social Control." *Contemporary Crises* 3:339–63.

———. 1983. "Social Control Talk: Telling Stories about Correctional Change." In Garland, D., and Young, P., eds., *The Power to Punish*, 101–29. London: Heinemann.

Cohn, Y. 1974. "Crisis Intervention and the Victim of Robbery." In Drapkin, I., and Viano, E., eds., *Victimology: A New Focus*, 2:17–28.

Conklin, J.E. 1972. *Robbery and the Criminal Justice System*. Philadelphia: Lippincott.

Connick, E. 1982. *Witness Intimidation: An Examination of the Criminal Justice System's Response to the Problem*. New York: Victim Services Agency.

Connick, E., Bryan, B., Grayson, D., Person, A., Chytilo, J., and Davis, R.C. 1982. *The Experiences of Women with Services for Abused Spouses in New York City*. New York: Victim Services Agency.

Connick, E., and Davis, R.C. 1981. *Case Disposition and Recidivism in Prior Relationship Cases in the Brooklyn Court System*. Report submitted to the Institute for Social Analysis, New York.

Cook, P.J., and Fischer, G.W. 1976. *Durham Urban Observatory Report: Citizen Cooperation with the Criminal Justice System*. Durham, N.C.: Duke University.

Cook, R.F., Roehl, J.A., and Sheppard, D.I. 1980. *Neighborhood Justice Centers Field Test—Final Evaluation Report*. Washington, D.C.: U.S. Department of Justice.

Cook, R.F., Smith, B.E., and Harrell, H.V. 1987. *Helping Crime Victims: Levels of Trauma and Effectiveness of Services*. Washington D.C.: U.S. Department of Justice.

Corbett, C., and Maguire, M. 1988. "The Value and Limitations of Victim Support Schemes." In Maguire and Pointing, J., eds., *Victims of Crime: A New Deal?* 26–39.

Cotterrell, R. 1992. *The Sociology of Law.* 2nd ed. London: Butterworths.

Covey, J.M. 1975. "Alternatives to a Compensation Plan for Victims of Physical Violence." 1956. In Hudson, J., and Galaway, B., eds., *Considering the Victim,* 220–37.

Cretney, A., and Davis, G. 1995. *Punishing Violence.* London: Routledge.

Cronin, R.C., and Bourque, B.B. 1980. *National Evaluation Program: Phase 1 Assessment of Victim/Witness Assistance Projects: Final Report.* Washington, D.C.: American Institute of Research/National Technical Information Service.

———. 1981. *Assessment of Victim/Witness Assistance Projects.* Washington, D.C.: U.S. Department of Justice.

Cullen, F.T., Clark, G.A., Cullen, J.B., and Mathers, R.A., 1985. "Attribution, Salience and Attitudes toward Criminal Sanctioning." *Criminal Justice and Behavior* 12:305–31.

Cullen, F.T., Cullen, J.B., and Wozniak, J.F. 1988. "Is Rehabilitation Dead? The Myth of the Punitive Public." *J. of Criminal Justice* 16:303–17.

Cullen, F.T., and Gilbert, K.E. 1982. *Reaffirming Rehabilitation.* Cincinnati: W.H. Anderson.

Curran, B.A. 1977. *The Legal Needs of the Public.* Chicago: American Bar Foundation.

Curtis, L. 1974. "Victim Precipitation and Violent Crime." *Social Problems* 21:594–605.

Damaska, M.R. 1985. "Some Remarks on the Status of the Victim in Continental and Anglo-American Administration of Justice." Paper presented at the 5th International Symposium on Victimology, Zagreb, Yugoslavia, August.

———. 1986. *The Faces of Justice and State Authority.* New Haven, Conn.: Yale University Press.

Danzig, R. 1973. "Towards the Creation of a Complementary Decentralized System of Criminal Justice." *Stanford Law Review* 26:1–54.

Davis, G. 1992. *Making Amends: Mediation and Reparation in Criminal Justice.* London: Routledge.

Davis, P.L. 1989. "The Crime Victim's Right to a Criminal Prosecution: A Proposed Model Statute for the Governance of Private Criminal Prosecutions." *De Paul Law Review* 38:329.

Davis, R.C. 1982. "Mediation: The Brooklyn Experiment." In Tomasic, R., and Feeley, M.M., eds., *Neighborhood Justice,* 154–72.

———. 1983. "Victim/Witness Noncooperation: A Selected Look at a Persistent Phenomenon." *J. of Criminal Justice* 11:287–99.

———. 1987. "Studying the Effects of Services for Victims in Crisis." *Crime and Delinquency* 33:520–31.

Davis, R.C., Chytilo, J., and Schraga, S. 1980. *Evaluation of Case Follow-up and Enforcement Activities by the Brooklyn Dispute Center.* New York: Victim Services Agency.

Davis, R.C., and Henley, M. 1990. "Victim Service Programs." In Lurigio, A.J., et al., eds., *Victims of Crime: Problems, Policies and Programs,* 157–71.

Davis, R.C., Henley, M., and Smith, B.E. 1990. *Victim Impact Statements: Their Effect on Court Outcomes and Victim Satisfaction: Summary.* New York: Victim Services Agency.

Davis, R.C., Russell, V., and Kunreuther, F. 1980. *The Role of the Complaining Witness in an Urban Criminal Court.* New York: Vera Institute and Victim Services Agency.

Davis, R.C., and Smith, B.E. 1994a. "The Effects of Victim Impact Statements on Sentencing Decisions: A Test in an Urban Setting." *Justice Quarterly* 11:453–69.

———. 1994b. "Victim Impact Statements and Victim Satisfaction: An Unfulfilled Promise?" *J. of Criminal Justice* 22:1–12.

Davis, R.C., Smith, B.E., and Hillenbrand, S. 1992. "Restitution: The Victim's Viewpoint." *Justice System J.* 15:746–58.

Davis, R.C., Tichane, M., and Connick, E. 1980. *First Year Evaluation of the Victim Involvement Project.* New York: Victim Services Agency.

Davis, R.C., Tichane, M., and Grayson, D. n.d. *Mediation and Arbitration as Alternatives to Prosecution in Felony Arrest Cases, An Evaluation of the Brooklyn Dispute Resolution Center (1st Year).* New York: Vera Institute of Justice.

Dawson, R.O. 1969. *Sentencing: The Decision as to Type, Length and Conditions of Sentence.* Boston: Little, Brown.

de Carufel, A. 1981. "Victim's Satisfaction with Compensation: Effects of Initial Disadvantage and Third Party Intervention." *J. of Applied Social Psychology* 11:445–59.

de Liege, M.-R. 1985. "La politique d'aide aux victimes en France." Paper presented at the 5th International Symposium on Victimology, Zagreb, August.

Denno, D., and Cramer, J.A. 1976. "The Effects of Victim Characteristics on Judicial Decision Making." In McDonald, W.F., ed., *Criminal Justice and the Victim,* 215–26. Beverly Hills, Calif.: Sage Publications.

Denton, A. 1979. "What They Think/What They Do: A Study of the Perceptions and Service Utilization of Victims of Violent Crimes." Ph.D. diss., Case Western Reserve University.

De Smith, S.A. 1980. *De Smith's Judicial Review of Administrative Action.* Ed. J.M. Evans. 4th ed. London: Stevens & Sons.

Deutsch, M. 1975. "Equity, Equality and Need: What Determines Which Value Will Be Used as the Basis of Distributive Justice?" *J. of Social Issues* 31:137–49.

Diamond, S.S. 1989. "Using Psychology to Control Law." *Law and Human Behavior* 13:239–52.

Dijk, J.J.M. Van. 1984. "State Assistance to the Victim of Crime in Securing Compensation: Alternative Models and the Expectations of the Victim." In *Towards a Victim Policy in Europe,* 80–84. Helsinki: Helsinki Institute for Crime Prevention and Control.

———. 1985. *Compensation by the State or by the Offender: The Victim's Perspective.* The Hague: Ministry of Justice.

———. 1988. "Ideological Trends within the Victims' Movement: An International Perspective." In Maguire, M., and Pointing, I., eds., *Victims of Crime: A New Deal?* 115–26.

Dijk, J.J.M. Van, and Mayhew, P. 1992. *Criminal Victimization in the Industrialized World*. The Hague: Ministry of Justice.

Dijk, J.J.M. Van, Mayhew, P., and Killias, M. 1990. *Experiences of Crime across the World*. Deventer: Kluwer.

Dijk, J.J.M. Van, Roell, A., and Steinmetz, C.H.D. 1983. *Bystanders Intervention in a Crime*. The Hague: Ministry of Justice.

Dijk, J.J.M. Van, and Steinmetz, C.H.D. 1988. "Pragmatism, Ideology and Crime Control: Three Dutch Surveys." In Walker, N., and Hough, M., eds., *Public Attitudes to Sentencing*, 74–83.

Doerner, W.G. 1977. "State Compensation Programs." *Victimology: An International Journal* 2:106–9.

———. 1979. "The Diffusion of Victim Compensation Laws in the U.S." *Victimology: An International Journal* 4:119–24.

Doerner, W.G., Knudten, M.S., Knudten, R.D., and Meade, A.C. 1976. "An Analysis of Victim Compensation Programs as a Time-Series Experiment." *Victimology: An International Journal* 1:295–313.

Doerner, W.G., and Lab, S.P. 1980. "The Impact of Crime Compensation upon Victim Attitudes toward the Criminal Justice System." *Victimology: An International Journal* 5:61–67.

———. 1995. *Victimology*. Cincinnati: Anderson.

Doerner, W.G., and Silverman, S.S. 1980. "The Diffusion of Victim Compensation in Canada." *Canadian J. of Criminology* 23:75–82.

Dolliver, J.M. 1987. "Victim's Rights Constitutional Amendment: A Bad Idea Whose Time Should Not Come." *Wayne Law Review* 34:87–93.

Doo, L.-W. 1973. "Dispute Settlement in Chinese American Communities." *American J. of Comparative Law* 21:627–33.

Douglas, R., Laster, K., and Inglis, N. 1994. "Victims of Efficiency: Tracking of Victim Impact Information through the System in Victoria, Australia." *International Review of Victimology* 3:95–110.

Drapkin, I., and Viano, E., eds. 1974. *Victimology*. Lexington, Mass.: Lexington Books.

———, eds. 1974–75. *Victimology: A New Focus*. 4 vols. Lexington, Mass.: Lexington Books.

Dubow, F.L., and Becker, T.M. 1976. "Patterns of Victim Advocacy." In McDonald, W.F., ed., *Criminal Justice and the Victim*, 147–64. Beverly Hills, Calif.: Sage Publications.

Duff, R.A. 1986. *Trials and Punishment*. Cambridge: Cambridge University Press.

Dunkel, F., and Rossner, D. 1989. "Law and Practice of Victim/Offender Agreements." In Wright M., and Galaway, B., eds., *Mediation and Criminal Justice*, 152–77.

Durham, A.M. 1993. "Public Opinion Regarding Sentences for Crime: Does It Exist?" *J. of Criminal Justice* 21:1–11.

Dussich, J.P.J. 1981. "Evolving Services for Crime Victims." In Galaway, B., and Hudson, J., eds., *Perspectives on Crime Victims*, 27–32. St. Louis: Mosby.

Dworkin, R. 1977. *Taking Rights Seriously*. Cambridge, Mass.: Harvard University Press.

Edelhertz, H., and Geis, G. 1974. *Public Compensation to Victims of Crime*. New York: Praeger.

Edelhertz, H., Schram, D., Walsh, M., and Lines, P. 1975. *Restitutive Justice: A General Survey and Analysis.* Seattle, Wash: Battelle Institute.

Eglash, A. 1958. "Creative Restitution." *J. of Criminal Law and Criminology* 48:619–22.

Ehrmann, H.W. 1976. *Comparative Legal Cultures.* Englewood Cliffs, N.J.: Prentice-Hall.

Eikenberry, K. 1989. "The Elevation of Victims' Rights in Washington State: Constitutional States." *Pepperdine Law Review* 17:19–33.

Elias, R. 1983a. "The Symbolic Politics of Victim Compensation." *Victimology: An International Journal* 9 (1–2): 213–24.

———. 1983b. *Victims of the System.* New Brunswick, N.J.: Transaction Books.

———. 1984. "Alienating the Victim." *J. of Social Issues* 40:107–16.

———. 1986. *The Politics of Victimization.* New York: Oxford University Press.

———. 1990. "Which Victim Movement? The Politics of Victim Policy." In Lurigio, A.J., et al., eds., *Victims of Crime: Problems, Policies and Programs,* 226–50.

———. 1993. *Victims Still: The Political Manipulation of Crime Victims.* Newbury Park, Calif.: Sage Publications.

Ellenberger, H. 1955. "Psychological Relationships between Criminal and Victim." *Archives of Criminal Psychodynamics* 2:257–90.

Emsley, C., and Storch, R.D. 1993. "Prosecution and the Police in England since 1700." *IAHCCJ Bulletin* 18:45–57.

Englard, I. 1993. *The Philosophy of Tort Law.* Aldershot: Dartmouth.

Epstein, R.A. 1977. "Crime and Tort: Old Wine in New Bottles." In Barnett, R.E., and Hagel, J., eds., *Assessing the Criminal: Restitution, Retribution, and the Legal Process,* 231–57. Cambridge, Mass.: Ballinger.

Ercman, S.L. 1985. "Right to Privacy and the Status of the Victim before Criminal Proceedings." Paper presented at the 5th International Symposium on Victimology, Zagreb, Yugoslavia, August.

Erez, E. 1990. "Victim Participation in Sentencing: Rhetoric and Reality." *J. of Criminal Justice* 18:19–31.

———. 1991. *Victim Impact Statements.* Canberra: Australian Institute of Criminology.

———. 1994. "Victim Participation in Sentencing: And the Debate Goes On. . . ." *International Review of Victimology* 3:17–32.

Erez, E., Roeger, L., and Morgan, F. 1994. *Victim Impact Statements in South Australia: An Evaluation.* Adelaide: South Australian Attorney-General's Department.

Erez, E., and Tontodonato, P. 1990. "The Effect of Victim Participation in Sentencing on Sentence Outcome." *Criminology* 28:451–74.

———. 1992. "Victim Participation in Sentencing and Satisfaction with Justice." *Justice Quarterly* 9:393–417.

Erickson, M.L., and Gibbs, J.P. 1979. "On the Perceived Severity of Legal Penalties." *J. of Criminal Law and Criminology* 70:102–16.

Erickson, W.H. 1978a. "New Directions in the Administration of Justice: Responses to the Pound Conference." *American Bar Association J.* 64:47–61.

———. 1978b. "The Pound Conference Recommendations: A Blueprint for the Justice System in the Twenty-First Century." *Federal Rules Decisions* 76:277–319.

Ervin, L., and Schneider, A. 1990. "Explaining the Effects of Restitution on Offenders: Results from a National Experiment in Juvenile Courts." In Galaway, B., and Hudson, J., eds., *Criminal Justice, Restitution and Reconciliation,* 183–206.

Etzioni, A. 1976. *Social Problems.* Englewood Cliffs, N.J.: Prentice-Hall.

Evaluation and Change. 1980. Special Issue.

Fagan, R.W. 1981. "Public Support for the Courts: An Examination of Alternative Explanations." *J. of Criminal Justice* 9:403–17.

Falandysz, L. 1982. "Victimology in the Radical Perspective." In Schneider, H-J., ed., *The Victim in International Perspective,* 105–27.

Fattah, E.A. 1967. "Towards a Criminological Classification of Victims." *International Criminal Police Review* 22:162–69.

―――. 1981. "Becoming a Victim: The Victimization Experience and Its Aftermath." *Victimology: An International Journal* 6:29–47.

―――, ed. 1986. *From Crime Policy to Victim Policy.* Basingstoke: Macmillan.

―――, ed. 1989. *The Plight of Crime Victims in Modern Society.* Basingstoke: Macmillan.

―――. 1991. *Understanding Criminal Victimization.* Scarborough, Ont.: Prentice-Hall.

―――. 1992. *Towards a Critical Victimology.* Basingstoke: Macmillan.

―――. 1994. *The Interchangeable Roles of Victim and Victimizer.* Helsinki: HEUNI.

Feeley, M.M. 1979. *The Process Is the Punishment.* New York: Russell Sage.

―――. 1983. *Court Reform on Trial: Why Simple Solutions Fail.* New York: Basic Books.

Feeley, M.M., and Krislov, S. 1990. *Constitutional Law.* 2nd ed. Glenview, Ill.: Scott, Foresman.

Feeley, M.M., and Simon, J. 1992. "The New Penology: Notes on the Emerging Strategy of Corrections and Its Implications." *Criminology* 30:449–74.

Feinberg, J. 1984. *Harm to Others.* New York: Oxford University Press.

Felstiner, W.L.F. 1974. "Influences of Social Organization on Dispute Processing." *Law and Society* 9:63–94.

―――. 1975. "Avoidance as Dispute Resolution: An Elaboration." *Law and Society Review* 9:695–706.

―――. 1984. "The Logic of Mediation." In Black, D., ed., *Toward a General Theory of Social Control,* 251–69. Orlando, Fla.: Academic Press.

Felstiner, W.L.F., Abel, R.L., and Sarat, A. 1980–81. "The Emergence and Transformation of Disputes: Naming, Blaming, Claiming. . . ." *Law and Society* 15:631–54.

Felstiner, W.L.F., and Drew, A.B. 1978. *European Alternatives to Criminal Trials and Their Applicability to the U.S.* Washington, D.C.: U.S. Department of Justice.

Felstiner, W.L.F., and Williams, L.A. 1978. "Mediation as an Alternative to Criminal Prosecution." *Law and Human Behavior* 2:223–44.

―――. 1980. *Community Mediation in Dorchester, Massachusetts.* Washington, D.C.: U.S. Department of Justice.

―――. 1982. "Community Mediation in Dorchester, Massachusetts." In Tomasic, P., and Feeley, M.M., eds., *Neighborhood Justice,* 111–53.

Field, H. 1978. "Juror Background Characteristics and Attitudes toward Rape: Correlates of Jurors' Decisions in Rape Trials." *Law and Human Behavior* 2:73–93.

Finn, P., and Colson, S. 1990. *Civil Protection Orders: Legislation, Current Court Practice, and Enforcement.* Washington, D.C.: U.S. Department of Justice.

Finn, P., and Lee, B. 1983. *Issues and Practices: Serving Crime Victims and Witnesses.* Cambridge, Mass.: Abt Associates.

Finnis, J. 1980. *Natural Law and Natural Rights.* London: Clarendon Press.

Fisher, P. 1984. "Preliminary Evaluation Results of the Victim Impact Demonstration Project in the Brooklyn Supreme Court." Paper presented at the Annual Meeting of the American Society of Criminology, Cincinnati.

Flanagan, T.J., and Maguire, K. 1992. *Sourcebook of Criminal Justice Statistics— 1991.* Washington D.C.: U.S. Department of Justice.

Flanagan, T.J., McGarrell, E.F., and Brown, E.J. 1985. "Public Perceptions of the Criminal Courts: The Role of Demographic and Related Attitudinal Variables." *J. of Research in Crime and Delinquency* 22:66–82.

Fleming, J.G. 1982. "Drug Injury Compensation Plans." *American J. of Comparative Law* 30:297–323.

Fleming, M. 1978. *Of Crimes and Rights.* New York: Norton.

Fletcher, G. 1978. *Rethinking Criminal Law.* Boston: Little, Brown.

Fogel, D. 1975. *"We Are the Living Proof . . .": The Justice Model for Corrections.* Cincinnati: W.H. Anderson.

Folger, R. 1984. "Emerging Issues in the Social Psychology of Justice." In Folger, ed., *The Sense of Injustice,* 3–24. New York: Plenum Press.

Forer, L.G. 1980. *Criminals and Victims.* New York: Norton.

Forst, B., and Wellford, C. 1981. "Punishment and Sentencing: Developing Sentencing Guidelines Empirically from Principles of Punishment." *Rutgers Law Review* 33:799–837.

Freedman, L. 1982. *State Legislation on Dispute Resolution—Special Committee on Alternative Means of Dispute Resolution.* Washington, D.C.: American Bar Association.

Freiberg, A., and O'Malley, P. 1984. "State Intervention and the Civil Offense." *Law and Society Review* 18:373–94.

Friedman, K., Bischoff, H., Davis, R., and Person, A. 1982. *Victims and Helpers: Reactions to Crime.* Washington, D.C.: U.S. Department of Justice.

Friedman, L.N., and Shulman, M. 1990. "Domestic Violence: The Criminal Justice Response." In Lurigio, A.J., et al., eds., *Victims of Crime: Problems, Policies and Programs,* 87–103.

Friedman, W. 1967. *Legal Theory.* 5th ed. London: Stevens & Sons.

Friedrichs, D.O. 1983. "Victimology: A Consideration of the Radical Critique." *Crime and Delinquency,* 29:283–94.

Fry, M. 1959. "Justice for Victims." *J. of Public Law* 8:191–94.

Fulton, F.M. 1991. *"A Duty to Warn": The Results of Fifteen Years of Tarasoff Warnings to the San Francisco Police Department.*

Galanter, M. 1974. "Why the 'Haves' Come Out Ahead: Speculations on the Limits of Legal Change." *Law and Society* 9:95–160.

———. 1984–85. *The Emergence of the Judge as a Mediator in Civil Cases.* Working paper, Disputes Processing Research Program, Madison, Wis.

———. 1991. "Punishment: Civil Style." *Israel Law Review* 25:759–78.

Galaway, B. 1984. "Restitution or Prison for Property Offenders: A Survey of the Views of the New Zealand Public." Paper presented at the Annual Meeting of the American Society of Criminology, Cincinnati.

———. 1985. "Preliminary Experiences of an Urban Victim Offender Reconciliation Project." Paper presented at the 5th International Symposium on Victimology, Zagreb, Yugoslavia, August.

———. 1988. "Restitution as Innovation or Unfulfilled Promise?" *Federal Probation* 52:3–14.

Galaway, B., and Hudson, J., eds. 1978. *Offender Restitution in Theory and Action.* Lexington, Mass.: Lexington Books.

———, eds. 1981. *Perspectives on Crime Victims.* St. Louis: Mosby.

———, eds. 1990. *Criminal Justice, Restitution and Reconciliation.* Monsey, N.Y.: Criminal Justice Press.

Galston, W.A. 1980. *Justice and the Human Good.* Chicago: University of Chicago Press.

Gandy, J.T. 1978. "Attitudes towards the Use of Restitution." In Galaway, B., and Hudson, J., eds., *Offender Restitution in Theory and Action,* 119–30.

Gandy, J.T., and Galaway, B. 1980. "Restitution as a Sanction for Offenders: The Public's View." In Hudson, J., and Galaway, eds., *Victims, Offenders and Alternative Sanctions,* 89–100.

Gardiner, M.R. 1981. "The Right to be Punished—a Suggested Constitutional Theory." *Rutgers Law Review* 33:838–64.

Garfinkel, H. 1956. "Conditions of Successful Degradation Ceremonies." *American J. of Sociology* 61:420–24.

Garofalo, J. 1977a. *Public Opinion about Crime: The Attitudes of Victims and Non-Victims in Selected Cities.* Washington, D.C.: U.S. Department of Justice.

———. 1977b. *The Police and Public Opinion: An Analysis of Victimization and Attitude Data from 13 American Cities.* Washington, D.C.: U.S. Department of Justice.

Garofalo, J., and Connelly, K.J. 1980. "Dispute Resolution Centers." Reprint from *Criminal Justice Abstracts.*

Garofalo, J., and McDermott, M.J. 1979. "National Victim Compensation—Its Cost and Coverage." *Law Policy Quarterly* 1:439–64.

Garofalo, J., and Sutton, L.P. 1977. *Compensating Victims of Violent Crime: Potential Costs and Coverage of a National Program.* Washington, D.C.: U.S. Department of Justice.

Garofalo, R. 1975. "Enforced Reparation as a Substitute for Imprisonment." 1914. In Hudson, J., and Galaway, B., eds., *Considering the Victim,* 43–53.

Geis, G. 1991. "Sanctioning the Selfish: The Operation of Portugal's New 'Bad Samaritan' Statute." *International Review of Victimology* 1:297–313.

Giliberti, C. 1991. "Evaluation of Victim Impact Statement Projects in Canada—a Summary of the Findings." In Kaiser, G., et al., eds., *Victims and Criminal Justice,* 51:703–18.

Gittler, J. 1984. "Expanding the Role of the Victim in the Criminal Action." *Pepperdine Law Review* 11:117–82.

Gobert, J.J. 1977. "Victim Precipitation." *Columbia Law Review,* 77:511–53.

Godfrey, B.W., and Lowe, C.A. 1975. "Devaluation of Innocent Victims: An Attribution Analysis within the Just World Paradigm." *J. of Personality and Social Psychology* 34:944–51.

Gold, A.R., Landerman, P.G., and Bullock, K.W. 1978. "Reactions to Victims of Crime: Sympathy, Defensive Attribution, and the Just World." *Social Behavior and Personality*, 295–304.

Goldsmith, J. 1978. "Victim Services and the Police." *Crime Prevention Review* 5:1–7.

Goldstein, A.S. 1974. "Reflections on Two Models: Inquisitorial Themes in American Criminal Procedure." *Stanford Law Review* 26:1009–25.

———. 1982. "Defining the Role of the Victim in Criminal Prosecution." *Mississippi Law J.* 52:515–66.

———. 1984. "The Victim and Prosecutorial Discretion: The Federal Victim and Witness Protection Act of 1982." *Law and Contemporary Problems* 47:225–48.

Gottfredson, D.M., and Gottfredson, M.R. 1988. *Decision-Making in Criminal Justice.* 2nd ed. New York: Plenum Press.

Grabovsky, P. 1985. "Crime Victims in Australia." In *Australian Discussion Papers*, 61–89. Canberra: Australian Institute of Criminology.

Gramatica, F. 1963. *Principes de defense sociale.* Paris: Cujas.

Green, E. 1961. *Judicial Attitudes in Sentencing.* London: Macmillan.

Green, S.P. 1988. "Private Challenges to Prosecutorial Inaction: A Model Declaratory Statute." *Yale Law J.* 97:488–507.

Greenberg, J. 1984. "On the Apocryphal Nature of Inequity Distress." In Folger, R., ed., *The Sense of Injustice,* 167–86. New York: Plenum Press.

Greenberg, M.S., and Ruback, R.B. 1992. *After the Crime: Victim Decision Making.* New York: Plenum Press.

Greenberg, M.S., Ruback, R.B., and Westcott, D.K. 1982. "Decision-Making by Crime Victims: A Multimethod Approach." *Law and Society Review* 17:47–84.

Greer, D.S. 1991. *Compensation for Criminal Injuries.* London: Sweet & Maxwell.

———. 1994. "A Transatlantic Perspective on the Compensation of Crime Victims in the United States." *J. of Criminal Law and Criminology* 85:333–401.

Greer, D.S., and Mitchell, V.A. 1982. *Compensation for Criminal Damage to Property.* Belfast: SLS Legal Publications.

Grey, T.C. 1983. *The Legal Enforcement of Morality.* New York: Knopf.

Griffiths, J. 1970. "Ideology in Criminal Procedure, or a Third Model of the Criminal Process." *Yale Law J.* 79:359–417.

Grube, E.J. 1993. "Punitive Damages: A Misplaced Remedy." *Southern California Law Review* 66:839–80.

Guidelines for Victim Support in Europe. 1989. Utrecht: Vereniging Landelijke Organisatie Slachtofferhulp.

Hadden, T. 1971. "Contract, Tort and Crime: The Forms of Legal Thought." *Law Quarterly Review* 87:240–60.

Hagan, J. 1980. *The Organizational Domination of Criminal Law: A Study of Victim Involvement in the Criminal Justice System.* Toronto: Center of Criminology.

Hall, D.J. 1975. "Role of the Victim in the Prosecution and Disposition of a Criminal Case." *Vanderbilt Law Review* 28:931–85.

————. 1991. "Victims' Voices in Criminal Court: The Need for Restraint." *American Criminal Law Review* 28:233–66.

Hall, J. 1943. "Interrelations of Criminal Law and Torts." *Columbia Law Review* 43:753.

Hamilton, V.L., and Rytina, S. 1980. "Social Consensus on Norms of Justice: Should the Punishment Fit the Crime?" *American J. of Sociology* 85:1117–44.

Hammer, J.H. 1989. *The Effect of Offender Punishment on Crime Victim's Recovery, and Perceived Fairness (Equity) and Process Control.* Ann Arbor, Mich.: University Microfilms.

Hannaford, K. 1991. "The Victim's Charter: A New Deal for Victims?" *Criminal Justice Matters* 5:4.

Harland, A.T. 1980. "Restitution Statutes and Cases—Some Substantive and Procedural Constraints." In Hudson, J., and Galaway, B., eds., *Victims, Offenders and Alternative Sanctions,* 131–40.

————. 1981. *Restitution to Victims of Personal and Household Crimes: Analytic Report.* Washington, D.C.: U.S. Department of Justice.

————. 1982. "One Hundred Years of Restitution: An International Review and Prospectus for Research." Paper presented at the 4th International Symposium on Victimology, Tokyo.

————. 1982. "Monetary Remedies for the Victims of Crime: Assessing This Role of the Criminal Courts." *U.C.L.A. Law Review* 30:52–128.

Harland, A.T., and Rosen, C.J. 1990. "Impediments to the Recovery of Restitution by Crime Victims." *Violence and Victims* 5:127–40.

Harlow, C. Wolf. 1989. *Injuries from Crime.* Washington, D.C.: U.S. Department of Justice.

Harrell-Bond, B., and Smith, A. 1983. "Dispute Treatment in an English Town." In Cain, M., and Kulcsar, K., eds., *Disputes and the Law,* 55–65.

Harrington, C.B. 1982. "Delegalization Reform Movements: A Historical Analysis." In Abel, R.L., ed., *The Politics of Informal Justice,* 1:35–71.

Harris, A.P. 1989. "Rereading Punitive Damages: Beyond the Public/Private Distinction." *Alabama Law Review* 40:1079–116.

Harris, D., Maclean, M., Genn, H., Lloyd-Bostock, S., Fenn, P., Corfield, P., and Brittan, Y. 1984. *Compensation and Support for Illness and Injury.* Oxford: Clarendon Press.

Hart, H.L.A. 1968. *Punishment and Responsibility.* Oxford: Clarendon Press.

Hassin, Y. 1979. "Making Money 'Work' and Post-Verdict Bargaining." *Israel Studies in Criminology* 5:205–23.

Hayden, R.M., and Anderson, J.K. 1978. "On the Evaluation of Procedural Systems in Laboratory Experiments: A Critique of Thibaut and Walker." *Law and Human Behavior* 3:21–58.

Heath, J. 1963. *Eighteenth Century Penal Theory.* London: Oxford University Press.

Heide, K.M. 1983. "An Empirical Assessment of the Value of Utilizing Personality Data in Restitution Outcome Prediction." In Laufer, W.S., and Day, J.M., eds., *Personality Theory, Moral Development and Criminal Behavior,* 251–78. Lexington, Mass.: Lexington Books.

Heinz, A.M. 1985. "Procedure versus Consequences." In Talarico, S.M., ed., *Courts and Criminal Justice,* 13–34. Beverly Hills, Calif.: Sage Publications.

Heinz, A.M., and Kerstetter, W.A. 1979. "Pretrial Settlement Conference: Evaluation of a Reform—Plea Bargaining." *Law and Society Review* 13:349–66.

———. 1980. "Victim Participation in Plea-Bargaining: A Field Experiment." In McDonald, W.F., and Cramer, J., eds., *Plea-Bargaining*, 167–77. Lexington, Mass.: Lexington Books.

Hellerstein, D. 1989. "The Victim Impact Statement: Reform or Reprisal?" *American Criminal Law Review* 27:391–430.

Henderson, J., and Gitchoff, T. 1981. "Using Experts and Victims in the Sentencing Process." *Criminal Law Bulletin* 17:226–33.

Henderson, L.N. 1985. "The Wrongs of Victims' Rights." *Stanford Law Review* 37:937–1021.

Henley, M., Davis, R.C., and Smith, B.E. 1994. "The Reactions of Prosecutors and Judges to Victim Impact Statements." *International Review of Victimology* 3:83–93.

Hentig, H. von. 1948. *The Criminal and His Victim*. New Haven, Conn.: Yale University Press.

Hermann, J. 1978. "Various Models of Criminal Proceedings." *South Africa J. of Criminal Law and Criminology* 2:3–19.

Hernon, J.C., and Forst, B. 1983. *The Criminal Justice Response to Victim Harm*. (Draft.) Washington, D.C.

———. 1984. *Criminal Justice Response to Victim Harm: Executive Summary*. Washington, D.C.: U.S. Department of Justice.

Hetherington, T. 1989. *Prosecution and the Public Interest*. London: Waterlow.

Heumann, M. 1978. *Plea Bargaining*. Chicago: University of Chicago Press.

Hillenbrand, S.W. 1989. "Legal Aid to Crime Victims." In Fattah, E., ed., *The Plight of Crime Victims in Modern Society*, 310–21.

———. 1990. "Restitution and Victim Rights in the 1980s." In Lurigio, A.J., et al., eds., *Victims of Crime: Problems, Policies and Programs*, 188–204.

Hillenbrand, S.W., and Smith, B.E. 1989. *Victims' Rights Legislation: An Assessment of Its Impact on Criminal Justice Practitioners and Victims*. Washington, D.C.: American Bar Association.

Hindelang, M.J. 1982. "Victimization Surveying: Theory and Research." In Schneider, H-J., ed., *The Victim in International Perspective*, 151–66.

Hindelang, M.J., and Gottfredson, M. 1976. "The Victim's Decision Not to Invoke the Criminal Justice Process." In McDonald, W.F., ed., *Criminal Justice and the Victim*, 57–78. Beverly Hills, Calif.: Sage Publications.

Hofrichter, R. 1980. "Techniques of Victim Involvement in Restitution." In Hudson, J., and Galaway, B., eds., *Victims, Offenders and Alternative Sanctions*, 103–19.

Hogan, R., and Emler, N.P. 1981. "Retributive Justice." In Lerner, M.J., and Lerner, S.C., eds., *The Justice Motive in Social Behavior*, 125–43. New York: Plenum Press.

Hogarth, J. 1971. *Sentencing as a Human Process*. Toronto: University of Toronto Press.

———. 1974. "Alternatives to the Adversary System." In Law Reform Commission of Canada, *Studies in Sentencing*, 35–89. Ottawa.

Hohenstein, W.F. 1969. "Factors Influencing the Police Disposition of Juvenile Offenders." In Sellin, T., and Wolfgang, M.E., eds., *Delinquency: Selected Studies*, 138–49. New York: Wiley.

Holmes, O.W. 1964. *The Common Law*. Boston: Little, Brown.

Holmstrom, L.L., and Burgess, A.W. 1978. *The Victim of Rape: Institutional Reactions*. New York: Wiley.

Holstein, J.A., and Miller, G. 1990. "Rethinking Victimization: An Interactional Approach to Victimology." *Symbolic Interaction* 13:103–22.

Homans, G.C. 1976. "Commentary." In Berkowitz, L., and Walster, E., eds., *Equity Theory: Toward a General Theory of Social Interaction*, 231–44.

Home Office. 1993. *Compensating Victims of Violent Crime: Changes to the Criminal Injuries Compensation Scheme*. London: HMSO.

Hospers, J. 1977. "Punishment, Protection and Retaliation." In Cederblom, J.B., and Blizek, W.L., eds., *Justice and Punishment*, 21–50. Cambridge, Mass.: Ballinger.

Hough, M. 1984. "The Impact of Victimization: Findings from the British Crime Survey." Paper prepared for the 3rd International Institute of Victimology, Lisbon, 1984.

Hough, M., and Mayhew, P. 1983. *The British Crime Survey: First Report*. London: HMSO.

Hough, M., and Moxon, D. 1985. "Dealing with Offenders: Popular Opinion and the Views of Victims: Findings from the British Crime Survey." *Howard J.* 24:160–75.

House of Commons. 1993. *Home Affairs Committee, Third Report: Domestic Violence*. Vol. 1. London: HMSO.

Howard, J. 1929. *The State of the Prisons*. First published 1777. London: Methuen.

Hudson, J., and Chesney, S. 1978. "Research on Restitution: A Review and Assessment." In Galaway, B., and Hudson, J., eds., *Offender Restitution in Theory and Action*.

Hudson, J., and Galaway, B., eds. 1975. *Considering the Victim*. Springfield, Ill.: Charles C. Thomas.

———, eds. 1977. *Restitution in Criminal Justice*. Lexington, Mass.: Lexington Books.

———. 1978. Introduction to Galaway and Hudson, eds., *Offender Restitution in Theory and Action*, 1–12.

———, eds. 1980. *Victims, Offenders and Alternative Sanctions*. Lexington, Mass.: Lexington Books.

———. 1980. "A Review of the Restitution and Community Service Sanctioning Research." In Hudson and Galaway, eds., *Victims, Offenders and Alternative Sanctions*, 173–84.

———. 1989. "Financial Restitution: Toward an Evaluable Program Model." *Canadian J. of Criminology* 31:1–18.

Hudson, J., Galaway, B., and Novack, S. 1980. *National Assessment of Adult Restitution Programs: Final Report*. Duluth, Minn.: University of Minnesota.

Hudson, P.S. 1984. "The Crime Victim and the Criminal Justice System: Time for a Change." *Pepperdine Law Review* 11:23–62.

Hulsman, L. 1985. The 'Right of the Victim' Not to Be Subordinated to the Dynamics of Criminal Justice." Paper presented at the 5th International Symposium on Victimology, Zagreb, Yugoslavia, August.

Hunter, C., and Frey, J. 1980. "Public Opinion in Juvenile Delinquency." *Nevada Public Affairs Review*, 45–49.

Jacob, B.R. 1970. "Reparation or Restitution by the Criminal Offender to His Victim: Applicability of an Ancient Concept in the Modern Correctional Process." *J. of Criminal Law, Criminology, and Police Science* 61:152–67.

Jacob, H. 1971. "Black and White Perceptions of Justice in the City." *Law and Society Review* 68–89.

Janoff-Bulman, R., and Frieze, I.H. 1983. "A Theoretical Perspective for Understanding Reactions to Victimization." *J. of Social Issues* 39:1–17.

Jeffery, C.R. 1969. "The Development of Crime in Early English Society." In Chambliss, W.J., ed., *Crime and the Legal Process*, 12–32. New York: McGraw-Hill.

Johnson, E., Jr. 1980. "Let the Trial Fit the Case—Establishing Criteria for Channeling Matters into Dispute Resolution Mechanisms" *Federal Rules Decisions* 80:166–201.

Johnson, E., et al. 1978. "Access to Justice in the United States: The Economic Barriers and Some Promising Solutions." In Cappelletti, M., ed., *Access to Justice*, 1:913–1023.

Jolowicz, H.F. 1939. *Historical Introduction to Roman Law*. Cambridge: Cambridge University Press.

Jolowicz, J.A. 1983. "The Dilemmas of Civil Litigation." *Israel Law Review* 18:161–77.

Jones, E.D., III. 1979. "The Costs of Victim Compensation." In Gray, C.M., ed., *The Cost of Crime*, 121–48. Beverly Hills, Calif.: Sage Publications.

Jones, K.S., and Gebhard, K.G. 1980. *Evaluation of Colorado Springs Neighborhood Justice Center—11/1/79–30/4/80*.

Jones, T., Maclean, B., and Young, J. 1986. *The Islington Crime Survey*. Aldershot: Gower.

Joutsen, M. 1984. "General Report on the Seminar." In *Towards a Victim Policy in Europe*, 1–13. Helsinki: Helsinki Institute for Crime Prevention and Control.

———. 1987. *The Role of the Victim of Crime in European Criminal Justice Systems*. Helsinki: HEUNI.

Kaiser, G., Kury, H., and Albrecht, H-J., eds. 1991. *Victims and Criminal Justice*. Vols. 50–52. Frieburg i. Br.: Max Planck Institute for Foreign and International Penal Law.

Kaiser, M. 1991. "The Status of the Victim in the Criminal Justice System According to the Victim Protection Act." In Kaiser, G., et al., eds., *Victims and Criminal Justice*, 51:543–77.

Kalogeropoulos, D., and Riviere, D. 1983. "Police Station Discourse." In Cain, M., and Kulcsar, K., eds., *Disputes and the Law*, 69–83.

Kalven, H., and Zeisel, H. 1966. *The American Jury*. Boston: Little, Brown.

Karmen, A. 1990. *Crime Victims: An Introduction to Victimology*. 2nd ed. 1st ed., 1984. Pacific Grove, Calif.: Brooks/Cole.

Kaufmann, W. 1977. "Retribution and the Ethics of Punishment." In Barnett, R.E., and Hagel, J., eds., *Assessing the Criminal: Restitution, Retribution and the Legal Process*, 211–30.

Kelly, D.P. 1982. "Victim's Reaction to the Criminal Justice Response." Paper prepared for the Annual Meeting of the Law and Society Association, Toronto.

Kennard, K.L. 1989. "The Victim's Veto: A Way to Increase Victim Impact on Criminal Case Dispositions." *California Law Review* 77:417–53.

Kenny, C.S. 1952. "The Nature of Crime." In Turner, J.W.C., *Kenny's Outlines of Criminal Law*, 16th ed., 530–47. London: Cambridge University Press.

Kerstetter, W.A., and Heinz, A.M. 1979. *Pretrial Settlement Conference: An Evaluation*. Washington, D.C.: U.S. Department of Justice.

Kidd, R.F., and Chayet, E.F. 1984. "Why Do Victims Fail to Report? The Psychology of Criminal Victimization." *J. of Social Issues* 40:39–50.

Kidd, R.F., and Utne, M.K. 1978. "Reactions to Inequity: A Perspective on the Role of Attributions." *Law and Human Behavior* 2:301–12.

Kidder, R.L. 1981. "Down-to-Earth Justice: Pitfalls on the Road to Legal Decentralization." In Lerner, M.J., and Lerner, S.C., eds., *The Justice Motive in Social Behavior*, 423–37. New York: Plenum Press.

Kigin, R., and Novack, S. 1980. "A Rural Restitution Program for Juvenile Offenders and Victims." In Hudson, J., and Galaway, B., eds., *Victims, Offenders and Alternative Sanctions*, 131–36.

Kilchling, M. 1991. "Interests of the Victim and Public Prosecution: First Results of a National Survey." In Kaiser, G., et al., eds., *Victims and Criminal Justice*, 52(1):29–65.

Kilpatrick, D.G., Resick, P.A., and Veronen, L.J. 1981. "Effects of a Rape Experience: A Longitudinal Study." *J. of Social Issues* 37:105–22.

Kilpatrick, D.G., Saunders, B.E., Veronen, L.J., Beit, C.L., and Von, J.M. 1987. "Criminal Victimization: Lifetime Prevalence, Reporting to the Police, and Psychological Impact." *Crime and Delinquency* 23:479–89.

King, M. 1981. *The Framework of Criminal Justice*. London: Croom Helm.

Kirchhoff, G.F. 1983–84. "The German Crime Victim Compensation Act (VCA)." *World Society of Victimology Newsletter* 3:17–36.

Klaus, P.A. 1994. *The Costs of Crime to Victims*. Washington, D.C.: Bureau of Justice Statistics.

Klaus, P.A., and Kalish, C. 1984. *The Severity of Crime*. Washington, D.C.: U.S. Dept. of Justice, Bureau of Justice Statistics.

Klein, J.F. 1978. "Revitalizing Restitution: Flogging a Horse That May Have Been Killed for Just Cause." *Criminal Law Quarterly* 20:383–408.

Klemmack, S.H., and Klemmack, D.L. 1976. "The Social Definition of Rape." In Walker, M.J., and Brodsky, S.L., eds., *Sexual Assault*. Lexington, Mass.: Lexington Books.

Knudten, R.D., Meade, A.C., Knudten, M.S., and Doerner, W.G. 1976. "The Victim in the Administration of Criminal Justice: Problems and Perceptions." In McDonald, W.F., ed., *Criminal Justice and the Victim*, 115–46. Beverly Hills, Calif.: Sage Publications.

Kobe, P. 1976. Paper presented at the Second International Symposium of Victimology, Boston.

Koch, P.K., and Bean, J.R. n.d. "Male-Female, Interviewer-Respondent Interaction in Observer Perceptions of Rape." Villanova University.

Koenig, D. 1980. "The Effects of Criminal Victimization and Judicial or Police Contacts on Public Attitudes toward Local Police." *J. of Criminal Justice* 8:243–49.

Kraintz, K.W. 1991. "Victimology Research in Austria." In Kaiser, G., et al., eds., *Victims and Criminal Justice*, 50:71–94.

Krapac, D., and Loncarevic, D. 1985. *Ostecenik Kao Tuzitely U Krivicnom Post-upku.* Zagreb: Zrinski.

Kress, J. 1976. "The Role of the Victim at Sentencing." Paper prepared for the 2nd International Symposium on Victimology, Boston, September.

Krohn, M., and Stratton, J. 1980. "A Sense of Injustice?" *Criminology* 17:495–504.

Krulewitz, J.E., and Nash, J.E. 1979. "Effects of Rape Victim Resistance, Assault Outcome and Sex of Observer on Attributions about Rape." *J. of Personality* 44:557–74.

Ku, R. 1977. *Victimization in Joliet and Peoria: A Baseline Survey.* Cambridge, Mass.: ABT Associates.

Kulcsar, K. 1983. "Social Aspects of Litigation in Civil Courts." In Cain, M., and Kulcsar, K., eds., *Disputes and the Law*, 85–118.

Kurczewski, J. 1983. "Dispute and Its Settlement." In Cain, M., and Kulcsar, K., eds., *Disputes and the Law*, 223–45.

LaFave, W.R. 1965. *Arrest: The Decision to Take a Suspect into Custody.* Boston: Little, Brown.

LaFree, G.D. 1989. *Rape and Criminal Justice: The Social Construction of Criminal Assault.* Belmont, Calif.: Wadsworth.

Lamborn, L.L. 1968. "Toward a Victim Orientation in Criminal Theory." *Rutgers Law Review* 22:733–68.

———. 1973a. "The Scope of Programs for Governmental Compensation of Victims of Crime." *University of Illinois Law Forum*, 21–87.

———. 1973b. "The Propriety of Governmental Compensation of Victims of Crime." *George Washington Law Review* 41:446–70.

———. 1979. "Reparations for Victims of Crime: Developments and Directions." *Victimology: An International Journal* 4:214–28.

———. 1987. "Victim Participation in the Criminal Justice Process: The Proposals for a Constitutional Amendment." *Wayne Law Review* 34:125–220.

———. 1988. "The United Nations Declaration on Victims: The Scope of Coverage." In Bassiouni, M.C., ed., *International Protection of Victims*, 105–11.

———. 1995. "Victims' Rights in the United States: From Statutory to Constitutional." In Kühne, H.H., ed. *Festschrift für Koichi Miyazawa*, 215–25. Baden-Baden: Verlags Gesellschaft.

Landau, S.F. 1977. "The Rape Offender's Perception of His Victim: Some Cross-Cultural Findings." (In Hebrew.) *Crime and Social Deviance* 5:1–20.

———. 1978. "Do Legal Variables Predict Police Decisions Regarding the Prosecution of Juvenile Offenders?" *Law and Human Behavior* 2:95–105.

Landau, S.F., and Freeman-Longo, R.E. 1990. "Classifying Victims: A Proposed Multidimensional Victimological Typology." *International Review of Victimology* 1:267–86.

Landau, S.F., and Sebba, L. 1991. "Victimological Research in Israel: Past and Current Perspectives." In Kaiser, G., et al., eds., *Victims and Criminal Justice*, 50:179–205.

Landes, W.M., and Posner, R.A. 1975. "The Private Enforcement of Law." *J. of Legal Studies* 4:1–46.

Landis, J.M., and Goodstein, L. 1986. "When Is Justice Fair: An Integrated Approach to the Outcome versus Procedure Debate." *American Bar Foundation J.*, 675–707.

Landis, P.H. 1956. *Social Control*. Chicago: Lippincott.

Laster, R. 1970. "Criminal Restitution: A Survey of Its Past History and an Analysis of Its Present Usefulness." *University of Richmond Law Review* 5:71–98.

Launay, G., and Murray, P. 1989. "Victim/Offender Groups." In Wright, M., and Galaway B., eds., *Mediation and Criminal Justice*, 113–31.

Law Reform Commission of Canada. 1986. *Private Prosecutions*. Ottawa.

Lawrence, R. 1990. "Restitution as a Cost-Effective Alternative to Incarceration." In Galaway, B., and Hudson, J., eds., *Criminal Justice, Restitution and Reconciliation*, 207–16.

Lejeune, R., and Alex, N. 1973. "On Being Mugged: The Event and Its Aftermath." *Urban Life and Culture* 2:259–87.

Lerner, M.J. 1970. "The Desire for Justice and Reactions to Victims." In Macaulay, J., and Berkowitz, L., eds., *Altruism and Helping Behavior*, 205–29. New York: Academic Press.

Lerner, M.J., Miller, D.T., and Holmes, J.G. 1976. "Deserving and the Emergence of Forms of Justice." In Berkowitz, L., and Walster, E., eds., *Equity Theory: Toward a General Theory of Social Interaction*, 133–61.

Lidstone, K.W., Hogg, R., and Sutcliffe, F. 1980. *Prosecutions by Private Individuals and Non-Police Agencies*. London: HMSO.

Lind, E.A., and Tyler, T.R. 1988. *The Social Psychology of Procedural Justice*. New York: Plenum Press.

Linden, A.M. 1975. "Victims of Crime and Tort Law." 1969. In Hudson, J., and Galaway, B., eds., *Considering the Victim*.

Llewellyn, K.N., and Hoebel, E.A. 1981. *The Cheyenne Way*. Norman: University of Oklahoma Press.

Lloyd, Lord, and Freeman, M.D.A., eds. 1985. *Lloyd's Introduction to Jurisprudence*. 5th ed. London: Stevens.

Longshore, D. 1979. "Equity in Criminal Justice: A Test of Two Constructs in Equity Theory." *Criminology* 17:242–50.

Lowenberg, D. 1981. "An Integrated Victim Services Model." In Galaway, B., and Hudson, J., eds., *Perspectives on Crime Victims*, 404–10.

Luginbuhl, J., and Frederick, J.T. 1978. "Experimental Research on Social Perceptions of Rape Victims: A Review and Critique." Paper presented at a meeting of the American Psychological Association, Toronto.

Lunderman, R.J., Sykes, R.E., and Clark, J.P. 1978. "Police Control of Juveniles: A Replication." *J. of Research in Crime and Delinquency* 15:74–91.

Lurigio, A.J. 1987. "Are All Victims Alike? The Adverse, Generalized, and Differential Impact of Crime." *Crime and Delinquency* 33:452–67.

Lurigio, A.J., and Davis, R.C. 1990. "Does a Threatening Letter Increase Compliance with Restitution Orders? A Field Experiment." *Crime and Delinquency* 36:537–48.

Lurigio, A.J., and Resick, P.A. 1990. "Healing the Psychological Wounds of Criminal Victimization: Predicting Postcrime Distress and Recovery." In Lurigio, A.J., et al., eds:, *Victims of Crime: Problems, Policies and Programs*, 50–68.

Lurigio, A.J., Skogan, W.G., and Davis, R.C., eds. 1990. *Victims of Crime: Problems, Policies and Programs*. Newbury Park, Calif.: Sage Publications.

Lynch, R.P. 1976. "Improving the Treatment of Victims: Some Guides for Action." In McDonald, W.F., ed., *Criminal Justice and the Victim*, 165–76. Beverly Hills, Calif.: Sage Publications.

Macaulay, S., and Walster, E. 1971. "Legal Structures and Restoring Equity." *J. of Social Issues* 27:173–88.

Mackay, H., and Hagan, J. 1978. "Studying the Victims of Crime: Some Methodological Notes." *Victimology: An International Journal* 3:135–40.

MacNamara, D.E.J., and Sullivan, J.J. 1974. "Composition, Restitution, Compensation: Making the Victim Whole." In Drapkin, I., and Viano, E., eds., *Victimology*, 221–30.

Maguire, K., Pastore, A.L., and Flanagan, T.J., eds. 1993. *Sourcebook of Criminal Justice Statistics—1992*. Washington D.C.: U.S. Department of Justice.

Maguire, M. 1980. "The Impact of Burglary upon Victims." *British J. of Criminology* 20:261–75.

———. 1989. "Matching Victim Assistance to Need." In *Guidelines for Victim Support in Europe*, 129–38.

———. 1991. "The Needs and Rights of Victims of Crime." *Crime and Justice: A Review of Research* 14:363–433.

Maguire, M., and Corbett, C. 1987. *The Effects of Crime and the Work of Victims' Support Schemes*. Aldershot: Gower.

Maguire, M., and Pointing, J., eds. 1988. *Victims of Crime: A New Deal?* Milton Keynes: Open University.

Maidment, S. 1983. "Civil v. Criminal: The Use of Legal Remedies in Response to Domestic Violence in England and Wales." *Victimology: An International Journal* 8:172–87.

Mann, K. 1992. "Punitive Civil Sanctions: The Middleground between Criminal and Civil Law." *Yale Law J.* 101:1795–873.

Mannheim, H. 1973. Introduction to Mannheim, ed., *Pioneers in Criminology*. 2nd ed. Montclair, N.J.: Patterson Smith.

Mapel, D. 1989. *Social Justice Reconsidered*. Urbana: University of Illinois Press.

Marek, A. 1985. "The Position of Crime Victim in Criminal Procedure." Paper presented at the 5th International Symposium on Victimology, Zagreb, August.

Marshall, T.F. 1985. *Alternatives to Criminal Courts*. Aldershot: Gower.

———. 1988. "Out of Court: More or Less Justice?" In Matthews, R., ed., *Informal Justice?* 25–50.

———. 1990. "Results of Research from British Experiments in Restorative Justice." In Galaway, B., and Hudson, J., eds., *Criminal Justice, Restitution, and Reconciliation*, 83–107.

Marshall, T.F., and Merry, S. 1990. *Crime and Accountability: Victim Offender Mediation in Practice.* London: HMSO.

Martinson, R. 1974. "What Works?—Questions and Answers about Prison Reform." *Public Interest* 35:22–54.

Martinson, R., Lipton, D., and Wilks, J. 1975. *The Effectiveness of Correctional Treatment.* New York: Praeger.

Marx, G.T. 1983. "Social Control and Victimization." *Victimology: An International Journal* 8 (3–4): 80–90.

Mason, A.T., Beaney, W.M., and Stephenson, D.G. 1983. *American Constitutional Law.* Englewood Cliffs, N.J.: Prentice-Hall.

Matthews, R., ed. 1988. *Informal Justice?* London: Sage Publications.

Mawby, R.I. n.d. "The Victim in a Mixed Economy of Welfare." Unpublished paper.

———. 1988. "Victims' Needs or Victims' Rights: Alternative Approaches to Policy-Making." In Maguire, M., and Pointing, J., eds., *Victims of Crime: A New Deal?* 127–37.

Mawby, R.I., and Gill, M.L. 1987. *Crime Victims: Needs, Services, and the Voluntary Sector.* London: Tavistock.

Mawby, R.I., and Walklate, S. 1994. *Critical Victimology.* London: Sage Publications.

Maxfield, M.G. 1984. "The London Metropolitan Police and Two Constituencies: Victim and Suspect Attitudes." Paper presented at the Annual Meeting of the American Society of Criminology, Cincinnati, November.

Mayhew, P. 1984. "The Effects of Crime: Victims, the Public and Fear." Report presented to the 16th Criminological Research Conference, Council of Europe, Strasbourg.

Mayhew, P., Elliott, D., and Dowds, L. 1989. *The 1988 British Crime Survey.* London: HMSO.

McAnany, P.D. 1978. "Restitution as Idea and Practice: The Retributive Process." In Galaway, B., and Hudson, J., eds., *Offender Restitution in Theory and Action,* 15–31.

McBarnet, D. 1976. "Victim in the Witness Box—Confronting the Stereotype." Paper presented at the 2nd International Symposium on Victimology, Boston, September.

McCabe, S., and Sutcliffe, F. 1978. *Defining Crime.* Oxford: Basil Blackwell.

McCleod, M. n.d. *The Authorization and Implementation of Victim Impact Statements, Draft Executive Summary.* Albany.

———. 1983. "Victim Non-Cooperation in the Prosecution of Domestic Assault." *Criminology* 21:395–416.

McCormack, R.J. 1991. "Compensating Victims of Crime." *Justice Quarterly* 8:329–46.

McCoy, C.S. 1987. *Plea Bargaining and Proposition 8 Politics: The Impact of the "Victims' Bill of Rights" in California.* Ann Arbor, Mich.: University Microfilms.

———. 1993. *Politics and Plea Bargaining.* Philadelphia: University of Pennsylvania Press.

McDade, R.J., and O'Donnell, K. 1992. "Parallel Civil and Criminal Proceedings." *American Criminal Law Review* 29:697–738.

McDonald, W.F. 1976a. "Notes on the Victim's Role in the Prosecutorial and Dispositional Stages of the American Criminal Justice Process." Paper prepared for the 2nd International Symposium on Victimology, Boston, September.

————. 1976b. "Criminal Justice and the Victim: An Introduction." In McDonald, ed., *Criminal Justice and the Victim*, 17–55. Beverly Hills, Calif.: Sage Publications.

————. 1977. "The Role of the Victim in America." In Barnett, R.E., and Hagel, J.H., eds., *Assessing the Criminal: Restitution, Retribution and the Legal Process*, 295–307. Cambridge, Mass.: Ballinger.

————. 1982. "The Victim's Role in the American Administration of Criminal Justice: Some Developments and Findings." In Schneider, H.-J., ed., *The Victim in International Perspective*, 396–402.

McDougal, M.S., Lasswell, H.D., and Chen, L.-C. 1980. *Human Rights and World Public Order*. New Haven, Conn.: Yale University Press.

McGillis, D. 1978. "Attribution and the Law: Convergences between Legal and Psychological Concepts." *Law and Human Behavior* 2:289–300.

————. 1986. *Crime Victim Restitution: An Analysis of Approaches*. Washington, D.C.: National Institute of Justice.

McGillis, D., and Mullen, J. 1977. *Neighborhood Justice Centers: An Analysis of Potential Models*. Washington, D.C.: U.S. Department of Justice.

McGillis, D., and Smith, P. 1983. *Compensating Victims of Crime: An Analysis of American Programs*. Washington, D.C.: U.S. Department of Justice.

Meador, B.J. 1982. *Re: Victims Bill of Rights Initiative*. Sacramento: ACLU.

Meier, J. 1992. "The Right to a Disinterested Prosecutor of Criminal Contempt: Unpacking Public and Private Interests." *Washington University Law Quarterly* 70:85–129.

Meiners, R.E. 1978. *Victim Compensation*. Lexington, Mass.: Lexington Books.

Melup, I. 1991. "United Nations: Victims of Crime—Report of the Secretary-General." *International Review of Victimology* 2 (1): 29–59.

Mendelsohn, B. 1974. "The Origin of the Doctrine of Victimology." In Drapkin, S., and Viano, E., eds., *Victimology*, 3–11.

Menlowe, M.A. 1993. "The Philosophical Foundation of a Duty to Rescue." In Menlowe and McCall Smith, A., eds., *The Duty to Rescue*, 55–91. Aldershot: Dartmouth.

Merigeau, M. 1991. "Evaluation of the Practice of Compensation within Recent Victim-Related Crime Policy in France." In Kaiser, G., et al., eds., *Victims and Criminal Justice*, 51:237–54.

Merrill, L.A. 1981. "The 1981 Oklahoma Crime Victim Compensation Act." *Tulsa Law J.* 17:260–305.

Merry, S.E. 1982. "Defining 'Success' in the Neighborhood Justice Movement." In Tomasic, R., and Feeley, M.M., eds., *Neighborhood Justice*, 172–93.

————. 1989. "Myth and Practice in the Mediation Process." In Wright, M., and Galaway, B., eds., *Mediation and Criminal Justice*, 239–50.

————. 1990. *Getting Justice and Getting Even*. Chicago: University of Chicago Press.

Merry, S.E., and Milner, N., eds. 1993. *The Possibility of Popular Justice*. Ann Arbor: University of Michigan Press.

Meschievitz, C.S., and Galanter, M. 1982. "In Search of Nyaya Panchayats: The Politics of a Moribund Institution." In Abel, R., ed., *The Politics of Informal Justice: Comparative Studies*, 2:47–77.

Michelman, F. 1969. "The Supreme Court 1968 Term: Foreword: On Protecting the Poor through the Fourteenth Amendment." *Harvard Law Review* 83:7–59.

———. [1975?]. "Constitutional Welfare Rights and a Theory of Justice." In Daniels, N., ed., *Reading Rawls*, 319–47. New York: Basic Books.

Miers, D. 1978. *Responses to Victimisation: A Comparative Study of Compensation for Criminal Violence in Great Britain and Ontario*. Abingdon, Eng.: Professional Books.

———. 1980. "Victim Compensation as a Labelling Process." *Victimology: An International Journal* 5:3–16.

———. 1983. "Compensation and Conceptions of Victims of Crime." *Victimology: An International Journal* 8:204–12.

———. 1990. *Compensation for Criminal Injuries*. London: Butterworths.

Miller, D. 1976. *Social Justice*. Oxford: Clarendon Press.

Miller, D.T., and Vidmar, N. 1981. "The Social Psychology of Punishment Reactions." In Lerner, M.J., and Lerner, S.L., eds., *The Justice Motive and Social Behavior*, 145–71. New York: Plenum Press.

Miller, F.W. 1969. *Prosecution: The Decision to Charge a Suspect with a Crime*. Boston: Little, Brown.

Miller, H.S., McDonald, W.F., and Cramer, J.A. 1978. *Plea Bargaining in the United States*. Washington, D.C.: U.S. Department of Justice.

Miller, R.E. 1983. "Erratum for 'Grievances, Claims and Disputes: Assessing the Adversary Culture.' " *Law and Society Review* 17:653–56.

Miller, T.I. 1981. "Consequences of Restitution." *Law and Human Behavior* 5:1–17.

Minow, M. 1993. "Surviving Victim Talk." *UCLA Law Review* 40:1411–45.

Miyazawa, K., and Ohya, M., eds. 1986. *Victimology in Comparative Perspective*. Tokyo: Seibundo.

Mnookin, R.H., and Kornhauser, L. 1979. "Bargaining in the Shadow of the Law: The Case of Divorce." *Yale Law J.* 88:950–97.

Molumby, T. 1984. "The Demise of Restitution in Iowa." Abstract in *American Society of Criminology Program and Proceedings*. Annual Meeting of the American Society of Criminology, Cincinnati, November, 121.

Monahan, J. 1981. *Predicting Violent Behavior*. Beverly Hills, Calif.: Sage Publications.

Morris, A. 1978. *Juvenile Justice?* London: Heinemann.

Morris, A., and Maxwell, G.M. 1993. "Juvenile Justice in New Zealand: A New Paradigm." *Australia and New Zealand J. of Criminology* 26:72–90.

Morris, A., Maxwell, G.M., and Robertson, J.P. 1993. "Giving Victims a Voice: A New Zealand Experiment." *Howard J.* 32:304–21.

Morris, N. 1974. *The Future of Imprisonment*. Chicago: University of Chicago Press.

Morris, N., and Tonry, M. 1990. *Between Prison and Probation: Intermediate Punishments in a Rational Sentencing System*. New York: Oxford University Press.

Moxon, D., Corkery, J.M., and Hedderman, C. 1992. *Developments in the Use of*

Compensation Orders in the Magistrates' Courts since October 1988. London: HMSO.

Mueller, G.O.W. 1977. *Sentencing: Process and Purpose*. Springfield, Ill.: Charles C. Thomas.

Mueller, G.O.W., and Cooper, H.H.A. 1974. "Society and the Victim: Alternative Responses." In Drapkin, I., and Viano, E., eds., *Victimology: A New Focus*, 2:85–101.

Murphy, J.G. 1990. "Getting Even: The Role of the Victim." In Paul, E.F., Miller, F.D., and Paul, J., eds., *Crime, Culpability and Remedy*, 209–25. Oxford: Blackwell.

Murphy, R.S. 1988. "The Significance of Victim Harm: *Booth v. Maryland* and the Philosophy of Punishment in the Supreme Court." *University of Chicago Law Review* 55:1303–33.

Myers, M. 1979. "Offended Parties' Official Reactions: Victims and the Sentencing of Criminal Defendants." *Sociological Quarterly* 20:529–40.

Nader, L., and Todd, H.F., eds. 1978. *The Disputing Process: Law in Ten Societies*. New York: Columbia University Press.

Naim, S. 1983. "Mediators and the Mediation Process in the Boulak District of Cairo." In Cain, M., and Kulcsar, K., eds., *Disputes and the Law*, 43–54.

National Association of Attorneys General and American Bar Association (NAAG/ABA). 1986. *Victims of Crime: Proposed Model*. Washington D.C.: U.S. Department of Justice.

National Conference of the Judiciary on the Rights of Victims of Crime. 1983. *Statement of Recommended Judicial Practices*. Washington, D.C.: U.S. Department of Justice.

National Organization of Victim Assistance (NOVA). n.d. *Campaign for Victim Rights*. Washington, D.C.

———. 1989. *Victim Rights and Services: A Legislative Directory 1988*. Washington, D.C.: U.S. Department of Justice.

National Victim Center. 1994. *Constitutional Amendments for Crime Victims' Rights: Update*. Arlington, Va.: Victims' Constitutional Amendment Network.

Naumova, S. 1983. "Formal and Informal Means of Dispute Treatment by Bulgarian Village Dwellers." In Cain, M., and Kulcsar, K., eds., *Disputes and the Law*, 175–82.

Nelken, D. Forthcoming. "Community Involvement in Crime Control: If Community Is the Answer, What Is the Question?" In Sebba, L., ed., *Social Control and Justice: Inside or Outside the Law?* Jerusalem: Magnes Press. An earlier version appeared in *Current Legal Problems* 38 (1985):239–67.

Nevares-Muniz, D. 1984. "The Eighth Amendment Revisited: A Model of Weighted Punishments." *J. of Criminal Law and Criminology* 75:272–89.

Newburn, T. 1988. *The Use and Enforcement of Compensation Orders in Magistrates' Courts*. London: HMSO.

———. 1989. *The Settlement of Claims at the Criminal Injuries Compensation Board*. London: HMSO.

Newton, A. 1976a. "Alternatives to Imprisonment: Day Fines, Community Service Orders, and Restitution." *Crime and Delinquency Literature*, NCCD Reprint.

————. 1976b. "Aid to the Victim, Part I: Compensation and Restitution; Part II: Victim Aid Programs." *Crime and Delinquency Literature*, NCCD Reprint.

Normandeau, A. 1983. "Project de charte de droits des victimes d'actes criminels." *Revue internationale de criminologie et de police technique* 36:25–29.

Note. 1955. "Private Prosecution: A Remedy for District Attorney's Unwarranted Inaction." *Yale Law J.* 65:209–34.

————. 1979. "Dispute Resolution." *Yale Law Journal* 88:905–9.

————. 1984. "Victim Restitution in the Criminal Process: A Procedural Analysis." *Harvard Law Review* 97:931–46.

Novack, S., Galaway, B., and Hudson, J. 1980. "Victim and Offender Perceptions of the Fairness of Restitution and Community Service Sanctions." In Hudson, J., and Galaway, B., eds., *Victims, Offenders and Alternative Sanctions*, 63–70.

Nozick, R. 1974. *Anarchy, State and Utopia*. New York: Basic Books.

O'Barr, W.M., and Conley, J.M. 1988. "Lay Expectations of the Civil Justice System." *Law and Society Review* 22:137–61.

O'Brien, V. 1992. *Civil Legal Remedies for Crime Victims*. OVC Bulletin. Washington, D.C.: U.S. Department of Justice.

Office for Victims of Crime. 1994. *Victims of Crime Act 1984 as Amended: A Report to the President and the Congress*. Washington, D.C.: U.S. Department of Justice.

Office of Justice Programs. 1986. *Four Years Later: A Report on the President's Task Force on Victims of Crime*. Washington, D.C.: U.S. Department of Justice.

O'Neill, T.P. 1984. "The Good, the Bad and the Burger Court: Victims' Rights and a New Model of Criminal Review." *J. of Criminal Law and Criminology* 75:363–87.

Oppenlander, N. 1982. "Coping or Copping Out." *Criminology* 20:449–65.

Paap, W.R. 1981. "Being Burglarized: An Account of Victimization." *Victimology: An International Journal* 6:297–305.

Packer, H.L. 1964. "Two Models of the Criminal Process." *University of Pennsylvania Law Review* 113:1–68.

Parent, D.G., Auerbach, B., and Carlson, K.E. 1992. *Compensating Crime Victims: A Summary of Policies and Practices*. Washington, D.C.: U.S. Department of Justice.

Parks, R.B. 1976. "Police Response to Victimization: Effects on Citizen Attitudes and Perceptions." In Skogan, W.G., ed., *Sample Surveys of the Victims of Crimes*. Boston: Ballinger.

Parnas, R.I. 1967. "The Police Response to Domestic Disturbance." *Wisconsin Law Review*, 914–60.

Parton, D.A., Hansel, M., and Stratton, J.R. 1991. "Measuring Crime Seriousness." *British J. of Criminology* 31:72–85.

Paternoster, R. 1984. "Prosecutorial Discretion in Requesting the Death Penalty: A Case of Victim-Based Racial Discrimination." *Law and Society Review* 18:437–78.

Paton, G.W. 1951. *A Textbook on Jurisprudence*. 2nd ed. Oxford: Clarendon Press.

Peachey, D.E. 1989. "The Kitchener Experiment." In Wright, M., and Galaway, B., eds., *Mediation and Criminal Justice*, 14–26.

Penley, V. n.d. "Public Opinion, Punishment and Rehabilitation: A Convergence of Ideologies." California State University, San Bernardino.

Pettit, P., with Braithwaite, J. 1993. "Not Just Deserts, Even in Sentencing." *Current Issues in Criminal Justice* 4:225–39.

Philips, C. 1981. *The Investigation and Prosecution of Criminal Offences in England and Wales.* London: HMSO.

Piliavin, I., and Briar, S. 1964. "Police Encounters with Juveniles." *American J. of Sociology* 70:206.

Pilon, R. 1978. "Criminal Remedies: Restitution, Punishment, or Both?" *Ethics* 88:348–57.

Pincoffs, E.L. 1977. "Are Questions of Desert Decidable?" In Cederblom, J.R., and Blizek, W.L., eds., *Justice and Punishment,* 75–88. Cambridge, Mass.: Ballinger.

Pitsela, A. 1991. "Results of Victim Survey Research in a Small Greek Town with Particular Reference to Attitudes towards Crime and the Criminal Justice System." In Kaiser, G., et al., eds., *Victims and Criminal Justice,* 50:731–62.

Plant, R., Lesser, H., and Taylor-Gooby, P. 1980. *Political Philosophy and Social Welfare.* London: Routledge and Kegan Paul.

Poister, T., and McDavid, J. 1978. "Victims' Evaluations of Police Performance." *J. of Criminal Justice* 6:133–49.

Polito, K.E. 1990. "The Rights of Crime Victims in the Criminal Justice System: Is Justice Blind to the Victims of Crime?" *Criminal and Civil Confinement* 16:241–70.

Posner, R.A. 1986. *Economic Analysis of Law.* 3rd ed. Boston: Little, Brown.

President's Commission on Law Enforcement and the Administration of Justice. 1967. *Field Surveys I and II.* Washington, D.C.: U.S. Government Printing Office.

President's Task Force on Victims of Crime. 1982. *Final Report.* Washington, D.C.

Primoratz, I. 1989. *Justifying Legal Punishment.* Atlantic Highlands, N.J.: Humanities Press.

Quinney, R. 1974. "Who Is the Victim?" In Drapkin, I., and Viano, E., eds., *Victimology,* 103–10.

Ramker, G.F., and Meagher, M.S. 1982. "Crime Victim Compensation: A Survey of State Programs." *Federal Probation* 46:68–76.

Ranish, D.R., and Shichor, D. 1985. "The Victim's Role in the Penal Process: Recent Developments in California." *Federal Probation* 49:50–57.

Rawls, J. 1971. *A Theory of Justice.* Cambridge, Mass.: Harvard University Press.

Reeves, H. 1985. "The Victim and Reparation." *World Society of Victimology Newsletter* 4:50–56.

———. 1988. Afterword to Maguire, M., and Pointing, J., *Victims of Crime: A New Deal?* 204–6.

Reiff, R. 1979. *The Invisible Victim.* New York: Basic Books.

Reiss, A.J. 1971. *The Police and the Public.* New Haven, Conn.: Yale University Press.

Rentmeister, F.R. 1979. *Profile of Crime in Brevard County, Florida.* Melbourne: Florida Institute of Technology.

Resick, P.A. 1990. "Victims of Sexual Assault." In Lurigio, et al., eds., *Victims of Crime: Problems, Policies and Programs*, 69–86.

Reynolds, D., and Blyth, D.A. 1976. "Occurrence, Reaction to, and Perception of Victimization in an Urban Setting: Analysis of a Survey of the Twin Cities Region." Sponsored by the Metropolitan Council of the Twin Cities, St. Paul, Minn.

Rice, P.R. 1979. "Mediation and Arbitration as a Civil Alternative to the Criminal Justice System—an Overview and Legal Analysis." *American University Law Review* 29:17–81.

Rich, R.F. 1981. "Evaluating Mental Health Services for Victims: Perspectives on Policies and Services in the United States." In Salasin, S.E., ed., *Evaluating Victim Services*, 128–42.

Rich, R.F., and Stenzel, S. 1980. "Mental Health Services for Victims: Policy Paradigms." *Evaluation and Change*, 47–54.

Riedel, M. 1975. "Perceived Circumstances, Inferences of Intent and Judgments of Offense Seriousness." *J. of Criminal Law and Criminology* 66:201–8.

Riggs, D.S., and Kilpatrick, D.G. 1990. "Families and Friends: Indirect Victimization by Crime." In Lurigio, A.J., et al., eds., *Victims of Crime: Problems, Policies and Programs*, 120–38.

Riley, P.J., and Rose, V.M. 1980. "Public vs. Elite Opinion on Correctional Reform: Implications for Social Policy." *J. of Criminal Justice* 8:345–56.

R.J.M. 1984. "The Constitutionality of the Victims' Restitution Provisions of the Victim and Witness Protection Act." *Virginia Law Review* 70:1059–81.

Robert, P. 1979. "The Extent of Public Information and the Nature of Public Attitudes towards the Social Control of Crime." In *Public Opinion on Crime and Criminal Justice*. Strasbourg: Council of Europe.

Roberts, A.R. 1990. *Helping Crime Victims*. Newbury Park, Calif.: Sage Publications.

Roberts, J.V. 1992. "Public Opinion, Crime and Criminal Justice." *Crime and Justice* 16:99–180.

Rock, P. 1986. *A View from the Shadows*. Oxford: Clarendon Press.

———. 1988. "Governments, Victims and Policies in Two Countries." *British J. of Criminology* 28 (1): 44–66.

———. 1990. *Helping Victims of Crime*. Oxford: Clarendon Press.

———. 1993. "The Victim in Court Project at the Crown Court at Wood Green." *Howard J.* 30:301–10.

Rodley, N.S. 1987. *The Treatment of Prisoners under International Law*. Oxford: Clarendon Press.

Roehl, J.A., and Cook, R.F. 1982. "The Neighborhood Justice Centers Field Test." In Tomasic, R., and Feeley, M.M., eds., *Neighborhood Justice*, 91–110.

Rosenbaum, D.P. 1987. "Coping with Victimization: The Effects of Police Intervention on Victims' Psychological Adjustment." *Crime and Delinquency* 33:502–19.

Rosenblum, R.H., and Blew, C.H. 1979. *Victim/Witness Assistance*. Washington, D.C.: U.S. Department of Justice.

Rossi, P.H., Waite, E., Bose, J.E., and Berk, R.E. 1975. "The Seriousness of Crimes: Normative Structure and Individual Differences." In Halleck, S.L., et al., eds.,

Aldine Crime and Justice Annual 1974. Chicago: Aldine Publishing Co. (Originally published in *American Sociological Review,* 1974.)

Rothbard, M.N. 1977. "Punishment and Proportionality." In Barnett, R.E., and Hagel, J., eds., *Assessing the Criminal: Restitution, Retribution and the Legal Process,* 259–70. Cambridge, Mass.: Ballinger.

Rothman, D.J. 1971. *The Discovery of the Asylum.* Boston: Little, Brown.

Rowley, M.S. 1990. "Comparison of Recidivism Rates for Delinquents Processed in a Restitution-Diversion Program to a Matched Sample Processed in Court." In Galaway, B., and Hudson, J., eds., *Criminal Justice, Restitution and Reconciliation,* 217–25.

Roxin, C. 1983. *Strafverfahrensrecht.* 18th ed. Munich.

Roy, S. 1990. "Offender-Oriented Restitution Bills: Bringing Total Justice for Victims?" *Federal Probation* 54:30–36.

Royal Commission on Criminal Justice. 1993. *Royal Commission on Criminal Justice: Report.* London: HMSO.

Rubel, H.C. 1986. "Victim Participation in Sentencing Proceedings." *Criminal Law Quarterly* 28:226–50.

Russell, J. 1990. *Home Office Funding of Victim Support Schemes—Money Well Spent?* Research and Planning Unit Paper 58. London: HMSO.

Sabatie, V. 1985. *Approche evaluative du comportement des victimes d'actes delictuels devant les tribunaux repressifs.* Tribunal de Grande Instance de Nanterre.

Sadurski, W. 1985. *Giving Desert Its Due.* Dordrecht: Reidel.

———. 1991. "Social Justice and the Problem of Punishment." *Israel Law Review* 25:302–31.

Saks, M.J. 1992. "Do We Really Know Anything about the Behavior of the Tort Litigation System—and Why Not?" *University of Pennsylvania Law Review* 140:1147–292.

Salasin, S., ed. 1981. *Evaluating Victim Services.* Beverly Hills, Calif.: Sage Publications.

Saleilles, R. 1911. *The Individualization of Punishment.* London: Heinemann.

Sales, E., Baum, M., and Shore, B. 1984. "Victim Adjustment Following Assault." *J. of Social Issues* 40:117–36.

Sampson, R.J., and Lauritsen, J.L. 1990. "Deviant Lifestyles, Proximity to Crime, and the Offender-Victim Link in Personal Violence." *J. of Research in Crime and Delinquency* 27:110–39.

Sander, F.E.A. 1976. "Varieties of Dispute Processing." *Federal Rules Decisions* 70:111–34.

Sander, F.E.A., and Snyder, F.E. 1982. *Alternative Methods of Dispute Settlement: A Selected Bibliography.* Updated version of 1979 ed. Washington, D.C.: American Bar Association.

Santos, B. de Sousa. 1982. "Law and Community: The Changing Nature of State Power in Late Capitalism." In Abel, R.L., ed., *The Politics of Informal Justice,* 1:249–66.

Sarat, A. 1988. "The 'New Formalism' in Dispute and Dispute Processing." *Law and Society Review* 21:695–715.

Sayles, S.L. 1991. "The Fight for Victims' Rights in Florida: The Realities of Social Reform." Ph.D. diss., Florida State University.

Schafer, S. 1968. *The Victim and His Criminal.* New York: Random House.

————. 1970. *Compensation and Restitution to Victims of Crime.* 1960. Montclair, N.J.: Patterson Smith.

————. 1976. "The Victim and Correctional Theory: Integrating Victim Reparation with Offender Rehabilitation." In McDonald, W.F., ed., *Criminal Justice and the Victim,* 227–36. Beverly Hills, Calif.: Sage Publications.

Scheingold, S.A., Olson, T., and Pershing, J. 1994. "Sexual Violence, Victim Advocacy, and Republican Criminology: Washington State's Community Protection Act." *Law and Society Review* 28:729–63.

Schneider, A.L. 1986. "Restitution and Recidivism Rates for Juvenile Offenders: Results from Four Experimental Studies." *Criminology* 24:533–52.

Schneider, A.L., Burcart, J.M., and Wilson, L.A. 1976. "The Role of Attitudes in the Decision to Report Crimes to the Police." In McDonald, W.F., ed., *Criminal Justice and the Victim,* 89–113. Beverly Hills, Calif.: Sage Publications.

Schneider, A.L., and Schneider, P.R. 1980. "Policy Expectations and Program Realities in Juvenile Restitution." In Hudson, J., and Galaway, B., eds., *Victims, Offenders and Alternative Sanctions,* 37–54.

————. 1981. "Victim Assistance Programs: An Overview." In Galaway, B., and Hudson, J., eds., *Perspectives on Crime Victims,* 364–73.

Schneider, H-J., ed. 1982. *The Victim in International Perspective.* Berlin: de Gruyter.

Schoenholz, K. 1980. "Holding Governments Strictly Liable for the Release of Dangerous Parolees." *New York University Law Review* 55:907–40.

Schulhofer, S. 1974. "Harm and Punishment: A Critique of Emphasis on the Results of Conduct in the Criminal Law." *University of Pennsylvania Law Review* 122:1497–607.

Schulz, J. 1982. *Beitrage zur Nebenklage.* Berlin: Duncker & Humblot.

Schur, E. 1973. *Radical Non-Intervention.* Englewood Cliffs, N.J.: Prentice-Hall.

Sebba, L. 1978. "Some Explorations in the Scaling of Penalties." *J. of Research in Crime and Delinquency* 15:247–65.

————. 1980. "Is Mens Rea a Component of Perceived Offense Seriousness?" *J. of Criminal Law and Criminology* 71:124–35.

————. 1982. "The Victim's Role in the Penal Process: A Theoretical Orientation." *American J. of Comparative Law* 30:217–40.

————. 1984. "Crime Seriousness and Criminal Intent." *Crime and Delinquency* 30:227–44.

————. 1994. "Sentencing the Victim: The Aftermath of Payne." *International Review of Victimology* 3:141–65.

————. Forthcoming. "Informal Modes of Dispute Resolution—the Debate Continues." In Sebba, L., ed., *Social Control and Justice: Inside or Outside the Law?* Jerusalem: Magnes Press.

Sebba, L., and Nathan, G. 1984. "Further Explorations in the Scaling of Penalties." *British J. of Criminology* 24:221–49.

Seligman, C., Brickman, J., and Koulack, D. 1977. "Rape and Physical Attractiveness: Assigning Responsibility to Victims." *J. of Personality* 45:554–63.

Sellin, T., and Wolfgang, M.E. 1978. *The Measurement of Delinquency.* 1964. Montclair, N.J.: Patterson Smith.

Separovic, Z.P., ed. 1989. *Victimology: International Action and Study of Victims.* 2 vols. Zagreb: University of Zagreb.

Sessar, K. 1984. "Public Attitudes towards Offender Restitution in Germany." Paper presented at the Annual Meeting of the American Society of Criminology, Cincinnati, November.

Shachar, Y. 1987. "The Fortuitous Gap in Law and Morality." *Criminal Justice Ethics* 6 (2): 12–36.

Shapiro, C. 1990. "Is Restitution Legislation the Chameleon of the Victims' Movement?" In Galaway, B., and Hudson, J., eds., *Criminal Justice, Restitution and Reconciliation*, 73–80.

Shapland, J. 1983. "Victim-Witness Services and the Needs of the Victim." *Victimology: An International Journal* 8:233–37.

———. 1984. "Victims, the Criminal Justice System and Compensation." *British J. of Criminology* 24:131–49.

———. 1986. "Victim Assistance and the Criminal Justice System: The Victim's Perspective." In Fattah, E.A., ed., *From Crime Policy to Victim Policy*, 218–33.

Shapland, J., Willmore, J., and Duff, P. 1981. *The Victim in the Criminal Justice System, Final Report to the Home Office.* Oxford: Centre for Criminological Research.

———. 1985. *Victims in the Criminal Justice System.* Aldershot: Gower.

Shaw, M. 1991. *International Law.* 3rd ed. Cambridge: Grotius.

Shaw, S. 1982. *People's Justice: A Major Poll in Public Attitudes on Crime and Punishment.* London: Prison Reform Trust.

Sheleff, L.S. 1978. *The Bystander.* Lexington, Mass.: Lexington Books.

Sheleff, S. 1977. "Victimology, Criminal Law and Conflict Resolution." *South African J. of Criminal Law and Criminology* 1:31–50.

Shelly, P.L., and Sparks, R.F. 1980. "Crime and Punishment." Newark, N.J.: School of Criminal Justice, Rutgers University.

Shenk, J.F., and Klaus, P.A. 1984. *The Economic Cost of Crime to Victims.* Washington, D.C.: U.S. Department of Justice.

Shonholtz, R. 1993. "Justice from Another Perspective: The Ideology and Developmental History of the Community Boards Program." In Merry, S.E., and Milner, N., eds., *The Possibility of Popular Justice*, 201–38.

Shotland, R.L. 1984. "Bystanders, Crime and an 'Obligation-to-Assist' Statute." Paper presented at the Annual Meeting of the American Society of Criminology, Cincinnati, November.

Shotland, R.L., and Goodstein, L.I. 1984. "The Role of Bystanders in Crime Control." *J. of Social Issues* 40:9–26.

Shuman, S.I. 1970. "Responsibility and Punishment: Why Criminal Law?" *American J. of Jurisprudence* 14:25.

Silver, R.L., Boon, C., and Stones, M.H. 1983. "Searching for Meaning in Misfortune: Making Sense of Incest." *J. of Social Issues* 39:81–101.

Silverman, R.A. 1974. "Victim Typologies: Overview, Critique and Reformulation." In Drapkin, I., and Viano, E., eds., *Victimology*, 55–59.

Silving, H. 1975. "Compensation for Victims of Physical Violence—a Round Table." 1959. In Hudson, J., and Galaway, B., eds., *Considering the Victim*, 198–219.

Singer, L.R. 1979. "Nonjudicial Dispute Resolution Mechanism: The Effects on Justice for the Poor." *Clearinghouse Review*, 569–82.

———. 1990. *Settling Disputes*. Boulder, Colo.: Westview Press.

Singer, R.G. 1979. *Just Deserts: Sentencing Based on Equality and Desert*. Cambridge, Mass.: Ballinger.

Singer, S.I. 1981. "Homogeneous Victim-Offender Populations: A Review and Some Research Implications." *J. of Criminal Law and Criminology* 72:779–88.

Skogan, W.G. 1981. "On Attitudes and Behaviors." In Lewis, D.A., ed., *Reactions to Crime*, 19–45. Beverly Hills, Calif.: Sage Publications.

———. 1987. "The Impact of Victimization on Fear." *Crime and Delinquency* 33:135–54.

———. 1990. *The Police and Public in England and Wales*. London: HMSO.

Skogan, W.G., Davis, R.G., and Lurigio, A.J. 1990. "Victims' Needs and Victim Services, Final Report to the National Institute of Justice." Washington, D.C.: National Institute of Justice.

———. 1991. "The Impact of Victim Services." In Kaiser, G., et al., eds., *Victims and Criminal Justice*, 97–114.

Skogan, W.G., and Maxfield, M.G. 1981. *Coping with Crime*. Beverly Hills, Calif.: Sage Publications.

Skogan, W.G., and Wycoff, M.A. 1987. "Some Unexpected Effects of a Police Service for Victims." *Crime and Delinquency* 33:490–501.

Slavin, L., and Sorin, D.J. 1984. "Congress Opens a Pandora's Box—the Restitution Provisions of the Victim and Witness Protection Act of 1982." *Fordham Law Review* 52:507–73.

Sluder, R.D., and del Carmen, R.V. 1990. "Are Probation and Parole Officers Liable for Injuries Caused by Probationers and Parolees?" *Federal Probation* 54:3–12.

Smale, G.J.A. 1984. "Psychological Effects and Behavioral Changes in the Case of Victims of Serious Crimes." In Block, R., ed., *Victimization and Fear of Crime: World Perspectives*, 87–92. Washington, D.C.: U.S. Department of Justice.

Smale, G.J.A., and Spickenhauer, H.L.P. 1979. "Feelings of Guilt and Need for Retaliation in Victims of Serious Crimes against Property and Persons." *Victimology: An International Journal* 4 (1): 75–85.

Smith, A.E., and Maness, D. 1976. "The Decision to Call the Police: Reactions to Burglary." In McDonald, W.F., ed., *Criminal Justice and the Victim*, 79–87. Beverly Hills, Calif.: Sage Publications.

Smith, B.E. 1983. *Non-Stranger Violence: The Criminal Court's Response*. Washington, D.C.: U.S. Department of Justice.

Smith, B.E., and Cook, R.F. 1984. "Crisis Intervention: How Effective Is It for Crime Victims?" Paper presented at the Annual Meeting of the American Society of Criminology, Cincinnati, November.

Smith, B.E., Cook, R.F., and Harrell, A.V. 1984. *Evaluation of Victim Services: Draft Final Report*. Washington, D.C.: U.S. Department of Justice.

Smith, B.E., Davis, R.C., and Hillenbrand, S.W. 1989. *Improving Enforcement of Court-Ordered Restitution*. Washington, D.C.: American Bar Association.

Smith, D.A., and Klein, J.R. 1984. "Police Control of Interpersonal Disputes." *Social Problems* 31:468–81.

Smith, D.N. 1978. "A Warmer Way of Disputing: Mediation and Conciliation." *American J. of Comparative Law* 26 (Suppl.): 205–16.

Smith, K.J. 1975. "A Cure for Crime." 1965. In Hudson, J., and Galaway, B., *Considering the Victim*, 340–50.

Smith, L.J.F. 1989. *Domestic Violence: An Overview of the Literature*. London: HMSO.

Smith, L.N., and Hill, G.D. 1991. "Victimization and Fear of Crime." *Criminal Justice and Behavior* 18:217–39.

Smith, P.E., and Hawkins, R.O. 1973. "Victimization, Types of Citizen-Police Contacts and Attitudes toward the Police." *Law and Society* 8:135–52.

Smith, S.R., and Freinkel, S. 1988. *Adjusting the Balance: Federal Policy and Victim Services*. New York: Greenwood Press.

Snyder, F.E. 1978. "Crime and Community Mediation—the Boston Experience: A Preliminary Report on the Dorchester Urban Court Program." *Wisconsin Law Review*, 737–95.

Sparks, R.F. 1982. *Research on Victims of Crime*. Rockville, Md.: National Institute of Mental Health and Human Services, Center for Studies in Crime and Delinquency.

Spaulding, D. 1980. "The Role of Victim Advocate." In Warner, C.G., ed., *Rape and Sexual Assault: Management and Intervention*, 199–212. Rockville, Md.: Aspen Systems Corp.

Spinellis, D.D. 1986. "The Civil Action: A Useful Alternative Solution to the Victims' Problems?" In Van Dijk, J.J.M., et al., *Criminal Law in Action*, 405–18. Arnhem: Gouda Quint Bv.

Stanko, E.A. 1981–82. "Impact of Victim Assessment on Prosecutors' Screening Decisions: The Case of the New York County District Attorney's Office." *Law and Society Review* 16:225-39.

Stark, J., and Goldstein, H.W. 1985. *The Rights of Crime Victims: An American Civil Liberties Union Handbook*. Toronto: Bantam Books.

Starkweather, D.A. 1992. "The Retributive Theory of 'Just Desert' and Victim Participation in Plea Bargaining." *Indiana Law J.* 67:853–78.

Statistics Division. 1984. *Awareness and Use of Crime Compensation Programs*. Ottawa: Ministry of the Solicitor General of Canada.

Stein, A. 1992. "Constitutionalizing the Rights of the Accused: Intrinsic Rights Strategy vs. the Balancing Approach." Paper presented at the Canada-Israel Law Conference on Chartering Human Rights.

Steinberg, A. 1984. "From Private Prosecution to Plea Bargaining: Criminal Prosecution, the District Attorney and American Legal History." *Crime and Delinquency* 30:568–92.

Steinmetz, C.H.D. 1988. "The Effect of Victim Assistance." Paper presented at the 10th International Congress on Criminology, Hamburg.

———. 1989. "The Effects of Victim Support." In *Guidelines for Victim Support in Europe*, 120–28.

Sterba, J. 1980. *Justice: Alternative Political Perspectives*. Belmont, Calif.: Wadsworth.

Stinchcombe, A.L., Adams, R., Heimer, C.A., Scheppele, K.L., Smith, T.W., and

Taylor, D.G. 1980. *Crime and Punishment—Changing Attitudes in America.* San Francisco: Jossey-Bass.

St. Louis, A. 1976. *Victims of Crime in Texas: The 1975 Texas Crime Trend Survey.* Texas Department of Public Safety.

Stoll, H. 1970. "Penal Purposes in the Law of Tort." *American J. of Comparative Law* 18:3–21.

Stuebing, W.K. 1984. *Crime Victims: Victims and Witnesses— Experiences, Needs, and Community/Criminal Justice Response.* Working Paper no. 9, Research and Statistics Section, Policy Planning and Development Branch, Department of Justice, Canada.

Sumner, C.J. 1987. "Victim Participation in the Criminal Justice System." *Australia and New Zealand J. of Criminology* 20:195–217.

———. 1994. "Taking Account of the Victim in Sentencing in South Australia." *International Review of Victimology* 3:111–19.

Sykes, G.M., and Matza, D. 1957. "Techniques of Neutralization: A Theory of Delinquency." *American Sociological Review* 22:664–70.

Symonds, M. 1980. "The 'Second Injury' to Victims." *Evaluation and Change,* 36–38.

Takooshian, H., and Stravitz, A. 1984. "Opinions on American Duty-to-Assist Legislation." Paper presented at the Annual Meeting of the American Society of Criminology, Cincinnati, November.

Talbert, P.A. 1988. "The Relevance of Victim Impact Statements to the Criminal Sentencing Decision." *UCLA Law Review* 36:199–232.

Tallack, W. 1900. *Reparations to the Injured: And the Rights of the Victims of Crime to Compensation.* London.

Teson, S.B. 1982. "Forgotten Victims: The Missouri Solution." *UMKC Law Review* 50:533–65.

Thibaut, J., and Walker, L. 1975. *Procedural Justice.* Hillsdale, N.J.: Lawrence Erbaum.

———. 1978. "A Theory of Procedure." *California Law Review* 66:541–66.

Thomas, C., and Hyman, J.M. 1977. "Perceptions of Crime, Fear of Victimization and Public Perceptions of Police Performance." *J. of Political Science and Administration* 5:305–17.

Thomas, D.A. 1967. "Sentencing—the Basic Principles." *Criminal Law Review,* 455–60.

Thomson, D.R., and Ragona, A.I. 1987. "Popular Moderation versus Governmental Authoritarianism: An Interactionist View of Public Sentiments toward Criminal Sanctions." *Crime and Delinquency* 33:337–57.

Thorvaldson, S.A. 1983. "Compensation by Offenders in Canada: A Victim's Right? Five Answers." Paper prepared for the 33rd International Course in Criminology, Vancouver.

———. 1990. "Restitution and Victim Participation at Sentencing: A Comparison of Two Models." In Galaway, B., and Hudson, J., eds., *Criminal Justice, Restitution and Reconciliation,* 23–36.

Thorvaldson, S.A., and Krasnick, M.R. 1980. "On Recovering Compensation Funds from Offenders." *Victimology: An International Journal* 5:18–29.

Tittle, C.R. 1978. "Retribution and Deterrence: An Evaluation of Compatibility."

In Galaway, B., and Hudson, J., eds., *Offender Restitution in Theory and Action*, 33–58.

Tomasic, R. 1982. "Mediation as an Alternative to Adjudication: Rhetoric and Reality in the Neighborhood Justice Movement." In Tomasic and Feeley, M.M., eds., *Neighborhood Justice*, 215–48.

Tomasic, R., and Feeley, M.M., eds. 1982. *Neighborhood Justice*. New York: Longman.

Tornblom, K. 1992. "The Social Psychology of Distributive Justice." In Scherer, K.R., ed., *Justice: Interdisciplinary Perspectives*, 177–236. Cambridge: Cambridge University Press.

Tsitsoura, A. 1984. "The European Convention on the Compensation of Victims of Violent Crimes." In *Towards a Victim Policy in Europe*, 133–45. Helsinki: Helsinki Institute for Crime Prevention and Control.

Tunc, A. n.d. "Introduction." *International Encyclopedia of Comparative Law*. Vol. 11, *Torts*, 17–24. Tubingen: Mohr.

Turpen, B., and Champagne, A. 1978. "Perceptions of Judicial Fairness." In Inciardi, J.A., and Haas, K.C., eds., *Crime and the Criminal Justice Process*, 260–69. Dubuque, Iowa: Kendall/Hunt Publishing Co.

Turpen, M.C. 1981. "The Criminal in the Justice System: An Overview of the Oklahoma Victims' Bill of Rights." *Tulsa Law J.* 1:253–59.

Tyler, T.R. 1984. "The Role of Perceived Injustice in Defendants' Evaluations of Their Courtroom Experience." *Law and Society Review* 18:51–74.

Umbreit, M.S. 1985. "Crime Victims Seeking Fairness, Not Revenge: Toward Restorative Justice." *Federal Probation* 53:52–57.

———. 1988. *The Meaning of Fairness to Victims in Victim Offender Mediation*. Ann Arbor, Mich.: University Microfilms.

———. 1989. "Violent Offenders and Their Victims." In Wright, M., and Galaway, B., eds., *Mediation and Criminal Justice*, 99–112.

———. 1994. *Victim Meets Offender: The Impact of Restorative Justice and Mediation*. Monsey, N.Y.: Criminal Justice Press.

U.S. Department of Justice. 1992. *Criminal Victimization in the United States, 1990*. Washington, D.C.: U.S. Department of Justice.

U.S. Sentencing Commission. 1987. *Sentencing Guidelines and Policy Statements*. Washington D.C.: U.S. Sentencing Commission.

———. 1994. *Guidelines Manual*. Washington, D.C.: U.S. Sentencing Commission.

Upson, L.A. 1987. "Criminal Restitution as a Limited Opportunity." *Criminal and Civil Confinement* 13:243–67.

Utne, M.K., and Hatfield, E. 1978. "Equity Theory and Restitution Programming." In Galaway, B., and Hudson, J., eds., *Offender Restitution in Theory and Action*, 73–88.

van den Haag, E. 1975. *Punishing Criminals: Concerning a Very Old and Painful Question*. New York: Basic Books.

Van Dine, S., Conrad, J.P., and Dinitz, S. 1977. "The Incapacitation of the Dangerous Offender: A Statistical Experiment." *J. of Research in Crime and Delinquency* 14:22-35.

Van Ness, D.N. 1993. "New Wine and Old Wineskins: Four Challenges of Restorative Justice." *Criminal Law Forum* 4:251–76.

Van Voorhis, P. 1983. "Theoretical Perspectives on Moral Development and Restitution." In Laufer, W.S., and Day, M., eds., *Personality Theory, Moral Development, and Criminal Behavior*, 411–39. Lexington, Mass.: Lexington Books.

———. 1985. "Restitution Outcome and Probationers' Assessment of Restitution." *Criminal Justice and Behavior* 12:259–87.

Veitch, E., and Miers, D. 1975. "Assault on the Law of Tort." *Modern Law Review* 38:139–52.

Vennard, J. 1976. "Victims' Views on Compensation and the Criminal Justice System." Paper presented at the 2nd International Symposium on Victimology, Boston, September.

———. 1978. "Compensation by the Offender: The Victim's Perspective." *Victimology: An International Journal* 3:154–60.

Verin, J. 1980. "La victime et le systeme penal." *Chronique de criminologie et des sciences de l'homme*, 763–71.

———. 1984. "La reparation due aux victimes d'infractions penales." In *Towards a Victim Policy in Europe*, 120–30. Helsinki: Helsinki Institute for Crime Prevention and Control.

Veronen, L.J., Kilpatrick, D.G., and Resick, P.A. 1979. "Treating Fear and Anxiety in Rape Victims: Implications for the Criminal Justice System." In Parsonage, W.H., ed., *Perspectives on Victimology*, 148–59. Beverly Hills, Calif.: Sage Publications.

Viano, E. 1978. "Victims, Offenders and the Criminal Justice System: Is Restitution an Answer?" In Galaway, B., and Hudson, J., eds., *Offender Restitution in Theory and Action*, 91–100.

———. 1979. *Victim/Witness Services: A Review of the Model*. Washington, D.C.: U.S. Department of Justice.

"Victims of Crime: Working Paper Prepared by the Secretariat." 7th UN Congress on the Prevention of Crime and the Treatment of Offenders, Milan, 1985.

Vidmar, N. 1981. "Justice Motives and Other Psychological Factors in the Development and Resolution of Disputes." In Lerner, M.J., and Lerner, S.C., eds., *The Justice Motive in Social Behavior*, 395–422. New York: Plenum Press.

Villmoare, E., and Neto, V.V. 1987. *Victim Appearances at Sentencing Hearings under the California Victims' Bill of Rights*. Washington, D.C.: U.S. Department of Justice.

Villmow, B. 1984. "Implications of Research on Victimization for Criminal and Social Policy." Report presented to the 16th Criminological Research Conference, Council of Europe, Strasbourg.

———. 1986. "The Application of the Victim Compensation Act in the Federal Republic of Germany." In Miyazawa, K., and Ohya, M., eds., *Victimology in Comparative Perspective*, 422–29.

von Hirsch, A. 1976. *Doing Justice: The Choice of Punishments*. New York: Hill & Wang.

———. 1982. "Constructing Guidelines for Sentencing: The Critical Choices for the Minnesota Sentencing Guidelines Commission." *Hamline Law Review* 5:164–275.

———. 1985. *Past or Future Crimes: Deservedness and Dangerousness in the Sentencing of Criminals*. New Brunswick, N.J.: Rutgers University Press.

von Hirsch, A., and Ashworth, A. 1992. "Not Not Just Deserts: A Response to Braithwaite and Pettit." *Oxford J. of Legal Studies* 12:83–98.

von Hirsch, A., and Jareborg, N. 1991. "Gauging Criminal Harm: A Living-Standard Analysis." *Oxford J. of Legal Studies* 11:1–38.

Wainstein, K.L. 1988. "Judicially Initiated Prosecution: A Means of Preventing Continuing Victimization in the Event of Prosecutorial Inaction." *California Law Review* 76:727–67.

Walker, N. 1969. *Sentencing in a Rational Society*. London: Allen Lane.

———. 1980. *Punishment, Danger and Stigma: The Morality of Criminal Justice*. Oxford: Basil Blackwell.

Walker, N., and Hough, M. 1988. Introduction to Walker, N., and Hough, M., eds., *Public Attitudes to Sentencing*, 1–15. Aldershot: Gower.

Walklate, S. 1989. *Victimology: The Victim and the Criminal Justice Process*. London: Unwin Hyman.

Waller, I. 1982. "Crime Victims: Needs, Services and Reforms—Orphans of Social Policy." Paper presented at the 4th International Symposium on Victimology, Tokyo.

———. 1984. *United Nations Declaration on the Protection and Assistance of Victims of Crime: Draft Explanatory Report and Draft Text*. Ottawa.

———. 1988. *The Role of the Victim in Sentencing and Related Processes*. Ottawa: Department of Justice.

Waller, I., and Okihiro, N. 1978. *Burglary: The Victim and the Public*. Toronto: University of Toronto Press.

Walsh, A. 1992. "Placebo Justice: Victim Recommendations and Offender Sentences in Sexual Assault Cases." 1986. In Fattah, E.A., ed., *Towards a Critical Victimology*, 295–310.

Walster, E. 1966. "Assignment of Responsibility for an Accident." *J. of Personality and Social Psychology* 7:73–79.

Walster, E., Berscheid, E., and Walster, G.W. 1976. "New Directions in Equity Research." In Berkowitz, L., and Walster, E., eds., *Equity Theory: Toward a General Theory of Social Interaction*, 1–42.

Walster, E., and Walster, G.W. 1975. "Equity and Social Justice." *J. of Social Issues* 31:21–43.

Ward. 1972. "Private Prosecution—the Entrenched Anomaly." *North Carolina Law Review* 20:117.

Warhaftig, P. 1981. "Dispute Resolution Retrospective." *Crime and Delinquency* 27:99–105.

———. 1982. "An Overview of Community-Oriented Citizen Dispute Resolution Programs in the U.S." In Abel, R.L., ed., *The Politics of Informal Justice*, 1:75–97.

Warr, M. 1989. "What Is the Perceived Seriousness of Crimes?" *Criminology* 27:795–821.

Weigend, T. 1986. "The Role of the Victim in the Criminal Process." In Miyazawa, K., and Ohya, M., eds., *Victimology in Comparative Perspective*, 160–70.

———. 1983. "Problems of Victim/Witness Assistance Programs, 1982." *Victimology: An International Journal* 8:91–101.

Weiss, P. 1980. "Idiocide." *Evaluation and Change*, 3.

Weitekamp, E. 1991. "Recent Developments in Restitution and Victim-Offender

Reconciliation in the U.S.A. and Canada: An Assessment." In Kaiser, G., et al., eds., *Victims and Criminal Justice*, 51:423–56.

———. 1993. "Calculating the Damage to Be Restored: Lessons from the National Survey of Crime Severity." Paper presented at the 11th International Congress on Criminology, Budapest.

Welling, S.N. 1987. "Victim Participation in Plea Bargains." *Washington University Law Quarterly* 65:301–56.

Wemmers, J. 1995. "Victims in the Dutch System: The Effects of Treatment on Victims, Attitudes and Compliance." *International Review of Victimology* 3:323–41.

White, G.E. 1980. *Tort Law in America: An Intellectual History*. New York: Oxford University Press.

White, G.F. 1975. "Public Responses to Hypothetical Crimes: Effects of Offender and Victim Status and Seriousness of the Offense on Punitive Reactions." *Social Forces* 53:411–19.

Williams, G.L.W. 1951. "The Aims of the Law of Tort." *Current Legal Problems* 4:137–76.

Williams, J.E. 1984. "Secondary Victimization: Confronting Public Attitudes about Rape." *Victimology: An International Journal* 9:66–81.

Williams, K.M. 1976. "The Effects of Victim Characteristics on the Disposition of Violent Cases." In McDonald, W.F., ed., *Criminal Justice and the Victim*, 177–213. Beverly Hills, Calif.: Sage Publications.

Willing, A. 1982. "Protection by Law Enforcement: The Emerging Constitutional Right." *Rutgers Law Review* 35:1–99.

Willis, B.L. 1984. "State Compensation of Victims of Violent Crimes: The Council of Europe Convention of 1983." *Virginia J. of International Law* 25:211–47.

Wilson, J.Q. 1975. *Thinking about Crime*. New York: Basic Books.

———. 1977. "The Political Feasibility of Punishment." In Cederblom, J.B., and Blizek, W.L., eds., *Justice and Punishment*, 107–23. Cambridge, Mass.: Ballinger.

———. 1978. *Varieties of Police Behavior: The Management of Law and Order in Eight Communities*. Cambridge, Mass.: Harvard University Press.

Wilson, J.Q., and Kelling, G.L. 1982. "Broken Windows: The Police and Neighborhood Safety." *Atlantic Monthly*, 29–38.

Winfield, P.H. 1931. *The Province of the Law of Tort*. Cambridge: Cambridge University Press.

Wolfgang, M.E. 1957. "Victim-Precipitated Criminal Homicide." *J. of Criminal Law, Criminology and Police Science* 48:1–11.

———. 1975. "Victim Compensation in Crimes of Personal Violence." 1965. In Hudson, J., and Galaway, B., eds., *Considering the Victim*, 116–29. Springfield, Ill.: Charles C. Thomas.

———. 1976. "Seriousness of Crime and a Policy of Juvenile Justice." In Short, J.F., ed., *Delinquency, Crime and Society*. Chicago: University of Chicago Press.

———. 1982. "Basic Concepts in Victimology Theory: Individualization of the Victim." In Schneider, H-J., ed., *The Victim in International Perspective*, 47–58.

———. 1989. "Victim Precipitation in Victimology and in Law." In Separovic, Z.P., ed., *Victimology: International Action and Study of Victims*, 1:33–42.

Wolfgang, M.E., Figlio, R.M., Tracy, P.E., and Singer, S.I. 1985. *The National Survey of Crime Severity*. Washington D.C.: U.S. Department of Justice.

Wolfgang, M.E., and Singer, S.I. 1978. "Victim Categories in Crime." *J. of Criminal Law and Criminology* 69:379–94.

Wootton, B. 1959. *Social Science and Social Pathology*. London: Allen & Unwin.

Woozley, A.D. 1983. "A Duty to Rescue: Some Thoughts on Criminal Liability." *Virginia Law Review* 69:1273–1300.

Wortman, C.B. 1983. "Coping with Victimization: Conclusions and Implications for Future Research." *J. of Social Issues* 39:195–221.

Wright, M. 1982. *Making Good: Prisons, Punishment and Beyond*. London: Burnett Books.

———. 1991. *Justice for Victims and Offenders*. Milton Keynes: Open University Press.

Wright, M., and Galaway, B. eds. 1989. *Mediation and Criminal Justice*. London: Sage Publications.

Yakovlev, A. 1985. "Criminal Justice as an Alternative in Dispute Settlement." Heuni, *Selected Issues in Criminal Justice*, 4. Helsinki, Finland.

Yngvesson, B. 1993. "Local People, Local Problems, and Neighborhood Justice: The Discourse of 'Community' in San Francisco Community Boards." In Merry, S.E., and Milner, N., eds., *The Possibility of Popular Justice*, 379–400.

Young, M. 1982. "Stress, Trauma and Crisis: The Theoretical Framework of Victimization Reconsidered." Paper presented at the 4th International Symposium on Victimology, Tokyo.

———. 1990. "Victim Assistance in the United States: The End of the Beginning." *International Review of Victimology* 1:181–99.

Young-Rifai, M.A. 1982. "Victimology: A Theoretical Framework." In Schneider, H-J., ed., *The Victim in International Perspective*, 65–79.

Zalman, M. 1991. "Review of the Domestic Violence Laws." Unpublished paper.

Zawitz, M.W., Klaus, P.A., Bachman, R., Bastian, L.D., De Berry, M.M., Rand, M.R., and Taylor, B.M. 1993. *Highlights from 20 Years of Surveying Crime Victims*. Washington, D.C.: U.S. Department of Justice.

Zedner, L. 1994. "Reparation and Retribution: Are They Reconcilable?" *Modern Law Review* 57:228–50.

Zehr, H. 1990. *Changing Lenses*. Scottdale, Pa.: Herald Press.

Ziegenhagen, E. 1976. "Towards a Theory of Victim-Criminal Justice System Interactions." In McDonald, W.F., ed., *Criminal Justice and the Victim*, 261–80. Beverly Hills, Calif.: Sage Publications.

———. 1977. *Victims, Crime and Social Control*. New York: Praeger.

———. 1989. "Crime Reporting and Services for Victims." In Fattah, E., ed., *The Plight of Crime Victims in Modern Society*, 277–88.

Ziegenhagen, E.A., and Benyi, J. 1981. "Victim Interests, Victim Services, and Social Control." In Galaway, B., and Hudson, J., eds., *Perspectives on Crime Victims*, 373–83. St. Louis: Mosby.

Zimmerman, S.E., Van Alstyne, D.J., and Dunn, C.S. 1988. "The National Punishment Survey and Public Policy Consequences." *J. of Research in Crime and Delinquency* 25:120–49.

Index

Volunteers, use in victim/witness assistance programs, 252, 259, 260, 263, 265

Von Bulow, Sunny, 1

Von Hirsch, Andrew, 158, 161, 203, 366 n. 7

VORPs (victim-offender reconciliation projects), 276, 279, 282, 287

Vulnerability, of victim, and seriousness of crime score, 163, 366 n. 8

Wages, prisoner's, and restitution, 173, 176, 177, 189, 379 n. 17

Wainstein, K.L., 195

Walker, L., 213, 294, 314, 324

Waller, Irvin, 7, 69, 73, 74

Walsh, A., 197, 199

Walster, E., 349, 382 n. 1

Washington State: Seattle survey on attitudes toward police, 89–90, 91; victim compensation programs, 231

Washington, D.C.: attitudes toward police, 95; attitudes toward prosecutors, 98; violations brought before prosecutors, 36

Wayne Law Review (1987), 11

Weapons, use, in committing a crime, 30, 36, 46

Weigend, T., 263, 312–13

Weinrib, E., 327

Weitekamp, E., 177, 179, 368 n. 25

Welden case (1984), on federal restitution provisions, 190–91

Welfare, victim's, 3, 4; services for, 17, 20, 148; and Fourteenth Amendment rights, 146–47

Welfare philosophy of law enforcement, and harm to victim, 30

Wellford, C., 165–67

Welling, S.N., 144–45

White, Byron R., 160

White-collar crime restitution, 173

Whites, attitudes toward police, 92, 94

Williams, K.M., 36

Williams, L.A., 284

Wilson, James Q., 5

Winston, T., 259

Wisconsin: attitudes toward police, 94; Victims' Bill of Rights, 267. *See also* Milwaukee, Wis.

Witnesses: noncooperation with prosecutors, 36, 114, 361 n. 39; protection of, 317; as victims during trials, 38–39, 40. *See also* Victim/witness assistance programs

Wolfgang, Marvin, 160–61, 204

Women, as victims: feminists' attention to, 6–7, 26; financial losses, 71; police activity, 31; psychiatric disturbances, 75, 79; and effect on sentencing, 48. *See also* Gender

World Society of Victimology, 2, 3, 12

Wortman, C.B., 74

Wright, M., 190, 331, 334, 380 n. 32

Wrongdoers. *See* Offenders

Wycoff, M.A., 256, 259

X and Y v. the Netherlands, 148

Young, Marlene, 7, 61, 268

Young v. United States ex rel. Vuitton et Fils (1987), use of private attorney as special prosecutor, 307

Zedner, L., 188

Zeisel, H., 41, 342

Zero-sum game: criminal justice as, 313; possibilities in informal modes of dispute resolution, 286

Ziegenhagen, E.A., 11, 32–33, 99, 106, 305, 378 n. 2

Zimmerman, S.E., 116